YOUTH ON TRIAL

A Developmental Perspective on Juvenile Justice

EDITED BY
Thomas Grisso and
Robert G. Schwartz

THE UNIVERSITY OF CHICAGO PRESS / CHICAGO AND LONDON

The University of Chicago Press, Chicago 60637
The University of Chicago Press, Ltd., London
© 2000 by The University of Chicago
All rights reserved. Published 2000
Printed in the United States of America
08 07 06 05 04 03 02 01 00   1 2 3 4 5
ISBN: 0-226-30912-6 (cloth)

Library of Congress Cataloging-in-Publication Data

Youth on trial : a developmental perspective on juvenile justice / edited by Thomas Grisso
and Robert G. Schwartz
    p. cm. — (The John D. and Catherine T. MacArthur Foundation series on mental
  health and development)
  Includes bibliographical references and index.
  ISBN 0-226-30912-6 (cloth : alk. paper)
    1. Juvenile justice, Administration of—United States.   2. Juvenile courts—United
  States.   3. Competency to stand trial—United States.   4. Criminal liability—United
  States.   5. Juvenile delinquents—Psychology.   6. Developmental psychology.
  7. Psychology, Forensic.   I. Grisso, Thomas.   II. Schwartz, Robert G.   III. Series.

HV9104 .Y685 2000
364.36′0973—dc21   99-055640

♾ The paper used in this publication meets the minimum requirements of the American
National Standard for Information Sciences—Permanence of Paper for Printed Library
Materials, ANSI Z39.48-1992.

YOUTH ON TRIAL

The John D. and Catherine T. MacArthur Foundation
Series on Mental Health and Development

CONTENTS

INTRODUCTION

At the dawn of the twentieth century, state legislatures in the United States embarked on a social experiment of sweeping proportion. States began to develop no less than a totally new and separate system of courts, laws, and correctional programs designed specifically for persons whose age placed them in a category called "juvenile."

This new juvenile justice system was fashioned to work more like a social-welfare agency than an institution of justice. With the authority of law, it would meet the needs of youths in a way that was expected to mitigate their continued involvement in criminal behavior when they reached adulthood. With rehabilitation and youth guidance as its objective, these courts would not need to meet all of the due process obligations of criminal courts. Even youths who committed serious offenses were considered "wayward," not criminally responsible, and they were to be assisted, not prosecuted.

Juvenile Justice at One Hundred Years

As the twentieth century reached its twilight years, however, legal responses to youths' offenses took a dramatic turn. Responding to an apparent increase in violent offenses by youths, most state legislatures moved to re-create juvenile laws to decrease the differences between dispositions of adolescent cases and the sentences of adults in criminal cases. Their response was based largely on their belief that the modern adolescent was more adultlike than adolescents of earlier generations and that the juvenile justice system was too lenient to be effective (Zimring 1998).

Beginning in the late 1980s, both of these perceptions led almost all states to expand the charges for which juveniles could be tried as adults in criminal courts, lower the age at which it could be done, and increase the

1

range of legal mechanisms that could be deployed to assure that more youths would be tried and sentenced as adults. Some states experimented with "blended sentencing," in which juveniles are accountable to both the juvenile and adult criminal justice systems. Many states changed the purposes of their juvenile codes to emphasize punishment and de-emphasize rehabilitation. Most states modified their programming accordingly, resorting to more punitive training schools and boot camps. Some states made courtrooms and juvenile records more accessible to the public (Torbet et al. 1996).

The consequences of these changes have been striking for both the criminal and juvenile justice systems. During the 1990s, many thousands of youths who in former years would have been dealt with in juvenile court were tried in adult criminal court and provided sentences formerly reserved for adults. The age at which youths may be tried in criminal court crept ever lower in many states, as low as ten or twelve in some and, in a few, no lower age limit at all. At its most extreme, the movement generated proposals such as that of a Texas legislator who advocated executing eleven-year-olds because "some of the kids that are growing up today . . . just aren't the *Leave It to Beaver* kids that I grew up with" (Coalition for Juvenile Justice 1998).

The juvenile justice system itself was transformed. Juvenile adjudications were used as predicates for subsequent decisions to transfer juveniles to criminal court and to enhance adult sentences. Juvenile records became less confidential and more available to the public.

Are Adolescents Adults?

Legislative reform moved forward quickly as the decade proceeded, fueled by the presumption that kids who engaged in "adult crimes" required "adult punishment." Even youths who were not transferred to criminal court would find that they were exposed to more adultlike consequences in the juvenile court. Yet as this book was being written, youth advocates were beginning to raise fundamental questions about the implications and assumptions of the reform, especially in light of the developmental status of adolescents. Two of these questions are the focus of this book.

Adolescents' Capacities as Trial Defendants

The first question addresses the process of justice. If youths are to be adjudicated as though they were adults, they must be afforded all of the rights and protections associated with due process in criminal cases. But compared to adults, are youths capable of participating in legal proceedings in a way that provides equal protection of their rights as defendants? The question is important for determining youths' competence to stand trial, without which a defendant cannot be adjudicated. It is important also for addressing the challenges that attorneys face in defending their youthful clients whose immaturity, even when youths meet legal criteria for competence to stand trial, may present unique challenges for attorney representation.

Adolescence and Culpability

The second question pertains to the more fundamental issue of blameworthiness. If youths are to be punished as adults for their offenses, they should be equally blameworthy with regard to the manner in which their offenses were committed. But are youths in fact adultlike in their cognitive abilities, decisions, judgment, and other psychological factors that pertain to the mental and emotional conditions that are relevant for understanding their crimes? Are they enough like adults to make appropriate a punitive social response that equals the sentences we provide to adults for their offenses?

The first question was never asked in the early juvenile justice system because the system's premises did not make many demands on youths' abilities to participate at trial or disposition. Nor was the second question seriously raised until recently. This was because the framers of the juvenile justice system chose not to respond to youths in proportion to their blameworthiness, but only in relation to their apparent need for rehabilitation in light of their offending.

Thus the recent changes in justice for juveniles raise fundamental questions about youths' capacities as adolescents that received little attention in former years. They may be addressed theoretically in a number of ways, and to some extent the answers depend on normative judgments. But a significant part of our consideration of these questions should depend on what we know empirically about the actual capacities of youths compared to those of adults.

The MacArthur Foundation Initiative

In this context the John D. and Catherine T. MacArthur Foundation identified society's need for a scientific initiative that would address the implications of adolescent development for the construction of rational juvenile justice policy and law. Beginning in 1995, the Foundation sponsored meetings of national experts in juvenile law and developmental psychology in order to identify what was known, and what needed to be learned, in order to achieve that end. Out of this process evolved the MacArthur Foundation's Research Network on Adolescent Development and Juvenile Justice, a collection of experts in psychology, sociology, public policy, law, and legal practice chaired by Laurence Steinberg, Ph.D., a developmental psychologist at Temple University.

At its inception in 1996, the Network was charged with engaging in a process that would eventually provide the information and tools that would assist in law, policy, and practice to address important issues of youth development that are raised by the current trends in juvenile law. Early in its process, the Network identified a number of important areas in need of research, two of which form the focus of this book—adolescents' capacities as trial defendants and the culpability of adolescent offenders.

As a first step toward fulfilling its mandate, the Network set for itself the following tasks:

- To produce the theoretical and conceptual foundation that was needed for applying developmental psychological knowledge to legal and policy analyses pertaining to youths capacities related to questions of trial participation and culpability.
- To thoroughly review what was known and not known about adolescent development that would address the two issues in question.
- Where information was lacking, to design a program of empirical research that would provide critical information about youths' development as it related to the two questions of youths' capacities in the legal context.

This book is built on the Network's conclusions after having completed the first phase of its work. The chapters were written not only by core members of the Network, but also by some of the scores of collaborators and consultants the Network engaged with during the completion of the above tasks. Among the larger group were developmental, clinical, and social psychologists; sociologists and criminologists; law scholars; juvenile justice advocates; juvenile defense and prosecuting attorneys; and juvenile court judges.

Whatever their discipline, each of the authors endeavored to communicate concepts and ideas in ways that could be read and used by an audience that would include social scientists, persons in juvenile law and policy, and professionals in legal and child clinical practice in the courts. Difficulties in interdisciplinary communication are well known, and every chapter in this volume naturally has its limitations in communicating equally well to all of these audiences. But if we were to wait until the members of a discipline could talk to others as well as they can communicate among their own members, no interdisciplinary discussion would ever be forthcoming.

These chapters are united by their fundamental assumption that an enlightened juvenile justice system must take into account the developmental psychological realities of adolescence. Part I lays the foundation for a developmental perspective on juvenile justice. Parts II and III then apply that perspective, respectively, to the issue of adolescents' capacities within the adjudicative process and to questions of culpability and mitigation when responding to the offenses of youths.

Youth on Trial

Youths are on trial today in two ways. In the first sense, whereas youths once faced delinquency hearings in juvenile courts, now with increasing frequency they stand trial in criminal courts. Those youths, like all other defendants in criminal court, must have capacities adequate to participate in their defense in order to ensure a just process. Do their capacities afford them adequate protection of their rights as defendants? Or are they disadvantaged in their defense as a consequence of their immaturity?

In the second sense, recent reforms in juvenile justice have placed the notion of youth itself on trial. Society's trend toward responding to adolescent offenders as adults asks that we set aside traditional presumptions about adolescence as a condition of immaturity that warrants mitigation. The ensuing debate highlights the need for evidence to address whether youths' capacities are sufficiently different from adults to warrant different legal responses to their transgressions.

We hope that the work that has begun here will eventually lead to a juvenile justice system that better serves the ultimate interests of society in its efforts to forge a rational and effective response to the needs, challenges, and promise of its youth.

Works Cited

Coalition for Juvenile Justice. 1998. *A celebration or a wake? The juvenile court after 100 years.* Washington, D.C.

Torbet, P., R. Gable, H. Hurst IV, I. Montgomery, L. Szymanski, and D. Thomas. 1996. *State responses to serious and violent juvenile crime.* Washington, DC: Office of Juvenile Justice and Delinquency Prevention.

Zimring, F. 1998. *American youth violence.* New York: Oxford University Press.

PART ONE

A Developmental Perspective
on Juvenile Justice

Youth on Trial begins with a focus on fundamentals, with the goal of discovering ways in which a developmental-psychological understanding of adolescents can assist us in addressing important questions in society's legal response to youthful offenders. To do this, we must first understand the fundamentals of developmental psychology as well as the juvenile justice system. Part I, therefore, offers a primer on adolescent development and juvenile justice.

Chapter 1 reviews the history of juvenile justice and discusses ways in which adolescent development is relevant to the various points of decision making in the juvenile justice system. It then provides an introduction to adolescent development, explaining in basic terms the way developmental psychologists understand adolescents' physical, intellectual, emotional, and social growth. It suggests that understanding the nature of psychological development during adolescence will help improve policymaking, judicial decision making, and legal practice.

Using principles of development to understand the circumstances of youthful offenders is complicated by an observation that has been widely accepted, even though research to support it has only recently evolved. Youths who are arrested for delinquent acts have a much higher prevalence of mental disorders than youths in general. Chapter 2 addresses mental disorders associated with adolescence, focusing especially on their interaction with developmental phenomena in ways that have implications for youths' capacities as defendants and as persons to whom culpability is attributed. Chapter 2 details the types of mental disabilities most often found among delinquent youths as well as their prevalence and comorbidity. Although recent studies offer clear warnings that we cannot ignore these findings, policymakers and practitioners continue to pay too little attention to the implications of mental disabilities for questions of justice, explanations for juvenile offending, and society's appropriate response. Chapter 2 gives an overview of the problem and, together with Chapter 1, establishes the developmental and clinical context in which the two main issues in Parts II and III must be considered.

CHAPTER ONE

Developmental Psychology Goes to Court

LAURENCE STEINBERG AND ROBERT G. SCHWARTZ

Few issues challenge a society's ideas about both the nature of human development and the nature of justice as much as serious juvenile crime. Because we neither expect children to be criminals nor expect crimes to be committed by children, the unexpected intersection between childhood and criminality creates a dilemma that most of us find difficult to resolve. Indeed, the only ways out of this problem are either to redefine the offense as something less serious than a crime or to redefine the offender as someone who is not really a child (Zimring 1998).

For the past hundred years, American society has most often chosen the first approach—redefining the offense—treating most juvenile infractions as matters to be adjudicated as delinquent acts within a separate juvenile justice system theoretically designed to recognize the special needs and immature status of young people and to therefore emphasize rehabilitation over punishment. Indeed, for much of the last century, states believed that the juvenile justice system was a vehicle to protect the public by providing a system that responds to children who are maturing into adulthood. States recognized that conduct alone—that is, the alleged criminal act—should not be dispositive in deciding when to invoke the heavy hand of the adult criminal justice system. They recognized that by providing for accountability, treatment, and supervision in the juvenile justice system—and in the community whenever possible—they promoted short-term and long-term public safety.

In recent years, however, there has been a dramatic shift in the way juvenile crime is viewed by policymakers and the general public. Rather than choosing to define offenses committed by youths as delinquent, society is increasingly opting to deal with young offenders more punitively in the juvenile justice system or to redefine them as adults and try them in adult criminal court. This trend is reflected in the growing number of juvenile offenses that are being adjudicated in adult criminal court, either by statute or through waiver; in the increasingly punitive response of our criminal justice system to juvenile offenders who are found guilty; and in what some observers have referred to as the "criminalization" of the juvenile justice system through increased use of punishment as a legitimate juvenile justice goal (Feld 1993).

The purpose of this volume is to integrate developmental considerations into moral, legal, political, and practical analyses of juvenile crime. This integration necessitates at least a rudimentary familiarity with the juvenile justice system and the study of psychological development. Our goal in this chapter is to introduce the reader to the most important concepts in both of these areas and, in so doing, to provide the background and context for the other chapters in this volume. We begin with a brief history of juvenile justice in America.

Juvenile Justice in America: An Overview

During much of the twentieth century, public rhetoric about how to respond to juvenile crime incorrectly posited clear, either-or positions from which policy choices should be made: child or adult, punishment or rehabilitation, judicial discretion or rigorous ironclad procedures. The reality has always been more ambiguous. Even though it is heuristically useful to divide this century's juvenile court experience into opposing epochs—the benign paternalism of the first part of the century versus the get-tough policies of recent decades—the actual lines between these orientations are far less clear.

It is also a mistake to think of the juvenile justice system as a single, self-contained unit operated by one entity (Guarino-Ghezzi and Loughran 1996). Every state has a different mix of decision makers and services, and each divides power over juveniles in different ways. It is rare that a coherent philosophy governs the component parts (Ayers 1997; Feld this volume).

These caveats notwithstanding, we can nevertheless divide the juvenile justice "system" between court and corrections: on the one hand is the judicial side that determines whether a juvenile is delinquent and enters orders of detention and disposition; on the other hand is that part of the system that rehabilitates, treats, supervises, or punishes young offenders.

This volume is, for the most part, concerned with the judicial part of the system, which historically was created well after decades of nineteenth-century experimentation with juvenile corrections. We begin, however, with the development of juvenile corrections policy during the nineteenth century, because many of the ideas that originated as a result of experimentation in corrections practices would influence the philosophy and organization of the juvenile court during the next century. As Jerome Miller has noted, "The [focus on the] establishment of the juvenile court in 1899 obscured the fact that another revolution in juvenile justice had occurred in the early 1800s. The earlier movement had resulted in increased institutionalization of juveniles, albeit in facilities different from adult jails and prisons" (Miller 1991).

The Origins of the Juvenile Justice System

Economic recessions in the early nineteenth century and the first wave of Irish immigrants pushed children out of work in America's new factory system during the industrial revolution. Concerns about poor children on the street led to the creation of institutional care for children. In New York City, the Society for Prevention of Pauperism in 1824 became the Society for the Reformation of Juvenile Delinquents, and in 1825 opened the nation's first House of Refuge. Boston followed a year later, and Philadelphia in 1828. These Houses of Refuge were designed to maintain class status and prevent unrest (Krisberg and Austin 1993; Platt 1977).

The concept of *parens patriae* provided the legal underpinning for the Houses of Refuge many years before it also provided a legal framework for the juvenile court. In ex parte *Crouse,* the Pennsylvania Supreme Court in 1838 affirmed the state's accepting Mary Ann Crouse from her mother and putting her into Philadelphia's House of Refuge. Mary Ann's father brought a writ of habeas corpus, rejected by the State Supreme Court. In now-famous language, the Court declared, "The object of the charity is reformation, by training its inmates to industry; by imbuing their minds with principles of morality and religion; by furnishing them with means to earn a living; and, above all, by separating them from the corrupting influence of improper associates. To this end, may not the natural parents, when unequal to the task of education, or unworthy of it, be superseded by the parens patriae, or common guardian of the community? . . . The infant has been snatched from a course which must have ended in confirmed depravity; and not only is the restraint of her person lawful, but it would have been an act of extreme cruelty to release her from it."

For the first time, parens patriae—a fifteenth-century concept for orphans—was applied to a poor child whose parents were still alive. By 1890, almost every state had some version of a reform school (Bernard 1992).

In 1899, Jane Addams and her Hull House colleagues established what is generally accepted to have been the nation's first juvenile court.

Juvenile court judges, in the early part of the twentieth century, "were authorized to investigate the character and social background of both 'pre-delinquent' and 'delinquent' children. They examined personal motivation as well as criminal intent, seeking to identify the moral reputation of problematic children" (Platt 1977). Ben Lindsey, of Denver, was the juvenile court judge whose practice most closely matched the rhetoric of the emerging juvenile court:

> We should make it our business to study and know each particular case, because it will generally demand treatment in some little respect different from any other case. . . . (a) Is the child simply mischievous or criminal in its tendencies? (b) Is the case simply an exceptional or isolated instance in which a really good boy or girl has gone wrong for the first time because too weak to resist a strong temptation? (c) Is the child a victim of incompetent parents? Does the home or parent need correction or assistance? (d) What of environment and association, which, of course, may embrace substantively all of the points of study? How can the environment be improved? Certainly by keeping the child out of the saloon and away from evil examples. (e) Is the child afflicted with what we call "the moving about fever"—that is, is he given to playing "hookey" from school, or "bumming" and running away, showing an entire lack of ambition or desire to work and settle down to regular habits (Platt 1977)?

Lindsey was the first to popularize "a highly personal approach to the children who came before him." The judge was like an idealized probation officer: visiting children's homes and schools, maintaining contact with employers, and becoming a confidant to the family. Lindsey saw himself as a therapeutic agent. He was the first to make the "highly personal and individualistic inquiry" that was the rhetorical hallmark of the juvenile court in the first half of the twentieth century (Fox 1997).

Judge Julian Mack, Chicago's second juvenile court judge, spoke glowingly of Lindsey in describing the idealized juvenile court. "The problem for determination by the judge is not Has this boy or girl committed a specific wrong but What is he, how has he become what he is, and what had best be done in his interest and in the interest of the state to save him from a downward career. It is apparent at once that the ordinary legal evidence in a criminal court is not the sort of evidence to be heard in such a proceeding" (Mack 1909).

Gault *and Its Impact*

At its most idealistic, the juvenile court of the first half of the century aimed to act as a benign parent would on behalf of a child. Several authors in this volume (Scott, for example) note the theoretically rehabilitative model for the pre-*Gault* juvenile court. The world of juvenile justice was altered forever in 1967 when the United States Supreme Court injected due process into the system as a consequence of the decision in *In re Gault* (387 U.S. 1 1967).

Gault involved a fifteen-year-old boy who was arrested for making calls to his next-door neighbor that the Supreme Court described as "of the irritatingly offensive, adolescent, sex variety." Gerald Gault was brought before a juvenile court judge, but he did not have notice of the charges against him, nor did he have a lawyer. The neighbor never appeared in court, but testimony was given by the arresting officer, who described what the neighbor had told him.

For an offense for which an adult could have received a fine of not more than fifty dollars or more than two months in jail, the juvenile court committed Gerald Gault to the Arizona State Industrial School for up to six years. Gerald challenged his adjudication of delinquency, and the U.S. Supreme Court held that the Fourteenth Amendment's Due Process clause applied to children. The Court held that in the context of adjudications of delinquency, children were persons within the meaning of the Fourteenth Amendment, and that no state could deprive them of liberty without due process of law. This meant that at trial juveniles had a right to notice of the charges, a right to counsel, and a right to confront witnesses against them.

The Court observed that "the highest motives and most enlightened impulses led to a peculiar system for juveniles, unknown to our law in any comparable context." The Court recalled the observation it made the year before in *Kent v. United States* (383 U.S. 541 1966), when it rejected the arbitrary transfer of a juvenile to criminal court: "There is evidence . . . that there may be grounds for concern that the child receives the worst of both worlds: that he gets neither the protections accorded to adults nor the solicitous care and regenerative treatment postulated for children." In words that rang for years in courthouses across America, the Court declared, "Under our Constitution, the condition of being a boy does not justify a kangaroo court."

The *Gault* decision thus ended benign neglect of the juvenile justice system and introduced a period in which juveniles were increasingly thought to be entitled to constitutional procedural protections similar to those of adults.[1] In a sense, this was a kind of "adultification" of the juvenile court.

During the mid-1990s, and motivated by very different concerns, a different sort of adultification occurred, one that moved the juvenile court away from its rehabilitative ideal and toward a retributive model that had much in common with the philosophy of the adult criminal court.[2] Almost every state changed its juvenile laws to respond to the large increase in violent juvenile crime between 1989 and 1993. States devised a variety of approaches to a) removing more juveniles from juvenile court jurisdiction, while placing them in criminal court; b) increasing the severity of juvenile court dispositions; and c) reducing the confidentiality of juvenile proceedings and records (Grisso 1996; Torbet et al. 1996).

It is unclear what impact the changes of the 1990s have had, or will have, on the day-to-day operations of the typical juvenile court. More juveniles are excluded from juvenile court than in previous times, but the vast majority of those who remain in juvenile court pass through a system that is not much different than the juvenile court of twenty years ago. Although the juvenile court of the late 1990s in practice is not as different as its predecessors, new punitive legislative policies have led some scholars to seek a middle ground between the "old" rehabilitative model of the idealized juvenile court and the "new" model of retributive justice. In the late 1980s, Dennis Maloney called for a "balanced approach" to juvenile probation in which probation would address public safety, accountability, and youth-competency development (Maloney, Romig, and Armstrong 1988). Maloney's work became part of the "restorative justice" movement of the 1990s, during which Gordon Bazemore, Mark Umbreit, and others called for a juvenile justice system in which attention would be paid to making the victim whole, involving communities in fashioning of dispositions, and teaching juveniles skills necessary to make the transition to responsible adulthood (Bazemore and Umbreit 1994).

Moving through the Contemporary Juvenile Justice Pipeline

It is useful to think of the juvenile justice system as similar to a pipeline (see fig. 1.1). Along the pipeline are diversion valves, which are the decision points at which children are either diverted from the pipeline or continue through its various gates and locks—these are the points of arrest, detention, adjudication, disposition, and disposition review. One of the signal characteristics of the juvenile justice system is its many diversion options: at every point of the system "valves" are available to send some children home, some to other systems, and others to noninstitutional care. Another characteristic that distinguishes the juvenile justice system from the adult system is the theoretical importance that the juvenile system places on a swift flow through the pipeline.[3]

For most of this century, juvenile court proceedings were held in courtrooms that were closed to the public. Juvenile records were sealed and unavailable to the public. In recent years, more states have opened juvenile court proceedings and made records available to law enforcement agencies, schools, and the criminal justice system when the juvenile is charged as an adult.

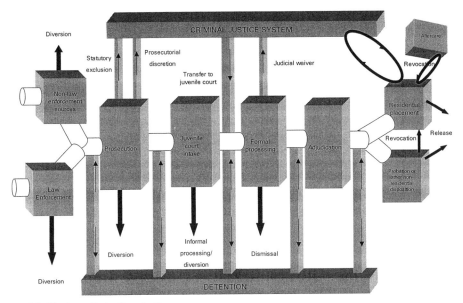

1.1. The juvenile justice pipeline

Each state has organized its justice system in slightly different ways, setting policies that determine which children are eligible for the juvenile justice system, which will be sent to the adult criminal justice system, and, within each system, which will go where and for how long. Idiosyncratic policies shape the particular structure of each state's system, and, in addition, each state operates idiosyncratically in the way those policies are implemented for individual juveniles. States may set different ages for a child's entry into the juvenile system (as young as seven, as old as ten) or exit from the system (as young as sixteen, as old as twenty-five). They may vary in placing burdens of proof on the juvenile or on the prosecutor, depending upon the decision to be made. And every state differs in the kinds of programs or services it offers at each stage of the process.

Critical Decision Points along the Pipeline

Despite whatever differences exist across jurisdictions in policies and practices, the points of decision are essentially similar: referral, intake, detention, transfer, adjudication, disposition, and release. Below we describe characteristics that can be found in many, if not all, juvenile justice systems. At each stage of the pipeline we give examples of youths' roles and responsibilities that are likely to unfold differently as they mature to adulthood.

Referral

Entrance into the pipeline begins with a referral to the juvenile justice system or a police arrest. Depending upon the state, a child may be too young or too old for the juvenile justice system. Children who are too young are most often diverted from the system or sent to the branch of juvenile court that has jurisdiction over neglected and abused children. Children who are too old are tried as adults. A juvenile may also be charged with an offense that results automatically in adult prosecution. If the juvenile is charged as an adult, most states allow for judges, after a hearing, to decide that the case should be transferred to juvenile court if the public interest requires it or if the juvenile can prove that he or she is amenable to treatment in the juvenile justice system.

Intake

If the child enters the juvenile justice system after being arrested, referred by a private petitioner (such as a school or next-door neighbor), or transferred from criminal court, there will be an intake decision. Should the case proceed or should the juvenile be diverted? If the latter, should it be an informal diversion without further involvement by the juvenile court or should the child be sent to a program—such as a community panel or teen court—and returned to juvenile court if he or she fails to obey a community-ordered disposition? Some cases are diverted to other systems, such as the mental health system. Some cases are dropped entirely, as intake officers decide that this particular combination of youth and offense does not belong in the juvenile justice system. Many factors thus enter into the decision to divert a case; the youth's age, prior history, the seriousness of the offense, and the youth's explanation or attitude will affect the intake decision.

Detention

If the intake officer (usually a juvenile probation officer) decides that the case should proceed to a hearing, the officer must decide whether the child should be sent home (with or without supervision) or should be detained, either in a maximum-security detention center or in a detention alternative. Juveniles and their parents will need to explain to an intake officer how pretrial supervision will occur, and they will have to convince the officer that the juvenile will appear for trial.

If the child is detained, there will be a court appearance within twenty-four to seventy-two hours. Most states call this first court appearance a detention hearing. Here a judge or referee will decide whether to continue the detention status. This is usually the first time that the child meets his or her attorney. Here the child must be able to discuss with counsel the circumstances of the arrest and out-of-court issues related to the detention decision (such as school attendance or the presence of an interested adult in the juvenile's life).

Transfer

Most persons under the age of eighteen who are tried as adults are done so because of statutory exclusion of their case from the juvenile justice system. As noted earlier, state law may exclude them because of their age—in New York, for example, a sixteen-year-old will be tried as an adult for any offense. Every state excludes some offenses from juvenile court jurisdiction if a child is of a certain age (for example, a state can decide that fifteen-year-olds who are charged with armed robbery will have their cases begin in adult criminal court). Some states permit prosecutors to file the juvenile's case directly in the adult system, where the juvenile may or may not have an opportunity to have the case transferred ("remanded" or "decertified") to juvenile court.

Every state also allows judges to transfer children of a certain age—usually fourteen, but in some instances, even younger—to criminal court if they are charged with an offense as serious as a felony.[4] In judicial transfer hearings, the state usually must prove that an offense occurred and that there is a prima facie case against the juvenile. States usually must prove that the juvenile is "not amenable to treatment" in the juvenile justice system in the time available to that system for treatment. Recently, state legislatures have made it easier for judges to transfer (or "waive" or "certify") juveniles to criminal court if it is "in the public interest" or if "public safety" requires it (Torbet et al. 1996). At transfer hearings, for example, it is important that the juvenile is able, for example, to discuss with counsel their recent placement history and its reason for failure. They should be able to understand the options available to them, such as proposed placements, counseling programs, or plea agreements.

Adjudication

If the child continues to be detained within the juvenile justice system, an adjudicatory hearing (comparable to the trial in criminal court) must be held within ten to thirty days. (While this is the general rule, in some states juveniles charged with high-profile crimes such as murder will have a longer time to wait until their trials.) Juveniles have no constitutional right to bail, although some states provide for bail by statute. If they are charged as adults, however, juveniles have the same right to bail as adults. Most states do not have speedy-trial requirements for conducting adjudicatory hearings if the juvenile is released before trial (Butts 1997).

At the adjudicatory hearing, the juvenile has a constitutional right to counsel. Many states provide a statutory right to counsel at all stages of the juvenile justice system, although the actual availability of counsel at the adjudicatory hearing or at other stages varies widely within states and between states (Feld 1988; Puritz 1995). Demands on juveniles at adjudicatory hearings are many: They will need to understand the nature of the charges against them and consult with counsel. They will have to weigh the costs and benefits of entering an admission (guilty plea). They should be able to help counsel identify potential witnesses, know whether an alibi or other defenses are available, and consult with counsel during cross-examination of state witnesses.

Disposition

If the juvenile admits to the offense or if the juvenile court finds by proof beyond a reasonable doubt that the child is found to have committed the offense, the court will proceed to disposition (comparable to the sentencing decision in adult court). Disposition must be done within a few weeks if the child is in detention. Juveniles are expected to assist counsel in presenting disposition options to the juvenile court. Assistance might include suggesting dispositions ("I think my grandmother will let me live with her," or "I'd like to be in a foster home") or helping the attorney and experts develop client-specific dispositions (which involve combining a number of services or programs to protect the public while meeting the needs of the child).

Juvenile dispositions historically have been aimed at providing "treatment, rehabilitation or supervision" in a way that best serves the needs of the juvenile. Such interventions have been thought to offer the best opportunity for public protection. In recent years, some legislatures have included incapacitation for public safety as a valid rationale for disposition. Others have required the juvenile court to balance public safety, accountability, and some version of treatment, or, as it is sometimes called, "competency development." Under any of the models, the juvenile court will have a range of discretion. In some states, such as Wisconsin or Pennsylvania, the juvenile court has wide latitude, from ordering that a child return home under supervision—that is, probation—to placing a child in maximum-security institutions, known as training schools, reform schools, or youth-development centers. In other states, such California or Massachusetts, that use a "youth authority" model, the court will either order probation or, if placement is warranted, transfer custody of the child to the youth authority, which will then determine the appropriate level of care.

Release

Most juvenile court dispositions are for indeterminate periods of time. However, they cannot be for a longer period of time than an adult would serve for a similar crime in the criminal justice system. In states in which the juvenile court controls all aspects of the juvenile's treatment, the court will usually review the juvenile's case every six to nine months. Sometimes the reviews are formal hearings and other times they are informal reviews of reports provided by probation officers or institutional staff. In states that have youth authorities, there will be administrative procedures to review the need for continued confinement.

Many juveniles in placement, particularly those with mental health needs or who are in inappropriate placements, end up being returned to juvenile court for a new disposition. Most often, those juveniles are placed in detention pending a new placement plan. These juveniles, too, are expected to assist counsel in preparing for a new disposition.

When juveniles are released from institutions, they are placed on "aftercare probation," which is analogous to parole. A juvenile who is on probation or aftercare probation status can have that status revoked, or "violated," for new offenses or for violating the terms of probation, such as associating with gang members, missing school, or missing curfew.

Relevance of Developmental Information to Decision Making

Although there are few decision points in the pipeline at which the developmental status of the juvenile is explicitly taken into account, at each decision juncture, information about the juvenile's stage of development should play an important role in the outcome of the decision. An understanding of child and adolescent development can be especially informative with respect to at least three fundamental questions:

- Is the juvenile sufficiently competent to participate in the adjudicative process?
- Is the juvenile sufficiently mature to be reasonably viewed as culpable for his or her behavior?
- Is the juvenile sufficiently malleable to be considered amenable to treatment?

A juvenile's developmental status is relevant with respect to the first question because a just and fair hearing requires the competent participation of the individual in his or her defense. As we noted earlier, at both the adjudication and transfer hearings certain competencies are expected to be in place, including those that potentially affect the juvenile's ability to understand the charges, assist counsel, and enter pleas. To the extent that these competencies are based on capabilities that develop over the course of childhood and adolescence, an accurate understanding of how and along what timetable these capabilities develop is crucial to deciding whether an individual possesses the skills necessary to participate in the process.

With respect to the second question, it is likely that the juvenile's appearance, behavior, and responses to questioning—all of which are influenced by the juvenile's stage of development—will influence the extent to which he or she is viewed by the various decision makers as culpable, which in turn will affect the nature of their decisions. At the detention, adjudication, or disposition hearings, for example, a juvenile who rightly or wrongly is perceived as being immature may be seen as less accountable for his or her actions and treated less harshly than one who comes across as more adultlike and is seen as having been responsible his behavior. Familiarity with the expected developmental timetables of phenomena such as self-control, moral reasoning, or judgment is therefore important for making determinations of culpability.

Finally, decision makers in the system often must make some assessment of the youngster's potential for change when making transfer or disposition decisions. Such determinations of developmental potential—what developmental psychologists call "plasticity"—are especially important at transfer hearings because a youngster who comes across as hardened and unlikely to profit from rehabilitation is more likely to be charged as an adult than one who is seen as malleable and amenable to intervention. Indeed, the transfer decision is one in which the juvenile's developmental status is supposed to be taken into account.

In order to make well-informed decisions about the treatment of juveniles who have entered the juvenile justice pipeline, therefore, policymakers, practitioners, and mental health professionals need to be familiar with the developmental changes that occur during childhood and adolescence in the capabilities and characteristics that are relevant to competence, culpability, and amenability. Legislators need this information in order to create age-related laws and statutes that are developmentally appropriate and scientifically reasonable: if, for example, we know that the ability to understand charges or enter pleas does not generally develop until a certain age, it makes little sense to draw age boundaries that would subject developmentally incompetent individuals to court proceedings that necessitate their participation in order to satisfy ordinary due process requirements.

Judges need this information in order to make wise and fair decisions in the courtroom: if we know that the capacity to regulate one's own behavior is unlikely to be present before a certain age, it is important that this information be taken into account at the time of sentencing or disposition. Mental health professionals need this information in order to perform accurate assessments and make appropriate treatment recommendations; individuals at different stages of development may need very different sorts of interventions. And attorneys need this information in order to practice law more effectively: prosecutors may consider a juvenile's developmental status in deciding when it is appropriate to charge an individual as an adult, and defense attorneys need to know how best to interact with clients who may not fully understand their situation. Understanding the nature of psychological development during adolescence, therefore, will likely improve policymaking, judicial decision making, forensic evaluation, and legal practice.

Understanding Adolescent Development: The Science of Developmental Psychology

Developmental psychology, broadly defined, concerns the scientific study of changes in physical, intellectual, emotional, and social development over the life cycle. Development is generally defined as change that is systematic, age-related, universal, predictable, enduring, and adaptive, in the sense that development usually involves some sort of lasting improvement in competencies and capabilities that occurs across the population around a given age. Development can be the result of biological forces (a process generally referred to as "maturation"), environmental forces (a process generally referred to as "learning"), or, as is usually the case, some combination of both.

Scholars of human development are mainly interested in the study of "normative" development (patterns of behavior, cognition, and emotion that are regular and predictable within the vast majority of the population of individuals of a given chronological age), but developmental psychologists are also interested in understanding normal individual differences in development (common variations within the range of what is considered normative for a given chronological age) as well as the causes and consequences of atypical or pathological development (development that departs significantly from accepted norms). The focus of the present discussion is on normative development because the logic of drawing distinctions between adolescents and adults either in policy or in practice must be based on age differences that characterize the population in general. Differences among individuals, whether normal or atypical, are often relevant to legal practice (such as a case in which a determination that an individual acted in a certain way because of mitigating circumstances or mental illness is relevant to his adjudication), but differences among individuals generally are not relevant to legal policy.

From the vantage point of developmental psychology, then, one asks whether the study of normative development indicates that there are scientific reasons to warrant the differential treatment of young people and adults within the legal system. Common sense and casual observation tell us that children and adolescents are different from adults in many respects, but without systematic information on those aspects of normative development that are relevant to the processing of juveniles within the justice system—in other words, those aspects of development that are relevant to issues of competence, culpability, and amenability—it is difficult to know whether any observed age differences between adolescents and adults are substantial and consistent enough to potentially shape either public policy or legal practice. This is not to say that developmental evidence should necessarily trump all other sorts of moral, legal, political, or practical arguments. However, what we know about normative development should be taken into account whenever changes in policy or practice are under consideration.

The majority of young people who commit serious offenses are teenagers. It is important, therefore, to consider how the nature of adolescent development in particular might inform policymaking and practice within the juvenile and criminal justice systems. Although delinquent and criminal acts are also committed by preadolescent children (those under twelve) and by young adults (those eighteen and older), the focus of the contemporary debate over how youthful offenders should be viewed and treated has been, and will continue to be, mainly on individuals between the ages of twelve and seventeen. Actuarially, although preadolescent crime generates tremendous media coverage, it remains an extremely rare occurrence with such low incidence that it would be an imprudent reason for sweeping revisions in our legal and social policies. And with regard to practical matters, although crime is relatively common among individuals between the ages of eighteen and twenty-four, the notion that offenders who are eighteen and older should be treated as adults under the law is so firmly in place that debates over how we treat late adolescent offenders are moot. Developmental psychology has potentially important things to say about the treatment of preadolescent children and young adults within the juvenile and criminal justice systems, but the present discussion, like the other chapters in this volume, focuses on the age range most under current political scrutiny.

The Nature of Adolescence in Contemporary Society

Today, most experts in developmental psychology agree that the period between twelve and seventeen occupies a crucial place in contemporary human development, for four interrelated reasons. Ironically, these very features of adolescence as a developmental period are simultaneously interesting to developmental psychologists and perplexing to policymakers and legal practitioners.

First, adolescence in modern society is an inherently transitional time during which there are rapid and dramatic changes in physical, intellectual, emotional, and social capabilities. We summarize some of the most important developments in each of these areas below; for now, suffice it to say that, other than infancy, there is probably no period of human development characterized by more rapid or pervasive transformations in individual competencies. As fascinating as this may be to scientists who study adolescence, the rapid, extensive, and transitional nature of development during this period makes it a poorly outlined, confusing, and moving target for policymakers.

Second, adolescence is a period of tremendous malleability, during which experiences in the family, peer group, school, and other settings have a great deal of influence over the course of development. Unlike infancy, during which much of development is dictated by biology and influenced only by extreme environmental variations, and unlike adulthood, by which time most intellectual, physical, emotional, and social development is more or less complete, adolescence is a period of tremendous plasticity in response to features of the environment. From the point of view of policymakers interested in intervention, the malleability of adolescence makes it a period of great opportunity.

A third, and in some ways paradoxical, point is that despite its malleability, adolescence is also an important formative period during which many developmental trajectories become firmly established and increasingly difficult to alter. While it would be an exaggeration to portray adolescence as a proverbial "last chance," it is not an overstatement to say that it is much easier to alter an individual's life course in adolescence than during adulthood. Events that occur in adolescence often cascade into adulthood, particularly in the realms of education and work, but also in the domains of mental and physical health, family formation, and interpersonal relationships. As a consequence, many adolescent experiences have a tremendous cumulative impact. The importance of this fact for the present discussion is that bad decisions or poorly formulated policies pertaining to juvenile offenders may have long-term consequences that are very hard to reverse. If incarceration during adolescence years makes it virtually impossible for an individual to enter the labor force after his release, for example, the long-term iatrogenic consequences of the punishment may be worse than the actions that precipitated the incarceration in the first place.

The final and most important point is that adolescence is a period of tremendous variability, both within and between individuals. Within any given individual, the developmental timetable of different aspects of maturation may vary markedly, such that a given teenager may be mature physically but immature emotionally, socially precocious but an intellectual late bloomer. In addition, development rarely follows a straight line during adolescence—periods of progress often alternate with periods of regression. This intraindividual variability makes it difficult, if not impossible, to make generalizations about an adolescent's "average" level of maturity on the basis of any one indicator alone. A tall, physically mature juvenile with an adult appearance may very well have the decision-making abilities of a child. An adolescent who carries himself like an adult today may seem like a child tomorrow. Variability between individuals is still more important; it is difficult to draw generalizations about the psychological capabilities of individuals who share the same chronological age.

Salient Features of Adolescent Development

Although there is considerable variability within the adolescent population, there are many normative developmental changes that occur during the adolescent years that distinguish adolescents from children or from adults. Our focus in this section is on those changes that are most relevant to the treatment of young people within the justice system. These changes occur across four distinct but interrelated domains: physical, intellectual, emotional, and social.

Physical Development

The physical changes of adolescence that take place during puberty transform the adolescent's appearance in dramatic ways. In addition to the spurt in height and weight—most individuals will grow more than a foot during puberty—there are also changes in facial and bodily features that transform the young person's appearance away from the characteristic appearance of the preadolescent child and toward the appearance of a fully grown adult. The most important of these changes include the appearance of secondary sex characteristics, increases in muscle mass and definition, and changes in the shape and characteristics of the face (a child's face is round, whereas adolescents and adults have a more angular face). For the most part, research on puberty and its impact on adolescent behavior indicates that the main way that puberty exerts its influence is through the changes it provokes in the adolescent's outward appearance and in the ways in which others respond to these changes. The popular notion that adolescents misbehave because they are under the influence of raging hormones has been firmly discredited. Misbehavior during adolescence is far more likely to be due to environmental than biological influence.

Although all physically healthy adolescents undergo this transformation in appearance, individuals differ in the timing and tempo of puberty: some may begin as early as nine, while others may not have even completed puberty by sixteen. As a consequence, youngsters who share the same chronological age may vary markedly in their outward physical appearance. More important, because there is no systematic relation between the timing of puberty and the timing of the normative intellectual, emotional, or social changes of adolescence, it is inappropriate to draw inferences about a juvenile's psychological or social maturity from his or her physical appearance. Because adults tend to do just this, early-maturing juveniles may be at a disadvantage in the courtroom, since their more adultlike appearance may suggest to adults a higher capacity for responsible decision making than is warranted. Recent research suggests that African-American youngsters are likely to go through puberty significantly earlier than other youths (Herman-Giddens et al. 1997), which would place them at special risk for the misattribution of psychological maturity on the basis of physical appearance.

For many years, psychologists believed that puberty is inherently stressful for young people. We now know that any difficulties associated with adjusting to puberty are minimized if adolescents know what changes to expect and have a positive attitude toward them. Although the immediate impact of puberty on the adolescent's self-image and mood may be very modest, however, the timing of physical maturation does affect social and emotional development in important ways. Early maturers are more likely to experience problem behaviors such as truancy, minor delinquency, and difficulties at school primarily because their appearance permits them to join up with older peer groups who may be involved in problem behavior.

Intellectual Development

A second salient aspect of adolescent development concerns the growth of intellectual abilities. Compared to children, adolescents think in ways that are more advanced, abstract, efficient, and effective. By the time they are seventeen, in fact, individuals' raw intellectual abilities are comparable to those of adults.

Three aspects of intellectual development during adolescence merit special comment here. First, although intellectual abilities toward the end of adolescence are not different from those observed during adulthood, intellectual functioning during the early years of adolescence (before age sixteen) may be more childlike than adultlike. Thus, in thinking about intellectual development during adolescence it is important to distinguish between older teenagers and their younger counterparts.

Second, although the raw intellectual abilities of older adolescents are comparable to those of adults, young people may have less experience to draw on than their elders. It is possible, therefore, that adolescents may have the necessary tools to engage in adultlike logical reasoning but lack the fund of information that is available to older individuals.

Finally, there is some evidence that adolescent judgment may differ from that of adults despite their comparable intellectual abilities. Decision making is influenced by a host of factors, of which intellectual ability is only one, and adolescents and adults may differ in many emotional and social respects that make teenagers' judgment less mature. Compared to adults, young people may be less future-oriented, less risk-averse, more impulsive, and more susceptible to the influence of others, and these differences may result in age differences in judgment. (See Chapter 12 in this volume.)

Emotional Development

In addition to being a time of biological and cognitive change, adolescence is also a time of emotional development and, in particular, a time of changes in the way individuals view themselves and in their capacity to function independently. As individuals mature intellectually and undergo the sorts of cognitive changes described earlier, their self-conceptions become more complicated and they become more able to see themselves in psychological terms. As a consequence, during adolescence individuals become better able to reflect on their own personality and explain their motivations and behaviors. Younger adolescents may have difficulties with such tasks.

Although conventional wisdom holds that adolescents have low self-esteem—that they are more insecure and self-critical than children or adults—most research says otherwise. Although teenagers' feelings about themselves may fluctuate, especially during early adolescence, their self-esteem remains fairly stable from about age thirteen on. If anything, self-esteem increases over the course of middle and late adolescence, and this is generally true for delinquent and nondelinquent youth. (There is no support for the notion that delinquent youths have low self-esteem.) Nor does it appear to be the case that teenagers typically go through the sort of "identity crisis" that was once thought to be the defining feature of emotional and social development during adolescence. Few individuals experience anything resembling an identity crisis much before the age of eighteen, and researchers now believe that most identity development takes place during the late teens and early twenties.

For most adolescents between the ages of twelve and seventeen, establishing a sense of autonomy, or independence, is probably a more important part of emotional development than is establishing a sense of identity. Of course, the process of establishing independence is not always smooth. Early adolescence, in particular, can be a difficult time for parents, teachers, and other adults in positions of authority because younger teenagers actually may be ambivalent about becoming independent, their braggadocio notwithstanding. As a consequence, many adolescents vacillate between childlike dependency and an exaggerated expression of cockiness and confidence. It is normative for young teenagers to express their emerging sense of autonomy by challenging or even opposing the influence of adults whose opinions they actually may value—almost as a way of proving to themselves that they are becoming independent. Along similar lines, at least some of the risk taking and precocious behavior that teenagers engage in is probably an attempt to convince themselves and others around them of their newfound status.

Social Development

Social development during adolescence is marked by an increase in the importance of peers, the emergence of interest in romantic relationships, and the onset of sexual activity. By far, the most important aspect of social development during adolescence to the present discussion concerns the growing importance of the peer group and changes in individuals' susceptibility to peer influence. Adolescents are, for the most part, pack animals, and their activities—whether harmless or worrisome—are typically pursued in group settings. (In some respects, gangs are simply adolescent peer groups whose identity and central activities revolve around antisocial behavior.) Understanding the importance of the peer group during adolescence is fundamental to understanding juvenile offending because the dynamic of the group may play a crucial role in drawing some youngsters into antisocial activities. As Zimring (1998) has pointed out, a much higher proportion of juvenile offending than adult offending occurs in groups.

Whatever importance the peer group has for the individual adolescent as a source of identity and companionship is exacerbated by an increase in susceptibility to peer pressure that occurs during the early adolescent years. Considerable research indicates that susceptibility to the influence of peers changes with development, increasing as youngsters move from childhood into early adolescence and declining as individuals move into late adolescence. In general, susceptibility to peer influence peaks between the ages of twelve and fifteen.

Concluding Notes on Adolescent Development and Juvenile Justice Policy

The transitional and variable nature of adolescence presents a problem for policymakers interested in drawing bright-line, age-defined boundaries between adolescence and adulthood. Indeed, as many historians of adolescence have pointed out, where we fix the boundary between adolescence and adulthood has depended to large measure on political expedience, practicality, and the social needs of the community. During wartime, for example, the very same individuals who had been labeled as too vulnerable to work in factories (mainly as a way of protecting adults' jobs from the threat of cheaper labor) are reborn as hardy enough to staff our armed forces, only to be magically transformed back into immature and incompetent youngsters when the war is over (Enright et al. 1987). Legal decision making is replete with similar instances of boundary-drawing by convenience; for example, adolescents have been found to lack the capacity to make certain medical decisions independently but to have the capacity to decide on their own whether to waive rights in police interrogations.

Historically, developmental psychology has had little or nothing to do with law-making; more often than not information about development is used post hoc to provide a rationale for laws that are erected to promote particular social aims. In general, we create age-related social policies from a utilitarian perspective in which regulating young people's behavior, rather than responding to their developmental needs or changing capabilities, is paramount. (See Chapter 4 in this volume.) Today, for example, there is a strong antidrug lobby that worries about exposing teenagers to the undocumented harms of experimenting with alcohol but there is no strong antidriving lobby that worries about exposing teenagers to the very well-documented risk of highway fatalities—so we set the drinking age at twenty-one and the driving age at sixteen even though we know that driving poses a much more serious threat to the health of teenagers than does beer.

The utilitarian perspective on the legislation of adolescence has resulted in a mix of social policies that may be practical or politically expedient but make no sense from the vantage point of developmental psychology. There is no scientific evidence on the nature of adolescent development, for example, that would support drawing different age boundaries between adolescence and adulthood for things such as driving (sixteen or younger in most states), attending R-rated movies (seventeen), voting (eighteen), or purchasing alcohol (twenty-one). Because it is likely that the same intellectual and emotional abilities that influence decision making behind the wheel also influence decision making in the voting booth, there is really no reason, from a developmental perspective, to have different ages for these two adult privileges. A developmental perspective on the treatment of juvenile offenders is important because without it it is all too easy to change our policies whenever the political winds blow in a different direction.

Debates over how society should respond to juvenile crime can be framed from many vantage points. Within a moral framework, one might very reasonably raise questions about fairness and justice and probe whether treating juvenile crime in a particular way strikes an acceptable balance between the rights of the offender, the interests of the offended, and the concerns of the community. Within a legal framework, the discussion might focus on the ways in which a given approach to juvenile crime fits within the broader compass of the law, and on the logic of the legal analysis that undergirds the proposed policy. From a political perspective, deciding how to respond to serious juvenile crime raises an entirely different set of concerns: what does the larger community want to accomplish, what sorts of social and legal policies might achieve these goals, which of the inevitable trade-offs are acceptable, and what are politicians willing to do to satisfy their constituents? And from a practical point of view, one might raise questions about the short- and long-term consequences of one set of policies versus another: does a given approach to juvenile crime strike a satisfactory balance among the community's legitimate but often conflicting interests in public safety, retribution, deterrence, and rehabilitation?

Regardless of the perspective one uses to examine the issues, however, the fact that juvenile crimes are committed by individuals who are not adults adds an element to the discussion that cannot be ignored. The moral, legal, political, and practical concerns that one brings to the table for a discussion of juvenile crime may be very different from those that are raised in a discussion of adult crime simply because of the developmental status of the offender. A fair punishment for an adult may seem unfair when applied to a child who may not have understood the consequences of his or her actions. The ways we interpret and apply laws may rightfully vary when the specific case at hand involves a defendant whose understanding of the law is limited by immaturity. The practical and political implications of treating offenders in a particular fashion may be very different when the offender is young than when he is an adult. Reasonable people may differ in their views of the extent to which, and the ways in which, an offender's age and developmental status should be taken into account in discussions of juvenile crime, but ignoring this factor entirely is like trying to ignore a very large elephant that has wandered into the room.

Works Cited

Ayers, W. 1997. *A kind and just parent: The children of juvenile court.* Boston: Beacon.

Bazemore, G. and M. S. Umbreit. 1994. *Balanced and restorative justice.* Washington, D.C.: Office of Juvenile Justice and Delinquency Prevention.

Bernard, T. J. 1992. *The cycle of juvenile justice.* New York: Oxford University Press.

Butts, J. 1997. Delays in Juvenile Court Processing of Delinquency Cases. Washington, D.C.: Office of Juvenile Justice and Delinquency Prevention.

Enright, R., V. Levy, D. Harris, and D. Lapsley. 1987. Do economic conditions influence how theorists view adolescents? *Journal of Youth and Adolescence* 16:541–560.

Feld, B. C. 1988. *In re Gault* revisited: A cross-state comparison of the right to counsel in juvenile court. *Crime and Delinquency* 34:393–424.

——. 1993. Criminalizing the American juvenile court. In *Crime and justice: an annual review of research,* edited by M. Tonry. Chicago: University of Chicago Press.

Fox, S. J. 1997. A contribution to the history of the American juvenile court to 1980. Paper presented at the National Council of Juvenile and Family Court Judges.

Grisso, T. 1996. Society's retributive response to juvenile violence: a developmental perspective. *Law and Human Behavior* 20:229–247.

Guarino-Ghezzi, S. and E. J. Loughran. 1996. *Balancing juvenile justice.* New Brunswick, N.J.: Transaction Publishers.

Herman-Giddens, M., E. Slora, R. Wasserman, C. Bourdony, M. Bhapkar, G. Koch, and C. Hasemeier. 1997. Secondary sexual characteristics and menses in young girls seen in office practice: A study from the Pediatric Research in Office Settings Network. *Pediatrics* 88:505–512.

Krisberg, B. and J. Austin. 1993. *Reinventing juvenile justice.* Thousand Oaks, Calif.: Sage Publications.

Mack, J. 1909. The juvenile court. *Harvard Law Review* 23:104–122.

Maloney, D., D. Romig, and T. Armstrong. 1988. Juvenile probation: The balanced approach. *Juvenile and Family Court Journal* 39:1–63.

Miller, J. G. 1991. *Last one over the wall: The Massachusetts experiment in closing reform schools.* Columbus: Ohio State University Press.

Platt, A. M. 1977. *The child savers: The invention of delinquency.* 2d ed. Chicago: University of Chicago Press.

Puritz, P. 1995. *A call for justice: An assessment of access to counsel and quality of representation in delinquency proceedings.* Chicago: American Bar Association.

Torbet, P., R. Gable, H. Hurst IV, I. Montgomery, L. Szymanski, and D. Thomas.

1996. *State responses to serious and violent juvenile crime.* Washington, D.C.: 1997. Office of Juvenile Justice and Delinquency Prevention.

Zimring, F. 1998. *The challenge of youth violence.* New York: Cambridge University Press.

Notes

1. In the years after *Gault,* the Supreme Court stopped short of making juveniles' rights identical to those of adults. While juveniles could only be adjudicated delinquent by proof beyond a reasonable doubt (*In re Winship,* 397 US 358 [1970]), and could avoid double jeopardy (*Breed v. Jones,* 421 US 519 [1975]), the Court held that they were not entitled to jury trials (*McKeiver v. Pennsylvania,* 403 US 528 [1971]), or to have strict Fourth Amendment procedures apply in schools (*T.L.O. v. New Jersey,* 469 US 325 [1985]). In addition, because children are always in some form of custody, the Supreme Court approved pretrial preventive detention for the child's own good (*Schall v. Martin,* 467 US 253 [1984]). Juveniles also have no constitutional right to bail or speedy trial.

2. Barry Feld suggests in this volume that the adultlike procedures introduced by the left worked in a spiral-like tandem with punitive measures introduced by the right to create an ungainly, harsh, and internally contradictory juvenile court.

3. While juvenile courts still operate more quickly than criminal courts, "delays in the juvenile justice system should be viewed from the perspective of an adolescent offender. Professional standards suggest that even the longest case should be processed within 90 days. Yet, a 90-day process means that a fourteen-year-old offender will wait the equivalent of a summer vacation for services or sanctions. In many of the Nation's juvenile courts, young offenders wait even longer" (Butts 1997).

4. The Institute of Judicial Administration-American Bar Association Standards would permit only judicial transfer for juveniles who are fifteen years old or older (IJA-ABA 1996).

CHAPTER TWO

Adolescent Development, Mental Disorders, and Decision Making of Delinquent Youths

ALAN E. KAZDIN

Adolescence has been characterized by competing and diametrically opposed views reflecting, on the one hand, a period filled with crisis, conflict, discontinuity, and turbulence (Hall 1904) or, on the other hand, gradual change, no necessary turmoil, and continuity with prior development (Hollingworth 1928). Together, these views capture the fact that there are different paths through adolescence and perhaps as well the possibility of considerable variability within a given adolescent over time. Adolescence is an extended period beginning with the onset of puberty (ten or eleven years of age) and ending with independence and entry into adulthood (eighteen to twenty-four years of age) (U.S. Congress 1991). This period encompasses several converging and interacting influences. These include physical maturation, sexuality, need for autonomy, increased influence of and sensitivity to peers, new or accentuated sources of stress (such as from relationships or concerns about physical attractiveness), and exposure to situations, circumstances, and opportunities that may place youths at risk for subsequent problems. The unique feature of adolescence, or at least early teenage years, is that multiple biological, psychological, and social systems are in transition. Even though there are continuities from childhood to adolescence, the transitions can lead to significant perturbations in adjustment and mark the emergence of new problems and trajectories that were not previously evident.

The multiple transitions and influences that converge are likely to influence the capacities of adolescents to make decisions—as, for example, in the context of engaging in illegal behaviors or participating in legal proceedings brought on by their delinquency. During "normal" adolescent development (when there are no major departures in mental and physical health and functioning) major questions are raised concerning the abilities of adolescents (as compared to adults) to consider options, weigh consequences, and make choices. Several of the chapters in this book examine developmental research for clues concerning what adolescents understand, how they think, and why they make the choices that they do.

An examination of decision-making abilities among delinquent youths must take into consideration the fact that, as a group, these youths have a much higher rate of mental disorders than do adolescents in general. These disorders can directly impair decision making insofar as symptoms of various mental disorders (such as impulsiveness and cognitive deficiencies) guide actions in everyday situations. Also, the disorders signal the presence of other personal, parent, family, and contextual influences that may foster poor decision making. In any case, research on decision making among adolescents in the community cannot be applied in a straightforward fashion to delinquent youths. Consideration must be given to the range of mental disorders delinquent youths may experience and how these can exert influence on decision making.

Psychiatric disorders and problem behaviors of adolescence raise special issues and serve as the focus of this chapter. During adolescence many emotional and behavioral problems (depression, eating problems, substance use, and vandalism) may emerge or greatly increase in severity. Many of these problems are somewhat normative in the sense that they characterize large segments of the population. The purpose of this chapter is to review major disorders and problem behaviors in adolescence, examine their prevalence in delinquent populations, and explore their relevance for understanding the potential effects of mental disorders on decision-making capacities. Research directions are also highlighted to elaborate the relation of multiple influences on the adolescent decision-making capacities.

Adolescent Mental Disorders
Overview of Disorders

Mental disorders refer to patterns of behavior that are associated with distress, impairment, or significantly increased risk of suffering, death, pain, disability, or an important loss of freedom (American Psychiatric Association 1994). The range of psychological dysfunctions or disorders that individuals can experience is enumerated in various diagnostic systems, such as the American Psychiatric Association's 1994 *Diagnostic and Statistical Manual of Mental Disorders* (DSM-IV) and the World Health Organization's 1992 *International Classification of Diseases* (ICD-10). The DSM-IV, the dominant system in use worldwide, recognizes several disorders that arise in infancy, childhood, or adolescence. These disorders are grouped into ten categories, which are listed in Table 2.1.

Table 2.1 omits many other disorders that are not considered to be

Table 2.1   Categories of major disorders first evident in infancy, childhood, or adolescence

1. Mental Retardation: Significant subaverage general intellectual functioning (an IQ of under seventy) associated with deficits or impairments in adaptive behavior (such as communication, self-care, social skills, and functional academic or work skills), with onset before the age of eighteen. Degrees of severity are distinguished based on intellectual impairment and adaptive functioning.

2. Learning Disorders: Achievement levels that are substantially below normative levels based on the individual's age, schooling, and level of intelligence. Separate disorders are distinguished based on the domain of dysfunction and include disorders of reading, mathematics, and written expression.

3. Motor Skills Disorder: Marked impairment in the development of motor coordination that interferes with academic achievement or activities of daily living and that cannot be traced to a general medical condition.

4. Communication Disorders: Impairment in the use of language that is substantially below normative levels of performance and interferes with daily functioning. Separate disorders are distinguished based on the domain of dysfunction and include disorders of expressive language, mixed receptive-expressive language, phonological (use of speech sounds) disorders, and stuttering.

5. Pervasive Developmental Disorders: Severe and pervasive impairment in several areas of development including social interactions, language and communication, and play (stereotyped behaviors, interests, and activities). These are usually evident in the first years of life. Separate disorders are distinguished based on the scope of impairment and time of onset and include autistic disorder, Rett's, Asperger's, and childhood disintegrative disorders.

6. Attention-Deficit Disorder and Disruptive-Behavior Disorders: Antisocial behavior or behaviors associated with inattention, impulsivity, overactivity, opposition and disobedience, provocativeness, and aggressiveness. Separate disorders are distinguished including attention-deficit/hyperactivity, conduct disorder, and oppositional-defiant disorder.

7. Feeding and Eating Disorders of Infancy or Early Childhood: Persistent eating and feeding disturbances such as eating nonnutritive substances (pica), repeated regurgitation and rechewing of food (rumination disorder), and persistent failure to eat adequately, resulting in significant failure to gain weight or weight loss (feeding disorder of infancy or early childhood).

8. Tic Disorders: Sudden, rapid, and recurrent stereotyped motor movement or vocalizations. Separate disorders are distinguished based on the scope of the tics (motor, vocal, or both) and their duration and include Tourette's, chronic motor or vocal disorder, and transient tic disorders.

9. Elimination Disorders: Dysfunction related to urination or defecation in which these functions appear to be uncontrolled and the client is beyond the age at which control has usually been established. Two disorders, enuresis and encopresis, are distinguished and require the absence of a medical condition in which these symptoms would emerge.

10. Other Disorders of Infancy, Childhood, or Adolescence: A collection of other disorders that are not covered elsewhere and include separation anxiety, selective mutism, reactive attachment, and stereotypic movement disorders.

Note: The disorders within each category have multiple inclusion and exclusion criteria related to the requisite symptoms, severity and duration, and patterns of onset. See the DSM-IV for more information, as details of the diagnoses are beyond the scope of this chapter.

unique to early development. Similar or identical diagnostic criteria are used across the life span. Major examples include anxiety, mood, eating, substance-related, sexual and gender identity, adjustment disorders, and schizophrenia. Table 2.2 highlights specific disorders within these categories to illustrate some of the more common diagnoses, particularly for children and adolescents. The information from both tables hints at some of the complexities. For example, a given type of disorder such as anxiety or eating may have different variations depending on the age of onset. Some disorders may emerge at any time, others primarily or exclusively emerge during childhood or adolescence.

To note that some disorders can emerge at any age does not necessarily mean that they are identical over the course of development. For example, depression can emerge during childhood, adolescence, or adulthood and can be diagnosed based on symptoms common across the life span. That there are common symptoms that point to the diagnosis does not mean that all symptoms, symptom patterns, or associated features are similar. For example, suicide attempt and completion are rarely evident in children, whether they are depressed or not; the rates increase significantly during adolescence and adulthood. Thus, a key feature of depression can change considerably over the life span.

For present purposes, it is useful to delineate four broad categories of disorders. First, externalizing disorders reflect problems that are directed toward the environment and others. They include oppositional, hyperactive, aggressive, and antisocial behaviors and are encompassed by the category Attention-Deficit Disorder and Disruptive-Behavior Disorders in Table 1. Among the externalizing disorders are conduct disorder (CD) and attention-deficit/hyperactivity disorder (ADHD). The symptoms of CD include many acts that are illegal, such as fighting, stealing, vandalizing, and fire-setting. ADHD is characterized by impulsivity and overactivity but overlaps with CD in other characteristics. For example, both CD and ADHD are associated with delinquency and criminal behavior, as discussed further below.

Second, internalizing disorders are directed toward inner experience and include anxiety, withdrawal, and depression. Depression and anxiety disorders, including posttraumatic stress disorder (PTSD), fall into the broad category of internalizing disorders. Internalizing disorders are usually not considered in discussions of how mental illness might influence delinquency or decision making. These disorders are disturbing to the individuals who experience them but are usually assumed to have little impact on the environment, particularly when compared to externalizing disorders. However, internalizing disorders can exert influence on both delinquency and decision making, as discussed later.

Third, substance-related disorders include impairment associated with

Table 2.2   Examples of disorders that may be evident at any point over the life span

Major Depressive Disorder: The appearance of depressed mood or loss of interest that lasts for at least two weeks and is associated with at least four additional symptoms: a change in appetite or weight; a change in sleep patterns and psychomotor activity; feelings of worthlessness or guilt; diminished energy; difficulty thinking, concentrating, or making decisions; and recurrent thoughts of death or suicidal ideation, plans, or attempts.

Posttraumatic Stress Disorder: Development of symptoms of anxiety after (a) exposure to an extreme traumatic event involving actual or threatened injury; (b) the witnessing of an event that involves death, injury, or a threat to the physical integrity of another person; or (c) learning about these events experienced by a family member. The events may include personal assault (sexual, physical, robbery), accidents, life-threatening illness, or a disaster (loss of one's home after a hurricane or tornado). Key symptoms involve intense fear, helplessness, horror, re-experience of the event (in thoughts or dreams), avoidance of stimuli associated with the event, numbing of general responsiveness (detachment, restricted affect), and persistent symptoms of increased arousal (difficulty falling or remaining asleep).

Eating Disorders: A disorder in which the individual does not maintain minimal normal body weight (he or she is less than 85 percent of normal body weight), is intensely afraid of gaining weight, and exhibits a significant disturbance in the perception of his or her body. Many methods of weight loss may be adopted such as self-induced vomiting, misuse of laxatives, and increased or excessive exercise.

Substance Abuse Disorder: A set of disorders (depending on the substance) characterized by a maladaptive use of the substance as evident in recurrent and significant adverse consequences (such as failure to fulfill role obligations at school, work, or home, and social and interpersonal problems). A period of twelve months is required of use and its associated consequences and continued use after untoward consequences (such as in role performance, legal problems, school expulsion) have occurred.

Schizophrenia: A disorder that lasts at least six months and includes two or more of these symptoms: delusions, hallucinations, disorganized speech, grossly disorganized catatonic behavior, and negative symptoms such as flat affect, poverty of speech (brief, empty replies), and inability to initiate or persist in goal-directed behavior. Significant dysfunction occurs in one or more areas of functioning including interpersonal relations, work, school, or self-care.

Adjustment Disorder: Development of clinically significant emotional or behavioral symptoms in response to an identifiable psychological stressor or stressors. The symptoms develop within three months of the event and are associated with marked distress or a reaction in excess of what might be expected within the context or culture. The symptoms of many other disorders may emerge (such as anxiety, depressed mood, or conduct problems).

Other Conditions: A set of problems are included that are not mental disorders but may serve as the focus of clinical attention. These may include relational problems (such as between parent and child, or between spouses), physical or sexual abuse of an adult or child, isolated antisocial behavior, bereavement, and many other problems that are not considered to be mental disorders but are brought to the attention of mental health professionals.

any of a variety of substances such as alcohol, illicit drugs, and tobacco (Weinberg et al. 1998). Problems associated with substance abuse can directly influence judgment and decision making. Indeed, a high proportion of criminal activity and behaviors that jeopardize physical health are carried out under the influence of alcohol and/or illicit substances.

Finally, learning and mental abilities (such as mental retardation and learning disorders from Table 1) include a range of problems related to intellectual and academic functioning. These problems are probably underestimated both in terms of prevalence and impact on behavior among delinquent youths because of the more salient externalizing problems. However, intelligence and mental retardation are likely to be of major significance in the decision-making process because mental abilities (that is, intelligence as measured by standardized tests) that predict academic functioning are also related to cognitive problem-solving strategies (such as selection of options and the consideration of consequences). In turn, these latter strategies relate to decision making in everyday life and to prosocial behavior.

The four categories omit several other disorders, including many of the more serious forms of psychopathology (such as schizophrenia and autism) that have a pervasive impact on the individual. These latter disorders are not emphasized here because they have relatively low base rates in the general population and probably in delinquent youths as well. The strong connection between mental disorders and delinquency are primarily found in the four categories delineated above, although, as noted later, the full range of disorders cannot be neglected.

Prevalence

There have been no large-scale national studies of adolescents that provide estimates of the disorders using current diagnostic criteria and rigorous assessment methods. Even so, several studies in the United States, Puerto Rico, Canada, and New Zealand have shown rather consistent results. Studies typically include children and adolescents (between the ages of four and eighteen) and indicate that between 17 and 22 percent suffer significant developmental, emotional, or behavioral problems (Costello 1989; Institute of Medicine 1989; U.S. Congress 1991; Zill and Schoenborn 1990). There are approximately sixty-eight million children and adolescents in the United States (U.S. Bureau of Census 1993). Assuming a prevalence rate of 20 percent, approximately thirteen and a half million of these youths have or have experienced significant impairment due to an emotional or behavioral problem. Focusing only on the thirty-five million adolescents (ages ten to nineteen), roughly seven million have significant impairment (Hollmann 1993). The estimates with adolescents are likely to be higher because rates of disorder among adolescents tend to be higher than the rates among children when these periods are distinguished (Zill and Schoenborn 1990).

Table 2.3 provides estimates of the prevalence of disorders among ado-

Table 2.3   Estimates in percent of prevalence of disorders among community and delinquent samples of adolescents

Mental Disorder	Community Samples (%)	Delinquent Samples (%)
Conduct disorder	2–10	41–90
Attention deficit disorders	2–10	19–46
Substance abuse and dependence	2–5	25–50
Mental retardation	1–3	7–15
Learning and academic disabilities	2–10	17–53
Mood disorders	2–8	19–78
Anxiety disorders	3–13	6–41
Posttraumatic stress disorder	1–3	32
Psychoses and autism	0.2–2	1–6
Any disorder present	18–22	80

Note: The data in the table are intended to present gross estimates of prevalence. Estimates are provided as ranges, except in instances where estimates were obtained from individual rather than multiple sources. For the majority of studies from which the delinquency data were drawn, standard diagnostic interviews were not used and samples were small and restricted to one location. The community-based data often surmounted these limitations with epidemiologically based samples and diagnostic interviews. Among the studies of delinquent and community youths, several factors that could readily influence prevalence rates—including the diagnostic criteria, the informant used, age, ethnicity, geographical local of the sample, and the period in which a diagnosis was present (past twelve months, current)—varied widely. Several sources were used to comprise this table, including reviews and individual investigations of prevalence (APA 1994; Cuffe et al. 1998; King et al. 1997; McGee et al. 1990, 1992; Otto et al. 1992; Steiner, Garcia, and Matthews 1997; Teplin, Abram, and McClelland 1998; U.S. Congress 1991; Weinberg et al. 1998; Zoccolillo 1993).

lescents based on studies derived from the prepubescent through the teenage years. The first column (community samples) provides estimates based on multiple studies with quite different samples, methods, and time frames. Youths included in the community samples are not clinically referred or adjudicated. Thus, the rates reflect approximations of the population at large.

Within a given category, more distinctions can be made. Prevalence rates can vary substantially for subtypes of the problem—for example, substance abuse among adolescents varies widely depending on the substance (less than 1 percent for hard drugs, 1 to 3 percent for marijuana, and 1 to 15 percent for alcohol) (Weinberg et al. 1998). The prevalence rates and patterns of dysfunction for psychiatric disorders are influenced by a variety of factors including, but by no means limited to, gender, poverty, race and ethnicity, parent education and marital status, and family constellation.

Several studies have estimated prevalence rates among delinquent youths in the juvenile justice system (Otto et al. 1992). The rates are highly variable among the studies. Table 2.3 provides the ranges to capture the findings for most of the studies, with the qualifications noted in the table. The prevalence estimates for delinquent youths require particular caution. Typically, diagnostic interviews have not been used with the delinquent samples, although this is considered to be the standard method for systematically evaluating the presence of mental disorders. A noteworthy exception was a comprehensive study of over twelve hundred delinquents (ages ten to seventeen) from a Cook County, Illinois juvenile detention facility (Teplin, Abram, and McClelland 1998). Using a standardized diagnostic interview (Diagnostic Interview Schedule for Children), the prevalence rates fell within the ranges provided in Table 2.3. Perhaps most significantly, 79.7 percent of the delinquent youths were found to have at least one mental disorder. This staggering figure could easily be an underestimate because several disorders (learning and academic disabilities, psychoses and autism) were not included. Even so, with the most conservative estimates, the prevalence rate of mental disorder is much higher—approximately four times higher—among delinquent youths than among community samples.

Important Considerations
Changes during Adolescence   The shift from childhood to adolescence, as marked by pre- and postpuberty, is associated with a number of changes in symptoms and disorders. First, several disorders increase markedly after the onset of puberty. Among these are mood disorders, eating disorders (anorexia nervosa), conduct disorder, substance abuse, and schizophrenia. For many of these disorders, though one can identify precursors in childhood the rates sharply increase during adolescence.

Second, a number of sex differences emerge or become more pronounced during adolescence. For example, rates of depression are low and similar in prepubescent boys and girls (Hammen and Rudolf 1996). With the onset of puberty, prevalence of depression is much higher for females than for males. Similarly, eating disorders, not very prevalent in preadolescence, emerge mostly after puberty and are much more common among females than males.

Third, characteristics of the disorder or its constituent symptoms may change. As mentioned previously, suicide attempt and completion, associated with depression, illustrates this change. Attempt and completion are quite rare before puberty. The rates increase with the onset of puberty, reaching a peak in the years between fifteen and nineteen (Cohen, Spirito, and Brown 1996). Attempted suicide is more common among females than males, although completion of suicide is more common among males than females. As another example, anxiety disorders change over the course of development. Animal phobias and separation anxiety are much more likely to emerge in young children than in adolescence. On the other hand, social phobias and agoraphobia are more likely to emerge in adolescents and are rare prior to puberty (Rutter 1990).

Age of onset of a disorder may have significant implications regarding etiological and risk factors, prevalence, and long-term outcome. Thus, the "same" disorder may be quite different depending on whether it emerges in early childhood or adolescence. Although this may apply to several different disorders (Rutter 1990), age of onset has been considered most frequently in the context of conduct disorder (Moffitt 1993; Patterson, DeBaryshe, and Ramsey 1989). CD can emerge in childhood or adolescence, but the prevalence rates are greater during adolescence. Also, sex differences in prevalence are evident. In childhood, CD is much more prevalent in boys than girls; during adolescence, the proportions are more evenly distributed. During adolescence, antisocial activity includes higher rates of vandalism and breaking into property than during childhood. Also, during adolescence these activities are likely to be completed in groups rather than by the individual acting alone. The peer group assumes much greater significance as a risk factor and direct influence on adolescent-onset than on child-onset conduct disorder. Child-onset CD is considered to have a much worse long-term prognosis (that is, it's more likely to be associated with later criminal activity) than adolescent onset conduct disorder, but further evidence is needed on this point. The influence of age of onset is not restricted to disruptive behavior disorders. For example, early onset of depression is associated with a more protracted and severe course of the disorder (Hammen and Rudolf 1996).

The above findings suggest that disorders, their characteristics, and presumably their impact can vary according to when the disorder emerges during a person's development. Unfortunately, changes in disorders over the course of childhood and adolescence are not well charted. The changes may have implications for decision making insofar as they influence problem solving, choices, and cognitive strategies quite differently depending on the onset of the disorder.

Comorbidity

Highlighting disorders and their prevalence rates does not fully represent the scope of impairment that adolescents experience. Many individuals meet criteria for two or more diagnoses, a phenomenon referred to as co-morbidity (Caron and Rutter 1991; Clark, Watson, and Reynolds 1995). Some combinations of disorders are more likely than others; a few disorders that are often seen together are ADHD and CD, CD and substance abuse disorder, anxiety disorder and depression, autism and mental retardation, and Tourette's syndrome and ADHD. Among community samples, comorbidity rates are relatively high. For example, among people ten to twenty years old, approximately half of the individuals with a substance abuse disorder also meet criteria for another disorder, including primarily disruptive behavior disorders (Cohen et al. 1993; Greenbaum, Foster-Johnson, and Petrila 1996). Among clinically referred and delinquent samples, the rates of comorbidity are much higher; among adolescents with a diagnosis of substance abuse, most (more than 70 percent) meet criteria for other disorders (Milin et al. 1991; Weinberg et al. 1998).

Comorbidity is significant in evaluating mental health and decision making. Many individuals may suffer significant impairment in multiple domains and areas of functioning. Without systematic evaluation, it is easy to ignore the secondary and tertiary diagnoses that are overshadowed by the delinquent acts that led to adjudication. Yet the comorbid conditions can have significant implications for the long-term functioning of the individual as well as responsiveness to interventions (Kazdin 1995; Rutter et al. 1994).

Comorbidity makes relevant for delinquency the entire spectrum of diagnoses. Although CD and ADHD are directly related to delinquent acts, other diagnoses, including internalizing disorders such as depression and anxiety, are relevant as well. It is likely that youths with these other diagnoses may have a comorbid externalizing or substance abuse disorder. For example, in community-based samples, among adolescents identified as depressed, 12 to 60 percent met criteria for disruptive behavior disorders (Anderson et al. 1987; Cohen et al. 1993; Lewinsohn et al. 1993). In delinquent samples, high rates of depression may be evident when systematically evaluated (Messier and Ward 1998). The implications of disorders such as depression on decision making are discussed later in this chapter.

Diagnostic Criteria and Assessment Methods

The prevalence rates are rather tentative. First, diagnostic systems have changed considerably over the past two decades. The disorders that arise in infancy, childhood, and adolescence have been modified in the revisions of the DSM. These changes include the emergence and elimination of various diagnostic categories as well as changes in the criteria for specific diagnoses, such as CD and ADHD. The different prevalence studies highlighted previously draw on these different systems depending on when they were completed. Nonetheless, the consistencies among the different studies (approximately 20 percent as the estimate of prevalence in community samples) are remarkable.

Second, different methods of assessment are used to assess prevalence and can lead to quite different results. Typically, diagnostic interviews are conducted with parents and children or adolescents. However, sometimes symptom checklists are used, and only parents are queried about the presence of the child's or adolescent's symptoms. Changes in the methods of assessing disorders lead to changes in the prevalence rates and in who is identified as meeting criteria for a disorder (Boyle et al. 1996; Kazdin 1989; Offord et al. 1996). There is no "gold standard" or means of unequivocally deciding if a disorder is present. Considerable differences exist among persons who provide the data regarding the presence and severity of the symptoms when different informants are consulted—such as adolescents, parents, teachers, and clinicians.

Third, it is likely that the prevalence rates significantly underestimate the range of mental disorders and impairment. Prevalence rates are determined by identifying youths who meet diagnostic criteria for a disorder. The criteria or threshold for a disorder in most cases has not been carefully established. Individuals who are subsyndromal, who fall below or fail to meet the diagnostic criteria, may still show significant impairment and untoward long-term prognoses. For example, adolescents who come close to, but who do not meet, criteria for major depression are much more likely to meet criteria for another disorder, to develop another disorder later, and to show impairment in psychosocial functioning than individuals with few or no depressive symptoms (Gotlib, Lewinsohn, and Seeley 1995). Similarly, CD seems to be represented better as a continuum or set of continua based on the number and severity of symptoms and the degree of impairment (Boyle et al. 1996; Offord et al. 1992). Here too, individuals who miss the cutoff criteria are likely to show impairment and poor long-term prognoses, although to a lesser extent as a function of the degree of dysfunction. Overall, these results convey that prevalence rates, when based on meeting criteria for diagnoses, may be conservative. Those identified with a disorder are likely to be impaired, but many youths who do not meet the criteria are also impaired and may have a poor long-term prognosis. The high prevalence rate of mental disorders among adolescents, and particularly those youths that are delinquent, clearly underestimates the scope of the problem.

Limitations of Current Research

The diagnostic and assessment issues noted previously are core issues that reflect challenges for work on the prevalence of disorders in general. It is worth commenting on issues that apply to studies of the prevalence of disorders among delinquent youths. In general, the available research on disorders among delinquent youths is sparse. Among existing studies, there are common weaknesses that greatly limit the knowledge base.

First, many of the studies include local samples—groups restricted to a given facility. This means that sampling issues can very much influence the rates of disorder. Also, local practices and resources related to arrest and adjudication and unique or special characteristics of the communities from which the samples are drawn (such as socio-occupational level or ethnic composition) may influence the rates and patterns of disorders. Large-scale studies are needed and samples need to be drawn from multiple sites, not merely to overcome the limits of local samples but also to understand factors that influence disorder and prevalence rates.

Second, standardized diagnostic assessment methods need to be used more frequently in delineating disorders among delinquent samples. Measures are available that are commonly used for prevalence studies in community and clinic samples. The measures are far from flawless, but they have been developed over several years and can provide prevalence estimates of lifetime and current rates of disorder. Some studies of delinquent samples have used standardized diagnostic interviews (Teplin, Abram, and McClelland 1998) and serve as a model for subsequent work.

Third, understanding the relation of mental disorders and delinquency will require studies of community samples as well as delinquent samples. Studying incarcerated or adjudicated samples is critically important because there is an urgent need to identify these disorders and understand their role in how the juveniles entered the systems and how they can be served once they are there. There is a great deal of delinquent behavior in the community that is not detected through formal adjudication or through participation of youths in the juvenile justice system. It is likely that the rate of mental illness among incarcerated samples (79.7 percent in the Teplin, Abram, and McClelland 1998 study) is greater than in community samples of youths that engage in delinquent behavior. Also, to understand the role of mental illness in delinquent acts, impairment, decision making, and entry into the juvenile justice system will require examining the relation of delinquency and mental illness among community samples. Mental illness may play a significant role in who is arrested, in light of the impairment with which clinical dysfunction is often associated. In general, studies of delinquent samples ought to draw on epidemiological methods of community studies of prevalence of disorders in terms of sampling and assessment. Studies of community samples typically draw on these methods but rarely include measures of delinquency. Increase in community studies with greater attention to delinquency would be extremely important when describing the relations of mental illness, delinquent behavior, adjudication, and decision making.

Problem and At-Risk Behaviors

Adolescence is associated with an increase in a number of activities that are referred to as problem or at-risk behaviors (DiClemente, Hansen, and Ponton 1996; Ketterlinus and Lamb 1994; U.S. Congress 1991). Problem behaviors overlap with psychiatric disorders and delinquency such as stealing and vandalism, but also include behaviors that may not be encompassed by either designation, such as unprotected sex or use (rather than abuse) of certain substances. The behaviors are delineated because they place the individual at risk for a variety of adverse psychological, social, and health outcomes. For example, alcohol use is associated with the three most frequent forms of mortality among adolescents: automobile accidents, homicides, and suicide (Windle, Shope, and Bukstein 1996); approximately 90 percent of automobile accidents among adolescents involve the use of alcohol.

The prevalence rates of problem behaviors are relatively high. In a summary of survey studies, Dryfoos (1990) estimated that among high school seniors:

- 12 percent engage in heavy cigarette smoking (more than half a pack per day);
- 15 percent in heavy drinking (more than five drinks in a row, three or more times in the past two weeks);
- 5 percent in regular use of marijuana (more than twenty times within the past thirty days); and
- 3 percent in frequent use of cocaine (more than three times within the past month).

Estimates of substance abuse vary because of the age ranges sampled, the range of substances included (such as inhalants), the assessment methods (self-report versus medical emergency visits), and the impact of many moderators (social class, ethnicity, and neighborhood). Even so, it is clear that substance use is relatively common; the points at which it can be referred to as abuse are not clear.

Even the rates of use are somewhat alarming. For example, in a recent survey, 50.8 percent of twelfth-grade students reported some alcohol use in the thirty days prior to the survey; 31.3 percent reported being drunk at least once; and 4.9 percent reported using marijuana daily or almost daily (Johnston 1996). Moreover, current data suggest that rates of substance use are increasing, a trend that began in the early 1990s (Weinberg et al. 1998). The direct and immediate health consequences and correlates of substance use—increased risk of death from overdose, injury and death while driving a vehicle, and sexually transmitted disease through unprotected sex—are serious. Adolescents who abuse the substances are at risk for subsequent school failure, poor occupational adjustment, crime, and mental disorders (Newcomb and Bentler 1988; U.S. Congress 1991).

Substance abuse is merely one example of at-risk behavior. A number of other examples have been identified including unprotected sexual activity and its risk for teen pregnancy or sexually transmitted diseases, including human immunodeficiency virus (HIV); delinquent, antisocial, and violent behavior; dropping out of school; and running away from home (DiClemente, Hansen, and Ponton 1996; Dryfoos 1990). Such behaviors are often associated with concurrent mental and physical health problems during adolescence as well as with subsequent problems in adulthood. The short- and long-term impact of problem behaviors on the adolescent are influenced by a variety of factors including severity and chronicity of the behavior or condition and a host of contextual factors such as family constellation and support system. For example, the use of illicit drugs per se may not expose a particular individual to adverse consequences. The specific substance and the level of use influence the risk for adverse outcomes (Newcomb and Bentler 1989).

Multiple problem behaviors often go together (Ketterlinus and Lamb 1994). This does not mean that drug abuse, delinquent behavior, and academic dysfunction invariably co-occur. Yet such behaviors often come in "packages." A sample of youths identified with one of the behaviors (such as early sexual activity) is likely to have higher rates of other behaviors (substance use and abuse, delinquent acts) than a comparison sample similar in age and sex. In an effort to estimate prevalence of high-risk behaviors, Dryfoos (1990) delineated groups based on the number and seriousness of at-risk behaviors and estimated rates of adolescents with these problems in the United States: 10 percent were at very high risk (multiple and serious problem behaviors); 15 percent were at high risk (two to three problem behaviors); and 25 percent were at moderate risk (one problem behavior). The cumulative percentage of youths characterized as high-to-moderate risk was 50 percent, which given the current census would translate to approximately seventeen million adolescents in the United States.

At-Risk Conditions and Contexts

Adolescents are dependent on living circumstances of their parents and families and hence are vulnerable to the impact of conditions well beyond their control. Many of these conditions have obvious bearing on the emergence of psychiatric disorders, problem behaviors, and delinquency. Research on the characteristics of the family illustrates the relation between conditions in which the child lives and mental disorders and delinquency. For example, harsh child-rearing practices, inconsistent (lax and harsh) practices, lack of parental supervision, limited involvement with the child, marital conflict, and parental criminal behavior place the child at risk for problem behaviors and delinquency (Kazdin 1995; Loeber 1990; Resnick et al. 1997; U.S. Congress 1991). Any one of these characteristics bears a relation to subsequent delinquency, but multiple characteristics in combination are particularly significant in increasing risk. On the more positive side, adolescents are less likely to abuse substances and to engage in sexual activity when they have a close relationship with and receive emotional support and acceptance from their parents (Fisher and Feldman 1998; Turner et al. 1993), when parents are authoritative (demanding and responsive) in their child-rearing (Baumrind 1991), and when they come from two-parent, rather than single-parent, families (Flewelling and Bauman 1990).

The relations of these family factors and delinquency are not always simple. For example, child victimization, including physical abuse, sexual abuse, and neglect, places children at risk for delinquency in adolescence (Widom 1994). Yet most individuals who experience some form of victimization do not become delinquent. The likelihood of subsequent delinquency depends on a variety of factors including the type, severity, and duration of victimization; sex of the child; and adaptive relations the child has with other (nonabusing) adults.

The peer group is another influence. Longitudinal studies have shown that association with deviant peers in early adolescence is strongly predictive of later criminal activity (Elliott, Huizinga, and Menard 1988; Patterson and Dishion 1985). A high proportion of delinquent behavior is often carried out with the peer group (Emler, Reicher, and Ross 1987). There are bidirectional influences of problem behavior of individuals and interactions with deviant peers. Individuals at risk for problem behaviors seek out deviant peers, and over time peer groups increase further deviance

(Thornberry and Krohn 1997). Association with deviant peers is related to disruption in parent-child interaction, poor bonding with the family, and rejection of normative peers early in life (Elliott, Huizinga, and Menard 1988; Patterson 1993).

Apart from interpersonal relations with the family and peers, living conditions to which the adolescent is exposed are relevant as well (Luthar in press). It has been known for some time that the neighborhood contributes to delinquency. Living in impoverished high-delinquency neighborhoods increases the likelihood of subsequent delinquent behavior (Simcha-Fagan and Schwartz 1986). More recently, attention has been accorded homelessness as a living condition among adolescents in light of the multiple physical and mental health consequences with which it is associated (Rotheram-Borus et al. 1996). Salient physical health consequences include chronic diseases, ailments resulting from exposure to the environment, poor nutrition and hygiene, and attendant conditions and diseases. Adverse mental health consequences associated with homelessness include elevated rates of emotional and behavioral problems (such as depression, anxiety, and substance abuse) and academic and developmental dysfunction (such as poor school attendance or dropping out of school) (Rafferty and Shinn 1991; U.S. Congress 1991). The rate of diagnosable psychiatric disorders has been estimated to be three times greater among homeless adolescents than among nonhomeless controls.

These examples are included to convey that contextual influences are critical to understanding and predicting externalizing and problem behaviors. They do not, of course, exhaust the range of influences that can be identified. Moreover, influences combine with individual difference variables of the adolescent and exert varying degrees of influence as a function of the outcome in question, whether it be violence, use of substances, or teen pregnancy (Resnick et al. 1997). The key point to underscore is that as a class of influences, interpersonal and environmental contexts in which adolescents function are relevant to behavioral paths and choices among adolescents, as discussed further below.

Implications for Decision Making and Choices by Adolescents
Mental Disorders and Problem Behaviors

Psychiatric disorders and problem behaviors relate directly to delinquent acts because of their core features or strong connection to these acts. For example, ADHD evident in childhood predicts delinquency and criminal behavior in adolescence (Farrington, Loeber, and Van Kammen 1990). Youths who engage in antisocial behavior and also meet criteria for

ADHD are more likely to show earlier onset of, and more enduring, delinquent behavior (Lahey and Loeber 1997).

Substance use and abuse disorders are related to delinquency, apart from the illegality of using many of the substances. Many delinquent acts are committed while, or immediately after, the adolescent has been consuming illicit substances. For example, in one survey 9 percent of institutionalized adolescent offenders (under eighteen years old) reported having committed the offense leading to institutionalization while under the influence of alcohol (U.S. Department of Justice 1988). In the same survey, 15.7 percent of the offenders reported having committed the offense while under the influence of an illicit drug, and 23 percent of the offenders used both alcohol and an illicit substance immediately before committing the offense. These comments do not suggest that substance abuse plays a causal role in delinquent acts. At the same time, substance abuse clearly fosters, promotes, and increases the likelihood of such acts by reducing inhibition or elevating bravado. If the individual is already predisposed to impulsive acts, perhaps due to the presence of a psychiatric disorder such as ADHD, then substance use may greatly increase the likelihood of delinquent behavior.

The extent to which disorders other than those associated with externalizing behavior and substance use increases the likelihood of delinquent behavior is unclear. In adults, the presence of psychiatric disorder, specifically when related to substance abuse, is associated with increased risk for violent behavior (Monahan 1997; Mulvey 1994). There has been little parallel work with adolescents that permits the evaluation of the relation of psychiatric disorder to delinquency with appropriate samples (community rather than adjudicated or incarcerated youths) and controls (controlling for sociodemographic characteristics with which psychiatric disorder and delinquency might be related).

Exposure to trauma (acute or chronic) might readily influence decision-making capacities. Posttraumatic stress disorder (PTSD) can result from exposure to a variety of events including natural disasters (such as earthquakes and hurricanes), death, injury, and violence. Many of these are chance events and are not necessarily associated with delinquent populations. Yet delinquent youths have relatively high (32 percent) rates of PTSD (Steiner, Garcia, and Matthews 1997). This results from the increased likelihood of exposure to physical abuse, sexual abuse, and domestic violence when compared to exposure to these experiences in nondelinquent samples. Exposure to trauma can lead to an increase in aggressive and antisocial behavior and ADHD (Fletcher 1996).

The precise role of mental disorders in the decision making of delinquent youths is insufficiently studied to permit firm conclusions. Even so, in many instances the core symptoms of disorders would be very likely to impair decision making. The most obvious example is the presence of ADHD. A central feature of this disorder is impulsiveness, as reflected in difficulty in resisting immediate temptations, inhibiting delay of gratification, or stopping an ongoing behavior (Barkley 1996). However, impulsiveness with or without ADHD can be increased by the presence of other disorders such as PTSD. Impulsiveness associated with or resulting from mental disorder could readily influence delinquent behavior and preempt deliberation, rational decision making, and selecting among alternative courses of action.

Associated Features

Features associated with mental disorders (as opposed to features that are the core or defining symptoms) are likely to be more relevant to decision making among adolescents. Core and associated features are important to delineate because even a careful diagnostic assessment of youths would not necessarily reveal key components that affect decision making. Individuals who meet criteria for the same diagnosis might differ considerably on the associated features and hence on many of the key factors that influence decision making. Consider some of the associated features of various disorders that are likely to have an impact on decision making.

Cognitive Processes and Mental Abilities

Externalizing symptoms and problem behavior are associated with a variety of cognitive processes, including beliefs, attributions, and problem-solving strategies. For example, adolescents with disruptive behavior disorders tend to be impulsive in their approach to situations, deficient in interpersonal problem-solving skills (such as generating solutions to problems, considering consequences of their actions, and accurately perceiving the cues of others), tend to attribute hostile intent to others, and believe that aggressive acts are likely to be associated with good outcomes such as tangible rewards, peer approval, and positive feelings (Dodge and Schwartz 1997; Shirk 1988). Cognitive processes can directly mediate interpersonal action and the completion of delinquent acts. For example, in situations in which the social cues and intentions of others are ambiguous, attribution of hostile intent to others is directly related to acts of aggression (Crick and Dodge 1994). Clearly, the cognitive processes associated with disruptive behavior disorders can directly influence aggression and violence. There are also more indirect effects that cognitive processes seem to play. Adolescents' beliefs about their strategies of coping with situations are also important. Those who believe that their strategies are unlikely to be effective are much more likely to engage in problem behavior (Allen, Leadbeater, and Aber 1994).

Internalizing disorders are also associated with deficiencies and distortions of cognitive processes, and these are likely to influence decision making. The most well-studied internalizing disorder in this regard is depression. Considerable research with children and adults, but to a lesser extent adolescents, has shown that depressed individuals, whether from clinic or community samples, tend to have negative cognitions about themselves, the world, and the future (Hammen and Rudolf 1996). Negative outcomes of events are more likely to be attributed to their actions. Depressed youths are also likely to have poor self-esteem.

In general, a great deal of evidence has conveyed that depression is associated with deficits and distortions in information processing, beliefs about causality of one's actions, and negative self-attributions. The precise implications for adolescent decision making is a matter of surmise. However, cognitive distortions among depressed adolescents are related to low levels of self- and peer-rated social competence and to greater dependence on others (Buhrmester 1990; Marton et al. 1993). Moreover, in children at least, depression is related to teacher and peer ratings of unpopularity and rejection (Hammen and Rudolf 1996). Some evidence suggests that depressed children may select more hostile problem-solving strategies to interpersonal problems (Rudolf, Hammen, and Burge 1994).

In general, cognitive processes associated with depression may not be of the impulsive type that characterizes those of externalizing disorders. Nevertheless, these processes reflect distortions of information-processing and problem-solving strategies. The fact that poor peer relations and dependency on peers are associated with depression and maladaptive cognitions may make such youths more vulnerable to peer influences. It is precisely those peer influences that play such a significant role in adolescent behavior. Decision making among youths with maladaptive cognitions is subject to a number of influences that could readily promote maladaptive and delinquent behavior and interfere with selection of rational strategies in the context of other decision-making opportunities.

PTSD disorder was mentioned previously because the symptoms resulting from exposure to trauma can increase impulsiveness as well as aggressive and antisocial behavior. A variety of other consequences of exposure to trauma include difficulty in concentrating, emotional detachment, and pessimism about the future (Fletcher 1996). Many of the cognitions that emerge are similar to those that are evident in depression. Other cognitions that emerge may be more directly related to choices and decision making in ways that promote delinquent behavior. For example, youths that have been sexually abused tend to believe that the world is a dangerous place, that their own behavior is not likely to have an impact, and that adults are not trustworthy (Wolfe et al. 1989, 1991). Some evidence also suggests that processes such as lowered personal restraint, impulse control, and the ability to inhibit aggressive behavior are also associated with PTSD among delinquent youths (Steiner, Garcia, and Matthews 1997). Overall, the range of cognitive processes associated with PTSD could readily influence decision making and limit the options that individuals consider to be viable for them. Although it is quite feasible that key cognitive processes underlying decision making are deleteriously influenced by exposure to trauma, direct evidence is not available to make this claim.

Academic deficiencies and low levels of intellectual functioning are also associated with externalizing behavior. This relationship has been demonstrated with diverse measures including verbal and nonverbal intelligence tests, grades, achievement tests, official school records, and parent, teacher, and adolescent reports (Kazdin 1995; Mandel 1997; Rutter and Giller 1983). Not all individuals with externalizing disorders or problem behavior have lower levels of intelligence or academic impairment. Those whose intelligence is lower are at greater risk for delinquency and a poor long-term prognosis. Limited intelligence is related to deficiencies in the cognitive problem-solving skills mentioned earlier, even though these can be distinguished. Also, poor school performance can result from or lead to deficits in bonding to conventional values and can foster stronger bonds to deviant peers. Intellectual and academic functioning are relevant to decision making through direct and indirect means. The direct means may reflect the effects of cognitive resources and problem-solving skills that are associated with intellectual functioning. The indirect effects may be evident through interpersonal influences such as associating with others who may not be functioning well in relation to conventional (such as academic) domains.

Biological Correlates/Substrates

There are many biological correlates of mental illness and delinquent behavior. Several of these correlates also can relate to influences on decision-making capacity. Genetic endowment, temperament, autonomic reactivity, pubertal development, various hormone levels (testosterone, sex-hormone-binding globulin, cortisol), and neurotransmitters (low serotonin turnover) relate to aggressive and antisocial behavior (Stoff, Breiling, and Maser 1997). As an example, persistent criminal activity in adolescents is much more likely among youths who show lower levels of autonomic reactivity (Magnusson, Klinteberg, and Stattin 1994). Although individual biological characteristics are useful to illustrate the relevance of this domain to delinquent behavior, it is likely that multiple characteristics contribute to any particular outcome. Consequently, many of the biological correlates are studied in combination with other influences, particularly psychosocial influences, to predict delinquent behavior. As an example, the impact of living conditions (is the father present, number of siblings in the home) on adolescent antisocial behavior can vary as a function of (interact with) levels of testosterone (Udry 1994).

Neuropsychological deficits are biological correlates that may be particularly relevant to adolescent decision making and delinquent behavior. Delinquents and youths with antisocial behavior have higher rates of neuropsychological deficits as reflected in language, verbal intelligence, working memory, and reading. Of special interest are deficiencies in "executive" functions that are served primarily by the frontal lobes of the brain and pathways to other brain systems. Executive functions include abstract reasoning, goal setting, anticipating and planning, self-monitoring and self-awareness, inhibiting of impulsive behavior, and interrupting an ongoing sequence of behavior in order to initiate a more adaptive behavior (Barkley 1996; Moffitt 1993). Higher rates of deficits in these areas are likely to be associated with delinquency and ADHD and to have direct implications for decision making. Adolescents with deficits in executive functions are not likely to be able to problem solve, select appropriate courses of action, and engage in self-control as well as those without such deficits. Clearly, neuropsychological deficits and the cognitive process with which these are associated are directly related to decision making and selecting among response alternatives.

Among delinquent youths, neuropsychological deficits are likely to occur in a broader context that is relevant to decision making. Thus, more complex relations are likely to operate to influence decision making than the presence or absence of one type of correlate or problem. For example, neuropsychological deficits of the type discussed here and adverse family environments each contribute to the likelihood of aggressive child behavior. However, when both of these influences are present, the likelihood of aggressive behavior is four times greater than it would be with either influence alone (Moffitt 1990). It is likely that prosocial and competent decision making is influenced in a similar way insofar as influences combine to increase or decrease the capacity to make sound choices.

Research on the relationship of biological characteristics such as hormones and neurotransmitters to behavior among children and adolescents has emerged relatively recently (Brain and Susman 1997). The research focuses on changes in mood, behavior, and biological rhythms, and how these may relate to broader characteristics such as antisocial behavior and peer relations. Among the features that are emerging are the important interactions of biological and environmental influences. For example, aggression in girls between the ages of ten to fourteen is related to the recent experience of negative life events and lower concentrations of adrenal androgens (dehydroepiandrosterone sulphate, or DHEAS). At higher levels of DHEAS concentrations, there is no relation between negative events and aggression. This work illustrates some of the complex interactions among biopsychosocial influences. The sequence of how these influences emerge and how they influence choice and decision making, or, indeed, are influenced by them, remains to be investigated.

In a discussion of biological substrates, it is important to mention in passing that significant advances are emerging in genetic and neuroimaging studies. For example, the relations of genetic factors, hormone receptors, and brain development may elaborate aspects of hyperactivity (Tannock 1998). Also, the study of structural and functional brain abnormalities through various techniques (such as computerized transaxial tomography, positron emission tomography, and functional magnetic resonance imaging) has revealed a number of areas that could serve as underpinnings for key characteristics such as cognitive deficits and hyperactivity. It is beyond the scope of the present chapter to elaborate on biological factors related to mental disorders and those disorders especially related to delinquency. However, the biological features, antecedents, and underpinnings of antisocial behavior are mentioned because they will need to be considered in conceptualizing the basis of delinquent acts and decision making.

Contextual Influences

The cognitive and biological associated features discussed previously pertain to characteristics within the individual that may affect decision making. No less significant are contextual influences, because these serve as factors that can enhance or impede an adolescent's competent decision making. From epidemiological research we know that several influences related to parents, the family, and peers can place a child at risk for psychiatric disorders, problem behaviors, and delinquency (Luthar 1999; Rutter and Giller 1983; Stoff, Breiling, and Maser 1997). This can be stated another way. Adolescents with psychiatric disorders are likely to live in contexts with a variety of characteristics. For example, adolescents with externalizing disorders or delinquent behavior are likely to have a parent with a lifetime or current mental disorder (such as antisocial behavior or substance abuse) and to be living in a home where there are marital conflicts, harsh child-rearing practices, and poor parental supervision. Externalizing problems are also associated with limited bonding to conventional values of the family and school that develop early in life (Elliott, Huizinga, and Menard 1988; Resnick et al. 1997).

Exposure to trauma and multiple trauma can influence later behavior in ways that may affect choice and decision making. For example, most boys who have been sexually abused themselves do not go on to become abusers. The likelihood of sexually abusing others is increased by witnessing family violence. Boys exposed to both sexual abuse and family violence are more likely to become abusers than those exposed to sexual abuse alone (Skuse et al. 1998). Early influences and contextual factors do not necessarily determine an individual's future behavior. However, as untoward influences accumulate, they can greatly affect the probability of engaging in maladaptive strategies and can decrease the likelihood that rational decision making plays a central role in selecting courses of action.

The family and peers are relevant influences for evaluating decision making by delinquent youths. Adolescents with externalizing problems are likely to live in contexts that do not provide prosocial resources on which to rely for decision making. Deficient bonding with the family is associated with subsequent bonding to peers, particularly delinquent peers. This means that the adolescent may have as a primary resource peers who promote deviant behavior. Deviant behavior is directly reinforced (reacted to positively) in conversations that antisocial adolescents have with each other; prosocial and more normative behaviors tend not to receive such attention among peers (Dishion and Patterson 1997). This work with peers is analogous to prior work in the family that showed how parents of antisocial youths unwittingly reinforce deviant behavior, ignore prosocial behavior, and in the process foster higher levels of deviance (Patterson 1982). Family and peer influences are relevant to current and future externalizing problems of delinquent youths and to evaluations of their decision making.

General Comments

Mental disorders among delinquents are quite relevant to decision making and delinquent behavior in at least two ways. First, core symptoms of mental disorders such as impulsiveness associated with ADHD can very much circumvent deliberation and thoughtful selection of appropriate plans of action. Also, substance abuse has been implicated on risk-taking behaviors among adolescents, as discussed previously. Second, the significance of mental disorder for understanding youths' choices to commit offenses stems from many of the features associated with the disorders rather than the core symptoms. Associated features of course vary with the disorders. For example, individuals with externalizing disorders are likely to show multiple problem behaviors and deficits in cognitive problem-solving skills, mental abilities, and self-control. Mental illness may be significant as a marker for many other characteristics of the adolescent, which may be equally or more relevant for understanding adolescents' capacities to make decisions about their behavior.

The term "decision-making capacity" draws attention to characteristics or abilities within the individual. However, as with the onset of mental disorder and delinquency, there are likely to be multiple contextual influences that are intertwined with individual characteristics. Characteristics of the parents and family, peer relations, living conditions, and settings are relevant. As an illustration, already mentioned were cognitive processes that mediate externalizing behavior. Although precisely how these cognitive processes emerge is incompletely understood, contextual influences play a significant role. Early experience of physical abuse plays a significant role in the development of cognitive processes that promote aggression as well as subsequent aggressive behavior (Dodge et al. 1995). Often contextual influences can play a critical role in conjunction with characteristics of the individual. For example, suicide (both ideation and attempt) among adolescents is related to depression, hopelessness, and stress, to mention a few of the key features. Suicide ideation and attempt (Resnick et al. 1997) and especially suicide completion (Brent et al. 1991), are influenced by the availability of the means (for example, guns in the home). The importance of context is underscored further by noting that reducing access to the means of committing suicide can reduce suicide rates (Clarke and Mayhew 1988).

The idea that mental illness is a risk factor for criminal activity is not new. However, recent evidence that there may be no critical threshold for deciding when a disorder is present may raise new considerations. In the context of a legal defense based on reason of insanity, the presence or absence of a diagnosable disorder may be difficult to justify. Subsyndromal levels of the disorder may be just as relevant. Even more noteworthy perhaps is that the features associated with mental illness are extremely relevant to decision making and criminal activity and in many cases are more relevant than the specific diagnosis. Meeting criteria for a psychiatric diagnosis is significant insofar as it serves as a marker or signal that associated features are likely to be present that impede decision making.

Research Implications

Several lines of research are needed to elaborate the relations of mental disorder and youths' decision-making capacities as an issue in juvenile justice. First, high priority must be given to studies of prevalence of mental disorders among delinquent youths. Systematic studies with standardized diagnostic assessments, across different age cohorts, settings, and geographical locales, are not yet available. The existing studies alert us to significant problems among delinquent adolescents, but the scope and patterns of disorders (such as comorbidity) warrant more systematic description.

Second, longitudinal studies of the relation of delinquency and mental illness are warranted. Are delinquent youths with any diagnosis of disorder, or some diagnoses rather than others, at greater risk for becoming career criminals? From research with clinical samples, it is clear that the presence of ADHD increases the risk for later criminal behavior. Yet a broad range of diagnoses, including internalizing disorders such as major depression and posttraumatic stress disorder, may be relevant to onset and long-term course of delinquent behavior. Moreover, among delinquent youths, the presence of disorders may have significant implications for recidivism, violent crime, and other outcomes pertinent to juvenile justice.

Third, conceptual and empirical work is needed to identify the range of characteristics of adolescents that are likely to influence their decision making. Many decisions that are part of adjudication and the trial process depend on cognitive competence and decision making on the part of adolescents (Grisso 1997). Very little evidence is available to understand the decision-making capacities of delinquent youths. Added to the influences on decision making that characterize adolescence in general are those factors raised by the high rates of mental illness among delinquent youths. Mental illness and problem behaviors are important characteristics, but features with which these are associated may be equally or even more significant for evaluating the youths' capacities to participate competently in their trials and understand their choices that lead to offending in the first place. Presence of a disorder in delinquent youths can signal a variety of other characteristics in the family, parents, and peer group. Which influences promote competent decision making, how they operate and influence each other, and how their influence varies in impact over the course of development are critical research questions. The decision-making process needs to be studied in interpersonal situations, particularly those situations that may be precursors to delinquent activity. For example, it would be very important to understand the factors that increase an individual's resistance to peer pressure for criminal activity, that reduce aggressive means of responding to others, and that increase inhibition in the face of antagonism from others. The influence of an individual's characteristics (such as decision-making capacity and mental illness) in conjunction with contextual influences (such as supportive family relations, absence of parental substance abuse, and psychopathology) affect the course of decision making. This is readily subject to empirical research.

From the standpoint of understanding youths' decision-making capacities, a profile of multiple characteristics needs to be assessed. It is an empirical question as to whether disorders or the many factors with which they are often associated are better indicators of decision-making capacities and deficits among delinquent youths. A comprehensive assessment of adolescents in principle could entail an unlimited number of domains. Research already points to several salient influences. Among the domains of the adolescents, cognitive processes, intellectual functioning, and bonding to conventional values are key domains to be assessed. Among the contextual domains, current or lifetime history of mental illness and criminality of the parents, conflict in the home, parent child-rearing practices, parent supervision, and peer relations are other such influences. Clearly, research is needed to evaluate the contribution of these influences on decision making; theoretical work is needed as well to pose questions regarding how these influences operate, what their precise role in decision making is, and where one might intervene to help develop effective decision-making capacities.

Conclusions

The prevalence rate of mental disorder in community samples of children and adolescents hovers close to 20 percent of the population. Research on the prevalence rate of mental disorders among delinquent youths has yielded quite varied results in light of differences in sampling methods and measures of identifying disorders. Even so, the rates far exceed those evident in community samples; an estimate based on one of the largest samples suggests a prevalence rate of 80 percent (Teplin, Abram, and McClelland 1998). Prevalence rates are useful to convey one facet of the problem, but the impact of mental illness on impairment, delinquent behavior, and decision making is not well represented by these rates. One reason is that there are likely to be high rates of comorbidity, that is, two or more disorders for the same individual. With delinquent samples, comorbidity of psychiatric disorders is less well studied than it is in studies of community samples. Another reason that prevalence rates can be misleading and conservative is that they focus on whether individuals meet criteria for various psychiatric diagnoses. In light of more recent evidence, it is clear that individuals who fall below but are close to meeting diagnostic criteria (subsyndromal dysfunction) may also show significant impairment and untoward long-term outcomes. In general, the scope of impairment among youths, delinquent youths in particular, is great even if one retains rather stringent criteria for making a diagnosis and omits a range of problem and at-risk behaviors.

Mental disorders play a twofold role as an influence on decision-making capabilities among delinquent youths. First, core symptoms of some of the disorders can directly interfere with decision making and also lead to delinquent behavior. Impulsiveness as a core feature of ADHD is clearly a prime example, but impulsiveness is a feature likely to be evident in any of the disruptive behavior disorders (conduct disorder and oppositional defiant disorder). Impulsiveness can emerge from other disorders (such as posttraumatic stress disorder) and hence one cannot assume that a single diagnosis is pertinent to impulsive behavior.

Second, the child, parent, family, and contextual influences with which the disorders are often associated also are relevant to adolescent decision making. Indeed, these influences are likely to be more relevant than core symptoms. Maladaptive cognitive processes, deficits in problem solving and self-regulation, distortions of processing information, and other cognitive abilities that directly affect decision making in interpersonal situations are evident in diverse externalizing and internalizing disorders including ADHD, CD, depression, and PTSD. These associated features can vary among individuals who meet a particular diagnosis. Parent, family, and contextual influences are critical to decision-making competencies of the child although the paths of influence may be indirect. Dysfunctional child-rearing (such as harsh discipline practices and poor supervision), exposure to trauma (both experience and observation of abuse), and exposure to and association with deviant peers all influence strategies that youths elect in their interpersonal behavior. While these influences are strongly associated with various forms of mental illness, they can be readily distinguished from the disorders themselves. Mental illness is a useful index insofar as it raises the prospect that several factors (associated features) other than the core symptoms may conspire to impair cognitive functioning, decision making, and selection of prosocial courses of action among delinquent youths.

Works Cited

Allen, L. P., B J. Leadbeater, and J. L. Aber. 1994. The development of problem behavior syndromes in at-risk adolescents. *Development and Psychopathology* 6:323–342.

American Psychiatric Association. 1994. *Diagnostic and statistical manual of mental disorders.* 4th ed. Washington, D.C.: American Psychiatric Association.

Anderson, J. C., S. Williams, R. McGee, and P. A. Silva. 1987. The prevalence of DSM-III disorders in pre-adolescent children: Prevalence in a large sample from the general population. *Archives of General Psychiatry* 44:69–76.

Barkley, R. A. 1996. Attention-deficit/hyperactivity disorder. In *Child psychopathology,* edited by E. J. Mash and R. A. Barkley. New York: Guilford.

Baumrind, D. 1991. The influence of parenting style on adolescent risk taking and substance abuse. *Journal of Early Adolescence* 11:56–95.

Boyle, M. H., D. Offord, Y. A. Racine, P. Szatmari, J. E. Fleming, and M. N. Sanford. 1996. Identifying thresholds for classifying psychiatric disorder: Issues and prospects. *Journal of the American Academy of Child and Adolescent Psychiatry* 35:1440–1448.

Brain, P. F., and E. J. Susman. 1997. Hormonal aspects of aggression and violence. In *Handbook of antisocial behavior,* edited by D. M Stoff, J. Breiling, and J. D. Maser. New York: Wiley.

Brent, D. A., J. A. Perper, C. J. Allman, G. M. Mortiz, M. E. Wartella, and J. P. Zelenak. 1991. The presence and accessibility of firearms in the homes of adolescent suicides: A case-control study. *Journal of the American Medical Association* 266:2989–2995.

Buhrmester, D. 1990. Intimacy of friendship, interpersonal competence, and adjustment during preadolescence and adolescence. *Child Development* 61:1101–1111.

Caron, C., and M. Rutter. 1991. Comorbidity in child psychopathology: Concepts, issues, and research strategies. *Journal of Child Psychology and Psychiatry* 32:1063–1080.

Clark, L. A., D. Watson, and S. Reynolds. 1995. Diagnosis and classification of psychopathology: Challenges to the current system and future directions. *Annual Review of Psychology* 46:121–152.

Clarke, R. V., and P. Mayhew. 1988. The British gas suicide story and its criminological implications. In *Crime and justice,* edited by M. Tonry and N. Morris. Vol. 10. Chicago: University of Chicago Press.

Cohen, P., J. Cohen, S. Kasen, C. N. Velez, C. Hartmark, J. Johnson, M. Rojas, J. Book, and E. L. Streuning. 1993. An epidemiological study of disorders in late childhood and adolescence. Part 1. *Journal of Child Psychology and Psychiatry* 34:851–867.

Cohen, Y., A. Spirito, and L. K. Brown. 1996. Suicide and suicidal behavior. In *Handbook of adolescent health risk behavior,* edited by R. J. Diclemente, W. B. Hansen, and L. E. Ponton. New York: Plenum.

Costello, E. J. 1989. Developments in child psychiatric epidemiology. *Journal of the American Academy of Child and Adolescent Psychiatry* 28:836–841.

Crick, N. R., and K. A. Dodge. 1994. A review and reformulation of social information processing mechanisms in children's social adjustment. *Psychological Bulletin* 115:74–101.

Cuffe, S. P., C. L. Addy, C. Z. Garrison, J. L. Waller, K. L. Jackson, R. E. McKeown, and S. Chilappagari. 1998. Prevalence of PTSD in a community sample of older adolescents. *Journal of the American Academy of Child and Adolescent Psychiatry* 37:147–154.

DiClemente, R. J., W. B. Hansen, and L. E. Ponton, eds. 1996. *Handbook of adolescent health risk behavior.* New York: Plenum.

Dishion, T., and G. R. Patterson. 1997. The timing and severity of antisocial behavior: Three hypotheses within an ecological framework. In *Handbook of antisocial behavior,* edited by D. M Stoff, J. Breiling, and J. D. Maser. New York: Wiley.

Dodge, K. A., G. S. Pettit, J. E. Bates, and E. Valente. 1995. Social information processing patterns partially mediate the effect of early physical abuse on later conduct problems. *Journal of Abnormal Psychology* 104:632–643.

Dodge, K. A., and D. Schwartz. 1997. Social information processing mechanisms in aggressive behavior. In *Handbook of antisocial behavior,* edited by D. M Stoff, J. Breiling, and J. D. Maser. New York: Wiley.

Dryfoos, J. G. 1990. *Adolescents at risk: Prevalence and prevention.* New York: Oxford University Press.

Elliott, D. S., D. Huizinga, and S. Menard. 1988. *Multiple problem youth: Delinquency, substance abuse, and mental health problems.* New York: Springer-Verlag.

Elmer, N., S. Reicher, and A. Ross. 1987. The social context of delinquent conduct. *Journal of Child Psychology and Psychiatry* 28:99–109.

Farrington, D., R. Loeber, and W. B. Van Kammen. 1990. Long-term criminal outcomes of hyperactivity-impulsivity-attention deficit and conduct problems in childhood. In *Straight and devious pathways from childhood to adulthood,* edited by L. N. Robins and M. Rutter. Cambridge: Cambridge University Press.

Fisher, L., and S. S. Feldman. 1998. Familial antecedents of young adult health risk behavior: A longitudinal study. *Journal of Family Psychology* 12:66–80.

Fletcher, K. E. 1996. Childhood posttraumatic stress disorder. In *Child psychopathology,* edited by E. J. Mash and R. A. Barkley. New York: Guilford.

Flewelling, R. L., and K. E. Bauman. 1990. Family structure as a predictor of initial substance use and sexual intercourse in early adolescence. *Journal of Marriage and Family* 52:171–181.

Gotlib, I. H., P. M. Lewinsohn, and J. R. Seeley. 1995. Symptoms versus a diagnosis of depression: Differences in psychosocial functioning. *Journal of Consulting and Clinical Psychology* 63:90–100.

Greenbaum, P. E., L. Foster-Johnson, and A. Petrila. 1996. Co-occurring addictive and mental disorders among adolescents: Prevalence research and future directions. *American Journal of Orthopsychiatry* 66:52–60.

Grisso, T. 1997. The competence of adolescents as trial defendants. *Psychology, Public Policy, and Law* 3:3–32.

Hall, G. S. 1904. Adolescence: Its psychology and its relations to physiology, anthropology, sociology, sex, crime, religion, and education. 2 vols. New York: Appelton.

Hammen, C., and K. D. Rudolf. 1996. Childhood depression. In *Child psychopathology,* edited by E. J. Mash and R. A. Barkley. New York: Guilford.

Hollingworth, L. S. 1928. *The psychology of the adolescent.* New York: Appelton.

Hollmann, F. W. 1993. U.S. population estimates by age, sex, race, and Hispanic origin: 1990–1992. Population Projections Branch, Population Division, U.S Bureau of the Census. Washington, D.C.

Institute of Medicine. 1989. *Research on children and adolescents with mental, behavioral, and developmental disorders.* Washington, D.C.: National Academy Press.

Johnston, L. D. 1996. The rise of drug use among American teens continues in 1996. *Monitoring the Future Study* (December). Ann Arbor, Mich.: University of Michigan.

Kazdin, A. E. 1989. Identifying depression in children: A comparison of alternative selection criteria. *Journal of Abnormal Child Psychology* 17:437–455.

———. 1995. *Conduct disorder in childhood and adolescence.* 2d ed. Thousand Oaks, Calif.: Sage Publications.

Ketterlinus, R. D., and M. E. Lamb, eds. 1994. *Adolescent problem behaviors: Issues and research.* Hillsdale, N.J.: Erlbaum.

King, B. H., M. W. State, B. Shah, P. Davanzo, and E. Dykens. 1997. Mental retardation: A review of the past 10 years. Part 1. *Journal of the American Academy of Child and Adolescent Psychiatry* 36:1656–1663.

Lahey, B. J., and R. Loeber. 1997. Attention-deficit/hyperactivity disorder, oppositional defiant disorder, conduct disorder, and adult antisocial behavior: A lifespan perspective. In *Handbook of antisocial behavior,* edited by D. M Stoff, J. Breiling, and J. D. Maser. New York: Wiley.

Lewinsohn, P. M., H. Hops, R. E. Roberts, J. R. Seeley, and J. A. Andrews. 1993. Adolescent psychopathology. Part 1. *Journal of Abnormal Psychology* 102:133–144.

Loeber, R. 1990. Development and risk factors of juvenile antisocial behavior and delinquency. *Clinical Psychology Review* 10:1–41.

Luthar, S. S. 1999. *Children in poverty: Risk and protective forces in adjustment.* Thousand Oaks, Calif.: Sage Publications.

Magnusson, D., B. A. Klinteberg, and H. Stattin. 1994. Juvenile and persistent offenders: Behavioral and physiological characteristics. In *Adolescent problem behaviors: Issues and research,* edited by R. D. Ketterlinus and M. E. Lamb. Hillsdale, N.J.: Erlbaum.

Mandel, H. P. 1997. *Conduct disorder and underachievement: Risk factors, assessment, treatment, and prevention.* New York: Wiley.

Marton, P., J. Connolly, S. Kutcher, and M. Korenblum. 1993. Cognitive social skills and social self-appraisal in depressed adolescents. *Journal of the American Academy of Child and Adolescent Psychiatry* 32:739–744.

McGee, R., M. Feehan, S. Williams, and J. Anderson. 1992. DSM-III disorders from age 11 to age 15 years. *Journal of the American Academy of Child and Adolescent Psychiatry* 31:50–59.

McGee, R., M. Feehan, S. Williams, F. Partridge, P. A. Silva, and J. Kelly. 1990. DSM-III disorders in a large sample of adolescents. *Journal of the American Academy of Child and Adolescent Psychiatry* 29:611–619.

Messier, L. P., and T. J. Ward. 1998. The coincidence of depression and high ability in delinquent youth. *Journal of Child and Family Studies* 7:97–105.

Milin, R., J. A. Halikas, J. E. Meller, and C. Morse. 1991. Psychopathology among substance abusing juvenile offenders. *Journal of the American Academy of Child and Adolescent Psychiatry* 30:569–574.

Moffitt, T. 1990. The neuropsychology of delinquency: A critical review of theory and research. In *Crime and justice,* edited by N. Morris and M. Tonry. Vol. 12. Chicago: University of Chicago Press.

———. 1993. The neuropsychology of conduct problems. *Development and Psychopathology* 5:135–151.

Monahan, J. 1997. Major mental disorders and violence to others. In *Handbook of antisocial behavior,* edited by D. M Stoff et al. New York: Wiley.

Mulvey, E. 1994. Assessing the evidence of a link between mental illness and violence. *Hospital and Community Psychiatry* 45:663–668.

Newcomb, M. D., and P. M. Bentler. 1988. *Consequences of adolescent drug use: Impact on the lives of young adults.* Thousand Oaks, Calif.: Sage Publications.

———. 1989. Substance use and abuse among children and teenagers. *American Psychologist* 44:242–248.

Offord, D., M. H. Boyle, Y. A. Racine, J. E. Fleming, D. T. Cadman, H. M. Blum, C. Byrne, P. S. Links, E. L. Lipman, H. L. MacMillan, N. I. Rae Grant, M. N. Sanford, P. Szatmari, H. Thomas, and C. A Woodward. 1992. Outcome, prognosis, and risk in a longitudinal follow-up study. *Journal of the American Academy of Child and Adolescent Psychiatry* 31:916–923.

Offord, D., M. H. Boyle, Y. A. Racine, P. Szatmari, J. E. Fleming, M. N. Sanford, and E. L. Lipman. 1996. Integrating assessment data from multiple informants. *Journal of the American Academy of Child and Adolescent Psychiatry* 35:1078–1085.

Otto, R. K., J. J. Greenstein, M. K Johnson, and R. M.Friedman. 1992. Prevalence of mental disorders among youth in the juvenile justice system. In *Responding to the mental health needs of youths in the juvenile justice system,* edited by J. J. Cocozza. Seattle, Wash.: National Coalition for the Mentally Ill in the Criminal Justice System.

Patterson, G. R. 1982. *Coercive family process.* Eugene, Ore.: Castalia.

———. 1993. Orderly change in a stable world: The antisocial trait as a chimera. *Journal of Consulting and Clinical Psychology* 61:911–919.

Patterson, G. R., B. D. DeBaryshe, and E. Ramsey. 1989. A developmental perspective on antisocial behavior. *American Psychologist* 44:329–335.

Patterson, G. R., and T. J. Dishion. 1985. Contributions of families and peers to delinquency. *Criminology* 23:63–79.

Rafferty, Y., and M. Shinn. 1991. The impact of homelessness on children. *American Psychologist* 46:1170–1179.

Resnick, M. D., P. S. Bearman, R. W. Blum, K. E. Bauman, K. M. Harris, J. Jones, J. Tabor, T. Beuhring, R. E. Sieving, M. Shew, M. Ireland, L. H. Bearinger, and J. R. Udry. 1997. Protecting adolescents from harm: Findings from the National Longitudinal Study on Adolescent Health. *Journal of the American Medical Association* 278:823–832.

Rotheram-Borus, M. J., M. Parra, C. Cantwell, M. Gwadz, and D. Murphy. 1996. Runaway and homeless youths. In *Handbook of adolescent health risk behavior,* edited by R. J. Diclemente, W. B. Hansen, and L. E. Ponton. New York: Plenum.

Rudolf, K. D., C. Hammen, and D. Burge. 1994. Interpersonal functioning and

depressive symptoms in childhood: Addressing the issues of specificity and comorbidity. *Journal of Abnormal Child Psychology* 22:355–371.

Rutter, M. 1990. Changing patterns of psychiatric disorders during adolescence.
In *Adolescence and puberty,* edited by J. Bancroft and J. M. Reinisch. New
York: Oxford University Press.

Rutter, M., and H. Giller. 1983. *Juvenile delinquency: Trends and perspectives.*
New York: Penguin Books.

Rutter, M., R. Harrington, D. Quinton, and A. Pickles. 1994. Adult outcome of
conduct disorder in childhood: Implications for concepts and definitions and
patterns of psychopathology. In *Adolescent problem behaviors: Issues and research,* edited by R. D. Ketterlinus and M. E. Lamb. Hillsdale, N.J.: Erlbaum.

Shirk, S. R., ed. 1988. *Cognitive development and child psychotherapy.* New York:
Plenum.

Simcha-Fagan, O., and J. E. Schwartz. 1986. Neighborhood and delinquency: An
assessment of contextual effects. *Criminology* 24:667–703.

Skuse, D., A. Bentovim, J. Hodges, J. Stevenson, C. Andreou, M. Lanyado,
M. New, B. Williams, and D. McMillan. 1998. Risk factors for development of
sexually abusive behaviour in sexually victimised adolescent boys: Cross sec-
tional study. *British Medical Journal* 317:175–179.

Steiner, H., I. G. Garcia, and Z. Matthews. 1997. Posttraumatic stress disorder in
incarcerated juvenile delinquents. *Journal of the American Academy of Child
and Adolescent Psychiatry* 36:357–365.

Stoff, D. M., J. Breiling, and J. D. Maser, eds. 1997. *Handbook of antisocial behavior.* New York: Wiley.

Tannock, R. 1998. Attention deficit hyperactivity disorder: Advances in cognitive,
neurobiological, and genetic research. *Journal of Child Psychology and Psychiatry* 39:65–99.

Teplin, L. A., K. M. Abram, and G. M. McClelland. 1998. Psychiatric disorders
among juvenile detainees. Paper presented at the Annual Conference on Criminal Justice Research and Evaluation, July, at the Bureau of Justice Assistance,
Office of Juvenile Justice and Delinquency Prevention, Washington, D.C.

Thornberry, T. P., and M. D. Krohn. 1997. Peers, drug use, and delinquency. In
Handbook of antisocial behavior, edited by D. M Stoff, J. Breiling, and J. D.
Maser. New York: Wiley.

Turner, R. A., C. E. Irwin Jr., J. M. Tschann, and S. G. Millstein. 1993. Autonomy,
relatedness, and early initiation of health risk behaviors in early adolescence.
Health Psychology 12:200–208.

Udry, J. R. 1994. Integrating biological and sociological models of adolescent
problem behavior. In *Adolescent problem behaviors: Issues and research,* edited by R. D. Ketterlinus and M. E. Lamb. Hillsdale, N.J.: Erlbaum.

United States Bureau of the Census. 1993. Current Population Reports. U.S. population estimates by age, sex, race, and Hispanic origin: 1980–1991. (P25-1095)
Washington, D.C.: U.S. Government Printing Office.

United States Congress, Office of Technology Assessment. 1991. Adolescent
health. (OTA-H-468) Washington, D.C.: U.S. Government Printing Office.

United States Department of Justice, Office of Justice Programs, Bureau of
Justice Statistics. 1988. Report to the nation on crime and justice. 2d ed.
(NCJ-105506M) Washington, D.C.: U.S. Government Printing Office.

Weinberg, N. Z., E. Rahdert, J. D. Colliver, and M. D. Glanz. 1998. Adolescent
substance abuse: A review of the past 10 years. *Journal of the American Academy of Child and Adolescent Psychiatry* 37:252–261.

Widom, C. S. 1994. Child victimization and adolescent problem behavior. In *Adolescent problem behaviors: Issues and research,* edited by R. D. Ketterlinus and
M. E. Lamb. Hillsdale, N.J.: Erlbaum.

Windle, M., J. T. Shope, and O. Bukstein. 1996. Alcohol use. In *Handbook of adolescent health risk behavior,* edited by R. J. Diclemente, W. B. Hansen, and L.
E. Ponton. New York: Plenum.

Wolfe, V. V., C. Gentile, T. Michienzi, L. Sas, and D. Wolfe. 1991. The children's
impact on traumatic events scale: A measure of post-sexual-abuse PTSD symptoms. *Behavioral Assessment* 13:359–383.

Wolfe, V. V., C. Gentile, and D. Wolfe. 1989. The impact of sexual abuse on children: A PTSD formulation. *Behavior Therapy* 20:215–228.

Zill, N., and C. A. Schoenborn. 1990. *Developmental, learning, and emotional
problems: Health of our nation's children, United States 1988.* Washington, D.C.:
National Center for Health Statistics.

Zoccolillo, M. 1993. Gender and the development of conduct disorder. *Development and Psychopathology* 5:65–78.

Note

The author gratefully acknowledges the Leon Lowenstein Foundation and the
William T. Grant Foundation, who provided grant support during the period in
which this chapter was written.

PART TWO

Adolescents' Capacities as Trial Defendants

As noted in the Introduction to this book, the issue of juveniles' capacities in the adjudicative process received only limited attention in law and legal or clinical practice prior to the last decade. Because of recent reforms pertaining to the adjudication of adolescents, questions of youths' capacities are now arising more frequently in reference to two important stages of the adjudication process.

Questions of Adjudicative Competence

One of these areas is the capacities of youths to waive Miranda rights voluntarily, knowingly, and intelligently during questioning by law-enforcement officers. This question was addressed with substantial frequency soon after *Gault,* both in the law and by researchers and clinicians who sought to provide reliable information for judicial decisions about youths' confessions.

The other important area is the capacity of youths to participate in the trial process, either in juvenile or criminal court. As the following chapters point out, recent reforms that subject youths to more punitive sentences have required the application of the concept of competence to stand trial to juvenile proceedings in many states, and have increased the frequency with which criminal courts have had to deal with incompetent youths who have been transferred to criminal court for trial. This has raised a host of new questions in light of youths' developmental immaturity, ranging from difficulties in applying legal definitions of competence in juvenile cases to questions about the proper ways to evaluate and describe youths' capacities as trial defendants.

Part II addresses Miranda waiver and the issue of competence to stand trial. Greater focus, however, is given to the latter question because historically it has received so much less attention in law and behavioral science research.

Why Juveniles' Capacities Are Important

Before introducing the chapters, it is worthwhile to reflect on why these questions matter. What difference does it make that defendants should have capacities associated with waiver of Miranda rights and participation in their trials? Three broad reasons for concern are relevant: assuring procedural justice, promoting effective representation, and facilitating youths' legal socialization.

Procedural Justice

The law has long required that defendants' confessions cannot be used against them unless they were preceded by the person's voluntary, knowing, and intelligent waiver of Fifth and Sixth Amendment rights (to avoid self-incrimination, and to legal counsel). For centuries the law has also prohibited trying defendants unless they are capable of defending themselves—that is, that they have the capacity to understand the nature of the proceedings against them as well as the capacity to assist counsel in their defense and make important decisions that they are likely to encounter in the trial process.

Law has recognized these rights as part of fundamental procedural justice for several reasons. It was considered unfair for the state to use its considerable powers to convict accused persons when they did not have the capacity to defend themselves. Moreover, the public's trust in the integrity of the justice system was jeopardized by the spectacle of trials of persons who were so disabled that they could not participate in their defense. Trying incompetent defendants and accepting their confessions as evidence might also contribute to inaccurate evidence, leading to erroneous convictions.

As Chapters 3 and 4 point out, these rights were not considered necessary in the early juvenile court because the juvenile justice system was predicated on the notion that delinquent youths were not held responsible for offenses in a manner associated with the punishment of crimes. Juveniles were identified as persons who needed the court's care and rehabilitative services. Recent reforms that have promoted the legal system's punitive response to delinquent youths, however, make all of the above matters of procedural justice applicable to youths who—whether in juvenile or criminal court—are confronted with consequences of convictions that involve substantial loss of liberty.

Thus one reason for concern about youths' capacities in the adjudicative process is to assure justice and the protection of fundamental legal rights of juveniles in an era in which youths face deprivations of liberty that often are no less consequential than the sentences of adult defendants to whom those rights have long been guaranteed. Several of the chapters in this section focus on these concerns. Chapter 3 (competence to stand trial) and Chapter 4 (juveniles' waiver of rights and confessions) examine the many issues of law and policy raised by the provision of these rights to youths in juvenile and criminal court. They provide a legal framework for considering the issues, discuss uncertainties in law that should address youths' competence as suspects and defendants, and offer directions for legal reform.

Chapters 5 and 6 examine empirical questions of youths' abilities relevant to their competence as trial defendants. Chapter 5 reviews current developmental and clinical knowledge about youths' capacities for comprehension, then applies that information. The chapter concludes by offering guidelines for the development of law, policy, and legal procedure that takes into account the actual capacities of youths. Those guidelines are tentative, however, because our knowledge of youths' capacities as trial defendants is quite incomplete. Chapter 6 describes the type of developmental psychological research that is needed to improve our understanding of the abilities and limits of youths as trial defendants, and that therefore would provide a more firm empirical basis for future law and policy regarding youths' competence to stand trial.

While lawmakers and behavioral-science researchers are struggling with these issues, courts must respond to the immediate need to identify youths whose capacities as trial defendants may be compromised by their developmental immaturity or mental disorders. Typically courts call upon mental health professionals to evaluate youths' capacities when their competence is questioned. Chapter 7 provides for courts, attorneys, and mental health professionals a perspective on the clinical assessment of those capacities.

Effective Representation

A second reason for our concern about these matters goes beyond the formal definitions and procedures related to legal competence and focuses on attorneys' capacities to provide effective representation of youths. Adolescents who meet the legal definition for competence to stand trial may nevertheless present challenges to their attorneys' abilities to counsel and defend them.

The attorney-client relationship, for example, is critically important for the development of a defense. The mere fact that a court believes that a youth has the requisite capacities to consult with his attorney tells us very little about the manner in which the youth will relate to his or her attorney. It tells us little about how youths will present themselves in court. It tells us nothing about the role of parents in developing a defense. All of these matters can be addressed in a developmental context, and developmental psychological information about youths should be used to assist attorneys in managing their relations with youthful clients such that the effectiveness of their representation is promoted.

We are far from being able to provide attorneys with definitive information for these purposes. Two of the chapters in this section, however, begin to explore these questions. Chapter 8 uses interviews with attorneys to describe the difficulties that they encounter while working with youthful clients who, although not considered incompetent to stand trial, present challenges associated with developmental characteristics of adolescence. Chapter 9 examines ways that attorneys can meet these challenges through a better understanding of their youthful clients' worldviews and adoption of approaches that take those views into account.

Legal Socialization

A third reason for our concern about youths' capacities in the adjudicative process is premised on the notion that their participation in their trials is part of a process of legal socialization. Youthful defendants are not merely objects in this process. What they see and experience as defendants subtly shapes their perceptions of the relationship between individuals and society. Their observations and experiences influence the development of their notions of law, rules, and agreements among members of society, and the legitimacy of authority to deal fairly with citizens who are charged with violating society's rules.

We should be concerned about youths' understanding and participation in their defense not only for reasons of procedural justice and effective representation, but also because only by comprehending the process—its meaning, the reasons for steps in the adjudicative process, and the system's attention to both rights and justice—can they learn by their experience as defendants the importance of those values for citizenship. Respect for the legal process and for society's rules is not likely to be engendered in a youth who is shuffled through the courts as a mere object about whom persons in authority make decisions. But taking steps to improve youths' grasp of the nature of the legal process they are enduring and assuring that the process is fair offers the possibility of promoting youths' respect for law and the beginning of a sense of citizenship.

This notion is not the focus of any specific chapter in this section, but it is woven into the fabric of several of them (for example, Chapters 5, 8, and 9). Moreover, it can be found just under the surface of several chapters in Part III, which deal with society's notions of youths' culpability, accountability, and responsibility.

CHAPTER THREE

Adjudicative Competence and Youthful Offenders

RICHARD J. BONNIE AND THOMAS GRISSO

In recent years the juvenile justice system has undergone substantial change. Legislatures have raised the penalties associated with adjudication of delinquency in juvenile court and have increased the number and types of youths whose cases are tried in criminal court with little or no regard for their developmental status. An increase in the stakes associated with the prosecution and punishment of youths as delinquent or criminal raises new reasons for concern about due process and fairness in the adjudication of charges against youthful offenders. Even after the U.S. Supreme Court ruled in *In re Gault* that youths in juvenile proceedings must have many of the same rights and protections as defendants in criminal court proceedings, many jurisdictions looked the other way when it came time to implement them, arguing that such protections were less important when the court's objective was to rehabilitate rather than to punish. Any rationale for that practice has eroded in the face of sentencing laws and practices that make little or no distinction between juvenile and adult defendants.

Adjudicative competence, or competence to stand trial, is one protection that has taken on new implications in this context. Concerns about the capacities of immature youths to understand the nature of the adjudication process and to make critical decisions related to it are being raised in legislatures and courts across the nation. Legal questions concerning youths' adjudicative competence have been raised in several specific ways. First of all, courts and commentators are uncertain about the significance of competence to stand trial in juvenile court proceedings where the concept has little history or precedent. Second, the traditional doctrine of adjudicative competence has an uncertain meaning when applied to youths being tried in criminal court, partly because immaturity has not usually been considered in adjudicative competence determinations.

Moreover, while defendants found to be incompetent are typically committed for restoration of competence, thereby enabling the proceedings to continue, the dispositional consequences of a finding that a youth is incompetent due to immaturity are less clear.

The purpose of this chapter is to review the foundation for the legal concept of adjudicative competence and to frame the questions about juveniles' competence that will be addressed in other chapters in this book. Part I develops the concept of adjudicative competence and describes its legal contours. Part II explores the question of youths' participation in criminal trials from a historical perspective, examining whether and how the concept of adjudicative competence has been applied to youths in the past. It also discusses conceptual problems inherent in applying to juveniles the competence criteria currently used in criminal cases and offers suggestions for dealing with these problems. Part III then argues for the application of adjudicative competence in juvenile courts in a limited range of cases.

Part I: Adjudicative Competence

At least since the fourteenth century, common-law courts have declined to proceed against criminal defendants who are "incompetent" to be brought before the court for adjudication.[1] As was true of so much of the common law, the "incompetency plea," as it developed, was rooted in an ancient legal formalism. A criminal prosecution could not proceed against someone who had not entered a plea (guilty or not guilty). A defendant who "stood mute" might be doing so willfully ("mute of malice") or due to deafness or madness ("mute by visitation of God"). Confinement in a small cell, starvation, or the pressure of heavy weights was used to induce a plea from strategically silent defendants, thereby allowing the process to move forward. However, the Crown could not proceed against a "lunatic" or "idiot" whose understanding of the proceedings was so diminished as to prevent a knowing plea. Even after the courts became willing to enter "not guilty" pleas on behalf of defendants who stood mute, the "incompetency plea" survived as an independent bar to adjudication.

The evolution of common-law doctrine is apparent in the court's description of the elements of "fitness to stand trial" in *R. v. Pritchard* in 1836, a famous case involving a defendant who was deaf and dumb:

> First, whether the prisoner is mute of malice or not; secondly, whether he can plead to the indictment or not; thirdly, whether he is of sufficient intellect to comprehend the course of proceedings on the trial, so as to make a proper defense—to know that

he might challenge [jurors] to whom he may object—and to comprehend the details of the evidence. . . . It is not enough that he may have a general capacity of communicating in ordinary matters.[2]

Although the medieval interest in whether a defendant remained "mute by malice" no longer has any legal importance, the two other key components of the *Pritchard* formulation (ability to understand the proceedings and to interact with one's attorney in a meaningful way) have continuing significance in applying the "incompetency plea." These two ideas are reflected in the "test" for adjudicative competence enunciated by the U.S. Supreme Court for use by the federal courts in *Dusky v. United States* in 1960: "whether the defendant has sufficient present ability to consult with his lawyer with a reasonable degree of rational understanding—and whether he has rational as well as factual understanding of the proceedings against him."[3]

Fifteen years after *Dusky,* in *Drope v. Missouri,* the Court held that the incompetence doctrine was "so fundamental to an adversary system of justice" that conviction of an incompetent defendant, or failure to adhere to procedures designed to assess a defendant's competence when doubt has been raised, violates the due process clause of the federal Constitution.[4] According to *Drope:* "It has long been accepted that a person whose mental condition is such that he lacks the capacity to understand the nature and object of the proceedings against him, to consult with counsel, and to assist in preparing his defense may not be subjected to a trial." And, it should be added, such a defendant is not competent to enter a plea of guilty in lieu of a trial.[5] The essential point is that incompetence bars adjudication, whether by plea or trial, and this includes any pretrial proceedings that could be adverse to the defendant's interests. For the sake of brevity, the term "adjudicative competence" will be used to refer to this requirement.

The concept of adjudicative competence described thus far conveys a fairly passive view of the defendant's role in criminal proceedings. A prosecution cannot proceed unless the defendant understands his jeopardy and is able to advise the lawyer who is representing him. In the picture that emerges, the defendant responds, consults, and assists, but the active adversaries in the litigation are the prosecutor and the defense attorney. This may be an accurate picture of many, if not most, criminal proceedings, but it is an incomplete picture of the *rights* accorded to the defendant under the Constitution and of the values embedded in the requirement of adjudicative competence. Under our system of criminal justice, certain decisions must be made by the defendant; they cannot be made by counsel acting on behalf of the defendant. The most important of these is whether to plead guilty. Others are whether to be tried before a jury and whether or not to testify if the case goes to trial. The defendant also is entitled to make decisions concerning the basic theory of the defense, including whether or not to raise a particular defense, and the attorney is bound to adhere to the defendant's instructions even if he or she believes that the defendant's interests would not be well served. The recent prosecution of Theodore Kaczynski revealed the tensions and difficulties that can arise when a defendant whose competence is questionable exercises the decision-making prerogatives accorded to him under our criminal justice system.[6]

When viewed from a contemporary perspective, the requirement of adjudicative competence in criminal proceedings serves three conceptually independent social purposes—preserving the dignity of the criminal process, reducing the risk of erroneous convictions, and protecting the defendant's decision-making autonomy. The dignity of the criminal process is undermined if the defendant lacks a basic moral understanding of the nature and purpose of the proceedings against him or her. The accuracy or reliability of the adjudication is threatened if the defendant is unable to assist in the development and presentation of a defense. Finally, to the extent that decisions about the course of adjudication must be made personally by the defendant, he or she must have the abilities needed to exercise decision-making autonomy.

Keeping in mind these three rationales for competence adjudication, and drawing on the language of *Dusky v. United States* and other appellate decisions that interpret and apply *Dusky,* it is possible to specify the competence-related abilities required for adjudicative competence.[7] Adjudicative competence encompasses two related but separable components. The first component refers to a foundational "competence to assist counsel." The minimum conditions legally required for participating in one's own defense generally include the capacity to do three things:

1. understand the charges and the basic elements of the adversary system (understanding),
2. appreciate one's situation as a defendant in a criminal prosecution (appreciation), and
3. relate pertinent information to counsel concerning the facts of the case (reasoning).

These abilities, taken together, make operational *Dusky*'s requirement that the defendant be able "to consult with counsel with a reasonable degree of rational understanding." The competence-to-assist-counsel component of adjudicative competence, summarized in this way, serves the dignity and accuracy rationales mentioned above, and the law clearly precludes any adjudication adverse to a defendant who lacks the abilities required to assist in his or her own defense. In this sense, competence to assist counsel is the foundational component of adjudicative competence.

The second component of adjudicative competence is decisional competence, because a defendant who is competent to assist counsel may not be competent to make the specific decisions regarding the defense of his or her case that are encountered as the process of criminal adjudication unfolds. Decision making clearly involves cognitive tasks in addition to those required for assisting counsel, but the abilities required to establish decisional competence have not yet been definitively established. The Supreme Court's 1993 decision in *Godinez v. Moran* acknowledged the significance of decisional competence, holding that a defendant's trial competence and competence to plead guilty should be addressed under a single standard (the *Dusky* standard) and that the defendant's decision-making abilities are encompassed within that standard. However, the Court did not articulate which abilities are required for decisional competence in criminal adjudication. Existing case law reflects four possible criteria that may be invoked in determining decisional competence:

1. the capacity to understand information relevant to the specific decision at issue (understanding),
2. the capacity to appreciate one's situation as a defendant confronted with a specific legal decision (appreciation),
3. the capacity to think rationally about alternative courses of action (reasoning), and
4. the capacity to express a choice among alternatives (choice).

Although some of the component abilities of adjudicative competence can be disaggregated and assessed using recently developed standardized instruments, there is no quantifiable test for deciding whether a defendant is or is not competent, or whether a particular ability is or is not fatally impaired. Not all competence-related abilities are amenable to standardized assessment. Moreover, whether the defendant's competence-related abilities are so significantly impaired as to preclude adjudication is a highly contextualized value judgment that depends on the circumstances of the particular case. As a result, competence assessment and adjudication tends to be a low-visibility, highly discretionary feature of the criminal process, rarely coming to public attention and rarely generating appealable error. In fact, most of the reported opinions on competence adjudication pertain to claims that defendants' attorneys failed to seek competence assessments or that trial judges failed to order them, rather than to claims that the trial judges misapplied the governing substantive criteria. Operationally, the salient truth about the law of adjudicative competence is that asking the question is more important than getting the "right" answer.

Participants in the criminal justice system have a variety of motivations for raising questions about the defendants' competence for adjudication other than those directly implicated by the rationales for the doctrine itself. Jail personnel may feel that the defendant needs mental health services that cannot be provided in the jail; in such cases referral for competence assessment serves as a mechanism for obtaining acute psychiatric care for defendants in detention. The prosecution or trial judge may feel that the defendant is mentally disordered and that the case should be directed to the mental health system; in such cases a commitment for competence evaluation and a finding of incompetence function as a surrogate for civil commitment. The prosecution may be seeking confinement of a defendant who would otherwise be released on bail; in such cases the incompetence commitment functions as a form of preventative detention. The defense attorney may be seeking consultation and assistance of mental health experts in deciding how to defend the case; in such cases the competence referral serves as a mechanism for obtaining more generalized forensic assistance.

In systemic terms the requirement of adjudicative competence plays a significant role in the administration of criminal justice. Although "procedural fairness" concerns (dignity, accuracy, and autonomy) may not be the main motivation for referral, they are embedded in the everyday practice of competence assessment and adjudication. Steadman and Monahan estimated, based on 1980 data, that at least twenty-five thousand felony defendants were referred for competence assessments during that year, with perhaps eight thousand of these evaluations being conducted on an inpatient basis.[8] The number of competence assessments is probably considerably higher today. Recent retrospective studies of a sample of closed criminal cases have indicated that attorneys express some doubt about their clients' competence in about 10 percent of felony cases, and that they seek evaluation in about half of these situations.[9] A conservative national estimate, based on referrals in 5 percent of 1.2 million felony indictments, would be sixty thousand pretrial competence assessments per year.[10]

Referral for a competence evaluation infrequently results in a finding of incompetence—perhaps 10 to 30 percent of defendants referred for evaluation are regarded as incompetent by evaluators and found to be so by the courts.[11] In these cases, defendants are committed for restoration of competence, usually to a forensic hospital, although treatment may also be administered on an outpatient basis. In the vast majority of such cases, the defendant is returned to the court for trial within six months. In a small number of incompetence commitments, typically involving severely and chronically mentally ill defendants or defendants with mental retardation, the defendants are found to be unrestorable and continued confinement must be predicated on the state's ordinary commitment or guardianship authority (and these criteria may not be met).[12]

In many states, the statutory criteria for incompetence do not explicitly require a finding of mental illness or mental retardation as a predicate for a finding of incompetence. As a practical matter, of course, deficits in competence-related abilities are usually associated with a mental disorder. However, some physical illnesses, such as those involving great pain or discomfort, can also impair a defendant's ability to consult with counsel and pay attention to the proceedings. Continuances are routinely granted in such cases on the ground that the defendant is not presently fit for trial. Although courts do not usually link such rulings to the competence requirement, they seem to reflect applications of the same principle.[13]

In the preceding pages, we have tried to summarize the law and practice of competence assessment and adjudication in criminal cases as a prelude to consideration of the implications of the concept of adjudicative competence in cases involving youthful offenders. As a final preliminary note, it is important to emphasize that, because a defendant's "incompetence" bars adjudication, any doubts about the defendant's mental status must be resolved before the case can proceed. In this respect, a claim that the defendant lacks competence to plead or stand trial must be distinguished from a defensive claim of mental disorder or "incapacity" that can be raised at trial. For example, a defendant who was competent to plead and to be brought to trial might nonetheless claim that he was insane *at the time of the alleged offense.* Such a claim bears on the defendant's criminal responsibility or liability and must be resolved by the jury (or the judge in a bench trial) on the basis of the evidence introduced at the trial. In sum, the doctrines of incompetence to proceed and insanity or nonresponsibility refer to two distinct connections between mental disorder and criminal adjudication—incompetence refers to a defendant's condition at the time of the adjudication and insanity or nonresponsibility refers to the defendant's condition at the time of the alleged crime.

Part II: The Adolescent in Criminal Court
Historical Overview
Before Emergence of the Juvenile Justice System

As just noted, the common-law doctrines of incompetence to plead and insanity, which serve distinct social purposes in criminal prosecutions of persons with mental disabilities, developed along separate paths. A priori, one might suppose that a similar distinction would have emerged in common-law doctrines governing the trial of children in criminal courts. First, one might expect to find that the common-law courts precluded adjudication in cases involving children too young to possess either a genuine understanding of the nature of the proceedings (or the nature of a plea) or the capacity to consult meaningfully with counsel in their own defense. Second, one might expect to find that, even if the child were able to plead, he might still be able to prove that he lacked the requisite capacity for criminal responsibility at the time of the offense. Interestingly, this is not what we find. Although a responsibility doctrine for juveniles (the "infancy" defense) was well-established by the fourteenth century, the case law reveals no doctrine barring adjudication based on immaturity equivalent to the incompetency plea.[14]

We find no evidence that the law categorically precluded the trial of young children. Indeed, legal historians have documented that criminal prosecutions of children younger than twelve were not uncommon in London and North America between 1750 and 1850. According to one commentator of the time, during a seven-year period (1822–1829), half of the persons convicted of crimes at the Old Bailey in London were under the age of twenty, and 370 of them were under twelve.[15] During that era, three thousand prisoners in London were under twenty, and half of those were under seventeen. Some of them were as young as six, and they were incarcerated at Newgate Prison with adults (although they were usually segregated) prior to and sometimes after their trials. Youths of nine and ten were often "sentenced to be burnt in the hand" or to be "transported" (to the colonies, usually Australia), and one review of cases indicates that youths were sometimes sentenced to death for crimes ranging from murder to arson or, in a few cases, theft (in one case, of a beaver hat). Death sentences usually were not carried out, but a few ten- to twelve-year-olds were executed in London and the United States during the early nineteenth century.[16]

Although youths were apparently brought to trial under the same procedures as adults, the courts recognized that youths' immaturity sometimes warranted special consideration in deciding whether they were criminally responsible. In these instances, judges were guided by common-law notions about the developmental capacities of children reflected in the so-called infancy defense. Ancient Saxon law had recognized twelve years as the age of possible discretion. In the mid-eighteenth century, Blackstone described the following stages of childhood employed in contemporary reasoning about the legally relevant capacities of children:

- birth to seven years, *infantia* or infancy,
- seven to fourteen years, *pueritia* or childhood (further distinguished as *aetas infantiae proxima* or the first stage of childhood at seven to ten and a half years, and *aetas pubertati proxima* or the second stage of childhood at ten and a half to fourteen years),
- fourteen and up, *pubertas* or adulthood.[17]

Youths below seven years, and in some historical periods up through the first stage of childhood (to about ten), were conclusively presumed to be incapable of criminal offenses because it was believed that they could not distinguish right from wrong and therefore could not have a *mens rea* (a guilty mind) or, to put it another way, were incapable of having a criminal intent. Youths over fourteen were presumed to have this capacity and therefore could be guilty of a felony. Youths in childhood (seven to fourteen) presented a special circumstance. These defendants were presumed to lack the necessary capacity, but this presumption was rebuttable if the state could demonstrate that the defendant was able to appreciate the consequence of the conduct with which he was charged. This approach allowed for considerable discretion by judges. As Blackstone described it, "By the law as it now stands . . . the capacity of doing ill, or contracting guilt, is not so much measured by years and days, as by the strength of the delinquent's understanding and judgment. For one lad of eleven years old may have as much cunning as another of fourteen . . ."[18]

The infancy presumptions seem to have been well established in colonial America. The earliest laws for the Massachusetts Bay Colony (1641) recognized immaturity (as well as idiocy, insanity, or ignorance of local laws and customs) as a basis for special "allowances" at the bar.[19]

Judges and juries, therefore, were sometimes required to decide whether individual youths in the age range from seven to fourteen had the developmental capacities to have formed criminal intent. However, the possible impact of immaturity on the ability to plead or stand trial seems to have received little attention from courts or commentators. If anyone gave any attention to youths' understanding of what was happening to them during adjudication or their understanding of decisions they had to make about pleading, typically it was the parish clergy, neighbors, parents, or schoolmasters who were moved by youths' distress.[20]

At least one account suggests that courts of that time sometimes simply could not avoid the question of children's developmental incapacities to participate in their adjudication. A schoolmaster at Newgate prison in London in the early 1800s recorded his observations of the trial in Old Bailey of a five-and-a-half-year-old boy (a prisoner at Newgate) for theft of a watch: "Nothing could be more ludicrous than the appearance of this child in court. There was the clerk reading over the indictment to this little urchin, whose chin did not reach the bar, concluding with, 'Are you guilty, or not guilty?' . . . the judge, essaying an air of extraordinary gravity . . . because [the youth] would call out, 'Not guilty, my lord.'"[21]

The judge and all attending were, in fact, "ashamed of the farce" of trying the youth, and they had conspired to assure that he would simply plead guilty and the judge would accept the plea, respite the sentence, and send the boy home with his mother.

"But the boys with whom he had been during his stay in prison had so drilled him in what he was to say when he came before the judge, telling him, if he said 'guilty' he would be hanged, that no power could induce him to say otherwise. . . . There was the minister of the parish . . . his mother, and other friends, together with the governor, all engaged in persuading this little fellow to plead guilty . . . [telling him] that he should have a tart if he would but pronounce the word 'guilty', without the addition of 'not.' But 'not guilty, my lord' was all they could get from him."

Their efforts having failed in the face of the youth's fearful obedience to the counsel of his peers, the court was required to accept his plea of not guilty. The case was then heard by a jury, which found the child not guilty "after all the gravest heads in the court had concerted a record of guilty."

In sum, the common law reflected a general recognition of the developmental incapacities of children and younger adolescents. Under the "defense" of infancy, evidence concerning the child's maturity could be admitted at the trial as a basis for excuse or mitigation. However, a diligent search has failed to reveal any case or statute enunciating a procedural bar to adjudication in criminal courts based on a defendant's immaturity.[22] In this respect the law relating to immaturity in criminal courts appears to have diverged from the law relating to mental disorder, which recognized separate doctrines of adjudicative competence and criminal responsibility. In any case, further development of the law was interrupted by the emergence of the juvenile court in the early twentieth century.

After Emergence of the Juvenile Justice System

With the advent of a juvenile justice system in the United States at the beginning of the twentieth century, youths of a certain age or younger (typically sixteen or seventeen was the maximum) were tried in a separate system of juvenile courts in lieu of criminal courts. The new juvenile court dispensed with the procedural formality and safeguards of criminal proceedings on the theory that juvenile delinquency adjudications had a rehabilitative objective, and that a delinquency disposition did not have the punitive purposes and consequences associated with a criminal conviction. However, even during the early period, when the rehabilitative ideal of the juvenile courts was most enthusiastically embraced, the architects of the juvenile court recognized that some youths would not be "amenable" to rehabilitation in services available to the juvenile courts. Some might present too great a risk of harm to other youths or the community, or they might appear too sophisticated or hardened in their pattern of crime to present a reasonable chance to be redirected prior to attainment of their adulthood. Therefore, even at its inception, the juvenile justice system allowed judges to waive juvenile court jurisdiction over certain youths who were judged not to be "fit and proper subjects" for rehabilitation services provided for youths. Waiver of jurisdiction by the juvenile court allowed charges against such youths to be filed in criminal court, where they would be tried as adults. Most states limited the option of waiver to youths who exceeded a certain age, typically fourteen, fifteen, or sixteen in various states. In addition, some states exempted a category of especially serious charges, particularly murder, from the exclusive jurisdiction of the juvenile court, allowing younger defendants to be tried in criminal courts under some circumstances.[23]

The continuing jurisdiction of the criminal courts over some youthful defendants charged with serious offenses raises the possibility that some youths transferred to criminal courts might be found to lack the capacities needed for the adjudication to go forward in criminal court. We did not expect to find many such cases. Juvenile court jurisdiction was usually exclusive in cases involving children and young adolescents, and even in states permitting juvenile courts to waive jurisdiction over young offenders (younger than fifteen), they tended not to do so. At least through the 1970s, the vast majority of youths who were waived to criminal court were near the maximum jurisdictional age for the juvenile justice system, having been charged in their sixteenth or seventeenth year.[24] Youths of that age rarely manifest serious deficits related to adjudicative competence that could be attributed to developmental immaturity. Moreover, juvenile court judges, who had nearly absolute discretion in most states, probably tended to retain jurisdiction over youths with the most serious developmental deficits, even if they were older or had been charged with serious offenses. If the offenses were less serious, these cases could sometimes be handled through arrangements with other social services (such as services for persons with mental retardation) among older offenders.

To say that waiver of less mature or more disturbed youths was probably very infrequent is not to say that it did not occur, however, and a few such cases appear in the appellate reports. Appellate courts showed some will-ingness to adopt safeguards not required for adults to protect juvenile de-fendants against ill-considered decisions such as pleading guilty or waiv-ing other rights in criminal proceedings.[25] However, occasional arguments that immaturity should be a presumptive basis for retaining juvenile court jurisdiction in a transfer proceeding were rejected,[26] and the possibility that a minor defendant might be regarded as incompetent to stand trial in a criminal court on grounds of immaturity appears to have been unex-amined by appellate courts (or legislatures) until the 1980s.[27]

Under Modern Juvenile Justice Reforms

Latent questions concerning the bearing of immaturity on criminal adju-dication have now become more pressing because of recent reforms in ju-venile law that have brought more youths, at younger ages, within the jurisdiction of criminal courts. Alarmed by an increase in violent offenses (especially gun homicides) by juveniles, most states during the past decade revised their codes pertaining to the adjudication of youths charged with serious and violent offenses.[28] Most states have utilized one or more of the following mechanisms:

1. lowering age of judicial waiver, and of criminal court juris-diction, permitting juvenile courts to waive jurisdiction in cases involving younger offenders;
2. statutory exclusion of certain offenses from juvenile court jurisdiction, allowing such charges to be filed automatically and exclusively in criminal court; and
3. conferring prosecutorial discretion to file charges against youths above specified ages in either juvenile or in criminal court.

Typically the scope of these laws is limited to charges against youths above a specified age (often thirteen or fourteen) who are arrested for certain serious offenses and/or who have a record of serious offenses in the past.

Most states combine judicial waiver with either statutory exclusion or prosecutorial discretion. Diversity in states' waiver laws is further in-creased by differences in minimum ages, types of offenses, and procedural and evidentiary requirements (such as burdens and standards of proof). As a consequence, the law governing waiver varies significantly from state to state. Overall, however, the trends in juvenile justice reform have had the general effects of curtailing the jurisdiction of juvenile courts, reduc-ing the discretion of juvenile court judges, enlarging the pool of young offenders subject to trial in criminal court, and subjecting to criminal prosecution offenders who are younger and less mature than before.

Empirical evidence indicates that these reforms have indeed increased the numbers of young offenders tried in criminal courts.[29] Whereas juvenile court judges formerly tended to retain jurisdiction over younger adolescents, new laws that provide automatically for criminal court jurisdiction over thirteen- or fourteen year olds charged with serious offenses, and that permit prosecutors to file criminal charges in such cases directly, have decreased the average age of youths seen in criminal court.[30] Most important, while there is less direct evidence, it is reasonable to expect that with the reduction in judicial discretion to screen youths whose cases will be adjudicated in criminal court, those who are seen there are psychologically more heterogeneous than under the previous generation of juvenile justice statutes. Criteria for jurisdiction that rely on age and offense alone are more likely to result in criminal adjudication of youths with developmental disabilities and mental illness who might have been screened out in states that formerly provided for waiver by judicial discretion alone. In light of these reconfigurations of the boundaries between juvenile and criminal adjudication, long latent questions regarding the significance of a defendant's immaturity must now be addressed. How the problem is addressed will depend on whether the case is initiated in the juvenile court or the criminal court.

Cases Initiated in Juvenile Court

In cases that are initially filed in juvenile court, judges are authorized to waive jurisdiction in cases involving younger offenders than before. Under traditional "amenability" criteria, juvenile judges apparently tended to retain jurisdiction in cases involving immature youths or those with developmental disabilities or mental or emotional disorders. In light of the statutory tendency to reduce juvenile court discretion and to establish presumptive criteria for waiver, the importance of taking into account the offender's competence to stand trial in the criminal court has finally been given explicit attention in several states. Under the Virginia waiver statute, a juvenile court must find that a defendant is competent for adjudication in criminal court before waiving jurisdiction to the criminal court.[31] Also, at least two state appellate courts have indicated that adjudicative competence should be taken into account in a transfer hearing.[32] In our view, considerations of both fairness and judicial economy suggest that the juvenile's competence to proceed in the criminal court should be a prerequisite for waiver of jurisdiction by the juvenile court.

Cases Initiated in Criminal Court

A more serious problem arises in those states that have authorized charges against younger offenders to be filed directly in the criminal court, bypassing the juvenile court entirely. Apparently recognizing the possibility that criminal adjudication might not be suitable for a subset of young offenders otherwise within the age/offense criteria, a few states have prescribed pretrial hearings in criminal court, allowing judges to remand some youths to juvenile court for adjudication when their cases have been filed directly in criminal court. In these states, the criteria for reverse waiver (waiving criminal court jurisdiction in favor of juvenile court jurisdiction) seem to represent the mirror image of the criteria governing waiver of jurisdiction by juvenile courts (transferring the case to criminal court).[33] In Maryland, for example, the criminal court may waive jurisdiction if it finds that doing so is "in the best interests of the child or society," taking into account, inter alia, "the mental and physical condition of the child."[34] In Wisconsin, the criminal court is directed to transfer jurisdiction if the child proves, inter alia, that he or she "could not receive adequate treatment in the criminal justice system."[35] In both states, the criminal courts have the flexibility to take into account the child's maturity, but even in these states the courts are not explicitly directed to take into account the youth's fitness for criminal adjudication. Again, it seems self-evident that the issue of adjudicative competence requires explicit attention early in the process when criminal charges are filed directly in criminal courts against youths younger than sixteen. As we will indicate below, we also think that a criminal court should ordinarily be required to waive jurisdiction to the juvenile court if it finds that a juvenile lacks competence for criminal adjudication.

Unresolved Issues Regarding the Competence of Youths in Criminal Court

When charges against youths are adjudicated in criminal court, at minimum the law should provide at least the same protections that are afforded to adults. According to the prevailing criteria of adjudicative competence, a criminal case may not proceed if the defendant's capacities to comprehend the nature of the proceedings, to assist counsel, or to make important decisions are significantly impaired. The due process clause also requires courts to take steps to assess the defendant's competence if a "good faith doubt" about the defendant's capacity has been raised. There are several reasons to be concerned, however, that a standard application of the current criteria and ways of thinking about adjudicative competence in criminal court may afford less protection to adolescents than to adult defendants.

Mental Disabilities and Youths

From a clinical and developmental perspective, mental illness is defined differently and is subject to greater error in identification for adolescents than for adults. If legal standards and procedures for adjudicative competence do not take adequate account of these differences, some youths with serious deficits in relevant capacities may incorrectly be regarded as competent. The basic problem is that some types of adolescent mental disorders do not meet the clinical thresholds typically employed in adult criminal cases. In everyday practice, findings of incompetence have been associated with schizophrenia or serious affective disorders.[36] But severe mental disorders in adolescents are not merely junior analogues of mental illnesses in adulthood. For example, some youths who are developing psychotic disorders do not manifest the classic symptoms—such as delusions and hallucinations in schizophrenia—until they enter adulthood.[37] Thus the early form of their disorder may be responsible for deficits in capacities associated with the standard for adjudicative competence (see Chapter 2 and Chapter 5 in this volume), yet may not be identified as the cause of the deficits if criminal courts are using as a guide the severity of disorders that they are accustomed to associating with adjudicative incompetence in adults. Moreover, for a number of reasons, clinicians themselves often cannot identify adolescents' serious mental disorders with the same degree of reliability that is typically achieved with adults.[38]

For these reasons, there is cause for concern that when mental disorders are responsible for youth's deficiencies in their abilities to participate in their adjudication, the mental disorder itself will not be identified.[39] This puts adolescents in general in a position of greater risk of an inappropriate finding of competence because courts and clinicians assume that a legal finding of incompetence must be predicated on a diagnosis of severe mental disorder, even if this is strictly true as a matter of law only in some states.

Developmental Immaturity

Some youths, especially those who are nearer to the minimum age for waiver to criminal court, may have significant deficits in competence-related abilities due not to mental disorder but to developmental immaturity. As noted earlier, few statutes or judicial decisions explicitly recognize developmental immaturity as a basis for adjudicative incompetence. Formalistic, disorder-oriented application of current standards, therefore, may result in unfair jeopardy for youths whose developmental incapacities impair their ability to participate in their defense.

Several commentators have drawn on the developmental literature to identify cognitive and psychosocial abilities that may be relevant to the adjudicative competence of adolescents, especially the decision-making abilities that bear on their waiver of important rights.[40] These reviews have made two points. First, even younger adolescents normally may be expected to have developed the cognitive capacities to comprehend legal proceedings in a manner that the competence doctrine seeks to ensure. Yet some younger adolescents may be temporarily delayed in their development, so that their cognitive capacities are more like those of children several years younger. (There is no reason to think that many adolescents lack the ability to understand the nature of the proceedings, but a substantial body of research suggests that, when compared with adults, delinquent youths tend to have an incomplete understanding of the concept of a right as an entitlement. Also, research suggests that younger adolescents may have more difficulty thinking strategically than older adolescents and adults. See Chapter 5 in this volume.) Second, even if their formal capacities for understanding and reasoning are adequately developed, the psychological context in which they perceive the legal process, or in which they weigh the consequences of their choices in that process, may affect their decisions in ways that are developmentally linked. This can result in choices that they would not make when they reach maturity. For example, reviews of normal developmental trends suggest that adolescents tend to focus on short-term consequences, favorable or unfavorable, and to discount long-term consequences of their actions. This tendency could lead them to make choices in the adjudicative process (about waiver of important rights or pleading, for example) that do not reflect the values that they would bring to bear on the judgment a few short years later when they become adults.[41]

Youths' developmental incapacities are presumably taken into account in traditional amenability determinations in the juvenile court, and might be taken into account in pretrial reverse-waiver hearings that some states require when charges are filed against youths directly in criminal court. But currently there is no evidence with which to weigh the adequacy of this mechanism as a safeguard, and existing law provides no formal basis for relying upon developmental immaturity as a reason for either reverse-waiver to juvenile court or a declaration of adjudicative incompetence.

Adolescent Status

Whatever their cognitive capacities, adolescent defendants in criminal court differ from adult defendants in an important way. Their trial "as an adult" does not change their social status as adolescents. This context of status difference between adolescent defendants and the adult world of their adjudication has potentially important implications for their participation in the trial process. Some of these implications are discussed in other chapters in this volume with a focus on youths' perceptions of their attorneys and attorney-youth communications, and on attorneys' and youths' perceptions of the role of youths in their defense.[42] Are youths as likely as adults, in general, to experience a sense of autonomy with regard to choices that they must make in the context of a trial as an adult? Are they at greater risk of failing to appreciate the impact of their appearance and demeanor on fact finders during the adjudication process? These discussions point out the need to examine ways in which youths' capacities and perspectives in social interactions, while potentially meeting the basic standards for adjudicative competence, might place them at a disadvantage relative to adult defendants in ways that may have an impact on legal decisions about their charges and their case dispositions.

Being Fair to Youths in Criminal Court

Subjecting youthful offenders to the jurisdiction of criminal courts is a controversial social policy, and there are many reasons for believing that the pendulum has swung too far in the direction of incapacitation and punishment. We tend to favor policies that would remake the juvenile court rather than abandon it or eviscerate its jurisdiction. Specifically, we believe that juvenile courts should have exclusive jurisdiction over offenders younger than fourteen and presumptive jurisdiction over those fourteen to fifteen. Among other reasons for this conclusion is deep concern about the risk of unfairness in criminal proceedings against youthful defendants. Although additional research is needed, current knowledge about adolescent development raises strong doubts about the capacities of youths thirteen or younger, in comparison with adults and older adolescents as a group, to assist effectively in their own defense and to make self-interested decisions.[43] The dignity of the criminal process might also be demeaned by the image of a thirteen-year-old defendant in the dock.

   Although concerns about immaturity per se diminish with age, the interaction of immaturity with mental disability highlights the risk of mandating criminal court jurisdiction in cases involving fourteen- or fifteen-year-old offenders as a class. Some flexibility for individualized as-sessment of the suitability of criminal prosecution should be preserved, either by the juvenile court or the criminal court. (As indicated above, we prefer that initial jurisdiction be lodged with the juvenile court, but the same principle would apply even if the charges were filed initially in crim-inal court.) Within that framework, judicial review of the defendant's competence for criminal adjudication should be mandatory in cases in-volving fourteen- to fifteen-year-old defendants.[44] To whatever extent the jurisdiction of criminal courts can be invoked against youthful offenders, courts will need to develop rules and practices to reduce the risk of un-fair adjudication.

Adjusting the Criteria of Adjudicative Competence

The first requirement is to recognize that the abilities required for adju-dicative competence can be affected by developmental factors. Thus, courts and legislatures should declare explicitly that a finding of incom-petence may be predicated on immaturity as well as mental disorder. Once courts have recognized that developmental factors have a bearing on an adolescent defendant's competence for criminal adjudication, they will need to adjust the criteria to take these factors into account. We do not claim that new or different criteria are necessary, but the usual criteria must be applied with sensitivity to the clinical realities of adolescent men-tal disorder and to the cognitive and psychosocial features of adolescent development reviewed in this volume.

Dispositional Consequences of a Finding of Incompetence

What should be done after a youth has been found incompetent for crim-inal adjudication? To the extent that the finding is predicated on psycho-pathology, treatment of the defendant's condition may be sufficient to re-store competence. However, what is to be done if the finding is predicated on developmental immaturity? Although the "condition" is remediable, the process of maturation cannot be accelerated by psychopharmacology or education. Although a six- to twelve-month delay in the criminal pro-ceedings might sometimes be sufficient to enable the defendant to grow up, a remedial legal disposition would be both illogical and ethically awk-ward in most cases. The design of alternative dispositions might turn on the nature of the defendant's deficit. For example, if the defendant's abil-ities to understand the proceedings and communicate with counsel were unaffected and the deficit related only to decision making, it might be pos-sible to proceed on the basis of default rules disallowing waivers of constitutional safeguards, together with other assurances of effective representation. In the absence of such a discrete deficit, however, the preferable disposition is for jurisdiction to be retained by, or transferred to, the juvenile court. As will be discussed below, the threshold for adjudicative competence in juvenile court should be lower than that required in criminal proceedings as long as the youth is not exposed to substantial jeopardy.

Beyond Adjudicative Competence

Because a finding of incompetence bars adjudication, the threshold for such a finding should not be set too low. However, even if they do not amount to legal incompetence, impairments or deficits in the defendant's competence-related abilities have important implications for effective advocacy by attorneys and for the design of procedural safeguards.

Effective Advocacy

The doctrine of adjudicative competence tends to focus on capacities of defendants that are constitutionally prerequisite to a fair adjudication. However, the demands of fairness also require attention to the interactive aspects of the relationship between the adolescent defendant and his or her attorney, and to the knowledge and skill required of attorneys who bear the heavy burden of representing adolescent defendants in criminal prosecutions.[45]

Particular attention should be paid to the adolescent defendant's understanding of the role and responsibilities of the attorney, especially in light of attitudes toward authority figures. Oppositional behavior toward authority could impair the adolescent's ability to trust the defense attorney and to assist in his or her own defense. Alternatively, viewing the attorney as an authority figure could lead to distorted communication and could also prevent the adolescent from appreciating his or her own role as an autonomous decision maker. Attorneys should also recognize that they may have to explain many aspects of the criminal proceedings that they may take for granted in representing adults, including the nature of a right.

Another important concern is the risk that adolescents may make decisions that they would not make several years later. This problem could arise because of a distorted time perspective and a tendency to discount long-term consequences (such as risk of long-term confinement) in favor of immediate consequences (such as looking "cool" in the eyes of peers). As noted earlier, developmental factors of this nature can affect the adolescents' interactions with their attorneys, their behavior in court, and their decisions regarding the defense or disposition of the case. Attorneys need to be alert to these possibilities in order to counteract them.

Procedural Protections

Many of the concerns mentioned earlier relate to developmentally linked psychosocial influences on the capacity of the adolescent to make self-interested decisions (decisions that he would make if he were an adult). These considerations can be taken into account in applying the traditional criteria of adjudicative competence. However, concerns about developmental immaturity can also be taken into account by rules and procedures that afford the adolescent greater protection than would be provided to (or would be appropriate for) adults. For example, the law could provide that adolescents being tried in criminal court are not permitted to waive counsel and are not permitted to plead guilty without counsel's consent. (Such a rule would not be permissible for competent adults under *Faretta v. California.*)[46] Or, in cases involving guilty pleas, trial courts might be required to undertake an elaborate colloquy probing the possible influence of developmental features of adolescence that can interfere with effective self-presentation and self-interested decision making. ("Why did you decide to plead guilty?" "What would be likely to happen if you didn't plead guilty?" "What did your mother or father want you to do?" "What did your attorney want you to do?" "What did your friend or co-defendant want you to do?")

It should be emphasized that safeguards against immature decision making by adolescents in criminal adjudication have been recognized by courts since early in the twentieth century, and that those protections are based in the deeply rooted traditions of Anglo-American law.[47] They should be strengthened whether or not immaturity is recognized as a basis for a finding of incompetence.

Summary

Our views regarding the procedures governing adjudication of minors in criminal court may be summarized briefly as follows:

- Juvenile court jurisdiction should be exclusive in cases involving defendants below the age of fourteen at the time of the alleged offense.
- For cases initiated in juvenile court in which judicial waiver is the applicable mechanism for invoking criminal court jurisdiction, a finding that the juvenile is competent for adjudication in criminal court should be a necessary predicate for transfer.

- For cases initiated in criminal court, a procedural mechanism for reverse waiver (for the court to decline jurisdiction and transfer the case to juvenile court) should be available for defendants younger than sixteen. A hearing on the defendant's competence for adjudication should be mandatory in any case involving a defendant younger than fourteen (if the criminal court has jurisdiction over such cases).
- If a criminal court finds that a juvenile defendant lacks the abilities required to understand the proceedings or assist counsel in criminal proceedings, the case should be transferred to juvenile court. In the event that the youth's deficits relate only to decision making, the case might be retained in the criminal court as long as safeguards are in place to assure that guilty pleas or other waivers of constitutional rights are in the defendant's best interests.

Part III: Adjudicative Competence in Juvenile Court
The Uncertain Status of Adjudicative Competence in Juvenile Court

Until the 1970s, the concept of adjudicative competence had little meaning in the juvenile court. Juvenile courts were developed in principle to provide rehabilitation, not punishment. Drawing on the *parens patriae* model of civil commitment, the architects of the juvenile court rejected the adversarial tradition of criminal adjudication in favor of an inquisitorial procedure in which all the parties were joined in a common effort to redirect the path of the wayward child.[48] According to the canon of juvenile court philosophy, delinquency proceedings did not pit the state against the child, and any intervention undertaken did not represent punishment for a criminal act. In this ideological environment, procedural safeguards designed to shield a defendant from the power of the state had no place. Even after adults were afforded counsel as a matter of right in criminal proceedings, delinquency adjudications were conducted in the informal manner of a social service case conference, without lawyers and unconstrained by the rules of evidence. Judges were given wide latitude to select a course of action in the child's best interests.

The three values underlying the doctrine of adjudicative competence in criminal cases are closely tied to the logic of the adversary system. First, prosecuting and convicting defendants who do not understand the nature of the proceedings or the jeopardy they face would demean the dignity of the criminal process and amounts to a senseless infliction of punishment. In a delinquency proceeding, by contrast, the state was said to be proceeding "in the interest" of the child, not against him or her, and the private, informal juvenile court hearing was meant to displace the formal spectacle of a public trial in criminal court. In a delinquency proceeding, a child's lack of understanding would not be an occasion for moral embarrassment; instead, it would highlight deficits that might properly bear on the child's diagnosis and treatment.

Second, a defendant's incompetence can weaken the reliability or accuracy of a criminal adjudication. A meaningful opportunity for a criminal defendant to confront the evidence against him or her, and to present his or her own case in defense, is an important safeguard against an unfair conviction. However, in the predictive context of the delinquency proceeding, whether or not a child committed the delinquent act was thought to be less important than the accuracy of the psychological assessment, which must be predicated on an understanding of all the child's behavior, not only on the particular act giving rise to the petition. Moreover, because the state's aims professed to be entirely rehabilitative, an unwarranted delinquency intervention could be characterized as less costly to the child and to society than an erroneous criminal conviction.

Third, because no decision-making role was envisioned for the child in a delinquency proceeding, developmental deficits or psychopathological symptoms were important only because of their possible bearing on treatment, not because they might compromise the child's capacity for decision-making autonomy.

All this changed drastically with the Supreme Court's seminal decision in *In re Gault*,[49] which challenged the ideological assumptions of the juvenile court and subjected delinquency adjudications to the requirements of the due process clause. Justice Fortas' opinion observed that the juvenile court had not lived up to its rehabilitative promise and that delinquency interventions had an inescapably punitive effect on the child even if the state had no punitive purpose. In subsequent rulings, the Court has subjected delinquency proceedings to virtually all of the safeguards of the criminal process except jury trial. Conceptually, the most revealing of these decisions for our purposes is *In re Winship*,[50] which required that the state prove the juvenile's guilt beyond a reasonable doubt—a decision that rests squarely on the premise that the cost of an erroneous finding of delinquency is equivalent to the cost of an erroneous criminal conviction.

None of the Supreme Court's decisions remaking the constitutional structure of juvenile court mentions the doctrine of adjudicative competence. However, the virtually inescapable conclusion is that the due process clause bars adjudication of delinquency against children who lack the minimum capacity to understand the proceedings and participate in their own defense.[51] As the Court said in *Drope v. Missouri*, the requirement of adjudicative competence is "fundamental to an adversarial system of justice"—the kind of system to which juvenile courts are now required to conform.[52] (As will be discussed below, this is not to say that the threshold of competence should be the same as that required for criminal proceedings.)

Although the implications of *Gault* and *Winship* for the doctrine of adjudicative competence seem readily apparent, the issue was not presented very often during the first twenty years after *Gault* was decided.[53] A few appellate cases dealt with youths suffering from mental illnesses, and one case appeared to recognize adjudicative incompetence due to developmental immaturity.[54] Overall, however, the issue was mainly of academic interest until the contemporary reforms of juvenile court statutes, beginning in the late 1980s, extended criminal-court jurisdiction over the most serious felony charges involving older adolescents and transformed the juvenile court's mission and authority in responding to the youths who remained within its jurisdiction.

The "purpose clauses" in juvenile courts legislation in some states were modified to make punishment, rather than rehabilitation, the primary objective of juvenile justice.[55] In addition, several types of reforms increased the punitive consequences of adjudication in juvenile court. First, juvenile court records began to "count" as prior convictions in adult sentencing, and some juvenile court proceedings became public. Second, determinate sentences were mandated for various offenses, thereby reducing juvenile judges' discretion to use probation or rehabilitative dispositions in cases that might warrant them. Third, new "youthful offender laws" in many states authorized juvenile court to sentence youths to periods of confinement that exceeded the juvenile court's typical jurisdictional age limits, thereby assuring that such youths would serve juvenile court sentences well into their adult years. Finally, some states lowered the jurisdictional age for delinquency adjudication, even including very young children between the ages of six to ten, for whom juvenile courts used to rely on rehabilitative options rather than formal adjudication.

Legislative efforts to reshape juvenile court adjudication in a more punitive mold—making punishment the avowed objective and empowering juvenile judges to mete out lengthy sentences similar to those imposed in criminal courts—appear to have called attention to the importance of adjudicative competence as a safeguard against unfair adjudication. More than half of the states have now explicitly recognized the requirement of adjudicative competence in delinquency proceedings, either by statute or case law.[56] Only one state, Oklahoma, has held (incorrectly, in our view) that the nonpunitive aspirations of the juvenile court continue to render the doctrine of adjudicative competence totally inapplicable.[57]

A recent Georgia Court of Appeals case illustrates the rationale that courts have employed in extending to defendants in juvenile court the protection of the adjudicative competence requirement.[58] The case involved a twelve-year-old boy, diagnosed with mental retardation, who was charged with aggravated sodomy of two younger children. The court noted that Georgia recognized many rights of juveniles in delinquency proceedings, among them the right to counsel and the privilege against self-incrimination, provision of which would be meaningless if a juvenile defendant were not capable of taking advantage of them. In this case, the juvenile defendant was unable to give a coherent or consistent account of the alleged event, preventing counsel from obtaining information critical for the boy's defense.

The Meaning of Adjudicative Competence in Juvenile Court

For the most part, statutes and judicial decisions recognizing the adjudicative competence requirement either do not prescribe a definition or incorporate the test used in criminal courts. This leaves many important questions unanswered. For example, are the criteria for adjudicative competence the same in juvenile proceedings as in criminal proceedings? More specifically, are the same abilities required? At the same level? What are the consequences of a finding that a juvenile is incompetent for delinquency adjudication? An underlying question is whether and under what circumstances a juvenile should be regarded as too immature even for juvenile delinquency adjudication.

Even if developmental considerations should affect the application of customary competence criteria to youths being prosecuted in criminal courts, it is not clear that the same should be true in juvenile courts. After all, *only* juveniles are subject to delinquency intervention. If a youth lacks sufficient competence to be adjudicated in criminal court, the default possibility is to retain juvenile court jurisdiction. But what is to happen if the youth is found to lack competence for juvenile court adjudication?

Few statutes address the connection between developmental considerations and the adjudicative competence requirement. The District of Columbia statute explicitly restricts the definition of incompetence to deficits existing "by reason of mental illness or at least moderate mental retardation. . . ."[59] Wyoming's statute not only predicates a finding of incompetence on mental illness or retardation, but ties it to involuntary commitment. By contrast, some states (Florida, for example) explicitly refer to the defendant's mental age. We are not aware of any statute that varies the meaning of competence according to the nature and severity of the dispositional consequences of a delinquency adjudication.

In our view, however, the meaning of adjudicative competence in delinquency adjudication should turn on the consequences of a delinquency finding (or conviction). If the jeopardy to which the juvenile is exposed in juvenile court is equivalent to the consequences of a criminal adjudication, the requirements of adjudicative competence should apply with full, undiluted force. However, if the juvenile is exposed to dispositions that expire at the age of majority, then the criteria of adjudicative competence should be limited to baseline cognitive abilities to understand the proceedings and communicate with counsel. In the rare situations in which the juvenile lacks even these abilities, delinquency jurisdiction would have to be foreclosed in favor of the residual parens patriae jurisdiction of the juvenile court (for example, PINS, or mental health commitment). We will elaborate on these points below.

Quasi-Criminal Dispositions

First, it seems self-evident, on grounds of fairness and efficiency, that a juvenile should not be subjected to the jeopardy of a transfer hearing unless he or she is competent for criminal adjudication. Second, even if juvenile court jurisdiction is retained, the defendant should not be subjected to a split sentence (part of which will be served in the criminal justice system), or to a sentence that extends the dispositional jurisdiction of the juvenile court beyond its adjudicative jurisdiction, unless he or she meets the undiluted criteria for adjudicative competence in criminal proceedings.

Adoption of this view should not pose significant barriers to adjudication in most situations. For adolescents, developmental lags are most likely to be associated with decision-making deficits rather than with diminished capacities to understand pertinent information, to appreciate the nature of the jeopardy, or to communicate rationally with counsel. In cases involving adolescents with diminished capacity for rational self-interested decision making, legislatures and courts can respond either by forsaking quasi-criminal dispositions or by adopting some of the protective rules and procedures described earlier in this chapter. (For example, guilty pleas and waivers of counsel could be foreclosed altogether, and other waivers of constitutional rights in juvenile court could be foreclosed without counsel's consent.)

In those cases where young defendants lack requisite ability to understand important information or appreciate the jeopardy they face, quasi-criminal dispositions would have to be foreclosed. However, delinquency jurisdiction, including exclusively juvenile dispositional options, would remain available.

Ordinary Juvenile Dispositions

As noted above, the constitutional logic of *In re Gault* and *In re Winship* entail a minimum requirement of adjudicative competence even in ordinary delinquency proceedings in which the court's dispositional authority expires at the age of majority. In our view, however, the criteria for competence in this setting are considerably less demanding than the criteria for competent participation in criminal proceedings. We say this because the competence requirement in juvenile adjudication serves the limited, though important, purpose of reducing the risk of an erroneous finding of guilt. An autonomous decision-making role by the minor is aspirational, not obligatory, and the youth's decisional competence therefore should not be regarded as a constitutional prerequisite to adjudication. Based on this analysis, adjudication should be permitted so long as the juvenile has a basic understanding of the purpose of the proceedings and is able to communicate rationally with counsel. Deficits in the juvenile's ability to appreciate counsel's role or to engage in reasoned decision making should not bar adjudication. In general, the measure of adjudicative competence in ordinary delinquency proceedings is exclusively cognitive; psychosocial aspects of adolescent development drop out of the equation altogether.

This is not to say that a juvenile who is competent in decision making should have no right to make important decisions bearing on defense strategy, or on the waiver or exercise of constitutional rights. The scope of a competent juvenile defendant's decision-making prerogatives merits independent attention, both as a matter of legal ethics and constitutional law. However, competence to make these decisions should not be regarded as a prerequisite for adjudication. In cases involving juveniles who are incompetent at decision making, waiver of constitutional rights would not be permitted and decisions about defense strategy would be made by the attorney (and/or the parent or guardian in consultation with the attorney).

Conclusion

In this chapter, we have attempted to transplant the ancient doctrine of adjudicative competence from its established surroundings in criminal proceedings to the shifting terrain of juvenile justice. This task has taken us down many doctrinal byways and has raised many unanswered questions. Perhaps we have made the problem more complicated than it needs to be, but recent efforts to reshape (or undermine) the juvenile justice system have also made juvenile adjudication more complicated than it needs to be. In any case, it would be a mistake to focus our attention exclusively on the symptom while bracketing the underlying problem. Legal recognition of the doctrine of adjudicative competence will not cure what ails the juvenile justice system and will do little to stem the flow of youthful offenders to correctional warehouses. But there is merit in rearguard actions, and raising the stakes also deepens the struggle for fairness.

Notes

1. Don Grubin, *Fitness to Plead Guilty in England and Wales* (East Sussex, U.K.: Psychology Press, 1996), 9.

2. *R. v. Pritchard,* 173 Eng Rep 135 (1836).

3. 362 US 402 (1960).

4. 420 US 162 (1975).

5. *Godinez v. Moran,* 509 US 389, 398 (1993), holds that the legal tests for competence to stand trial and competence to plead guilty (and waive counsel) are the same.

6. Although he eventually pleaded guilty to the many charges against him, the Unabomber and his attorneys battled for months over control of the case. The defendant, diagnosed as having paranoid schizophrenia, resisted an insanity plea and apparently was opposed to the introduction of any evidence that would show that he was mentally ill, even at the capital-sentencing phase of his trial (if the case had been tried).

7. This analysis of the components of adjudicative competence is set forth in Richard J. Bonnie, "The Competence of Criminal Defendants: Beyond Dusky and Drope," *Miami Law Review* 47 (1993): 539–601.

8. Henry J. Steadman and John Monahan, eds., *Mentally Disordered Offenders* (New York: Plenum Press, 1983).

9. Steven K. Hoge, Richard J. Bonnie, Norman Poythress, and John Monahan, "Attorney-Client Decision Making in Criminal Cases: Client Competence and Participation as Perceived by Their Attorneys," *Behavioral Sciences and the Law* 10 (1992): 385–394. Norman Poythress, Richard J. Bonnie, Steven R. Hoge, John Monahan, and Lois Oberlander, "Client Abilities to Assist Counsel and Make Decisions in Criminal Cases: Findings from Three Studies," *Law and Human Behavior* 18 (1994): 437–452.

10. The estimate of 1.2 million felony indictments is based on extrapolation from figures from two publications of the Bureau of Justice Statistics on criminal adjudication in state courts in 1994: Brian A. Reaves, "Felony Defendants in Large Urban Counties, 1994." In *Bureau of Justice Statistics, Executive Summary* (January 1998). Patrick A. Langan and Jodi M. Brown, "Felony Sentences in State Courts, 1994." In *Bureau of Justice Statistics, Bulletin* (January 1997).

11. Gary Melton, John Petrila, Norman Poythress, and Christopher Slobogin, *Psychological Evaluations for the Courts,* 2d ed. (New York: Gilford Press, 1997), 135. In the remaining cases, however, a pretrial competence evaluation has two important practical effects: it provides an opportunity for mental health consul-

tation for an attorney representing a client with mental disability, and it serves to "cleanse" the case of a possible ground for setting aside a conviction based on a claim that the attorney or the court failed to recognize or explore the possibility of incompetence.

12. *Jackson v. Indiana,* 406 US 715, 738 (1972).

13. Those cases typically arise in appeal when the defendant claims that the trial court's refusal to grant a continuance was an abuse of discretion. When appellate courts reverse convictions in such cases—which is atypical—the decision is grounded in concerns that the defendant's illness impeded his ability to assist counsel in preparation for trial or in the conduct of trial. (*Ward v. State,* 142 Fla. 238, 194 So. 637 (1940) [heart condition]; *State v. Wilson,* 181 La. 61, 158 So. 621 (1935) [gunshot wound].) Occasionally, a court will invoke the due process clause (*Miller v. Commonwealth,* 197 Ky. 703, 247 S.W. 956 [1923]) or the *Dusky* criteria (*State v. Kaiser,* 74 N.J.Super. 257, 181 A.2d 184 [1962]).

14. Richard J. Bonnie, Anne Coughlin, John Jeffries, and Peter Low, *Criminal Law* (Westbury, NY: Foundation Press, 1997), 420.

15. Wiley B. Sanders, ed., *Juvenile Offenders for a Thousand Years* (Chapel Hill: University of North Carolina Press, 1970), 21–42, 135.

16. Information in this paragraph is drawn from Thomas Bernard, *The Cycle of Juvenile Justice* (New York: Oxford University Press, 1992), 24; and Sanders, 21–38 and 320–22.

17. Sir William Blackstone, *Commentaries on the Laws of England, In Four Books,* vol. 4 (Chicago: University of Chicago Press, 1979), 22.

18. Ibid., 23.

19. The law stated, under the heading "Tryals" that "Children, Ideots, distracted persons, and all that are Strangers or new comers to our Plantation, shall have such allowances, and dispensations in any case, whether Criminal or others, as Religion and Reason require." Sanders, 317, provides the following citation: "*The General Laws and Liberties of the Massachusetts Colony: Revised and Re-printed, By Order of the General Court Holden at Boston, May 15th, 1672,* p. 152."

20. For example, see accounts of children's trials at the Old Bailey in Sanders, 146–149.

21. This account is from Sanders, 147–148, who cites an anonymous author of a work published in London in 1833. No explanation is provided concerning this criminal trial of a youth who was below the age of seven and who therefore, according to the infancy presumption of the common law as described by Blackstone, could not lawfully have been found guilty.

22. There is some indication, however, of a judicial inclination to require procedural protections for juveniles beyond those required for adults in criminal proceedings. *Ledrick v. United States,* 42 App.D.C. 384, 387 DC (1914) (requiring plea colloquy for minor pleading guilty); *State v. Oberst,* 127 Kan. 412, 273 P. 490 (1929) (precluding guilty plea by minor without advice of counsel).

23. Richard J. Bonnie, "Juvenile Homicide: A Study in Legal Ambivalence," in *Juvenile Homicide,* edited by Elissa Benedek and Dewey Cornell. (Washington, D.C.: American Psychiatric Press, 1989).

24. The juvenile court statutes in most states required that if youths were retained in juvenile court and found delinquent, the court was required to release them from custody at the juvenile system's maximum jurisdictional age. For youths charged with serious offenses at sixteen or seventeen, this would cause their release within a few months of their potential juvenile adjudication. Under the circumstances, judges often had no difficulty ruling that the time remaining prior to those youths' mandatory release would not be enough to assure their rehabilitation in the juvenile justice system.

In fact, research showed that for various serious felonies by juveniles, age sixteen or seventeen was overwhelmingly the best predictor of waiver. Margaret Bortner, "Traditional Rhetoric, Organizational Realities: Remand of Juveniles to Adult Court," *Crime and Delinquency* 32 (1986): 53.

25. *State v. Oberst,* 127 Kan. 412, 273 P. 490 (1929) (precluding uncounselled guilty plea); *Ridge v. State,* 25 Okla.Cr. 396, 220 P. 965, 966 (1923) (precluding waivers of procedural protections in the absence of specific finding that minor comprehends the notion of the waiver).

26. *Matter of Charles E. Smith,* 548 P.2d 647 (1976); *Matter of Thomas Stapelkemper,* 172 Mont. 192, 562 P.2d 815 (1977); *Commonwealth v. Williams,* 514 Pa. 62, 522 A.2d 1058 (1987); *People v. M.D.,* 100 Ill.2d 73, 461 N.E.2d 367 (1984).

27. The first case to address the question squarely seems to be *Bettleyoun v. Talbott,* 286 N.W.2d 526 (S.D. 1980) (affirming trial-court finding that defendant was incompetent to stand trial based on immaturity). Five years later, in *W.S.L. v. State,* 470 So.2d 828 (Fla. 1985), the Florida Supreme Court held that a juvenile defendant was entitled to a hearing on his competence to stand trial based on a psychologist's report indicating that he "did not have an understanding of the adversary nature of the criminal justice system and had no ability to assist his attorney in planning a defense because of his age and intellect." Only one state statute explicitly addresses the problem. Under Va. Code Ann., § 16.1–269.1 (Michie, 1996) juvenile court judges may not waive jurisdiction and transfer a juvenile to criminal court unless the juvenile is found competent to stand trial.

28. Patricia Torbet et al. *State Responses to Serious and Violent Juvenile Crime* (Washington, D.C.: U.S. Dept. of Justice, Office of Justice Programs, Office of Juvenile Justice and Delinquency Prevention, 1996); Howard Snyder and Melissa Sickmund, *Juvenile Offenders and Victims: A National Report* (Washington, D.C.: U.S. Dept. of Justice, Office of Justice Programs, Office of Juvenile Justice and Delinquency Prevention, 1995); Eric Fritsch and Craig Hemmens, "Juvenile Waiver in the United States: 1979–1995: A Comparison and Analysis of the State Waiver Statutes," *Juvenile and Family Court Journal* 46 (Summer 1995): 17. Kirk A. Heilbrun et al., "A National Survey of US Statutes on Juvenile Transfer: Implications for Policy and Practice," *Behavioral Sciences & the Law* 15 (1997): 125.

29. For example, between 1988 and 1992, the number of youths facing adjudication in criminal courts rose almost 100 percent for all categories of offense except property offenses: Melissa Sickmund, "How Juveniles Get to Criminal Court," in *OJJDP Update on Statistics* (Washington, D.C.: US DOJ, 1994), 1.

30. See Carol J. DeFrances, *Juveniles Prosecuted in State Criminal Courts: National Survey of Prosecutors, 1994* (Washington, D.C.: BJS, 1997), Table 5, which indicates that the number of transferred cases increased from 7,000 in 1988 to 12,300 in 1994. (Survey of prosecutors indicated that, among cases waived to criminal court, the proportion of offenders under sixteen had doubled, from 6 percent to 12 percent.)

31. Va. Code Ann. § 16.1–269.1 (Michie, 1996).

32. *Ex parte Brown,* 540 So. 2d 740, 745 (Ala. 1989); Matter of LeBlanc, 430 N.W. 2d 780, 783 (Mich. App. 1988).

33. A recent summary of state laws indicates that twenty-two states have "reverse waiver" provisions. See Patricia Torbert et al., supra note 26. However, it appears that most of these statutes merely allow prosecutors to change their minds or allow criminal courts to transfer a case to juvenile court upon determining that they lack jurisdiction. Thus, under many of these statutes, the criminal court's authority to transfer the case to juvenile court is limited to circumstances in which it finds that the case fails to meet the prescribed age/offense/prior record jurisdictional criteria.

34. Md. Ann. Code of 1957, Art. 27, Sec. 594 A (a) and (c)(2).

35. Wisc.Stat.Ann. 970.032 (2)(a).

36. Robert Nicholson and R. Kugler, "Competent and Incompetent Defendants: A Quantitative Review of Comparative Research," *Psychological Bulletin* 109 (1991): 355.

37. American Psychiatric Association, *Diagnostic and Statistical Manual of Mental Disorders,* 4th ed. (Washington, D.C.: American Psychiatric Association, 1994), 37; Thomas Grisso, *Forensic Evaluation of Juveniles* (Sarasota, Fla.: Professional Resource Press, 1998); Thomas Grisso, "Society's Retributive Response to Juvenile Violence: A Developmental Perspective," *Law and Human Behavior* 20 (1996): 229, 237–238.

38. E. Dulit, "Adolescent Psychological Development: Normal and Abnormal," in *Juvenile Psychiatry and the Law,* edited by R. Rosner and H. Schwartz (New York: Plenum, 1989), 219–236; Jonathan J. F. Mattanah et al., "Diagnostic Stability in Adolescents Followed Up Two Years after Hospitalization," *American Journal of Psychiatry* 152 (1995): 889, 892.

39. The problem of "underidentification" may be accentuated in cases involving mental retardation because of the offender's tendency to mask his or her deficits. See Richard J. Bonnie, "The Competence of Defendants with Mental Retardation to Participate in Their Own Defense," *Journal of Criminal Law & Criminology* 81 (1990): 419.

40. See chapters 5, 11, and 12 in this volume. See also Thomas Grisso, "The Competence of Adolescents as Trial Defendants," *Psychology, Public Policy, & Law* 3 (1997): 3; Thomas Grisso, "Juvenile Competency to Stand Trial," *Criminal Justice* 12 (1997): 4; Elizabeth S. Scott et al., "Evaluating Adolescent Decision Making in Legal Contexts," *Law and Human Behavior* 19 (1995): 221; Laurence Steinberg and Elizabeth Cauffman, "Maturity of Judgment in Adolescence: Psychosocial Factors in Adolescent Decision Making," *Law and Human Behavior* 20 (1996): 249.

41. See supra, note 34, especially Scott (1995) and Steinberg and Cauffman (1996).

42. See Chapters 8 and 9 in this volume; see also Emily Buss, "'You're My What?' The Problem of Children's Misperceptions of Their Lawyers' Roles," *Fordham Law Review* 64 (1996): 1699.

43. Grisso, "Competence," 23.

44. Ibid., 24.

45. Increased awareness of issues relating to adjudicative competence should also have the salutary effect of raising the standard of practice for representation of adolescent defendants.

46. 422 US 806 (1975).

47. *Ledrick v. United States* 42 App.D.C. 384 (D.C. 1914); *State v. Oberst* 127 Kan. 412, 273 P. 490 (1929). See also Chapter 10 in this volume.

48. Anthony M. Platt, *The Child Savers* (Chicago: University of Chicago Press, 1969).

49. 387 US 1 (1967).

50. 397 US 358 (1970).

51. *In the Interest of S.H., a Child,* 469 S.E.2d 810 (Ga. Ct. App. 1996). But see *G.J.I. v. State,* 778 P.2d 485 (Okl.Crim. 1989).

52. 420 US 162, 172 (1975).

53. The actual extent to which juvenile defense attorneys or courts raised the issue of youths competence to stand trial in juvenile court is difficult to discern owing to the absence of documentation. When evaluations of competence to stand trial were requested, often courts were motivated merely by a desire to place youths under psychiatric observation in order to obtain diagnostic or treatment services, rather than obtaining information about competence as a substantive matter; Thomas Grisso et al., "Competency to Stand Trial in Juvenile Court," *International Journal of Law and Psychiatry* 10 (1987):1.

54. *Briones v. Juvenile Court of Denver,* 534 P.2d 624 (Co. 1975); *In re Two Minor Children,* 592 P.2d 166 (Nev. 1979).

55. The Minnesota Juvenile Court legislation provides that "the purpose of the laws relating to children alleged or adjudicated to be delinquent is to promote the public safety and reduce juvenile delinquency by maintaining the integrity of the substantive law prohibiting certain behavior and by developing individual responsibility for lawful behavior." Minn.Stat.Ann. § 260.011; The Washington statute states that juvenile adjudication shall "make the juvenile offender accountable for his or her criminal behavior; [and] provide for punishment commensurate with the age, crime, and criminal history of the juvenile offender." Rev. Wash. Code Ann. § 13.40.010 (2)(c), (d).

56. Lynda Frost, "Adjudicative Competence in Juvenile Court: A Review of the Law," manuscript on file with the authors. The impact of recent reforms is evident in the fact that only one-third of the states explicitly recognized the requirement a decade earlier. See Thomas Grisso et al., op.cit., note 43.

57. *G. J.I. v. State,* 778 P.2d 485, 487 (Okla. Cr. 1989).

58. *In the Interest of S.H., a Child,* 469 S.E.2d 810 (Ga. Ct. App. 1996).

59. D.C. Code Ann. § 44-23-410 (Law. Coop. 1985).

CHAPTER FOUR

Juveniles' Waiver of Legal Rights: Confessions, *Miranda,* and the Right to Counsel

BARRY C. FELD

Procedure and substance intertwine inextricably in juvenile courts. Progressives reformers envisioned a procedurally informal court that made dispositions in the "best interests" of the child. The Supreme Court in *In re Gault* emphasized the disjunctions between rehabilitative rhetoric and punitive reality and engrafted greater procedural safeguards onto juvenile courts' individualized sentencing schema.[1] Although *Gault* provided the impetus for a procedural convergence between juvenile and criminal courts, a substantial gulf remains between theory and reality, between the law on the books and the law in action. In theory, the Constitution and states' laws entitle delinquents to the privilege against self-incrimination, to formal trials, and to the assistance of counsel. In reality, juveniles receive a very different version of procedural justice. Oftentimes, delinquents waive *Miranda* rights without appreciating the legal significance of confessing, and relinquish their right to counsel prior to trial and face the power of the state alone and unaided.

Three decades ago, the Supreme Court in *Kent v. United States* observed that "the child receives the worst of both worlds: he gets neither the protections accorded to adults nor the solicitous care and regenerative treatment postulated for children."[2] In the contemporary "worst of both worlds" of juvenile justice, youths receive neither therapy nor procedural justice but instead punishment without criminal due process.[3] Despite the criminalizing of juvenile courts, most states provide neither special procedures to protect juveniles from their own immaturity and vulnerability nor the full panoply of adult criminal procedural safeguards. Rather, states treat juveniles just like adult criminal defendants when formal equality redounds to their disadvantage and use less adequate juvenile court safeguards when those deficient procedures provide a comparative advantage to the state.[4] This procedural disparity occurs because American culture and law contain two competing and conflicting images of young people. On the one hand, legal culture views young people as innocent, vulnerable, fragile, and dependent children whom their parents and the state should protect and nurture. On the other hand, legal culture perceives young people as vigorous, autonomous, responsible, almost adult-like people from whose criminal behavior the public needs protection. Juvenile justice jurisprudence attempts to reconcile the fundamental ambivalence and conflicted impulses engendered by these competing social constructs of innocence and responsibility when a child is a criminal.

The "jurisprudence of youth" serves to maximize the social control of young people. This explains the seeming contradiction between treating youths just like adults defendants in some procedural contexts—presuming autonomy and responsibility—and using "special" protective juvenile court procedures in other instances—invoking images of immaturity and incompetence. The cultural and legal assumptions weigh youths' claims against adults' interests, skew the respective valuations and balances, and justify denial of rights to young people. By manipulating fluid concepts like childhood or rehabilitation, as the Supreme Court did in *McKeiver v. Pennsylvania,* for example, juvenile court law readily subordinates young peoples' legal claims to procedural parity.[5] Without recognizing any contradiction, in the same term the Supreme Court asserted that adolescents lacked the capacity to make sound, self-regarding decisions and delegated to their parents the authority "voluntarily" to confine them in institutions, and simultaneously ruled that minors possess sufficient capacity to invoke or waive their Fifth Amendment *Miranda* rights without any assistance from parents or lawyers, and insisted that they must do so with adultlike technical precision.[6]

This chapter analyzes judicial decisions and laws that govern youths' waivers of the privilege against self-incrimination and the right to counsel. In most jurisdictions, states' juvenile and criminal justice systems use the adult legal standard of "knowing, intelligent, and voluntary" under the "totality of the circumstances" to assess the validity of juveniles' waivers of legal rights. Effectively, these policies characterize young people as autonomous and responsible even though many youths do not possess the capacity of adults to exercise or relinquish their constitutional rights in a "knowing and intelligent" manner. The chapter also analyzes policies employed in some states that recognize the developmental limitations of youths in their dealings with the juvenile justice system and the adequacy of those protections. Finally, the chapter analyzes legal-policy implications of accommodating "youthfulness" in the legal process.

Waiver of the Right to Remain Silent

In re Gault involved the delinquency adjudication and institutional confinement of a youth who allegedly made a lewd telephone call of the "irritatingly offensive, adolescent, sex variety."[7] Police took fifteen-year-old Gerald Gault into custody, detained him overnight without notifying his parents, and required him to appear at a juvenile court hearing the following day. A probation officer filed a pro forma petition that alleged simply that Gault was a delinquent minor in need of the care and custody of the court. No complaining witness appeared and the juvenile court did not take sworn testimony or prepare a transcript or formal memorandum of the proceedings. The judge interrogated Gault about the alleged telephone call and he apparently made incriminating responses. The judge did not advise Gault of a right to remain silent or the right to counsel and did not provide him with the assistance of an attorney. Following his hearing, the judge returned Gault to a detention cell for several days. At the dispositional hearing the following week, the judge committed Gault as a juvenile delinquent to the State Industrial School "for the period of his minority [that is, until twenty-one], unless sooner discharged by due process of law." If Gault had been convicted as an adult, a criminal court judge could have sentenced him to a maximum of a fifty-dollar fine or up to two months' imprisonment.

Rather than accepting uncritically the rehabilitative rhetoric of Progressive juvenile jurisprudence, the Supreme Court examined the realities of juvenile justice administration. The Court reviewed the history of the juvenile court and the traditional rationales to deny procedural safeguards to juveniles. Progressive reformers characterized delinquency proceedings as informal and civil rather than as adversarial or criminal, and asserted that because the State acted as parens patriae, the child should receive custody rather than liberty. Although the Court hoped to retain the potential benefits of the juvenile process, it candidly appraised the claims of the juvenile court in the light of its high rates of recidivism, the failures of rehabilitation, the stigma of a delinquency label, the breaches of confidentiality, the arbitrariness of the process, and the realities of juvenile institutional incarceration.[8] For youths charged with crimes and facing confinement, the Court mandated elementary procedural safeguards—advance notice of charges, a fair and impartial hearing, assistance of counsel, an opportunity to confront and cross-examine witnesses, and the privilege against self-incrimination.

Although the Court emphasized the realities of the juvenile justice system to justify providing procedural safeguards, it narrowly limited its holding to the adjudicatory hearing—the trial—at which a juvenile court decided whether a child committed a criminal act.[9] In the *Gault* case, the Court held that juvenile proceedings required some adversarial procedural safeguards both to determine the truth of allegations and to limit the power of the State and to preserve individual freedom. *Gault* did not restrict juvenile courts' substantive jurisdiction or dispositional authority, and the Court insisted that providing procedural safeguards would not adversely affect their unique approach to processing and treating juveniles. The Court specifically held that "[w]e do not in this opinion consider the impact of these constitutional provisions upon the totality of the relationship of the juvenile and the state. We do not even consider the entire process relating to juvenile 'delinquents.'"[10]

In contrast to its narrow holding, the Court relied upon the Fourteenth Amendment's broad, general guarantees of "due process" and "fundamental fairness," rather than the specific requirements of the Bill of Rights. For example, the Court required juvenile courts to provide delinquents with notice of charges, assistance of counsel, and an opportunity to confront and cross-examine witnesses as a matter of "due process" rather than because the Sixth Amendment explicitly enumerated those rights.[11] On the other hand, the Court relied upon the specific provisions of the Fifth Amendment to import the privilege against self-incrimination into delinquency proceedings.

> It would be entirely unrealistic to carve out of the Fifth Amendment all statements by juveniles on the ground that these cannot lead to 'criminal' involvement. In the first place, juvenile proceedings to determine delinquency, which may lead to commitment to a state institution, must be regarded as criminal for purposes of the privilege against self-incrimination . . . commitment is a deprivation of liberty. It is incarceration against one's will, whether it is called civil or criminal.[12]

As a consequence of *Gault*'s application of the privilege against self-incrimination to delinquency proceedings, states no longer could characterize juvenile courts either as "noncriminal" or "nonadversarial." The Fifth Amendment privilege against self-incrimination, more than any other provision of the Bill of Rights, serves as the fundamental guarantor of an adversarial process, places the defendant "off limits" as a source of evidence, and maintains a balance between the State and the individual.[13] Once a child admits to criminal involvement, the other procedural rights *Gault* made available at trial retain little practical significance for determining guilt or innocence.

Gault's extension of the self-incrimination protection provides the clearest example of the dual functions of procedural safeguards in juvenile court adjudications: to assure accurate fact-finding and to protect against government oppression. If the Court in *Gault* had been concerned solely with the reliability of juvenile confessions and the accuracy of fact-finding, then other safeguards, such as the requirement that juveniles confess voluntarily, would have sufficed. In *Gallegos v. Colorado* and *Haley v. Ohio,* for example, the Supreme Court employed the Fourteenth Amendment's "voluntariness" test to determine the admissibility of confessions made by juveniles and concluded that youthfulness constituted a special circumstance that required close judicial scrutiny.[14] Although the Fifth Amendment functions, in part, to ensure accurate fact-finding and reliable confessions, *Gault* recognized it served also to limit governmental overreaching and to maintain a proper balance between the individual and the State:

> The privilege against self-incrimination is, of course, related to the question of the safeguards necessary to assure that admissions or confessions are reasonably trustworthy, that they are not mere fruits of fear or coercion, but are reliable expressions of the truth. The roots of the privilege are, however, far deeper. They tap the basic stream of religious and political principle because the privilege reflects the limits of the individual's attornment to the state and—in a philosophical sense—insists upon the equality of the individual and the state. In other words, the privilege has a broader and deeper thrust than the rule which prevents the use of confessions which are the product of coercion because coercion is thought to carry with it the danger of unreliability. One of its purposes is to prevent the state, whether by force or by psychological domination, from overcoming the mind and will of the person under investigation and depriving him of the freedom to decide whether to assist the state in securing his conviction.[15]

In this respect, *Gault* represents a premier example of the Warren Court's belief that expanding constitutional rights and the adversary process would restrict the coercive powers of the State, assure the regularity of law enforcement, and thereby reduce the need for continual judicial scrutiny. "Surely one of the most distinctive tendencies of the Warren Court was its allegiance to the adversary theory of criminal justice. Thus, a large part of the Court's work in the criminal area consisted of its efforts to revitalize the adversary process in those areas of the system in which it was always supposed to flourish. . . . Even more striking, however, are the cases in which the Court extended the adversary process into areas of the system in which, theretofore, adversary proceedings were unknown or rarely employed."[16]

When *Gault* applied the privilege against self-incrimination to delinquency proceedings, the "warning" safeguards developed in *Miranda v. Arizona* also became available to juveniles.[17] Courts evaluate the validity of juveniles' waivers of Fifth Amendment rights and other constitutional rights such as the right to counsel, and the voluntariness of any confessions obtained by assessing whether the youth made a "knowing, intelligent, and voluntary" waiver under the "totality of the circumstances."[18]

Even before *Miranda* and *Gault,* the United States Supreme Court cautioned trial judges to be particularly sensitive to the effects of a youth's age and inexperience on the validity of waivers and the voluntariness of confessions. In *Haley v. Ohio,* police interrogated a fifteen-year-old "lad" in relays beginning shortly after midnight, denied him access to counsel, and confronted him with confessions by codefendants until he finally confessed at five in the morning. The Supreme Court reversed his conviction and ruled that a confession obtained under these circumstances was involuntary:

> What transpired would make us pause for careful inquiry if a mature man was involved. And when, as here, a mere child—an easy victim of the law—is before us, special care in scrutinizing the record must be used. Age 15 is a tender and difficult age for a boy. . . . He cannot be judged by the more exacting standards of maturity. That which would leave a man cold and unimpressed can overawe and overwhelm a lad in his early teens. This is the period of great instability which the crisis of adolescence produces. . . . [W]e cannot believe that a lad of tender years is a match for the police in such a contest. He needs counsel and support if he is not to become the victim first of fear, then of panic.[19]

In *Gallegos v. Colorado,* the Court reiterated that the age of the accused constituted a special circumstance that affects the voluntariness of confessions and reemphasized the vulnerability of youths. "A 14-year-old boy, no matter how sophisticated, . . . is not equal to the police in knowledge and understanding . . . and is unable to know how to protect his own interests or how to get the benefits of his constitutional rights. . . . A lawyer or an adult relative or friend could have given the petitioner the protection which his own immaturity could not. . . . Without some adult protection against this inequality, a 14-year-old boy would not be able to know, let alone assert, such constitutional rights as he had."[20] The Court in *In re Gault* repeated that "admissions and confessions of juveniles require special caution," and suggested that "even greater protection might be required where juveniles are involved, since their immaturity and greater vulnerability place them at a greater disadvantage in their dealings with police."[21] Thus, the Court long had recognized that youths are not the equals of adults in the interrogation room and that they require greater procedural safeguards than adults, such as the presence of counsel, to compensate for their vulnerability and susceptibility to coercive influences.

Subsequently, however, in *Fare v. Michael C.,* the Supreme Court retreated from its earlier solicitude for youths, at least for a sixteen-year-old offender with several prior arrests who had "served time" in a youth camp.[22] *Fare* reaffirmed that the adult "totality of the circumstances" test constituted the appropriate standard by which to evaluate the validity of waivers of *Miranda* rights and the admissibility of juvenile confessions. *Fare* held that a youth's request to speak with his probation officer when police interrogated him constituted neither a per se invocation of his *Miranda* privilege against self-incrimination nor the functional equivalent of a request for counsel that would have required further questioning to cease.[23] The Court used the discretionary adult "totality" approach to provide trial judges with the flexibility necessary to protect juveniles who lacked sufficient capacity or who succumbed to coercive police practices more readily than adults without unduly interfering with the ability of police to interrogate more sophisticated juveniles. *Fare* concluded that

> there are no persuasive reasons why any other approach is required where the question is whether a juvenile has waived his rights, as opposed to whether an adult has done so. The totality approach permits—indeed, it mandates—inquiry into all the circumstances surrounding the interrogation. This includes evaluation of the juvenile's age, experience, education, background, and intelligence, and into whether he has the capacity to understand the warnings given him, the nature of his Fifth Amendment rights, and the consequences of those rights.[24]

In subsequent interpretations of *Miranda,* the Court in *Moran v. Burbine* clarified that a valid waiver required both voluntariness and a "knowing and intelligent" awareness of the right relinquished. "Only if the 'totality of the circumstances surrounding the interrogation' reveal both an uncoerced choice and the requisite level of comprehension may a court properly conclude that the *Miranda* rights have been waived."[25] However, courts interpret comprehension to mean only an understanding and awareness of the *Miranda* rights themselves, that is, a right not to speak and to have counsel present, rather than an appreciation of the ramifications and legal consequences of a waiver.[26] A youth's minimal awareness that police would not compel him to talk but would use his statements against him would constitute an adequate understanding of the right to remain silent.[27] And, in *Colorado v. Connelly,* the Court held that in the absence of police coercion, a defendant's mental state alone would not render a confession involuntary.[28] *Connelly* emphasized that a "voluntariness" inquiry properly focused on police conduct rather than the subjective susceptibility of the defendant. Thus, courts' assessments of *Miranda* waivers—"knowing, intelligent, and voluntary under the totality of the circumstances"—focus narrowly on the suspect's awareness of and ability to comprehend the *Miranda* warnings, and coercive police conduct that deprives the suspect of the freedom to choose to exercise or to waive those rights.

The *Fare* Court held that a child's request to speak with someone other than an attorney comprised simply one of many factors affecting the validity of a *Miranda* waiver, and expressly declined to give children greater procedural protection than adults.[29] Rather, the Court insisted that children invoke their legal rights with adultlike technical precision and denied that young people were inherently incapable of validly waiving their constitutional rights. The Court rejected the view that "adult and child are members of binary, dichotomous categories whose inherently differing cognitive capacities justify separate waiver rules." By endorsing the adult waiver standard, the Court rejected the view that developmental or psychological differences between juveniles and adults justified or required different rules or special procedural protections.[30]

The "totality" approach gives trial judges discretion to consider a youth's immaturity, but imposes minimal interference with police investigative work. Most states allow juveniles to waive constitutional rights such as *Miranda* and the right to counsel without restriction or assistance, and to confront the power of the State alone and unaided. Thus, *Fare* employs a "liberationist" rather than a "protectionist" construction of adolescence, affirms adolescents' ability to make autonomous legal decisions without additional special procedures, and enables police interrogators to take advantage of their manifest social-psychological limitations relative to adults.

Most states follow *Fare,* use the adult "totality of the circumstances" test, and allow juveniles to waive *Miranda* rights and other constitutional rights.[31] As the California Supreme Court held in the leading case of *People v. Lara,* "a minor has the capacity to make a voluntary confession, even of capital offenses, without the presence or consent of counsel or other responsible adult, and the admissibility of such a confession depends not on his age alone but on a combination of that factor with such other circumstances as his intelligence, education, experience, and ability to comprehend the meaning and effect of his statement." Judges typically focus on characteristics of the juvenile such as age, education, and I.Q., and on circumstances surrounding the interrogation, such as methods and length of the questioning, when they evaluate the validity of any waivers or the admissibility of any statement.[32] Several leading cases have elaborated extensive lists of factors for trial judges to consider when assessing the validity of juveniles' waiver decisions—age, education, physical condition, presence of or opportunity to consult with parent or other adult, length of interrogation, method of interrogation, knowledge of the charges, subsequent repudiation of the statement, understanding of the warnings given, warning of possible transfer to criminal court, and the like.[33]

While appellate courts have identified many relevant factors that bear on determinations of "voluntariness," they do not assign controlling weight to any particular element and instead remit the weighing of different factors to the unfettered discretion of the trial court.[34] Without clear-cut rules to protect children who lack the maturity or knowledge of adults, the totality approach leaves judges' discretion virtually unlimited and unreviewable. When judges actually apply the test, they exclude only the most egregiously obtained confessions and then only on a haphazard basis.[35] Although a few courts closely scrutinize youths' awareness of the meaning of *Miranda* rights, most tend to apply the "totality" standard very conservatively.[36] Courts routinely find valid *Miranda* waivers when police testify that they advised the juveniles of their rights and they answered "yes" when asked if they understood them.[37] Even overtly coercive police interrogation techniques and a youth's very young age or mental deficiencies do not prevent trial judges from finding and appellate courts from upholding a waiver to be voluntary.[38] Courts readily admit the confessions of illiterate, mentally retarded juveniles with I.Q.s in the sixties whom psychologists characterize as incapable of abstract reasoning.[39] *Fare* accepted police interrogation as legitimate law enforcement tool, posited coerciveness as a fact question in each case, declined to unduly restrict law enforcement with brightlines, and provided police with considerable latitude to exploit youths' vulnerability. Susceptibility to interrogation, in turn, adversely affects youths' subsequent dispositions. Juvenile court judges appear to sentence more severely youths who admit their criminal involvement than those who deny it.[40]

Despite *Fare*'s adherence to the "totality of the circumstances" approach to relinquishing constitutional rights, reasons exist to question whether a typical juvenile's waiver decision is, or even can be, "knowing, intelligent, and voluntary." Empirical studies that evaluate juveniles' comprehension of their *Miranda* rights indicate that most juveniles who receive a *Miranda* warning may not understand it well enough to waive their constitutional rights in a "knowing and intelligent" manner. Professor Thomas Grisso conducted tests to determine whether juveniles could paraphrase the words in the *Miranda* warning, whether they could define six critical words in the *Miranda* warning such as "attorney," "consult," and "appoint," and whether they could give correct true-false answers to twelve rewordings of the *Miranda* warnings.[41] He administered structured interviews, designed by a panel of psychologists and lawyers, to three samples of juvenile subjects and to two samples of adult subjects, and compared the juveniles' performances with the adult norms. Most juveniles who received the warnings did not understand them well enough to waive their constitutional rights "knowingly and intelligently." Only 20.9 percent of the juveniles, as compared with 42.3 percent of the adults, demonstrated adequate understanding of the four components of a *Miranda* warning, while 55.3 percent of juveniles as contrasted with 23.1 percent of the adults exhibited no comprehension of at least one of the four warnings.[42] Juveniles most frequently misunderstood the *Miranda* advisory that they had the right to consult with an attorney and to have one present during interrogation. Younger juveniles exhibited even greater difficulties understanding their rights. "As a class, juveniles younger than fifteen years of age failed to meet both the absolute and relative (adult norm) standards for comprehension. . . . The vast majority of these juveniles misunderstood at least one of the four standard *Miranda* statements, and compared with adults, demonstrated significantly poorer comprehension of the nature and significance of the *Miranda* rights."[43] Although "juveniles younger than fifteen manifest significantly poorer comprehension than adults of comparable intelligence," the level of comprehension exhibited by youths sixteen and older, although comparable to that of adults, left much to be desired.

A replication of Grisso's study in Canada reported that very few juveniles fully understood their warnings and that the youths who lacked comprehension waived their rights more readily. "[I]t seems likely that many if not most juveniles who are asked by the police to waive their rights do not have sufficient understanding to be competent to waive them."[44] Another study reported that youths interpreted the warning that "anything can and will be used against you in a court of law" to mean that "any disrespectful words directed toward police would be reported to the judge."[45] A study of urban, black high school students who participated in a year-long course in street law reported that education about *Miranda* rights did not improve students' understanding or comprehension in ways that would enable them to take meaningful advantage of their rights.[46]

Moreover, research conducted under "ideal" laboratory conditions may fail to capture sufficiently the individual characteristics, social context, and stressful coercive conditions associated with actual police interrogation. Responses to hypothetical questions in a relaxed atmosphere do not replicate adequately the conditions created by police who "can be gentle or tough, can explain the rights well or poorly, and in many ways can exert varying amounts of pressure to comply." Typically, delinquents come from lower-income households and may possess fewer verbal skills or less of a capacity to understand legal abstractions than the youths who participated in these studies. Moreover, children from poorer and ethnic-minority backgrounds often express doubt that law enforcement officials will not punish them for exercising their legal rights.[47] Immaturity, inex-

perience, and lower verbal competence than adults render youths especially vulnerable to police interrogation tactics.

Youths' social status relative to adult authority figures such as police
also render them more susceptible than adults to the coercive pressures
of interrogation. Children's greater dependence upon adults and societal
expectations of youthful obedience to authority also make youths more
vulnerable to police interrogation techniques. Most people believe that
answering the police in a respectful and cooperative manner will benefit
them, at least in the short run. Inexperienced youths may waive their rights
and speak to the police in the short-sighted and unrealistic belief that their
interrogation will end more quickly and secure their release. Many people
from traditionally disempowered communities, such as females, African-
Americans, and youths, pragmatically use indirect patterns of speech in
order to avoid conflict in their dealings with authority figures. People with
lower social status than their interrogators typically respond more passively, "talk" more readily, acquiesce to police suggestions more easily,
and speak less assertively or aggressively.[48] Thus, *Fare*'s requirement that
youths invoke *Miranda* rights forthrightly and with adultlike precision
runs contrary to the normal and predictable social reactions and verbal
styles of most delinquents subjected to custodial interrogation.

Minors' lack of comprehension and vulnerability to coercive pressures
raises questions about the adequacy of the *Miranda* warning as a procedural safeguard at interrogation. The Court intended the *Miranda* warnings to inform and educate defendants, to enable them to assert their
rights, and to ensure that they made waivers "knowingly and intelligently." If most juveniles lack the cognitive capacity to understand the
warning or the psychosocial ability to invoke or exercise rights, then ritualistic recitation of a *Miranda* litany hardly accomplishes those purposes.

States' laws recognize that younger people have different social and
psychological competencies than adults and paternalistically impose a
host of legal disabilities on children to protect them from their own limitations in contexts other than criminal law enforcement. For example, states
limit youths ability to enter contracts, convey property, marry, drink,
drive, file a law suit, or even donate blood.[49] Some states recognize this developmental reality and restrict youths' ability to waive legal rights. Courts
explain that special procedural safeguards at interrogation, such as the
"interested adult" rule, are designed

> to afford protection to juveniles . . . disadvantaged by the imma-
> turity occasioned by their youth. The rationale underlying this
> per se rule is that the immaturity of the juvenile significantly af-
> fects both the ability of the juvenile to understand fully his or her
> rights and the susceptibility of the juvenile to the compelling at-
> mosphere of police interrogation, and that special protections

are thus required to protect the juvenile from incompetently waiving his or her rights. It is believed that the interested adult can remedy the shortcomings resulting from immaturity by providing advice to enhance the juvenile's understanding of his or her rights and by being present during custodial interrogation to protect the child from the compelling atmosphere of custodial interrogation.[50]

Other courts explain that "The law presumes different levels of responsibility for juveniles and adults and, realizing that juveniles frequently lack the capacity to appreciate the consequences of their actions, seeks to protect them from the possible consequences of their immaturity. Moreover, by providing the juvenile with the opportunity for meaningful consultation with an informed adult, these procedures prevent the warnings from becoming merely a ritualistic recitation wherein the effect of actual comprehension by the juvenile is ignored."[51]

A few states have experimented with alternative strategies to compensate for youths' special vulnerabilities during interrogation. These jurisdictions use concrete guidelines or per se rules to assure the validity of a juvenile's waiver of rights or confession. They typically require either the presence of an "interested adult," such as a parent, or consultation with an attorney.[52] The per se approach excludes any waiver of rights or confession made by a juvenile if the police failed to adhere to the required procedural safeguards. The per se approach presumes that most juveniles lack maturity or legal competence and hence require special safeguards to protect them from their own limitations. "The concept of establishing different standards for a juvenile is an accepted legal principle since minors generally hold a subordinate and protected status in our legal system. . . . It would indeed be inconsistent and unjust to hold that one whom the state deems incapable of being able to marry, [or] purchase alcoholic beverages . . . should be compelled to stand on the same footing as an adult when asked to waive important Fifth and Sixth Amendment rights at a time most critical to him and in an atmosphere most foreign and unfamiliar."[53]

States use several variants of an "interested adult" per se strategy to provide juveniles with greater protections at interrogation than those afforded youths by *Miranda* and *Fare*. Some require police to inform the juvenile and the interested adult of the youth's *Miranda* rights, to provide them with an opportunity to consult, and demand both to consent to any subsequent waiver.[54] Others require, in addition, that the interested adult actually be present at the time of interrogation, and bar statements obtained after police warned both the juvenile and parent and provided an opportunity to consult, but then excluded, the parent.[55] Other states require a juvenile below the age of fourteen years actually to consult with an interested adult, but provide older juveniles only with an opportunity to consult with an interested adult as a prerequisite to a valid waiver.[56] Several state's statutes also incorporate variations of these "interested adult" requirements.[57] Although these per se strategies provide additional safeguards to protect the vast majority of unsophisticated juveniles who need them, they may afford unnecessary protection for the occasional sophisticated youth who does not.

States that require consultation with an interested adult or parents' presence at interrogation offer a variety of rationales. They contend that these safeguards will mitigate the dangers of untrustworthiness, reduce coercive influences, and provide an independent witness who can testify about any coercive practices that police used. They assert that parental presence will assure the accuracy of any statements obtained, involve parents in the process at the initial stages, ensure that police fully advise and a juvenile actually understand those advisories, and relieve police of the burden of making judgments about a youth's competency.[58] States that require parental presence at interrogation recognize that most juveniles lack the maturity to understand their rights and the competence to exercise or waive them without prior consulting with a knowledgeable adult. Proponents believe that parental presence reduces a juvenile's isolation and fear and provides them with access to legal advice.

Courts that require parental presence as a prerequisite to a juvenile's waiver of rights assume that parent and child share an identity of interests and that parents can adequately understand the legal situation and can function as effective advisors. However, the presence of parents during interrogation may not provide the envisioned benefit for the child and may increase, rather than decrease, the coercive pressures on a youth. Parents' potential conflict of interest with the child, emotional reactions to their child's arrest, or their own intellectual or social limitations may prevent them from playing the supportive role envisioned. Court cases report many instances in which parents coerce their children to confess to the police.[59] Research indicates that most parents did not directly advise their children about the waiver decision and that those that did almost always urged the child to waive rights.[60] Parents appear predisposed to aggravate rather than to mitigate coercive police pressures at interrogation and to urge their children to waive the right to silence. Moreover, research on adults' ability to understand and intelligently exercise their own *Miranda* rights casts doubt upon even well-intentioned parents' competence to assist their children.[61] Parents seldom have legal training and may not understand or appreciate the legal problems their child faces.

> The most serious objections to this [parental presence] alternative concerns the ability of layman to provide effective assistance

in a preinterrogation setting. Commentators have observed that many parents do not care, and that "often the parents are, at best, only equal in capacity to the child and therefore poorly equipped to comprehend the complexities confronting them." . . . When [the] finding [of parents' attitudes towards juveniles' rights in interrogation] are coupled with those of the instant studies, which indicated that many adults do not themselves adequately understand their *Miranda* rights, the "interested adult" alternative becomes even less attractive.[62]

Finally, because a juvenile's privilege against self-incrimination is a personal right, it seems inconsistent to allow others, even parents, to assert or waive it.

Courts and commentators have proposed other safeguards, besides parental presence, to bolster protection of youths' *Miranda* rights. If juveniles' lack of understanding or comprehension confounds assessments of waiver decisions, then police could administer a "dumbed-down" version of a *Miranda* warning "in language understandable to a child."[63] Some suggest that states require police to videotape all interrogations of juveniles as a middle ground between the discretionary "totality" approach and stricter per se requirements.[64] At least two state Supreme Courts require police to record their interrogation of adult defendants in order to resolve the "swearing match between the law enforcement official and the defendant," and many more routinely videotape drunk-driving suspects.[65] Other analysts propose a conclusive presumption that younger juveniles lack the capacity to waive rights and would require an "informed consent" dialogue to assure that older juveniles possess the cognitive competency to make a valid waiver decision.[66] However, judicial hostility toward youthful law-breakers and the increased burdens that an "informed consent" dialogue would impose on an overloaded justice system makes such an extended inquiry unlikely.

Instead of relying on judges to review the "totality of the circumstances" or parents to assist a youth at interrogation, states could require the presence of an attorney and consultation with counsel prior to any juveniles' waiver of *Miranda* or the right to counsel. Waivers of *Miranda* rights and the right to counsel involve tactical and strategic considerations as well as an abstract awareness of the rights themselves. A per se requirement of consultation with counsel prior to any waiver of rights recognizes youths' immaturity and lack of experience with law enforcement, and provides the only effective means to protect their interests. Unlike most parents, only attorneys possess the skills and training necessary to assist the child in the adversarial process.

Many professional groups have endorsed the appointment of and consultation with counsel as a prerequisite to any waiver of rights. The President's Commission on Law Enforcement and Administration of Justice recommended appointment of counsel for juveniles as a matter of course whenever the possibility of coercive state action existed.[67] The National Advisory Committee Task Force on Juvenile Justice recommended that during police interrogation, states prohibit juveniles from "waiv[ing] the right against self-incrimination without the advice of counsel."[68] The American Bar Association's Juvenile Justice Standards recommend that "the right to counsel should attach as soon as the juvenile is taken into custody . . . , when a petition is filed . . . , or when the juvenile appears personally at an intake conference, whichever occurs first."[69] In addition, the juvenile should have "the effective assistance of counsel at all stages of the proceeding" and this right to counsel is mandatory and nonwaivable. These various proposals recognize juveniles' need for legal counsel where a waiver of rights likely will affect subsequent proceedings. In *Fare,* the Supreme Court elaborated on the crucial role of counsel by noting that

> the lawyer occupies a critical position in our legal system because of his unique ability to protect the Fifth Amendment rights of a client undergoing custodial interrogation. Because of this special ability of the lawyer to help the client preserve his Fifth Amendment rights once the client becomes enmeshed in the adversary process, the Court found that "the right to have counsel present at the interrogation is indispensable to the protection of the Fifth Amendment privilege under the system" established by the Court. . . . The per se aspect of *Miranda* was thus based on the unique role the lawyer plays in the adversary system of criminal justice in this country.
>
> Whether it is a minor or an adult who stands accused, the lawyer is the one person to whom society as a whole looks to as the protector of the legal rights of that person in his dealings with the police and the courts.[70]

A few states require juveniles to be represented by an attorney at interrogation and bar youths from waiving the right to counsel.[71] In order to assure the availability of counsel, states could have defense attorneys on call, and police could summon a lawyer to the police station prior to any custodial interrogation of a juvenile.

Mandatory, nonwaivable appointment of counsel protects the rights of the juvenile and also helps the courts efficiently handle cases and assure that any decisions a juvenile makes truly are "knowing" and "intelligent." Clearly, a rule requiring courts to appoint counsel for juveniles prior to interrogation as well as throughout the process could substantially affect juvenile justice administration. The ability of police to obtain waivers from and interrogate youths likely would decrease. Indeed, courts decry the adverse effects that such procedural safeguards and per se rules would have on police interrogation and the efficient repression of crime and share the "societal outrage against crime."[72] "It is apparent most courts, required to deal pragmatically with an ever-mounting crime wave in which minors play a disproportionate role, have considered society's self-preservation interest in rejecting a blanket exclusion for juvenile confessions."[73] A decade ago, Pennsylvania abandoned its "interest adult" rule in favor of a "totality" approach, observing that "protection of juveniles against the innate disadvantages associated with the immaturity of most youth may . . . be achieved in a manner that affords more adequate weight to the interests of society, and of justice."[74] Thus, most states categorically reject the only recognized and effective procedural safeguard to protect youths from their own vulnerability during interrogation and instead adopt a policy that functionally disadvantages youths.

Despite the adverse impact that the presence of counsel would have on police's ability to interrogate youths, however, *Gault* and *Miranda* already assure juveniles' access to counsel during interrogation and throughout the juvenile justice process if the youths know and are capable enough to request one. Only an ill-informed, inexperienced, or overwhelmed young person will cooperate with the police to his or her own detriment. Only an attorney can redress the imbalance between a vulnerable youth and the state. The issue is not one of entitlement, but rather the ease or difficulty with which courts find that juveniles waive their *Miranda* and counsel rights, which, in turn, affects every other aspect of juvenile justice administration. According to *Fare,* the Constitution does not require mandatory appointment of counsel for juveniles, prohibit them from waiving their Fifth Amendment rights without consulting with their attorneys, or prevent them from confronting the coercive power of the state without the assistance of counsel. *Fare* spurned the "protectionist" policy option to safeguard youths from the consequences of their own immaturity. As a result, most states reject the only truly effective safeguard for juveniles at interrogation—assistance of counsel—in favor of "totality of the circumstances" approach exactly because the latter enables police to take advantage of youths' characteristic developmental susceptibility. The decision to put young offenders on the same procedural footing as adult criminal defendants results in practical inequality and a distinct disadvantage because of their relative inexperience and vulnerability to adult coercion. A "liberationist" policy that denies youths special safeguards to protect them from the adverse consequences of their own immaturity makes perfect sense as a crime-control strategy that maximizes their social control.

Waiver of the Right to Counsel in Juvenile Court

Procedural justice hinges on access to and the effective assistance of counsel. *Gault* observed that juvenile courts' informality often resulted in arbitrary and erroneous decisions, and that benevolent discretion provided an inadequate substitute for fair procedures.[75] The Court based its decision to grant juveniles the right to counsel on the Fourteenth Amendment due process clause rather than the language of the Sixth Amendment that explicitly provides for counsel in criminal proceedings. The Court asserted that as a matter of Fourteenth Amendment Due Process, "a proceeding where the issue is whether the child will be found to be 'delinquent' and subjected to the loss of his liberty for years is comparable in seriousness to a felony prosecution. The juvenile needs the assistance of counsel to cope with problems of law, to make skilled inquiry into the facts, to insist upon the regularity of the proceedings, and to ascertain whether he has a defense and to prepare and submit it."[76]

Gault quoted extensively from the Report of the President's Commission on Law Enforcement and the Administration of Justice and endorsed its recommendations:

> No single action holds more potential for achieving procedural justice for the child in the juvenile court than provision of counsel. The presence of an independent legal representative of the child, or of his parent, is the keystone of the whole structure of guarantees that a minimum system of procedural justice requires. The rights to confront one's accusers, to cross-examine witnesses, to present evidence and testimony of one's own, to be unaffected by prejudicial and unreliable evidence, to participate meaningfully in the dispositional decision, to take an appeal have substantial meaning for the overwhelming majority of persons brought before the juvenile court only if they are provided with competent lawyers who can invoke those rights effectively. . . .[77]

While *Gault* recognized that the presence of lawyers would make juvenile court proceedings more formal and adversarial, the Court asserted that their presence would impart "a healthy atmosphere of accountability."[78] However, *Gault* did not require judges automatically to appoint counsel whenever delinquents appeared in juvenile court, but only held that "the child and his parents must be notified of the child's right to be represented by counsel retained by them, or if they are unable to afford counsel, that counsel will be appointed to represent the child."[79]

When *Gault* granted juveniles the right to counsel, it manifested the Warren Court's beliefs that adversarial procedures protected constitutional rights, limited the coercive powers of the state, assured the regularity of law enforcement, and preserved individual liberty and autonomy.

Several years earlier in *Gideon v. Wainwright,* the Warren Court incorporated the Sixth Amendment's guarantee of counsel and required states to appoint counsel for indigent adult defendants in felony proceedings.[80] "[I]n our adversary system of criminal justice, any person haled into court, who is too poor to hire a lawyer, cannot be assured a fair trial unless counsel is provided for him."[81] Because *Gault* based its decision on the Fourteenth Amendment rather than on the Sixth Amendment and *Gideon,* some ambiguity remained whether juvenile court judges must appoint counsel in all delinquency proceedings.[82] As a matter of due process, the "special circumstances" of "youthfulness" could require courts to appoint counsel even in less serious and nonincarceration cases if children appear unable to prepare an adequate defense because of the inherent disabilities of their youth, substandard intelligence, or the complexities of particular case. Most states' juvenile codes provide juveniles with a statutory right to court-appointed counsel even in misdemeanor cases that potentially may result in confinement, although delinquents may waive their right to counsel.[83]

Implementation of Gault

When the Supreme Court decided *Gault,* attorneys rarely appeared in delinquency proceedings, by some estimates in fewer than five percent of cases.[84] Historically, juvenile court judges declined to appoint lawyers for indigents, often attempted to discourage parents from retaining counsel, and frequently obstructed lawyers who appeared in their courts.[85] *Gault* did little initially to alter that judicial antipathy. Even in the 1960s, "a number of attorneys who had appeared in juvenile court cases discovered that the right to engage counsel could be an empty one under the procedures they encountered. Furthermore, as many as half the judges in the state [of California] were ill-disposed to the appearance of attorneys in juvenile court."[86]

Despite *Gault*'s formal ruling, the actual delivery of legal services to juveniles continued to lag behind. In the aftermath of *Gault,* several observers monitored juvenile courts' compliance with the decision and reported that the judges neither adequately advised juveniles of their right to counsel nor appointed lawyers for them.[87] In the three decades since *Gault,* the promise of representation at all, much less effective assistance of counsel, still remains unrealized. In many states, half or fewer of all juveniles receive the assistance of counsel to which the law entitles them.[88] The only study that includes both complete statewide information from several states and makes interstate comparisons of the delivery of legal services reported that in three of the six states surveyed, lawyers represented only 37.5 percent, 47.7 percent, and 52.7 percent of juveniles charged with delinquent and status offenses.[89] As one might expect, rates of representation varied with the seriousness of the offense; judges appoint lawyers more often for youths charged with felonies than for those charged with misdemeanor or status offenses. The General Accounting Office (GAO) analyzed rates of representation in certain counties in three states and found that rates of representation varied among the states, within each state, and across offense and offense histories within each state. In 1990 and 1991, attorneys represented more than 90 percent of all youths in the "high representation" states of California and Pennsylvania, but less than two-thirds (64.9 percent) of those in Nebraska, patterns similar to those reported half a decade earlier.[90] Although the GAO attempted to ascertain the quality of juvenile representation, it interviewed only a few juvenile court judges and prosecutors, both of whom had a professional stake in affirming the quality of juvenile defense representation.

The American Bar Association (ABA) recently published two reports on the legal needs of young people.[91] In *America's Children at Risk*, it reported that "Many children go through the juvenile justice system without the benefit of legal counsel. Among those who do have counsel, some are represented by counsel who are untrained in the complexities of representing juveniles and fail to provide 'competent' representation."[92] The ABA concluded that providing competent counsel for every youth charged with a crime would help to alleviate some of the problems endemic to juvenile justice, for example, overcrowded conditions of confinement, racial disparities in processing, and inappropriate adjudication or transfer of youths to adult courts. In a second study that focused on the quality of representation in juvenile courts, the American Bar Association reported that defense attorneys who represented their clients vigorously and enthusiastically constituted the exception rather than the rule, and most juvenile defenders worked under conditions that often significantly compromised youths' interests and left many of them literally defenseless.[93] Defense lawyer-respondents also reported that many youths waived counsel and appeared in juvenile courts without representation.

Several reasons explain why so many youths in so many jurisdictions remain unrepresented. Parents may refrain from retaining an attorney or accepting appointment of a public defender for their child. Some parents may not appreciate the legal consequences of a delinquency adjudication. Others may feel that if their child is guilty, he or she should admit it rather than contest the matter. Juvenile public-defender legal services often may be inadequate or nonexistent in nonurban areas. Some judges encourage and readily find a waiver of the right to counsel in order to ease their courts' administrative burdens or because they remain committed to a traditional, rehabilitative role. Judges often give cursory and misleading advisories that inadequately convey the importance of the right to counsel and suggest that the waiver litany constitutes a meaningless technicality. Despite *Gault,* a continuing judicial hostility to an advocacy role persists in traditional treatment-oriented courts. "An attorney in traditional courts will find himself within a legal system which still considers itself non-adversary and seeks to serve goals not usually associated with other branches of law . . . [H]e will face formal and informal pressures to conform his manner of participation in delinquency hearings to the values of these courts—for example, to be less of an advocate for the child's best interests."[94] Many judges and probation officers believed that their informal and extralegal methods performed satisfactorily and resented *Gault*'s implications that they trampled on juveniles' rights. Judges also may dispense with an attorney if they predetermine that they will not incarcerate a youth after finding him delinquent. Whatever the reasons and despite *Gault*'s promise of counsel, many juveniles never see a lawyer, waive their right to counsel without consulting with an attorney, fail to appreciate the legal consequences of relinquishing counsel, and appear in juvenile court without professional assistance.

Waivers of the Right to Counsel

Waiver of counsel constitutes the most common explanation for why so many youths appear without a lawyer. As with waivers of *Miranda* rights, most jurisdictions use the adult legal standard to assess whether a juvenile validly made a "knowing, intelligent, and voluntary" waiver under the "totality of the circumstances."[95] In *Johnson v. Zerbst,* the Supreme Court held that a valid waiver of counsel required an intentional relinquishment of a known right.[96] In *Faretta v. California,* the Supreme Court held that an adult defendant in a state criminal trial had a constitutional right to proceed without counsel and to represent himself when he "voluntarily and intelligently" elects to do so. *Faretta* emphasized that the right to counsel guarantees to a willing defendant the "assistance of counsel," and not "an organ of the State interposed between an unwilling defendant and his right to defend himself personally."[97] By endorsing the adult totality test as the appropriate standard to evaluate juveniles' waivers of rights, *Fare* eroded Progressives' protectionist assumptions that children differ from adults and that courts should treat them more solicitously. Rather, *Faretta* and *Fare* allow juveniles to waive counsel, presume that youths possess the same degree of autonomy and competence as adult defendants, and permit and encourage youths to make legal decisions that ultimately redound to their detriment. The majority of states analogize to *Miranda* waivers and focus on whether a youth waived the right to counsel in a "knowing and voluntary manner" under the "totality of the circumstances."[98]

The crucial issue for juveniles, as for adults, is whether they can voluntarily and intelligently waive counsel, especially if they have not previously consulted with a lawyer. The problem becomes more acute when judges who advise youths about their right to an attorney seek a predetermined result, waiver of counsel, which influences both the information they convey and their interpretation of the juvenile's response. Although appellate courts emphasize that "exceptional efforts must be made in order to be certain that an uncounselled juvenile fully understands the nature and consequences of his admission of delinquency," many judges do not exert "exceptional efforts" and engage in only cursory colloquies with youths prior to deciding that they "knowingly, intelligently, and voluntarily" waived counsel.[99]

Although young people lack the technical competence of an attorney or even the ability of most pro se adult criminal defendants to represent themselves, courts offer several reasons to allow juveniles to waive their right to counsel. A requirement of mandatory, nonwaivable representation, for example, might "frustrate a principle goal of juvenile law of encouraging children to accept responsibility for their transgressions and take an active role in their rehabilitation."[100] Because representation by counsel may reduce juveniles' sense of involvement in their case and foster a perception that they are passive spectators rather than active participants in the proceedings, allowing them to waive counsel "can be a significant rehabilitative moment."[101]

Many analysts extensively criticize the "totality" approach to juveniles' waivers of their right to counsel as another instance in which treating juveniles just like adults places them at a practical procedural disadvantage.[102] The research previously reviewed on juveniles' waivers of *Miranda* rights provides compelling evidence that youths, especially younger juveniles, do not possess the competence of adults to waive constitutional rights "knowingly and intelligently." Research on juveniles' understanding of legal language and the justice process also raises questions about their ability either to relinquish counsel without consulting an attorney or to participate meaningfully without the assistance of counsel. Interviews conducted with delinquents shortly after they appeared at a hearing (and after their lawyers had explained to them what occurred) indicated that 80 percent did not understand many of the legal and technical words used in the proceedings.[103] Juveniles' lack of understanding can have serious legal consequences, increase their dependency upon probation officers for explanations, erode protection of juveniles' rights, and deprive the court of any moralizing or educational effects. Interviews with delinquents in Colorado's juvenile courts resulted in findings that many youths found the court process confusing and that many youths experienced difficulty understanding legal vocabularies, rules, and procedures.[104] Age, class or ethnic differences, and linguistic or cognitive deficiencies render young people more vulnerable than adults in legal proceedings.

Even if juveniles understand the language, court processes, and role of an attorney, many do not expect that their lawyers will help them.[105] Many question the reality of attorney-client confidentiality, particularly if their parents retained or the court appointed their lawyer. Others doubt that lawyers will provide a vigorous adversarial defense. Lawyers frequently lack the training or skill to develop rapport with juveniles, to explain their functions in ways that youths can understand, or to listen and perceive the situation as experienced by the youth.[106] Youths' skepticism may simply reflect lawyers' self-presentation. It may also reflect juveniles' experience with the performance of lawyers, many of whom often share the juvenile court's "benevolent" perspective and act as agents on its behalf. In one study, only one-third (34 percent) of delinquents spoke positively of their defense lawyers and the majority complained that "their attorneys gave up, would not explain what was happening, would not tell the judge what the youth wanted and was not on the youths' side. These youths had never met their attorneys before their court appearances."[107]

A few states use different procedures or a higher standard to gauge juveniles' waivers of counsel at trial than the totality approach used to assess *Miranda* and *Faretta* waivers.[108] These states, as a matter of court decision or rules of procedure, require juvenile court judges to discuss with a youth prior to any waiver of counsel the nature of the charges and the proceeding; the range of possible sentences; the role of counsel in presenting a defense or marshaling favorable materials at disposition; the role of counsel in enhancing the exercise of other trial rights, such as confrontation and cross-examination; and the dangers of self-representation.[109] Minnesota bolsters this colloquy and the delivery of legal services by requiring that the child "be fully and effectively informed of the child's right to counsel and the disadvantages of self-representation by an in-person consultation with an attorney, and counsel shall appear with the child in court and inform the court that such consultation has occurred."[110] Requiring consultation with counsel and the presence of counsel in court prior to any waiver of counsel assures that the juvenile receives the attorney advisory from a lawyer acting on behalf of the juvenile. Requiring counsel to meet with the juvenile prior to any court appearance assures the practical availability of lawyers to delinquents. Finally, for any youth charged with a criminal offense, Minnesota requires juvenile court judges to appoint counsel or stand-by counsel if the youth waives the right to defense representation, and bars any out-of-home placement of an unrepresented youth.[111] Several other states also preclude youths from appearing in delinquency proceedings without the mandatory appointment of either an attorney or stand-by counsel, if the juvenile insists on waiving counsel.[112] Research on the delivery of legal services confirms that when state laws mandate nonwaivable appointment of counsel, lawyers represent virtually all juveniles in their justice systems.[113]

More than three decades after *Gault,* simply getting an attorney into juvenile court remains problematic in many jurisdictions. The appropriate role for attorneys to play once they appear also poses difficulties. Analysts question whether attorneys can function as adversaries in juvenile courts grounded in a parens patriae ideology and, yet, whether any utility exists for their presence in any other role.[114] To a greater degree than do their criminal-court counterparts, juvenile court judges dominate the entire justice process. In a closed, discretionary proceeding, they can mobilize a variety of pressures to induce defense attorneys' cooperation. "The defense lawyer who is seen as obstreperous in her advocacy will be reminded subtly, or overtly if necessary, that excessive zeal in representing her juvenile clients is inappropriate and counter-productive. If she ignores these signals to temper her advocacy, the appointed defense lawyer is vulnerable to direct attacks, such as having her fees slashed or being excluded from the panel of lawyers from which the court makes indigent appointments. . . . For most defense lawyers, withstanding the psychological debilitation attendant upon being the sustained focus of judicial and prosecutorial disapproval is hopeless."[115]

Apart from the institutional pressures to cooperate, some defense lawyers resist simply transplanting the adversarial role of criminal defense counsel into delinquency proceedings. They perceive differences between adult and juvenile defendants, or between punitive criminal court sentences and therapeutic juvenile court dispositions. The legacy of parens patriae encourage some lawyers to sacrifice their clients' legal rights to their perceived long-term "best interests." The ideology of childhood encumbers some attorneys with moral qualms that do not plague them with respect to somewhat older criminal defendants, and limit their abilities to vindicate young peoples' legal rights. The cultural baggage of childhood and organizational co-optation incline lawyers to negotiate or mediate rather than to advocate as an adversary in a criminal proceeding.

Most juvenile courts hear delinquency cases informally, behind closed doors, and without a jury. The juvenile justice process places young people at a considerable disadvantage because they do not possess the linguistic or legal capacities of adults. Judges, court personnel, and other authority figures easily overwhelm them in an alien and intimidating judicial environment. Legal terminology goes over their heads, and they passively acquiesce to the suggestions of judges to "expedite" proceedings by waiving counsel. Even when lawyers appear to represent youths, organizational co-optation and the low visibility of the proceedings allows lawyers working under the pressure of crushing caseloads to cut corners. Judges seeking to expedite the processing of cases may tacitly encourage lawyers to cooperate and avoid challenge.[116] The juvenile court functions with a small cadre of co-opted "regular" public defenders, and very few "outsiders" penetrate its closed system. The realities of bureaucratic imperatives and administering caseloads without challenge prevail over idealized professional responsibilities.

Conclusion

Gault engrafted some formal procedures at trial onto the juvenile court's individualized sentencing schema, and thereby fostered their procedural and substantive convergence with criminal courts. *Gault* shifted the focus of a delinquency hearing from an inquiry about a child's "real needs" to proof of legal guilt in an adversarial proceeding. By focusing initially on a youth's criminality rather than "best interests," *Gault* formalized the connection between criminal conduct and coercive intervention. As a result, the juvenile court has become a wholly owned subsidiary of the criminal justice system. Providing a modicum of procedural safeguards legitimated greater punitiveness in juvenile court. The historical irony of these changes is that race provided the impetus for the Supreme Court's focus on procedural rights to protect minorities' liberty interests, but now the more punitive juvenile court sentences fall disproportionately heavily on minority offenders.

Despite juvenile courts' convergence with criminal courts, *Gault* constitutes an incomplete procedural reform, a "due process revolution" that failed. The legal system manipulates the fluid concepts of childhood and treatment to provide youths with fewer procedural safeguards than those accorded adult criminal defendants. States treat juveniles just like adults when formal equality procedures practical inequality, and use less adequate juvenile court procedures when they provide an advantage to the state. States' legal policies on waivers of *Miranda* and the right to counsel illustrate the inequality that results from judging youths by the legal standards employed for adults. But most states resist providing youths with greater procedural protections than those afforded adults in order to achieve equality because doing so would frustrate the primary crime control functions of the juvenile court.

Notes

1. 387 US 1 (1967).
2. 383 US 541, 556 (1966).

3. Barry C. Feld, *Criminalizing the American Juvenile Court,* 17 Crime and Justice 197 (1993); Barry C. Feld, *The Transformation of the Juvenile Court,* 75 Minn L Rev 691 (1991); Barry C. Feld, *The Juvenile Court Meets the Principle of Offense: Punishment, Treatment, and the Difference It Makes,* 68 BUL Rev 821 (1988).

4. Barry C. Feld, *Criminalizing Juvenile Justice: Rules of Procedure for Juvenile Court,* 69 Minn L Rev 141 (1984).

5. 403 US 528 (1971). Juveniles have no constitutional right to a jury trial in delinquency trials, because "due process" requires only "accurate fact-finding," a requirement that a judge can satisfy as well as a jury.

6. Compare *Parham v. J.R.,* 442 US 584 at 603 (1979) with *Fare v. Michael C.,* 442 US 707 (1979).

7. 387 US at 4.

8. 387 US at 14–17. The Court appraised the claims of the juvenile court: 387 US at 21.

9. Irene Merker Rosenberg, *The Constitutional Rights of Children Charged with Crime: Proposal for a Return to the Not So Distant Past,* 27 UCLA L Rev 656 (1980); Feld, *Criminalizing Juvenile Justice;* Francis Barry McCarthy, *Pre-Adjudicatory Rights in Juvenile Court: An Historical and Constitutional Analysis,* 42 U Pitt L Rev 457 (1981).

10. 387 US at 13.

11. 387 US 1 at 30.

12. 387 US at 49–50.

13. In other decisions, the Court described the policies of the Fifth Amendment as reflecting "our preference for an accusatorial rather than an inquisitorial system of criminal justice . . . [and] our sense of fair play which dictates a 'fair state-individual balance by requiring the government to leave the individual alone until good cause is shown for disturbing him and by requiring the government in its contest with the individual to shoulder the entire load.'" *Murphy v. Waterfront Commission,* 378 US at 52 (1964).

14. *Gallegos:* 370 US 49 (1962); *Haley:* 332 US 596 (1948).

15. 387 US at 47.

16. Francis A. Allen, *The Judicial Quest for Penal Justice: The Warren Court and the Criminal Cases,* University of Illinois Law Forum 518, 530–31 (1975).

17. 384 US 436 (1966). Although the Supreme Court has never explicitly held that *Miranda* applies to juvenile proceedings, the Court, in *Fare v. Michael C.,* 442 US at 717 n. 4 (1979), "assume[d] without deciding that the *Miranda* principles were fully applicable to the present [juvenile] proceeding." See also Elizabeth J. Maykut, *Who Is Advising Our Children: Custodial Interrogation of Juveniles in Florida,* Fla St U L Rev 1345 (1994); Larry Holtz, *Miranda in a Juvenile Setting: A Child's Right to Choose,* 78 J Crim L & Criminology 534 (1987).

18. Feld, *Criminalizing Juvenile Justice,* 169–190; *Fare v. Michael C.,* 442 US 707 (1979).

19. 332 US at 599-601.

20. 370 US at 54.

21. 387 US at 45, 55.

22. 442 US 707 (1979).

23. Compare with *Edwards v. Arizona*, 451 US 477 (1981). Earlier, the California Supreme Court had held in *People v. Burton*, 6 Cal 3d 375, 491 P2d 793, 99 Cal Rptr 1 (1971) that when a child who is in custody and who is interrogated without the presence of counsel requests to see one of his or her parents, then further questioning must cease. In *In re Michael C.*, 21 Cal 3d 471, 579 P2d 7, 146 Cal Rptr 358 (1978), rev'd sub nom, *Fare v. Michael C.*, 442 US 707 (1979), the California Supreme Court extended Burton's "parental request" rule to a youth's request to consult with his probation officer. The Supreme Court in *Fare* rejected this position and distinguished the role of counsel from that of probation officers in the *Miranda* process. Id. at 718–24.

24. *Fare*, 442 US at 725–26.

25. *Moran v. Burbine*, 475 US 412 at 421 (1986). Waiver has two distinct elements—"voluntary in the sense that it was the product of a free and deliberate choice rather than intimidation, coercion, or deception" and that it was "made with a full awareness of both the nature of the right being abandoned and the consequences of the decision to abandon it."

26. *People v. Cheatham*, 453 Mich 1 at 29, 551 NW2d 355 at 367 (Mich 1996) "The test is not whether [the defendant] made an intelligent decision in the sense that it was wise or smart . . . but whether his decision was made with the full understanding that he need say nothing at all."

27. *People v. Bernasco*, 138 Ill2d 349, 562 NE 2d 958, 964 (1990). For *Miranda* purposes, intelligent knowledge "means the ability to understand the very words used in the warnings. It need not mean the ability to understand far-reaching legal and strategic effects of waiving one's rights, or to appreciate how widely or deeply an interrogation may probe, or to withstand the influence of stress or fancy." *State v. Knights*, 482 A2d 436 (Me 1984).

28. 449 US 157 at 164 (1986). "While a defendant's mental condition may be a significant factor in determining the 'voluntariness' of a confession, this factor alone does not justify a conclusion that the mental condition, apart from its relation to any alleged coercion by police, should dispose of the voluntariness issue."

29. 442 US 707, 725 (1979). See also Irene Merker Rosenberg, *The Constitutional Rights*; Francis Barry McCarthy, *Pre-Adjudicatory Rights*; Feld, *Criminalizing*.

30. Janet E. Ainsworth, *Re-Imagining Childhood and Reconstructing the Legal Order: The Case for Abolishing the Juvenile Court*, 69 NCL Rev 1083, 1116 (1991); Thomas Grisso, *Juveniles' Waivers of Rights: Legal and Psychological Competence* 209 (1981).

31. *Quick v. State*, 599 P2d 712 Alaska (1979) (juvenile may waive *Miranda* rights without consulting parent or other adult); *Carter v. State*, 697 So 2d 529, 533,34 Florida (1997) (affirming "totality" approach and upholding trial court exclusion of "Grisso test" used to measure juvenile's ability to comprehend Miranda warnings); *Dutil v. State*, 606 P2d 269 Washington (1980) (declining to adopt per se rule requiring presence of parent, guardian or counsel); *State v. Bobo*, 585 NE 2d 429, 432–32 Ct App Ohio (1989) (applying "totality test" and holding that parental presence is "only one factor in the totality of the circumstances").

32. "A minor has the capacity . . .": *People v. Lara*, 432, P2d 202, 215 Cal (1967), cert denied, 392 US 945 (1968). "Judges typically focus . . .": *West v. United States*, 399 F2d 467, 469 5th Cir (1968); *People v. Lara*, 67 Cal 2d 365, 367–77, 432 P2d 202, 217–18 (1967).

33. *Fare v. Michael C.*, 442 US at 725; *State v. Benoit*, 126 NH 6, 15, 490 A2d 295, 302 (1985); *State v. Riley*, 237 Ga 124, 226 SE 2d 922, 926 (1976).

34. A survey of juvenile-waiver decisions between 1948 and 1979 concluded that no single factor determined the validity of a waiver because courts typically cited constellations of variables in conjunction with one another to justify their decisions. See also Thomas Grisso, *Juveniles' Capacities to Waive Miranda Rights: An Empirical Analysis*, 68 Calif L Rev 1134, 1138 (1980).

35. See Feld, *Criminalizing Juvenile Justice* 176; and *In re W.C.*, 657 NE 2d 908 Ill (1995) (upholding validity of waiver by thirteen-year-old who was "illiterate and moderately retarded with an IQ of 48 . . . the equivalent developmentally of a six- to eight-year-old . . . [and] possessing the emotional maturity of a six- to seven-year-old").

36. In *State v. Bernasco*, 562 NE 2d 958 (Ill Sup Ct 1990), the Court described the type of awareness required for a valid *Miranda* waiver as "being cognizant at all times of the State's intention to use [one's] statements to secure a conviction, and of the fact that one can stand mute and request a lawyer." The Court further stated that "if intelligent knowledge in the Miranda context means anything, it means the ability to understand the very words used in the warnings. It need not mean the ability to understand far-reaching legal and strategic effects of waiving one's rights, or to appreciate how widely or deeply an interrogation may probe, or to withstand the influence of stress or fancy; but to waive rights intelligently and knowingly, one must at least understand basically what those rights encompass and minimally what their waiver will entail." (Id. at 964.)

The Court invalidated the confession made by a seventeen-year-old youth with subnormal intelligence, no prior police experience, and a ninth-grade education because he did not have a "normal ability to understand questions and concepts." Id.

37. Wallace J. Mlyniec, *A Judge's Ethical Dilemma: Assessing a Child's Capacity to Choose*, 64 Fordham L Rev 1873, 1902 (1996) (at hearing to determine admissibility of statements, "police officers frequently relate that they read the *Miranda* warnings and that the child agreed to talk").

38. See *W.M. v. State*, 585 So 2d 979 Fla 4th DCA (1991). Appellate courts cannot substitute their own evaluations of facts for those of a trial judge unless they find them to be "clearly erroneous" or an "abuse of discretion," or without substantial support in the record. As a result, courts often uphold trial judges' decisions based on extreme "facts." According to the dissent in *W.M.*, the Court held that "a 10-year old boy with an IQ of 69 or 70, who had been placed by school authorities in a learning disability program and was described by one of his teachers as having difficulty understanding directions, who had no prior record with the police, who was crying and upset when taken into custody, and who was then held by police for nearly 6 hours . . . without any nonaccusatorial adult present, could

in the end knowingly and voluntarily confess to nearly every unsolved burglary on the police blotter."

39. See *People v. Cheatham*, 453 Mich 1,36, 551 NW 2d 355, 370 Mich (1996) (court upheld waiver by an intellectually limited, illiterate juvenile with an IQ of 62 because "low mental ability in and of itself is insufficient to establish that a defendant did not understand his rights"); see also *State v. Cleary*, 161 Vt 403, 641 A2 102 Vt (1994) (court upheld waiver by juvenile with only a limited ability to read or write and an IQ of 65).

40. R. Barry Ruback and Paula J. Vardaman, *Decision Making in Delinquency Cases: The Role of Race and Juveniles' Admission/Denial of Crime*, 21 Law and Human Behavior 47 (1997). Judges sentenced more severely those youths who admitted committing crimes than those who denied involvement.

41. See Grisso, *Juveniles' Waivers;* Grisso, *Juveniles' Capacities,* and Thomas Grisso, *Juveniles' Consent in Delinquency Proceedings,* in *Children's Competence to Consent,* edited by Gary B. Melton, Gerald P. Koocher, and Michael J. Saks (New York: Plenum Press, 1983).

42. Grisso, *Juveniles' Capacities,* 1153–54. An earlier study found that over 90 percent of the juveniles whom police interrogated waived their rights, that an equal number did not understand the rights they waived, and that even a simplified version of the language in the *Miranda* warning failed to cure these defects. Ferguson and Douglas, *A Study of Juvenile Waiver,* 7 San Diego L Rev 39, 53 (1970).

43. Grisso, *Juveniles' Capacities* 1160.

44. Rona Abramovitch, Karen Higgins-Biss, and Stephen Biss, *Young Persons' Comprehension of waivers in Criminal Proceedings,* Canadian Journal of Criminology 309, 319 (1993).

45. *Novak v. Commonwealth,* 457 SE 2d 402 Va Ct App (1995); Ellen R. Fulmer, *Novak v. Commonwealth: Are Virginia Courts Providing a Special Protection to Virginia's Juvenile Defendants,* 30 U Rich L Rev 935, 955 (1996).

46. Chevon M. Wall and Mary Furlong, *Comprehension of Miranda Rights by Urban Adolescents with Law-Related Education,* 56 Psychological Reports 359 (1985).

47. Abramovitch, *Young Persons' Comprehension,* 319; Grisso, *Juveniles' Consent,* 139. Gary B. Melton, *Taking Gault Seriously: Toward a New Juvenile Court,* 68 Nebraska L Rev 146 (1989).

48. Janet E. Ainsworth, *In a Different Register: The Pragmatics of Powerlessness in Police Interrogation,* 103 Yale L J 315, 316 (1993); Edwin Driver, *Confessions and the Social Psychology of Coercion,* 82 Harvard L Rev 42, 56 (1968).

49. *Thompson v. Oklahoma,* 487 US 815 (1988). In *Lewis v. State,* 259 Ind 432, 347–38, 288 NE 2d 138, 141–42 (1972), the Court recognized the contradiction between protectionist policies in other contexts and waiver procedures. "It would indeed be inconsistent and unjust to hold that one whom the State deems incapable of being able to marry, purchase alcoholic beverages, or even donate their own blood, should be compelled to stand on the same footing as an adult when asked to waive important Fifth and Sixth Amendment rights at a time most critical to him and in an atmosphere most foreign and unfamiliar."

50. *State v. Benoit,* 126 NH 6, 15, 490 A2d 295, 301 NH (1985).

51. *Commonwealth v. A. Juvenile,* 389 Mass 128 at 132, 449 NE 2d 654 at 656 Mass (1983).

52. *State in the interests of Dino,* 359 So 2d 586 La Sup Ct (1978); *Commonwealth v. Smith,* 372 A2d 797 (1977); *Lewis v. State,* 259 Ind 431, 288 NE 2d 138 (Ind Sup Ct 1972); *Freeman v. Wilcox,* 167 SE 2d 163 (1969); *People v. Saiz,* 620 P2d 15 (Colo 1980); *Commonwealth v. A Juvenile,* 449 NE 2d 654, 657 (Mass. 1983) (in order to demonstrate knowing an intelligent waiver by a juvenile, Commonwealth must show that "a parent or interested adult was present, understood the warnings, and had the opportunity to explain his rights to the juvenile so that the juvenile understands the significance of these rights"). In *In re E.T.C.,* the Vermont Supreme Court held that the state constitution imposed three criteria to establish a valid waiver by a juvenile: the youth "must be given the opportunity to consult with an adult . . . that adult must be one who is not only generally interested in the welfare of the juvenile but completely independent from and disassociated with the prosecution, e.g. a parent, legal guardian, or attorney representing the juvenile; and . . . the interested adult must be informed and aware of the rights guaranteed to the juvenile." Several states provide the right to the presence of a parent or "interested adult" by statute. See, for example, Ind Code § 31-6-7-3(a)(1982), and infra note.

53. *Lewis v. State,* 259 Ind 431, 439, 288 NE 2d 138, 141–42 (Ind Sup Ct 1972) (absence of per se guidance forces police to speculate about court's later assessment of youth's capacity and admissibility of statements).

54. Ibid., 142 (1972) (barring admissibility of confession unless both juvenile and "his parents or guardian were informed of his rights to an attorney, and to remain silent. Furthermore, the child must be given an opportunity to consult . . . as to whether or not he wishes to waive those rights"). See also *Commonwealth v. A Juvenile,* 389 Mass at 134, 449 NE 2d at 657 (Mass. 1983).

55. Conn Gen Stat § 46b–137(a)(West Supp 1986) (bars statements "unless made by such child in the presence of his parent" and after both were advised of their rights). Connecticut courts strictly have construed this "parental presence" provision and barred statements obtained when police separated the juvenile from his parent. See, e.g., *In re Robert M.,* 22 Conn App 53, 56–7, 576 A2d 549 (1990).

56. *Commonwealth v. A. Juvenile,* 389 Mass 128, 449 NE 2d 654, 657 (1983); *Commonwealth v. Berry,* 410 Mass 31, 570 NE 2d 1004 (1991).

57. Colo Rev Stat § 19-2-210(1) (1996) (Parent present at interrogation and advised of juvenile's *Miranda* rights); Conn Gen State § 46b-137 (1981); Ind Code Ann § 31-32-5-1 (Waiver only with counsel or after "meaningful consultation" with and in the presence of parent or guardian who "has no interest adverse to the child"); Mont Code Ann § 41-5-303(2) NM Stat Ann § 32A-2-14(E) (F) (1987) (Confessions by child under thirteen years of age inadmissible, rebuttable presumption of inadmissibility by any child thirteen or fourteen); Okla Stat Tit 10, § 1109(a)(1981); Tex Fam Code Ann § 51.09 (Vernon 1997) (Waiver by child and attorney, unless juvenile previously presented to and received *Miranda* warning from a magistrate); W Va Code § 49-5-2(l) (Supp 1996) (Statements by juvenile under fourteen years of age inadmissible unless made in parents' presence).

58. *In re Dino*, 359 So 2d 586 (La 1978), cert den'd 439 US 1047 (1978) (Court concluded that parental presence would help "overcome the pressure of the interrogation" and assure that "the juvenile knows he is free to exercise his rights" and "can mitigate the dangers of untrustworthiness." "The likelihood that the police will practice coercion is reduced, and if coercion is nevertheless exercised the adult can testify to it in court. The presence of such an adult can also help to guarantee that the accused gives a fully accurate statement and that the statement is rightly reported by the prosecution at trial . . . a rule will relieve the police from having to make a subjective judgment in each case").

In *State v. Fernandez*, 712 So.2d 485 (La. 1998), the Louisiana Supreme Court overruled *Dino* and reinstated the "totality" approach. The court considered the three reasons offered by *Dino*—a perceived growing trend toward an interested adult standard, empirical studies, and the public policy to protect juveniles—and concluded that none justified a departure from the "totality" analysis. "Under a totality of circumstances standard, the special needs of juveniles can be accommodated in a manner that affords protection not only to juveniles, but also to the interests of society and of justice. [c] Excluding an otherwise valid confession of guilt just because the accused was a few months away from achieving non-juvenile status is simply too high a price to pay for the arguable benefit of more easily administering a *per se* rule . . ."

59. Feld, *Criminalizing Juvenile Justice*, 182; *Anglin v. State*, 259 So 2d 752 (Fla Dist Ct App 1972) (Mother repeatedly urged her fifteen-year-old boy "to tell the truth" or "she would clobber him," but the court concluded that "the motherly concern for . . . the basic precepts of morality are to be commended . . . [and there was no] threat or coercion on [her] part."); *In the Matter of C.P.*, 411 A2d 643 (DC Ct Ap 1980) (Court admitted juvenile's statement, which was not the result of police interrogation but rather of well-intentioned parental influence, when the mother "told him to tell the truth. I kept telling him to tell the truth, more than once I know . . . I just repeating to him to tell the truth, tell the man the truth, tell what happened."); *Commonwealth v. Philip S.*, 611 NE 2d 226 (Massachusetts Sup Jud Ct 1993) ("Our interested adult rule, which we conclude was satisfied in this case, is not violated because a parent fails to provide what, in hindsight and from a legal perspective, might have been optimum advice.")

60. Grisso, *Juveniles' Capacities;* Grisso, *Juveniles' Waivers.*

61. Driver, *Confessions;* J. Griffiths and B. E. Ayres, *A Postscript to the Miranda Project: Interrogation of Draft Protesters*, 77 Yale L J 300 (1967); Project, *Interrogations in New Haven: The Impact of Miranda*, 76 Yale L J 1519 (1967); Richard A. Leo, *Inside the Interrogation Room: A Qualitative and Quantitative Analysis of Contemporary American Police Practices*, 86 J Crim L & Criminology 621 (1996).

62. Grisso, *Juveniles' Capacities*, 1163.

63. *State v. Benoit*, 490 A2d 295, 304 (NH 1985); Larry E. Holtz, *Miranda In a Juvenile Setting: A Child's Right to silence*, 78 J Crim L & Criminology 534 (1987); National Advisory Committee for Juvenile Justice and Delinquency Prevention, Standards for the Administration of Juvenile Justice § 2.247 (1980) (Miranda warnings administered and "explained in language understandable by the juvenile.")

64. Lawrence Schlam, *Police Interrogation of Children and State Constitutions: Why Not Videotape the MTV Generation?:*, 26 U Tol L Rev 901, 923 (1995) (Use of states' constitutions as basis for requiring videotaping of interrogations of juveniles.)

65. *Stephan v. State,* 711 P2d 1156, 1181 (Alaska 1985); *State v. Scales,* 518 NW 2d 587, 592 (Minn 1994) ("All custodial interrogation including any information about rights, any waiver of those rights, and all questioning shall be electronically recorded where feasible and must be recorded when questioning occurs at a place of detention."); *Pennsylvania v. Muniz,* 496 US 582 (1990) (Admissibility of statements on video-tape made by drunk driver.)

66. Mlyniec, *Judge's Ethical Dilemma,* 1909.

67. President's Commission on Law Enforcement and Administration of Justice, The Challenge of Crime in a Free Society 87 (1967).

68. National Advisory Committee on Criminal Justice Standards and Goals, Report of the Task Force on Juvenile Justice and Delinquency Prevention 212 (OJJDP, Washington, DC: 1976).

69. American Bar Association-Institute of Judicial Administration, *Juvenile Justice Standards Relating to Pretrial Court Proceedings* 89 (Cambridge, MA: Ballinger, 1980).

70. *Fare v. Michael C.,* 442 US at 719 (1979).

71. Wis Stat § 938.23 (1996) (No out-of-home placement of any youth who waived counsel; no waivers allowed by juveniles under fifteen years of age.); Iowa Code § 232.11 (1996) (No waiver of counsel at interrogation by a juvenile under sixteen years of age without written consent of parent.)

72. Wallace J. Mlyniec, *A Judge's Ethical Dilemma,* 910-11. (Courts find most juvenile confessions to be knowing, intelligent and voluntary despite overwhelming research evidence to the contrary on juveniles' capacity to waive.)

73. *In re Thompson,* 241 NW 2d 2, 5 (Iowa 1976). See also *State v. Francois* 197 So 2d 492, 495 (Fla 1967). ("We feel, too, that 'self-confessed criminals should be punished, not liberated on the basis of dubious technicalities' even though they may be young.")

74. *Commonwealth v. Christmas,* 502 Pa 218, 465 A2d 989, 992 (Pennsylvania 1983).

75. *Gault,* 387 US at 18.

76. Ibid. at 36-37.

77. Ibid. at 38, n.65.

78. Ibid. at 38.

79. Ibid. at 41.

80. 372 US 335 (1963).

81. *Gideon,* 372 US at 344 (1963).

82. In *Argersinger v. Hamlin,* 407 US 25 (1972), the Court considered whether the Sixth Amendment required states to appoint counsel for an indigent adult defendant charged with and imprisoned for a minor offense, and held that "absent a knowing and intelligent waiver, no person may be imprisoned for any offense, whether classified as petty, misdemeanor or felony unless he was represented by counsel." Id. at 37. In *Scott v. Illinois,* 440 US 367 (1979), the Court clarified *Arger-*

singer and limited adult misdemeanants' constitutional right to court-appointed counsel to cases in which the trial judge actually sentenced the defendant to some form of incarceration. Prosecutors do not charge most juveniles delinquents with felony-level offenses (Howard Snyder and Melissa Sickmund, *Juvenile Offenders and Victims: A National Report* ([1995]), and Scott limited misdemeanants' right to court-appointed lawyers to cases of actual imprisonment.

83. Barry C. Feld, *Justice For Children: The Right to Counsel and Juvenile Courts* (1993); American Bar Association, *A Call for Justice: An Assessment of Access to Counsel and Quality of Representation in Delinquency Proceedings* (1995); United States General Accounting Office, *Juvenile Justice: Representation Rates Varied as Did Counsel's Impact on Court Outcomes* (1995); Tory J. Caeti, Craig Hemmens, Velmer S. Burton, *Juvenile Right to Counsel: A National Comparison of State Legal Codes,* 23 Am J Crim L 611 (1996).

84. Note, *Juvenile Delinquents, the Police, State Courts, and Individualized Justice,* 79 Harvard L Rev 775 (1966); Edwin Lemert, *Social Action and Legal Change: Revolution Within the Juvenile Court* 172 (1970).

85. Steven Schlossman, *Love and the American Delinquent* (1977); David Rothman, *Conscience and Convenience: The Asylum and Its Alternatives in Progressive America* (1980).

86. Lemert, *Social Action,* 99.

87. Norman Lefstein, Vaughan Stapleton, and Lee Teitelbaum, *In Search of Juvenile Justice: Gault and Its Implementation,* 3 Law & Soc'y Rev 491 (1969); Vaughan Stapleton and Lee Teitelbaum, *In Defense of Youth* (1972). A 1968 study of juvenile court records found that lawyers represented only 27 percent of delinquents, that lawyers appeared in only 37.5 percent of the hearings observed, and that attorneys did not actively participate in two thirds (66.7 percent) of those cases in which they appeared. Elyce Zenoff Ferster and Thomas Courtless, *Predispositional Data, Role of Counsel and Decisions in a Juvenile Court,* 7 Law & Soc'y Rev 195 (1972). A post-*Gault* nationwide survey of 234 juvenile courts "revealed an astonishing disregard for due process by judges and very little activity by attorneys." Rosemary Sarri and Y. Hasenfeld, *Brought to Justice? Juveniles, The Courts, and the Law* 136 (1976). Only 17 percent of courts employed lawyers full time, another 11 percent employed them part time, and in most instances, lawyers had minimal influence on the trial process.

88. Barry C. Feld, *In re Gault Revisited: A Cross-State Comparison of the Right to Counsel in Juvenile Court,* 34 Crime & Del 393 (1988); Barry C. Feld, *The Right to Counsel in Juvenile Court: An Empirical Study of When Lawyers Appear and the Difference They Make,* 79 J Crim L & Criminology 1185 (1989); Feld, *Justice.* In 1978, the juvenile defender project represented only 22.3 percent of juveniles in Winston-Salem, NC, and only 45.8 percent in Charlotte, NC Stevens H. Clarke and Gary G. Koch, *Juvenile Court: Therapy or Crime Control, and Do Lawyers Make a Difference?,* 14 Law & Soc'y Rev 263 (1980). Other studies in the 1980s reported rates of representation of 26.2 percent and 38.7 percent in two southeastern jurisdictions, David Aday, *Court Structure, Defense Attorney Use, and Juvenile Court Dcisions,* 27 Sociological Q 107 (1986), of 32 percent in a large north central city, James D Walter and Susan Ostrander, *An Observational Study of a*

Juvenile Court, 33 Juv & Fam Ct J 53 (1982), and 41.8 percent in a large, Midwestern county, M. A. Bortner, *Inside a Juvenile Court* (1982). In Minnesota, throughout the 1980s and early 1990s, a majority of all juveniles appeared without counsel. See Feld, *Criminalizing;* Feld, *Right to Counsel;* Barry C. Feld, *Violent Youth and Public Policy: A Case-Study of Juvenile Justice Law Reform,* 79 Minn L Rev 969 (1995). Rates of representation varied from county to county within Minnesota, ranging from nearly 100 percent in a few counties to less than 5 percent in several others. Feld, *Justice.* A substantial minority of youths removed from their homes (30.7 percent) or confined in state juvenile correctional institutions (26.5 percent) lacked representation at the time of their adjudication and disposition. Feld, *Right to Counsel.* A virtually identical pattern prevailed in Missouri: lawyers represented only 39.6 percent of urban youths and 5.3 percent of rural juveniles, rates of representation varied substantially in different judicial circuits, and judges removed from their homes a significant minority of all the youths who appeared without counsel. Kimberly Kempf, Scott Decker, and Robert Bing, *An Analysis of Apparent Disparities in the Handling of Black Youth Within Missouri's Juvenile Justice Systems* (1990).

89. Feld, *In re Gault Revisited.*

90. United States General Accounting Office, *Juvenile Justice,* 12.

91. American Bar Association, *America's Children at Risk: A National Agenda for Legal Action* (1993); American Bar Association, *A Call for Justice.*

92. ABA, *Children at Risk,* 60.

93. ABA, *A Call for Justice,* 41–2.

94. Stapleton and Teitelbaum, *In Defense of Youth,* 38.

95. *Johnson v. Zerbst,* 304 US 458 (1938); *Fare v. Michael C.,* 442 US 707 [1979]; Feld, *Criminalizing;* Grisso, *Juveniles' Waivers.*

96. 304 US 458 at 464 ("The determination of whether there has been an intelligent waiver of the right to counsel must depend, in each case, upon the particular facts and circumstances surrounding that case, including the background, experience, and conduct of the accused.")

97. 422 US 806 (1975); 422 US at 820.

98. *McElmore v. Cubley,* 569 F2d 940 (5th Cir 1978); *People v. Kitley,* 59 Mich App 71, 228 NW 2d 834 (1975).

99. *In re John D.,* 479 A2d 1173 at 1178 (RI 1984); *K.M. v. State,* 448 So2d 1124, 1125 (Fla Dist Ct App 1984) (requiring a thorough inquiry as to whether juvenile made waiver of counsel voluntarily and intelligently, "at least equal to that accorded an adult"); *State ex rel. Jones,* 372 So2d 779, 780 (La Ct Ap 1979) (finding that a mentally retarded fifteen-year-old "lacked capacity to intelligently waive his right to counsel"). ABA, *Call for Justice,* 45.

100. *In re Manuel R.,* 207 Conn 725, 734, 543 A2d 719,722 (Conn 1988).

101. *Manuel R.,* 207 Conn at 736, 543 A2d at 724.

102. Rosenberg, *Constitutional Rights;* Grisso, *Juveniles' Capacity;* Feld, *Criminalizing Juvenile Justice;* Melton, *Taking Gault Seriously.*

103. Trudie Smith, *Law Talk: Juveniles' Understanding of Legal Language,* 13 J Crim Justice 339 (1985).

104. Regina Huerter and Bonnie Saltzman, *What Do "They" Think? The*

Delinquency Court Process in Colorado as Viewed by the Youth, 69 Denver U L Rev 345, 353 (1992).

105. Grisso, *Juveniles' Consent,* 143–5.

106. ABA, *Call for Justice.*

107. Huerter and Saltzman, *What Do "They" Think?,* 354.

108. Two states, Iowa and Texas, prohibit juveniles' waivers of counsel. Iowa Code Ann § 232.11(2)(199); Texas Family Code Ann § 51.10(b)(1996). Other states require an extensive judicial inquiry into the validity of the waiver, such as Virginia Supreme Court Rule 8:17 (1997); New York Family Court Act § 249-1 (1987). Some states require a juvenile to consult with her parent or guardian prior to waiving counsel. *State in interest of Jones,* 372 So 2d 779 (La App 1979); *Edwards v. Collings,* 193 Mont 426, 632 P2d 325 (1981); *Williams v. States,* 433 NE 2d 769 (Ind. 1982); *In re Appeal in Navajo County Juvenile Action No. JV-94000086,* 898 P2d 517 (Ariz App 1993).

109. Maryland Rule of Juvenile Court Procedure 906; Connecticut Practice Book § 961; *In re Manuel R.,* 207 Conn at 737, 543 A2d at 725: "The validity of a child's waiver of counsel depends upon furnishing the child full information not only about the child's own legal rights but also about the overall nature of the proceeding against him or her. . . . Only a full colloquy between the court and the child can . . . provide a solid basis for the intelligent exercise or waiver of the right to counsel . . . [and] permit the court to make an accurate determination of whether a child who professes to wish to proceed pro se, without counsel has the developmental and cognitive ability to undertake a realistic assessment of the consequences of such an action."

110. Minnesota Rules of Juvenile Procedure 3.04. *State ex rel. M. v. Taylor,* 166 W Va 511, 276 SE 2d 199 (W Va 1981) (waiver invalid unless informed by advice of counsel); *State v. Doe,* 95 NM 302, 621 P2d 519 (NM 1980) (mandatory initial consultation with counsel).

111. Minn Stat § 260.155 (West 1995); Minn Rules of Juv Proc 3.02.

112. Cal Welf & Inst Code § 634; Cal R Juv Proc 1412(g)(h); NM Stat Ann § 32A-2-14; New Mexico Child Ct Rule 10-205; NY Jud Law §§ 241, 249, 249-a; 42 Pa Cons Stat Ann § 6337.

113. Feld, *In re Gault Revisited;* General Accounting Office, *Juvenile Justice.*

114. Lefstein, Stapleton and Teitelbaum, *In Search;* ABA, *Call for Justice.*

115. Ainsworth, *Re-Imagining,* 1129.

116. Ibid, 1128.

CHAPTER FIVE

What We Know about Youths' Capacities as Trial Defendants

THOMAS GRISSO

This chapter uses behavioral and social science knowledge to review what we know and can infer about youths' capacities for participation in their trials in juvenile and criminal court. Its purpose is to provide a benchmark in an ongoing process of research to improve our knowledge in this area. Chapter 6 in this volume (Researching Juveniles' Capacities as Defendants, by Woolard and Reppucci) uses this information to describe directions for research that will meet that objective.

In Chapter 3, Bonnie and Grisso defined adjudicative competence and its relevance for adolescent defendants. Recent changes in laws have increased the number of youths, especially of younger ages, who are tried in criminal court and receive sanctions formerly reserved for adults. New laws pertaining to juvenile court proceedings are also of concern. They confront more juveniles with juvenile court transfer or waiver proceedings that may carry with them the potential for criminal court adjudications. In addition, new laws have significantly increased the severity of penalties that youths may receive when adjudicated delinquent in juvenile court for certain serious offenses. These changes in law have raised important questions about youths' capacities to participate in their defense.

The legal concept of competence to stand trial is defined as a defendant's "sufficient present ability to consult with his lawyer with a reasonable degree of rational understanding" and a "rational as well as factual understanding of proceedings against him" (*Dusky v. U.S.*, 362 U.S. 402 [1960]). Defendants who have serious deficits in their abilities to assist counsel in a defense, or to understand and appreciate the significance of the legal process against them, may be found incompetent to proceed to trial. Often these defendants have serious mental disorders, and the trial is then postponed while efforts are made to remediate deficits in their relevant abilities by providing psychiatric treatment. When their capacities are restored, the trial proceeds.

As described in Chapter 3 in this volume, the role of adjudicative competence in juvenile cases is uncertain in several ways. Juveniles who are transferred to criminal court are protected by the same right to be competent at trial as are adults. But current law is unclear regarding how to respond to youths' potential deficits in the requisite abilities when the deficits are due to immaturity rather than mental illness or mental retardation. In juvenile court, where adjudicative competence was not traditionally required for most of this century, a number of states recently have recognized the legal requirement of competence to stand trial in juvenile proceedings (see Chapter 3 for a review), but its meaning is uncertain.

The application of legal criteria for competence to stand trial is not the only reason to be concerned about youths' capacities in the trial process. Even youths who meet those legal criteria may present special issues for attorneys who represent them, because their immaturity may influence their participation in their trials in ways that have potential consequences for the quality of their representation. The distinction between formal competence criteria and broader concerns about youths' participation in their trials is outlined and discussed in Part I of this chapter.

Part I also identifies the relevant abilities associated with capacities as a defendant, adolescent populations about which we are concerned, and areas of theory and research that are relevant for review. Part II then reviews research describing youths' capacities relevant for their participation in their trials. Part III identifies what can be inferred from the review and suggests implications for policy, law, and practice.

Part I: Legal and Psychological Definitions of Competence
What Is Adjudicative Competence?

As noted above, adjudicative competence typically is associated with the formal legal concept of competence to stand trial as defined in *Dusky v. U.S.*: whether a defendant has sufficient ability to understand and appreciate the significance of the criminal proceedings, and whether the defendant can assist counsel in a defense. As a legal concept, adjudicative competence refers to the individual's capacity to understand, believe, or do those things that are considered necessary *at minimum* for undertaking the role of defendant (Grisso 1986). When defendants do not meet this minimum requirement, they do not proceed to trial.

This legal definition of adjudicative competence, however, is not the only framework within which we should be concerned about youths' capacities as defendants. There is another reason that is less bounded by formal requirements of law. Among defendants who are considered legally competent to stand trial, there are considerable individual differences in their capacities to participate meaningfully in their defense; they vary in what they can contribute to the quality of their representation at trial. To distinguish this second issue of youths' capacities from the issue of adjudicative competence, I will refer to it as *effectiveness of participation*.

Many of the same types of abilities might be involved in concerns about adjudicative competence and about effectiveness of participation. But their implications may differ. For example, a defendant's capacity to manage his or her behavior in the courtroom is of concern for questions of adjudicative competence only if the defendant's behavior, perhaps due to a mental disorder, threatens to disrupt the trial process. Yet there is much more to the question of a defendant's ability to manage behavior in the courtroom when regarded from the attorney's perspective of effectiveness of participation: for example, the impression that the defendant's lack of attentiveness to the trial process might have on the judge or jury. Even when defendants have sufficient ability in these areas to meet legal standards for adjudicative competence, they may vary in the strength of those abilities that can contribute to—or when weak, can inhibit—the effectiveness of their contribution to their defense.

Both meanings of competence are relevant for justice in the adjudicative process, but in different ways. Adjudicative competence directs us to examine the degree to which defendants are at risk of having deficits that seriously jeopardize their defense in ways that have constitutional implications, and the decision regarding this question is binary: the individual either is or is not competent to proceed to trial. In contrast, effectiveness of participation focuses us on a continuum of lesser to greater capacities for contributing to one's defense, and it provides a foundation for seeking ways to maximize defendants' effectiveness.

Just as youths may differ from adults normatively in reference to adjudicative competence, legally competent youths may also differ from legally competent adults in their relative degrees of effectiveness in assisting counsel. The present review focuses on what we know about adolescents' capacities in comparison to adults' capacities for both of these forms of competence in the context of their participation in their trials. The adjudicative competence perspective will be of primary relevance for legislative definitions and judicial decisions about youths' competence to stand trial. The broader issue of effectiveness of participation is of special interest to youth advocates and defense attorneys who are concerned not only with youths' competence to stand trial, but also with developmental characteristics that may affect the quality of youths' defense.

How Is Adjudicative Competence Conceptualized?

Seeking to clarify *Dusky's* legal standard for adjudicative competence, courts and mental health professionals have identified several types of abilities that are relevant for the two broad capacities to which *Dusky* refers. The best known is a list developed by McGarry and associates (Laboratory of Community Psychiatry 1973), rearranged here into four categories not provided in McGarry's original design:

Understanding of Charges and Potential Consequence

1. Ability to understand and appreciate the charges and their seriousness
2. Ability to understand possible dispositional consequences of guilty, not guilty, and not guilty by reason of insanity
3. Ability to realistically appraise the likely outcomes

Understanding of the Trial Process

4. Ability to understand, without significant distortion, the roles of participants in the trial process (for example, judge, defense attorney, prosecutor, witnesses, jury)
5. Ability to understand the process and potential consequences of pleading and plea bargaining
6. Ability to grasp the general sequence of pretrial/trial events

Capacity to Participate with Attorney in a Defense

7. Ability to adequately trust or work collaboratively with attorney
8. Ability to disclose to attorney reasonably coherent description of facts pertaining to the charges, as perceived by the defendant
9. Ability to reason about available options by weighing their consequences, without significant distortion
10. Ability to realistically challenge prosecution witnesses and monitor trial events

Potential for Courtroom Participation

11. Ability to testify coherently, if testimony is needed
12. Ability to control own behavior during trial proceedings
13. Ability to manage the stress of trial

Bonnie (1992) has developed a different but complementary way to conceptualize adjudicative competence. He suggested that it has two primary components: competence to assist counsel, and decisional competence. Competence to assist counsel is a threshold concept that refers to the defendant's capacity to grasp the meaning of the legal procedure and to participate in it with the assistance of counsel. Decisional competence refers to the capacity to engage in cognitive and judgment processes in making important decisions that defendants must make for themselves: for example, concerning pleading and weighing plea agreements. Bonnie uses four types of abilities in examining the degree to which defendants are competent in these two ways, including the abilities to: (a) understand the legal process; (b) appreciate the significance of legal circumstances for one's own situation; (c) communicate information; and (d) use reasoning and judgment in making decisions.

The following review of youths' capacities as trial defendants will use both of these ways of conceptualizing the abilities that are relevant for legally competent trial participation. They will direct us to theory and research that may be relevant in characterizing youths' capacities in general (for example, the development of functions required for problem solving and judgment) and in the specific context of trials (such as their ability to reason about plea bargains).

Reports by juvenile defense attorneys, however, suggest that there are some capacities beyond those traditionally considered for adjudicative competence that need attention in a review of youths' psychological abilities relevant for questions of effectiveness of participation and the quality of their defense (American Bar Association 1995; Buss 1996, Chapter 9 this volume; Tobey, Grisso, and Schwartz Chapter 8 this volume). For example, even when they are legally competent to stand trial, youths will vary in their abilities to:

- Take an active role in decision making and monitoring the trial process, in contrast to an entirely passive and blindly acquiescent role;
- Consider both short-range and long-range consequences when making decisions;
- Respond to assistance offered by parents and attorneys; and
- Manage their behavior both inside and outside the courtroom in a manner that is in their best interest.

Adults also may vary in these abilities. What is of special interest, therefore, is whether youths are at any comparatively greater risk of reducing the effectiveness of their defense as a consequence of developmental characteristics that diminish these abilities.

Neither adjudicative competence nor effectiveness of participation, however, is judged by an examination of individuals' abilities alone. Competence in a specific situation involves a dynamic interaction between a person with a certain level of abilities and a situation or environment that can facilitate or inhibit the realization of those abilities. Effectiveness of an individual's adaptation may be impaired if the social context that the individual faces presents unusual barriers to performance. Conversely, performance may be more effective in meeting the demands of a situation if the individual is offered what Vygotsky (1978) called *scaffolding:* structure and support that allows the individual to perform up to potential given his or her current level of development. This view of competence is recognized in law as well, such that a person whose performance appears to be seriously deficient may nevertheless be found competent to proceed to trial if circumstances can be created that will augment the individual's functioning during the trial process (Grisso 1986).

This interactive feature of competence suggests that we need to be cautious in interpreting whatever evidence we find for youths' abilities to participate in their trials, both in reference to adjudicative competence and effectiveness of participation. For example, we should not conclude that youths are as competent as adults based simply on similarities between their performance on relevant ability measures. That evidence might not indicate whether youths are able to perform in the same manner as adults if they were in the actual circumstances of a trial, the demands of which might inhibit or interfere with deployment of the abilities that they manifest in the research setting.

By the same token, we should not conclude that youths are incompetent based simply on their poor performance on relevant ability measures. They might perform more effectively if provided "scaffolding" that accommodates to their deficits and assists them in contributing to their defense: for example, providing youths with defense attorneys who are especially prepared to understand youths' capacities and needs for assistance in their role as defendant. As Masten and Coatsworth (1998, 206) aptly comment, "Although a child must act to demonstrate competence, it is also true that environments afford competence." The interactive quality of competence urges us to look for ways in which effective adaptation is enhanced by environments that can compensate for individuals' apparent deficits.

Finally, some studies I will review have tested individuals' capacities when presented with content that is related to trials and legal procedures, while other studies examined youths' abilities in a general or abstract sense. Both are relevant for understanding youths' adjudicative competence, but special weight is given here to the former type of study. It is well known that youths' abilities do not develop uniformly across all life domains. Youths may begin to manifest certain cognitive or social abilities in one context (for example, school or peer interactions) while failing to apply it to a new context until some time later in their development. The fact that youths can think strategically in general tests of problem solving, for example, does not necessarily mean that they can do so with regard to a proposed plea agreement offered to their attorney by a prosecutor in the midst of a trial process involving their potential waiver to criminal court. We need to pay special attention, therefore, to research that directly examines youths' understanding, reasoning, and other abilities in the context of the role of a defendant in juvenile or criminal court, while seeking additional guidance from studies of these abilities in the abstract.

What Populations Are Relevant?

We are concerned about the capacities of youths whose alleged offenses are sufficiently serious to warrant delinquency charges or waiver (transfer) to criminal court. Such youths will range in ages from about ten to seventeen, with questions of competence more likely to be raised for those who are fifteen or younger. Compared to general populations of adolescents, delinquent populations have greater proportions of males; minorities; youths with academic, intellectual, and neuropsychological deficits; and youths with mental, emotional, and attentional disorders (Cocozza 1992; Elliott et al. 1983; Howell et al. 1995; Otto et al. 1992). Therefore, information on the developmental capacities of adolescents in general cannot necessarily be used to affirm the capacities or deficits of youths who encounter the justice system. Moreover, youths in the justice system have greater exposure to the demands of the system itself, raising the possibility that they will be better adapted to it (for example, may know more about the trial process) than youths of the same age in the general population.

Therefore, research that examines relevant abilities among delinquent youths themselves is especially important. This does not mean that research on general youth samples is irrelevant for addressing questions of adjudicative competence. Such research does provide a developmental baseline that may help us to understand certain deficits that may be found in delinquent samples.

Part II reviews what is known about youths' capacities as trial defendants. It uses Bonnie's (1992) model to organize an examination of adolescents' capacities in five sections: their abilities to (a) *understand* the legal process, (b) *appreciate the significance* of legal circumstances for their own situations, (c) *communicate* information, and (d) *reason* about choices. To these I add a fifth category, in light of recent theories offered to explain potential differences between youths and adults in the quality of their decisions: (e) immaturity in adolescents' *judgment* when making decisions, as a consequence of psychosocial developmental characteristics rather than differences in cognitive abilities. (This review is based on my 1997 publication "The competence of adolescents as trial defendants." Its organization has been modified and its content revised to include research that has been published subsequent to the original review.)

Part II: Empirical Review of Youths' Adjudicative Capacities
Understanding the Legal Process

Central to adjudicative competence and youths' effectiveness of participation is the capacity to understand the nature of legal proceedings, one's rights in that process, and the roles of individuals in the legal process. A review of research on youths' capacities in this area reveals two broad types of studies: those that examine youths' knowledge (in other words, what they bring to the trial process), and those that examine youths' acquisition of information (that is, what they can learn if they are told about matters that are not part of their cognitive repertoire).

Youths' Knowledge of Trials and Their Participants

Elementary and preadolescent children's answers to direct questions about courtroom matters ("What does a judge do?") indicate that by around age thirteen most children accurately identify most of the trial participants' roles and the purposes of trials, at least at a fundamental level (Cashmore and Bussey 1990; Melton 1980; Melton et al. 1992; Saywitz 1989; Warren-Leubecker et al. 1989). For example, Warren-Leubecker et al. (1989) found that 90 percent of thirteen-year-olds understood that jurors decide whether the person is guilty or not guilty based on what they hear in court. Defense counsel as helper or advocate appears to be understood by about as many thirteen-year-olds (80-90 percent) as older teens and adults (Grisso 1981; Lawrence 1983; Read 1987).

Peterson-Badali and Abramovitch (1992) and Peterson-Badali, Abramovitch, and Duda (1997), however, found substantial increases in trial knowledge between ages seven and thirteen, suggesting that it is relatively undeveloped in the preadolescent years. Moreover, they found that thirteen-year-olds provided less evidence of knowledge of trials than in some other studies noted above. Their method, however, analyzed adolescents' spontaneous responses to open-ended inquiries to describe what happens in trials. Therefore, whereas other studies suggest that definitions for various elements of the trial are known by most early adolescents, organization and integration of this knowledge may continue to develop beyond early adolescence.

Using a structured method for assessment of competence to stand trial, the Competency Screening Test (Laboratory of Community Psychiatry 1973), Savitsky and Karras (1984) found that people fifteen to seventeen years old in public schools and in juvenile detention centers obtained significantly lower scores than did adult nondefendants, and significantly better scores than those who were twelve.

In a similar study, Cooper (1997) gave the Mississippi State Hospital's version of the Georgia Court Competency Test (Nicholson, Briggs, and Robertson 1988) to 112 youths, ages eleven to sixteen, who were recently adjudicated delinquent. Cooper found a significant age effect, with youths thirteen or younger performing more poorly than youths who were fourteen, fifteen, or sixteen. Using a cut-off score judged by expert consultants to represent a reasonable index below which competence was questionable, only two of the 112 youths obtained scores above the cut-off. The youths' performance could not be compared confidently with adult norms on the instrument, however, because its administration to youths required modification of several test items. Using the same measure as in Cooper's study, Schnyder and Brodsky (1998) found a significant relationship between understanding of trial-related information and age in a sample of delinquent youths who were between twelve and twenty.

The studies in this area do not provide clear answers to questions about the relation of youths' ages to knowledge that they might bring to their trials. Cross-study comparison is difficult because of differences between studies in sample characteristics (delinquent or nondelinquent) as well as methods of measurement. At best the studies suggest that youths below age fourteen are less likely than older adolescents to be familiar with more than the most rudimentary of trial-related matters. The results of the studies by Cooper and by Savitsky and Karras raise the question of whether fourteen- to sixteen-year-old delinquent youths as a group bring as much knowledge to their trials as do adults, but neither study provided direct comparisons to adult defendants. Schnyder and Brodsky's study showed a significant age effect, but their method of reporting their statistical analysis did not indicate whether their "adults" (youths over the usual juvenile jurisdictional age of seventeen) performed significantly differently than youths in the younger half of their age range (twelve to twenty).

Even if adolescent defendants were found to have less knowledge of trials than do adults, this would not mean that they are necessarily incompetent to stand trial or less effective in their participation in the role of defendant. One would want to know whether adolescents might be able to learn what they do not know if appropriately instructed. This question is addressed later in this chapter.

Conceptualization of a Right

Understanding the legal process and one's choices in it requires knowing not only that one has certain rights, but also knowing what a right is. Defendants' decisions about waiving the right to avoid self-incrimination (for example, in the context of a guilty plea) or waiving the right to a jury trial will be ill-informed if they do not conceptualize a right as a legal entitlement, providing protection that authorities in the justice system cannot arbitrarily set aside.

According to theoretical views of children's development of conceptualizations of law and rules (Tapp and Kohlberg 1971; Tapp and Levine 1974), most preadolescent children are expected to have a *preconventional* view of laws as mandates that are made and controlled by persons in authority. Cognitive and social development early in adolescence makes possible the capacity, although not automatically or uniformly realized, for development of a *conventional* concept of law. This perspective conceptualizes laws as consensual agreements among members of society for the collective benefit. A third, more abstract conceptualization of law as derived from universal principles also is possible *(postconventional)*.

Melton (1980) found that public school children below age thirteen or fourteen did indeed tend to have a preconventional view of rights as bestowed by authority and therefore retractable by authority as well. By fourteen, however, most of the youths in Melton's study were able to provide a conventional definition of a right as an entitlement guaranteed by societal agreement. There apparently are no data on the development of the concept of rights during the remainder of adolescence. But research on the more general concept of law (Tapp and Kohlberg 1971) suggests that only a minority of persons (even in adulthood) develop a postconventional conceptualization that functions consistently in their views of legal entitlements.

Other findings suggest caution when applying these theoretical guides to delinquent adolescents. Read (1987) found that about one third of delinquent fifteen- to sixteen-year-olds saw rights as conditional rather than automatic. In two studies with a broad age range of delinquent adolescents (Grisso 1981; Lawrence 1983), less than one quarter (compared with about one half of adult ex-offenders; Grisso 1981) defined a right in a way that indicated that it was an entitlement ("You can do it no matter what"). They tended more often to construe a right as something one is "allowed" to do. Thus, when asked "what should happen" if a judge at a hearing discovers that a youth "wouldn't talk to the police," one-half to two-thirds of adolescents (but only 30 percent of adults) did not recognize that the court should not penalize a defendant for having asserted a right to avoid self-incrimination (Grisso 1981; Wall and Furlong 1985). Only about four in ten adolescents in the former study recognized that defendants do not have to make statements about their offenses even if a judge were to order them to do so. (Many adults, however, also failed to recognize this.)

These comparisons of delinquent adolescents with adults suggest that a larger proportion of delinquent youths bring to the defendant role an incomplete comprehension of the concept and meaning of a right as it applies to adversarial legal proceedings. The difference between these results and those of Melton (1980), who found most fourteen-year-olds had a conventional, adultlike sense of a right as an entitlement, may be due to the fact that Melton did not use a delinquent sample. For example, Melton found that his general conclusion did not hold as well for youths of lower socioeconomic status, which is typical for delinquent samples.

Acquiring Information One Is Given

Defendants with little knowledge of the trial process or their rights need not be considered incompetent to participate if they are capable of acquiring information. If adolescents can learn what they need to know from their attorneys, then this may diminish the significance of any deficits in knowledge that they bring to their trials.

The only data related to this question come from a few studies that examined youths' comprehension of the Miranda warnings (concerning the right to avoid self-incrimination and the right to counsel). In these studies, typically, the warnings were given and adolescents were asked to describe what they mean, their answers being scored on objective criteria.

In general, these studies found good understanding for a majority of sixteen-to-nineteen-year-olds. (A study of nondelinquents was performed by Abramovitch, Peterson-Badali, and Rohan 1995; a study of delinquents and nondelinquents by Ferguson and Douglas 1970; and a study of delinquents by Grisso 1980, 1981). Younger adolescents, however, often misconstrued the right to silence; for example, they understood it to mean that they should remain silent until they were told to talk. Many who grasped that they could have an attorney did not understand the Miranda statements that offer them the opportunity to obtain an attorney "now" without financial cost (Abramovitch, Higgins-Biss, and Biss 1993; Grisso 1981). Comparing delinquent youths with adult ex-offenders, the latter study found that 45 percent of adolescents compared with 74 percent of adults demonstrated at least partial understanding of all four Miranda warnings on a reliable measure of Miranda comprehension. Scores were significantly poorer for ten- to twelve-year-olds than for thirteen- to fifteen-year-olds, the former group performing at a level similar to that of adults with mental retardation in a more recent study by Fulero and Everington (1995) using the same measure. The thirteen- to fifteen-year-olds performed significantly more poorly than the seventeen- to twenty-three-year-old group. A wide range of scores was found at every age, however, related to differences within age groups on variables such as intellectual functioning (as described in the next discussion).

Could adolescents' abilities to comprehend legal information be improved if they were given information in ways that compensated for their poor comprehension? Two studies have addressed this question by providing adolescents the Miranda warnings in simplified words and phrases (Ferguson and Douglas 1970; Manoogian 1978). Neither study demonstrated a significant increase in juveniles' understanding compared to their performance with the standard Miranda warnings. In a study described earlier, after testing delinquent youths' knowledge of trials, Cooper (1997) used a fifty-minute videotaped training session to teach the youths about trials, their participants, and trial consequences. In posttraining testing, the mean scores of all age groups were improved, especially for youths thirteen or younger. Only about 10 percent, however, achieved posttraining scores that were above the study's cut-off score for questionable competence.

Even if one could achieve better results with more systematic teaching methods, they would be of practical significance only if attorneys were careful to use such methods. In contrast, evidence suggests that in many jurisdictions, lawyers who defend delinquent youths are deficient in their abilities or motivation to augment their clients' knowledge of the legal proceedings that they face (for a review, see American Bar Association Juvenile Justice Center 1995; Federle 1988). If this is so, then one cannot presume that adolescent defendants will know more about the trial process than they bring to the situation. Some parents, of course, may be of assistance in helping their children understand the trial process. But there is no empirical information regarding parents' knowledge of the trial process and defendants' rights.

Understanding and Individual Characteristics

Thus far the present review has focused on the relation between age and defendants' knowledge and acquisition of information about trials and

rights. Some studies have examined adolescents' understanding in relation to other individual characteristics.

Legal Experience   Do youths with more prior experience in the juvenile
justice system have better knowledge of legal procedures, rights, and
attorneys? Some studies have suggested that they do not. Savitsky and
Karras (1984) found no difference between delinquent and nondelinquent adolescents in their scores on a psychometric test of information
related to trial competence. Knowledge of rights, pleas, and other court-
related matters typically have been found to be unrelated to whether or
not adolescents had a record of delinquency (Cowden and McKee 1995;
Lawrence 1983), a greater number of prior arrests or offenses (Grisso
1981), or direct experience in courtrooms (Saywitz 1989; but note that this
study involved preadolescents as witnesses). In one study (Vermeulen
1998), correct knowledge of the meaning of a guilty plea was actually *negatively* correlated with the number of times youths had appeared in court
and with the length of their custody.

Two studies, however, reported exceptions to those findings. My 1981
study found a relation between an understanding of defendants' rights
and a record of at least three prior felony referrals, but this greater experience with courts was related to better understanding among White adolescents and poorer understanding among African American adolescents. Ferguson and Douglas (1970) found better understanding of rights
among delinquent youths who were examined while in juvenile justice institutions than among youths in public schools. The result, however, may
have been related to the experimental procedures. All research participants were brought from their classroom or work settings without explanation, given the Miranda warnings, and questioned about their understanding. Thus one wonders whether the procedure may have been more
unexpected and frightening for adolescents in the public school setting,
producing a related decrement in performance.

Intellectual Functioning   Poorer comprehension of legal information and
concepts has been found for delinquent youths with lower intelligence-
test scores (Grisso 1981; Shepard and Zaremba 1995; Zaremba 1992),
lower scores on a verbal-ability test (Peterson-Badali and Abramovitch
1992; nondelinquent sample), remedial or problematic educational histories (Cowden and McKee 1995; Lawrence 1983), and learning disabilities
(Zaremba 1992). Intelligence may be a stronger correlate of an understanding of legal information than is age. On measures of comprehension
of defendants' rights with delinquent youths, my 1981 study found that the
mean performance for fifteen- to nineteen-year-olds of low I.Q. (seventy

or below) was poorer than that of ten- to twelve-year-olds with an average I.Q.

Ethnicity and Socioeconomic Status   Studies have reported poorer knowledge of relevant legal information among African American (Zaremba 1992) and Hispanic (Lawrence 1983) youths than among White youths, and among adolescents with lower socioeconomic backgrounds (Melton 1980, among fourteen-year-olds; Wall and Furlong 1985, in an African American adolescent sample). Examining ethnicity and socioeconomic status together, my 1981 study found that the only reliable and substantial race difference in Miranda rights comprehension occurred among delinquent youths of lower socioeconomic status with I.Q. scores below ninety; for that group alone, African American youths manifested poorer comprehension than White youths.

Mental Disorder   A study of the understanding of health-care information found no differences between adolescents with and without mental disturbances (Mulvey and Peeples 1996). Cowden and McKee (1995), however, found that delinquent youths whom clinicians judged incompetent to stand trial were more likely to have severe mental disorders.

In summary, the studies of understanding in relation to individual variables other than age suggest that adolescents with various intellectual and emotional problems are at risk of having a poor understanding of legal matters because of cognitive and psychosocial disadvantages. This is true of adults as well, however. For addressing matters of policy, we need to know whether the understanding of older adolescents with such disadvantages is affected differently than for adults with similar disadvantages. Little research addresses that question, but my 1981 study of Miranda comprehension suggests that disabilities and development interact to produce poorer functioning for disabled delinquent adolescents than for disabled criminal adults. For example, I found that at average I.Q. levels, fifteen- and sixteen-year-olds performed as well as adults of similar intelligence; but with IQ scores below eighty, fifteen- and sixteen-year-olds had a poorer understanding than did adults of similar intelligence.

Summary

Current evidence suggests that compared with adults, youths under age fifteen are at greater risk of having a poor knowledge of matters related to their participation in trials. For adolescents fifteen and older, on average their understanding may be more like that of adults. When they have a poor understanding, it is likely to be related to disabilities and social disadvantages that produced delays in their cognitive development. There is some evidence that these variables affect adolescents differently than they do adults with similar disabilities. Caution must be used when interpreting the results of this collection of studies, because some of them did not examine delinquent youths, who are most likely to become defendants. Those that did, however, usually found levels of performance that were no better (and often poorer) than the performance found in studies using nondelinquent samples.

Appreciating the Significance of Legal Circumstances

Defendants who understand the meanings of events, participants, and rights in the trial process sometimes fail to appreciate that these actually apply to their own circumstances. Typically this element of adjudicative competence becomes critical when delinquents' mental illness is responsible for disorientation or delusions, causing them to have irrational notions about the purpose of their trial or the motives of defense counsel (Grisso 1986; Melton et al. 1997). The paranoid psychotic defendant who understands that trials are supposed to be fair and impartial hearings but who believes that his attorney is conspiring with the prosecution is not prepared to assist counsel in his defense.

Similar questions are raised, however, when certain nonpathological, developmental characteristics of adolescents influence their ability to appreciate the significance of legal circumstances in their trials even when their understanding of relevant concepts is adequate. Serious deficits in these characteristics may have significance for youths' legal competence. Beyond questions of the minimal capacity required for legal competence, developmental characteristics associated with diminished appreciation of the significance of trial circumstances may have implications for the quality of youths' representation to the extent that they compromise youths' meaningful participation. Two characteristics associated with appreciation of the significance of legal circumstances are reviewed below: beliefs about jeopardy associated with the trial and beliefs about defense counsel.

Beliefs about Jeopardy

To be prepared to attend to and decide carefully about their situations, defendants must appreciate the seriousness of the penalties they face as well as the probability of those penalties happening. Are adolescents at any greater risk than adults of failing to appreciate the dangers they face?

As a group, adolescents have a greater tendency than adults to take risks that endanger them (Arnett 1992). This suggests that something about adolescence as a developmental stage causes them to be less sensitive to jeopardy. For example, Elkind (1967) proposed that adolescents have a tendency to believe in their own invulnerability as a consequence of "egocentrism" associated with the adolescent developmental process ("Maybe for others, but it won't happen to me"). Several studies have tested the invulnerability hypothesis (for a review, see Quadrel, Fischhoff, and Davis 1993), producing mixed results; it is not clear empirically that a sense of invulnerability is a reliable characteristic of adolescence. In contrast, a number of studies of adolescents' perceptions of the risks associated with driving, drinking, and sexual behavior provide considerable evidence that adolescents are aware of the risks they take (Alexander et al. 1990; Hingson, Strunin, and Berlin 1989; Phelps 1987).

Only two studies have addressed the question in the context of legal charges. Using hypothetical situations with public school students, Peterson-Badali and Abramovitch (1993) found no differences in adolescents' decisions about pleading guilty in relation to variations in seriousness of charges (at any age from ten to nineteen). This might suggest a certain insensitivity to degrees of jeopardy. My 1981 study, however, found that delinquent adolescents did associate more serious charges with more negative legal consequences; the effect was not related to age.

Thus, there is no empirical evidence suggesting that adolescent defendants are more likely than adult defendants to fail to believe that they are in jeopardy during their participation in legal proceedings against them.

Beliefs about Legal Counsel

Studies reviewed earlier indicated that even most young adolescents understand that defense counsel plays an advocacy role. But does this necessarily mean that they believe that this advocacy is available in their own cases? Rafkey and Sealey (1975) found that a majority of high school students believed that attorneys and police officers are dishonest. A majority of juvenile defendants in several studies voiced disappointment in their lawyers' advocacy after delinquency hearings (Catton 1978; Catton and Erickson 1975; Connor 1972; Walker 1971), and many have said that they trusted their probation officers more than their attorneys (Stapleton and Teitelbaum 1969; see *Fare v. Michael C.,* 442 U.S. 707 [1979] for an example). Such attitudes are not conducive to collaborative interactions between lawyers and adolescent clients.

Other studies have documented adolescents' more specific misbeliefs or distortions of the attorney-client role that might interfere with their collaboration. Peterson-Badali and Abramovitch (1992) found that, compared with nineteen-year-olds, a greater number of younger adolescents (and a substantial proportion of sixteen-year-olds as well) incorrectly believed that the attorney was authorized to tell judges or police officers what was discussed in confidential attorney-defendant conversations. When I asked detained juveniles in my 1981 study why defendants must be truthful with their lawyers, about one third of them (but only about 10 percent of adult ex-offenders) believed that this was necessary so that the lawyer could decide whether or not to advocate the defendant's interests, whether to report the defendant's guilt to the court, or whether to "let him go or send him up" (Grisso 1981, 119). Adolescents often seem to believe that defense attorneys defend the innocent but become more like police officers for the guilty.

There are several ways to explain these findings. A developmental explanation would focus on adolescents' frequent difficulties in relating to or trusting adults in authority. The evidence that mistrust of authority is age-related, however, is mixed (Reicher and Emler 1985; Rigby and Rump 1981). Schnyder and Brodsky (1998) found that age was unrelated to the degree of mistrust that adolescent and young adult offenders expressed about their lawyers.

Alternatively, adolescents' skepticism about their attorneys might simply be a consequence of their experience. Federle (1988) claimed that defense attorneys for juveniles sometimes are not adept in relating to youths. Schnyder and Brodsky (1998), for example, found that youths expressed less mistrust of their attorneys when they were represented by private counsel than by public defenders, which might be a consequence of more zealous advocacy among the former types of attorneys in the jurisdiction where the study was performed. The hypothesis that youthful defendants' perceptions of attorneys are responsive to the quality of lawyering that they receive is supported by Tobey, Grisso, and Schwartz's interview study of a small number of attorneys and youths subsequent to disposition of the youths' delinquency cases (Chapter 8, this volume). In this sample, most of the youths were represented by highly specialized juvenile defense attorneys who tended to spend more time in direct contact with their youthful clients and in their preparations of a defense. In these cases, youths usually expressed a considerable degree of trust in the attorney, as well as a sense of satisfaction with their attorneys' performance, independent of the specific case outcome.

Summary

Whether due to developmental characteristics of early adolescence or to the quality of lawyering for juveniles, studies report that juvenile defendants often are skeptical about the intended benefits of legal counsel and of rights when applied to their own situations. When this occurs, it could interfere with attorney-client collaboration. There is no evidence, however, that adolescents' attitudes toward attorneys are any different than one might find among adult defendants.

Communicating Information

The role of defendant requires the ability to provide relevant information about crime events, personal feelings, and social background when working with counsel to develop a defense. Serious deficits in this ability are relevant for legal competence in that defendants who cannot provide information to counsel may experience an unfair disadvantage in developing a defense. Less serious but substantial deficits in this area may simply make communications more difficult between defendant and legal counsel, thus placing an added burden on representation. If youths' capacities to express themselves are typically less adequate than those of adults, this would represent a disadvantage that is faced more often by attorneys in defense of juveniles than in defense of adult defendants.

Fundamental abilities of sensation, perception, and memory ordinarily have matured by early adolescence, suggesting that adolescents should be as capable as adults of providing accurate information from their experience. Nevertheless, the status differences between adolescent defendants and attorneys, due to age and to the attorney's position of authority, presents other potential sources of communication difficulties.

The review in the previous section concerning adolescents' mistrust of attorneys suggests that some adolescents might resist disclosing critical information to their attorneys. Results of two studies support this notion (Read 1987; Walker 1971), finding that about one third of adjudicated delinquent youths reported that they did not tell their attorneys some things related to their defense. In contrast, Tobey, Grisso, and Schwartz (Chapter 8, this volume) obtained evidence that this need not be the case; most juveniles in that study showed little sign of withholding information from their attorneys.

Research by Gudjonsson (1992; Gudjonsson and Singh 1984) suggests that adolescents are more prone to offer inaccurate information to persons in authority when they are pressured. Gudjonsson created conditions in which an authority figure expressed disbelief and disapproval at subjects' descriptions of an event, insisting that they try to be more accurate. Younger adolescents were significantly more likely than adults to change their stories, resulting in answers that were less accurate than their original descriptions. This suggests that if such pressures were to arise in the client-attorney context, younger adolescents would be at greater risk of providing distorted information to their attorneys.

The ability to take another person's perspective is important for effective communication. It allows one to accept that others may hold different points of view, to consider that others' perspectives may also have value, and to gauge what another person will think of one's own ideas or decisions. Immature development of these abilities could reduce the effectiveness of attorney-client communications. There is evidence that the ability to take another person's perspective has matured for most youths by middle adolescence, but is less reliably found in early adolescence (Selman 1980).

In summary, there is tentative evidence suggesting that younger adolescents may be at risk of experiencing difficulties in communication, as a consequence of developmental immaturity, that could interfere with their assistance to counsel. Current studies, however, do not address whether these risks are any greater for middle and older adolescents than for adult defendants.

Reasoning

Reasoning ability refers to cognitive capacities to process information when arriving at a decision. Defendants may be considered legally incompetent if they have serious deficits in their reasoning abilities. For example, the ability to make decisions must be sufficiently intact to allow one to make choices concerning how to plead and whether to accept proposed plea agreements. When defendants are not so impoverished in their reasoning abilities as to require a finding of incompetence, they may nevertheless manifest deficits in reasoning that are less extreme yet may affect the quality of their participation in the trial process and therefore the quality of their representation.

Effective decision making requires the development of certain formal cognitive abilities such as transitive thinking and the ability to think in abstractions and hypotheticals. In addition, models of everyday problem solving identify a core of functions that promote more adaptive processing of information to make practical decisions (Beyth-Marom et al. 1993; D'Zurilla and Goldfried 1971; Frisch and Clemen 1994; Hogarth 1987; Janis and Mann 1977; Spivack and Shure 1974). With some consistency, these models note the importance of being able to:

- imagine alternative courses of action,
- think of potential consequences of these hypothetical actions,
- estimate the probabilities of their occurrence,
- weigh their desirability according to one's preferences, and
- engage in comparative deliberation about alternatives and consequences.

A number of studies (none of them with delinquent youths) have found few differences between adolescents and adults in these formal decision-making functions (Ambuel and Rappaport 1992; Garrison 1991; Lewis 1980; Scherer 1991; Weithorn and Campbell 1982). Reviewers have concluded that at least by age fifteen, adolescent-adult differences in cognitive capacities associated with decision making are minimal (Beyth-Marom et al. 1993; Furby and Beyth-Marom 1990; Grisso and Vierling 1978; Mann, Harmoni, and Power 1989; Weithorn 1983). This conclusion, however, is based primarily on studies involving adolescents' processing of hypothetical problems, not real circumstances. None of the above studies examined decision making about matters related to trials. Moreover, many of the studies investigated the performance of adolescents with average intelligence or middle socioeconomic status, unlike the norms for delinquent youths.

Other studies of specific problem-solving functions have reported differences between younger adolescents and older adolescents or adults. For example, some studies have found young (nondelinquent) adolescents less capable of imagining risky consequences during hypothetical problem solving (Kaser-Boyd, Adelman, and Taylor 1985; Lewis 1981; but for different results, see Ross 1981; Beyth-Marom et al. 1993). My 1981 study found similar results when delinquent adolescents were asked to make and explain their decisions about how to respond to police questioning in hypothetical arrest circumstances. Among White youths, a more constricted number and range of consequences were considered by younger than by older adolescents. African American youths showed no age effect but were more constricted generally than were White youths in the alternatives and consequences they foresaw.

A study by Peterson-Badali and Abramovitch (1993) suggested that younger (nondelinquent) adolescents faced with pleading decisions are less likely to adjust their decisions in response to odds. They presented adolescents with four hypothetical legal cases that varied in terms of the seriousness of the offense charged and the strength of the evidence against the defendant. When asked how defendants should plead in each situation, most adolescents thought strategically, pleading guilty less often when police had only weak evidence of guilt. The ten- and thirteen-year-olds, however, were significantly less likely to use this strategy than were older adolescents. Similar results were found in a replication of the above study with youths between seven and twelve (Peterson-Badali, Abramovitch, and Duda 1997), and in a study with similar methods but with a focus on the decision to consult a lawyer about one's charges (Abramovitch, Peterson-Badali, and Rohan 1995).

Even when adolescents' cognitive capacities are similar to adults' capacities, theory suggests that they will deploy those abilities with less dependability in new, ambiguous, or stressful situations, because the abilities have been acquired more recently and are less well established (Guerra, Nucci, and Huesman 1994; Mann 1992; Scott, Reppucci, and Woolard 1995; Steinberg and Cauffman 1996). Moreover, empirical studies have demonstrated that we should not expect adolescents' newly developed abilities to be manifested uniformly across different domains of social problem solving (Flavell 1985; Seigler 1991).

Emotions, mood, and stress often have a negative influence on decision making, causing a constriction in the range of options considered or consequences foreseen (Janis 1982; Mann 1992). Mulvey and Peeples (1996), for example, found that adolescents seen in a mental health clinic for emotional disturbances performed more poorly than same-age community controls on reasoning tasks involving health-care decisions. To the extent that moodiness (and variation in mood) is more characteristic of adolescents than adults (Steinberg and Cauffman 1996), greater inconsistency in problem-solving effectiveness would be expected among adolescents. Unfortunately, we know little empirically about the actual effects of these variables on delinquent or nondelinquent adolescents' abilities to process information, compared with those of adults.

In summary, existing studies suggest that formal reasoning or problem-solving abilities continue to improve through adolescence, but normatively they may not be substantially different from adults' abilities after age fourteen or fifteen. Beyond those ages, dissimilarity between adolescents' and adults' decision-making abilities is more likely to be related to differences in motivation, in functioning under stress, and in individual differences in rates of cognitive development.

Judgment and Decision Making

Scott (1992; Scott, Reppucci, and Woolard 1995) and Steinberg and Cauffman (1996) have suggested that whether or not there are systematic differences between adolescents' and adults' cognitive capacities to make decisions, cognitive abilities are not the whole story when we are considering how people make choices. Even when people are capable of considering all of the options and consequences, and even when they are able to weigh the consequences logically, they make different choices because of differences among them in the importance that they attach to various possible consequences of their decisions. Stated simply, if two people have equal decision-making capacities in choosing a life course, but one values money and luxury while the other values rustic living, they are likely to make different choices on the basis of those values. Ordinarily we do not discount the choices of either of them as bad or incompetent, even if we would not wish them for ourselves, as long as the cognitive processes by which they were made had integrity.

But what if the individual's choices reflected preferences based on a temporary set of values sure to change in a short time? For example, if an adult makes a life-changing choice that is influenced by a serious depression in the midst of a process of mourning the death of a loved one, we may worry about the choice (despite the intact quality of the person's abilities to reason) because the person's perspective is likely to change. When the mourning process has run its course, our friend might look back at the decision with regret as a choice that did not reflect his or her actual desires.

Similarly, Scott, Reppucci, and Woolard (1995) and Steinberg and Cauffman (1996) posit that adolescents are under the influence of values and preferences that are in transition. They point to the maturation of various dimensions of attitudinal and social perspective that they call "psychosocial" developmental characteristics. Scott, Reppucci, and Woolard have focused on three developmental characteristics that could influence youths' judgment negatively: (a) conformity to peers, (b) attitudes toward and perceptions of risks that change with increasing development, and (c) changes in youths' time perspective from relatively short-term to longer-term.

Steinberg and Cauffman have conceptualized the relevant developmental psychosocial characteristics in transition during adolescence within three broad categories: responsibility (identity and ego development), temperance (including several factors associated with risk taking), and perspective (future time perspective, decentration). These psychosocial characteristics in transition are said to influence how youths perceive the importance or likelihood of various consequences when they are making choices. To the extent that their psychosocial perspectives on these dimensions are in transition—that is, are not what they will be when they mature—adolescents' choices sometimes (and more often than is the case for adults) will constitute what is commonly called poor judgment, not reflecting that which they would choose for themselves a few years hence when their perspective has matured.

For example, imagine a fourteen-year-old youth being tried for a murder on which there is substantial evidence to convict him. His attorney is offered a plea agreement by the prosecutor that would allow the youth to avoid waiver to criminal court (and the jeopardy of a life sentence if tried in criminal court) if the youth will plead guilty in juvenile court and receive a sentence there that would extend to age twenty-one. The youth appears to have excellent cognitive capacities to understand and reason about such matters. But he refuses to plead guilty because it wouldn't appear "cool" to his friends and, besides, he's always wanted to see what it's like to be the center of attention in the courtroom. Were he an adult, he would be allowed to make this choice, no matter how ill-advised it might be. Scott's theory, however, would posit that as an adolescent, the boy may be making the choice under the influence of immature perspective associated with psychosocial factors that are still in transition, causing him to make a choice that he might well not make were his developmental process nearer to completion.

A good deal of theory, and some research, supports the general proposition that youths are in transition with regard to various psychosocial characteristics that could influence their preferences when they make choices. Not all of the psychosocial characteristics identified by Scott, Reppucci, and Woolard and by Steinberg and Cauffman are necessarily relevant for the present context of adolescents' choices as trial defendants. One characteristic that is relevant and worthy of consideration, however, is the developmental nature of *future orientation, risk perception, and risk preference,* all of which might be important in making choices about pleading and dealing with plea agreements.

There is evidence that the tendency to be oriented generally to the future and to take into account future consequences of actions one is considering increases from childhood to adolescence and that it continues to develop between adolescence and young adulthood (Greene 1986; Nurmi 1991). But whether this ability is manifested very differently by adolescents than by adults is less clear. For example, as noted earlier in this chapter, there is considerable evidence that adolescents on average are aware of risks that they take, even longer-range risks (Alexander et al. 1990), and some studies (e.g., Beyth-Marom et al. 1993) have found only equivocal or situation-specific differences between adolescents and adults in their tendency to imagine long-range consequences. Nevertheless, more recent studies (Cauffman and Steinberg 1999) have suggested that adolescents not only differ from adults on measures of time perspective (less future orientation), but also that those differences are related to choices that can be construed as less adaptive.

There is also evidence that adolescents on average may differ from adults in the weights that they give to potential positive and negative outcomes. For example, theory and research suggests that adolescents are more likely than adults to give greater weight to anticipated gains than to possible losses or negative risks (Benthin, Slovic, and Severson 1993; Furby and Beyth-Marom 1990; Gardner 1993; Gardner and Herman

1990), especially when the gains are more immediate. They also appear to be more willing to take physical and social risks for the sake of experiencing novel and complex sensations (Arnett 1994).

Reasons for a foreshortened time perspective and a tendency to discount the importance of long-range future risks have been offered specifically for delinquent youths. Growing up in environments that provide little opportunity, delinquent youths often give less weight to long-range consequences when making life decisions (Gardner 1993; Jessor 1992a, 1992b). Thus, I found (1981) that when delinquent youths were asked to imagine any consequences of waiving or asserting rights to silence when questioned by police, the consequence mentioned most frequently was the immediate response of the police ("If I talk, they'll let me go home tonight"). An index of time perspective in this study indicated significant age differences in interaction with intelligence; among adolescents with I.Q. scores below eighty, those who were fourteen or younger were more likely than those who were older to focus one-sidedly on short-range consequences.

Despite some pieces of evidence about differences between adults and youths in their consideration of longer-range consequences, the gaps in our knowledge in this area are considerable. It is not possible to say with certainty at this time that we should expect youths to have a substantially different way of regarding long-range consequences of their choices in the adjudicative process than do adults, but evidence is beginning to mount in that direction.

Part III: Summary and Implications

It is apparent from this review that the abilities of youths as trial defendants and the decision-making capacities of adolescents in general have not received much study. Substantive recommendations for law, policy, and practice in this area will be limited until research on adolescents' capacities as defendants has filled these gaps. Woolard and Reppucci (Chapter 6, this volume) indicate the directions in which such research should proceed. Therefore, this chapter concludes with a summary of trends in current findings and a discussion of their implications for policy and practice if future research indicates that these trends are reliable.

Trends in Findings Regarding Adolescents' Trial Capacities

The data now available suggest that certain types of youths may be at risk of significant deficits in abilities related to adjudicative competence. If further research supports these suggestions, the results should play a role in policy debates concerning the need for special protections to avoid adolescents' incompetent participation in their trials.

Specifically, for youths who are under fourteen years old, the balance of evidence discussed in this chapter suggests that as a group they are at greater risk than most adults for deficits in abilities associated with adjudicative competence. Significant differences between this age group and older adolescents or adults have been found in most types of abilities reviewed thus far. Youths of that age who have defendant abilities similar to those of adults represent a significant exception to the norm.

In contrast, among adolescents who are fourteen to sixteen years old, age itself tends to be a poor indicator of abilities associated with the defendant role. By about fourteen to fifteen years of age, some youths appear to have developed legally relevant cognitive abilities that approximate those of older adolescents. Many other youths at those ages, however, continue to develop more slowly and will achieve their adult capacities at a later age, nearer to the late teens. This developmental delay is seen especially in delinquent populations, which have a greater proportion of adolescents with intellectual deficits, learning disabilities, emotional disorders, and reduced educational and cultural opportunities. These characteristics tend to slow the pace of cognitive and psychosocial development. Therefore, some adolescents appear to have matured sufficiently to have the capacity to perform more or less as they will in their adult years, while others have not reached the level of ability and psychosocial maturity that they will manifest when they reach young adulthood.

Even among fourteen- to sixteen-year-olds who have achieved their adult capacity for understanding and reasoning, some may not have the ability to maintain or use those capacities consistently across situations and under stress in ways that they will achieve on entering their adult years. Moreover, despite adequate cognitive abilities, their judgment in using information to make decisions may not be like that of most adults. This remains a theoretical speculation, however, in the absence of research to test it.

Implications for Law and Policy

The current state of research on adolescents' capacities as defendants does not provide a definitive basis for recommending changes in law and policy to protect youths from incompetent participation in their trials. Nevertheless, the results suggest that we should begin to consider legal changes that may be needed if further research supports current findings.

If future studies affirm those reviewed here, arguments could be made for a legal presumption of incompetence to stand trial for youths younger than fourteen, when they face proceedings that may lead to criminal adjudications (including juvenile court transfer hearings). Similar arguments have been made for the protection of other rights of adolescent defendants, such as the automatic exclusion of confessions based on the unassisted waiver of Miranda warnings by youths younger than fourteen (Grisso 1980). Moreover, many states already exclude juveniles younger than fourteen from adjudication in criminal court, and in states that allow transfer at lower ages the number of youths transferred at ages below fourteen is relatively small. Youths under fourteen still could be competent to participate in trials leading to dispositions within the juvenile justice system, presuming that the threshold for competence in such hearings is lower than the threshold applied for criminal proceedings.

For youths who are fourteen to sixteen years of age, current research suggests that learning disabilities or emotional disorders often produce delays in cognitive or psychosocial development that reduce their capacities related to adjudicative competence. Of course, not all such youths need to be found incompetent, even if they manifest significant trial-related deficits in an evaluation; some will respond adequately to special efforts to assist them in their decisions as defendants, such as being taught by their attorney. For some, however, important deficits in defendant abilities will persist. These conclusions suggest the need to enhance the courts' attention to the potential for adjudicative incompetence in this age group, possibly by mandating a review of competence for all adolescents prior to their participation in criminal court proceedings or in juvenile proceedings that may lead to criminal adjudication.

Reform might have to go further, however, if youths are to be protected from deficits in their capacities as defendants due to their developmental immaturity. Current standards for competence to stand trial in criminal court identify incompetence as deficits in trial-related abilities when they are produced by serious mental illness (such as psychoses) or mental retardation. Youths whose abilities are impaired by these conditions would be protected by these same standards from incompetent participation in their trials. The current review, however, suggests that some adolescents' capacities to participate in their trials may be impaired for other reasons. For some fourteen- to sixteen-year-olds, cognitive and social development is delayed by learning disabilities or emotional disturbances. Some of these youths may not yet have achieved the level of development typical for peers their age, and they will achieve adult levels of capacity later than their peers. Others have emotional disorders of adolescence that are not the equivalent of serious mental illnesses manifested in adulthood, yet their disorders may nonetheless impair their functioning as defendants no less than psychotic disorders. With the appearance of an increasing number of juveniles in criminal court, it could be argued that immature or deficient development of cognitive and social abilities, as well as emotional disorders of adolescence, should be formally recognized as relevant bases for incompetence.

Implications for Practice

Questions about adolescents' adjudicative competence and effectiveness of participation in their defense will arise with increasing frequency as new laws bring greater numbers of adolescents of all ages into the criminal courts. The results reviewed in this chapter offer some guidance for attorneys, forensic mental health examiners, and courts who will be asked to respond to these circumstances. (See also Chapter 7 of this volume [Clinical and Forensic Evaluation of Competence to Stand Trial in Juvenile Defendants, by Richard Barnum]; Grisso 1998.)

For attorneys representing youths, the review identifies the types of deficits they should be aware of as they interact with their adolescent clients. Identification of serious deficits in a youth's trial-related abilities, however, does not necessarily require that one formally raise the question of the youth's competence to stand trial. The attorney's first responsibility is to take steps to try to augment the youth's understanding or reasoning through, for example, careful explanations and additional discussion that may clarify the youth's misunderstanding. Attorneys are in need of systematic guidance for fulfilling this objective. As more is known about adolescents' deficits as trial defendants, it might be possible to translate this information into concrete methods with which attorneys could improve their juvenile clients' abilities as defendants.

If the attorney's remedial efforts are not fruitful and the legal question of competence must be raised, forensic mental health examiners often will be expected to perform more formal evaluations of youths' competence to stand trial. No methods for doing this have been developed specifically for adolescents. Forensic examiners can adapt current methods, developed for use with adult defendants, that provide guidance concerning the types of information to obtain (Golding, Roesch, and Schreiber 1984; Grisso 1986, 1988, 1998; Grisso, Miller, and Sales 1987; Laboratory of Community Psychiatry 1972; Melton et al. 1997). Research is needed, however, to provide examiners with adolescent norms for performance on these instruments.

Examiners should recognize that the interpretation of their data will require attention to developmental factors not often considered in the evaluation of adult defendants. This chapter provides some theoretical and empirical guidance for that interpretative process.

Finally, as defense attorneys' claims about their youthful clients' adjudicative incompetence increase in frequency, courts will more often be faced with questions of youths' developmental capacities to participate in their trials. The research reviewed here, imperfect as it is, provides courts with the only empirical guidance that psychology has to offer until such time as research focused specifically on adjudicative capacities of adolescents offers more definitive information.

Works Cited

Abramovitch, R., K. Higgins-Biss, and S. Biss. 1993. Young persons' comprehension of waivers in criminal proceedings. *Canadian Journal of Criminology* 35:309–322.

Abramovitch, R., M. Peterson-Badali, and M. Rohan. 1995. Young people's understanding and assertion of their rights to silence and legal counsel. *Canadian Journal of Criminology* 37:1–18.

Alexander, C., Y. Kim, M. Ensminger, K. Johnson, B. Smith, and L. Dolan. 1990. A measure of risk taking for young adolescents: Reliability and validity assessments. *Journal of Youth and Adolescence* 19:559–569.

Ambuel, B., and J. Rappaport. 1992. Developmental trends in adolescents' psychological and legal competence to consent to abortion. *Law and Human Behavior* 16:129–154.

American Bar Association Juvenile Justice Center. 1995. A *call for justice: An assessment of access to counsel and quality of representation in delinquency proceedings.* Washington, D.C.: Author.

Arnett, J. 1992. Reckless behavior in adolescence: A developmental perspective. *Development Review* 12: 339–373.

———. 1994. Sensation seeking: A new conceptualization and a new scale. *Personality and Individual Differences* 16:289–296.

Benthin, A., P. Slovic, and H. Severson. 1993. A psychometric study of adolescent risk perception. *Journal of Adolescence* 16:153–168.

Beyth-Marom, R., L. Austin, B. Fischhoff, C. Palmgren, and M. Jacobs-Quadrel. 1993. Perceived consequences of risky behaviors: Adults and adolescents. *Developmental Psychology* 29:549–563.

Bonnie, R. 1992. The competence of criminal defendants: A theoretical reformulation. *Behavioral Sciences and the Law* 10:291–316.

Buss, E. 1996. "You're my what?" The problem of children's misperceptions of their lawyers' roles. *Fordham Law Review* 64:1699.

Cashmore, J., and K. Bussey. 1990 . Children's conceptions of the witness role. In *Children's evidence in legal proceedings: An international perspective,* edited by J. Spencer, G. Nicholson, R. Flin, and R. Bull. Cambridge, England: University of Cambridge, Faculty of Law.

Catton, K. 1978. Children in the courts: A selected empirical review. *Canadian Journal of Family Law* 1:329–362.

Catton, K., and P. Erickson. 1975. *The juvenile's perception of the role of defense counsel in juvenile court.* Unpublished manuscript, University of Toronto, Center for Criminology, Toronto, Ontario, Canada.

Cauffman, E., and L. Steinberg. 1999. (Im)maturity of judgment in adolescence: Why adolescents may be less culpable than adults. Unpublished manuscript.

Cocozza, J, ed. 1992. *Responding to mental health needs of youth in the juvenile justice system.* Seattle, Wash.: National Coalition for the Mentally III in the Criminal Justice System.

Connor, W. 1972. *The juvenile court: Its impact on children adjudged to be delinquent.* Unpublished master's thesis, University of Toronto, Center for Criminology, Toronto, Ontario, Canada.

Cooper, D. 1997. Juveniles' understanding of trial-related information: Are they competent defendants? *Behavioral Sciences and the Law* 15:167–180.

Cowden, V., and G. McKee. 1995. Competency to stand trial in juvenile delinquency proceedings: Cognitive maturity and the attorney-client relationship. *Journal of Family Law* 33:629–660.

D'Zurilla, T., and M. Goldfried. 1971. Problem solving and behavior modification. *Journal of Abnormal Psychology* 78:107–126.

Elkind, D. 1967. Egocentrism in adolescence. *Child Development* 38:1025–1034.

Elliott, D., S. Ageton, D. Huizinga, B. Knowles, and R. Canter. 1983. *The prevalence and incidence of delinquent behavior: 1976–1980 (The National Youth Survey Report No. 26).* Boulder, Colo.: Behavioral Research Institute.

Federle, K. 1988. Overcoming the adult-child dyad: A methodology for interviewing and counseling the juvenile client in delinquency cases. *Journal of Family Law* 26:545–578.

Ferguson, A., and A. Douglas. 1970. A study of juvenile waiver. *San Diego Law Review* 7:39–54.

Flavell, J. 1985. *Cognitive development.* Englewood Cliffs, N.J.: Prentice Hall.

Frisch, D., and R. Clemen. 1994. Beyond expected utility: Rethinking behavior decision research. *Psychological Bulletin* 116:45–54.

Fulero, S., and C. Everington. 1995. Assessing competency to waive Miranda rights in defendants with mental retardation. *Law and Human Behavior* 19:533–545.

Furby, L., and R. Beyth-Marom. 1990. *Risk taking in adolescence: A decision-making perspective.* Washington, D.C.: Office of Technology Assessment.

Gardner, W. 1993. A life-span rational-choice theory of risk taking. In *Adolescent risk taking,* edited by N. Bell and R. Bell. Thousand Oaks, Calif.: Sage.

Gardner, W., and J. Herman, 1990. Adolescents' AIDS risk taking: A rational choice perspective. In *Adolescents in the AIDS epidemic,* edited by W. Gardner, S. Millstein, and B. Wilcox. San Francisco, Calif.: Jossey-Bass.

Garrison, E. 1991. Children's competence to participate in divorce custody decisions. *Journal of Clinical Child Psychology* 20:78–87.

Golding, S., R. Roesch, and J. Schreiber. 1984. Assessment and conceptualization of competency to stand trial: Preliminary data on the Interdisciplinary Fitness Interview. *Law and Human Behavior* 9:321–334.

Greene, A. 1986. Future-time perspective in adolescence: The present of things future revisited. *Journal of Youth and Adolescence* 15:99–113.

Grisso, T. 1980. Juveniles' capacities to waive *Miranda* rights: An empirical analysis. *California Law Review* 68:1134–1166.

——. 1981. *Juveniles' waiver of rights: Legal and psychological competence.* New York: Plenum.

——. 1986. *Evaluating competencies: Forensic assessments and instruments.* New York: Plenum.

——. 1988. *Competency to stand trial: A manual for practice.* Sarasota, Fla.: Professional Resource Press.

——. 1997. The competence of adolescents as trial defendants. *Psychology, Public Policy, and Law* 3:3–32.

——. 1998. *Forensic evaluation of juveniles.* Sarasota, Fla.: Professional Resource Press.

Grisso, T., M. Miller, and B. Sales. 1987. Competency to stand trial in juvenile court. *International Journal of Law and Psychiatry* 10:1–20.

Grisso, T., and L. Vierling. 1978. Minors' consent to treatment: A developmental perspective. *Professional Psychology* 9: 412–427.

Gudjonsson, G. 1992. *The psychology of interrogations, confessions, and testimony.* New York: Wiley.

Gudjonsson, G., and K. Singh. 1984. Interrogative suggestibility and delinquent boys: An empirical validation study. *Personality and Individual Differences* 5:425–430.

Guerra, N., L. Nucci, and L. Huesman. 1994. Moral cognition and childhood aggression. In *Aggressive behavior: Current perspectives,* edited by L. Huesman. New York: Plenum.

Hingson, R., L. Strunin, and B. Berlin. 1989. AIDS transmission: Changes in knowledge and behaviors among adolescents. *Pediatrics* 85:24–29.

Hogarth, R. 1987. *Judgment and choice.* New York: Wiley.

Howell, J., B., Krisberg, J. Hawkins, and J. Wilson, eds. 1995. *Serious, violent, and chronic juvenile offenders.* Thousand Oaks, Calif.: Sage.

Janis, I. 1982. Decision-making under stress. In *Handbook of stress: Theoretical and clinical aspects,* edited by L. Goldberger and S. Breznitz. New York: Van Nostrand Reinhold.

Janis, I., and L. Mann. 1977. *Decision-making.* New York: Free Press.

Jessor, R. 1992a. Reply: Risk behavior in adolescence: A psychosocial framework for understanding and action. *Developmental Review* 12:374–390.

——. 1992b. Risk behavior in adolescence: A psychosocial framework for understanding and action. In *Adolescents at risk: Medical and social perspectives,* edited by D. Rogers and E. Ginzburg. Boulder, Colo.: Westview Press.

Kaser-Boyd, N., H. Adelman, and L. Taylor. 1985. Minors' ability to identify risks and benefits of therapy. *Professional Psychology: Research and Practice* 16:411–417.

Laboratory of Community Psychiatry, Harvard Medical School. 1973. *Competency to stand trial and mental illness.* Rockville, Md.: Department of Health, Education and Welfare.

Lawrence, R. 1983. The role of legal counsel in juveniles' understanding of their rights. *Juvenile and Family Court Journal* 34:49–58.

Lewis, C. 1980. A comparison of minors' and adults' pregnancy decisions. *American Journal of Orthopsychiatry* 50:446–453.

——. 1981. How adolescents approach decisions: Changes over grades seven to twelve and policy implications. *Child Development* 52:538–544.

Mann, L. 1992. Stress, affect, and risk taking. In *Risk-taking,* edited by J. Yates. New York: Wiley.

Mann, L., R. Harmoni, and C. Power. 1989. Adolescent decision-making: The development of competence. *Journal of Adolescence* 12:265–278.

Manoogian, S. 1978. *Factors affecting juveniles' comprehension of Miranda rights.* Unpublished doctoral dissertation, Saint Louis University, Department of Psychology, Missouri.

Masten, A., and J. Coatsworth. 1998. The development of competence in favorable and unfavorable environments. *American Psychologist* 53:205–220.

Melton, G. 1980. Children's concepts of their rights. *Journal of Clinical Child Psychology* 9:186–190.

Melton, G., S. Limber, J. Jacobs, and L. Oberlander. 1992. *Preparing sexually abused children for testimony: Children's perceptions of the legal process.* Unpublished report, University of Nebraska-Lincoln, Center for Children, Families, and the Law.

Melton, G., J. Petrila, N. Poythress, and C. Slobogin. 1997. *Psychological evaluations for the courts.* 2d ed. New York: Guilford.

Mulvey, E., and F. Peeples. 1996. Are disturbed and normal adolescents equally competent to make decisions about mental health treatments? *Law and Human Behavior* 20:273–287.

Nicholson, R., S. Briggs, and H. Robertson. 1988. Instruments for assessing competency to stand trial: How do they work? *Professional Psychology: Research and Practice* 19:383–394.

Nurmi, J. 1991. How do adolescents see their future? A review of the development of future orientation and planning. *Developmental Review* 11:1–59.

Otto, R., J. Greenstein, M. Johnson, and R. Friedman. 1992. Prevalence of mental disorders among youth in the juvenile justice system. In *Responding to the mental health needs of youth in the juvenile justice system,* edited by J. Cocozza. Seattle, Wash: National Coalition for the Mentally Ill in the Criminal Justice System.

Peterson-Badali, M., and R. Abramovitch. 1992. Children's knowledge of the legal system: Are they competent to instruct legal counsel? *Canadian Journal of Criminology* 34:139–160.

——. 1993. Grade related changes in young people's reasoning about plea decisions. *Law and Human Behavior* 17:537–552.

Peterson-Badali, M., R. Abramovitch, and J. Duda. 1997. Young children's legal knowledge and reasoning ability. *Canadian Journal of Criminology* 39:145–170.

Phelps, C. 1987. Risk and perceived risk of drunk driving among young drivers. *Journal of Policy Analysis and Management* 6:708–714.

Quadrel, M., B. Fischhoff, and W. Davis. 1993. Adolescent (in)vulnerability. *American Psychologist* 48:102–116.

Rafkey, D., and R. Sealey. 1975. The adolescent and the law: A survey. *Crime and Delinquency* 21:131–138.

Read, A. 1987. *Minors' ability to participate in the adjudication process: A look at their understanding of court proceedings and legal rights.* Unpublished master's thesis, University of Toronto, Toronto, Ontario, Canada.

Reicher, S., and N. Emler. 1985. Delinquent behaviour and attitudes to formal authority. *British Journal of Social Psychology* 24:161–168.

Rigby, K., and E. Rump. 1981. Attitudes toward parents and institutional authorities during adolescence. *Journal of Psychology* 109:109–118.

Ross, J. 1981. The measurement of student progress in a decision-making approach to values education. *The Alberta Journal of Educational Research* 27:1–15.

Savitsky, J., and D. Karras. 1984. Competency to stand trial among adolescents. *Adolescence* 19:349358.

Saywitz, K. 1989. Children's conceptions of the legal system: "Court is a place to play basketball." In *Perspectives on children's testimony,* edited by S. Ceci, D. Ross, and M. Toglia. Springer-Verlag.

Scherer, D. 1991. The capacities of minors to exercise voluntariness in medical treatment decisions. *Law and Human Behavior* 15:431–449.

Schnyder, C., and S. Brodsky. 1998. *The importance of trust in the attorney-juvenile client relationship.* Paper presented at the convention of the American Psychology-Law Society, Redondo Beach, Calif.

Scott, E. 1992. Judgment and reasoning in adolescent decision making. *Villanova Law Review* 37:1607–1669.

Scott, E., N. Reppucci, and J. Woolard. 1995. Evaluating adolescent decision-making in legal contexts. *Law and Human Behavior* 19:221–244.

Seigler, R. 1991. *Children's thinking.* 2d ed. Englewood Cliffs, N.J.: Prentice Hall.

Selman, R. 1980. *The growth of interpersonal understanding: Developmental and clinical analyses.* New York: Academic Press.

Shepard, R., and B. Zaremba. 1995. When a disabled juvenile confesses to a crime: Should it be admissible? *Criminal Justice* 9:31–32.

Spivack, G., and M. Shure. 1974. *Social adjustment of young children: A cognitive approach to solving real-life problems.* San Francisco, Calif.: Jossey-Bass.

Stapleton, W., and L. Teitelbaum. 1969. *In defense of youth.* New York: Holt, Rinehart, & Winston.

Steinberg, L., and E. Cauffman. 1996. Maturity of judgment in adolescence: Psychosocial factors in adolescent decision-making. *Law and Human Behavior* 20:249–272.

Tapp, J., and L. Kohlberg. 1971. Developing senses of law and legal justice. *Journal of Social Issues* 27:65–91.

Tapp, J., and E. Levine. 1974. Legal socialization: Strategies for an ethical legality. *Stanford Law Review* 27:1–72.

Vermeulen, S. 1998. *Young offenders' and high school students' plea decision-making capabilities.* Paper presented at the convention of the American Psychology-Law Society, Redondo Beach, Calif.

Vygotsky, L. 1978. *Mind in society: The development of higher psychological processes.* Cambridge, Mass.: Harvard University Press.

Walker, S. 1971. The lawyer-child relationship: A statistical analysis. *Duquesne Law Review* 9:627–650.

Wall, S., and M. Furlong. 1985. Comprehension of Miranda rights by urban adolescents with law-related education. *Psychological Reports* 56:359–372.

Warren-Leubecker, A., C. Tate, I. Hinton, and N. Ozbek. 1989. What do children know about the legal system and when do they know it? In *Perspectives on children's testimony,* edited by S. Ceci, D. Ross, and M. Toglia. New York: Springer-Verlag.

Weithorn, L. 1983. Involving children in decisions affecting their own welfare. In *Children's competence to consent,* edited by G. Melton, G. Koocher, and M. Saks. New York: Plenum.

Weithorn, L., and S. Campbell. 1982. The competency of children and adolescents to make informed treatment decisions. *Child Development* 53:1589–1598.

Zaremba, B. 1992. *Comprehension of* Miranda *rights by 14-18 year old African American and Caucasian males with and without learning disabilities.* Unpublished doctoral dissertation, College of William and Mary, School of Education, Williamsburg, Virginia.

CHAPTER SIX

Researching Juveniles' Capacities as Defendants

JENNIFER L. WOOLARD AND N. DICKON REPPUCCI

This chapter identifies studies that need to be done to learn about juveniles' capacities as trial defendants, and the methodological issues that must be addressed in designing those studies. Throughout this chapter we will use juveniles' participation as an overarching construct including both the broader abilities as well as the more narrowly drawn issues of competence to stand trial. Much of the existing research, particularly clinical and developmental research on competence to stand trial and adolescents' decision-making abilities, is summarized in the preceding chapter. This chapter will draw on that summary to identify the limitations of the extant research and the conceptual and methodological issues for future research.

Over the past twenty years, numerous authors have called for developmental research that examines adolescent choices in legal contexts (Grisso 1996; Grisso and Lovinguth 1982; Melton 1981; Reppucci et al. 1984; Scott, Reppucci, and Woolard 1995; Steinberg and Cauffman 1996; Wald 1976; Woolard, Reppucci, and Redding 1996). Because the law has traditionally limited minors' participation in the legal system based at least in part on their presumed incompetence (Melton 1983; *Parham v. J.R.* 1979), early research on juveniles' participation focused primarily on setting forth legal standards of competent decision making and testing adolescents' performance on such standards. Legal and social interest in adolescent abortion (*Belloti v. Baird* 1979; *H.L. v. Matheson* 1981) as well as other medical and mental health decisions encouraged research into presumptions of adolescent incapacity and incompetence to make choices about treatment. At the same time, juvenile justice reform was in full swing and psychological research on juveniles' capacities as defendants emerged (Grisso 1981).

The 1990s have brought a new wave of changes in processing juveniles.

As adult processing and penalties are increasingly directed at larger numbers of juvenile defendants, researchers have called on the field to examine the presumption that juveniles have adultlike capacities to understand
and participate meaningfully in the adjudicative process, specifically in
terms of competence to stand trial (adjudicative competence). Although
research on juvenile's capacities as defendants is underway and a small literature on adjudicative competence is being established, legal presumptions and policy changes affecting juvenile defendants have outpaced our
empirical knowledge. Research must be developed to respond to changes
in both practice and theory because empirical analysis is vital to clarify the
ways in which adolescents are similar to, and different from, adult defendants. In the next section we review the limitations of the extant research.
Then, we elaborate on goals of a research agenda on juvenile defendants'
capacities and provide an overview of directions for future research.

Limitations of Extant Research

There have been two major criticisms of the past literature on youths' capacities: concerns about what capacities have been studied and how the
studies have been designed. The first criticism suggests that methodological weaknesses in sampling and measurement limit the conclusions that
can be drawn from prior research. The second criticism holds that prior research has been limited by a focus on adult criteria for competence, overlooking additional developmental factors that might affect juvenile capacities. Although a number of these concerns have been raised since the
inception of this research endeavor (Grisso and Lovinguth 1982; Melton
1981), these limitations persist in the field and constrain the generalizability of the research and its potential to have an impact on policy and
practice.

Study Design and Implementation

Much of the previous research relevant to juveniles' capacities as defendants is not directly related to participation in one's defense and did not
focus on juvenile defendants per se. With some exceptions, the majority
of studies did not focus on youths that were defendants or who matched
in some way the demographic and experience characteristics of juvenile
defendant populations. The resulting samples, comprised of predominantly white, middle- to upper-class high school students with average or
above average intellectual or academic skills, do not represent populations
of juveniles that are likely to come into contact with the justice system.
The number of dimensions on which these participants differ from delinquent samples substantially weakens the validity of any generalizations

to offender populations and does not even adequately represent normative development in the general population.

Although they may have greater generalizability to the population of juvenile defendants, samples that are from the justice system are obtained from different points of system penetration, including juveniles placed in detention centers (Savitsky and Karras 1984), referred for clinical competence evaluation (Cowden and McKee 1995), or who are adjudicated delinquent (Cooper 1997; Peterson-Badali et al. in press). These studies contribute to our knowledge about juvenile defendants but, because a proportion of juvenile defendants is screened out at each stage of processing, they need to be replicated and extended to defendants at multiple points of system processing. Moreover, most sampling strategies do not include comparison samples of adults who are either representative of the adult offender population or matched in some way to the demographic and experience characteristics of the juvenile defendants. Imputing developmental change in defendants' capacities from cross-sectional sampling is difficult, but the task is made even more difficult when adult samples are nonexistent or incomparable to the juvenile samples.

Much of the existing research on juveniles' capacities is based on self-reports of knowledge or behavioral intentions in hypothetical vignettes under nonstressful circumstances. Several concerns arise here. First, due to a fundamental lack of descriptive research on the realities of system processing, it is unclear whether the vignettes adequately incorporate the key dimensions and complexity of juvenile defendants' experience. With the exception of Grisso (1981), most early studies used vignettes about mental health or medical contexts, not justice system processes. Recent research has turned to issues of competence and participation in the justice system context (Abramovitch, Higgins-Biss, and Biss 1993; Cooper 1997; Peterson-Badali et al. in press; Woolard and Reppucci 1998), but further elaboration on the multiple points at which competence-related abilities are relevant is needed. Second, the reduced ecological validity of such designs is particularly important because it may affect performance (Woolard, Reppucci, and Redding 1996). The juvenile who demonstrates adequate understanding or decision-making skills in the research interview may not perform as well under other situational constraints such as heightened emotional affect and stress, time pressures, or limited contact with attorneys. Little if any research documents whether the vignette responses relate to a defendant's actual behavior in legal contexts.

Capacities of Interest

The existing research base has focused primarily on cognitive aspects of juvenile capacities, and most of the research that is directly on point has focused on aspects of competence to stand trial as enumerated for adult criminal court. Early measures of adult competence to stand trial such as the Competency Screening Test (Lipsitt, Lelos, and McGarry 1971) and the Georgia Court Competency Test (Wildman 1978) consist of a brief number of questions focusing on broad understanding and/or capacity to confer with counsel. The Interdisciplinary Fitness Interview uses a semi-structured interview protocol to assess knowledge and mental distur-bance, but does not contain normative scores or standard scoring criteria (Golding, Roesch, and Schreiber 1984). More recently, the MacArthur Competence Assessment Tool for Criminal Adjudication (Otto et al. in press) improves the state of the field by using a semistructured interview with objective scoring criteria to assess existing knowledge and the capac-ity for understanding, as well as reasoning and appreciation. Some of these assessment tools have recently been used to assess competence to stand trial in juvenile defendants (Cooper 1997; Savitsky and Karras 1984).

Past researchers who have examined adolescents' abilities related to competence to stand trial have been guided by the traditional cognitive framework that evolved when the concept was applied only to adults in criminal trials. This approach fails to account for the fact that develop-mentally related abilities other than cognitive ones may make adoles-cents' performances different from that of adults. Several authors have proposed categories of capacities that are normally excluded under adult tests of competence but, because they are changing throughout the course of adolescence, may have an impact on an adolescent defendant's effective participation (Scott, Reppucci, and Woolard 1995; Steinberg and Cauff-man 1996). Psychosocial factors, or abilities relating to social and emo-tional maturity, are changing during adolescence and have been linked to decision making in some general developmental studies (see Chapter 5 in this volume). Clinical factors such as mental retardation and mental ill-ness are associated with incompetence and may interact with age to im-pact defendants' capacities and functioning on competence-related tasks (Barnum this volume; Cowden and McKee 1995; Lexcen and Reppucci in press). A limited amount of research has begun to test these theories, but much work remains to be done.

Questions for Research on Juveniles' Capacities as Defendants

In general, two broad goals define the structure of an empirical inquiry into juveniles' capacities as defendants: identifying the capacities and ca-pabilities relevant to the law, specifically adjudicative competence, and identifying juveniles' performance under a variety of relevant conditions and contexts. Juveniles' capacities and performance are a function of the

adolescents themselves, the legal-system context within which they operate, and the interaction between capacity and context; that is, both the person and environment (Bronfenbrenner 1979; Lerner 1991; Lewin 1951).
This ecological approach to research requires an examination of the task
demands placed on youths as they are processed through the legal system
as well as the capacities that youths must have in order to meet those demands. Limits of youths' capacities as defendants, whether developmental, clinical, or contextual, can be considered risk factors or barriers to
competent participation. With these issues in mind, the goals of future research on juveniles' capacities as defendants can be summarized in three
broad substantive questions.

*Do juvenile defendants possess the capacities constitutionally required
of adults for adjudicative competence and considered necessary for effective participation?* As summarized by several authors (Bonnie 1993;
Grisso 1997, this volume; Barnum this volume), the capacities subsumed
by the legal construct of competence to stand trial have been well described in the adult criminal justice context and have recently been extended to concerns about juvenile defendants. Competence to stand trial
sets the minimum standard for defendants' capacities that are required
for their cases to go forward, although whether an individual will be found
to meet the standard for competence to stand trial depends on evidence
regarding the person's abilities as well as judicial interpretation of that evidence.

In general, a competent defendant must have capacities to understand
information and participate in the justice system process. These include
the capacities to acquire and use information about the nature of the
charges, trial process, and potential outcomes; appreciate the significance
of this information for one's own situation; and communicate with and assist counsel in one's own defense, including participation in the trial process and decision making about relevant trial issues. Included in the question about juveniles' capacity is the issue of whether mental illness and
mental retardation, the clinical factors responsible for most adult impairments, operate similarly for adolescents.

Effective participation goes beyond the consideration of constitutionally required capacities to include those capacities that may affect the nature and quality of a defendant's participation but do not cross the threshold of incompetence to stand trial (see Chapter 3 in this volume). Legal
and clinical scholars have commented on the importance of these capacities and behaviors for the nature and quality of interaction between the
juvenile and attorney (Bonnie and Grisso this volume; Buss this volume;
Federle 1996; Barnum this volume). Grisso, in Chapter 5, offers several
examples of these capacities, including the ability to take an active role in

the defense process and to manage one's behavior in court-related settings to maximize the likelihood of a quality defense.

Although the research question is phrased in a policy-relevant manner, that is, comparing juvenile defendants to adult defendants, the question can be reinterpreted to ask whether there are developmental differences in competence-related abilities across adolescence into adulthood. Either perspective requires age-based comparisons of capacities between adolescents and adults, as well as more refined comparisons within the span of adolescence (between younger and older adolescents).

Do developmental factors influence youths' exercise of these capacities in legal contexts? Several authors hypothesize that developmental constructs that are not captured by traditional competence assessments may influence the nature of juveniles' participation in the justice system. Cognitive and psychosocial factors may affect the way that adolescents use and value information, resulting in increased risk of impairments to their effective participation as defendants. These factors are reviewed in greater detail elsewhere in this volume, such as Chapter 5, but include future orientation, risk perception, risk preference, self-efficacy, and susceptibility to peer influence, among others. Future research faces the task of analyzing these factors for the justice system context and evaluating their role in juvenile defendants' performance. Moreover, these developmental factors may interact with other possible barriers to competence such as mental illness and mental retardation to exacerbate capacity deficits, but these effects have yet to be studied.

Do contextual factors influence youths' capacities as defendants? Early studies on adolescent competence focused primarily on the cognitive abilities and deficits that the adolescents brought to their roles as defendants. Although the multiple and interactive influences of context on adolescent development has received increasing attention in the developmental literature (Lerner and Galambos 1998), little research has specifically examined the role of contextual factors as barriers or facilitators of juveniles' effective participation in the justice system. Because competence and effective participation are interactive, they depend to some degree on the match between the contextual demands and adolescents' capacities—the way in which aspects of the context influence adolescents' performance or use of their capacities (Woolard, Reppucci, and Redding 1996). Context can include the types and characteristics of people whom a defendant must interact with (such as attorney, judge, and parents) as well as the conditions under which those interactions take place (stress, time pressure, and amount and weight of evidence available). The justice system context also consists of larger macrosystem parameters such as overrepresentation of minorities in the system and availability of resources to assist juvenile defendants that may indirectly influence the way an individual defendant is processed. These broad structural factors may vary across jurisdictions and have an effect on the attitudes and behaviors of justice system officials. Variations in these factors also may interact with an adolescent's existing capacities to shape his or her participation as a defendant.

Methodological Issues

A number of methodological issues arise when designing research to meet the aforementioned goals. The complexity of sampling and research design requires attention to the characteristics of age-based comparisons within the justice system and comparison samples from the community. The potential contributions of cross-sectional, longitudinal, and intervention designs need to be identified. The need for improved ecological validity by incorporating contextual factors at multiple levels (personal, relational, and systemwide) should be taken into account. Finally, directions for the measurement and analysis of competence-relevant capacities need to be identified.

The Complexity of Sampling and Research Design

As previously mentioned, few studies have focused on juvenile defendants per se, and the resulting samples do not represent juvenile populations likely to have contact with the justice system. Attention must be given to sampling within the justice system context, to longitudinal designs, to comparison samples outside the justice system, and to the development of experimental/intervention designs.

Sampling within the Justice System Context

Juvenile defendants are not a homogenous category; samples drawn from the population will have different characteristics depending on their status in the system process and the system/laws under which they are processed. That is, there may be different populations of offenders depending on their age and where they are in the system. Conceivably, research on juveniles' capacities as defendants could be sampled at a number of different points in the system, including arrest, charging (or petition filing), pretrial detention, adjudication, postadjudication, and special proceedings such as transfer/waiver hearings or referrals for competence evaluations. Each level or degree of system penetration acts as a gatekeeper, screening out (or in) only a proportion of the defendant population. For example, research on competence to stand trial may sample juveniles held in pretrial detention. Approximately 21 percent of youths are detained prior to adjudication (Poe-Yamagata 1997) and the reasons for detention are likely to vary across age. Anecdotal information from one study suggested that the youngest adolescents were likely to have committed quite serious crimes (for their age) or had committed lesser offenses but had difficult or unsafe family situations (Woolard and Reppucci 1998). Older adolescents were committed to detention for a wider range of seriousness of offenses. State-level variations in the processing of juveniles are evident through the myriad of changes in juvenile justice legislation, particularly with respect to transfer to adult court (Redding 1997). Descriptive studies of case-processing highlight local and regional variations in the predictors of transfer (Poulos and Orchowsky 1994) that may largely determine the types of adolescents involved in the legal system.

Research also suggests that juvenile defendant samples may be qualitatively different from adult defendant samples drawn from the criminal justice system. A cross section of adolescents selected for research while in pretrial detention may include a variety of types of offenders. Some are on a path to continued delinquency and crime, and others are engaging in normative types of delinquency that will desist late in adolescence—the groups Moffitt (1993) has identified as "life-course persistent" and "adolescence-limited," respectively. Adult samples presumably include higher proportions of persistent offenders.

These issues have important implications for sampling strategies. First, it is unclear where lines for age-based categories should be drawn. Recent reviews on cognitive and psychosocial factors suggest important developmental changes throughout adolescence (Graber and Petersen 1991; Scott, Reppucci, and Woolard 1995; Steinberg and Cauffman 1996), but do not provide definitive guidance for psychologically meaningful and policy-relevant age categories. Prior research suggests that youths in late adolescence may look like adults under some research circumstances but not others. It may be more appropriate to consider age as a continuous variable, in the tradition of identifying age-based trends and trajectories, with legally relevant age-based categories created to answer specific questions.

Second, even when the boundaries for age-based comparisons are drawn, cross-sectional sampling strategies within a single jurisdiction may result in qualitatively different samples of adolescents and adults. Given the factors that influence system involvement and penetration, the assumption of between-age comparability of participants may not be met. These one-time sample designs will need to consider, and perhaps match, the various age-based samples on system experience and history characteristics as well as demographic variables such as race and gender that are correlated with system processing. When cross-sectional designs are used, researchers must recognize that sampling at a particular point of system involvement, for example, will result in a priori sample selections effects that may covary with age. Moving toward longitudinal designs could reduce the impact of these effects on age-based comparisons.

Longitudinal Designs

Although more difficult and expensive, longitudinal designs could track defendants through multiple points of system involvement on a single incident, or track reentry into the system over the course of adolescence into adulthood. Such age-related repeated measurement designs would facilitate the study of intraindividual change in competence-related abilities (changes within an individual across time) as well as the identification of interindividual patterns of intraindividual change (differences between individuals in the pattern or timing of change) (Baltes and Nesselroade 1979). A longitudinal design is also the most effective way to examine patterns of change among several variables of interest. In competence research, a longitudinal design could elaborate on the relationship among changes in cognitive and psychosocial factors across age. These types of studies are useful for identifying risk factors for incompetence or reduced participation effectiveness by testing the association between risk factors and competence-related outcomes across time. Risk factors can either be fixed (those characteristics that are unable to be changed, such as race and gender) or variable (such as knowledge and skills that can be changed over time). Both types of factors are important to include in longitudinal studies. The practical costs of longitudinal methodology, including expense, sample attrition, and length of data collection, may require initial cross-sectional studies of panel designs to refine methodology and evaluate competence-related outcomes before a longitudinal study is implemented.

Comparison Samples outside the Justice System

Whether cross-sectional or longitudinal designs are used, research on juveniles' capacities should also include studies of community-based samples of people not currently involved with the justice system. Particularly when developmental factors are hypothesized to be significant components affecting juveniles' capacities, understanding normative development is an important research goal. The portrait of development created by a justice system sample does not reflect adolescents as a population, but a particular segment of adolescents. Policy regarding adolescents as a class may be more usefully informed by an understanding of the capacity and performance of both groups—adolescents who are likely to enter the system as well as adolescents generally. Random samples of community adolescents would provide information on normative developmental trajectories on capacities of interest such as cognitive and psychosocial factors. Community samples matched on demographic characteristics to justice system samples could elucidate the ways in which contextual factors might affect juveniles' performance.

The Need for Experimental/Intervention Designs

For both justice system and community samples, intervention studies provide a rigorous method for evaluating risks and/or contributors to incompetence and ineffective participation. Hypotheses about the role and relative strength of risk factors can be ultimately evaluated by experimental or intervention studies (Offord 1997). If a variable risk factor (that is, a factor able to be changed) in the individual or the justice system context is associated with varying degrees of competence or participation effectiveness, then it should be possible to design interventions that change this factor and evaluate its impact. For example, interventions designed to change attorneys' interactions with juvenile clients, educate the court on the developmental aspects of adolescent behavior, or institute an education program to teach adolescents the knowledge required for competent participation all rest on the theory that modifications to the justice system context or the juvenile defendant can enhance the effectiveness of juveniles' participation. Theory-based interventions that target risks for reduced competence located in the individual as well as the context will provide a strong test of juvenile capacities for competence and participation.

Ecological Validity and Contextual Factors

Because competence and effective participation are interactive, they depend on the capacities that the juvenile defendants bring to their role as defendants as well as the match between the contextual demands and the adolescents' capacities. In other words, how do aspects of the context influence the adolescents' performance or use of their capacities (Woolard, Reppucci, and Redding 1996)? Contextual demands can occur within a defendant's actual experience, such as the relationship with his or her attorney, or at a more global level, such as the systemwide parameters that affect how issues of capacity and competence are managed.

Juvenile defendants must manage interactions with a variety of adult professionals during their justice system involvement. Scholars in law (Buss 1996; Federle 1996) and psychology (Barnum this volume; Tobey, Grisso, and Schwartz this volume) have described the complexity of the relationship between an attorney and his or her juvenile client. Defendants in juvenile court may have additional personnel such as social workers and probation officers involved, as well as family members, each with potentially conflicting interests in the juvenile's case outcome (Stanger 1996).[1] Adult defendants also manage a variety of relationships with professionals, but juveniles may be less able than adults to identify the interests of each professional, solicit advice, and manage the additional adult-child status differential (Lewis 1981).

Juveniles' abilities to work with professionals and make decisions about their cases may also be differentially affected by stress. The justice system context can be a very stressful and emotion-laden experience, and stress has been shown to impair decision-making functions (Driskell and Salas 1996). Adults also face stress and emotional experiences in the criminal justice system, but some research suggests that juveniles may generally experience more variability and volatility of mood than adults (Larson, Csikszentmihalyi, and Graef 1980; Larson and Lampman-Petraitis 1989). Little existing research on juvenile defendants has incorporated stress or affect into the design or measurement, however, either through assessments of current emotional/affective state or by varying the conditions or degrees of stress. Future studies should specifically examine the implications of these developmental differences for juveniles' interactions with justice system officials and their performance as defendants in the justice system process.

In addition to the number of interactions and relationships that juveniles must manage, the very nature of the interaction with an adult may be different because the client is a juvenile, but little data speak to these issues. For example, the attorney-client relationship is arguably a critical component of a juvenile defendant's context. Aspects of this relationship that could affect juvenile defendants' participation include the role attorneys assume when defending juvenile clients and their sensitivity to developmental issues. Federle (1996) offers two models of attorney representation—an empowerment model in which the attorney facilitates decision making by the juvenile client, and a best-interests model in which the attorney takes the lead in decision making on behalf of the client. Juveniles may need varying types and levels of skill to operate as an effective defendant because the two models require different thresholds of engagement. However, we have no systematic data on the strategies that defense attorneys use with various types of juvenile cases and clients.

Furthermore, the attorney's knowledge of and sensitivity to issues of development generally, and competence to stand trial specifically, may drive whether competence issues are appropriately raised and alternatives to formal competence evaluations are utilized. There is some precedent for examining these issues empirically. Using a structured interview with attorneys and adult clients to study clients' participation in their cases, Poythress et al. (1994) found that attorneys who doubted their clients' competence rated them as less helpful but often used alternatives to formal competence evaluations to resolve competence questions. Extending this type of research to juvenile clients would elucidate the connections between attorney-client perceptions and questions of competence and whether any additional concerns are raised due to the client's age.

Beyond the case-level interactions that juveniles must manage, larger macrosystem variables affect how incapacity and incompetence, whatever the causes, are identified and managed with juvenile clients in the justice system. Factors such as caseloads of defense attorneys, availability of mental health professionals trained in juvenile forensic issues, legal requirements for mental health screening, or competence evaluations at various points in the juvenile and criminal justice proceedings all set the stage for the salience of competence issues for juvenile defendants. The availability of resources for enhancing the quality of juveniles' participation, whether to meet minimum standards of competence or to improve their effectiveness as defendants, will also determine in part how juveniles' capacities are appraised and what formal or informal assistance is utilized. A study of amenability to treatment demonstrated that ratings of amenability and appropriate treatments varied according to the respondent's professional role (mental health, probation, attorney) and the resources available in that jurisdiction (Mulvey and Reppucci 1988).

Although case studies, commentaries, and system-level statistics provide some insight into the inner workings of juvenile court, research must extend this work to identify the important dimensions of the justice system context that may shape juveniles' performance as defendants. At a basic level, observational, focus group, and interview methods should be used to identify the important characteristics of context. Recent studies have examined the experiences of juvenile defendants in the justice system (Koegl 1997; Peterson-Badali et al. in press; Tobey, Grisso, and Schwartz this volume). In a descriptive study of young offenders' experiences with the police and legal counsel, Peterson-Badali et al. asked young offenders to describe their interactions with police and legal counsel. This descriptive study provides important information about offenders' understanding and assertion of due process rights (rights to silence and counsel) as well as their perceptions of their custody and interrogation experiences. Approximately one-third of the participants cited specific police practices such as intimidation, coercion, and promises of leniency as important factors in their decision about remaining silent and contacting a lawyer.

Studies about the justice system context and youths' experiences can be useful in two main ways. First, they can inform the development of ecologically valid assessments of juveniles' capacities that incorporate the key dimensions of context. Second, these contextual variations underscore the importance of documenting system-level characteristics and building them into explanatory models, and caution us to consider carefully the generalizability of single-jurisdiction studies.[2]

The Measurement and Analysis of Competence-Relevant Capacities

As noted earlier, major criticisms of prior research on juveniles' capacities as defendants centered in part on the types of capacities included and the ways in which those capacities were measured. Future research can improve the measurement of competence-relevant capacities and respond to both of these criticisms. Studies should: (1) include improved measures of context-specific capacities as well as general measures of the same capacities; (2) utilize multiple methods of assessment that go beyond traditional self-report methods; and (3) incorporate several approaches to data analysis.

Capacity Measures That Are General and Context-Specific

The prior research on medical, mental health, and justice system decision making by adolescents often provided context-specific hypothetical vignettes requiring participants to demonstrate their existing knowledge about relevant issues and to explain their rationale for various decisions such as accepting a plea agreement or asserting the right to remain silent. Some aspects of the decision-making process were explored, such as reasons for choosing a particular outcome or perceived consequences for possible decision choices, but many of the psychosocial factors hypothesized above to be relevant to juvenile competence were not included. Future research should examine the role of these factors within decision contexts, as well as the consistency of the decision-making processes and choices across decision contexts. For example, are younger adolescents who are likely to waive Miranda rights also likely to accept a plea bargain? If so, are the rationales consistent across the decisions, and how do they compare to older adolescents or adults?

Although the focus on context-specific decision making is important, the inclusion of noncontextual assessments of cognitive and psychosocial factors establishes a critical link to questions regarding development. As reviewed elsewhere in this volume, some existing developmental research provides support for the notion that psychosocial factors link to decision making and demonstrate age-related changes. However, little research establishes the connection between these general developmental constructs and specific responses to legally relevant contexts. Likewise, if context-specific assessments of psychosocial factors do demonstrate age-related differences in their relation to defendants' capacities, it would not be clear whether the differences were a result of the context in which they were measured or underlying changes in the development of the factors themselves. Incorporating both general (noncourt context) measures and context-specific measures in the same study would strengthen any conclusions about developmental changes (or stability) in psychosocial factors and their relationships with competence.

The need to use both contextual and noncontextual measures across a potentially broad age range (in developmental terms) calls for attention to assumptions about equivalency of measures across age and ability levels. Questions of both psychometric properties and content validity arise. For example, measures of competence to stand trial that refer to juries would not make sense in a juvenile justice system that does not use juries. In these situations, modifications to the original measures, either through the deletion of items or the creation of items about comparable situations in the juvenile court context, may be required.

Multiple Methods, Multiple Reporters

One of the limitations of prior research is that it quite often relied on a battery of self-report items and hypothetical vignettes to assess juveniles' capacities. Although it is difficult to implement data collection in applied settings of the legal system, particularly when working with juveniles and adults who are awaiting trial on charges, it would be useful to obtain information on dimensions of capacity from multiple reporters such as attorneys, probation officers, and parents. For example, Tobey, Grisso, and Schwartz (this volume) obtained reports from both juveniles and their attorneys regarding the collaboration process and the nature of juveniles' participation. The sample size was limited, but the study provides a starting point for examining the consistency of attorney-client perceptions. This type of design could extend and strengthen the validity of self-report information and vignette-based assessments with multiple reports of juveniles' actual experiences and decisions in the legal process (for example, did they actively participate in their defense or accept a plea bargain?). In addition to using multiple sources of information, alternative methods of data collection could augment traditional self-report and interview paradigms. Context-specific assessments of juvenile capacities could be obtained from observation of the juvenile's activities as a defendant. Systematic rating and classification schemes could be developed to analyze an attorney-client interview or a court appearance. Practical constraints such as access and ethical issues of client confidentiality would have to be addressed but may not be insurmountable. Alternative paradigms for collecting noncontextual information are also available. Gardner and Herman (1991) used a computer-based gambling game to assess risk preferences among adolescents and adults, and Costanza and Shaw (1966) created a simulated peer-conformity situation that tested the influence of false information on subjects' self-reports. These types of paradigms may provide additional venues for gathering information about juveniles' capacities that could be used in conjunction with other methodologies and context-based assessments.

Analytical Strategies for Measuring Change

Questions of juveniles' capacities as compared to those of adults lend themselves quite naturally to a mean-differences analytic strategy. Prior research has usually compared younger and older adolescents on the average scores or levels of understanding (Abramovitch, Peterson-Badali, and Rohan 1995; Grisso 1981), reasoning about plea-bargaining (Peterson-Badali and Abramovitch 1993), or on the percentage of respondents selecting a particular decision outcome. This strategy has utility for comparing average performance across age groups. However, it does not capture equally important issues of within-group and between-group variability. There is likely to be considerable variability in capacities within age groups of interest (individual differences) as well as substantial differences between age groups (age-related or developmental differences).

Ultimately it is the relationship between background characteristics (demographics and justice system experience), capacities (both cognitive and psychosocial) and decision outcomes that is most important. Rather than searching for dichotomous outcomes or classifications (for example, competent or incompetent), we should focus on factors or patterns that place youths at greater risk than adults for deficits in their competence-related capacities. Because of the interest in change over age, models of capacity could be tested for the structural and metric equivalence of relationships between age groups, or change could be modeled across a continuous age distribution.

Summary and Conclusion

Clearly, a number of serious issues face researchers who are developing research on juveniles' capacities as defendants. Although limited, prior work in clinical, developmental, and law-related psychology has provided the theoretical and empirical foundation for such an initiative. Future work must overcome the limitations of the extant literature and develop new ways of assessing juveniles' capacities in an ecologically valid, socially relevant manner. The research agenda outlined in this chapter attempts to integrate psychological theory about juveniles' capacities with a legal framework of competence and effective participation to evaluate juveniles' capacities as defendants. Such an initiative will hopefully provide an empirical foundation from which psychological theory about juveniles' capacities can be evaluated in the context of the legal system, and interventions can be designed to improve both adolescents' abilities to negotiate the legal system and the system's response to the particular needs and characteristics of adolescent offenders.

Works Cited

Abramovitch, R., Higgins-Biss, K. L., and Biss, S. R. 1993. Young persons' comprehension of waivers in criminal proceedings. *Canadian Journal of Criminology* 35:309–22.

Abramovitch, R., Peterson-Badali, M., and Rohan, M. 1995. Young people's understanding and assertion of their rights to silence and legal counsel. *Canadian Journal of Criminology* 37:1–18.

Baltes, P. B., and J. R. Nesselroade. 1979. History and rationale of longitudinal research. In *Longitudinal research in the study of behavior and development*, edited by P. Baltes and J. R. Nesselroade. New York: Academic Press.

Bellotti v. Baird, 443 U.S. 622. 1979.

Bronfenbrenner, U. 1979. *The ecology of human development: Experiments by nature and design*. Cambridge: Harvard University Press.

Bonnie, R. J. 1993. The competence of criminal defendants: Beyond Dusky and Drope. *University of Miami Law Review* 47:539–601.

Buss, E. 1996. "You're my what?" The problems of children's misperceptions of their lawyers' roles. *Fordham Law Review* 64:1699–1762.

Cooper, D. K. 1997. Juveniles' understanding of trial-related information: Are they competent defendants? *Behavioral Sciences and the Law* 15:167–80.

Costanza, P. R., and M. E. Shaw. 1966. Conformity as a function of age level. *Child Development* 37:967–75.

Cowden, V. L., and G. R. McKee. 1995. Competency to stand trial in juvenile delinquency proceedings: Cognitive maturity and the attorney-client relationship. University of Louisville Journal of Law 33:629–51.

Driskell, J. E., and E. Salas, eds. 1996. *Stress and human performance*. Mahwah, N.J.: Lawrence Erlbaum.

Federle, K. H. 1996. The ethics of empowerment: Rethinking the role of lawyers in interviewing and counseling the child client. *Fordham Law Review* 64:1655–97.

Gardner, W., and J. Herman. April 1991. Developmental change in decision-making: Use of multiplicative strategies and sensitivity to losses. Paper presented at the Biennial Meeting of the Society for Research in Child Development, Seattle, WA.

Golding, S., R. Roesch, and J. Schreiber. 1984. Assessment and conceptualization of competency to stand trial: Preliminary data on the Interdisciplinary Fitness Interview. *Law and Human Behavior* 8:321–34.

Graber, J. A., and A. C. Petersen. 1991. Cognitive changes at adolescence: biological perspectives. In *Brain maturation and cognitive development: Comparative and cross-cultural perspectives,* edited by K. R. Gibson and A. C. Petersen. New York: Aldine de Gruyter.

Grisso, T. 1981. *Juveniles' waiver of rights: Legal and psychological competence.* New York: Plenum.

———. 1996. Society's retributive response to juvenile violence: A developmental perspective. *Law and Human Behavior* 20:229–48.

———. (1997). The competence of adolescents as trial defendants. *Psychology, Public Policy, and Law* 3:3–32.

Grisso, T. and T. Lovinguth. 1982. Lawyers and child clients: A call for research. In *Children and the law,* edited by J. Henning. Springfield, IL: Charles C. Thomas.

H.L. v. Matheson, 450 U.S. 398. 1981.

Koegl, C. J. 1997. Contextual and motivational factors affecting young offenders' use of legal rights. Unpublished master's thesis.

Larson, R., M. Csikszentmihalyi, and R. Graef. 1980. Mood variability and the psychosocial adjustment of adolescents. *Journal of Youth and Adolescence* 9: 469–90.

Larson, R., and C. Lampman-Petraitis. 1989. Daily emotional states as reported by children and adolescents. *Child Development* 60:1250–60.

Lerner, R. M. 1991. Changing organism-context relations as the basic process of development: A developmental contextual perspective. *Developmental Psychology* 27:27–32.

Lerner, R. M., and N. L. Galambos. 1998. Adolescent development: Challenges and opportunities for research, programs, and policies. *Annual Review of Psychology* 49:413–46.

Lewin, K. 1951. *Field theory in social science.* New York: Harper and Row.

Lexcen, F., and N. D. Reppucci. In press. *Effects of psychopathology on adolescent medical decision making.* Chicago: University of Chicago Law School Roundtable.

Lipsitt, P., D. Lelos, and A. L. McGarry. 1971. Competency for trial: A screening instrument. *American Journal of Psychiatry* 128:137–41.

Lewis, C. C. 1981. How adolescents approach decisions: Changes over grades seven to twelve and policy implications. *Child Development* 52:538–44.

Melton, G. 1981. Psycholegal issues in juveniles' competency to waive their rights. *Journal of Clinical Child Psychology* 10:59–62.

———. 1983. Toward "personhood" for adolescents: Autonomy and privacy as values in public policy. *American Psychologist* 38:99–103.

Moffitt, T. E. 1993. Adolescence-limited and life-course persistent antisocial behavior: A developmental taxonomy. *Psychological Review* 100:674–701.

Mulvey, E. P., and N. D. Reppucci. 1988. The context of clinical judgment: The effect of resource availability on judgments of amenability to treatment in juvenile offenders. *American Journal of Community Psychology* 16:525–46.

Offord, D. R. (1997). Bridging development, prevention, and policy. In D. Stoff, J. Brieling, and J. D. Maser, eds., *Handbook of antisocial behavior.* New York: John Wiley and Sons.

Otto, R. K., N. G. Poythress, R. A. Nicholson, J. F. Edens, J. Monahan, R. J. Bonnie, S. K. Hoge, and M. Eisenberg. in press. Psychometric properties of the MacArthur Competence Assessment Tool-Criminal Adjudication (MacCAT-CA). Psychological Assessment.

Parham v. J.R., 442 U.S. 584. 1979.

Peterson-Badali, M., and R. Abramovitch. 1993. Grade-related changes in young people's reasoning about plea decisions. *Law and Human Behavior* 17:537–552.

Peterson-Badali, M., R. Abramovitch, C. J. Koegl, and M. D. Ruck. in press. Young people's experience of the Canadian Youth Justice System: Interacting with police and legal counsel. *Behavioral Sciences and the Law.*

Poe-Yamagata, E. 1997. Detention and delinquency cases, 1985–1994. Fact Sheet. Washington DC: Office of Juvenile Justice and Delinquency Prevention, U.S. Department of Justice.

Poulos, T. M., and S. Orchowsky. 1994. Serious juvenile offenders: Predicting the probability of transfer to criminal court. *Crime and Delinquency* 40:3–17.

Poythress, N. G., R. J. Bonnie, S. K. Hoge, J. Monahan, and L. B. Oberlander. 1994. Client abilities to assist counsel and make decisions in criminal cases. *Law and Human Behavior* 18:437–52.

Redding, R. E. 1997. Juveniles transferred to criminal court: Legal reform proposals based on social science research. *Utah Law Review* 1997:709–63.

Reppucci, N. D., L. A. Weithorn, E. P. Mulvey, and J. Monahan, eds. 1984. *Children, mental health, and the law.* Beverly Hills: Sage.

Savitsky, J., and D. Karras. 1984. Competency to stand trial among adolescents. *Adolescence,* 19:349–58.

Scott, E. S., N. D. Reppucci, and J. L. Woolard. 1995. Evaluating adolescent decision making in legal contexts. *Law and Human Behavior* 19:221–44.

Stanger, L. A. 1996. Note: Conflicts between attorneys and social workers representing children in delinquency proceedings. *Fordham Law Review* 65:1123–60.

Steinberg, L. and E. Cauffman. 1996. Maturity of judgment in adolescence: Psychosocial factors in adolescent decision making. *Law and Human Behavior* 20:249–72.

Wald, M. (1976). Legal policies affecting children: A lawyer's request for aid. *Child Development* 46:1–5.

Wildman, R. (1978). The Georgia Court Competency Test (GCCT): An attempt to develop a rapid, quantitative measure of fitness for trial. Unpublished manuscript.

Woolard, J. L., and N. D. Reppucci. August, 1998. Juvenile competence: Judgment and decision making in legal context. Paper presented at the American Psychological Association Convention, San Francisco, CA.

Woolard, J. L., N. D. Reppucci, and R. E. Redding. 1996. Theoretical and methodological issues in studying children's capacities in legal contexts. *Law and Human Behavior* 20:219–28.

Notes

1. Stanger discusses the conflicts between two types of professionals commonly involved with juvenile defendants—social workers and attorneys. Social workers trying to obtain services for a juvenile may recommend pleading guilty as a mechanism for receiving services, whereas the attorney may recommend pleading not guilty to prevent the ramifications of a conviction. Clients must consider these varying perspectives and motivations as defendants.

2. It is important to note that single-jurisdiction studies should be undertaken because most investigators can neither afford nor have the facility or human resources to complete multijurisdiction studies. Once in the literature, the various investigations can be compared and contrasted in order to pinpoint the most salient variables.

CHAPTER SEVEN

Clinical and Forensic Evaluation of Competence to Stand Trial in Juvenile Defendants

RICHARD BARNUM

The tradition of clinical consultation for juvenile courts has focused on broad clinical issues of risk of future violence and treatment planning. In contrast, an assessment for competence to stand trial addresses a technical forensic evaluation question, presenting challenges for the standard practice models of the clinical consultant in juvenile court. Competence evaluation in juvenile court differs from other juvenile court evaluations in that it addresses a more specific issue relevant to the legal process, but it differs from competence evaluation for criminal court in that other clinical and dispositional issues will more often be involved in addition to the technical question of competence. The consultant must understand the issue of competence itself, especially as it applies to juveniles, understand that concept with special reference to the ambiguous demands of juvenile court proceedings, and gain clinical information relevant to the concept. The consultant must also recognize the various ways that raising the question of competence may fit into the overall case, and be prepared to address the other related clinical and dispositional questions that arise in juvenile matters.

This chapter will offer a detailed account of the clinical-practice issues involved in responding to questions about competence in juvenile defendants. Its focus will be on the assessment of competence to stand trial in juvenile court, but it will also consider some issues relevant to assessment of juvenile defendants standing trial in adult criminal court. It will include some cursory reviews of definitional issues (addressed in greater detail elsewhere in this book), with special reference to how these inform the evaluation agenda (Keilitz 1984). It will explore what clinical information is likely to be relevant to answering specific referral questions (Delineating Questions) and how it may be obtained (Acquiring Information), and it will touch briefly on issues of reporting results and opinions (Reporting Evaluation Results). My purpose is to provide specific articulation for clinicians and lawyers of what a juvenile competence assessment should address, but by exploring the clinical issues in concrete detail, this chapter also suggests to scholars and policymakers the variety of special concerns that arise in applying the concept of competence to stand trial to juvenile delinquency proceedings.

Delineating Questions

As with any juvenile forensic evaluation, understanding referrals about a juvenile's competence to stand trial will require attention to three types of questions: forensic, clinical, and systems (Barnum 1986). A wide variety of potential customers may have an interest in the evaluation beyond the explicit referral source. It is appropriate to consider who these may be, and to what extent any evaluation will attend to concerns beyond those presented explicitly by the referral source. For example, a case may be referred by an attorney with an explicit forensic concern about a juvenile's competence to understand the proceedings. The child's parent may wish for clarification of the child's clinical diagnosis, and the local school department and mental health agency may be in dispute about the child's eligibility for special services within their different systems. In every case it is important for the consultant to recognize the range of potential issues that may arise and to contract carefully with the referral source regarding which of these questions the assessment will address.

Forensic Questions
Adult Standards

The basic forensic questions in any referral concerning a juvenile's competence to stand trial are drawn from adult case law and from the literature of adult forensic psychiatry and psychology. (As detailed elsewhere in this book, this is only because there is no adequate legal guidance regarding a more appropriate way to define the questions in a juvenile case.) The adult standard for competence is generally that the defendant understand the charges against him, and be able to consult rationally with counsel in his defense (*Dusky v. U.S.* 1960).

A common appropriate way to articulate this standard operationally is to examine:

- the defendant's specific understanding of such issues as the charges against him and the potential consequences of those charges, and his understanding of the workings of the proceeding itself, including such issues as the roles of the participants, the nature of evidence, the various possible pleadings and findings, and the process of negotiated settlement; and

- the nature of the defendant's interaction with counsel in such areas as communication, understanding, trust, and decision making, on such points as whether to speak with police, whether to testify, how to plead, and (most importantly) how to evaluate the benefits of various potential negotiated solutions (McGarry 1973; Grisso 1986).

Juvenile Adjustments

To the extent that the circumstances of juvenile proceedings may be significantly different from those of adult proceedings, it is appropriate to expect that the actual application of legal standards for competence in juvenile proceedings will differ. Among the ways in which juvenile proceedings may vary are the following.

The traditional stakes of delinquency proceedings are rehabilitative rather than retributive. Despite very appropriate concerns about increasing explicit punitiveness in juvenile proceedings (Grisso 1998a) and about the risks to juveniles of involvement even in ostensibly rehabilitative services (Soler 1987), many delinquency proceedings really do have effective treatment as a primary goal. It is important to consider the juvenile's understanding of the goals of the proceedings, not just regarding the potential for aversive sanctions but also regarding the potential for involvement in further services. Some juvenile defendants will find service involvement less onerous than detention or other punishment; others will feel exactly the opposite.

Procedures for juveniles also tend to differ from those for adults. Delinquency adjudication hearings are often more informal than criminal trials, may be private, and in most places do not involve juries. Some juvenile procedures, however, are at least as complex as a criminal trial, and may be more so. A high-stakes juvenile transfer hearing can be as procedurally elaborate as a major criminal trial; such a hearing actually presents the juvenile defendant and counsel with some decisions that are more complex than those in a criminal trial, especially concerning the defendant's potential admissions of guilt and involvement in clinical evaluation (Barnum 1990).

Even when transfer is not an issue, the very informality of the juvenile process can present very complex decision challenges in areas of pretrial clinical evaluation and in negotiating pleas and dispositions. For example, juvenile courts often prefer to accept plea bargains in cases involving sexual offenses against younger children, to spare the young victim the stress of giving testimony and in the hope that treatment will be an appropriate resolution. How well a juvenile defendant can understand the potential benefits and risks of offering an admission in the context of a pretrial evaluation to assess the appropriateness of such a plea bargain, and whether the juvenile actually understands what may be involved in elaborate probation agreements and treatment contracts, may be critical issues in determining his competence to take part in a negotiated solution.

Certainly the child's level of development will affect her capacity to cope with the demands of being a defendant. As detailed elsewhere in this book, adolescent norms in various areas of cognition, judgment, and emotional functioning may be quite different from those for adults. These differences may have compelling impacts on adolescents' capacities to achieve a sound understanding of the potentially complex issues in the trial process, to communicate effectively with counsel, and to further their true interests in making decisions in this context. Furthermore, developmental differences between adolescents and adults in the expression of psychopathology may also affect adolescent competence (see Chapter 2 in this volume). Uncertainty as to whether a specific area of functional impairment represents a transient developmental problem or is an early sign of a more serious mental illness adds to the difficulty of establishing the proper adjustments to the operational standards for competence with juvenile defendants.

Ambiguity in role relationships involving adolescents contributes to a potential need to adjust standards of competence for adolescents. Unlike adults, adolescents are not considered autonomous agents in most contexts under the law. They are subject to their parents' authority, have special obligations (such as school attendance) that adults do not have, and experience a variety of limits on their freedom of action and decision making owing specifically to their age. The law expects that for important decisions an adolescent's parents will essentially act on the child's behalf, bringing appropriate adult judgment and mature advocacy for the child's interest to the decision in question.

Case law in delinquency makes some reference to the expectation that adolescent defendants differ from adults in their need for this sort of adult involvement in their decision making (*Fare v. Michael C.* 1979). However, the relative absence of explicit statutory and case law guidance in this area leaves a default expectation that in acting as a defendant, a juvenile needs to be competent autonomously; if he is thought not to be competent, he does not have the right to have an appropriate substitute decision maker act on his behalf (Grisso, Miller, and Sales 1987). Transferring to juvenile court the absolute requirement that a defendant be competent to stand trial in order for proceedings to go forward leaves the juvenile defendant without the usual protection of reliance on adult judgment. Furthermore, it leaves the juvenile's parent without the usual right to take action on the child's behalf.

Traditional juvenile proceedings do tend to take account of a parent's appropriate interest in a child's well-being by informally including the parent in the attorney-client relationship. But parents vary considerably in terms of how they approach delinquency prosecution and how they advise their children in this context (Grisso and Ring 1979), and no ordinary, commonly accepted procedures exist for assessing the appropriateness of parental involvement in an adolescent's defense (Barnum 1997a).

The Problem of Adult Sanctions

Increasing concerns about juvenile violence have led to a general increase in the exposure of juvenile defendants to adult sanctions (Flicker 1981; Bernard 1992). The most common type of exposure is through some preadjudication transfer of the case to criminal court (either by a statutory requirement for specific charges, direct prosecutorial filing of adult charges, or a court hearing with judicial discretion). A few states have begun to experiment with other means of exposing juveniles to adult sanctions. The "trial first" approach (Schwartz et al. 1995) replaces the judicial transfer hearing process with an initial adjudication followed by a dispositional process in which either juvenile or adult sanctions may be imposed, based on characteristics of the individual case. The "second look" approach exposes certain juveniles who have been adjudicated and committed to youth-corrections agencies to an additional process at the end of their commitment period (Podkopacz and Feld 1995). This process examines how they have responded to treatment and whether they are indeed rehabilitated; further commitment to adult prison can result if the youth is found not to have responded sufficiently to treatment.

Thus juvenile defendants may be involved in three different types of proceedings: juvenile proceedings with no possibility of adult sanctions (ordinary delinquency proceedings); juvenile proceedings with some chance of adult sanctions as a consequence; and adult criminal trials with adult sanctions, as a result of either legislative, prosecutorial, or judicial waiver. In the second and third of these possibilities, the elevated stakes of the proceedings (including the possibility of adult sanctions) may indicate that fairness would require that a juvenile have a right to be competent.

However, more important than this general point is an appreciation in each individual case of what the true potential stakes of the matter may be. Regardless of rhetoric about rehabilitation, some cases involving purely juvenile proceedings and consequences may have substantially higher stakes in areas such as loss of liberty and aversive conditions of confinement than will many purely adult cases. Young juveniles may routinely face confinement of many years in juvenile facilities, even on charges that might not in themselves be considered a basis for extended sentences in adult court, depending on the individual circumstances of the case.

As with any competence question, evaluation of a juvenile's competence to stand trial needs to attend to both individual abilities and context. The legal standard is as yet inexplicit, but it is reasonable to attend to both developmental issues and the broad range of potential proceedings and stakes to which juveniles may be subjected.

Clinical Questions

Any evaluation of competence must include a basic clinical assessment, sufficient to characterize the subject's overall cognition and psychopathology. With juvenile defendants the assessment will appropriately attend to the role of developmental processes in any deficits present. This basic assessment is necessary for establishing the cause of any deficits in competence, and also as a basis for offering any opinions and recommendations concerning remediation of deficits (Grisso 1998b).

Some jurisdictions specifically require the consultant to attend to broader clinical treatment recommendations in the context of clinical assessment of competence. Even when such broader issues are not explicit, they are frequently implicit in the referral, and addressing them may be both helpful to the youth and helpful in resolving the case. On the other hand, in some circumstances addressing issues of clinical treatment may go beyond the appropriate scope of the evaluation (Melton et al. 1987). In order to respond to broader clinical questions in a competence evaluation properly, the consultant should be careful in delineating the scope and tasks of the evaluation with the referral source and (as appropriate) with other interested customers. Reaching consensus on what the scope should be is important; if consensus is not possible, differences should be resolved before beginning the evaluation. It may be appropriate for certain information in the evaluation to be subject to limits on its availability or use, such as defendant communications that might be self-incriminating.

Some competence questions may arise in the context of conducting ordinary clinical evaluations of delinquency defendants. Courts are often interested in gaining a general assessment of a defendant for the purpose of aiding the court in dispositional planning, and they will sometimes request such an assessment early in the process, well before adjudication, and often before a youth has even had a chance to develop a relationship with an attorney. When issues arise spontaneously in the context of such evaluation as to the youth's understanding of the nature of the proceedings or her ability to collaborate with a lawyer, it is appropriate to bring these concerns to the attention of the court early on; the court may then wish to seek further more specific evaluation on this point or may determine that the issue does not warrant that sort of attention.

Systems Questions

A competence evaluation will not in itself provide treatment. However, it is appropriate for the consultant to recognize treatment needs when they exist, and to be familiar enough with the workings of the specific mental health and legal systems to be able to help others meet those needs. The consultant must be familiar with the potential consequences of a determination of competence or incompetence for access to mental health care. Though sometimes a determination of incompetence will lead directly to dismissal of the delinquency charge, in other circumstances the court may prefer to hold the charge pending and seek services for restoring competence, as with an adult defendant. In either event, the consultant may need to be involved in obtaining additional services, such as referring the child for hospitalization or determining special eligibility characteristics for more specialized programs.

Sometimes the court will prefer to find a way to adjudicate the case, even if the defendant has significant deficits, by steering the legal process away from areas in which the defendant's weaknesses are most significant. For example, if a defendant has a basic understanding of the delinquency charges but doesn't seem able to cope with the complexities of negotiating a plea, the court might simply order that the defendant enter a plea of not delinquent and proceed with an adjudicatory hearing (Barnum and Grisso 1994). The consultant will provide a better individual evaluation by being aware of such possibilities. It is important to be clear about the various procedural routes that a case might take and to comment specifically on how the defendant might cope with the various challenges of each route, regarding both competence and other clinical implications of different procedural pathways. A legal process with many delays, for example, might interfere with timely access to treatment for an acute condition; or a public process might bring greater emotional stress and damage (regardless of issues of capacity) than would a private one; or a plea-bargained settlement in which a defendant admits to a lesser charge may lead to future problems in efforts at rehabilitation, with the defendant avoiding full treatment accountability for the actual offense (Wexler 1993).

Acquiring Information

The only general rules that apply to all evaluations in determining juveniles' competence to stand trial are that the clinical assessment needs to be detailed enough to address the specific questions of the individual case, and each individual case is different. The evaluation should provide an overall diagnostic assessment and additional detailed characterization of the defendant's specific functioning in the areas relevant to competence. The appropriate level of clinical thoroughness and detail will vary with the intrinsic clinical complexity of the case, with the legal context and stakes, and with the consultant's role in the legal system (Keilitz 1989; Grisso et al 1994). Before beginning the evaluation it is important to be sure that the rules and limits of confidentiality for the evaluation are clear and that the child and family understand them (Barnum, Silverberg, and Nied 1987).

Clinical Data

The likely appropriate sources for obtaining clinical data relevant to assessment of a juvenile's competence to stand trial will include a variety of historical records, a range of interviews and other observations, and (in some cases) some specialized tests. General clinical background will appropriately be more detailed in cases where the referral question explicitly includes a request for clinical diagnosis and treatment recommendations in addition to assessment of competence, and less so where the evaluation is expected to address competence alone. In any case, clinical background needs to be sufficient to provide a basis for conclusions as to the nature of the youth's disorder (if any), her level of development, and the relationships between disorder and development (on the one hand) and competence abilities (on the other).

It will be important to review available records of the child's school functioning, past clinical assessment and treatment history, and past legal involvements. Clinical interviewing for general background history needs to include both the child and the family and should address ordinary issues of family and developmental history; family, school, and peer functioning; substance abuse; trauma exposure; and history of clinical disorder and treatment. Interviewing should also include some structured observations regarding current psychological functioning, or mental status, both for the youth and for important family members. Structured instruments (such as checklists, rating scales, structured diagnostic interviews, and psychological and medical tests) can sometimes add important clinical information beyond that provided by interviews alone.

Specific Data concerning Functional Capacities

The main focus of the competence evaluation concerns the youth's abilities to understand and cope with the legal process. Following the adult standard, these abilities generally involve an understanding of the charges and procedures and a capacity to collaborate rationally with counsel. This information generally comes from three sources: direct questioning of the defendant, inferences from functioning in other areas, and direct observation of the defendant's behavior and interactions with others.

Understanding the Charges and Legal Process

The first element of competence is the youth's basic knowledge and rational perception of the overall legal process. This includes his understanding of what he is charged with and what the consequences may be, and of the specific procedures and players within that process.

Charges   The most essential ingredient of competence to stand trial is awareness that one is indeed charged with a crime, is on trial, and is therefore at risk for aversive state intervention. It is useful to begin inquiry in this area with general questions about the defendant's court involvement, looking for spontaneous expressions from defendant and family regarding their understanding of the basis for that involvement and the nature and seriousness of the circumstances. It can then be helpful to inquire about the name of the charge (or charges) faced. Understanding this technicality may not be essential to the defendant's understanding of her jeopardy and it may be entirely irrelevant to a delinquency prosecution in which any finding of delinquency (regardless of the charge) triggers a rehabilitative response based on need rather than offense. However, this information can provide an indication of the youth's sophistication about the legal process, and accurate understanding of this issue may in some cases be an important element of negotiating a resolution (see below). This is especially true where an adjudication on specific types of charges (such as sex offenses) may have specific consequences (such as sex-offender registration and mandated offender specific treatment).

One should learn the defendant's understanding of what she is actually accused of doing because, in contrast to the name of the charge, this report offers a more concrete indication of the defendant's detailed understanding of the allegations against her. An appreciation of the defendant's detailed understanding of what is alleged, on what basis, by whom, and with what supporting evidence, is a good indication of how clearly she may understand the basis for the legal process against her. It can also be helpful to gain an explicit account from the defendant of what she actually did, both to judge the coherence of this account and the defendant's likely capacity to discuss it with counsel, and also to detail the defendant's understanding of differences between this account and others' allegations.

Consequences   As another specific indication of the defendant's understanding of the process, it is useful to inquire about his expectations regarding what the consequences of the court involvement may prove to be.

In traditional evaluations of adults' competence to stand trial, the essential issue is to be sure that the defendant appreciates that any criminal charge brings with it some risk of aversive sanctions, and that it is thus appropriate to be cautious and to take care to protect one's rights. This is certainly a very relevant issue in juvenile justice as well, since juvenile charges may indeed have extremely aversive consequences, especially in cases involving the possibility of adult sanctions. However, it also happens that delinquency prosecution can be undertaken with genuinely benign intentions that seek to make the defendant's life better, sometimes resulting in access to care and rehabilitation that leads to dramatic improvements in the youth's safety, education, social functioning, mental and physical health, and future prospects.

Because the course of juvenile proceedings can vary so widely and the consequences can vary from extremely aversive to extremely beneficial, rational understanding of the likely consequences in most cases will include a high degree of uncertainty. The clinical evaluation of the youth's understanding of the consequences of facing charges will ideally not stop with accepting the youth's declaration that she "might have to do some time." Instead, it will explore in considerably more detail the youth's knowledge of the potential directions that the individual case might take; her perceptions about which of these directions is relatively likely, which less so, and why; her understanding of the potential risks of exposure to probation supervision, detention, secure placement, or adult sanctions; and also her knowledge of the potential benefits of involvement with juvenile justice services, such as protection from dangerous gang conflicts or family violence, and involvement in services that might reduce her risk of facing incarceration again in the future. How a youth might evaluate and weigh these potential risks and benefits is addressed later in this chapter, under "Decision Making."

Roles   Like the consequences of juvenile justice involvement, the juvenile hearing and adjudication process varies widely in its elaborateness and formality. It can be helpful to explore with a defendant the typical roles played in a trial process (such as judge, prosecutor, defense lawyer, and witness) to gain an indication of the youth's basic appreciation of the fact that the manner in which his case may be decided can be quite formal and adversarial. A youth who does not understand these basic roles—who believes, for example, that the prosecutor is acting entirely in the youth's interest and that the judge has no role in the process other than to bang a gavel—may be lacking a fundamental understanding of his risk and how he might protect himself.

However, most juvenile cases are not actually resolved by this formal adjudication process, and it is important to explore with the youth the roles that others might play in contributing to a less formal resolution. A probation officer or court intake worker might have significant influence on an early determination to divert the case from formal prosecution. In another case a detention-based mental health screening might determine the presence of risk factors that contribute to a prosecutor's decision to move for transfer. Even the competence evaluation itself can play a major role in determining what sort of course the case may take. Thorough evaluation of a youth's appreciation of important roles would explore all these issues. A youth who has a basic understanding of how things work in a television-like trial may have some appreciation of being at risk from the state, but a youth who understands something more about these informal procedures and about how he can relate productively to the individuals involved in them will be more competent at furthering his interests in the process.

Evidence and Proof   The juvenile defendant's understanding of issues of evidence and standards and burdens of proof can provide important insight into her appreciation of how the formal adversary process works to resolve disputes. Knowing what a witness is, what different kinds of witnesses there may be, and specifically who may be expected to give testimony shows an understanding that the allegations need to be based on specific accounts and need to be proven. Exploring these issues in some detail can also help to clarify the more salient question of how the defendant understands the relative strength of the state's case. A full understanding of these issues will also include recognition of the role of physical evidence and of expert's reports and testimony, as well as understanding that the state bears the burden of proving the allegations and needs to prove the case beyond a reasonable doubt.

Pleadings and Findings   Here, there are two areas of basic knowledge that are important for a defendant: an awareness that the defendant has the option of answering the charges in a variety of ways (she should at least understand "guilty or not guilty," and possibly others such as "no contest" or "not guilty by reason of insanity," depending on the circumstances), and the awareness that either a judge or a jury will ultimately make a finding, based on the evidence presented. It is important that the defendant appreciate that although a "not guilty" plea will likely result in a more formal and longer-lasting process, it may sometimes result in a "not guilty" finding, while a "guilty" plea may expose the youth to a variety of intrusive interventions without her having the opportunity to mount a defense.

Though knowledge of these formal procedural issues may be important, in many juvenile cases (as in many adult cases) what really matters in how a case is decided is a process of negotiation. This process is broadly known as "plea bargaining," though it usually involves negotiation not just of charges and pleas but also of processes and dispositions. For example, it may be relatively common in some juvenile court settings for prosecutors to set a low threshold for bringing actions with adult-sanction consequences, and then to negotiate the dismissal of that process (or the elimination of adult sanctions) in response to the defendant offering a guilty plea and accepting a juvenile disposition. In this negotiation, the juvenile may accept a more onerous juvenile disposition (such as extended commitment to juvenile corrections custody) than she might have expected if the prosecution had not raised the ante by bringing a transfer or other adult-sanctions process.

Even entirely within the juvenile realm, similar negotiations are common. Sometimes they involve disposition only, such as when a youth agrees to plead delinquent in exchange for accepting a term of probation rather than youth-corrections commitment. Sometimes they involve the actual finding, such as when a youth may admit to sufficient facts for a finding of delinquency, but the court continues the case without a finding for a specified period and sets conditions of probation, agreeing to dismiss the case without a finding of delinquency at the end of that period if the youth keeps the conditions of probation. Sometimes they involve the specific charges, such as when a youth is charged with a sexual assault and agrees to plead delinquent to simple assault in order to avoid the risk of having to register as a sexual offender; or when a youth is charged with a violent offense that on a finding of delinquency would lead to mandatory confinement, and pleads delinquent to a less violent offense without the same mandatory requirement.

The details of all these negotiations can be very complex. True competence for taking part in this sort of negotiation requires an appreciation that it is a genuine negotiation in which there are two sides (the state and the defendant) represented by counsel (prosecutor and defense lawyer) who each have something to gain and something to give up in the negotiation process. True competence also requires some ability to understand important areas of uncertainty, such as weighing the strength of the state's case and the cost to the state of formal prosecution. It requires an understanding of the significance of stakes, such as the value to the youth of avoiding sex-offender registration, and it requires that the youth make a decision as to whether a proposed deal is a good one for him or not.

Careful assessment of the youth's capacities in this area requires detailed, explicit inquiry as to the youth's understanding in each of these areas. Does she understand the concept of give and take in making a deal? What other examples of this process is she familiar with or has she taken part in? For example, some youths will be familiar with negotiating chores or allowance with parents or others at home; some will have experience in making deals with friends in trading personal items back and forth. Some will have had experience in negotiating employment relationships or conditions. Some youths' experience with negotiation will be primarily in crime-related areas such as making drug deals or negotiating territorial disputes with rival gangs. Sometimes a youth's experience with negotiation will be better discussed as responses to threats, such as agreeing to clean up the kitchen in response to the threat of being beaten if she doesn't.

Knowing what experience in these areas a youth has had will help to clarify his cognitive understanding of give and take and will also inform the consultant as to the range of emotional stances that the youth may bring to the negotiating process. Some youths will be readily intimated; others may tend to be defensive, antagonistic, or feel a sense of entitlement. Still others may be more flexible, adjusting their stance to the specific circumstances of a negotiation. Recognizing these emotional characteristics and their sources and degree of persistence may be relevant to understanding the youth's ability to take part in negotiations in this context. The issue of how the youth makes a decision in responding to a proposed plea bargain is addressed in further detail later in this chapter, under "Decision Making."

Collaboration with Counsel

The second basic element of competence is the youth's ability to work together with counsel in a rational manner to protect his own interests. The assessment of the youth's understanding of roles in the process will have established whether the youth understands that he has a lawyer, knows who that person is, and understands that that person's job is to protect him and advocate for his interests in the legal process. This part of the evaluation is more concerned with aspects of how the youth's actual psychological functioning affects his ability to use a lawyer successfully. Addressing this element involves exploration of the youth's specific relationship with his lawyer as well as his own decision-making process in responding to his lawyer's advice.

Communication, Understanding, and Trust   Assessing the communication between lawyer and youth includes attention to intrinsic characteristics of the youth as well as issues specific to the interaction between the individual youth and lawyer.

Factors specific to the youth will include aspects of his overall clinical

condition and development such as general cognitive level, specific communication skills and deficits, and the presence of psychopathology that
might undermine effective communication and understanding. Problems
with attention or distractibility may interfere with a youth's ability to
master complicated issues of law or process. Depression may interfere
both with attention and with motivation to understand. Paranoid pre-
occupations or delusions may result in compelling distortions of information presented by an attorney. Intrusive thoughts or anxieties may be
distracting and may bring distress in response to specific issues, which
could lead the youth to avoid dealing with those issues when raised by
counsel. Even when a youth has been able to attend to the attorney's information and advice, depression, isolation, or paranoia may be sufficient
to make her discount the attorney's advice as either careless and incompetent or as based in a fancied collusion between the lawyer and the state.

It is also important to attend to what the youth's actual experience with
her attorney has been and what she has learned from it. If she has met the
lawyer one time, for five minutes in a courtroom corridor, at a point in the
case when the details about what could be expected to develop as issues
in the case were unclear, then deficits in the youth's understanding may
not be ascribable to whatever clinical or developmental problems she
may have. On the other hand, if the case has been ongoing for some time,
if she knows the lawyer well, and if they have spent hours together discussing the issues, then deficits may be more reasonably laid to problems
with the youth.

As part of this inquiry, it is important to explore how much of the
youth's understanding of the legal issues in her case actually comes from
her lawyer's advice and information versus how much comes from other
sources. A youth who is entirely familiar with the criminal justice system
from watching trials on television or from discussions with peers in detention may not have important knowledge deficits in the basics of the
trial process, but at the same time may not really understand very much
about the specific issues in her own case and may not have established the
sort of relationship with counsel that might enable her to learn about
these issues successfully.

It should be obvious that interviewing regarding these issues should include both the defendant and the attorney. The attorney's impressions of
the youth's strengths and weaknesses in communication and understanding may accord with the consultant's independent impressions, but they
may be different. A lawyer may perceive the youth to have a higher degree of understanding than the youth appears to the consultant to have.
If this is the case, the youth may have malingered deficits with the consultant, or perhaps was in a more deteriorated condition when seen by

the consultant than he was when he met with the lawyer. Or, perhaps there are simply differences between the consultant and the lawyer in their standards for recognizing deficits. Lawyers may have noticed that courts generally tend to set fairly low expectations of defendants in determining issues of competence, and they may not attend to indications of deficit that are less than egregious. Clinical consultants, on the other hand, may be accustomed to noting small differences in capacity and may consider such differences to be positive findings. In this case, both parties may be right, and the issue becomes how significance in this area is determined. This is addressed further in the section "Reporting Evaluation Results."

Alternatively, a lawyer may have the impression that a youth suffers substantial impairments in functioning that compellingly interfere with his capacity to understand and respond to the attorney's advice. As above, this difference may simply reflect different sensitivities; in this case the lawyer may take a more aggressively protective advocacy stance, and may argue that even relatively subtle deficits are significant enough to interfere with the youth's fundamental ability to understand and cope with the proceedings. Alternatively, the consultant may have been too superficial in undertaking clinical and forensic assessment, having been satisfied with a youth's general social interaction and basic knowledge of ordinary legal proceedings; she may have missed indications in the youth of deficits in language and communication that the youth has learned to cover for, and may not have been careful enough in exploring the youth's detailed understanding of the issues in the individual case.

Another possible explanation of this sort of difference between the attorney's and the clinician's perceptions of a youth's capacities concerns issues of "match" between client and attorney. If a youth is relatively young or has more serious developmental difficulties or psychopathology, then it may be reasonable to expect lawyers without much experience or training in dealing with children, or with these sorts of deficits, to have greater difficulty in establishing effective communication with the youth. A clinical consultant who actually does have training and experience in these areas can naturally be expected to communicate more effectively. It is therefore very important for the consultant to gain a sense of the attorney's skills in dealing with difficult youths, and to be as clear (and polite) as possible in noting that communication problems may rest largely with the attorney's lack of experience in the area. Most attorneys will not in fact be troubled by this and will be eager to learn from the consultant.

Obviously, it is also important to address the match between youth and attorney in areas of language and culture. Even though simple language issues may be addressed through translation, more basic cultural differences may engender problems in trust, which may be difficult to overcome. Such problems do not result from psychopathology or developmental deficits in the youth, but they may lead to significant reduction in the effectiveness of the attorney-client collaboration. Equally important, the consultant herself needs to understand fundamental issues in the youth's culture and family, especially as they affect dealings with both the legal system and mental health professionals. Familiarity with the youth's culture will help the consultant be sure that she is seeking and obtaining the appropriate information for a full understanding of the youth's clinical condition and can enable the consultant to help overcome deficits in understanding between the youth and the attorney that may have a cultural basis.

Decision Making   Defending against delinquency or criminal charges requires the defendant to make a number of decisions; some of these are fairly explicit and others may be harder to notice. Examples of important explicit decisions include how to plead (including whether to offer psychological evidence as excuse or mitigation), whether to waive the rights to counsel or to a jury trial (when offered), whether to offer testimony, and, most importantly, whether to accept a negotiated settlement. Other important decisions that may be more subtle, or may arise only in some circumstances, include how much information to convey to counsel, whether to offer testimony against others in the hope of mitigation, and whether and how much to cooperate with clinical assessments at various points in the process.

While it is important to explore the youth's understanding of his attorney's advice in these areas, it is also important not to mistake that advice for the youth's own judgment. The decisions themselves belong to the defendant. Though disagreement between a defendant and a lawyer on any of these points may raise appropriate concerns as to the effectiveness of the collaboration between defendant and counsel, it does not necessarily indicate any incapacity; the youth may understand her attorney's advice perfectly, may consider it carefully, and may decide rationally for her own reasons not to follow it. On the other hand, that the youth agrees with her lawyer's advice (or at least tacitly complies with it) is no guarantee that she has made a competent decision to do so. Juvenile defendants (as well as many adults) quite often will not have a very good understanding of these issues or may be unable to think effectively about them, and will blindly comply with an attorney's advice. Such circumstances may not often come to the court's attention, but they can lead to important failures of justice.

Taking a juvenile defendant's decision-making capacity seriously requires attention to several issues. Whether a decision is competent depends on whether it is voluntary, whether it is informed, and whether it is rational (Appelbaum and Grisso 1988).

The issue of voluntariness concerns the extent and power of compelling influences on the youth that may pressure him to make a decision in a particular way. These influences can include the desires of parents, other relatives or close adults, or probation or other court staff; they can include potentially serious threats from peers in gang-related circumstances; or they can include pressure from the attorney to decide an issue in a particular way.

How well-informed a decision is depends in part on the extent of the youth's knowledge of the options involved and of what may reasonably be expected as a result of choosing any of these options. The youth needs to understand that there are options in the first place, and that there is a decision to be made. He needs to know what the specific range of options is in a particular circumstance and he needs to have some notion of how choosing any of them may affect the progress of his case and his long-term interests.

The rationality of a decision concerns the nature of the thought process that supports it. Does that process include some actual consideration of options, some coherent basis for weighing the likely benefits and risks of particular choices, and a choice that seems to follow in some logical manner from that weighing? Or does the youth's way of thinking seem to be garbled, idiosyncratic, or otherwise unreasonable?

Potential impairments in rationality may stem from psychopathology or from problems in development, as detailed elsewhere in this book (see Chapters 2 and 5 in this volume). Potentially relevant problems include inattention, depression, or psychotic disorganization that interferes with the youth's ability to deliberate alternatives; hopelessness such that the youth feels the decision doesn't matter; delusional or otherwise fixed and irrational beliefs that falsely influence the youth's understanding of options and of their likely outcomes; and idiosyncrasies of perception, judgment, or moral reasoning specific to adolescent development.

Evaluating a juvenile defendant's decision-making capacity involves exploration with the teen of each of these areas of functioning. The consultant should consider the issue of voluntariness by focusing on specific decisions and asking the youth whether others in her life have ideas about what she should do. If that is the case, the consultant should follow up with questions about what the ideas are, how powerfully they are held, whether the youth feels obliged or pressured to conform to those ideas, and what she thinks might happen if she failed to do so. The extent of the youth's information regarding decisions she may need to make will in part be clear from the exploration of her basic knowledge of the legal process generally, but it is also important to inquire directly as to what she actually expects would be the likely outcomes of her case if she followed through with specific decisions one way or the other.

Assessing the rationality of the youth's decision-making process can include an examination of how the youth makes decisions in other contexts and an exploration of the specific decision (or decisions) he faces in the current legal process. This especially involves examining his process of gathering information and weighing it, and trying to determine whether there is some understandable and consistent basis for his making particular choices.

Conduct during Trial

Sometimes concerns about a youth's conduct may be raised as potentially significant to his competence. A youth may be characteristically impulsive, loud, angry, or disruptive, and it may be suggested that these tendencies may undermine the formality or integrity of the proceedings. In addressing this question it is important to be clear about the general clinical basis for any expected functional problems with disruptiveness and, even more importantly, to be clear about specific implications of potential disruptiveness for the relevant features of competence. If a youth's impulsiveness may be expected to interfere with his attention to the proceedings in the courtroom, and if his attention to those proceedings actually matters to his understanding and effective collaboration with counsel, then it will be important to characterize these expectations and their implications. If he is so angry and disruptive that he seems unable to sit and confer with counsel, this may have important implications for his ability to understand the issues and respond helpfully to them; the consultant needs to attend to these issues and show how they stem (or do not stem) from clinical disorder or developmental deficits. On the other hand, if the only consequence of the youth's expected disruptiveness is that it will be irritating and distracting to others, it is not clear that this impact would warrant consideration of the disruptiveness as an impairment to the youth's competence.

Special Evaluation Techniques

With younger children or with cognitively limited adolescents, it can be important to adapt techniques of interviewing for forensic data that are similar to usual methods of interviewing children for clinical information. Using drawings or props for dramatic play such as dolls and puppets can help children be more comfortable expressing themselves and will sometimes help them convey their knowledge and feelings more fully than will direct questioning.

No specific tests, instruments, or procedures are either necessary or sufficient for generating the clinical data relevant to competence evaluation. Some specialized instruments, primarily for use with adults, are available to help the consultant gather the relevant information. These include checklists that serve primarily to screen for areas that may need more careful attention (Lipsitt, Lelos, and McGarry 1971; Nicholson et al. 1988) and structured interview protocols to ensure thorough coverage of the relevant breadth of clinical data regarding competence itself (McGarry 1973; Roesch, Webster, and Eaves 1994). A newer instrument (Hoge et al. 1997) includes an objective scoring system (though such a system may risk conveying the false impression that legal competence is somehow measurable by such a test). However, since the reality of juvenile court proceedings is not always like that of adult proceedings, to rely on the simple transfer from adult settings of such instruments for gathering the basic required information about a youth's understanding and collaboration risks missing areas of strength and weakness that may be relevant to the youth's participation in the juvenile case.

No specific instruments exist to help with the assessment of the functional areas specifically relevant to juvenile defendants' competence to stand trial. One adult-competence screening measure has been modified to make it easier for adolescents to use (Cooper 1997), and another screening instrument developed for mentally retarded adult defendants may be useful in gathering information with adolescents (Everington 1990). Some instruments exist to help with the assessment of children's decision-making abilities as they may affect issues of informed consent (Weithorn 1985), and in some cases consultants might find it helpful to use such instruments in clarifying these specific abilities.

In addition to interviews and tests, it can also be very useful to observe the defendant directly, in a variety of settings, in the process of responding to the legal process.

The consultant should observe interaction between the youth and the attorney; this is the best means of gaining insight into the nature and basis of any deficits in communication and understanding between them. It is important to attend to the youth's capacity to pay attention, his ability to express uncertainty when he does not understand and put in his own words what he does understand, how forthcoming he can be in response to questions from the attorney, and whether he can ask questions and avoid extremes of either resistance or compliance. The consultant should note changes in these capacities over the course of the observation, either from fatigue or boredom or in response to specifically difficult or anxiety-provoking issues. Just as important is observing the attorney's specific approach to the discussion, attending especially to his abilities to help the youth feel comfortable, encourage him to be open, and adjust to the youth's level of language and abstraction in offering explanations of issues in the legal process. Similar conversations between the child and parents and other potentially significant sources of advice and support should be observed.

What is the youth's demeanor in court? Depending on the case circumstances, the courtroom may be intrinsically more anxiety-provoking and distracting than a lawyer's office or conference room. The youth's ability in this setting to comport herself properly, control emotional disruptions, and pay adequate attention to the testimony of witnesses and to other courtroom activities may in some cases be relevant to the question of competence. Direct observation of any difficulties in these areas can help the consultant offer more meaningful understanding of the nature of such problems and of their potential relevance to issues of competence.

Evaluation of the Family and Significant Others

One of the most fundamental differences between evaluating an adult defendant's competence and that of a juvenile is the importance of the family's involvement in the juvenile evaluation. Parents and other family members are usually the best sources of information about a wide range of clinical issues regarding the youth. In addition, parents and other family members will in most cases be the most important continuing resources for undertaking any further efforts at treatment for the child. Parental involvement in the evaluation can legitimize the evaluation process for the youth and can make it more comfortable and easier for him to take part.

More specifically related to the problem of a juvenile's competence to stand trial is the parent's right to make decisions on behalf of a child. In other circumstances, children are generally assumed to be legally incompetent, and parents are entitled to make decisions on their behalf. This parental entitlement is based partly on an assumption that the parent knows the child best, cares about her well-being, and is best informed about her actual condition and needs. It is also based in part on the traditional notion that the parents have a property interest in the child and can thus (within broad limits) direct the child as they see fit.

In the delinquency context, parents do not seem to have such a clear right to advocate for their children. However, some case law respects the appropriateness of parental advice to children in the delinquency context (*Commonwealth v. a Juvenile* 1983), and the tradition of juvenile court proceedings implicitly does allow the parent to contribute to the child's defense. Parental involvement in the clinical assessment of competence is critical for understanding the nature and quality of this contribution, and specifically for assessing its likely success in remediating incapacities on the part of the youth.

Assessing the quality of a parent's understanding of a child's capacities and needs can be an elaborate and cumbersome process (Barnum 1997b). However, when there is doubt about the juvenile defendant's autonomous competence, it is appropriate to examine the parent's ability to provide appropriate support and advice to make up for the youth's deficits. This examination involves subjecting the parent to essentially the same series of inquiries as the defendant, both in terms of the parent's general clinical functioning and the specific issues related to an understanding of the process and the ability to collaborate with counsel.

Evaluation should also include attention to the interaction between parent and youth, specifically concerning the parent's ability to understand her needs, the effectiveness of communication and advice from the parent, and the presence of any differences of opinion between the two regarding specific decisions to be made. Evaluation should also attend to the relationship between the parents and the attorney for the defendant. Since the law is unclear, the best a consultant may be able to offer in such a situation is a clear and detailed characterization of the relevant strengths and weaknesses of parent and defendant and of the history of advocacy for the defendant by the parent, so that the court can determine how these features may be relevant to a decision on the child's competence.

Issues of Remediation

In the event that a juvenile defendant appears to have deficits in knowledge or ability to collaborate, trying to provide help in these areas is appropriate as part of the evaluation process. If, at the conclusion of the evaluation, the court determines that the youth is not competent, then more elaborate efforts at remediation may be appropriate.

Remediation as Part of the Evaluation

Most juvenile defendants referred for evaluation of competence to stand trial will have some deficits in either knowledge of the proceedings or in communication and collaboration with counsel. These deficits in most cases will stem from either a lack of sufficient preparation of the defendant at the time of referral regarding specific process details or from counsel's lack of understanding of and effective response to the defendant's developmental and clinical problems.

The simplest form of remediation is to teach the defendant information about the legal proceedings. When the inquiry into the defendant's understanding of charges, consequences, and trial roles and procedures shows incomplete knowledge, the consultant should explain the point, ensure that the defendant understands, and then come back to it at a later point in the evaluation to determine if the youth has retained the information. If the problem appears to be one of communication and understanding between youth and attorney, the consultant should help the attorney understand the special needs of the youth in these areas and suggest methods for improvement. Often very simple advice such as taking more time with the youth, meeting in quiet spaces, meeting for shorter periods with frequent breaks, being careful to use simple language, and encouraging the youth to ask questions and repeat his understanding in his own words can lead to remarkable improvements in a youth's ability to understand and respond fruitfully to information and advice from counsel. Parents or other supportive family members can take part in this process, to improve the youth's comfort and add to the resources for supporting and clarifying his communication.

When the youth's deficits stem from treatable mental disorders, treating them can also result in substantial improvements in the client's capacity. When an evaluation can be extended over a period of time and is conducted under physical and legal circumstances that allow for treatment to be provided, then treatment should not wait for the conclusion of the evaluation but should be undertaken with one goal of the treatment being improvement in the youth's competence abilities. Obviously, treatment requires appropriate consent, usually from a parent, and it is important for the youth, parent, attorney, court, and mental health professional to be clear about the indications for treatment and the relationship between the treatment and the youth's court involvement. Ideally, specific treatment for mental disorder is undertaken by a clinician other than the consultant performing the evaluation, to avoid potential conflicts and confusion regarding roles and agency.

These efforts undertaken within the context of the evaluation serve two important functions. First, they can help solve easily remediable competence deficits quickly, reduce confusion and uncertainty about the case, and allow proceedings to continue without unnecessary delays. Second, they provide an important source of information for the evaluation itself as to the nature and responsiveness of the youth's deficits. Showing that a youth can learn and retain information appropriate to the case, or improve communication with support or treatment (or documenting that she does not seem able to), helps the court and attorneys understand the youth's condition and prognosis better.

Longer-Term Remediation

In cases where a juvenile defendant has substantial deficits in knowledge or collaboration and where simple efforts at remediation in the context of evaluation do not prove successful, the youth might be determined legally to be incompetent to stand trial. This determination will likely trigger a series of further legal, placement, and treatment consequences, depending on court preference and on local law and custom.

Treatment

When incompetence stems from deficits owing to such treatable mental disorders as depression, psychosis, PTSD, and ADHD, it is usually possible to treat the disorder with combinations of psychosocial and pharmacological interventions. The specific aim of treatment is to provide sufficient improvement in symptoms that the specific impairments to competence become less salient. However, it will usually be important to involve the defendant in other efforts at specific remediation of competence deficits as well, such as teaching about the legal process, supporting and consulting with counsel regarding effective communication, and facilitating support and advocacy from parents and other potentially helpful and trusted adults. The consultant may articulate specific treatment plans and other recommendations for treatment and should be clear in distinguishing between plans and goals for overall clinical care and treatment versus specific treatment and education aimed just at establishing competence.

Advocacy and Support

Some juvenile defendants may be found incompetent to stand trial on the basis of deficits that may not easily respond to teaching, help with communication, or treatment. They may function at cognitive levels that do not allow for effective teaching, or suffer from disabling mental disorders that do not respond well to treatment. A young defendant might possibly be considered incompetent solely on the basis of immaturity in cognition, perspective, and decision-making capacity, for which time, growth, and experience would be the only effective remedies.

For some such defendants, the charges may be serious enough that they are not likely to be dismissed, leading to a potential extended period of ambiguous legal status. This ambiguity may be stressful and actually deleterious to further development. Sometimes it may be more in the defendant's interest to be able to be adjudicated, especially if the alternative to adjudication is extended delay and uncertainty in a stressful or inappropriate placement. In some cases it may be necessary for the juvenile to be adjudicated in order to be eligible for specialized treatment. In such circumstances, exploring legal remedies to incompetence can potentially be in the child's interest. The consultant may be able to help in this effort by characterizing the capacity of a parent to act on the youth's behalf in negotiating a settlement, arranging for further help to improve the appropriateness and effectiveness of parental advocacy, or by contributing to the discovery or establishment of other relationships between the youth and competent, trusted adults. Any of these actions could help improve the youth's connections with others, potentially supporting her functioning so that she could be considered competent and able to move on to more appropriate placement and care.

Interpretation and Opinion

At the end of the evaluation process, the consultant needs to organize the clinical data and help the court and attorneys understand what it means. This interpretation generally has three steps: diagnosis, functional characterization, and linkage.

The first interpretive task is entirely clinical. Based on the range of historical, mental status, and test data gathered, the consultant arrives at diagnoses to account for the youth's overall condition. Though impressions vary, various mental disorders appear to be significantly overrepresented in the delinquent population (Otto et al. 1992), especially mood disorders, impulse control disorders, substance abuse, learning problems, and posttraumatic disorders. Problems with cognitive development are also prevalent (Murray 1976; Rutter and Giller 1984). Youths in this population commonly suffer from more than one disorder. The consultant's task is to consider the significant history along with current signs and symptoms and arrive at the most reasonable combination of diagnoses to account for the youth's individual presentation.

Increasingly, the issue of competence to stand trial arises in juvenile cases not because of concerns about a clinical disorder but simply on a developmental basis (see Chapters 3 and 5 in this volume). The important clinical issue for the consultant may therefore in some cases not be clinical diagnosis, but rather developmental assessment. The important questions concern the youth's maturity, not just in terms of cognitive development but also in areas of social and emotional development. Delays in these areas—or even normative development for the youth's age—may result in relative deficits (compared with adults) in his understanding, his interaction with counsel and other advisers, and his decision-making process. The consultant should describe how the youth's functioning in these areas compares with that of other youths of similar age and with adults, taking account of the growing research base in this area described elsewhere in this volume (see Chapter 6 in this volume).

The next interpretive task is more traditionally forensic. It involves collecting the range of observations specifically relevant to the youth's strengths and weaknesses in competence abilities, and using them as a basis for summary opinions about the youth's functioning in the basic areas of knowledge and collaboration. It is important to note strengths as well as deficits in this characterization, and to include specific consideration of the interaction among the youth's abilities, the demands of the specific legal case, and the nature and effectiveness of the support available to the youth.

Finally, the consultant needs to be as specific as possible in developing opinions about the linkage between specific diagnoses of mental disorder or developmental problems on the one hand, and functional deficits in competence abilities on the other. He or she should attend to the possibility that functional impairments may be malingered rather than genuinely linked to disorders (McCann 1998), as well as to the possibilities that deficits in communication and collaboration may rest as much with counsel's unfamiliarity with the youth or his disorders as with the youth himself. It is also important to include more general consideration of the issue of motivation. A youth who does not understand the proceedings or does not communicate with counsel may be poorly motivated by reason of anxiety, suspiciousness, or depression; or he may simply be motivated to keep the proceedings from going forward so that he might avoid adjudication.

Reporting Evaluation Results

When the consultant is done with the gathering of clinical and forensic information and with formulating opinions regarding clinical issues and specific competence questions, the final phase of the evaluation process is to provide some kind of report to the court, attorney, or agency making the referral, and possibly to others as well.

Informal Consultation

One of the first issues to clarify when accepting a referral for evaluation is whether or not a written report will be required, and what specific expectations may apply regarding structure and dissemination of a report (Melton, Weithorn, and Slobogin 1985; Fein et al. 1991). Even in cases where a formal written report is not desired, drafting a report helps the consultant review data and articulate clear opinions. Such a draft also provides documentation for the consultant to refer back to in the future in the event that proceedings are extended or the case returns at a later point.

Written Reports

Written reports have the advantage of a standard format, which helps the consultant be sure that she has considered all the relevant questions and provides a familiar structure for readers. They allow all those with access to the report to have the same understanding of the information that the consultant has developed, and of how that information supports (or may not support) the opinions provided. They provide explicit documentation of the subject's condition at the time of the evaluation, and can be helpful in providing a basis for undertaking treatment, either specifically to establish competence or for broader rehabilitative purposes.

Disadvantages of written reports mostly concern costs. It takes time to write a report, and of course a more detailed report takes more time than a less detailed report. In addition, written reports may make information more readily available under conditions that may put a defendant at inappropriate risk. Information intended for limited use in the context of determining competence can sometimes be harmful if available in the context of transfer or adjudication. Some jurisdictions have explicitly forbidden court-ordered evaluation of clinical issues in the context of a transfer hearing, since clinical information can be used to address issues of risk and amenability to treatment, and can thus expose the youth to transfer (*R.H. v. Alaska* 1989; *Commonwealth v. Wayne W.* 1993). Even when consultants and attorneys are careful to pursue appropriate protection of information in competence reports, written information is more prone to adversarial discovery or to inadvertent or deliberate leakage.

The usual format for competence reports follows a common basic structure (Melton et al. 1987), which should be followed for the sake of consistency and clarity:

1. identifying information and referral questions;
2. a description of the structure of the evaluation, including sources and a notation of the confidentiality expectations;

3. the provision of clinical and forensic data; and
4. discussion and presentation of opinions.

Clinical data can be organized by source, by area of function, or by historical chronology; no single way of organizing clinical history works best for every case. Forensic data are best presented in two sections, reflecting knowledge and understanding of charges and proceedings, and communication and collaboration with counsel.

In conveying clinical and forensic data in a written report, it is important to be careful about including communications from the youth, family, or counsel concerning the specifics of the offense itself or details of defense strategy. In some circumstances it may be appropriate to include this information, especially with defense approval. But this is one circumstance in which the risks of full reporting of data may outweigh the benefits. Including the details of the defendant's account of the offense and of her understanding of her attorney's advice on specific points will likely help the reader develop a much more explicit understanding of the strengths and weaknesses of the defendant's collaboration with counsel, but it may also fundamentally undermine the essential confidentiality of the defendant's communication with her attorney.

Opinions regarding various elements of the youth's competence follow directly from the clinical and forensic data, in a separate section of the report. This section should provide clear statements of the strengths and weaknesses of the youth in the areas relevant to the specific case. Opinions on competence abilities need to draw on explicit connection between areas of deficit and the specific clinical or developmental condition that causes it, and should include additional statements about the likely effect that parental advice, support, and direction may have upon any relative deficits in a juvenile's functioning. Opinions should note the parent's extent of understanding of the issue in question, the relative degree of understanding about how resolution of the issue will affect the youth's interests, and the relative strength or weakness of communication between parent and child and of the child's ability to rely on parental advice.

However, mental health professionals should avoid giving an opinion on the ultimate legal question of competence to stand trial. No absolute standards for legal competence exist. Each circumstance in which an individual's competence may be questioned includes different demands, complexities, and stakes; whether a specific profile of skills and deficits is adequate to the specific tasks of a specific individual's circumstances must be an individual-case determination. Most importantly, the ultimate determination of competence is not within clinical expertise. The ultimate question is whether deciding that a specific defendant is competent will result in a fair proceeding, in light of that defendant's specific skills and deficits and considering the demands of the proceeding. The determination of adequate fairness is a moral and legal one, not a clinical one.

In the relatively new and ambiguous area of competence of juveniles, it is especially important that experts maintain the position of careful adherence to this ethical principle. It is very reasonable to expect that judges and attorneys will find claims of adolescent incompetence puzzling, since both the psychopathological and developmental bases upon which such claims might rest may be unfamiliar, and since the appropriate legal remedies for incompetence may not be entirely clear. In the face of this puzzlement, judges and lawyers might put greater pressure on experts to come up with answers that might resolve ambiguity and offer clearer direction. Courts will press experts to say whether an individual juvenile is competent or not; whether an individual parent's contribution to the juvenile's understanding and judgment is sufficient to render the youth competent; and whether a specific degree of communication among lawyer, family, and child is sufficient to make the youth's decisions competent ones. The only proper response to these questions is to be as clear and explicit as possible about issues that are within clinical expertise (including quantifying relative degrees of capacity and impairment), and to be respectful and deferential to the court and counsel in explaining why judgments on these fundamentally ambiguous issues of legal and moral judgment must not be made by experts and can only be made by the court.

Finally, though it is not proper to offer opinions about the legal issue of competence, it is proper and usually helpful to offer both opinions and specific recommendations regarding a youth's further care and treatment. The scope of such opinions and recommendations needs to be made clear at the start of the evaluation. They may need to be limited to recommendations concerning the establishment of competence (if the youth is found incompetent), or they may include broader recommendations for clinical placement and treatment in a variety of realms.

The form in which the consultant offers clinical recommendations in this area needs to take account of the ambiguity regarding competence. Having carefully avoided offering an opinion as to the ultimate opinion of competence, the consultant may introduce new confusion if she offers a clinical recommendation that is available only to an adjudicated delinquent. Such a recommendation may be understood either as reflecting an implicit opinion that the defendant should be found competent and adjudicated delinquent, or as reflecting a lack of understanding of the proceedings by the consultant; neither of these would be helpful.

The proper form for offering clinical recommendations is conditional. The report should state, "If the defendant is found incompetent," and then go on to list placement and treatment recommendations that would be appropriate to this finding. It should go on to state, "If the defendant is found competent," and list the appropriate placement and treatment recommendations in that event. Usually, treatment recommendations for a defendant found competent will not need to include consideration of treatment specifically addressed to establishing competence, and, often, placement options may be different for competent and incompetent defendants. In most cases, however, the fundamental clinical treatment recommendations will be the same.

Conclusion

Introducing the concept of competence to stand trial in juvenile proceedings presents challenging questions to the forensic mental health consultant. Evaluation in this area requires special care so the consultant can understand the complex procedures and stakes in matters involving juvenile defendants and the variety of clinical and forensic questions that may arise. Assessment must be based on adequate clinical expertise with children and families, and needs to be flexible in its level of detail, reflecting the variety of potential circumstances in which competence questions may arise. Evaluation needs to recognize the complexities of role relationships involving juvenile defendants, and must especially appreciate the fundamental and potentially ambiguous responsibilities of parents in contributing to the juvenile's defense. Consultants need to appreciate the systems implications of competence questions and must be able to provide opinions and recommendations that match the legal and systems circumstances of individual cases.

The area is full of uncertainty, and the complexity of these challenges can sometimes seem overwhelming. But in responding carefully and thoughtfully to questions in this area, consultants can contribute to the development of a potentially important area of legal and clinical practice and arrive at solutions to difficult and challenging cases.

Works Cited

Appelbaum, P., and Grisso, T. 1988. Assessing patients' capacities to consent to treatment. *New England Journal of Medicine* 319:1645–1638.

Barnum, R. 1986. Integrating multiple perspectives in forensic child psychiatry consultation. *Journal of the American Academy of Child Psychiatry* 25:718–723.

———. 1990. Self incrimination and denial in the juvenile transfer evaluation. *Bulletin of the American Academy of Psychiatry and the Law* 18:413–428.

———. 1997a. Competence to stand trial in juvenile court. Keynote address for the Massachusetts Association of Guardians ad Litem annual conference, Boston, Mass.

———. 1997b. A suggested framework for forensic consultation in cases of child abuse and neglect. *Journal of the American Academy of Psychiatry and the Law* 25:581–594.

Barnum, R., and T. Grisso. 1994. Competence to stand trial in Massachusetts: Issues of therapeutic jurisprudence. *New England Journal of Civil and Criminal Confinement* 20:321–344.

Barnum, R., J. Silverberg, and D. Nied. 1987. Patient warnings in court-ordered evaluations of children and families. *Bulletin of the American Academy of Psychiatry and the Law* 15:283–300.

Bernard, T. 1992. *The cycle of juvenile justice.* New York: Oxford University Press.

Commonwealth v. a Juvenile, 389 Mass. 128, 449 N.E. 2d 654, 657 (1983).

Commonwealth v. Wayne W. 414 Mass. 218 (1993).

Cooper, D. K. 1997. Juveniles' understanding of trial-related information: Are they competent defendants? *Behavioral Sciences and the Law* 15:167–180.

Dusky v. U.S. 362 U.S. 402 (1960).

Everington, C. 1990. The competence assessment for standing trial for defendants with mental retardation (CAST-MR). *Criminal Justice and Behavior* 17:147–168.

Fare v. Michael C., 442 U.S. 707 (1979).

Fein, R. A., K. Appelbaum, R. Barnum, P. Baxter, T. Grisso, and N. Leavitt. 1991. The designated forensic professional program: A state government-university partnership to improve forensic mental health services. *Journal of Mental Health Administration* 18:223–230.

Flicker, B. 1981. Prosecuting juveniles as adults: A symptom of a crisis in the juvenile courts. In *Major issues in juvenile justice information and training: Readings in public policy,* edited by J. Hall. Columbus, Ohio: Academy of Contemporary Problems.

Grisso, T. 1986. *Evaluating competencies: Forensic assessments and instruments.* New York: Plenum.

———. 1998a. Society's retributive response to juvenile offenders: A developmental perspective. *Law and Human Behavior* 20:229–247.

———. 1998b. Forensic evaluation of juveniles: A manual for practice. Sarasota, Fla.: Professional Resources Press.

Grisso, T., and M. Ring. 1979. Parents' attitudes toward juveniles' rights in interrogation. *Criminal Justice and Behavior* 6:221–226.

Grisso, T., M. O. Miller, and B. Sales. 1987. Competency to stand trial in juvenile court. *International Journal of Law and Psychiatry* 10:1–20.

Grisso, T., J. Cocozza, H. Steadman, W. Fisher, and A. Greer. 1994. The organization of pretrial forensic evaluation services: A national profile. *Law and Human Behavior* 18:377–393.

Hoge, S., N. Poythress, R. Bonnie, J. Monahan, M. Eisenberg, and T. Feucht-Haviar. 1997. The MacArthur adjudication competence study: Diagnosis, psychopathology, and adjudicative competence-related abilities. *Behavioral Sciences and the Law* 15:329–345.

Keilitz, I. 1984. A model process for forensic mental health screening and evaluation. *Law and Human Behavior* 8:355–369.

———. 1989. *An interorganizational analysis of mental health expert services provided to trial courts.* Williamsburg, Va.: National Center for State Courts.

Lipsitt, P., D. Lelos, and A. L. McGarry. 1971. Competency for trial: A screening instrument. *American Journal of Psychiatry* 128:105–109.

McCann, J. 1998. *Malingering and deception in adolescents: Assessing credibility in clinical and forensic settings.* Washington, D.C.: American Psychological Association.

McGarry, A. L. 1973. *Competency to stand trial and mental illness* (Publication No. ADM #77-103). Rockville, Md.: Department of Health, Education and Welfare.

Melton, G. B., L. Weithorn, and C. Slobogin. 1985. *Community mental health centers and the courts: An evaluation of community-based forensic services.* Lincoln, Nebr.: University of Nebraska Press.

Melton, G. B., J. Petrila, N. Poythress, and C. Slobogin. 1987. *Psychological evaluations for the courts.* New York: Guilford Press.

Murray, C. 1976. *The link between learning disabilities and juvenile delinquency: Current theory and knowledge.* Washington, D.C.: US Government Printing Office.

Nicholson, R., H. Robertson, W. Johnson, and G. Jenson. 1988. A comparison of instruments for assessing competency to stand trial. *Law and Human Behavior* 12:313–321.

Otto, R., J. Greenstein, M. Johnson, and R. Friedman. 1992. Prevalence of mental disorders among youth in the juvenile justice system. In *Responding to youth with mental disorders in the juvenile justice system,* edited by J. J. Cocozza. Seattle, Wash.: National Coalition for Mental and Substance Abuse Health Care in the Justice System.

Podkopacz, M. R., and B. C. Feld. 1995. Judicial waiver policy and practice: Persistence, seriousness and race. *Law and Inequality: A Journal of Theory and Practice* 14:73–178.

R. H. v. Alaska, 777 P. 2nd 204 (1989).

Roesch, R., C. Webster, and D. Eaves. 1994. *The fitness interview test revised: A method for examining fitness to stand trial.* Burnaby, Canada: Department of Psychology, Simon Fraser University.

Rutter, M., and H. Giller. 1984. *Juvenile delinquency: Trends and perspectives.* New York: Guilford Press.

Schwartz, I. M., R. Van Vleet, F. A. Orlando, and S. McMurphy. 1995. *A study of New Mexico's youthful offenders.* Philadelphia: Center for the Study of Youth Policy.

Soler, M. 1987. Horrors and healers: New directions for child advocacy. Address to the American Psychological Association division for child, youth, and family services, New York.

Weithorn, L. 1985. Children's capacities for participation in treatment decision making. In *Emerging issues in child psychiatry and the law,* edited by D. Schetky and E. Benedek. New York: Brunner/Mazel.

Wexler, D. B. 1993. Therapeutic jurisprudence and the criminal courts. *William and Mary Law Review* 35:279–299.

CHAPTER EIGHT

Youths' Trial Participation as Seen by Youths and Their Attorneys: An Exploration of Competence-Based Issues

ANN TOBEY, THOMAS GRISSO, AND ROBERT SCHWARTZ

A great deal has been written about lawyering for delinquent children (*Fordham* 1996), yet little attention has been paid to issues of adolescent development and mental disorders that influence a child's ability to be an effective client. Instead, much of the debate over the role of lawyering for children, especially in the years immediately following *In re Gault* (1967), focused on the role of counsel—for example, whether lawyers should serve as guardians ad litem, in the best interests of their clients, or as pure advocates (Stapleton and Teitelbaum 1972; Davis 1993; Platt 1977). Since the late sixties and early seventies, when *Gault's* mandate became the law across the country (Feld 1988), the weight of professional opinion has settled on the "lawyer as advocate" role in delinquency cases (Institute of Judicial Administration 1980; Puritz et al. 1995; *Fordham* 1996).

Lawyers for alleged delinquent children are still struggling, however, to give meaning to their advocacy. Commentators have recognized that even the most zealous advocates for juveniles must know how to be effective counselors in ways that differ significantly from representation of adults (Davis 1993; Melton 1989). Platt (1977) observed that many lawyers, arriving for the first time in juvenile court in the years after *Gault,* found traditional defense tactics "complicated by the unpredictability of juvenile clients who 'have poor memories,' 'don't have the social and intellectual maturity of an adult,' are likely to 'blurt out and convict themselves,' and easily 'spill the beans.'" Melton (1989) has noted, "Effective representation of juveniles does not imply simply an increased allotment of time to counseling. The nature of the counseling also may be qualitatively different."

Some observers have recognized the importance of low caseloads that allow lawyers to better perform their counseling function at various stages of the juvenile justice process (Edwards 1993; Higginbotham and Ross

1993; Platt 1977; Puritz et al. 1995). Other commentators have illustrated ways in which developmental issues should affect the lawyer-client relationship (Guttman 1995).

As the number of lawyers for children has burgeoned in the last few decades, the academic community has called upon lawyers to learn about how to work more appropriately with their young clients. However, there has been little empirical research to delineate for lawyers (a) the specific ways in which children's differences make them less effective as clients, and (b) the kinds of competency issues that may require lawyers and the legal system to change the way they work with juveniles.

The information in this chapter derives from a study that we intended as a first step toward delineating these issues. Designed as an exploratory project with a small number of cases, the study focused on the types of competence issues that attorneys have observed in their day-to-day work representing delinquent youths in juvenile court. In addition, we sought to explore youths' recollections and perceptions of their experiences within the legal process by talking to the youths that were represented by the attorneys in the study.

We made no predictions and no hypotheses were tested. We used a systematic and semistructured interview procedure that involved primarily open-ended questions. We hoped to learn more about this unfamiliar terrain in order to guide future design of more controlled studies and to shed light on potential policy and training issues.

The Research Method

Attorneys were recruited from a pool of juvenile public defenders practicing in and around a large urban area of the eastern United States. Attorneys were contacted via telephone, using a roster of attorneys who were known to have specialized in the public defense of juveniles in delinquency cases. We explained the purpose and nature of the study, as well as what attorneys would be expected to do if they agreed to participate. Specifically, each attorney was asked to choose one youth whom he or she had represented over the past year, whose case was completed and whom the attorney had had some difficulty representing for reasons related to the youth's capacities to participate as a defendant in the trial process. It was not necessary for the question of competence to stand trial to have been raised formally in the adjudication process. The youth simply needed to have presented some difficulty for the attorney with regard to the youth's ability to participate meaningfully in the trial process, perhaps due to emotional disturbance, intellectual deficits, or developmental issues.

When the attorney agreed to participate and chose a youth, we asked the attorney to contact the youth to gain consent to participate in the study. For youths in Department of Youth Services facilities, caseworker consent to participate was also obtained. Following consent procedures with attorneys and youths, interviews were conducted separately, first with the attorney and then the youth. Youths were paid ten dollars for volunteering their time to the study. All subjects were informed of potential risks and procedures employed to protect anonymity. It was explained that information shared with the interviewer would not be shared with the respective attorney or youth in the case.

A total of ten attorneys participated in the study, involving interviews with ten youths. Attorney experience ranged from six months to twenty-eight years, with a mean of eight years' experience representing juveniles. Three of the ten attorneys were female, and the attorney group was racially and ethnically mixed, although predominantly Caucasian.

The ten youths (one female and nine males) ranged in age from eleven to sixteen years at the time of arrest, with a mean age of fourteen years, seven months. Seven of the ten youths were being held in facilities at the time of the interview, and the remaining three were interviewed in the community.

To provide some standardization of the interviews across attorneys and across youths, we developed a lengthy semistructured interview schedule that controlled the sequence of topics and questioning while providing much flexibility regarding exploration and spontaneous responses by participants. The sequence of content areas was similar for attorneys and youths, although the questions within these content areas were somewhat different for attorneys than for youths as was appropriate for their different roles in the attorney-client relationship and the trial process. Almost all questions were open-ended in order to allow participants to make observations that the interviewers might not have anticipated in this relatively unexplored area.

More specifically, interviews with youths included background questions about the youth and the case; questions to develop a basic chronology of the pretrial and trial process; and questions regarding the youth's perceptions of the legal process, including cognitive/verbal issues (fund of knowledge, receptive abilities, memory/attention issues, expressive abilities), relationship and trust issues, youth's participation, and youth's decision-making capabilities. Finally, the interview contained a checklist of specific defendant abilities similar to those functional abilities (such as understanding of charges and decision-making capacity) typically considered in evaluations of defendant competence. Overall, the interview provided ample opportunity and stimuli for encouraging the youths to report on their past thoughts and behaviors during the trial process and to reflect on the trial process and the behaviors of their attorneys.

Interviews with attorneys followed a similar format but contained further background descriptions of the youths, questions related to attorney experience, attorney's reflections on the youth's behaviors and capacities, and a consideration of differences between the youth and the average adult defendant. Interviews ranged in length from forty-five minutes to two hours.

Interviews were interpreted qualitatively to examine the characteristics of the youths that attorneys were identifying and the nature of youths' deficits, and to generate examples of problems faced by youths and attorneys in representing this population. No formal scoring or coding procedures were employed.

Results of the Interviews
Overview of Types of Youths Selected

The group of youths chosen by attorneys was of inherent interest because it indicated the diversity in the types of youths about whom attorneys may have doubts concerning their abilities as trial participants. Interestingly, youths were somewhat older than might have been expected. At the time of arrest, five youths were sixteen, two were fifteen, two were thirteen, and one was eleven. It was likely that the urban locations and issues raised by English as a second language skewed the racial and ethnic composition of the sample. Five youths were African American, four were Latino, and one was Caucasian.

In general, the youths were identified by the attorneys for quite diverse reasons. One youth with very serious charges was seen by his attorney as very passive regarding participation and decision making in his case. Another youth with serious cognitive limitations was unable to keep appointments or develop an adequate relationship with his attorney, grasp the nature or gravity of the situation, or conform his behavior out of court during the pretrial stage of the proceedings. Yet another youth's cognitive limitations made it difficult for him to retain information, and his relationship with his attorney deteriorated as the case was repeatedly delayed.

Other youths had mental or emotional disturbances. One youth of average intelligence was especially of concern to his attorney due to his serious depression, passivity, and lack of parental support, which left the attorney in a position of providing the only adult guidance this young defendant had. In another case a particularly young client with serious emotional and behavioral disturbances had great difficulty expressing his knowledge of the legal process and participants, was unable to conform his behavior both in and out of court, and had great difficulty paying attention to his attorney. Finally, a youth with very poor parental supports and poor emotional stability became quite overwhelmed by the legal process. He was unable to follow through with any demands made on him and was uncommunicative with his attorney. He sometimes sat faced away from his attorney, sucking his thumb and rocking his body. He could not bring himself to answer the judge, and this apparently angered the judge. This youth reported that he wished the judge had been more understanding.

All but one youth experienced poor school functioning. Those with school problems were not attending school, were failing school, or were in special-education programs for learning problems, behavior problems, or both. Two youths had tested within the "mentally deficient" range on a standard intelligence test, and three were described as "nonreaders."

Although diagnostic information was not available on all youths, two of them were known to hold diagnoses of mental retardation, two had previously been diagnosed with attention deficit hyperactivity disorder (ADHD), one was diagnosed with posttraumatic stress disorder (PTSD) and depression, and another with bipolar disorder. The majority of youths described themselves or were described as marijuana users.

One part of the interview inquired about other events in the youth's life during the legal process, especially events that might engender added stress. Four of the nine males reported becoming fathers while they were awaiting or participating in their legal process, while a fifth reported that his girlfriend miscarried their baby. Other stressful events while awaiting resolution of their cases included maternal mental illness, loss of family support, and transfers between facilities, especially transfers that increased the distance between themselves and their families.

In only two of the ten cases was an evaluation for competency requested, and in both instances the attorney raised the request. The reason for evaluation in one case was that the youth was clearly mentally retarded with significant problems in comprehension and expression. In the other case the youth was quite young and had severe ADHD. In neither case did the course of the legal process include a competency hearing. In the former case the lack of dispositional alternatives available seemed to influence the judge, who felt that it would send the wrong message to the youth if he "got off" as incompetent. In the latter case a mental health screening deemed that the youth would probably be competent if provided some interventions that did not require treatment, and the question was not pursued further.

There were a variety of charges and legal circumstances. Charges included murder, possession of drugs, receiving a stolen motor vehicle, assault and battery with a deadly weapon, indecent assault and battery, statutory rape, attempted murder, armed robbery, unarmed robbery, arson of a dwelling, and kidnapping. One case involved a juvenile transfer hearing (waiver to criminal court) and a jury trial in juvenile court, four involved superior court indictments of youths as "youthful offenders" (which can result in sentences that extend into the adult years), and five cases were juvenile delinquency proceedings, two of which involved probation surrenders. Case outcomes involved seven decisions to plead guilty to lesser charges and two probation surrenders, while in the case involving a transfer hearing the youth was retained in the juvenile court and acquitted by a jury.

Attorneys' and youths' comments regarding specific types of deficits in functional abilities related to trial participation are described below.

Fund of Information

Some interview questions focused on the fund of legal knowledge that youths brought with them to the legal experience. Youths reported learning about court from various sources, including their prior legal involvement, family legal involvement, television court programs, and school. Prior legal involvement did not necessarily help youths understand their present cases. For instance, the two most cognitively impaired youths seemed to have learned very little from prior involvement. Not only did they know very little about the system, but they also failed to learn from past mistakes—much to the frustration of their attorneys, they picked up new charges during the pretrial process by continuing to engage in illegal behaviors.

Receptive Abilities

The most salient issue cited by both youths and attorneys was deficits in youths' receptive capacities, meaning their ability to understand what others tried to explain to them about their ongoing cases. Attorneys observed that youths "didn't comprehend," or "just didn't get it." Youths made statements such as, "I kinda got the idea" or "I had trouble understanding." Some youths said that they attempted to gain better understanding by asking a parent or their attorney, but according to both youths and attorneys, most seemed to have done nothing to seek further explanation.

In several cases youths reported that it was particularly helpful when parents explained things. Unfortunately, attorneys observed that in some of these cases parents were trying to help but did not seem to fully understand the circumstances themselves. In some cases, therefore, attorneys had to contend with the fact that parents were misinforming their clients.

One youth reported that he was able to understand his attorney "because she would talk real slow." Youths especially had difficulty understanding the judge, and didn't know "what all those terms and words mean." They cited terms such as "commitment," "surrender," and "youthful offender" as words they did not understand.

Both attorneys and youths reported that youths' understanding improved with time, although some admitted that it was "still fuzzy" even at the end. In general, at the time of interviewing it was apparent that most of the youths still had only a marginal grasp of legal concepts and the roles of participants. Nevertheless, all but the most compromised youths were attuned to their charges and the penalties for their charges. It is important to note that the majority of attorneys who participated in the study reportedly spent more time with these youths than was typically the case. Most made numerous visits and phone calls during the pretrial process and spent a good deal of time reviewing concepts with these young clients.

Memory and Attention

Youths' difficulties in retaining information were often cited by attorneys as a major problem. For example, one attorney recalled that although the youth seemed to grasp information during a particular meeting, when he saw the youth again a week or so later "it was as if we never had the previous conversation." It was necessary to start all over again in explaining the same information. Attorneys described having to repeat the same information numerous times across many encounters, especially with the most cognitively compromised youths.

Attention was also cited as a problem. Vulnerability to distraction and loss of attention led to poor demeanor both in and out of the courtroom and an inability to attend to significant events as they occurred. One youth who had been very depressed at the time of adjudication reported that the whole process was "boring" to him (despite the serious potential consequences of the case) and he didn't pay much attention because he "didn't really care that much." Others reported that it was hard to pay attention because of overwhelming emotions ("felt like crying," "felt like blowing up") or because things went on too long and they didn't really understand so they just stopped paying attention. For instance, one youth reported that "sometimes I'd put my head down and not listen . . . It was hard to be in court, I'd be hungry and tired and sayin' 'I'm gettin' tired of all this.'" In another instance, a particularly young defendant with a diagnosis of ADHD had an especially difficult time tolerating the long wait for her turn in court. On two occasions, after she and her mother came to the courthouse at the appointed early-morning time and the case was not heard before lunch, she became very agitated and irritable. In each case she left the courthouse and did not come back after lunch, which negatively affected her case.

Language and Culture

English as a second language and the vernacular of the courtroom added to youths' problems in understanding the legal process. In one case a youth expressed that he had to really concentrate to understand English in the first place, and it was especially hard because of the language used by the lawyers and judges in the courtroom.

Parents who did not speak English had a very difficult time being actively involved and supportive of their children in the English-only setting of the courts. Interpreters apparently were only occasionally used in court and almost never used outside of court.

Expressive Abilities

Several youths felt they had difficulties expressing themselves in court and to their attorneys. In several cases emotional issues, despite reasonable intelligence, impaired youths' communication. For instance, one youth reported that it was very difficult to tell the story to the attorney because it was too emotional to recount. Another youth reported that it "was hard to figure out how to put it out there and what to say." This youth found it virtually impossible to express himself to his attorney and to the judge in court.

Only one youth (who was probably the most cognitively limited participant) admitted that it was hard to get his ideas across to his attorney due to problems with expressive language. Knowing his attorney from a previous case helped one youth with serious expressive-language problems feel more comfortable in getting information across. In addition, his attorney described taking much time and several meetings to elicit the requisite information from the youth.

Relationship with Attorney

The interview focused at various points on youths' experiences and attorneys' reflections concerning youths' degree of trust in the relationship as well as their dependency. Youths generally reported trusting their attorneys, and to varying degrees they reportedly (and, it appeared, actually) understood that their attorneys were there to help them with their cases. Judging from youths' discussions of this topic, it appeared to be very important to them that they had developed a relationship and felt a connection with their attorneys. When they expressed liking their attorneys, inquiry about the reasons elicited observations that the attorney was "cool," was able to "chit chat," or went out of their way to contact and visit their client. For instance, one youth reported that he knew his attorney was there to help him because she came to see him at home and spent a lot of time talking to his mother. Despite his own lack of interest in his case, he was able to appreciate his attorney's efforts.

In contrast, in some cases youths seemed to "shut down" when their cases did not move quickly enough or did not move in their favor. In these cases, what had originally been reasonably good attorney-client relationships deteriorated. In one case this seemed due to the youth's lack of understanding of the legal process, which gave him unrealistic expectations of his attorney. In another case the youth felt ignored by his attorney, who rarely called or came to see him as the case dragged on.

One case provided a particularly good example of the way that youths sometimes interpret attorneys' behaviors across linguistic, ethnic, and cultural divides in a manner that affects the relationship without the attorney's knowledge of how or why. The youth reported that sometimes he didn't want to tell his attorney things because it seemed to him that the attorney always agreed with the other side. This particular attorney had a habit of responding to courtroom interactions by saying "okay" at the conclusion of the opposing attorney's comments, as a conversational marker but not necessarily as an exclamation of agreement. The youth interpreted this as a sign that the attorney was not an advocate who could be trusted.

In another case a very emotionally fragile youth reported that he was unable to communicate with his attorney at first because he "didn't know her." By the time his case was closed he had begun to feel more comfortable and was beginning to talk to her. Unfortunately, the court did not understand the nature of this youth's serious emotional fragility, seemed to interpret his lack of participation as defiance, and treated him accordingly.

A major concern of attorneys was the dependency and passivity of their clients, which they felt was substantially more pronounced in their adolescent clients than in their adult client population. Some attorneys felt that the youths they represented were overly trusting and dependent on their recommendations; in some cases they felt that youths were not really making autonomous decisions at all but were simply relying on attorney recommendations. This was seconded by the reports of the young defendants who claimed that decision making was easy because they just went along with what the attorney recommended. One attorney observed that it would be very easy for counsel to mislead and/or take advantage of most adolescent clients because of their passivity.

Decision Making and Participation

Of particular concern were decisions made while in police custody when counsel was not available. Youths had great difficulty understanding Miranda rights. One youth described waiving his right to remain silent because he did not understand it was his decision to make. Regarding his confession to the police, another youth remarked, "They the police, you do what they say."

Youths lacked appropriate decision-making capacity for a number of reasons, including immaturity, failure to appreciate the complexity of a situation, lack of basic understanding of the process, and emotional complications. While several youths appreciated the complexity of the decision, one said that he simply wanted to hurry up the court process. The most cognitively compromised youth admitted that he did not understand why he had pled guilty. Another youth, the attorney reported, was so depressed that he seemed not to really care and simply went along with what the attorney suggested. Despite potentially adequate cognitive capacity, his functioning and decision making were quite poor. Attorneys observed that several youths, even when they could generally understand what was going on, had very little capacity to weigh alternatives and consider the variety of outcomes.

Many of the defendants were driven by the desire to "get it over with" or avoid the negative consequence of the immediate moment, with little regard for long-term issues. For instance, when one youth was asked for the "most important reason" that he had decided to plead guilty he responded, "I was too tired of waiting for court . . . I don't want to wait to stay in court." This youth's decision to plead guilty resulted in a split sentence, meaning a commitment to age twenty-one in the juvenile system, with the potential for an adult state prison sentence of another five to seven years that may be suspended dependent on the youth's behavior during the first phase. His attorney stated, "Kids see the short term . . . they take the option of the Department of Youth Services to avoid prison today and don't really understand that one screw-up will land them in prison. They have no perspective and nothing to compare it to. [He] has never been on probation so he doesn't really know what he has to do [to avoid the adult phase of the sentence] . . . to him it seemed like less time." As another youth stated, "The most important thing [in his decision to plead guilty] was what would get me home the soonest." Pleading guilty in order to get home quickly was more important for this youth than the fact that he would have to endure being publicly registered as a sex offender for years to come.

There was evidence from several youths that their beliefs about society's attitudes toward them affected their decision making. For instance, one youth commented that going into the legal process he believed he would not get a fair trial because he was a Black teenager from a "bad" neighborhood who had committed a serious crime against a White person. In another case, a major part of a youth's decision to plead guilty was that he felt others would not believe him and his codefendants because they were "three Hispanics who supposedly beat up a White guy." In another instance, a youth reported that although he denied some of the charges he decided to plead guilty because he "wanted to get off the street anyway." As he described the situation, he had many enemies on the street and felt safer in the locked facility.

Interestingly, typical adolescent risk-taking behavior did not seem to play a major role in legal decision making. Youths who maintained a "don't care" attitude were those who seemed to be suffering from significant emotional disturbances such as depression and/or neurological issues, whereas most youths were very worried and concerned about the legal outcome. Despite their impatience with the process, youths were hardly cavalier in their attitudes regarding outcome. Even so, an orientation to short-term consequences played a major role in their decision making.

Youths' actual participation in the pretrial and trial processes was typically described by youths and attorneys as limited but nevertheless important. They had to tell the facts of the case to the attorney, had to behave themselves in and out of court, and had to make a decision to plead or go to trial. In most cases attorneys felt there was no way their youthful clients would have been able to testify if it had been necessary. In only one case did a youth actually testify.

For several youths the only role that they could describe for themselves in the trial process was that of showing up at court and avoiding acting inappropriately. Others were aware that it was also their job to stay out of trouble outside the courtroom while their cases were in progress.

Parents' Roles

Although parents' involvement varied, positive involvement seemed to make a difference in some defendants' abilities to eventually grasp the concepts necessary to work with their attorneys. Alternately, parental un-involvement often made the process much more difficult for youths to navigate. For instance, in one case, the lack of parental support (at least in part) eventually caused a child to be locked up "for services" on a pro-bation surrender, following numerous missed appointments and contin-ued truancy. In another case a youth became more depressed when her only family member left the state. This left the youth heavily reliant on her attorney, who, in turn, felt very responsible for helping her with le-gal and personal decision making, stating she "leaned on me heavily for guidance."

What Do the Results Show?

We do not know whether the small sample of youths and attorneys in-volved in this exploratory study provided a balanced or complete view of the difficulties attorneys and youths encounter regarding youths' capaci-ties to participate as defendants in their juvenile court trials. Moreover, the attorneys participating in this study specialized in juvenile defense and, as a group, were far more involved in their young clients' cases than one is led to expect is the average involvement among legal counsel for juveniles nationally (Puritz et al. 1995).

Nevertheless, the observations made here do demonstrate that the rea-sons for youths' deficits in trial participation are extremely diverse. More-over, certain patterns and generalizations regarding attorneys' concerns and ways to deal with youths' deficits in trial participation do begin to emerge even from this small sample. We discuss these below, followed by comments for further research and for attorney training.

Attorneys' Concerns

First, we noted that when we initially posed the task to attorneys to select a case that presented problems because of the youth's deficits in trial par-ticipation, some attorneys had difficulty thinking of a youth that met our criteria. It was clear that attorneys did not have caseloads full of youths with trial-related deficits. We wondered whether this was because they had become accustomed to accommodating to youths' lesser capacities due to immaturity. For example, despite their difficulties in identifying problem cases, virtually all of the attorneys noted that there was a marked difference between the capacities of their adolescent clients and adult de-fendants whom they had represented in the past. Formal competence to stand trial has not been a traditional concern for juvenile courts, and it is likely that attorneys who represent juveniles have become accustomed to accepting a lower level of competence in their clients. We suspect, there-

fore, that the cases that were nominated represented problem cases in relation to other juvenile cases, not in relation to adults. Posing an adult
standard might have caused attorneys to perceive more youths as having
significant deficits in trial participation.

Even if the proportion of youths with special problems in representation was relatively small, attorneys reported that the defendants whom
they nominated put particular strains on them. They spent far more time
trying to get these clients to appointments, developing relationships, and
educating them and their families so they could begin to make decisions.
For instance, in a particularly difficult case a very cognitively limited youth
with a number of charges had never kept a scheduled appointment with
an attorney and continued to violate his probation. His attorney, in conjunction with a social worker, made extra efforts to pick up the youth and
bring him and his mother to meet with the attorney. Additionally, calls
were made to remind the youth to attend appointments, go to school, and
stay out of trouble. This youth also required numerous meetings with his
attorney for repeated attempts to explain the proceedings, and eventually
with a psychologist for an evaluation of competency.

Second, we were struck by the anxiety that many attorneys felt regarding the implications of their youthful clients' passivity when important
and presumably autonomous decisions had to be made. Several of them
spoke of walking an ethical tightrope regarding who, in fact, was making
the decision about such matters as pleading, and feeling that the line between client autonomy and incompetence was unclear. They often questioned whether youths really appreciated the potential ramifications, especially the long-term implications, of the options they had to decide on.

Why, then, did attorneys formally raise the issue of their clients' competence to stand trial in only two of these ten cases? Apparently there
were several reasons. In some cases attorneys appeared not to recognize
youths' difficulties in decision making as a potential basis for incompetence to stand trial. If the youth had a basic understanding of the legal
process and communicated adequately with the attorney, attorneys may
have felt that the formal legal criteria for competence to stand trial were
satisfied. The notion that a nonautonomous decision maker is a competent defendant seems logically suspect, but the actual role of autonomous
decision making as a requirement for competence in juvenile court is as
yet an unsettled matter (see Chapter 3 in this volume). Sometimes attorneys appeared to make a distinction between competence to stand trial
and the difficulties they were facing.

In other cases attorneys appeared to believe that raising the issue of
competence to stand trial was not good strategy from a defense standpoint. When the issue was raised, attorneys reported that it met with re-

sistance from the judiciary, thus risking negative outcomes for the case. One case, however, provided an interesting twist in this regard. In that case, the attorney did not particularly want to raise the issue but felt it necessary. According to the attorney, the judge conducted a "leading" colloquy and deemed the youth competent. The attorney then requested a competency evaluation and formal hearing on the issue. Without the attorney's intention, this move became a "bargaining chip." The youth was of very limited intelligence, and it was questionable whether a finding of incompetence could ever result in remediation that would raise the youth's capacities to a level constituting competence to stand trial. Therefore, the judge feared that a finding of incompetence would, as restated by the attorney, be "giving him a free pass for life." To avoid this, the judge eventually provided a lighter disposition than would otherwise have been likely, and the competence issue was never formally tested.

"Assisted Competence"

At each point during the course of the legal process there were demands placed upon the youths that required them to understand and participate appropriately. The youths in the study had a variety of deficits that made it difficult for them to function in their own best interests as defendants. Raising the question of competence to stand trial was not the only way to respond to their questionable capacities as trial defendants. Another response, the one typically preferred by these attorneys, was to try to augment youths' capacities by providing structure, support, or other mechanisms to create what might be called "assisted competence." Sometimes this assistance helped, but the attorneys also provided many examples of instances in which it did not solve the problems they faced. Situations in which the youths seemed to have the most difficulty included the time of arrest and police interrogation, waiver of rights, decision to plead guilty, and the plea colloquy. Notably, there were few mechanisms for assisted competence prior to arraignment, and it was not uncommon for youths to waive their Miranda rights and make self-incriminating statements to police.

When youths encountered difficulties understanding legal terms or making decisions, they relied primarily on the availability and quality of their attorney and, to some extent, their parents. Again, these attorneys often went the extra mile to improve their clients' understanding. But if they were rushed, unavailable, or related poorly to their young clients, the youth suffered in their ability to grasp and work with the process.

Parents, when available and accurate in their understanding, were a resource to youths in helping them understand what was happening during the trial process. Nevertheless, there were serious limitations to parents' ability to contribute to their youths' assisted competence, even if they were an adequate resource. As more than one attorney stated, parents cannot make the ultimate decisions, because those decisions involve claiming or relinquishing important rights (pleading guilty involves waiver of rights to trial and to avoid self-incrimination) that can only be waived by the defendant. In addition, parents cannot sit next to their children and advise them when they are in the courtroom.

Moreover, parents were functionally unavailable for a variety of reasons such as substance abuse, mental illness, or lack of facility with the English language. Additionally, at times youths were placed in detention facilities far from access to their parents or in facilities where they could not have any physical contact with them. These situations created further stress on the young defendants when, as compromised youths, they required supports, not stressors.

Parents as aids to youths worried some attorneys. Although the law frequently presumes that parents are "interested adults," attorneys often observed that parents' interests conflicted with the wishes of the young defendants. In addition, parents sometimes had difficulty understanding the process appropriately and sometimes miscommunicated information to their children. In other cases attorneys felt that their attempts to elicit parents' help would have required that they infringe on their clients' confidentiality.

Occasionally circumstances that were unrelated to attorneys' interventions had effects that created assisted competence, or at least helped to avoid negative consequences that sometimes arise as a result of youths' poor judgment. Specifically, some youths that we interviewed had been held in pretrial detention while awaiting adjudication, while others had been staying at home and spending time on the street while waiting for trial dates. In the latter cases, youths sometimes had difficulty complying with rules of probation or maintaining good behavior, thus jeopardizing their cases. Others awaiting trials while in the community sometimes failed to attend scheduled appointments with attorneys, creating difficulties in the development of the attorney-client relationship. These problems typically did not arise when youths were being held in detention, where greater structure provided less opportunity for them to engage in behaviors that would harm their cases and where they had little choice but to be available when their attorneys wanted to see them. We are not suggesting that youths should be in secure detention as an assisted-competence strategy. The above observations, however, do suggest that when working with youths who are not in secure detention prior to their trials, attorneys might sometimes need to reinforce natural external controls (such as parents' attention to a youth's curfew) that will augment youths' capacities to stay out of the sort of trouble that could jeopardize their defense.

The ways that court proceedings were conducted often compromised youths' capacities to participate effectively in their trials. Youths frequently mentioned the fast pace of the proceedings (and, as noted earlier, the legal vernacular) as presenting difficulties that affected their understanding or their ability to attend to what was happening. The objectives of assisted competence probably could be promoted by adjusting some of these conditions. Only one youth reported that the judge sometimes interrupted the proceedings to make sure the youth understood what was going on. In contrast, in another case, a youth felt completely alienated by a judge who demanded that he speak despite his very apparent emotional fragility. There is considerable potential to design legal procedures that accommodate youths' deficits to allow meaningful participation in their juvenile court cases.

Implications
Directions for Research

Other chapters in this volume describe research that is necessary to better understand youths' capacities and deficits as participants in their trials. Observations from this exploratory study provide some additional guidance.

First, attorneys in this study were more concerned with their clients' abilities to make autonomous decisions than their abilities to understand the trial process. While some youths were deficient in the latter, almost all were seen as too acquiescent, passive, or naive—compared to most adults—in their approach to decisions about pleas. Research on competence to stand trial of adults has tended to focus heavily on what Bonnie (1992) has called "competence to proceed," meaning defendants' abilities to understand the trial process and to assist counsel in a defense. In contrast, less attention has been paid to "decisional competence," which seems to be precisely the ability attorneys in this study were most concerned about. Future research that compares adolescents to adults on only their abilities to understand the basics of trials and to talk to or trust their attorneys is likely to miss many of the real differences between adolescent and adult defendants.

Second, although very young adolescents may present problems of trial competence, it is clear from our study that immaturity associated with early adolescence is not the only variable to consider. Most of the youths nominated by our attorneys were in middle adolescence but experienced a variety of cognitive and emotional problems. It will be important for future research on youths' abilities as defendants to include samples of youths that, although they are older adolescents, manifest deficits and delays in emotional, cognitive, and interpersonal development.

Finally, research might also identify ways to improve youths' capacities as trial defendants through assisted competence. Would parent-and-child classes on legal matters augment youths' capacities while they are awaiting trial in detention centers? Could juvenile-court trial procedures be modified to better match the cognitive and interpersonal capacities of youths while still respecting the basic requirements of legal due process?

Implications for Attorney and Judicial Training

We noted that attorneys rarely referred youths for competence-to-stand-trial evaluation despite the relative seriousness of some of the cases. Perhaps this was due to trial strategy in some instances, but it might also suggest that attorneys often fail to recognize the extent of their youths' incapacities or the nature of incapacities that would seem to be a basis for further investigation. Attorneys may need better training regarding how to identify potentially incompetent clients and when to make a referral.

Our observations also reinforce the suggestions offered by Buss (Chapter 9 in this volume) regarding the special-training needs of attorneys who work with juvenile clients. Attorneys can be encouraged to think about ways to explain things to young people in simpler terms. Success in improving communications to youthful clients has been reported with methods that involve diagrams, using parents, role playing, and repeating information excessively. Mental health professionals, given their knowledge of developmental, clinical, and applied interviewing strategies, are likely to be better prepared to teach lawyers these skills than are other lawyers.

Finally, we also encourage judicial training regarding the capacities of youths as trial defendants. The courtroom that juvenile court judges manage is more than a place to mete out punishment, and youths that face trials have more to learn than the negative consequences of their offenses. The legal process that youths face offers an opportunity to teach them how a society that respects an individual's rights deals with its citizens' offenses—that the law is not applied arbitrarily, but surely and dispassionately. Like the conclusion of a wise and fair parent, a juvenile court's guilty verdict should not be easily dismissed by a youth as merely the consequence of authority's anger or an abusive use of power. But youths who pass through this process without an adequate understanding of its meaning, as passive and uncomprehending observers, learn nothing about the law and acquire no reason to respect it. Judges, as well as lawyers, have a chance to teach that respect (as well as improve the youths' grasp of the legal process) if they are better able to understand the limited capacities of youthful defendants.

Works Cited

Bonnie, R. 1992. The competence of criminal defendants: A theoretical reformulation. *Behavioral Sciences and the Law* 10:291–316.

Davis, S. M. 1993. The role of the attorney in child advocacy. *University of Louisville Journal of Family Law* 32:817–831.

Edwards, L. P. 1993. A comprehensive approach to the representation of children: The child advocacy coordinating counsel. *Family Law Quarterly* 27:417–431.

Feld, B. C. 1988. *In re Gault* revisited: A cross-state comparison of the right to counsel in juvenile court. *Crime and Delinquency* 34:393–424.

Fordham Law Review. 1996. "Special Issue on Ethical Issues in Legal Representation of Children." *Fordham Law Review* 44.4 (March).

Guttman, C. R. 1995. Listen to the children: The decision to transfer juveniles to adult court. *Harvard Civil Rights-Civil Liberties Law Review* 30:507–42.

Higginbotham, Jr., A. L., and C. J. Ross. 1993. *America's children at risk: a national agenda for legal action.* Chicago: American Bar Association.

In re Gault, 387 U.S. 1 (1967).

Institute of Judicial Administration-American Bar Association. 1980. *Standards relating to counsel for private parties.* Chicago: American Bar Association.

Melton, G. B. 1989. Taking *Gault* seriously: Toward a new juvenile court. *Nebraska Law Review* 68: 146–181.

Platt, A. M. 1977. *The child savers: The invention of delinquency,* 2d ed. Chicago: University of Chicago Press.

Puritz, P., S. Burrell, R. Schwartz, M. Soler, and L. Warboys. 1995. *A call for justice: An assessment of access to counsel and quality of representation in delinquency proceedings.* Chicago: American Bar Association.

Stapleton, W., and L. Teitelbaum. 1972. *In defense of youth: A study of the role of counsel in American juvenile courts.* New York: Russell Sage.

CHAPTER NINE

The Role of Lawyers in Promoting Juveniles' Competence as Defendants

EMILY BUSS

Whether in juvenile court or the adult criminal court, minors accused of crimes are granted the same right as adult defendants to counsel and, through counsel, to participate in the trial process.[1] The law's extension of these adult rights to juveniles is grounded in simple notions of fairness: where juveniles face equal, or even greater, infringements on their liberty, surely they are entitled to the same level of legal assistance and involvement in the process as adults.[2] What the law has failed to take into account, however, is developmental differences between juveniles and adults that may impair juveniles' ability to exercise their participation rights. Others have argued, in this volume (see Chapters 3, 5, and 8) and elsewhere, that children's immaturity impairs their trial competence, their ability to understand the adjudicative process and to participate in decision making regarding their own defense (Grisso 1997; Cowden and McKee 1994-95). My purpose in this chapter is not to cover that ground again, but rather to consider how lawyers representing children might enhance the trial competence of their clients.

I will begin by organizing issues of minors' adjudicative competence into three basic categories that raise different questions for their lawyers. Minors' diminished understanding of their rights, greater confusion about the trial process and the roles of the various participants within that process, and less-developed decision-making skills can all undermine their ability to participate effectively and assist with their defense, whether in juvenile or criminal court. I will next address whether lawyers would, in fact, serve their minor clients' interests if they could succeed in enhancing their adjudicative competence. Finally, I will address what lawyers can do, in conceptual and in more concrete terms, to enhance the trial competence of their child clients.

Obstacles to Minors' Effective Participation

In other chapters of this volume, authors go into considerable detail about what the law requires to establish an adult standard of trial competence and why we might expect adolescents, particularly younger adolescents, to fail to meet that standard. Here, I merely set out with a broad brush the categories of impairments that are likely to interfere with children's effective participation in the adjudicatory process. The purpose of my categorization is to set the stage for my subsequent analysis of the lawyer's role in diminishing those impairments in trial competence. How much a lawyer can do, I will suggest, will vary with the kind of impairment at issue.

The competency problems addressed in the literature can be roughly divided into three categories, with significant overlap and interconnection among them. Juveniles are said to lag behind adults in (1) their ability to understand their rights; (2) their ability to understand the adjudicatory process (including the role of their attorneys in the process); and (3) their ability to make decisions that serve their own (particularly long-term) interests. Of course, these capacities change over time, and there is no reason to think that a typical seventeen-and-a-half-year-old's trial competence will be any different from that of the typical eighteen-year-old. Because the focus of this chapter is on those adolescents who have not yet achieved adult-level capacities in these areas, I will focus my developmental discussion on the end of the spectrum where capacities diverge from adult capacities most sharply. While, for simplicity's sake, I will not ascribe age ranges to the children whose capacities I am describing, it is always safe to assume that these comments apply most strongly to the youngest adolescents, and least strongly to the oldest.

Minors' Understanding of Their Rights

Studies of juveniles' understanding of their rights reveal that younger adolescents have difficulty grasping the abstract concept of rights as well as the particular workings of the rights implicated in the criminal process (Melton 1980; Melton 1982; Grisso 1981). In thinking about rights, in general, children have considerable difficulty understanding rights as entitlements that are within their exclusive control to assert or to waive. This difficulty reflects a broader cognitive resistance to the internalization of control: young children tend to attribute the cause of relevant events to sources other than themselves (most commonly authoritative adults). As they age, children become increasingly likely to perceive themselves as having influence over outcomes, but this "internalization" of the "locus of control" (Rotter 1966; Nowicki and Strickland 1973; Rosenberg 1985) comes more slowly for children of disadvantaged backgrounds who have fewer opportunities to exercise control over their lives (Lefcourt 1976). In the juvenile justice context, even younger adolescents have been shown to think of rights as opportunities granted to them not by a system of laws but by the adults in their lives. This confusion about the source of their rights translates into confusion about the durability of their rights. If adults dole out rights, they can just as easily withhold them, perhaps because they have determined that the minor is somehow unworthy, or better served, without them.

Minors' dual confusion about the concept of rights, in the abstract, is reflected in their confusion about the significance of the specific rights at stake in the criminal process. Their understanding of the right to remain silent, to the effective assistance of counsel, and to have one's guilt proved beyond a reasonable doubt are all susceptible to distortion by their misperception of rights as discretionary and externally controlled. This potential for distortion, in turn, raises questions about whether a waiver of any of these rights can be said to be knowing and voluntary.

Take, for example, the minor who is informed, at the time of his arrest, that he has a right to remain silent. If the minor interprets the police officer's statement to mean "I won't make you talk" (rather than "I can't make you talk"), then he is likely to perceive the officer's subsequent invitation to talk as a change in the officer's message ("now you have to talk"), rather than as an invitation to waive his right ("you can talk, but you don't have to"). Similarly, a minor is less likely to detect subsequent police conduct (such as the attempted coercion of a confession) as a rights violation (Belter and Grisso 1984), for such behavior is also likely to be interpreted as a change in, or explication of, the rules, which is perceived as coming straight from the rulemaker.

Sadly, children's understanding of their rights appears to be only further confused by their actual experience with the criminal justice system (Cowden and McKee 1994-95; Grisso 1981). Perhaps particularly in the juvenile justice system (Ainsworth 1991), minors are likely to see rampant rights violations—counsel that is, at best, ineffective and, at worst, nonexistent (Puritz 1995); cases in which judges find against the accused on thin evidence presented in a procedurally inappropriate manner; and pleas induced by pressure from the judge. Even a minor old enough to possess the capacity to grasp the concept of a right as an absolute and irrevocable entitlement may learn, from his experience, a very different, more contingent, message about rights.

Minors' cognitive difficulty conceptualizing their rights has received considerable attention. Less studied, I think, is the likely complement: minors' valuation of their rights is likely to fall short of adults' as well. It is my untested conjecture that minors are more likely than adults to trade off rights for other interests (say, an interest in pleasing parents, on whom they depend for physical and emotional security) and that this difference is only partly accounted for by adults' and minors' different conception of rights.[3] When we turn to our consideration of how we might enhance minors' competence, we should ask not only how we can help minors understand the nature of their rights but also whether we want to encourage them to value those rights over other interests that may be compromised in their exercise.

Minors' Understanding of the Trial Process

Minors' confusion about the nature of their rights is necessarily intertwined with their confusion about the adjudicatory process and the role of their lawyers in that process, for both the process and the role rest upon assumptions about minor's rights that minors frequently do not share. What is being decided at the trial, by whom, on what grounds, and according to what rules are all questions whose answers depend, in part, on an understanding of the rights afforded the criminal accused. Minors' difficulty understanding the process may stem from a more superficial confusion as well: the minor may simply not understand the role of key players (such as prosecutors, testifying witnesses, and probation officers), the purpose of various procedures, or the range of potential consequences that may flow from a proceeding.

In this context, too, there is an issue of valuation. Even if minors understand the nuts and bolts of the adjudicatory process, they are unlikely to participate meaningfully or effectively if they have not, at least to some extent, embraced the validity of the process. This issue does not apply exclusively to minors (Tyler 1984), but there is some reason to think that minors' immaturity might exacerbate more age-generic resistance to the legitimacy of the process. According to at least some developmentalists, perceiving the social system as a primary unit of moral evaluation, and oneself as a member of that social system, comes fairly late in a child's moral development (Kohlberg 1986) and comes particularly late, if at all, to many minors engaged in delinquent behavior (Prothrow-Stith 1991). Unless and until minors are mature enough to perceive our laws and procedures as the legitimate enforcer of a social order of which they are a part, minors are likely to feel particularly alienated from this process, and this alienation, in turn, will further undermine their participation (Melton 1980; Reicher and Emler 1985).

The Special Importance of Understanding the Role of the Attorney

Nothing is more important to the minor's understanding of the adjudicatory process than his understanding of his lawyer's role in that process. Whether tried in adult criminal court or in the juvenile justice system, a minor is entitled to the same zealous advocacy as is afforded adult criminal defendants. Just as with the adult client, the lawyer must take direction from the minor client and advocate for his objectives—as identified by him—after counseling him on the various options and the potential consequences of those options.[4] If the minor truly understands that his lawyer is his champion and will zealously advocate his desired ends, his ability to understand other aspects of the adjudicatory process becomes somewhat less important, for he should at least be able to entrust to his lawyer the translation of his goals into an effective trial strategy. Moreover, as I will discuss below, a lawyer cannot expect to facilitate her client's trial competence unless the client has a good grasp of the lawyer-client relationship.

As I have discussed elsewhere, however (Buss 1996, 1999), acquiring this understanding of the lawyer-client relationship may be far more elusive than acquiring an understanding of the general purposes of the proceeding, the roles of the other relevant players, or even the court's basis for decision making. The minors' difficulty comprehending the role of his attorney tracks the difficulty he has conceptualizing his rights. In both contexts, minors' conceptual limitations reflect their understanding, gained through a child-life of experience, that adults are in control. In the context of rights, it is hard for a minor to comprehend that his rights exist, wholly independent of adult authority. In the context of the lawyer-client relationship, it is hard for a minor to comprehend that his own authority eclipses that of the adult.[5] In the rights context, the perception of external controls grows out of this life experience coupled with developmental limitations on minors' ability to think abstractly. In the lawyer-client context, the same perception of external control reflects life experience bolstered by sociocognitive immaturity: children must be fairly far along in their sociocognitive development before they are capable of understanding not only that each individual has his own point of view (this comes earlier), but that one individual would, in essence, cede control over that point of view to serve a principled purpose (here, the effective legal representation of a client) (Selman 1980).

Here, again, minors' past experience with the juvenile justice system is likely to undermine, rather than enhance, this understanding. Lawyers, often buried under caseloads of five hundred or more each year, frequently fail to provide a level of attention to their clients that comports with zealous advocacy (Puritz 1995). Moreover, while there is strong support among commentators and jurists for the traditional "zealous advocate" model of representation in this context, many individual attorneys in fact expressly or surreptitiously press for what they think is best for their clients, whether or not their clients agree (Moss 1987). They may directly press their minor clients to change their positions with a paternalistic zeal (and employing paternalistic arguments) that they would never use with adult clients. Or they might ignore (or avoid) their clients' positions altogether in order to advocate their own positions in court.

Minors' experience with adult authority in general, and with lawyers in the juvenile justice system in particular, joined with the complexity of the proper lawyer-client relationship all make that relationship particularly difficult for a minor to comprehend. Facilitating that comprehension is crucial, however, for if a minor fails to understand his lawyer's role in the process, the lawyer cannot engage in effective representation. Absent such an understanding of this aberrationally deferential role, a minor is unlikely to credit claims of loyalty and, more particularly, a commitment to confidentiality. And where such commitments are not believed, the counseling provided by the lawyer will not be perceived as the giving of advice, to help the minor make a more informed decision, but rather as the directions of yet another adult telling him what to do. Under such circumstances, the lawyer's communications to her client are likely to be tuned out by the client, bringing him no closer to an understanding of the trial process.

Communications from client to lawyer are likely to be equally useless. Laboring under a misperception of the lawyer's role, a minor will withhold important information for fear that it will be used against him by the lawyer (Grisso 1983). He will either refuse to answer the lawyer's inquiries or breezily agree with the lawyer's suggestions (as a socially expedient, consequence-free act). He will not seek out counsel when he sees trouble on the horizon (perhaps when he violates a condition of his probation, or when a former criminal associate begins to pressure him to engage in additional criminal activity) for fear that such information will just earn the lawyer's disapproval and undermine the lawyer's commitment to his defense. And in the juvenile justice system in particular, where the dispositional remedy is aimed at treatment rather than punishment, the minor unconvinced of his lawyer's allegiance may forgo a critical opportunity to participate in the development of a workable treatment plan, not to mention a plan that meets his needs. The minor's confusion of his lawyer with the rest of the law-enforcement system may make him eager to convey his willingness to comply with the dispositional terms the lawyer proposes, rather than test those terms against his better knowledge of himself.

Where the minor misperceives his lawyer's role, conversations between lawyer and client can be torturously awkward, and there is no reason to think that the products of such conversations accurately capture the views and choices of the client. In sum, unless a lawyer can overcome these misperceptions, the minor will have no meaningful opportunity to participate in his own defense.

Minors' Decision Making Competence

Much attention has, properly, been devoted to assessing the decision-making competence of juveniles. On this subject, there appears to be a growing consensus that minors' decision-making capacity can be impaired in two conceptually distinct ways. First, pre- and young adolescents may lack the basic cognitive capacity to think abstractly and assess the relative merits of a range of hypothetical outcomes and the likelihood that such outcomes will be achieved. These children can be said to lack the ability to engage in a rational decision-making process that would be required of patients authorized to control decision making in the context of medical treatment (Applebaum, Lidz, and Meisel 1987; Roth, Meisel, and Lidz 1977). Second, even after children have acquired this capacity, they may lack the psychosocial maturity necessary to ensure that they use their cognitive decision-making skills to reach what adults consider to be good decisions (Cauffman and Steinberg 1995; Scott, Reppucci, and Woolard 1995). In particular, studies suggest that minors tend to discount and undervalue risk, overvalue short- as compared to long-term consequences, and are more subject than adults to peer influences. We worry about the first form of impairment because it produces an infirm decision-making process (which, in turn, can be expected to generate problematic judgments), whereas we worry about the latter form of impairment purely because it produces unsatisfactory decision-making outcomes.

In the context of adults, the adjudicative competence inquiry is centered on the first form of impairment: the concern is not whether defendants' trial participation is sensible or effective, but rather whether it reflects a rational engagement. In *Dusky v. U.S.,* the Court asked whether the defendant had "sufficient present ability to consult with his lawyer with a reasonable degree of rational understanding," and in *Godinez v. Moran,* the Court asked whether the waiver of rights was "knowing and voluntary."[6] Assuming that the adult, rationality-focused inquiry applies to assessments of children's competence as well, the poor quality of the accused's choices, standing alone, would not be sufficient to prevent the trial from going forward on competency grounds. But this all-or-nothing inquiry is not, of course, the only competency inquiry that matters for the lawyer representing a juvenile. In making decisions about whether to waive rights or about what dispositional terms to seek, it is clearly preferable for minors to exercise good judgment, take risks seriously, give adequate weight to long-term consequences, and reach decisions based on their own sense of best results rather than out of concern for how these decisions will be received by peers. Facilitating good judgments is unquestionably an appropriate role for the juvenile's lawyer, whether needed to render the juvenile trial-worthy or not.

The three forms of impairment discussed here act together to undermine the adjudicative competence of juvenile defendants. First, juveniles' limited understanding of their rights raises serious questions about their ability to waive those rights knowingly and voluntarily and suggests that their understanding of the trial process itself is incomplete at best. Second, their particular confusion about the role of their lawyer (and their right to be represented by a lawyer who behaves in a particular way) may prevent the formation of a successful lawyer-client relationship, which is essential to the minor's meaningful trial participation. Finally, minors' impaired decision-making capacity will, at a minimum, raise questions about the soundness of the minors' choices and, at the other extreme, may prevent "rational" participation altogether.

Responding to Diminished Competence

Where mental illness or mental retardation accounts for a defendant's inability to participate in the trial process, the trial is adjourned pending treatment for the mental deficiency. Where competency can be established (or restored) with medication or a regime of therapy, such treatment is administered by the appropriate professionals, and the trial resumes when an adequate level of competence is achieved. Where the mental deficiency cannot be corrected within the foreseeable future, the case is dismissed and other systems are left to take responsibility for ongoing problems created by the deficiency.[7] This response to mental deficiencies need make no distinctions between the cases of children and adults. Like adults, children with mental illness or mental retardation that renders them incompetent to participate in the adjudicatory process must either be rendered competent through appropriate treatment or protected from adjudication altogether.

But how should the system respond to a minor's incompetence generated not by mental deficiencies but by immaturity? Should the system wait for the child to grow up? While theoretically coherent, such a response would disserve the goals of both the criminal and juvenile justice systems; the state's case against the defendant and the effectiveness of re-habilitation, deterrence, or punishment would all be weakened by the pas-sage of time. Abandoning the cases altogether would surely be perceived as an even less satisfactory solution. If these cases are to go forward in a reasonable amount of time, juveniles' trial competence must be enhanced or the trial process adjusted to meet the juvenile's level of competence. As the professional charged with safeguarding the minor's rights, cham-pioning his causes in the trial process, and assisting him with legal deci-sion making, the minor's lawyer may be particularly well positioned to enhance the minor's level of competence. Before considering how the lawyer might do so, however, I want to consider, briefly, whether doing so is even in the minor clients' interest.

Children's impaired ability to participate in the adjudicative process might be addressed either by modifying children (at the hands of their lawyers or otherwise) to equip them for the process, or by modifying the process to meet children on their own terms. At least hypothetically, ju-veniles could be adjudicated in a process that bore so little resemblance to the criminal process that competence would be irrelevant, or, more properly, would be measured in entirely different terms. If, for example, allegations against juveniles were referred to a mediator who only had authority to facilitate a conversation between the victim and the accused, we would not have the same concerns about liberty in jeopardy, nor would we be as concerned about whether a minor could track what was going on.

As conceived, the juvenile court was to be such a distinct system, fo-cused on identifying and "fixing" troubled children rather than assigning guilt and meting out punishments. Pointing to the distinct mission of the juvenile court, some argue that the solution to juveniles' adjudicative in-competence is simply to keep incompetent juveniles out of the adult crim-inal court—to keep them in juvenile court regardless of the seriousness of the charges against them (see Chapter 3 in this volume). The argument can be grounded in logic (what sense does it make to set up a separate sys-tem for minors to accommodate their immaturity, and then screen them out of that system on the grounds of immaturity?) or in justice (it is fair to demand less in the way of competence in a system aimed at treatment rather than punishment). Both the logic and the justice of the position are considerably undermined, however, by the shrinking of the distinction be-tween the procedures and consequences of the two systems.

This convergence of the two systems was dramatically acknowledged by the Court in *In re Gault,* and has only accelerated in recent years. As juvenile proceedings are opened to the public and produce sentences that extend past the defendant's minority and count in subsequent sentencing as an adult, few distinctions remain that reflect the grounding of the juvenile justice system in the accused's immaturity. Indeed, the biggest remaining difference between the two systems—the lack of a right to a jury trial in the juvenile system—may well produce greater burdens on a juvenile's comprehension of and participation in the juvenile system than in the adult criminal system. Lawyers and judges accommodate juries by slowing things down and making efforts to present testimony and explain their arguments in laymen's terms. In contrast, the overtaxed judge-run juvenile system runs in high gear. Cases are whisked before the judge and presented in summary terms that make sense only to the "regulars"—the lawyers, probation officers, and judges. In the name of informality, cases tend to be stripped of the procedural trappings that can help a defendant track what is happening. The presentation of opening and closing statements, the swearing in of witnesses one at a time, and the giving of testimony in a designated spot are all often dispatched with in the interest of expediency. We should be careful not to exaggerate either the greater comprehensibility of the juvenile justice system to juveniles, or the lesser detriment imposed on juveniles by this system.

That said, it is still the prevailing view of those with the interest and expertise that the juvenile system is more benign than the adult criminal system. Faced with a choice, most juveniles, and most lawyers representing juveniles, would choose adjudication in juvenile court over the adult criminal court without hesitation. If a finding of incompetence could secure the minor's adjudication in juvenile court, a lawyer should think twice about engaging in efforts to enhance her client's trial competence in adult court.

States are funneling ever-increasing numbers of children into the adult criminal system. In state after state, legislatures are reducing the age and increasing the list of crimes that qualify a minor for transfer to adult court, while shifting decision-making authority for transfer from juvenile judges to prosecutors or eliminating discretion altogether. In this political atmosphere, minors' participatory incompetence may be their last line of defense, both in their individual cases and in the legislative arena. In individual cases, participatory incompetence may offer a defense against transfer. In the legislative arena, minors' lesser ability to exercise their rights and participate in their own defense may offer one of the more politically palatable justifications for diverting minors into a separate, child-focused, system of adjudication.

To the extent that courts and legislatures are willing to draw the analogy between incompetence grounded in mental impairments and incompetence grounded in immaturity, juveniles may be better off the more plausibly they can claim to be without the requisite capacities. Like guaranteeing capital defendants counsel on appeal (which thereby dissipates defendants' opportunity to bring subsequent, life-prolonging habeas claims), juveniles may lose at least as much as they gain in the way of strategic advantage from lawyers' attempts to shore up their trial competence. Enhancing trial competence could give developmental coherence to the trend arguably started with *Gault,* and clearly embraced with increasing zeal in recent years, to make no allowance for childhood in our response to criminal conduct.

Many would suggest, however, that the trend is already so far advanced that developmentally grounded arguments of incompetence will fall on deaf legislative and judicial ears. If arguments of incompetence will produce no benefits for minors, then facilitating competence becomes an unambiguous good.

The Lawyers' Opportunities for Influence: Mechanisms to Facilitate Competence

In considering how lawyers for juveniles can facilitate trial competence, we should ask, first, what means are available to lawyers to accomplish this goal and, second, in light of these means, over which aspects of minors' competence lawyers are likely to have the greatest influence. Of course, these inquiries are necessarily intertwined.

Speaking broadly, lawyers can facilitate trial competence in two basic ways: they can facilitate through instruction and through the development of a relationship.

The Lawyer as Instructor

Instruction offers the most straightforward approach: lawyers can explain rights, processes, options, and likely consequences; they can also connect their clients to others (judges, social workers, and probation officers) who might be better prepared to provide the explanation.

To the extent that instruction can work, the approach is unassailable — lawyers should surely make every effort to improve their client's understanding by communicating how the system works and what is at stake. The Model Rules of Professional Conduct, which govern the conduct of lawyers in most states, place heavy emphasis on lawyer/client communication, directing lawyers to "explain . . . matter[s] to the extent necessary to permit the client to make informed decisions regarding the representation."[8] Any effort to facilitate competence should begin with careful efforts to explain the issues in language minors can understand and in a manner that encourages them to feel comfortable asking questions or noting areas of confusion. At least part of the problem, for some juveniles, is that their lawyers do not even provide them with these basic explanations. Indeed, lawyers, if they appear at all, often meet their clients for the first time immediately before a court appearance, with only minutes to cover everything the lawyer might need to know to defend the case (Puritz 1995).

Even lawyers with the time and dedication necessary to provide thorough explanations at every stage of the proceedings, however, are unlikely to have much effect on trial competence through words alone. Instruction by itself is an ineffective tool in part because, as a practical matter, instruction will go unheeded, absent the necessary relationship ("why should I listen to her?"), and in part because, as a matter of psychological development, instruction by itself is insufficient to produce maturation.

While no studies have addressed the efficacy of instruction in this particular context, there is a striking degree of consensus among developmental psychologists and learning theorists about the limited usefulness of instruction, applied in isolation, as a tool to foster enhanced competence of any sort (Wood 1988; Sylva and Lunt 1982). Educational theorists encourage teachers to minimize formal instruction and to facilitate learning through exploration and experience. Straight instruction, argue these "discovery learning" theorists, fosters unthinking conformity with procedures and rules without the grasping of important, underlying concepts. In recent years, however, growing attention has been given to the value of instruction that occurs in the context of a minor's social and cultural world. Children, the argument goes, do benefit from instruction, where that instruction occurs in the course of natural interactions with adult models who play an important role in their lives (Vygotsky 1978, 1962; Rogoff 1990).

The Lawyer as Friend

This insight about how children learn leads to the second approach available to lawyers: the enhancement of adjudicative competence through relationship-building. While lawyers have no particular credibility as instructors, they do have tremendous specialized authority to build a very distinctive and powerful relationship with their minor clients. Lawyers are authorized to delve into important, secret subjects with their clients, and to use those secrets only to serve the interests of those clients. They have access equal to that of parents to information about their minor clients and have authority to share that information with their clients, with or without parental consent. Lawyers are authorized to oppose parents, the government, and all other interested parties on their minor clients' behalf. When a minor is detained, his lawyer has greater access to him than any other individual not affiliated with the detention facility, even his parents. All this power puts the lawyer in a unique position to establish a relationship of some significance with the child.

Note how closely method relates to a piece of adjudicative competence itself: a lawyer who succeeds in forming a close relationship with his client has probably succeeded in communicating the lawyer's unique role to his client. My consideration of the method of relationship-building, however, has a different focus than the goal of client-driven representation. Indeed, the commitment to relationship-building I am calling for, even where pursued only through means that comport with a lawyer's professional obligations, represents an extension beyond the ordinary scope of the lawyer's efforts on behalf of his client.

In 1976, Charles Fried wrote an article entitled "The Lawyer as Friend" that likened a lawyer's loyalty to his client (even an immoral one) to the loyalty we show our friends. Whether or not one finds the analogy entirely compelling (many critics have not) the basic message is surely right: a fundamental premise of the lawyer-client relationship is that clients, particularly clients in trouble, can show a friendlike trust in their lawyers—they can go to their lawyers with confidential, compromising information and they can rely on their lawyers to get them through scrapes and fight for their interests over those of others, no matter how deserving. While this friendlike trust will not be reflected in all adult client-lawyer relationships, we're generally comfortable assuming that where it is lacking the client has made a conscious choice that such a relationship is not necessary to meet the aims of the legal representation. Adults seek out lawyers with specific goals in mind.

We can make no such assumption, however, when it comes to children. Children will have no expectation of a friendlike relationship of trust with their lawyer. This is in part because the client-lawyer relationship is so far from their understanding of how children and adults relate, and in part because minors engaged in delinquent behavior tend, more generally, to have difficulty forming relationships of trust. As Robert Selman and his collaborators point out in their extensive exploration of childhood friendships, children with adjustment problems need considerable assistance in learning how to establish healthy friendships with anyone (Selman, Watts, and Schultz 1997; Selman and Schultz 1990). While their focus is on the fostering of healthy relationships between peers, their twin goals of intimacy and autonomy in friendship bear a striking resemblance to the two goals of successful lawyer-client relationships, namely trust and client-directed decision making. Professional lawyer-client friendships will not be achieved in the delinquency context unless lawyers work to cultivate them. If they can achieve this professional friendship, they will be in a position to facilitate minors' trial competence in significant ways.

Building the Professional Friendship

Before considering how this relationship can lead to enhanced trial competence, I want to consider how such relationships can be established in the first place. These inquiries are, again, intertwined. A consideration of the process by which such relationships can be forged starts to account for the facilitative effect of such relationship-building.

In focusing on the establishment of the lawyer-client friendship, it is important to understand what kind of relationship I am advocating. I am not calling for lawyers to become big brothers or basketball buddies to their clients. Indeed, such nonlawyer relationships run the risk of confusing client and lawyer alike. The client has no sense of how to distinguish his lawyer from other state agents, volunteers, and family members who are involved in his life, and will therefore apply the same rules about trust and lines of authority that he applies to whichever of these groups seems to offer the best fit. The lawyer may develop a parentlike attachment to the minor, making it harder for her to defer to her client when she fears the consequences of his choices. Rather, the friendship the lawyer should seek to foster is a professional friendship, grounded on and focused exclusively on the task at hand: securing the ends identified by the client through the trial process.

So how do lawyers get there? It is clearly not easy, and probably cannot be done at all without a serious commitment of time. With time, a lawyer can do a number of things to help establish and define the relationship. She can give the client a sense of the mechanics of the process and the nature of the decisions to be made by involving him directly in trial preparation. More importantly, she can give the client a sense of the unique nature of the lawyer-client relationship in the course of this involvement by demonstrating her commitment to keeping client confidences and putting his own view of his interests before those of his parents. Finally, she can reinforce these real-life lessons about the mechanics and obligations of the lawyer's role through role-playing activities.

Enhanced Client Involvement   Involving the minor in the litigation process means much more than soliciting his viewpoints and representation of facts. Indeed, as already noted, such solicitations in the absence of a relationship of trust are unlikely to yield complete or reliable information. To help the client understand the mechanics of the lawyer's role and the workings of the justice system more generally, the lawyer should engage him in extensive discussions about the various issues, strategic as well as substantive, that may arise at trial, and should bring him into the trial preparation process. She should share with the minor her review of important documents, and should have the minor present and involved during interviews with significant witnesses. At all hearings, the lawyer should keep the client by her side to enhance his awareness and understanding of the process and to facilitate his involvement at all stages of the proceeding.

Demonstrations of Loyalty   The lawyer should also seek out opportunities (whether at court hearings or in informal negotiations with the prosecutor or probation staff) to demonstrate her friendlike loyalty to the minor's position. While any zealous advocacy, particularly of controversial positions, will help to convey the message of the lawyer's allegiance, there are two related demonstrations that a lawyer can make that will convey this message especially clearly, in large part because these demonstrations will so contradict the minor's expectations. First, the lawyer can demonstrate a commitment to confidentiality, particularly in the face of pressure on the lawyer to reveal information. Second, the lawyer can demonstrate a willingness to exclude the minor's parents from the conversation and, indeed, from the entire lawyer-client relationship. In fact, these two demonstrations may be most effective when combined: in all likelihood, the minor will experience the keeping of secrets from parents as particularly extraordinary.

As a general matter, minors have little control over their own private information. Their parents not only have a right of access to records containing sensitive information (including medical records, mental health records, and school records) but also often have unlimited authority to share this information, as well as the secrets told to them directly by their children, with whomever they think is appropriate. Informing a minor that a lawyer's professional duties include the obligation to keep secrets will convey, as much as any words can, that the lawyer's role diverges from the role of other adults. Of course, far more important than the making is the honoring of the pledge. When the lawyer demonstrates her willingness to keep secrets, even secrets about the minor's misconduct that governmental and familial authorities would clearly want to know, she cultivates the relationship of trust that is essential to the successful facilitation of the minor's understanding of and participation in the adjudicatory process.[9]

Courts and legislatures have, particularly in the interrogation context, looked to parents to safeguard their children's rights. Because parents are thought to be in a good position to assess their children's interests and to offer their children wise counsel, some states require a parent's presence before a juvenile can be found to have waived his right to remain silent or consult with an attorney.[10] In those states, as well as others that impose no per se requirement, parental presence is viewed as strong evidence that the waiver of rights (usually reflected in the making of a confession) was voluntary. (Grisso 1981). While others have raised questions about whether parents offer meaningful assistance to their children in this context and whether they are committed to protecting their children's rights in the justice system (see Chapter 4 in this volume), I wish to suggest a further reason for distancing minors from their parents in the course of legal representation.

While many minors will be well served by the involvement of their parents, lawyers will undermine their relationship with their clients if they do not take pains to separate their interaction with the minor, as client, from their interaction with parents, as potential assistants to their clients. To help the minor understand the special relationship between client and lawyer, the minor must be made to understand the counterintuitive lesson that the lawyer will do the minor client's bidding regardless of the parents' wishes. Parental inclusion in the relationship should come, if at all, not because it is good for children to involve their parents but because the child has expressly chosen to value that involvement. As with the demonstration of a commitment to confidentiality, a demonstrated willingness not to include parents in discussions, not to share the minor's viewpoints with the parents, and not to take the parents' advice about how to proceed (if one or all of these exclusions is desired by the child) will all help impress the minor that he does, in fact, have his attorney's undivided loyalty.[11]

Once so impressed, the minor may be more inclined to be candid in his disclosure of facts and concerns to his lawyer, and to take the time to assist his lawyer in developing his case. He may seek out his lawyer for advice when he anticipates trouble, including trouble with his parents that weakens his litigation position.[12] He may insist on his lawyer's presence if he faces the police again. To foster this level of involvement, however, the lawyer must be within easy reach of the defendant when the defendant decides to put some trust in the relationship. Lawyers should make it possible for minors to call them at any time (or reach them indirectly through an answering service or beeper system), for a minor seized with the rare impulse to talk to his lawyer may not retain that impulse until the next business day. Even more important, a minor faced with a law-enforcement emergency (classically an arrest) will need legal advice immediately in order for that advice to be useful. Lawyers must also keep cases. High turnover, or rotating coverage, undermines any message of loyalty and dependability (Puritz 1995). Indeed, as I have heard from so many minor clients, a frequent change of lawyers gives the clients a clear message that they do not matter and that no one cares enough about their case to remember it from the last hearing, or to see it through to the next. Finally, lawyers must be prepared to continue to give considerable time to each case. While lawyers tend to devote disproportionate resources to the adjudicatory phase of proceedings, minors tried in the delinquency system may need their lawyers most when a disposition is being developed or reviewed.

If the approach sounds aggressive, it should. Lawyers representing juveniles too often conflate their obligation to take direction from their client with an obligation to take the delinquent's expressed views at face value. They equate pursuing a "normal client-lawyer relationship" with simply following the expressed choices of the client, without inquiring whether the client's perception of the relationship bears any likeness to the normal client-lawyer relationship.[13] If those expressions derive from the minor's lack of understanding, and therefore commitment, to the professional friendship, they cannot be relied upon any more than if the client has confused his lawyer with his truant officer. The lawyer must establish the relationship before the relationship can be expected to work.

Enhancing Competence through Relationship-Building

Clearly, without the relationship we can have no effective client control of representation, a core piece of adjudicative competence. But this is not the only sort of adjudicative competence that will be enhanced by the creation of the relationship. Indeed, for related but distinct reasons, the juvenile's understanding and exercise of his rights, and his understanding of the adjudicative process as a whole, will be enhanced by the successful creation of the professional friendship. To some extent, the relationship will also create opportunities to improve the quality of the minor's decisions, though, in my view, lawyers should consider this aspect of adjudicative competence the least amenable to lawyer influence. Finally, the forging of the relationship may also have the effect of enhancing minors' "valuation competence," that is, their ascribing of adultlike value to the exercise of their rights, to their participation in the trial process, and to the process itself.

Facilitating Minors' Understanding of Rights   Learning to take on the role of decision maker and, particularly, to take that role away from an adult with authority, gives the minor a concrete experience with internalization of control that can assist him in conceptualizing his rights. Where minors are inclined to perceive their rights as provided at the discretion

of powerful adults, the ceding of control to them by one of those powerful adults, the lawyer, may make the cession of control over rights seem
more plausible. Indeed, for some minors, the lawyer may be perceived as
the most direct controller of those rights. If the child learns to believe that
his lawyer exercises no control over him, the lesson about rights may be
learned along the way. As discussed earlier, minors' resistance to a proper
conceptualization of rights is tied only in part to their understanding of
adult authority. The other source of confusion is the level of abstraction
at which we must think to understand rights as entitlements established
by law rather than privileges bestowed by people. Inhibitions on abstract
thinking are unlikely to be directly overcome by forging a relationship
with the client. Indirectly, however, the transfer of authority within the relationship may serve to illustrate in concrete terms what is accomplished
more abstractly through our allocation of rights.

Transforming the Usefulness of Instruction   Forging a successful professional friendship is also likely to transform instruction—an impotent
mechanism in the absence of a relationship—into an effective additional
tool. I have rejected instruction as a means in itself to facilitate competence for two reasons, both of which are addressed in the context of the
relationship. First, minors have little to no incentive to listen to or care
about the information and advice provided by a lawyer in the absence
of a relationship of caring and trust. Second, instruction alone is a fairly
week tool in stimulating development—but instruction combined with
experience may be the most effective teacher.

If you watch minors in the delinquency system, you'll see they don't
lack for direction and advice. Indeed, at times it seems as though the only
kind of communication ever directed to them is of this nature: court officials bark orders, judges lean over the bench and sound a warning against
future misdeeds, probation officers run through the conditions with which
the minor is required to comply. Who is the lawyer? Just another person
with a word or two of advice of her own, another piece of this system that,
looked at most charitably, wants to do everything it can to keep the juvenile from messing up again. The system is full of finger-wagging lecturers,
and the minor has every reason to expect precisely the same from his
lawyer. Indeed, that is usually precisely what he gets. These lectures may
all be well meaning, but a minor, on the defensive and angry with authority, will have little interest in listening to, let alone crediting, the advice
provided.

If the lawyer succeeds in establishing the relationship, however, the minor will have every reason to listen. He will probably have developed
some respect for the views of the lawyer, but, even short of that, he will
know the motivation behind the information and advice. He will know

that the voice of the lawyer is distinct from the punishing system. He will also know that the advice is offered to aid in his own decision making and is not an attempt to overpower his own judgment.

Lev Vygotsky, a prominent Russian developmentalist whose influence in the West has grown in recent years, has focused considerable attention on the role of supportive adults in facilitating developmental progress (1978). He relies on the metaphor of scaffolding to illustrate how adults help children move from one level of understanding to the next. To borrow and distort his metaphor for my own purposes, let me suggest the following: one's willingness to climb onto the scaffolding built by another depends upon one's confidence that the scaffolding will hold and a belief that it will take one where one wants to go. Vygotsky's scaffolding is, most classically, built by parents, teachers, or adults within a child's cultural community. In this context, a child has every reason to trust the edifice. In our context, however, the juvenile will have to get to know the builder before he will be willing to climb on.

Many forms of trial competence might be particularly well facilitated by instruction and the giving of advice, assuming the instructor/advisor has a willing listener and that the instruction can be backed up with other learning aids, such as observation and participation. The trial process, the issues at stake, the parties involved, and the strategic decisions to be made all will be captured most completely and with greatest nuance where observation and participation can be reinforced and embellished through verbal description.

Facilitating Good Decision Making   The quality of the minor's decisions (about trial strategy and the ultimate goals of representation) might also be influenced by discussion with the lawyer, but here, I think, a lawyer's expectation for influence should be modest. To the extent that the poor quality of adolescent decision making reflects not a flawed decision-making process but rather a different weighing of the options, a lawyer should take care in how forcefully she pushes to persuade her client to reweigh. A lawyer who has gained the respect of her client will have more credibility when she pushes her client to reassess his priorities, but there is only so far that a lawyer can push in that direction without undermining precisely the relationship on which the respect is grounded. The ultimate choices must be those of the client, and any resistance expressed by the lawyer that focuses on the ends chosen, rather than the process of decision making, threatens to undermine the client's belief in his control.

There is one form of client decision making against which the lawyer's demonstration of resistance is appropriate. Where minors choose not to get involved, to avoid even conveying to their lawyers a coherent story of their behavior at the time of the arrest or the reported commission of the crime, the lawyer should resist the client's choice of apathy or disengagement vigorously. Again, the building of the relationship interrelates with the enhancement of adjudicative competence once the relationship is built. After a professional friendship is formed, a client is far less likely to try to opt out of participation and engagement, but where the client does make such choices, it is not only appropriate but essential for the lawyer to push the client to reconsider.

Facilitating Value   This last scenario brings us back to my speculation that minors place less value on their trial rights and on the adjudicatory process than do adults. If this is in fact the case, it seems sensible to conclude that the development of a professional friendship between lawyer and client is likely to increase the minor's appetite for the exercise of rights, particularly participatory rights. While it is difficult to make the point without sounding trite, an adolescent who has had the experience of being shown respect and deference may begin to see himself as someone who has something to say that people ought to hear and to see the process as one that listens. Learning from the lawyer that his view is important is likely to translate into a greater commitment on his part to making that view heard. This valuing of participation may, in turn, translate into a greater valuing of individual rights, for it is through these rights that control over one's own participation is exercised. It may also translate into a stronger sense of connection to the entire justice system—a system perceived as inclusive and fair in large part because of its grounding in a system of legal representation that provides the accused with a zealous advocate who, in the context of the litigation, embraces the accused's goals as her own.

Conclusion

In the end, I reach the unremarkable conclusion that lawyers must spend more time with their clients in order to facilitate their competence. I want to emphasize again, however, that it's not just any kind of time, but rather time spent drawing the child into the professional friendship. Increasing time spent preparing for court that doesn't involve the client directly may improve the quality of lawyering, but it will do nothing to enhance a minor's competence. Increasing the time spent with the minor on matters not related to the case may enhance feelings of affection between lawyer and client, but could just as easily undermine as enhance the minor's understanding of the trial process and his rights therein.

   Calling for lawyers to spend more time with their clients is generally perceived as politically unachievable—lawyers cannot spend more time with their clients unless their caseloads are dramatically reduced, which would require states to pay for many more lawyers for this unpopular group. In recognition of the fact that giving lawyers the time to forge professional friendships with their clients may not be achievable, I should also state my thesis in the negative: in the absence of true lawyer-client professional relationships, lawyers can expect to have little, if any, effect on their client's trial competence. Indeed, where the lawyer fails to forge professional friendships, she is likely affirmatively to undermine adjudicative competence by introducing minors to yet another player who reinforces the minors' silence and confusion.

Works Cited

Ainsworth, J. 1991. Re-imagining childhood and reconstructing the legal order: The case for the abolishing the juvenile court. *North Carolina Law Review* 69:1083.

Appelbaum, P. S., C. N. Lidz, and A. Meisel. 1987. *Informed consent: Legal theory and clinical practice.* New York: Oxford University Press.

Belter, R., and T. Grisso. 1984. Children's recognition of rights violations in counseling. *Professional Psychology: Research and Practice* 15:899–910.

Buss, E. 1996. You're my what? The problem of children's misperception of their lawyer's roles. *Fordham Law Review* 64:1699–1762.

———. 1999. Confronting developmental barriers to the empowerment of child clients. *Cornell Law Review* 84:895–966.

Cauffman, E. and L. Steinberg. 1995. The cognitive and affective influences on adolescent decision-making. *Temple Law Review* 68:1763–89.

Cowden, L., and G. McKee. 1994–95. Competency to stand trial in juvenile delinquency proceedings—cognitive maturity and the attorney-client relationship. *Journal of Family Law* 33 (3): 629–60.

Fried, C. 1976. The lawyer as friend: The moral foundations of the lawyer-client relation. *Yale Law Journal* 85:1060–89.

Grisso, T. 1981. *Juveniles' Waiver of Rights.* New York: Plenum Press.

———. 1983. Children's consent in delinquency proceedings. In *Children's competence to consent,* edited by G. Melton, G. Koocher, and M. Saks. New York: Plenum Press.

———. 1997. The competence of adolescents as trial defendants. *Psychology, Public Policy, and Law* 3:3–32.

Kohlberg, L. 1986. *The psychology of moral development.* New York: Harper and Row.

Lefcourt, H. 1976. *Locus of control: Current trends in theory and research.* Hillsdale, N.J.: Lawrence Erlbaum Associates.

Melton, G. 1980. Children's concepts of their rights. *Journal of Clinical Child Psychology* 9:186–90.

———. 1982. Teaching children about their rights. In *The rights of children: Legal and psychological perspectives,* edited by J. Henning. Springfield, Ill.: Charles C. Thomas.

Moss, D. 1987. *In re Gault* now 20, but. . . . *American Bar Association Journal* 29.

Nowicki, S. and B. Strickland. 1973. A locus of control scale for children. *Journal of Consulting and Clinical Psychology* 40:148–54.

Prothrow-Stith, D. 1991. *Deadly consequences.* New York: Harper Collins.

Puritz, P. 1995. *A call for justice.* Washington, D.C.: American Bar Association Juvenile Justice Center.

Reicher, S. and N. Emler. 1985. Delinquent behavior and attitudes to formal authority. *British Journal of Social Psychology* 24:161–68.

Rogoff, B. 1990. *Apprenticeship in thinking: Cognitive development in social context.* New York: Oxford University Press.

Rosenberg, M. 1985. Self-concept and psychological well-being in adolescence. In *The development of the self,* edited by R. Leahy. Orlando, Fla.: Academic Press, Inc.

Roth, L. H., A. Meisel, and C. W. Lidz. 1977. Tests of competency to consent to treatment. *American Journal of Psychiatry* 134:279–84.

Rotter, J. B. 1966. Generalized expectancies for internal versus external control of reinforcement. *Psychological Monographs* 80 (1) Whole no. 609.

Scott, E., N. Reppucci, and J. Woolard. 1995. Evaluating adolescent decision making in legal contexts. *Law and Human Behavior* 19:221–44.

Selman, R. 1980. *The growth of interpersonal understanding.* New York: Academic Press.

Selman, R. and L. Schultz. 1990. *Making a friend in youth: Developmental theory and pair therapy.* Chicago: University of Chicago Press.

Selman, R., C. Watts, and L. Schultz, eds. 1997. *Fostering friendship: Pair therapy for treatment and prevention.* New York: Aldine de Gruyter.

Sylva, K. and I. Lunt. 1982. *Child development: A first course.* London: G. McIntyre.

Tyler, T. 1984. The role of perceived injustice in defendant's evaluations of their courtroom experience. *Law and Society Review* 18:51–74.

Vygotsky, L. 1978. *Mind in society: The development of higher psychological processes.* Cambridge: Harvard University Press.

———. 1962. *Thought and language.* Cambridge: The M.I.T. Press and John Wiley and Sons, Inc.

Wood, D. 1988. *How children think and learn.* Oxford: Basil Blackwell.

Notes

1. See *In re Gault,* 387 US 1 (1967).

2. In *In re Gault,* the Court grounded its recognition of a juvenile's right to counsel in part on the conclusion that minors, like Gerald Gault, often faced far more severe restrictions on their liberty than their adult counterparts.

3. In fact, it may be somewhat artificial to separate the grasp of the concept from the understanding of the concept's value. Where a child's sense of the importance of adults' viewpoints produces deference to adults in the exercise of rights, that experience, in turn, reinforces a minor's sense that rights are not absolute.

4. This is the consensus position among practitioners and scholars about the role of counsel in delinquency proceedings and, in my view, reflects the most co-

herent interpretation of the right to counsel recognized in *Gault.* There are, however, courts that have ascribed to counsel for juveniles the role of identifying the child's best interests and advocating those interests, even against the client's wishes, before the court. See *In Interest of K.M.B.* 462 N.E.2d 1271 (Ill. App. 1984).

5. See Thomas Grisso, 1983. Juveniles' consent in delinquency proceedings. In *Children's Competence to Consent,* edited by Gary B. Melton et al., 131, 143, which reported the results of a study that suggested that children were three times as likely as adults to believe that their lawyer would stop advocating on their behalf if they admitted their guilt to the lawyer.

6. *Dusky:* 362 US 402 (1960); *Godinez:* 509 US 389, 400 (1993).

7. See *Jackson v. Indiana,* 406 US 715, 738 (1971): State may hold defendant found to lack the capacity to stand trial only for "the reasonable period of time necessary to determine whether there is a substantial probability that he will attain that capacity in the foreseeable future."

8. ABA Model Rules of Professional Conduct Rule 1.4(b).

9. Again, reference to children's development of intimate friendships in the peer context is illuminating. See, for example, Dennis Barr, 1997. Friendship and Belonging in Fostering Friendship: Pair Therapy for Treatment and Prevention, edited by R. Selman, C. Watts, and L. Schultz. "When friends disclose personal information to one another, the friendship is reaffirmed and strengthened by their willingness and capacity to maintain the privacy of the information." See also William Damon, The Social World of the Child 161–62, suggesting that the basis of friendship in adolescence is the "sharing with each other [of] innermost thoughts, feelings, and other secrets."

10. See, for example, Conn. Gen. Stat. Ann. § 46b–137 (West 1998).

11. Lawyers can demonstrate this deference to their clients during their initial interview (if parents are present) by first talking to the child alone and then offering the child the option of inviting his parents in for a second phase of discussion. Where the minor indicates his willingness to include his parents, the lawyer should then walk him through each matter discussed between them, to determine on which subjects the minor wishes to receive parental input and/or knowledge and to reinforce the lesson of child control.

12. Such troubles can have a dramatic effect on his case by, for example, undermining his ability to remain in the community or threatening his compliance with probationary conditions.

13. Model Rules 1.14.

PART THREE

Culpability and Youths' Capacities

The law has always recognized circumstances or cases in which individuals were not fully culpable for the offenses with which they were charged. Criminal law, for example, has long recognized reduced culpability (resulting in dispositions of "not guilty by reason of mental illness" or "diminished responsibility") for some persons whose mental illnesses or developmental disabilities impaired their capacities in ways that related to their ability to appreciate or control their actions.

As several chapters in Part III explain, the developmental immaturity of children has also been a basis for presuming reduced culpability under various circumstances in the tradition and history of law. Children younger than seven, for example, have generally not been seen as capable of forming the necessary intent for acts that would otherwise be considered crimes. Thus they have not been considered culpable at all within the framework of criminal law.

But how society has construed the culpability of children has been more variable for youths in later childhood and the adolescent years. The topic received little attention during the first half of the twentieth century, largely because the question of youths' culpability was conceptually irrelevant. In the early juvenile justice system, youths were not given sentences that reflected the full culpability that society assigned to adults who committed similar acts. Largely within the past decade, however, many state legislatures have made it possible for younger adolescents, when alleged to have committed certain offenses, to be charged automatically under criminal law, tried in adult court, and receive sentences formerly reserved for adults.

Under these circumstances, it is necessary for society to raise questions about youths' culpability that were not so pressing earlier in the century. When youths engage in illegal behaviors, do they do so with the same capacities as adults? For example, do they have the same abilities as adults for anticipating the consequences of their actions? Are they responding to developmentally related motivations—for example, the strong influence that peers have on adolescents' choices and behaviors—that should be weighed when we are considering their degree of culpability? Indeed, what capacities are relevant to consider when examining questions of mitigation regarding youths' culpability and the legal responses that are appropriate? At what age is it reasonable to assume that those capacities have matured sufficiently to warrant attributions of culpability that we associate with "full" punishment under the law?

These are the questions addressed in Part III. Chapter 10 explores the logic for a proportionately different legal response to youths' transgressions than that provided to adults. The historical legal notion of culpability is discussed, and the chapter introduces the social and psychological rationale for a system of justice that recognizes youths' reduced culpability as a matter of law and policy. This logic is continued in Chapter 11 with a closer examination of the developmental and psychological characteristics of adolescence that can inform policy regarding reduced culpability when adolescents are accused of offenses. Much of the rationale is found to be based on developmental theories that have not yet been tested in empirical research on relevant developmental characteristics. For example, developmental theory suggests that the ability or inclination to consider long-range consequences of one's behavior is not fully developed in adolescence. Yet there has not been sufficient research to support or question this assertion. Chapter 12 examines research that has addressed such questions and describes further research that will be needed to provide a solid foundation for society's decisions concerning whether to punish youths in a manner that presumes their culpability to be adultlike.

The remaining two chapters in Part III consider questions of culpability from specific theoretical perspectives derived from developmental psychology, social psychology, and sociology. Chapter 13 examines the potential application of social-cognitive (attribution) theory to further our conceptualization of the issue of youths' culpability. For example, to what extent do adolescents attribute their own behaviors to circumstances that they can or cannot avoid, and is there a developmental difference between adolescents and adults in this regard? Chapter 14 offers a perspective based on the notion of scripts for adolescents' presentation of self in social situations, and uses this theoretical platform to explore factors that may influence youths' decisions in everyday life. Both chapters have implications for the debate about the degree to which youths' developmental status warrants a different assignment of culpability to their illegal behaviors than is typically attributed to adults.

Several concepts unite the chapters in this section. One is the nature of youths' choices, especially cognitive and attitudinal characteristics that influence their decisions and that may still be in the process of developing to the level that is typical for adults. The other is the contextual nature of those choices. The way in which youths approach decisions on the street and in other aspects of everyday life is influenced by social factors, such as peer and parent influences, that have a developmental quality differing from the social contexts in which most adults make choices about their behaviors.

Whether society's responses to youthful offenders *should* recognize their reduced culpability is a larger question than the one addressed in Chapters 10 through 14. In Chapter 15, however, a former juvenile court judge looks at the research and suggests ways in which the existence of the juvenile court recognizes that adolescents are, indeed, less culpable than adults. The author suggests that the complexity of adolescent crime, combined with questions of competence, require the existence of a juvenile court that provides strong procedural safeguards. The need for searching inquiry requires a well-trained coterie of juvenile court personnel, low caseloads, unwaivable right to counsel, and prompt appellate review. Properly run, it is argued, the juvenile court remains a suitable agent of justice for adolescent offenders.

Taken together, these chapters explore the developmental and social psychological foundation upon which a legal policy of reduced culpability could be based, and they identify what more we need to know in order to complete that foundation. Once that is done, society will have the information about adolescent development that should be weighed, along with other societal concerns, in shaping a rational legal response to adolescents and their offenses.

CHAPTER TEN

Penal Proportionality for the Young Offender: Notes on Immaturity, Capacity, and Diminished Responsibility

FRANKLIN E. ZIMRING

At its core, Anglo American criminal law is about punishment—about the intentional infliction of harm on persons who have committed blameworthy acts. We punish because we believe such harm is morally deserved by a particular individual for a particular act. To do this, the criminal law needs to make sense as a language of moral desert, punishing only those who deserve condemnation, punishing the guilty only to the extent of their individual moral desert, and punishing the range of variously guilty offenders it apprehends in an order that reflects their relative blameworthiness. Of course the perfect satisfaction of these standards is always beyond human capacity, but the legitimacy of a system of criminal punishment depends on recognizing the moral obligations of penal proportionality and attempting to meet them. To the extent that institutions of criminal and juvenile justice make punishment decisions about young law violators, they must be servants of the moral obligations of penal proportionality.

The harm caused by a particular criminal act is one important measure of the seriousness of an offense and thus of the amount of punishment it deserves, but the role of harm done in determining deserved criminal punishment is much less dominant than the influence of harm done in the measure of compensation due or owing in civil law. The level of harm suffered determines compensation in the civil system once a liability threshold has been satisfied. But desert is a measure of fault that will attach very different punishment to criminal acts that cause similar amounts of harm.

The Anglo American law of homicide is a spectacular demonstration of the large range of punishments that await persons culpable in causing a death, even though the harm caused is a near constant. The full range in the United States for criminal homicide is typically from probation to capital punishment with a number of intermediate stops (Zimring, Eigen, and O'Malley 1976). An intentional and culpable killing may be first-degree murder, second-degree murder, or voluntary manslaughter (LaFave and Scott 1986, 605–683). Recklessness and negligence lead to multiple categories of criminal liability. Blameworthy intended killings under circumstances of provocation or unreasonable mistake may generate less punishment than some categories of reckless conduct that cause death. A host of subjective elements affect judgments of deserved punishment even though the victim is just as dead in each different case.

This chapter considers one set of subjective personal factors that influence the extent to which adolescent defendants deserve punishment for particular blameworthy acts. I will argue that even when a particular young person possesses the cognitive capacities and social controls necessary to eligibility for punishment, immaturity should continue to be a mitigating circumstance for some time.

This chapter is organized under four parts. Part I attempts to create mutually exclusive definitions of capacity and diminished responsibility to avoid a persisting confusion between threshold issues of capacity and questions of the proper level of punishment for an immature offender. Part II argues that juvenile courts in the United States have been a recognized part of a punishment system for at least a generation. Part III first distinguishes between two separate reasons for smaller punishment of the immature—penal proportionality and theories of youth as a protected and privileged status. The diminished-responsibility doctrine in penal theory is then developed at some length and contrasted to changes in adolescent punishment based on youth policy. Part IV addresses the relationship between assumptions about immaturity that animate various conceptions of diminished responsibility and other legal doctrines that govern adolescence in modern industrial states.

Part I: Immaturity and Desert

One fundamental distinction in the criminal law is between conditions that negate criminal liability and those that might mitigate the punishment deserved under particular circumstances. Very young children and the profoundly mentally ill lack the minimum capacity necessary to justify punishment under a system where blameworthiness is punishment's sine qua non. Those exhibiting less profound handicaps of the same kind that serve as excuses will often qualify for a lesser level of deserved punishment even though they meet the minimum conditions for some punishment.

Those who were searching for illustrations of the difference between excuse and mitigation in the early months of 1998 needed look no further than the sad but well-publicized plea bargain of Theodore Kaczynski, the infamous Unabomber sentenced to life in prison after a negotiated plea of guilty on the eve of his death-penalty trial. A psychiatric diagnosis of this defendant clearly established the existence of serious psychosis. Just as clearly, the defendant was not sufficiently removed by illness from the capacity for moral judgment to excuse his conduct from criminal liability under current law. Under the circumstances of this case, the trial judge would not even have allowed the defense team to raise the defendant's profound mental illness as an absolute defense to the criminal charges.

The general principle that mental illness that should not excuse can mitigate is well established (see American Law Institute 1980 Model Penal Code 210.3[1][b]). Thus, the same disease conditions that could not excuse Kaczynski's conduct might well mitigate his deserved punishment, and this was the prospect that could justify the government in agreeing to a less-than-death sentence. With respect to the death penalty there are common law, constitutional, and statutory discussions of mitigation not found in current law on imprisonment or other punishments.

Immaturity, like mental disease or defect, might serve both as an excuse and as a mitigation in the determination of just punishment. But this double duty has frequently led to confusion between the criteria and proper ages for immaturity to function as an excuse, and the criteria and proper age boundaries for mitigation. Part of this confusion is solely linguistic. Terms such as "capacity," "culpability," and "responsibility" are quite slippery. For the purposes of this chapter, I wish to use the term "capacity" rather restrictively, to refer to the cognitive- and experientially based abilities that are necessary at minimum before punitive sanctions may properly be imposed in either a juvenile or a criminal court.

In a simple world, the matter of capacity could be a totally binary concept, something a particular youth either has for all purposes or lacks. In the real world, different thresholds of competence may apply, depending first on the kind of court and kind of punishment involved and, second, on the type of task that a finding of competence applies to. But my use of the term "competence" restricts it to binary determinations of minimum conditions of punishment eligibility.

I want to restrict the term "diminished responsibility" to circumstances where the minimum abilities for blameworthiness and thus for punishment exist but the immaturity of the offender still suggests that less punishment is justified by reason of the offender's immaturity. While the elements of capacity were limited in the previous discussion to moral reasoning and minimal social information and experience, the personal deficits that could count toward immaturity as a mitigation of punishment might be more numerous.

The use of restrictive and mutually exclusive definitions makes it possible to make two points that are no less important to legal policy because of their simplicity. In the first place, a finding of minimal capacity is in no way logically inconsistent with concluding that an offender's immaturity is a reason for mitigating the punishment imposed on him or her. The definitions I've imposed would make any argument of this kind a confusion between capacity concerns (excuse in relation to liability) and diminished-responsibility concerns (mitigation of punishment).

The second preliminary point is not quite so simple, but involves the systematic relationship between standards for competence and the theoretical and practical importance of diminished responsibility in criminal sentencing. Once personal capacity is relevant to the moral measure of punishment, we should expect to observe an inverse relationship between whether a minimum-capacity test screens out troublesome cases and the importance of assessing diminished responsibility for punishment purposes. The more significant the capacity stage, the less significant will be the role of diminished-responsibility concerns in keeping the punishment system morally coherent.

The criminal law of mental illness provides an illustration of this theory of inverse importance. Assume two competing standards for when mental illness excuses persons who commit forbidden behaviors from criminal liability. Under a very restrictive McNaughton standard, relatively few mentally ill persons will be excused from criminal liability since the standard requires that a defendant not appreciate the wrongfulness of his conduct before the excuse will hold. Under the much more liberal Durham rule, a larger proportion of mentally ill defendants will be excused from any criminal liability because the excuse will apply whenever it is found that the otherwise criminal act was the product of a mental disease. If serious mental illness is a moral concern relevant to punishment, where will the law and procedure relating to mitigating punishment by reason of mental illness be more important, in a liberal Durham jurisdiction or in a restrictive McNaughton jurisdiction?

The relative importance of diminished responsibility should be greater in the McNaughton jurisdiction, because the more liberal rules of excuse in a Durham jurisdiction will divert many more defendants away from being eligible for a criminal sentence, including a large number of those defendants with the most profound mental illnesses. By contrast, the more restrictive McNaughton rule will push a much larger proportion of its mentally ill defendants through to criminal sentencing, including many of the sickest. There will be a larger number of cases to consider for mitigation of punishment, and a larger range of types and severity of mental illness to be measured against the moral compass of the criminal law of sentencing. The stricter the standard of excluding the mentally ill, the more important the doctrines and procedures that calibrate mitigations of punishment. (On this reasoning, the maximum importance for a diminished-responsibility system would come in a system that rejects a defense of insanity but admits the relevance of mental illness. See Norval Morris, *Madness and the Criminal Law.*)

With regard to the punishment of the immature, the same inverse-importance principle applies. If no offender under eighteen was eligible for punishment because the system diverted all below that age out at the capacity stage, the role of diminished responsibility would be much less important than if a system found minimum capacity at age twelve or thirteen. The younger the age at which we deemed kids eligible for some punishment, the more important would be the role of principles of mitigation of punishment based on immaturity.

The implications of any such inverse relationship between excuse and mitigation for immaturity are substantial in the United States at this moment in our history. Every trend in recent legislation in this country seems calculated to increase the importance of doctrines of mitigation on account of immaturity as an influence on sentencing. Mandatory and discretionary waiver of adolescent offenders to criminal courts, lowering of the minimum ages for eligibility for transfer from juvenile to criminal court, and increasing the severity and penal context of sanctions administered within juvenile courts all have the tendency to put additional pressure on doctrines of mitigation to avoid injustice in the punishment of young offenders. The collective impact of all three trends is to place unprecedented importance on the ability of American criminal and juvenile courts to generate coherent doctrines of diminished responsibility on account of immaturity for the huge and diverse assortment of young offenders who are now regarded to be eligible for some punishment. Every new reduction in the threshold of penal capacity makes the role of the diminished-capacity doctrine more important in maintaining a system of penal proportionality.

But what should be the content and boundaries of such doctrines? What aspects of American adolescence are relevant to the proper punishment for crimes committed by the young? This is a question of not only analytic matters, but rather an issue that requires hands-on knowledge of youth and youth policy to answer. After a short discussion of further conceptual distinctions in Part II, such an empirically informed assessment is discussed in the third section of this chapter.

Part II: Delinquency and the Aims of the Juvenile Court

Is there an age or level of capacity below which no child should be subjected to the delinquency jurisdiction of the juvenile court? The answer to this question depends on whether the delinquency docket of the juvenile court should be regarded as punitive in nature. If not, there is no need to find any minimum standard of accountability or ability to assist a defense counsel. No minimum age or level of capacity is necessary for a juvenile court to take dependency jurisdiction or to investigate neglect. If the sole aim of delinquency jurisdiction were the assistance and the best interests of the minor, then kids of any age and capacity would be eligible for such help, no matter the level of their comprehension.

For this reason, the original theory of juvenile justice probably would not have required any minimum level of comprehension or desert prior to a delinquency finding (Zimring 1982, 31–40). Just as clearly, the U.S. Constitution now requires some minimum level of penal responsibility and comprehension prior to affixing the delinquency label. The constitutional precedent for this requirement is *In re Gault,* a case more often noted for its procedural rulings than for the substantive assumption at the heart of the ruling. What juvenile courts do to young persons classified as delinquent was enough like punishment in the view of the *Gault* Court so that a large number of criminal-style procedural regularities were necessary to satisfy the due process guarantee of the Fifth Amendment.

As a matter of constitutional law, then, we have known for a generation that those who administer juvenile court delinquency dockets are in the business of punishing adolescent law violators. Once this is conceded, it is also apparent that juvenile and criminal courts in the United States have been operating a large system with relatively low standards of penal capacity but with reduced sanctions that fit closely to a model of diminished responsibility in juvenile courts and probably in criminal courts as well. If this reading of the juvenile court is correct, the dominant impact of immaturity on punishment in the United States is reduction of punishment on account of diminished responsibility.

What is extraordinary about this huge diminished-responsibility system operating across two large and independent judicial branches is the absence of either explicit recognition of this fact or any legal standards for describing this diminished-responsibility system.

Indeed, many observers deny the character of the system. Transfer to criminal courts is often debated as if it were a precondition for punishing young persons arrested for crime. What the juvenile court does in this view is not "real" punishment, however that term might be defined. The confusion here may be between the character of a sanction and its quantity. Delinquents in juvenile courts may be receiving punishment, but not as much punishment as is administered to older offenders in other courts. But the lower dose does not change the fundamental character of the medicine.

In the United States, there is a massive establishment that administers punitive sanctions short of full adult penalties for proportionality reasons that never get mentioned or analyzed. In terms of the inverse significance of capacity and diminished responsibly discussed in the previous section, the major operating principle at work in this country, at least since the 1960s, is diminished capacity—all the more reason to wonder about the substantive standards being used in this unarticulated and unself-conscious punishment enterprise.

What should be the articulated standards for such a system? That is the topic of the next section.

Part III: Foundations of Special Punishments for Adolescents

For a variety of reasons, little has been written about the substantive arguments that support a separate policy toward crimes committed by young offenders. Part of the problem is that debate about procedures and jurisdiction crowds out any issues of the substantive content of a youth-crime policy (Zimring 1998), and another part of the problem is that juvenile- and criminal-court issues are usually considered separately, so that there's little pressure exerted to examine the same questions across different procedural settings. A further deterrent to substantive analysis is that separate treatment of children seems intuitively right in a way that does not invite further scrutiny from its advocates. Of course kids who violate laws should be treated differently; should we imprison six-year-olds? Legal nuance and complexity might seem beside the point in this context. For all these reasons, no sustained analysis of the factors that justify separate treatment of adolescent offenders is in the literature to measure against the known facts on serious youth violence.

Some years ago, I suggested that two general policy clusters were at work in youth-crime policy: diminished responsibility due to immaturity and special efforts designed to give young offenders room to reform in the course of adolescent years. The issues grouped under the "diminished capacity" heading relate to the traditional concerns of the criminal law; these matters tell us why a criminal lawyer might regard a younger offender as less culpable than an older offender. The cluster of policies under the heading of "room to reform" are derived from legal policies toward young persons in the process of growing up. They do not concern penal desert.

Dimensions of Diminished Responsibility

The consideration of immaturity as a species of diminished responsibility has some historic precedent but little analytic history. Children below seven were at common law not responsible for criminal acts by reason of incapacity while those between seven and fourteen were the subject of special inquiries with respect to capacity. Capacity in this sense was not a question of degree, but an "all or nothing" matter similar to legal insanity as discussed in Part I. Yet diminished-culpability logic argues that even after a youth passes the minimum threshold of competence that leads to a finding of capacity to commit crime, the barely competent youth is not as culpable and therefore not as deserving of a full measure of punishment as a fully qualified adult offender. Just as psychiatric disorder or cognitive impairment that does not render a subject exempt from the criminal law might still mitigate the punishment to be imposed, so a minimally competent adolescent should not be responsible for the whole of an adult's desert for the same act.

Part I argued that this notion of diminished culpability as a limiting influence on criminal punishment is not an isolated element of juvenile jurisprudence but rather one expression of a core value in Anglo American criminal law—the notion of penal proportionality.

Yet the absence of analysis about penal proportionality for early- and middle adolescents is particularly puzzling. Despite the universal acceptance of immaturity in doctrines of infancy and the widespread acceptance of reduced levels of responsibility in early teen years, there has been little analysis of the aspects of immaturity that are relevant to mitigation of punishment. Again, the intuitive appeal of the result and the separate categories of juvenile and criminal jurisprudence may have deferred the analysis of its rationale. Yet the specific attributes of legal immaturity must be discovered before judgments can be made about what ages and conditions are relevant to reducing punishment on this ground.

Part II argued that the entirety of the delinquency jurisdiction of the juvenile court can be seen as an institutional expression of the diminished culpability of youthful offenders. The lesser maximum punishments of serious crime in juvenile court can be seen as testimony to the belief in youthful diminished culpability, but this set of practices is at best mute testimony, lacking any statement of principles that can be analyzed and criticized. Further, when this concept of proportionality is expressed only in the institutional output of one court system, the transfer of offenders from the juvenile to criminal court would risk changing the applicable penal principles without justification.

What characteristics of children and adolescents might lead us to lessen punishment in the name of penal proportionality? An initial distinction needs to be drawn between diminished responsibilities and the poor decisions such impairments encourage. Most teenaged law violators make bad decisions, but so do most adults who commit major infractions of the criminal law. Anglo American criminal law is designed to punish bad decisions in full measure. But persons who through no fault of their own lack the abilities observed in the common citizen either to appreciate the difference between wrong and allowable conduct or to conform their conduct to the law's requirements may be blameless because of their incapacity. Even when sufficient cognitive skill and emotional control is present to pass the threshold of criminal capacity, a significant deficit in the ability to appreciate or control behavior would mean the forbidden conduct is not as much the offender's fault as it would otherwise be, and the quantum of appropriate punishment is less.

How might fourteen-, fifteen-, and seventeen-year-olds who commit crimes be said to exhibit diminished responsibility in moral and legal terms? There are three different types of personal attributes that influence adolescents' decisions to commit crimes. In each case, the adolescents may lack full adult skills and therefore also full adult moral responsibilities when the law is violated.

First, older children and younger adolescents may lack fully developed cognitive abilities to comprehend the moral content of commands and to apply legal and moral rules to social situations. The lack of this kind of capacity is at the heart of infancy as an absolute defense to criminal liability. This ability to comprehend and apply rules in the abstract requires a mix of cognitive ability and information. A young person who lacks these skills will not do well on a paper-and-pencil test to assess knowledge about what is lawful and unlawful behavior and why. Very young children have obvious gaps in both information and the cognitive skills to use it. Older children have more subtle, but nonetheless significant, deficits in moral-reasoning abilities. For most normal adolescents, the ability to reason in an adult style is present by age sixteen or, at the latest, seventeen (Steinberg and Cauffman 1996, 268).

The ability to pass paper-and-pencil tests in moral reasoning may be one necessary condition for adult capacity of self-control, but it is by no means a sufficient condition. A second skill that is required to transform cognitive understanding into the fully developed capacity to obey the law is the ability to control impulses. This is not the type of skill that can be tested well on abstract written or oral surveys. Long after a child knows that taking property is wrong, the capacity to resist temptation may not be fully operational.

To an important extent, self-control is a habit of behavior developed over a period of time—a habit dependent on the experience of successfully exercising self-control. This particular type of maturity, like so many others, takes practice. While children must start learning to control impulses at a very early age, the question of how long the process continues until adult levels of behavioral control are achieved is an open one.

Impulse control is a social skill not easily measured in a laboratory. We also do not know the extent to which lessons to control impulses are generalized, nor do we know how context-specific habits of self-control are. Kids must learn not to dash in front of cars at an early age. How much of that capacity for self-control carries over when other impulses—say the temptation to cheat on a test—occur in new situations? The assessment of self-control in field settings is not a thick chapter in current psychological knowledge. The developmental psychology of self-control has been studied by question-and-answer hypotheticals and not by the observation of behavior in natural settings.

There may also be an important distinction between impulse control in the context of frustration and impulse control in temptation settings. If so, the frustration context may be the more important one for study of the determinants of youth violence. When should we expect adult levels of control of violent impulses while angry? Almost certainly the developing adolescent can only learn his or her way to fully developed control by experience. This process will probably not be completed until very late in the teen years.

To the extent that new situations and opportunities require new habits of self-control, the teen years are periods when self-control issues are confronted on a series of distinctive new battlefields. The physical controls of earlier years are supplanted by physical freedoms. New domains—including secondary education, sex, and driving—require not only the cognitive appreciation of the need for self-control in a new situation but also its practice. If this normally takes a while to develop, the bad decisions made along the way should not be punished as severely as they are for adults, who have already had full opportunity to develop habits of self-control in a variety of domains relevant to the criminal law. To the extent that inexperience is associated with being error prone, this inexperience is partially excusable in the teen years whereas it is not in later life. That is the basis for a mitigation for adolescents that is not available for most adults.

The ability to resist peer pressure is yet another social skill that is a necessary part of legal obedience not fully developed in many adolescents. A teen may know right from wrong and may even have developed the capacity to control his or her impulses while alone, but resisting temptation while alone is a different task than resisting the pressure to commit an offense when adolescent peers are pushing for misbehavior and waiting to see whether or not the outcome they desire will occur. Most adolescent decisions to break the law take place on a social stage where the immediate pressure of peers is the real motive for most teenage crime. A necessary condition for an adolescent to stay law-abiding is the ability to

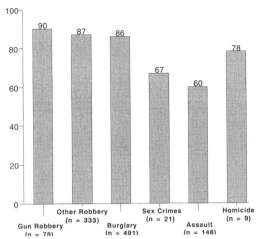

10.1 Multiple offender cases as a percentage of total juveniles charged, by crime, New York City. Source: Zimring 1981.

deflect or resist peer pressure. Many kids lack this crucial social skill for a long time.

Figure 10.1 shows the percentage of juvenile defendants who were accused of committing a crime with at least one confederate in the New York City juvenile courts of the 1970s. These offenders were all under sixteen at the time the act was committed. The percentage of total defendants who acted with a confederate ranged from 60 percent for assault to 90 percent for robbery.

The cold criminological facts are these: the teen years are characterized by what has long been called "group offending." No matter the crime, if a teenager is the offender, he is usually not committing the offense alone. When adults commit theft, they usually are acting alone. When kids commit theft, it's usually in groups. When adults commit rape, robbery, homicide, burglary, or assault, they usually are acting alone. When adolescents commit the same offenses, they usually do so accompanied by other kids (Zimring 1981). The setting for the offenses of adolescents is the presence of delinquent peers as witnesses and collaborators.

No fact of adolescent criminality is more important than what sociologists call its "group context," and this fact is important to a reality-based theory of adolescent moral and legal responsibility for criminal acts.

When an adult offender commits rape, his incitement to action may be rage or lust or any number of other things. When a teen offender in a group setting commits rape, an important part of the motive is social—usually "I dare you," or "Don't be a chicken." Fear of being called "chicken" is almost certainly the major cause of death and injury from youth violence in the United States—the explicit or implicit "I dare you" leads kids to show off and deters them from publicly backing out of committing crimes even if they would prefer to. "I dare you" is the reason that "having delinquent friends" both precedes an adolescent's involvement in violence and is a discriminant predictor of future violence (Howell and Hawkins 1998; Elliott and Menard 1996).

How does this propensity for group crime amount to diminished responsibility? That social settings account for the majority of all youth crime suggests that the capacity to deflect or resist peer pressure is a crucially necessary dimension of being law-abiding in adolescence. Dealing with peer pressure is another dimension of capacity that requires social experience. Kids who do not know how to deal with such pressure lack effective control of the situations that place them most at risk of crime in their teens. This surely does not excuse criminal conduct. But any moral scheme that gives mitigational recognition to other forms of inexperience must also do so for a lack of peer-management skills that an accused has not had a fair opportunity to develop. This is a matter of great importance given the reality of contemporary youth crime as group behavior.

I do not want to suggest that current knowledge is sufficient for us to measure the extent of diminished capacity in young offenders, nor do I want to express in detail the types of understanding and control that are important parts of a normative developmental psychology. We have a great deal of social psychology homework ahead of us here before achieving an understanding of the key terms in adolescent behavioral controls relevant to criminal offending in field settings.

There are, however, two important points to be made about age and diminished responsibility even in the current state of partial knowledge. The first principle about adolescent development and age boundaries for diminished responsibilities is that the ages where the legal system can expect adult-level abilities depends on the range of experience that is regarded as important. If only the cognitive capacity to make judgments in paper-and-pencil exercises is important, then adolescents are usually well equipped by their sixteenth birthdays. But if social experience in matters such as anger and impulse-management also counts, and a fair opportunity to learn to deal with peer pressures is regarded as important, expecting the experienced-based ability to resist impulses and peers to be fully formed prior to age eighteen or nineteen would seem on present evidence to be wishful thinking. Becoming an adult is a gradual process in modern industrial societies. Ironically, the process may start earlier but still take longer to complete than in earlier eras (Zimring 1982, 17–22). Partial responsibility for law violation may come at a young age but full responsibility should take longer.

The second thing to remember about diminished responsibility is that it is not merely a doctrine of juvenile justice but a principle of penal proportionality. The nature of adolescent immaturity would raise the same issues we now confront in juvenile justice even if all young offenders were tried in criminal courts. In other words, even if there were no separate youth policy to consult in making decisions about younger offenders and even if there were no juvenile court, the just punishment of young offenders would still be a distinctive moral and legal problem. So, changes in the jurisdictional boundaries of juvenile and criminal courts do not remove the necessity of determining variations in moral desert.

Room to Reform in Youth-Development Policy

The notion that children and adolescents should be the subject of special legal rules pervades the civil as well as criminal laws of most developed societies. There are a multiplicity of different policies reflected in different legal areas, and also important differences throughout law in the treatment of younger and older children. Under these circumstances, referring to a single "youth policy" generally risks misunderstandings about both the subjects of the policies and the age groups covered.

The policies I refer to in this chapter concern adolescence, a period that spans roughly from ages eleven or twelve to about age twenty-one. This is also the only segment of childhood associated with high rates of serious crime. This span has been described as a period of increasing semi-autonomy in which kids acquire adult liberties in stages and learn their way toward adult freedoms along the way (Zimring 1982).

At the heart of this process is a notion of adolescence as a period of "learning by doing" in which the only way competence in decision making can be achieved is by making decisions and making mistakes. For this reason, adolescence is mistake-prone by design. The special challenge here is to create safeguards in the environments of adolescents that reduce the permanent costs of adolescent mistakes. Two goals of legal policy are to facilitate "learning by doing" and to reduce the hazards associated with expectable errors. One important hallmark of a successful adolescence is survival to adulthood, preferably with the individual's life chances intact.

There is a popular theory about the etiology of youth crime that provides a rationale for a room-to-reform policy. The theory is that the high prevalence of offense behavior in the teen years and the rather high rates of incidence for those who offend are transitory phenomena associated with a transitional status and life period (Elliott 1994). Even absent heroic interventions, the conduct that occurs at peak rates in adolescence will level off substantially if and when adolescents achieve adult roles and status.

That assumption carries three implications. First, it regards criminal offenses as a more or less normal adolescent phenomenon, a by-product of the same transitional status that increases the risks of traffic accidents, accidental pregnancies, and suicidal gestures. This view of youth crime tells us, therefore, that policy toward those offenses that are a by-product of adolescence should be a part of larger policies toward youth.

A second implication of the notion that high rates of adolescent crime can be outgrown is that major interventions may not be necessary to reorient offenders. The central notion of what has been called "adolescence-limited" offending is that the cure for youth crime is growing up.

Related to the hope for natural processes of remission over time is the tendency for persons who view youth-crime policy as a branch of youth-development policy to worry that drastic countermeasures that inhibit the natural transition to adulthood may cause more harm than they are worth. If a particular treatment carries risks of severe side effects, it usually should only be elected if failure to use it would risk even more. Those who regard youth crime as a transitional phenomenon see problems of deviance resolving themselves without drastic interventions and are prone to doubt the efficacy of high-risk interventions on utilitarian grounds. So juvenile justice theories with labels such as "radical nonintervention" and "diversion" are a natural outgrowth of the belief that long-term prospects for most young offenders are favorable.

But what about the short term? The current costs of youth crime to the community at large, to other adolescents, and to the offending kids are quite large. How would enthusiasts for juvenile court nonintervention seek to protect the community? Is a room-to-reform policy inconsistent with any punitive responses to adolescent law violation?

The emphasis in youth-development policy is on risk management over a period of transitional high danger. As we have seen, the legal theory that adolescents are not fully mature allows a larger variety of risk-management tactics than are available for dealing with adults. Minors cannot purchase liquor, acquire handguns, buy cigarettes, or pilot planes. Younger adolescents are constrained by curfews and compulsory-education laws. There are special age-graded rules for driving motor vehicles and entering contracts and employment relationships. Many of these rules are to protect the young person from the predation of others. Many are to protect the young person from herself. Many are to protect the community from harmful acts by the young. So there is a rich mixture of risk-management strategies available to reduce the level of harmful consequences from youth crime.

Does this mix of strategies include the punishment of intentional harms? The answer to this question is "yes" from all but the most extreme radical noninterventionists, but attaching negative consequences to youthful offenders is regarded as good policy only up to a point. Youth-development proponents are suspicious of sacrificing the interests of a young person in order to serve as a deterrent example to other youth if the punished offender's interests are substantially prejudiced. Punishing a young offender in ways that significantly diminish later life changes compromises the essential core of a youth-protection policy. There may be circumstances in which drastic punishment is required, but such punishments always violate important elements of youth-development policy and can be tolerated only rarely, in cases of proven need. In this view, punishment begins to be suspicious when it compromises the long-term interests of the targeted young offender.

Part IV: Punishment and the Legal Construction of Adolescence

The account of diminished responsibility and immaturity presented above is only one of a number of competing proposals for measuring the liability of adolescent offenders. It is a characteristic of the current era that there are sharply different proposals for punishment policies toward young offenders that explicitly or implicitly make quite different assumptions about the moral responsibilities of adolescents.

One of the most discouraging features of this continuing debate about punishing youth crime in the United States is the extent to which it is isolated from consideration of other law-related policies toward growing up. When the issue is transfer from juvenile to adult court or the maximum punishment that juvenile courts with blended jurisdiction should have the power to impose, there is rarely much reference to the age boundaries used in other areas of law, or whether the assumptions about adolescent development that particular crime policies advance are consistent with the assumptions about ages of maturity that are made in other regulatory domains. There is, instead, an ad hoc quality to youth-crime policy discussions as if the way in which the juvenile and criminal courts treat young offenders is not related in important ways to other areas of law or to the legal conceptions of adolescent nonoffenders.

I wish to defend a contrary proposition that one measure of the merit of a punishment policy toward young offenders is the degree to which the legal policy on this topic is consistent with the assumptions about adolescent competencies that can be found in other areas of the law. Even if the crime-policy preferences we express are in fact made on an ad hoc basis, one important test of the quality of any punishment policy is whether it says the same things about the nature of growing up in the United States as the legal rules that govern the advancement to adult status in other legal categories.

If consistency with other legal doctrines on age is the criterion, the trend toward early full-penal responsibility is problematic. Failing to regard persons under the age of eighteen as anything other than significantly less mature than adults who meet the full adult standard for punishment contradicts the laws regarding the age of majority in every state in every area of nonpenal law. Yet despite the fact that every state in the United States has legislated some circumstances where persons under eighteen face the criminal courts without any explicit recognition that their young age merits a reduction of the punishment, there is no mention in legislative debate of the fact that persons treated as nonadult for all other purposes are presumably held to adult standards upon criminal conviction. Why is this?

There are two circumstances in which the gap between criminal-liability standards and other legal standards might be other than problematic, but neither saving circumstance is plausible in the United States of the 1990s. In the first place, it could be argued that serious criminal offenders are much more mature than their noncriminal age peers. Of course, to take this seriously would be to suggest that kids who commit serious crimes should be able to drink alcohol and purchase firearms at an earlier age than ordinary teens. The closest example I have seen to this sort of tribute to the maturity of the targets of social control was in an article entitled "In Venezuela 'Year of Rights,' the Police Kill More Youths," published in the *New York Times,* 6 December 1997, in which a Venezuelan official justified his country's jailing policy by alleging that "Latin American minors are not like European minors. Mentally they are adults." Are juvenile armed robbers in the United States also to be considered a discrete category of precocious mental adults?

The second proposition that could harmonize full punishment at young ages with higher ages of privilege and majority is concluding that immaturity on account of youth should not influence the level of punishment deserved by any persons capable of committing crimes. To the extent that immaturity deprives a person of penal capacity, this theory of the irrelevancy of youth would give way to common-law requirements of minimal responsibility, as discussed in Part I. But once capacity is established, why not just treat all lesser levels of immaturity the way the penal law treats bad judgments by adults?

But why would any legal system wish to treat offenses that were partly the result of immaturity as if the immaturity that co-occurs with childhood and adolescence were wholly the young person's fault? One searches in vain for a principled argument to make immaturity a step function of tremendous importance in determining a capacity threshold for punishment but irrelevant thereafter. It may be said that terrible crimes are committed by youths and there is a social necessity for punishment. Whether there is a social necessity for the same level of punishment as for adults is usually not discussed in this context. The implicit assumption is that only two polar alternatives, full penal responsibility or no responsibility, are the field of choice. Certainly the political slogan associated with unmitigated penalties is something of a non sequitur: If you are old enough to do the crime, you are old enough to do the time. (Read literally, this refrain would also remove any requirement of capacity prior to punishment.)

The lack of principle on this question is not limited to the realm of politics. The United States Supreme Court has made important constitutional law on the matter of diminished responsibility by reason of youth in connection with capital punishment with a distressing lack of substantive analysis. *Thompson v. Oklahoma* and *Stanford v. Kentucky* are the two leading cases on youths and capital punishment, and the results in these cases are much easier to state than the principles on which they rest. No state may execute a person for an offense committed under the age of sixteen even though the defendant might properly be found guilty of the highest grade of murder at a younger age than sixteen *(Thompson v. Oklahoma)*. The states may, if they choose, subject persons otherwise guilty of a capital crime to the death penalty if the defendant was over sixteen at the time of the offense *(Stanford v. Kentucky)*.

With respect to the death penalty, then, the prohibition against cruel and unusual punishment in the Eighth Amendment mandates lesser maximum punishment for fifteen-year-old murderers than for adults. But not for sixteen-year-old murderers. The age boundaries imposed in these two cases were, to some extent, related to public attitudes as expressed through state legislative standards of minimum age (at the time of the crime) for execution. But there was no attempt to relate the age boundary selected for the death penalty to the views of maturity reflected in other legal rules. As a matter of minimum constitutional standards, a youth can become eligible for what has properly been called the "ultimate penalty in criminal law" five years before he is old enough to purchase alcohol or handguns and two years before the general age of majority in any state. Some theory of proportionality is at work here, for why else would the Court prohibit imposition of a punishment on a fifteen-year-old defendant who is properly liable for first-degree murder? But how this implicit theory of penal proportionality can be rationalized with the other age boundaries of growing up in American law is a continuing mystery.

If immaturity on account of youth is relevant to penal desert, then proposing a particular age or set of conditions as appropriate for full punishment should be accompanied by the advancement of a theory of maturity—a set of assumptions that should be tested against other legal principles that implicitly or explicitly make assumptions about how and when adolescents reach adulthood.

The conception of adolescent punishment discussed in Part II of this chapter is consistent by design with a theory first advanced some years ago (Zimring 1982) that sees adolescence as a long period of semiautonomy in which adolescents learn their way toward adult levels of responsibility gradually. This notion is also consistent with relatively early ages of partial accountability—an early age of capacity to be punished—but long periods of diminished responsibility that incrementally approach adult standards in the late teens. The major emphasis of this approach is not the capacity threshold but the less-than-adult punishments that gradually approach adult levels during the late teen years. This system is consistent with the extension of some privileges such as driving and voting prior to full adulthood, because these privileges are extended to allow young persons to exercise their responsibility, a "learning by doing" theory (Zimring 1982, 89–96). It is also consistent with staggering ages of majority throughout adolescence rather than making all transitions effective upon a single magic birthday. This is not a view of growing up in American law that would make sixteen-year-olds eligible for lethal injection as punishment for crime.

Conclusion

Once immaturity is relevant to the punishment that young offenders deserve, there is an inverse relationship between the importance of threshold determinations of capacity and the importance of diminished responsibility in keeping punishments proportional to the blameworthiness of offenders. If the juvenile court is best viewed as an agency that assigns punishment to delinquents, then the major emphasis in the American system is on diminished responsibility. But no explicit doctrine of diminished responsibility can be found in the statute books and case reports of modern American law.

This analysis has argued for two doctrinal developments in the penal law of youth crime. The first is a sliding scale of responsibility based on both judgment and the practical experience of impulse management and peer control. The second is for establishing as a requirement—for any theory governing punishment for young offenders—an attempt to harmonize assumptions about the nature of adolescent development and responsibility with other legal regulations of the transition to adulthood. The rules of penal responsibility for the young should not be permitted to remain an isolated anomaly in the legal landscape.

Works Cited

Elliott, Delbert. 1994. Serious violent offenders: Onset, developmental course, and termination—the American Society of Criminology 1993 presidential address. *Criminology* 32:1.
Elliott, Delbert, and Scott Menard. 1996. Delinquent friends and delinquent

behavior: Temporal and developmental patterns. In *Delinquency and crime: Current theories,* edited by J. David Hawkins. New York: Cambridge University Press.

Howell, James C., and David Hawkins. 1998. Prevention of youth violence. In *Crime and justice: An annual review of research,* edited by Michael Tonry and Mark Moore. Chicago: University of Chicago Press.

In re Gault. 387 U.S. 1, 87 S.Ct. 1428 (1967).

LaFave, Wayne R., and Austin W. Scott, Jr. 1986. *Criminal Law.* 2d ed. St. Paul, Minn.: West Publishing Co.

Morris, Norval. 1982. *Madness and the criminal law.* Chicago: University of Chicago Press.

Stanford v. Kentucky. 492 U.S. 361, 109 S.Ct. 2969 (1989).

Steinberg, Laurence, and Elizabeth Cauffman. 1996. Maturity of judgment in adolescence: Psychosocial factors in adolescent decision making. *Law and Human Behavior* 20:249–272.

Thompson v. Oklahoma. 487 U.S. 815, 108 S.Ct. 2687 (1988).

Zimring, Franklin E. 1981. Kids, groups, and crime: Some implications of a well-known secret. *Journal of Criminal Law and Criminology* 72:867–885.

———. 1982. *The changing legal world of adolescence.* New York: The Free Press.

———. 1998. *American youth violence.* New York: Oxford University Press.

Zimring, Franklin, Joel Eigen, and Sheila O'Malley. 1976. Punishing homicide in Philadelphia: Perspectives on the death penalty. *University of Chicago Law Review* 43:227.

CHAPTER ELEVEN

Criminal Responsibility in Adolescence: Lessons from Developmental Psychology

ELIZABETH S. SCOTT

During the past one hundred years, the legal response to juvenile crime has undergone three dramatic periods of reform. The first period began with the establishment of the first juvenile court in Chicago in 1899, and extended into the 1960s. The Progressive reformers at the turn of the century envisioned a court that would rehabilitate rather than punish errant youth, attending to the individual needs of young offenders rather than to the seriousness of their criminal acts (Ryerson 1978). By the 1960s this system, and its foundational principle of rehabilitation, were under attack from all sides. In 1967, the Supreme Court issued the landmark opinion of *In re Gault,* introducing procedural regularity to delinquency proceedings, and initiated a second period of reform. Courts, legislatures, and law-reform groups struggled to create a new model of juvenile justice, which afforded juvenile defendants procedural protections and acknowledged the accountability of young offenders while at the same time maintaining the special character of a separate justice system for youth.

We are currently in the midst of a third wave of reform, as policymakers at the state and federal level respond to public fear and anger at what is perceived to be an epidemic of youth violence, including an alarming increase in juvenile homicide (FBI Uniform Crime Reports 1995). The direction of this reform movement is toward subjecting young offenders to the same punishment as adults for the harms they cause (Fritsch and Hemmens 1996; House 1996, 14–15). The next step, which many are quite ready to take, is to abolish the separate juvenile justice system.

One way to think about the evolution of the juvenile justice system through these periods of reform is in terms of the empirical account of adolescence that is expressed by the reformers. During each reform period, a distinctive story of the characteristics of typical young offenders emerges from the rhetoric of politicians, advocates, academics, and judges, and is interwoven with proposed legal reforms. Implicitly, at least, the central theme of each account concerns whether and in what ways young offenders differ from their adult counterparts. The changing descriptions of adolescence over the past century have functioned in important ways both to shape and to justify juvenile justice reforms. Thus, the way in which the justice system has described its youthful "clientele" over the course of the twentieth century offers useful insights about the evolving legal response to juvenile crime. It also provides a standard by which to evaluate the legal regimes.

Through this lens, the traditional (pre-*Gault*) juvenile court was shaped in important ways by a conception of errant youths as childlike, relatively innocent, and malleable. On this view, the job of the court was not to punish criminals but to promote the welfare of misguided youths. With the post-*Gault* reforms of the 1970s and 1980s, a less idealized view of adolescence emerged, together with a growing skepticism about adolescents' potential for rehabilitation. Juvenile offenders were seen as less culpable than adults, but not as blameless children. Lacking experience and judgment, young offenders needed lessons in accountability. A perusal of the current landscape of juvenile justice reform suggests a view of delinquent youths as appropriately subject to adult punishment and procedures, thus indistinguishable in any important way from their adult counterparts.

My purpose in this chapter is to examine these changing accounts through the lens of developmental psychology. This perspective provides a scientific measure of the empirical assumptions, intuitions, and predictions about adolescence that have always played a large role in the formation of juvenile justice policy. Most importantly, perhaps, it challenges two assumptions underlying the contemporary punitive reforms. The first is what might be called the "competence assumption"—that no significant differences distinguish adolescents and adults charged with crimes. Modern developmental psychology provides substantial, if indirect, evidence that adolescent choices about involvement in criminal activity may reflect cognitive and psychosocial immaturity. This evidence challenges modern justice policies that assume youthful offenders can be held fully accountable for their crimes without undermining generally endorsed principles of criminal responsibility.

Developmental psychology also challenges a second premise implicit in the recent reforms. The "utilitarian assumption" qualifies the competence assumption, holding that even if developmental differences distinguish adolescent and adult offenders, those differences must be ignored in formulating a legal response to delinquency because of the enormous social cost of youth crime. This assumption is contested by evidence about the role of delinquent behavior in adolescent development. The modern punitive reforms tend to treat adolescent offenders as though most are young career criminals. This premise is true of only a small group of young offenders; the criminal activity of most adolescents, in contrast, reflects a relatively typical inclination to engage in antisocial behavior during this developmental stage—a tendency that desists with maturity (Moffitt 1993). Thus, policies that focus solely on the harm caused by youthful offenders fail to calculate the long-term social costs of categorical punishment, particularly the costs incurred by diminishing the prospects for productive adulthood of those offenders whose delinquent behavior reflects transient developmental influences.

Part I of this chapter briefly sketches the changing conceptions of adolescence in the three periods of juvenile justice reform during the twentieth century. Part II presents a developmental framework in which to examine these accounts. First, I describe the role of antisocial conduct in adolescence, and then offer a decision-making model that incorporates cognitive and psychosocial developmental factors that may distinguish adolescents from adults. I then apply this framework, examining the impact of developmental factors on decisions to engage in criminal conduct. Part III explores the possible implications of developmental knowledge for evaluating the criminal culpability of youth, and concludes that developmental-psychology evidence supports a presumption of youthful diminished responsibility for younger and mid-adolescents. The developmental framework is then employed to challenge the utilitarian argument that societal protection necessitates severe penalties for youthful offenders. Instead, the framework indicates that punitive policies may not be the optimal means to achieve the instrumentalist goals of their proponents. Part IV examines the lessons of the developmental perspective for juvenile justice policy and suggests some directions for policy that is formulated in a developmental framework.

Part I: Three Accounts of Adolescence in Criminal Justice Reform

Offenders as Children: The Traditional Court

The creation of a separate juvenile court at the end of the nineteenth century was grounded firmly in the belief that youthful offenders were different from their adult counterparts (Holl 1971). Advocates described as "an outrage against childhood" that youths of seven years of age and older could be tried and punished as adults (Lindsey and O'Higgins 1970, 85; Levine and Levine 1970; Walkover 1984). In framing the idealistic policies that shaped the new juvenile court, the Progressive reformers were influenced by the new science of psychology, which contributed to a heightened awareness of psychological differences between youths and adults (Fox 1970; Kett 1977; Ryerson 1978).

The new juvenile court was grounded in a commitment to the rehabilitation of young offenders and a rejection of retribution as a legitimate purpose of state intervention (Mack 1909; Zimring 1982; Teitelbaum 1991). The goal of rehabilitation came in part out of the late-nineteenth-century understanding of the nature of criminal conduct as a symptom of an underlying condition in the individual that required treatment, rather than as bad conduct warranting punishment (Mack 1909). This model also influenced adult criminal sentencing reform, generating indeterminate sentencing policies that dominated adult criminal corrections for more than a century (Von Hirsch 1976; Bonnie 1977; Feld 1987). However, the Progressives were more successful in advocating policies based on rehabilitation for juveniles, because the claim that punishment is not an appropriate response to crime was more palatable when applied to this group. Moreover, because juveniles were immature and malleable, they were believed to be ideally suited to a regime grounded in rehabilitation (Forst and Blomquist 1991; Mack 1909).

Youthful offenders should not be subject to criminal punishment, the reformers argued, because they were neither morally or criminally responsible for the harm they caused. Their criminal conduct reflected youthful immaturity and poor parental guidance (Lindsey and O'Higgins 1970; Zimring 1982). State officials involved in delinquency interventions—judges, social workers, and probation officers—were parent surrogates, providing caring discipline and treatment to wayward children. Their role was to diagnose and to prescribe treatment that responded to the individual needs of young offenders. Thus, proceedings were informal and not adversarial, and dispositions (like treatment for medical conditions) were indeterminate (Feld 1987; Forst and Blomquist 1991).

Given this vision of the juvenile justice system, it is not surprising perhaps that the Progressive reformers tended to describe young offenders in childlike terms (Mack 1909; Levine and Levine 1970; Larson 1972). Judge Ben Lindsey, a prominent early reformer, recounted heartwarming tales of himself as the fatherly judge, putting his arm around the shoulders of young miscreants and guiding them from their wayward paths. Lindsey rejected any notion of assigning criminal responsibility to young offenders, arguing that "Our laws against crime were as inapplicable to children as they would be to idiots" (Lindsey and O'Higgins 1970, 133). In part, this characterization may have reflected a tendency to exaggerate the differences between adult and youthful offenders by advocates who sought to underscore the appropriateness of a very different legal response. Moreover, the reformers, in fact, may have been imagining younger offenders. The jurisdiction of juvenile courts in the early years ended at age fourteen or sixteen, and the real victory for reformers was that children between the ages of seven and fourteen were no longer tried as adults (Larson 1972; Walkover 1984).

Under the rehabilitative model of juvenile justice, young offenders were thought to have different capacities and needs than adults, but the qualities that made juveniles less culpable were not articulated with any precision. Because punishment by the state generally is justified on the ground that criminal acts represent the free and rational choice to "do the bad thing," a rejection of retribution implicitly reflected a view that juveniles were developmentally unable to make this choice. Some observers pointed to the impulsiveness and malleability of youths as traits that were the basis of limited criminal responsibility (Forst and Blomquist 1991; Lindsey and O'Higgins 1970). Impulsiveness presumably contributes to incapacity because it impedes the ability to weigh the consequences of behavior; it might also make youths less deterrable. If youths were more malleable than adults, they might be more vulnerable to bad influences, particularly from peers.

The rehabilitative approach of the traditional juvenile court presumed that state intervention could have either negative or positive effects on youthful offenders, and it emphasized the importance of preserving the future prospects of young offenders (*State v. Benoit* 1985). The Progressive view, however, did not seem to be that criminal conduct reflected developmental influences that would attenuate with age. Rather, the belief was that the delinquent youth was on a path to a criminal career, from which he could be diverted through rehabilitation, or toward which he would proceed without appropriate intervention (Mack 1909).

The Second Reform Period: The Wake of Gault

In 1967, the Supreme Court changed the juvenile court forever, and initiated a second period of juvenile justice reform. In *In re Gault,* the Court extended to juveniles in delinquency proceedings many procedural rights accorded to adult criminal defendants. *Gault* not only reformed the procedures of the juvenile court, it also shattered the myth that the state's primary objective in delinquency cases was to promote the welfare of youngsters charged with crimes. As Justice Fortas suggested, these youths got the worst of both worlds. They were not accorded the procedural protections to which adult criminal defendants were entitled; at the same time they received little in the way of treatment as promised under the rehabilitative model.

Gault reflected mounting skepticism about the core premises of the traditional juvenile justice system. First, many critics doubted that rehabilitation was effective with youthful offenders, and argued that protection of society should be acknowledged as an important objective of intervention (Institute 1980a; Feld 1987). Moreover, post-*Gault* reformers rejected the childlike image of young offenders that was so integral to the Progressive account that shaped the traditional court. The modern reformers thought that adolescent offenders, while not fully mature, were more like adults than the traditional model recognized, and thus should be held accountable (at least to some extent) for their offenses (Zimring 1978; Zimring 1982; Institute 1980a).

During this period, major law-reform initiatives grappled with the challenge of constructing a juvenile justice system in which assigning criminal responsibility and protecting public safety were legitimate goals, but that at the same time recognized the youth and immaturity of young offenders (Zimring 1978; Institute 1980a; Maloney, Romig, and Armstrong 1988). In general, the post-*Gault* reformers concluded that juveniles should be held responsible for their criminal acts because they have sufficient capacity for moral judgment and self-control to justify this response (Zimring 1978; Walkover 1984). Moreover, lessons in accountability were important preparation for adulthood (Zimring 1982). However, due to developmental immaturity, the criminal choices of juveniles were seen as less culpable and thus less deserving of punishment than were those of adults (Juvenile Justice Standards 1980; Zimring 1978). Thus, dispositions, under principles of fairness and proportionality, should be based on the seriousness of the offense and not on individual traits of the offender. However, dispositional duration could be categorically reduced for juveniles, because youth was presumed to be a basis for diminished responsibility (Institute 1980b).

Some post-*Gault* reformers, such as Franklin Zimring, recognized that developmental traits of adolescence not only make young offenders less culpable than their adult counterparts, but also contribute to a tendency to engage in criminal conduct. On this view, high crime rates among youths were linked to psychological and biological factors associated with this developmental stage, and many adolescents predictably would desist from crime with maturity (Zimring 1978). Thus, a dispositional response that differentiated between adults and youth was also justified as a means to preserve the future life prospects of young delinquents.

Although the influence of developmental factors on criminal conduct was mostly presumed rather than analyzed, post-*Gault* reformers suggested that several adolescent traits both contribute to criminal conduct and render adolescents less blameworthy. As compared to adults, minors were assumed to be more impulsive (to have less capacity for self-control), to lack experience, and to be more inclined to focus on immediate rather than long-term consequences of their choices (Zimring 1978). Observers also pointed to the importance of peer approval (and peer pressure), rebellion against parental authority and restrictions, and the inclination of adolescents to experiment and engage in risk taking as developmentally linked factors that contributed to youth crime. In combination, these traits were taken to characterize adolescence itself, and therefore to justify a conclusion that youthful criminal conduct was less culpable (Zimring 1978).

These reform initiatives contributed to significant changes in legal policy. In the post-*Gault* generation, many jurisdictions have enacted statutes in which the purpose of public protection is explicit and the seriousness of the present offense and the juvenile's prior record have become central factors in legislative sentencing provisions (Feld 1991). A "balanced approach" adopted by a number of states placed new emphasis on accountability and public safety. 1 Nevertheless, these statutory reforms also generally reflected the reformers' core prescription limiting punishment—that most juveniles, because of developmental immaturity, should be subject to less punishment than adult criminals and that they should be dealt with in separate courts and correctional facilities.

The Era of Punitive Reforms—Obscuring the Developmental Lines

We are currently in a third period of reform, in which the limits on punishment that were important to the post-*Gault* reformers have become less of a constraint. The emphasis today is on social control—on protecting society from the harms inflicted by young offenders—and the clear trend has been toward punishing adolescents, especially those who commit violent crimes, as adults (Grisso 1996; Stepp 1994). These policies explicitly or implicitly present adolescent offenders as indistinguishable from adult counterparts, and reject the importance of youthful immaturity in assessments of criminal responsibility. As one advocate of "get tough" policies put it, juvenile offenders "are criminals who happen to be young, not children who happen to be criminal." (Regnery 1985).

Some supporters of this trend challenge the notion that tough young criminals are less culpable or less mature than their adult counterparts, and argue that the juvenile justice system coddles young criminals. Contemporary reformers argue that the traditional account of immature youngsters getting into scrapes with the law simply does not describe the savvy young offenders committing serious crimes today (Daly 1995, Regnery 1985; Dowie 1993). Indeed, the capacities of young offenders are not simply those of ordinary adults—they are "superpredators" (Bennett, Di-iullio, and Walters 1996). On this view, minors who inflict serious harm are engaging in adultlike criminal conduct and thus are presumed to be sufficiently mature to be tried and punished as adults. According to one critic, "Society may wish to be lenient with first offenders, particularly for lesser crimes, but there is no reason that society should be more lenient with a sixteen year old offender than a thirty year old offender." (Regnery 1985).

Several legislative strategies have been employed, on both the state and federal level, to treat juvenile offenders more like their adult counterparts. Many state statutes provide for increasingly broad authority to adjudicate juveniles charged with serious offenses in adult criminal court, either through judicial transfer, legislative waiver, or prosecutorial discretion. The age of transfer has been lowered in many jurisdictions, and a broader range of felonies can lead to adjudication as an adult (Grisso 1996; Fritsch and Hemmens 1995). Moreover, youthful offenders in broad categories based on offense and age increasingly are statutorily defined as adults and excluded from juvenile court jurisdiction (Feld 1987). Under "direct file" statutes, prosecutors can opt to bring charges for serious offenses against minors in adult criminal court. Finally, under "rollover" sentencing laws, juveniles are subject to stiff statutory minimum sentences in juvenile court for certain offenses, then transferred to prison to complete the sentence when they reach adulthood (Grisso 1996). The upshot is that today in many states, juveniles who have not reached adolescence can be tried as adults and confined in adult prisons—serving "adult time for adult crime," as many advocate (Stepp 1994).

Criminal courts also appear to have adopted the view that youth is not an important factor in distinguishing juveniles from adults. Despite some predictions to the contrary, many criminal courts do not seem to respond to juvenile offenders more leniently than they do to adult criminals. Studies have found that adolescents charged with serious offenses are convicted at about the same rate as adults and, if convicted, receive sentences of similar severity (Grisso 1996).

The modern reformers presume that there are no psychological differences between adolescent and adult offenders that are important to criminal responsibility. Usually the issue is not addressed, and the argument for tough sanctions focuses on the harm caused by youthful predators (Regnery 1985). However, not only do those who would treat young offenders as adults adamantly reject the traditional account of adolescent offenders as children, they also appear to assume that any legal standard for maturity that might be required to hold young offenders fully responsible for their crimes is almost always met.

Although the trend toward imposing full criminal responsibility on juvenile defendants seems inexorable, the account of adolescence that is embedded in the punitive reforms has generated discomfort and controversy. This discomfort can be acute when highly publicized cases arise involving preadolescent offenders who commit serious violent crimes (McCormick 1994). Many observers continue to emphasize that youthful immaturity mitigates criminal culpability (Grisso 1996; Forst and Blomquist 1991; Springer 1991; Teitelbaum 1991; Gardner 1989; Melton 1989). Even some proponents of abolition of the juvenile court, such as Barry Feld, argue that minors are less capable of sound judgment because of impulsiveness and a reduced capacity to appreciate the consequences of their acts and are thus less culpable than adult offenders (Feld 1997; Ainsworth 1991; Federle 1990). Feld and others conclude that the immaturity of juvenile offenders can be accommodated at sentencing (Feld 1997, Ainsworth 1991, Melton 1989). Thus, the intuitions about the immaturity of youths that drove the early Progressive founders of the court and (in a moderate form) the post-*Gault* reformers continue to be expressed today. Currently, these concerns tend to be overwhelmed in the debate by accounts of the social costs of a system that fails to restrain young offenders whose age alone distinguishes them from adult criminals.

Part II: Youthful Offending in a Developmental Framework

The three juvenile justice reform movements of the twentieth century provide different accounts of youthful offenders and the extent to which they differ from their adult counterparts. To an important degree, these accounts are at the heart of each reform movement and justify the recommended response to youthful criminal conduct. Thus, if offenders are children, as the Progressives held, then it makes sense to conclude that they are not criminally responsible. On the other hand, if no important differences distinguish adult and juvenile offenders, then they can appropriately be subject to the same sanctions, as modern punitive reformers argue.

Developmental psychology provides a useful purchase from which to test the accuracy of the various accounts of adolescence and to evaluate the legal responses that are based in part on empirical assumptions about whether and how adolescents who become involved in criminal activity differ from adults. The developmental inquiry has two parts. The first explores the role that delinquent behavior may play in adolescence. Many youths engage in criminal activity during this period but do not persist in this behavior into adulthood, a pattern that can be explained most satisfactorily in developmental and social terms. The second part of the inquiry focuses on developmental influences on decision making that may distinguish the choices of adolescents from those of adults. My interest here is in factors that may affect the understanding, reasoning, and—perhaps most importantly—the judgment of youths who engage in criminal conduct.

Antisocial Behavior as a Part of Adolescence

Many adolescents become involved in criminal activity in their teens and desist by the time they reach young adulthood. Research demonstrates that criminal behavior is rare in early adolescence; it increases through age sixteen and declines sharply from age seventeen onward (Jessor and Jessor 1977, Farrington 1983, Moffitt 1993). Self-report studies indicate that most teenage males engage in some criminal conduct, leading criminologists to conclude that participation in delinquency is "a normal part of teen life" (Moffitt 1993). For most adolescent delinquents, desistance from antisocial behavior also seems to be a predictable part of the maturation process (Mulvey and La Rosa 1986; Hirschi and Gottfredson 1983; Moffitt 1993; Blumstein and Cohen 1987; Farrington 1986). Only a small group of young offenders will persist in a life of crime (Moffitt 1993; Wolfgang, Figlio, and Sellin 1972).

Terrie Moffitt has offered a taxonomy of adolescent antisocial conduct in which a representative sample of adolescents involved in criminal activity would include a large group whose antisocial conduct is "adolescence limited" and a much smaller group whose conduct is "life-course persistent" (Moffitt 1993, Mulvey and Aber 1988). Of this latter group, some will initiate antisocial behavior in adolescence (Loeber and Stouthamer-Loeber 1998); however, many display a variety of problem behaviors that begin early in life and persist through adolescence into adulthood (Moffitt 1993; Wolfgang, Figlio, and Sellin 1972; Elliott 1993). Of this latter group, many, although certainly not all, will become career criminals. However, as Moffitt points out, most youths who engage in delinquent behavior have little notable history of antisocial conduct in childhood; nor will the conduct continue into adulthood. Involvement in criminal activity and other antisocial behavior begins in adolescence and tends to follow a "natural onset and recovery process" (Mulvey and Aber 1988).

The forces that contribute to the onset and desistance of delinquent adolescent behavior are not well understood. Moffitt (1993) offers an etiological theory under which the tendency of adolescents to engage in antisocial behavior is linked to the gap experienced by contemporary youths between early biological maturity and late social maturity and independence (Kett 1977). She argues that adolescents strive for elusive autonomy from parental and adult authority in a context in which most privileges of adult status are withheld. Many adolescents may be inclined to mimic their antisocial peers, who appear to have attained adult status in many ways: they are sexually active at an earlier age, less subject to parental and adult authority, and are able to attain possessions through theft and other illegal activity. Through antisocial conduct, the normative adolescent attenuates the ties of childhood and demonstrates that he can act independently. Under Moffitt's theory, youthful antisocial risk-taking acts are personal statements of independence by individuals who are not yet permitted to assume legitimate adult roles. Desistance in young adulthood is explained as the adaptive response to changed contingencies as more legitimate adult roles become available. Delinquent behavior becomes costly rather than rewarding, as many young adults perceive that it threatens now-available conventional opportunities and may foreclose future goals. In short, they come to realize that they have something to lose (Moffitt 1993).

Reasoning and Judgment in Adolescent Decision Making

A general account of the role of antisocial conduct in adolescence suggests that youthful criminal conduct is best understood in a developmental context. In this section, I turn to particular developmental influences on individual decision making that may interact to shape the choices of youthful actors in ways that distinguish them from adults (Mann, Harmoni, and Power 1989, Furby and Beyth-Marom 1990). These endogenous factors could be important in understanding why adolescents frequently get involved in criminal activity and desist as they mature. To a large extent, this framework complements Moffitt's theory, but it focuses on internal dynamic influences on adolescent decision making that are associated with this developmental stage, whereas Moffitt's emphasis is on changing external contingencies.

The most familiar developmental influences on decision making are elements of cognitive development—reasoning and understanding. Probably more salient to decisions about participation in criminal conduct are psychosocial influences such as peer influence, time perspective (a tendency to focus on short-term versus long-term consequences), and risk perception and preference, factors that may affect decision making in powerful ways that distinguish juveniles from adults. I designate these psychosocial influences as "judgment" factors, and argue that immature judgment in adolescence may contribute to choices made about involvement in crime (Scott 1992; Scott, Reppucci, and Woolard 1995; Steinberg and Cauffman 1996; Cauffman, in press).

Understanding and Reasoning

It is generally recognized that decision-making capacities increase through childhood into adolescence and that, although there is great variability among individuals, preadolescents and younger teens differ substantially from adults in their abilities. Development occurs along several lines. The capacities to process information and to think hypothetically develop into adolescence, and cognitive performance improves generally due to knowledge gained in specific domains. Moreover, cognitive skills acquired earlier mature and develop in adolescence (Flavell, Miller, and Miller 1993; Siegler 1991).

The question of how adolescents' capacities for understanding and reasoning in decision making compare with those of adults has received much attention among policy analysts and children's rights advocates in recent years—although largely not in the context of juvenile justice policy. Proponents of broader self-determination rights for minors, drawing on child-development theory and empirical research, have argued that, by about age fourteen, adolescents' cognitive decision-making abilities are similar to those of adults (Melton 1983; Billick 1986; American Psychological Association 1990; American Psychological Association 1987). This argument holds that adolescents are capable of making informed and competent decisions about medical treatment and other matters, and should have the legal authority to do so (Scott 1992). The evidence for these claims is drawn in part from Piaget's stage theory of cognitive development (Flavell, Miller, and Miller 1993; Inhelder and Piaget 1958; Scott 1992), and from several empirical studies that focus on minors' ability to understand and reason about medical and abortion decisions (Ambuel and Rappaport 1992; Weithorn and Campbell 1982), treatment issues in psychotherapy (Kaser-Boyd, Adelman, and Taylor 1985; Kaser-Boyd et al. 1986), and their Fifth Amendment rights and the meaning of Miranda waivers (Grisso 1981; Grisso 1980). The advocates argue that the research supports a conclusion that younger teens differ from adults in their cognitive capacities, but their reasoning and understanding appears to be similar to that of adults by mid-adolescence.

Together, this scientific evidence indicates that adolescents are more competent as decision makers than has been presumed under paternalistic legal policies, but the research does not demonstrate that youthful cognitive decision-making capacity is like that of adults (Gardner, Scherer, and Tester 1989; Scott 1992). First, cognitive psychologists no longer accept Piaget's theory that cognitive development is strictly stagelike in the sense that children at a given stage engage in characteristic reasoning across task domains. Rather, skills seem to develop at different rates in different domains, and competence to make one kind of decision can not be generalized (Siegler 1991; Flavell, Miller, and Miller 1993). Beyond this, the research evidence supporting the advocates' claim is sketchy; the studies are small and mostly involve middle-class subjects of average intelligence. Only a handful compare the decision making of minors with that of adults. Finally, the studies of adolescent decision making have been conducted in laboratory settings in which the decision is hypothetical and preframed in the sense that all relevant information is provided to the subjects (Scott 1992). Thus, the findings are only modestly useful in understanding how youths make decisions in informal and unstructured settings (such as the street) in which they must rely on their own experience and knowledge in making choices. Moreover, research offers little evidence of how minors may function relative to adults in stressful situations in which decisions have salience to their lives (Steinberg and Cauffman 1996; Cauffman 1996).

In sum, scientific authority indicates that, in general, the cognitive capacity for reasoning and understanding of preadolescents and many younger teens differs substantially in some regards from that of older teens and adults. Tentative authority also supports the conclusion that, by mid-adolescence, youthful capacities for reasoning and understanding approximate those of adults. Whether and how these capacities are employed, however, may be quite variable, and adolescent performance is not necessarily like that of adults in various contexts. Because the research was largely undertaken in structured settings, the findings may be more useful in shedding light on questions about competence to stand trial than on cognitive capacity as it affects choices relevant to criminal conduct.

Judgment Factors in Decision Making

Other psychological factors may also influence adolescent decision making in ways that are relevant to criminal responsibility. Psychosocial and experiential factors such as conformity and compliance in relation to peers, attitude toward and perception of risk, and time perspective seem particularly salient in this context (Scott, Reppucci, and Woolard 1995, Steinberg and Cauffman 1996). If these factors influence decision making, the impact is not on reasoning and understanding but rather on judgment (as the term is used in common parlance, rather than in cognitive psychology) (Scott, Reppucci, and Woolard 1995). Judgment may be affected by differences in experience and knowledge; it also reflects differences in values and preferences that are driven by psychosocial influences.

Whereas cognitive competence affects the process of decision making, immature judgment is reflected in outcomes. This is so because psychosocial developmental factors influence values and preferences, which in turn shape the cost-benefit calculus, which determines outcomes. The influence of these factors will change as the individual matures and values and preferences change—resulting in different choices. The traditional presumption (in juvenile justice and in many other policy areas) that minors are not fully accountable and need legal protection rests in part on a widely shared assumption that children and adolescents have immature judgment and will make unwise choices. In essence, the intuition is that developmentally linked predispositions and responses systematically affect youthful decision making in ways that may lead to harmful choices.

Peer Influence   It is widely assumed (and the research supports) that teens are more subject to peer influence than are adults (Scott 1992; Scott, Reppucci, and Woolard 1995; Steinberg and Cauffman 1996; Steinberg and Silverberg 1986) and that peer influence plays an important role in adolescent crime (Reiss Jr. and Farrington 1991). Peer influence seems to operate through two means: social comparison and conformity. Social comparison refers to adolescents' tendency to measure their own behavior by comparing it to others (Sprinthall and Collins 1988). Social conformity, which peaks at about age fourteen, influences adolescents to adapt their behavior and attitudes to that of their peers (Berndt 1979; Coleman 1961; Costanza and Shaw 1966). Peer influence could affect adolescent decision making in several ways. In some contexts adolescents might make choices in response to direct peer pressure or coercion. More indirectly, adolescent desire for peer approval could affect their choices without any direct coercion. Finally, as Moffitt suggests, peers may provide models for behavior that adolescents believe will assist them in accomplishing their own ends.

Risk Perception and Preference   Research evidence also suggests that adolescents differ from adults in their perception of and attitude toward risk (Finn and Bragg 1986; Gardner 1992; Gardner and Herman 1991; Matthews and Moran 1986; Tester, Gardner, and Wilfong 1987). Adolescents and young adults generally take more risks with health and safety than do older adults, by engaging more frequently in behavior such as unprotected sex, drunk driving, and criminal conduct (Furby and Beyth-Marom 1990). It is possible that this inclination may result from differences in risk perception. Adolescents, perhaps because they have less knowledge and experience, are less aware of risks than are adults (Lewis 1981; Elkind 1967). They also may calculate the probability of risks differently or value them differently (Furby and Beyth-Marom 1990; Gardner and Herman 1991). Adolescents seem to be less averse to risk than are adults, tending to focus less on protection against losses and more on opportunities for gains in making choices (Gardner and Herman 1991; Lopes 1987).

Time Perspective   Attitude toward risk is related to differences in temporal perspective (Scott, Reppucci, and Woolard 1995). Adolescents seem to discount the future more than adults do, and to weigh more heavily short-term consequences of decisions (both risks and benefits)—a response that in some circumstances can lead to risky behavior such as smoking or engaging in unprotected sex (Gardner and Herman 1991). In part, this tendency may reflect the difference in experience between teens and adults. Adolescents may be less likely than adults to contemplate the meaning of a consequence that will have an impact ten or fifteen years into the future (Gardner 1992). Alternatively, adolescents may simply attach more weight to short-term consequences because they seem more salient to their lives.

In general, the fact that adolescents have less experience and knowledge than adults seems likely to affect their decision making in tangible and intangible ways. Although the relative inexperience of adolescents has not been contested as a general proposition, the relevance of inexperience to decision making and judgment is uncertain.

Developmental Factors and Decision Making about Offending

Any assertions about the effect of cognitive and psychosocial immaturity on adolescent decision making must be very tentative (Scott, Reppucci, and Woolard 1995; Cauffman 1996). With this caveat, it seems probable that developmental factors associated with adolescence could affect decision making in several ways (Scott 1992; Scott, Reppucci, and Woolard 1995). First, adolescents may use information differently from adults. They may consider different or fewer options in thinking about their available choices or in identifying consequences when comparing alternatives (Lewis 1981). The extent and sources of the differences in use of information are unclear. It is plausible that dissimilar and more limited experience and knowledge, as well as attitudes toward risk, temporal perspective, and peer influence, are all implicated. To the extent that differences are linked to knowledge and experience, they may be most evident in unstructured and informal settings where information is not provided and individuals must make choices based on their own knowledge and experience (Scott 1992).

Secondly, substantial theoretical arguments hold that while older adolescents may have adultlike capacities for reasoning, they may not deploy those capacities as uniformly across different problem-solving situations as do adults (Flavell, Miller, and Miller 1993; Siegler 1991), and they may do so less dependably in ambiguous or stressful situations (Steinberg and Cauffman 1996; Mann 1992; Janis 1982). Finally, adolescents, for developmental reasons, could differ from adults in the subjective value that is assigned to perceived consequences in the process of making choices (Furby and Beyth-Marom 1990; Gardner and Herman 1991; Scott 1992; Kulbok, Earls, and Montgomery 1988). Influenced by the psychosocial developmental factors that I have described, adolescents may weigh costs and benefits differently, sometimes even viewing as a benefit what adults would consider to be a cost (Benthin, Slovic, and Severson 1993, Hampson et al. 1992).

Developmental factors could affect choices about participating in crime. Consider the following example. A youth hangs out with his buddies on the street. Someone suggests holding up a nearby convenience store. The boy has mixed feelings about the proposal, but cannot think of ways to extricate himself—although perhaps a more mature person might develop a strategy. The possibility that one of his friends has a gun, and the consequences of that fact, may not occur to him. He goes along with the plan partly because he fears rejection by his friends—a consequence that he attaches to a decision not to participate—and that carries substantial weight in his calculus. Also, the excitement of the holdup and the possibility of getting some money are attractive. These considerations weigh more heavily in his decision than the cost of possible apprehension by the police, or the long-term costs to his future life of conviction of a serious crime (Scott, Reppucci, and Woolard 1995).

This account suggests how psychosocial developmental factors could affect adolescents' choices to engage in criminal conduct. The choice may be based on limited knowledge and experience, but it may not otherwise reflect purely cognitive immaturity, because the youth may be rationally choosing the option that promotes subjective utility, given his values. The decision does, however, implicate immaturity of judgment. At least from a societal perspective, it is an unwise choice because it causes harm to a victim and threatens harm to the youth himself.

If these influences on decision making are developmental and not simply reflective of individual idiosyncratic preferences for risk taking, they should abate with maturity. This prediction is consistent with the well-documented pattern of desistance from delinquent conduct in late adolescence or early adulthood. In general, it is reasonable to argue that the developmental factors of peer influence, time perspective (discounting the future), and risk perception and preference contribute to delinquent behavior and that their declining influence contributes to desistance. Although the factors contributing to desistance have not been adequately studied, researchers have linked desistance to a longer time perspective and to changing patterns of peer relationships (Mulvey and La Rosa 1986). As Moffitt postulates (1993), young adults may cease to commit crimes because they come to understand that the decision to offend carries the risk of lost future opportunities. In other words, a cost-benefit calculus leads to a conclusion that choosing crime no longer maximizes subjective utility.

What is not clear is whether the source of the change is exogenous or endogenous. Moffitt seems to suggest that the calculus shifts because external contingencies change. A focus on psychosocial influences that contribute to immaturity of judgment suggests that desistance can be linked to developmental maturation. A plausible hypothesis, based on the developmental research and theory, is that much adolescent participation in crime is the result of interaction between developmental influences on decision making and external contingencies that affect individuals during this stage. Recent studies have begun to demonstrate the relation between psychosocial developmental factors and the quality of youths' choices compared to that of adults (Cauffman 1996). Further research is required, however, to determine the degree to which these developmental factors directly affect the decisions of youths participating in delinquent activity.

Part III: The Developmental Framework and Criminal Punishment
Criminal Responsibility and Psychological Immaturity

Developmental influences relating to understanding and judgment seem likely to affect adolescent choices to commit crime in ways that distinguish most young offenders from their adult counterparts. Although individual adult and juvenile offenders vary, decision-making factors associated with age that affect decision making provide a basis for differentiating between the two categories of offenders. Moreover, the fact that delinquent behavior desists for most adolescents as they approach adulthood strongly suggests that criminal conduct, for most youths, is linked to factors peculiar to adolescence as a developmental stage. The evidence from developmental psychology challenges the account of adolescence offered by the modern punitive reformers who generally do not accept that relevant differences exist between youthful and adult offenders. This evidence also suggests that the Progressive's account of young offenders as blameless children in need of treatment is distorted. When analyzed in the framework of conventional criminal-excuse doctrine, the developmental evidence supports a presumption of diminished responsibility for adolescent offenders—but not a lack of responsibility.

The argument for a presumption of diminished responsibility for young offenders is compatible with conventional justifications for criminal responsibility. The criminal law posits that the offender is a rational actor, autonomously choosing to commit a crime on the basis of personal values and preferences (Bonnie et al. 1997; Morse 1976). The legitimacy of punishing an offender as a blameworthy moral agent is undermined if criminal choices depart substantially from this autonomy model (Walkover 1984). The evidence from developmental psychology indicates that youthful choices to offend may be based on an immature capacity to make decisions or may be driven by transient developmental influences. If this is so, then the presumptions of autonomy, free will, and rational choice on which adult criminal responsibility is based become weaker, making the criminal conduct of juveniles less blameworthy than similar criminal acts of adults. Under the principle of proportionality, punishment should be based in part on the blameworthiness of the offender; youths are less blameworthy than adults and should be subject to less punishment.

It is important not to exaggerate the practical importance of whatever differences may exist between the criminal choices of adolescents and adults. Although criminal law abounds in rhetoric about free will and blameworthy choice, defenses that fully excuse actors from responsibility are very narrowly drawn under established doctrinal standards for evaluating the quality of criminal choice. For example, many adult defendants whose choices reflect serious psychological impairment or exogenous coercion nevertheless are convicted and punished for their crimes. Although mental disability and disorder are not uncommon among criminals (Monahan 1997), the modern insanity defense is available only to defendants with such severe cognitive impairment that they are unable to understand or appreciate the nature of their wrongful conduct (Bonnie et al. 1997; Steadman et al. 1993). In short, despite the law's theoretical commitment to conditions of free will and rational choice, in practice only a small group of offenders whose choices are extremely compromised are fully excused from criminal liability.

The upshot is that the developmental psychology evidence does not support the Progressive stance that notions of accountability simply do not apply to juvenile offenders as a group (Lindsey and O'Higgins 1970). Analyzed in the framework of criminal-law doctrine, developmental differences affecting decision making are likely to be substantial enough to provide categorical excuse from responsibility only for very young juveniles, who are qualitatively different from adults in moral, cognitive, and social development. Certainly by midadolescence, adolescents differ from adults in ways that are more subtle than those that distinguish the adult offenders whose crimes are fully excused under current law from other adult offenders. Thus, the categorical presumption of adolescent nonresponsibility at the heart of the traditional juvenile justice system cannot be defended on grounds of immaturity (Regnery 1985).

On the other hand, the developmental psychology and criminology evidence also challenges the arguments of modern advocates of punitive policies. A claim that juvenile offenders and adults deserve equivalent punishment presumes that no substantial differences exist that undermine the legitimacy of imposing equal measures of blame and punishment on the two groups (Regnery 1985). On this point, the scientific evidence disputes the conclusion that most delinquents are indistinguishable from adults in any way that is relevant to culpability, and supports the creation of adult and juvenile culpability categories—although, of course, there will be outliers in both groups. In short, the predispositions, psychosocial influences, and behavioral characteristics that are associated with the developmental stage of adolescence are factors that support a policy of diminished criminal responsibility for juvenile offenders.

The developmental evidence supports the position of the post-*Gault* reformers of the 1970s that a presumptive diminished-responsibility standard be applied to juveniles. Adolescents are not innocent children, but, as a group, their criminal choices reflect immaturity and inexperience and are driven by developmental factors that will change in predictable and systemic ways. A legal response that holds young offenders accountable, while recognizing that they are less culpable than their adult counterparts, serves the purposes of criminal punishment without violating the underlying principle of proportionality. As Franklin Zimring has argued, adolescence can usefully be conceptualized as a probationary period in which young decision makers learn to make responsible choices without bearing the full costs of their mistakes (1982). Zimring's approach argues for a legal response that signals that criminal choices have consequences and that bad behavior is punished, but does not punish youths as severely as older offenders, who have been given the opportunity to learn to make better choices.

Given the principles that define criminal responsibility, it is not surprising perhaps that some of the same themes can be discerned in the punishment of adult offenders whose conduct suggests reduced culpability. The behavioral traits and inexperience that in general characterize youthful offenders as a group may be relevant for grading purposes at sentencing of adult criminals. The "immature" offender whose acts were influenced by others, who is a first offender, or who "made a mistake" out of inexperience and can be expected to have "learned her lesson" may receive a reduced sentence based on an official judgment that her crime is less culpable and deserves less punishment than does that of a seasoned criminal (Von Hirsch 1976; *Lockett v. Ohio;* Federal Sentencing Guidelines 1996).

In the case of adults, leniency acknowledges a deficiency in the individual offender—a failure to attain an adult level of maturity and experience. For utilitarian reasons, however, such leniency will be cautiously exercised, lest the presumption of free will completely collapse. Most adults are presumed to act on the basis of individual values and preferences, and to have had adequate opportunity to acquire maturity and experience. Minors have not had this opportunity, and their criminal choices are presumed less to express individual preferences and more to reflect the behavioral influences characteristic of a transitory developmental stage generally shared with others in the age cohort. This difference supports drawing a line based on age and subjecting adolescents to a categorical presumption of reduced responsibility.

Adolescent Development and the Social Cost of Crime

Many policymakers are persuaded that society cannot afford to punish youthful offenders more leniently than adults because of the enormous social cost of juvenile crime (Snyder and Sickmund 1995; Allen-Hagen and Sickmund 1993). A developmental perspective challenges this utilitarian assumption underlying current policies, and reveals that punitive policies are shortsighted, even in terms of the reformers' goal of protecting society. On purely instrumentalist grounds, effective policy will attend to the developmental character of much youth crime and to the divergent patterns of offending represented by the two groups described earlier—those youths whose criminal behavior is limited to adolescence and those whose delinquency is part of a life-course persistent pattern.

The Utilitarian Argument for Punitive Policies

Political arguments for tough juvenile sanctions combine a retributive claim that juvenile and adult offenders deserve similar punishment with a utilitarian argument that such policies will reduce crime. Modern punitive reformers might even acknowledge that youthful criminal choices reflect immaturity, but argue that the goal of protecting society is simply more important (Regnery 1985; Van den Haag 1975; Dowie 1993; Baker 1996). Although only the most fervent advocates of punitive policies would punish children regardless of age like their adult counterparts, many more conclude that policies that generally ignore the impact of immaturity on adolescent criminal choices do not unduly strain the principles limiting criminal punishment.

On this view, any modest developmental claim for leniency seems to be far outweighed by the importance of reducing the social threat of adolescent crime. Some observers suggest that the traditional differential response to the criminal conduct of minors may have made sense in a more peaceful time (Daly 1995), but today the stakes are too high to retain a system that sacrifices social protection (Steadman et al. 1993). In general, criminal law balances autonomy-based constraints on retribution against the social cost of excusing conduct that inflicts harm; how the balance is struck depends in part on the magnitude of the perceived harm. Thus, for example, only negligence or recklessness (rather than purpose) need be shown to establish criminal intent for most crimes (Model Penal Code 1962). Employing this instrumentalist calculus, recent legal reforms have shifted the balance toward greater social protection. In response to a perception that violent youth crime has escalated in recent years, the conventional limits on punishment of juveniles have been relaxed.

From an instrumentalist perspective, the argument for discounting youth as a mitigating factor in applying criminal sanctions is particularly compelling because the developmental factors at issue are likely to contribute to the inclination to commit crimes. If adolescents tend to be risk-preferring actors who discount future consequences in favor of immediate gratification, they present a greater threat than do older offenders, and the social interest in constraint is more compelling. On this view, a system that responds leniently to its most dangerous offenders appears to be muddled and inefficient.

Utilitarian Policies through a Developmental Lens

The utilitarian assumption underlying the current trend holds that a rigorously punitive approach is the optimal means of reducing the social cost of youth crime. At one level the "cure" seems promising, given the objectives. Young offenders who are incarcerated cannot be on the streets committing crimes. The developmental analysis in Part II, however, suggests that the utilitarian assumption is flawed and that categorically punitive policies are not the best means to limit the costs of juvenile crime.

The utilitarian assumption is flawed because it fails to account for the substantial societal interest in facilitating desistance in delinquents whose crimes are driven by developmental influences and in preserving their future prospects. Most delinquent conduct is "adolescence limited"; young offenders will mature into useful (or at least not criminal) citizens if they survive adolescence without destroying their life chances. When and whether they assume conventional adult roles is likely to be at least in part a function of the system's response to their adolescent criminal conduct (Moffitt 1993). It seems likely, although it has not been demonstrated, that categorically imposing adult criminal penalties on adolescents will increase the likelihood that they will become career criminals or at least that it may delay desistance (Fagan in press). Moreover, a criminal sentence is likely to have both direct and indirect negative effects on the future educational, employment, and social productivity of those youths whose crimes represent adolescent-limited antisocial behavior. Policy that attends to this developmental pattern would give these delinquent minors room to reform, protecting them from the most severe consequences of choices based on immature judgment (Zimring 1982, 1978).

Developmental analysis supports a modest claim that the broad use of adult criminal penalties against youths may carry social costs that have been ignored, when such penalties are applied to normative adolescent offenders. The social benefits that proponents of tough penalties promise are not likely to be realized because two implicit assumptions underlying the policies appear to be erroneous: that most youths who commit serious crimes are young career criminals (Wolfgang, Figlio, and Sellin 1972; Elliott 1993), and that adult penalties will not generate severe iatrogenic effects that harm those who would otherwise outgrow their inclination to engage in criminal conduct (Fagan in press).

But what is the optimal response to the crimes of the small group of delinquents whose conduct is more likely to persist into adulthood? The research suggests that these youths are likely to offend at an earlier age and that their criminal conduct is frequent, chronic, and more likely to be violent than is that of their delinquent peers (Farrington, Ohlin, and Wilson 1986; Wolfgang, Figlio, and Sellin 1972). Thus, purely on instrumentalist grounds, early and severe punitive sanctions may seem to be justified, once a "differential diagnosis" identifies an offender as belonging to this group. However, such a response may be shortsighted—even aside from the formidable problem of false positive identification—given our current level of knowledge and the constraints on punishment of the youngest offenders. Lifelong careers in crime carry enormous social cost—as does lifelong imprisonment. Thus, a societal investment in developing early and comprehensive remedial interventions may ultimately yield more social benefit than the alternative response that is in vogue today. Although knowledge currently is inadequate to the task and simple prescriptions seem unlikely, a long-term strategy for dealing with this group that relies only on punishment is not likely to be cost-effective.

Rejection of a punitive approach on utilitarian grounds does not signify that the optimal legal response to youth crime is "benign neglect." Although some sociologists have advocated a minimalist approach to intervention as the best means to avoid turning delinquents into career criminals (Schur 1973), this is not a desirable response on several grounds. First, the prediction on which it is premised is simply wrong as applied to life-course-persistent offenders, the group threatening the greatest harm. Further, young offenders cause social harm, which is not mitigated by the prediction that most will desist with maturity. This social cost may be contained through carefully designed sanctions. Finally, as to the larger group of normative adolescent offenders, lessons in accountability are important. As Franklin Zimring has argued (1982), adolescents need to learn from their foolish youthful choices so that they can successfully assume adult roles.

Part IV: Lessons for Juvenile Justice Policy

The developmental perspective may be usefully employed in formulating legal responses to juvenile crime. In this part, I will sketch a few policy lessons that can be taken from the analysis, and suggest directions for future innovation and research. My aim is not to provide a detailed policy blueprint, but rather to suggest the contours of a system for responding to juvenile crime that is informed by developmental knowledge. As a starting point, I assume that a central objective of any viable contemporary system is to reduce the social cost of youth crime through means that conform to conventional limits on retribution. These goals function as constraints on the generation of policies under a developmental model of juvenile justice.

My observations are based on a few points taken from the developmental-psychology evidence that seem to me to be the most important in shaping juvenile justice policy. First, on average, adolescents' decision-making abilities, especially those related to judgment, have not matured to a level characteristic of adults, and these developmental differences are relevant to assessing youthful culpability. This gap is likely to be substantial with younger teens, and for this group may include immaturity in understanding and reasoning as well as judgment. Second, the category of juvenile offenders includes two very different kinds of youths with different prognoses and often with different histories. For example, the evidence indicates that offenders who initiate criminal behavior at a younger age are likely to present a higher risk of becoming career criminals than are teens who first become involved in criminal activity in mid-adolescence. For most adolescents, delinquent behavior is shaped by developmental influences and it desists with maturity into adulthood. In the following sections, I suggest some ways in which an optimal legal response to youth crime will attend to these developmental considerations.

Responding to Crimes of Younger Adolescent Offenders

The developmental psychology evidence supports a conclusion that, as a general matter, younger teens are sufficiently different from adults in cognitive and psychosocial development that they should not be tried or punished in the adult criminal justice system. The argument for diminished criminal responsibility is particularly compelling as applied to these youths, who come close to the Progressive description of young offenders as "childlike." To be sure, it is difficult to define precisely the minimum age at which adult punishment does not violate widely shared moral constraints on retribution, and the issue will not be decided on developmental evidence alone. However, thirteen-year-old offenders simply are substantially less capable decision makers than are adults, and subjecting them to the same criminal punishment offends the principles that define the boundaries of criminal responsibility.

This is not to say that a minimalist response to the offenses of this group is indicated, because, as I have suggested, these youths are at considerable risk of becoming chronic serious offenders. As compared to adolescents who first offend a few years later, the criminal conduct of younger teens (and preadolescents) is less likely to be part of a typical developmental process that will progress to a stage of natural recovery and desistance. Their behavior is more likely to reflect a nascent personality disorder, developing over time through the interaction of individual vulnerabilities and environmental factors (Moffitt 1993). Currently, we cannot predict in the early stages which young adolescent offenders will proceed to criminal careers. Further research is needed to distinguish these youths from young juveniles whose crimes reflect transient developmental influences (Loeber 1982; Moffitt 1993; Lynam 1996). Nonetheless, preadolescent and early adolescent criminal conduct is a sufficiently important predictor so as to place these youths in a high-risk category that warrants serious attention (Elliott 1993).

In responding to these young offenders, the traditional goal of rehabilitation can be revitalized to play an important role in a contemporary model of juvenile justice. A modern rehabilitative model would function quite differently from the traditional response by focusing intensive rehabilitative interventions on the youngest offenders. In some sense, the traditional dispositional regime is backward in its tendency to intervene minimally with younger offenders and more assertively with older adolescents. This response misses the opportunity to remediate at a point when the possibility of change is more promising than it will be when these offenders are older and well launched on a criminal career (Moffitt 1993; Loeber 1982).

It is fair to say that we have not yet developed effective rehabilitative interventions for these very young offenders, although a few delinquency programs employing an intensive multisystemic approach have reported promising results (Tate, Reppucci, and Mulvey 1995; Henggeler et al.

1983). On the whole, we have not yet invested substantially in developing and providing comprehensive interventions directed at the interrelated and complex psychological, familial, and educational problems that these youths face (Henggeler et al. 1983). Such an effort requires a serious long-term commitment of societal resources, and until it is undertaken it cannot be said that "nothing works" (Martinson 1974). Given the long-term social cost of failure to make the investment—costs that include both the wasted lives of these youths and the harm they inflict on society—the effort seems well worth it.

If comprehensive remediation efforts are unsuccessful, at some point society's interests in protection through incapacitation will dominate in determining the legal response. However, since rehabilitative intervention with persistently antisocial youths is unlikely to result in a "quick fix," this determination of failure should not be made prematurely. A commitment to rehabilitation reinforces the constraints on punishment of the very young offenders that I have described, making a powerful case against subjecting fourteen-year-old repeat offenders to adult criminal punishment.

Policies for Responding to Adolescence-Limited Offenders

An important insight of the developmental analysis is that neither the traditional rehabilitative model (with its treatment focus) nor the modern criminal justice model (with its single-minded focus on punishment) provides the conceptual tools to describe accurately or to respond effectively to the largest category of adolescent offenders: those whose first offenses occur in the midadolescent years and whose crimes are driven by developmental influences. These offenders are not childlike and blameless, but their decisions to become involved in crimes are likely to reflect immature judgment, influenced by the psychosocial developmental factors that I have described. Thus, their criminal choices differ from those of adults in ways that are relevant to culpability and they should not be held to adult standards of criminal responsibility.

In the contemporary context, many are ready to ignore these somewhat subtle differences in assigning criminal responsibility. Thus, perhaps a more important practical implication of adopting the developmental framework is the recognition that imposing severe sanctions on adolescents whose crimes reflect transient developmental influences (i.e., "adolescent-limited" offenders) is unlikely to serve the interest of either society or offenders. In policy terms, this should translate into a presumption against adult criminal adjudication and sanctions for first offenses, even for serious crimes. Contrary to the assumption of current law, if reducing social cost is important, then the case for this more "lenient" response holds as powerfully for older (and thus presumably more culpable) youths as for younger adolescents. Indeed, the research indicates that the midadolescent first offender with no prior history of problem behavior is less likely than his younger counterpart (with such a history) to represent a substantial threat to society later in adulthood.

Under a developmental model, delinquency interventions directed at adolescents whose crimes are likely to reflect transient developmental influences would be shaped to serve multiple purposes. First, a developmental model recognizes the importance of lessons in accountability; slaps on the wrist fail to serve this purpose. Second (and linked to the first), the objective of protecting society would not be discounted. The fact that many youthful offenders will desist in their criminal activity as they mature does not create a license to offend during adolescence. Moreover, diminished responsibility does not mean nonresponsibility. The failure of the Progressives to recognize this was a fatal flaw in the traditional model of juvenile justice. Third, the systemic response would be tailored to protect rather than damage the prospects for a productive future of adolescents whose desistance is probable.

Some states have undertaken statutory-law reform that embodies the lessons of the developmental model. Pennsylvania, for example, in enacting its new Juvenile Act in 1995 adopted a "balanced approach" that embraces three goals: community protection, accountability, and competency development (to enable juveniles to leave the system more capable of "being responsible and productive members of the community") (Juvenile Court 1997; Bazemore and Umbreit 1995).

The future opportunities of juvenile offenders can be protected in several ways, including some that were designed to serve this purpose under the traditional juvenile justice system. For example, policies of maintaining the anonymity of juvenile defendants in the press and of giving accused juveniles the right to choose a closed hearing may limit the stigma of delinquency status and its lasting impact. The sealing of juvenile justice records reduces the likelihood that the young adult who has desisted from crime will be haunted by the mistakes of his youth in employment and educational contexts (On the other hand, societal protection justifies access to juvenile records if the criminal conduct persists in adulthood.) Dispositional programs that emphasize education and the acquisition of job skills will contribute to future productivity and may facilitate the process of assuming adult roles.

The developmental model also suggests directions for future innovations in juvenile justice research and policy. First, research on how the criminal choices of adolescents differ from adults and what roles developmental factors play in youthful involvement in crime will be important in refining the concept of diminished responsibility in this context. Further understanding could also allow policymakers to draw on developmental knowledge to structure incentives that could influence decisions about participation in criminal activity. Currently, we can only hypothesize about the factors that influence decision making in this context, based on knowledge of traits that shape adolescent choices in other settings. A better understanding of the process by which adolescents make choices to participate in crime could be useful in formulating prophylactic responses. Indeed, some current policies that seem to be directed toward deterrence are based on intuitions about the influences affecting juvenile choices. For example, curfew regulations discourage youths from gathering together at night, partly in recognition of the role that peer influence may have on choices that lead to trouble. A more sophisticated understanding of adolescent decision making can contribute to more effective efforts to influence youthful choices about involvement in crime.

Another important research agenda would focus on desistance from a developmental perspective. Criminological research to date has focused on the etiology of delinquency; little attention has been directed toward the process of "maturing out" of delinquency or of the mechanisms that contribute to desistance (Mulvey and Aber 1988; Farrington et al. 1988). The developmental framework clarifies the importance of seeking to understand this process and of beginning to develop interventions that may accelerate desistance—or at a minimum that do not delay the process (Moffitt 1993).

Differential Treatment in a Separate System

The most effective means of implementing the lessons from developmental psychology is to maintain a system of adjudication and disposition that is separate from the adult criminal justice system. First, a juvenile court is more likely to sustain a commitment to the principle of diminished responsibility in responding to young offenders, and to resist political pressures to subject young offenders to adult punishments. Moreover, a separate juvenile correctional system is more likely to utilize dispositional strategies, goals, and approaches that are grounded in developmental knowledge. The development of intensive rehabilitative interventions for young offenders and of responses that protect the future prospects of youths whose crimes are adolescent-limited are two strategies that promise to be more cost-effective in the long run than the blanket punitive policies that are currently in vogue. It is unlikely that either juvenile offenders or society will be better served by a unified criminal justice system—even one that treats minors more leniently for sentencing purposes (see Chapter 4 in this volume). However, the ability or inclination of the criminal justice system to tailor its response to juvenile crime so as to utilize the lessons of developmental psychology is questionable. The evidence suggests that political pressure functions as a one-way ratchet, in the direction of ever-stiffer penalties. Programs designed for adolescents and sentencing distinctions between adults and juveniles will be much harder to maintain in a unified system in which juveniles are otherwise treated as adults; it seems predictable that the lines between age groups will become blurred.

The argument for separate treatment of juvenile offenders becomes weaker when youths get older and persist in serious criminal activity. Policies regarding the adjudication of chronic serious adolescent offenders in the criminal justice system are subject to considerable debate, which generally reflects political and ideological differences. As to the optimal policy for dealing with older adolescent repeat offenders, the empirical evidence and theoretical insights from developmental psychology and criminology provide no answers.

For a broad range of juvenile offenders, however, utilitarian and retributive arguments converge to support adjudication and disposition in a separate juvenile justice system. Such a system, grounded in developmental principles, can function more coherently and effectively than a unitary system to achieve the complex societal objectives at stake. It also stands as a powerful symbol that most young offenders are different from their adult counterparts. The developmental-psychology evidence reveals that the Progressive reformers who created the traditional juvenile court a century ago exaggerated these differences in depicting young offenders as irresponsible children. Nonetheless, their core intuition, which has been obscured recently, was sound. Modern policymakers should attend to the lesson that social welfare is promoted through justice policies that recognize the immaturity of young offenders.

Works Cited

Ainsworth, J. 1991. Re-imagining childhood and reconstructing the legal order: The case for abolishing the juvenile court. *North Carolina Law Review* 69:1083–1133.

Allen-Hagen, B., and M. Sickmund. 1993. Juveniles and violence: offending and victimization. *Juvenile Justice Digest* 21:1–5.

Ambuel, B., and J. Rappaport. 1992. Developmental trends in adolescents' psychological and legal competence to consent to abortion. *Law and Human Behavior* 69:129–154.

American Psychological Association. 1990. Brief for Amicus Curiae, in support of appellees. *Hodgson v. Minnesota,* 497 U.S. 417.

——. 1987. Brief for Amicus Curiae, in support of appellees. *Zbaraz v. Hartigan,* 484 U.S. 171.

Baker, P. 1996. Va. bill takes hard line on youth crime. *Washington Post,* 1 February.

Bazemore, G., and M. Umbreit. 1995. *Balanced and restorative justice for juveniles, a national strategy for juvenile justice in the 21st century. The balanced and restorative justice project.* U.S. Dept. of Justice. Office of Juvenile Justice and Delinquency Prevention.

Bennett, W., Diiullio, Jr., J., and J. Walters. 1996. *Body count.* New York: Simon and Schuster.

Benthin, A., P. Slovic, and H. Severson. 1993. A psychometric study of adolescent risk perception. *Journal of Adolescence* 16:153–168.

Berndt, T. J. 1979. Developmental changes in conformity to peers and parents. *Developmental Psychology* 15:608–616.

Billick, S. 1986. Developmental competency. *Bulletin of the American Academy of Psychiatry* 14:301.

Blumstein, A., and J. Cohen. 1987. Characterizing criminal careers. *Science* 237:985–991.

Bonnie, R. 1977. Trends in juvenile justice reform. In *Psychiatrists and the legal process: diagnosis and debate.* New York: Insight Publishing Company.

Bonnie, R., A. Coughlin, J. Jeffries, and P. Low. 1997. *Criminal Law.* Westbury, N.Y.: The Foundation Press.

Cauffman, E. In press. (Im)maturity of judgment in adolescence: Why adolescents may be less culpable than adults. *Behavioral Sciences and the Law.*

Coleman, J. 1961. *The adolescent society.* New York: The Free Press.

Costanzo, P. R., and M. Shaw. 1966. Conformity as a function of age level. *Child Developmen* 37:967–975.

Daly, M. 1995. House toughens juvenile justice: Lawmakers back bill to try youths as adults in some violent crimes. *Hartford Courant,* 4 June.

Dowie, M. 1993. Tough justice: When kids commit adult crimes, some say that they should do adult time. *California Lawyer* 13:54–58.

Elkind, D. 1967. Egocentrism in adolescence. *Child Development* 38:1025–1034.

Elliott, D. 1993. Youth violence: An overview. Center for the Study of Youth Policy, University of Pennsylvania.

Fagan, J. In press. The comparative advantages of juvenile verses criminal court sanction on recidivism among adolescent felony offenders. Journal of Law and Social Policy.

Farrington, D. P. 1986. Age and crime. In *Crime and justice: An annual review of research,* edited by M. Tonry and N. Morris. Chicago: University of Chicago Press.

——. 1983. Offending from 10 to 25 years of age. In *Prospective studies in crime and delinquency,* edited by K. Teilman, Van Deusen, and S. A. Mednick. Boston: Nijhoff Pub.

Farrington, D., B. Gallagher, L. Morley, R. St. Ledger, and D. West. 1988. A 24 year follow-up of men from vulnerable backgrounds. In *The abandonment of delinquent behavior: Promoting the turnaround,* edited by R. L. Jenkins and W. Brown. New York: Praeger.

Farrington, D., L. Ohlin, and J. Q. Wilson. 1986. *Understanding and controlling crime.* New York: Springer-Verlag.

FBI Uniform Crime Reports. 1995. *Guide for implementing the comprehensive strategy for serious, violent, and chronic juvenile offenders.* Office of Juvenile Justice and Delinquency Prevention 1.

Federal Sentencing Guidelines, 28 U.S.C.A. Sect. 994 (1996).

Federle, K. H. 1990. The abolition of the juvenile court: A proposal for the protection of children's rights. *Journal of Contemporary Law* 16:23–51.

Feld, B. 1997. Abolish the juvenile court: Criminal responsibility and sentencing policy. *Journal of Criminal Law and Criminology* 88:68–136.

———.1991. The transformation of the juvenile court. *Minnesota Law Review* 75:691–725.

———.1987. The juvenile court meets the principle of the offense: Legislative changes in juvenile waiver statutes. *Journal of Criminal Law and Criminology* 78:471–533.

Finn, P., and B. Bragg. 1986. Perception of the risk of an accident by young and older drivers. *Accident Analysis and Prevention* 18:289–298.

Flavell, J., P. Miller, and S. Miller. 1993. *Cognitive development.* 3d ed. Englewood Cliffs, N.J.: Prentice-Hall.

Forst, M. and M. Blomquist. 1991. Cracking down on juveniles: The changing ideology of youth corrections. *Notre Dame Journal of Law, Ethics and Public Policy* 5:324–35.

Fox, S. 1970. Juvenile justice reform: An historical perspective. *Stanford Law Review* 22:1187–1239.

Fritsch, E., and C. Hemmens. 1996. An assessment of legislative approaches to the problem of serious juvenile crime: A case study in Texas 1973–1995. *American Journal of Criminal Law* 23:563–609.

———. 1995. Juvenile waiver in the United States 1979–1995: A comparison and analysis of state waiver statutes. *Juvenile and Family Court Journal* 46:17.

Furby L., and R. Beyth-Marom. 1990. Risk taking in adolescence: A decision-making perspective. *Development Review* 12:1–44.

Gardner, M. R. 1989. The right of juvenile offenders to be punished: Some implications of treating kids as persons. *Nebraska Law Review* 68:182–215.

Gardner, W. 1992. A life span theory of risk taking. In *Adolescent and adult risk taking: the eighth Texas Tech symposium on interfaces in psychology,* edited by N. Bell. Thousand Oaks, Calif.: Sage.

Gardner, W., and J. Herman. 1991. Adolescents' AIDS risk taking: A rational choice perspective. In *Adolescents in the AIDS epidemi,* edited by W. Gardner, S. Millstein, and B. Wilcox. San Francisco: Jossey-Bass.

Gardner, W., D. Scherer, and M. Tester. 1989. Asserting scientific authority: Cognitive development and adolescent legal rights. *American Psychologist* 44:895–902.

Grisso, T. 1980. Juveniles' capacities to waive Miranda rights: An empirical analysis. *California Law Review* 68:1134–1166.

———. 1981. *Juveniles' waiver of Miranda rights: Legal and psychological competence.* New York: Plenum.

———. 1996. Society's retributive response to juvenile violence: A developmental perspective. *Law and Human Behavior* 20:229.

Hampson, S., W. Burns, H. Severson, and P. Slovic. 1992. Adolescent alcohol-related risk taking: Exploring structural relations among risk perceptions, personality, and risk taking. Unpublished manuscript.

Henggeler, S., G. Melton, L. Smith, S. Schoenwald, and J. Hanley. 1983. Family preservation using multisystemic treatment: Long-term followup to a clinical trial with serious violent offenders. *Journal of Child and Family Studies* 2:283.

Hirschi, T. and M. Gottfredson. 1983. Age and the explanation of crime. *American Journal of Sociology* 89:552–584.

Holl, J. 1971. *Juvenile reform in the progressive era.* 1909. Reprint, Ithaca, N.Y.: Cornell University Press.

In re Gault 387 U.S. 1 (1967)

Inhelder, B., and J. Piaget. 1958. *The growth of logical thinking from childhood to adolescence.* New York: Basic.

Institute of Judicial Administration-American Bar Association. 1980a. Juvenile Justice Standards, Standards Relating to Dispositions.

———. 1980b. Juvenile Justice Standards, Standards Relating to Juvenile Delinquency and Sanctions.

Janis, I. 1982. Decision-making under stress. In *Handbook of stress: Theoretical and clinical aspects,* edited by L. Goldberger and S. Breznitz. New York: Free Press.

Jessor, R., and S. Jessor. 1977. *Problem behavior and psychological development: A longitudinal study of youth.* New York: Academic Press.

Juvenile Court Judges' Commission. 1997. Balanced and restorative justice in Pennsylvania: a new mission and changing roles within the juvenile justice system.

Kaser-Boyd, N., H. S. Adelman, and L. Taylor. 1985. Minors' ability to identify risks and benefits of therapy. *Professional Psychology: Research and Practice* 16:411–417.

Kaser-Boyd, N., H. S. Adelman, L. Taylor, and P. Nelson. 1986. Children's understanding of risks and benefits of psychotherapy. *Clinical Child Psychology* 15:165–171.

Kett, J. 1977. *Rites of passage: Adolescence in America—1790 to present.* New York: Basic Press.

Kulbok, P., F. Earls, and A Montgomery. 1988. Life style and patterns of health and social behavior in high-risk adolescents. *Advances in Nursing Science* 11:22.

Larson, C. 1972. *The good fight: the life and times of Ben. B. Lindsey.* Chicago: Quadrangle Books.

Levine, M., and A. Levine. 1970. *A social history of helping services.* New York: Appleton-Century-Crofts.

Lewis, C. 1981. How adolescents approach decisions: Changes over grades seven to twelve and policy implications. *Child Development* 52:538–544.

Lindsey, B., and H. O'Higgins. 1970. *The beast.* 1909. Reprint, Seattle: University of Washington Press.

Lockett v Ohio 438 US 586, 597 (1978).

Loeber, R. 1982. The stability of antisocial and delinquent child behavior: A review. *Child Development* 53:1431–32.

Loeber, R. and M. Stouthamer-Loeber. 1998. Developments of juvenile aggression and violence: Some common misconceptions and controversies. *American Psychologist* 52:242–259.

Lopes, L. 1987. Between hope and fear: the psychology of risk. *Advances in Experimental Social Psychology* 20:255–275.

Lynam, D. 1996. Early identification of chronic offenders: Who are the fledgling psychopaths? *Psychological Bulletin* 120:209.

Mack, J. 1909. The juvenile court. *Harvard Law Review* 23:104–122.

Maloney, D., D. Romig, and T. Armstrong. 1988. Juvenile probation: The balanced approach. *Juvenile and Family Court Journal* 39.

Mann, L., R. Harmoni, and C. Power. 1989. Adolescent decision-making: The development of competence. *Journal of Adolescence* 12:265.

Mann, L. 1992. Stress, affect, and risk taking. In *Risk-taking behavior,* edited by J. Yates. New York: Wiley.

Martinson, R. 1974. What works—questions and answers about prison reform. *Public Interest* 35:22–54.

Matthews, M. L., and A. R. Moran. 1986. Age differences in male drivers' perception of accident risk: The role of perceived driving ability. *Accident Analysis and Prevention* 18:299–313.

McCormick, J. 1994. Death of a child criminal. *Newsweek* 45 (12 September).

Melton, G. B. 1983. Toward 'personhood' for adolescence: Autonomy and privacy as values in public policy. *American Psychologist* 38:99–103.

———. 1989. Taking *Gault* seriously: Toward a new juvenile court. *Nebraska Law Review* 68:146–200.

Model Penal Code, Art. II, Sect. 2.01 (1962). American Law Institute.

Moffitt, T. 1993. Adolescent-limited and life course persistent antisocial behavior: A developmental taxonomy. *Psychological Bulletin* 100:674–700.

Monahan, J. 1997. Clinical and actuarial predictions of violence. In *Modern scientific evidence: The law and science of expert testimony,* edited by D. Faigman, D. Kaye, D. Saks, M. and J. Sanders. St. Paul, Minn.: West Publishing Co.

Morse, S. 1976. The twilight of welfare criminology: A reply to justice bazelon. *Southern California Law Review* 49:1247–1268.

Mulvey, E., and M. Aber. 1988. "Growing out" of delinquency: Development and desistance. In *The abandonment of delinquent behavior: Promoting the turnaround,* edited by R. L. Jenkins and W. Brown. New York: Praeger.

Mulvey, E., and J. La Rosa. 1986. Delinquency cessation and adolescent development. *American Journal of Orthopsychiatry* 56(2):212–224.

Regnery, A. S. 1985. Getting away with murder: Why the juvenile justice system needs an overhaul. *Policy Review* 34:65–69.

Reiss Jr., A., and D. Farrington. 1991. Advance knowledge about co-offending: Results from a prospective longitudinal survey of London males. *Journal of Criminal Law and Criminology* 82:360–395.

Ryerson, E. 1978. *The best laid plans—America's juvenile court experiment.* New York: Hill and Wang.

Schur, E. M. 1973. *Radical nonintervention: Rethinking the delinquency problem.* Englewood Cliffs, N.J.: Prentice-Hall.

Scott, E. 1992. Judgment and reasoning in adolescent decision making. *Villanova Law Review* 37:1607–1669.

Scott, E., N. D. Reppucci, and J. Woolard. 1995. Evaluating adolescent decision making in legal contexts. *Law and Human Behavior* 19:221–244.

Siegler, R. 1991. *Children's thinking.* 2d ed. Englewood Cliffs, N.J.: Prentice-Hall.

Snyder, H., and M. Sickmund. 1995. Juvenile offenders and victims: National report. National Center of Juvenile Justice, Pittsburgh.

Springer, C. 1991. Rehabilitating the juvenile court. *Notre Dame Journal of Law, Ethics and Public Policy* 5:397–420.

Sprinthall, N., and W. A. Collins. 1988. *Adolescent psychology: A developmental view.* New York: Random House.

State v Benoit 490 A2d 295 (N.H. 1985).

Steadman, H., M. McGreevy, J. Morrissey, L. Callahan, P. Robbins, and C. Cirincione. 1993. *Before and after Hinckley: Evaluating insanity defense reform.* New York: Guilford Press.

Steinberg, L., and E. Cauffman. 1996. Maturity of judgment in adolescence: Psychosocial factors in adolescent decision making. *Law and Human Behavior* 20(3).

Steinberg, L., and S. Silverberg. 1986. The vicissitudes of autonomy in early adolescence. *Child Development* 57:841–851.

Stepp, L. 1994. The crackdown on juvenile crime: Do stricter laws deter youth? *Washington Post,* 15 October.

Tate, D., N. D. Reppucci, and E. Mulvey. 1995. Violent juvenile delinquents: Treatment effectiveness and implications for future action. *American Psychologist* 50:777–81.

Teitelbaum, L. 1991. Youth crime and the choice between rules and standards. *Brigham Young University Law Review* 351–402.

Tester, M., W. Gardner, and E. Wilfong. 1987. Experimental studies of the development of decision-making competence. Paper presented at symposium, Children, Risks, and Decisions: Psychological and Legal Implications. Annual Convention of the American Psychological Association, New York.

U.S. House. 1996. Virginia Commission on Youth to the Governor and General Assembly. Study of Juvenile Justice Reform. H. Doc. 37.

Van den Haag, E. 1975. *Punishing criminals: Concerning a very old and painful question.* New York: Basic Books.

Von Hirsch, A. 1976. *Doing justice.* New York: Hill and Wang.

Walkover, A. 1984. The infancy defense in the new juvenile court. *University of California at Los Angeles Law Review* 31:503–562.

Weithorn, L., and S. Campbell. 1982. The competency of children and adolescents to make informed treatment decisions. *Child Development* 63:1589–1598.

Wolfgang, M., R. Figlio, and T. Sellin. 1972. *Delinquency in a birth cohort.* Chicago: University of Chicago Press.

Zimring, F. 1978. *Twentieth century fund task force on sentencing policy toward young offenders: Confronting youth crime.* New York: Holmes and Merger Publishers.

———. 1982. *The changing legal world of adolescence.* New York: The Free Press.

Note

1. Wash. Rev. Code Ann. Sect. 13.40.0io(2)(1990); N.C. Gen. Stat. Sect. 7A-646 (1993); N.J. Stat. Ann. Sect.2A:4A-43(a); Tex. Fam. Code Ann. Sect. 54.04 (1991); Ohio Rev. Code Ann. Sect. 2151-355 (1992); Ind. Code Ann. Sect. 36-6-1-1- (1987); Cal. Welf. and Instit. Code CODE Sect. 202(a)(1990). See also, for example, Pennsylvania's Juvenile Act, 42 Pa.P.S. Sect. 6301.

CHAPTER TWELVE

Researching Adolescents' Judgment and Culpability

Elizabeth Cauffman and Laurence Steinberg

The existence of a juvenile justice system separate from that for adults is based on two fundamental principles (Scott and Grisso 1997). The first tenet is that children are not fully matured and should not, therefore, be held fully responsible (or culpable) for their behavior. The second is that children are developing persons who are capable of change, and they are thus proper targets for rehabilitation rather than punishment alone. These tenets have shaped a twentieth-century jurisprudence that required judicial responses to fit the child, not the crime. This model rejected proportional punishment of the adult criminal justice system in favor of a treatment, or medical, model. The treatment model in turn required juvenile courts to make individually tailored decisions based on perceptions of each offender's degree of culpability.

Since culpability refers to the extent to which a person can be considered blameworthy or deserving of punishment for a given behavior, the evaluation of cupability is ultimately a moral decision that relies on one's notion of justice. Nevertheless, if any such moral standard is to be applied to offenders of varying levels of maturity, it is important that evaluations of maturity (and subsequent determinations of culpability) be grounded in an accurate understanding of the factors that influence how adolescents make decisions.

In recent years, legislatures and courts have placed greater emphasis on proportionality—choosing the punishment according to characteristics of the crime, rather than the offender—resulting in more frequent transfers of juveniles to adult criminal court. This trend further emphasizes the need for research on how adolescents make the choices that get them involved in offenses, and on whether young offenders' immaturity in that regard should be taken into account when society evaluates their culpability. This consideration is necessary to ensure that sanctions placed on juveniles are appropriate for their individual circumstances, as well as to ensure that youths whose offending is a consequence of immature capacities are sanctioned less harshly than adults who commit the same offenses but whose decision-making capacities are fully matured.

Despite these very important theoretical and practical concerns, there is little empirical research on the psychological attributes most relevant to these issues of culpability, especially within juvenile populations. Even in the arena of the adult justice system, there is very little systematic research regarding the extent to which various components of the insanity defense (the inability to appreciate the wrongfulness of one's acts or to conform one's conduct to the requirements of the law) are in fact related to mental illness. Among juveniles, studies linking psychological factors directly to criminal accountability are virtually nonexistent. Although our understanding of how a number of potentially relevant cognitive and psychosocial factors evolve during adolescence has grown considerably in recent years, the implications of these findings for decision-making in legal settings remain largely theoretical. The goal of this chapter is to review the literature on the psychological changes occurring during adolescence that are likely to be most relevant to questions of culpability.

Although culpability is a construct that has psychological underpinnings, the term rarely appears within the scientific literature on psychological development during adolescence. A number of related constructs have been studied by developmental psychologists, however, and research on these aspects of development, such as responsibility or maturity, is relevant to the present discussion. In addition to identifying the legal implications of such research, we shall also discuss research areas that warrant additional attention, as well as a number of methodological issues associated with ensuring that future research is applicable to the shaping of juvenile justice policy.

Maturity of Judgment

Many questions concerning adolescent culpability can be reframed as questions about decision-making and judgment, two aspects of human behavior that have received at least some attention from developmental psychologists. The term "decision-making" is generally used in studies of the actual choices that individuals make, while "judgment" refers to the underlying cognitive, emotional, and social processes involved in making these choices. "Maturity of judgment" refers to the degree of complexity and sophistication of these underlying processes. To the extent that adolescents' decision-making or judgment is comparable to that of adults, one might argue that youthful offenders should be judged by similar standards of culpability. On the other hand, if it can be demonstrated that adolescents' decision-making abilities are less than fully developed, or their judgment immature, one could assert that young offenders should, as a class, be viewed as having diminished responsibility. Consistent with this logic, a guiding assumption within the juvenile justice system is that both rehabilitation and individualized sanctioning are appropriate precisely because minors are not yet fully mature, their characters are not yet fully formed, and the degree of accountability to which they can be held is therefore lower than that for adults. Given the widespread use of the construct of immaturity to distinguish between adolescents and adults under current law—and in light of growing questions about the wisdom of this practice, as reflected in the growth of policies designed to ease the transfer of juvenile offenders to adult court—there is good reason to examine the relevant psychological evidence on the issue.

Roughly speaking, explanations of adolescents' immaturity of judgment within the developmental literature on decision-making may be classified into two broad categories: those that attribute youthful immaturity to cognitive differences between adolescents and adults (deficiencies in the fundamental mechanics of how adolescents think), and those that attribute immaturity to psychosocial differences (deficiencies in adolescents' social and emotional functioning that affect how their cognitive capabilities are used). These cognitive and psychosocial differences are assumed to result in differences in maturity of judgment and, therefore, in corresponding differences in decision-making. While the terms "judgment" and "decision-making" are closely related and are often used interchangeably, we believe that "judgment" better captures the mix of cognitive and psychosocial processes of interest than does "decision-making," a term that traditionally has had a more purely cognitive flavor within the psychological literature.

Three points about what we mean by "maturity of judgment" warrant some additional elaboration. The first is that "maturity," within the framework we offer in this chapter, refers to the process of decision-making, and not to any particular decision outcome. Separating the two—distinguishing between the quality of adolescents' decisions and the quality of their decision-making—is as difficult as it is important. In the eyes of adults, teenagers make many bad decisions: they drive too fast, they have sex without using contraception, they spend money impulsively, they experiment with drugs, they drink alcohol to excess, and so on. What is not obvious, however, is that these and other sorts of adolescent risk taking reflect deficiencies in the process of decision-making. In terms of the determination of culpability, the issue is not solely whether adolescents make bad decisions; the issue is also whether adolescents make decisions badly. For example, both a six-year-old and a thirty-six-year-old who shoot someone may be said to have made a bad decision. Yet one may be held blameless and the other fully responsible because of our different presumptions about the process by which the decision to shoot someone was made. Accordingly, any evaluation of an individual's culpability ought to depend upon the degree of maturity of the process through which his or her decision was made.

The second point about maturity of judgment has to do with the term "judgment" as opposed to "maturity." Within the framework we have advanced, judgment is neither exclusively cognitive nor exclusively psychosocial; it is a by-product of both sets of influences. Accordingly, an individual can exhibit poor judgment because of some sort of intellectual deficiency such as faulty logic or ignorance of some crucial piece of information, or because of some emotional shortcoming such as impulsivity or panic. Thus, one would argue that a young teen who robs a liquor store with his friends exhibits poor judgment regardless of whether he does so because he is unaware of the risks or because he feared the disapproval of his friends. (If, however, the teen's actions were motivated by cognitive and psychosocial processes similar to those of adults, the decision might still be bad but the decision-making process itself would not be.)

To date, most research on adolescent judgment and decision-making, and on whether adolescents' judgment is less mature than that of adults, has focused on the cognitive processes involved and has more or less ignored emotional and social influences on decision-making. In fact, the legal basis for limiting the autonomy of minors is borrowed from the medical doctrine of informed consent, which holds that patients have the right to make decisions regarding their treatment as long as these decisions are made knowingly, competently, and voluntarily (Culver 1982; Grisso and Vierling 1978; Marks 1975; Meisel, Roth, and Lidz 1977; Murphy 1979; Wadlington 1983, 57–74). Research regarding the capacities of adolescents to provide informed consent has relied almost exclusively on assessments of cognitive aspects of decision-making, in order to avoid the difficulties associated with performing studies in which the maturity of a decision is not determined by the choice itself. As we shall argue, such a narrow perspective may not allow for a full appreciation of the differences between adolescent and adult judgment.

The third and final point about maturity of judgment is that it grows both as a function of maturation (that is, changes in individuals' inherent capacities and competencies that are attributable to development) and experience (that is, changes in individuals' knowledge about the world that are attributable to exposure to any number of activities or situations). Differences in judgment between adolescents and adults, to the extent that they exist, could be due to maturational factors, experiential factors, or a combination of the two. Although it may be important in theory to ask whether any argument for the diminished culpability of adolescents as a class is more compelling if the argument is based on maturational imma- turity than if it is based on experiential immaturity, as a practical matter such distinctions are virtually impossible to make, since experience and maturation almost always go hand in hand. In the literature on automobile safety, for example, it has proven difficult to disentangle developmental differences from experiential ones in explaining why adolescents have more accidents than adults.

The commonly held belief that adolescents show poorer judgment than adults is, in all likelihood, linked to their frequent participation in dan- gerous activities. For example, adolescents, when compared with other age groups, are the most likely to be involved in automobile accidents, drug use, and unprotected sex (Arnett 1992). Arrest rates peak between the ages of fifteen and eighteen (Gottfredson and Hirschi 1990). The very fact that young people engage in these and other risky behaviors at a higher rate than adults is often taken as prima facie evidence of the in- herent immaturity of adolescent judgment—an argument that is ques- tionable. By the same token, the fact that rates of involvement in these same risky behaviors decrease as individuals develop beyond adolescence is often interpreted as evidence that individuals' judgment becomes more mature during the transition into adulthood—an equally questionable argument.

The problem in drawing inferences about judgment from evidence about risk taking inheres in the distinction between making bad decisions and making decisions badly. After all, the argument that adolescents ought to be viewed under the law as less culpable than adults hinges on showing that young people's judgment is less mature, not merely that young people take more chances or make less desirable decisions than their elders. Demonstrating that adolescents take more risks than adults is straightforward. Demonstrating that adolescents' higher incidence of risk taking is due to developmental differences in judgment is not.

In point of fact, most efforts to identify the underlying influences on judgment and decision-making that account for age differences in risk taking have not been successful (Fischhoff 1992, 133–162; Furby and Beyth-Marom 1992). Contrary to the stereotype of adolescents as mark- edly egocentric, for example, or as doomed by deficiencies in logical abil- ity, studies show that adolescents (at least, from age fifteen on) are no more likely than adults to suffer from the "personal fable" (the belief that one's behavior is somehow not governed by the same rules of nature that apply to everyone else, such as when a cigarette smoker believes that he is immune to the health effects of smoking) and no less likely than adults to employ rational algorithms in decision-making situations (Jacobs-Quadrel, Fischhoff, and Davis 1993). In fact, there is substantial evidence that adolescents are well aware of the risks they take (Alexander et al. 1990), and ample evidence suggesting that increasing adolescents' awareness of various risks has little impact on their decision-making outside the laboratory (Office of Technology 1991; Rotheram-Borus and Koopman 1990, 29–36). There is little evidence that growth in logical abilities occurs in any systematic way much past age sixteen.

The failure of researchers to find strong evidence of cognitive differences between adolescents and adults that might account for developmental differences in risky decision-making has led to two very different sorts of speculation. One line of reasoning, derived from behavioral decision theory, is that adolescents and adults employ the same logical processes when making decisions but differ in the sorts of information they use and the priorities they hold; adolescents may make bad decisions, but they do not make decisions badly, or, at least, any differently than would an adult with the same priorities. According to this view, for example, adolescents engage in unprotected sex more often than adults not because adolescents suffer from a personal fable that permits them to deny the possibility of pregnancy or because they are misinformed about the risks of the activity, but because in the calculus of a sixteen-year-old, the potential benefits of unprotected sex (spontaneity, heightened physical pleasure) simply outweigh in value the potential costs. Within this model, age differences in risky decision-making stem from differences in concerns, not competencies (Beyth-Marom et al. 1993; Furby and Beyth-Marom 1992; Gardner and Herman 1990, 17–34).

The distinction between concerns and competencies has important applied, as well as theoretical, implications. It also is directly relevant to the present discussion of adolescent culpability. Indeed, the failure of researchers to document systematic differences between adolescents and adults on measures of the cognitive processes underlying decision-making has led many to challenge the long-standing view of adolescents as inherently less culpable than adults, a view that, as we have noted, undergirds the very existence of a separate juvenile justice system. The absence of systematic data showing that adults outperform adolescents on assessments of cognitive abilities consequently has raised concerns about the appropriateness of laws and legal decisions that historically have been grounded in this perspective, whether those laws govern access to medical care (where youth advocates have argued, for example, that adolescents ought to be able to make their own health care decisions, without parental consent, on the ground that adolescents are just as competent as adults) or the adjudication of criminal conduct (where advocates of harsher treatment of juvenile offenders have used the same evidence to argue against the presumption of diminished responsibility among youth).

In other words, there is little evidence, at least from studies of cognitive development, to support the assertion that adolescents, once they have reached sixteen, should be viewed as less culpable than adults. This is not the end of the story, however, nor should it mean the end of the juvenile justice system. The second line of reasoning on the question of age differences in risky decision-making has been suggested by several writers who have argued that there may be developmental differences between adolescents and adults in noncognitive realms that account for age differences in behavior and that may have implications for assessments of culpability (Cauffman and Steinberg 1995; Scott, Reppucci, and Woolard 1995; Steinberg and Cauffman 1996). We and others have suggested, specifically, that differences in risky decision-making between adolescents and adults may well reflect differences in aptitudes, but that the particular aptitudes involved are not those that are assessed by measures of logical reasoning. According to our view, there may well exist psychosocial factors that affect the sorts of decisions individuals make, that follow a developmental progression between adolescence and adulthood, and that bear on the question of adolescent culpability.

In several publications (Cauffman and Steinberg 1995; Steinberg and Cauffman 1996), we have proposed a model of maturity of judgment that emphasizes three broad categories of psychosocial factors that are likely to affect the ways in which individuals make decisions, including decisions to commit antisocial or criminal acts. These three categories of psychosocial factors include *responsibility,* which encompasses such characteristics as self-reliance, clarity of identity, and healthy autonomy; *perspective,* which refers to the ability to understand the complexity of a situation and place it in a broader context; and *temperance,* which refers to the ability to limit impulsivity and to evaluate situations before acting. Although systematic data on the developmental course of each of these phenomena, their interrelations, and their joint and cumulative impact on decision-making are lacking, most major theories of adolescent psychosocial development suggest that there are significant developmental changes in several aspects of responsibility, perspective, and temperance over the course of adolescence. More important, there is reason to suspect that developments in these areas may potentially affect individuals' decision-making and risk taking in ways that ought to be taken into account in making culpability determinations. In other words, there is reason to believe that adolescents, as a class, may warrant the characterization of diminished responsibility not because of cognitive immaturity or otherwise impaired reasoning, but because of deficiencies in responsibility, perspective, and temperance.

The relative importance of cognitive versus psychosocial characteristics in evaluating culpability is not clear, nor is it certain if particular psychosocial factors ought to be weighed more heavily than others. It is clear, however, that judges are often required to consider the "totality of circumstances" when evaluating options for juveniles. Our reading of relevant rulings, moreover, suggests that when American legal opinions refer to individuals' maturity (or immaturity) of judgment, the courts have in mind something close to the virtues of responsibility, perspective, and temperance. For example, in the landmark case *Kent v. United States* (1966), the Supreme Court reviewed the District of Columbia's statutory criteria for waiver to adult court, which included such factors as "the sophistication and maturity of the juvenile as determined by consideration of his home, environmental situation, emotional attitude, and pattern of living."

Although there has been some research to date on the development of various aspects of responsibility, perspective, and temperance during adolescence (Steinberg and Cauffman 1996), few studies have compared adolescents and adults directly on these dimensions, and fewer still have attempted to examine the relations between these psychosocial elements of judgment and decision-making in situations relevant to legal concerns. We recently completed a study designed to explore the relations between judgment and several aspects of psychosocial maturity within a sample of over a thousand individuals ranging in age from ten to forty-eight (Cauffman and Steinberg, in press). In this research, we looked at age differences in individuals' performance on a series of hypothetical judgments designed to assess the participants' likelihood of engaging in criminal behavior (shoplifting, smoking marijuana, joyriding in a stolen car); individuals' performance in these hypothetical judgments has been shown to be predictive of actual criminal behavior (Brown et al. 1993). We also examined age differences in responsibility, perspective, and temperance, and the relations between judgment and psychosocial maturity, both within and across age groups.

Three overall patterns of findings from this study are relevant to the present discussion of culpability and maturity of judgment. First, we found clear and significant age differences on the measure of decision-making in antisocial situations, with adults significantly less likely than adolescents to respond to the dilemmas in ways indicative of antisocial inclinations. Second, we found consistent age differences on a wide array of measures of responsibility, perspective, and temperance. Compared with adults, for example, adolescents scored lower on measures of self-restraint, consideration of future consequences, and self-reliance, three widely cited components of psychosocial maturity. Third, and most importantly, individuals who scored higher on the measures of psychosocial maturity were more likely to make socially responsible decisions in the hypothetical situations than those who were less psychosocially mature. Once the differences in responsibility, perspective, and temperance were accounted for, age was no longer a significant predictor of judgment. In other words, although adults tended to make more socially responsible decisions than adolescents, this difference in decision-making was due to differences in psychosocial maturity. On average, adolescents make poorer (more antisocial) decisions than adults because they are more psychosocially immature.

Although we did discover broad and consistent age trends in both decision-making and psychosocial maturity, we could not identify a clear-cut chronological age at which the increase in maturity is so dramatic that a bright-line age distinction would be warranted. Nevertheless, it is clear that important progress in the development of psychosocial maturity continues to occur during late adolescence, beyond the point in development when age differences in purely logical abilities seem to disappear. Moreover, it certainly appears as if these changes in psychosocial maturity have an effect on individuals' ability to make consistently mature decisions when tempted by situations that could have legal ramifications.

As developmental psychologists, it is difficult for us to say just how these findings ought to affect decisions about adolescents within legal contexts. The decisions about whether an individual is mature enough to be held culpable for his or her actions are moral, not scientific. We do believe, however, that our work challenges the widely reported presumption derived from recent work on the development of logical decision-making that adolescents are just as competent as adults. With regard to important aspects of psychosocial functioning that affect judgment—such things as self-reliance, the consideration of future consequences, and self-restraint—adolescents, even those who are seventeen or eighteen, are not equivalent to adults. Much more, and better, research is certainly needed, but it surely appears as if a great deal of development continues to take place during middle and late adolescence within the realm of judgment that is not picked up in research that equates the study of judgment with the study of logical reasoning.

Unanswered Research Questions

As we have noted, the standard approach to the psychological study of the development of legal competence has been to investigate age differences, different aspects of cognitive functioning, and, in particular, the logical-reasoning abilities presumed to undergird decision-making. Typically, individuals of different ages are asked to respond to hypothetical vignettes that require them to analyze information and make a decision. In some versions of this research, the nature or amount of information presented in the vignettes is systematically varied, and individuals' responses are examined in light of this variation. For example, in a study concerning sexual risk taking, in which individuals are asked whether they would use a particular form of contraception, the probability of the contraceptive failing might be varied within the vignette to see whether individuals' decision-making differed in response to that particular piece of information. In this sort of research, respondents may also be asked a series of open-ended questions about a decision in order to reveal further clues about the logical processes they employ. For example, in a study by Beyth-Marom et al. (1993), subjects were presented with several behaviors and asked to think about a range of possible outcomes. For instance, "Your friends asked you to come along with them for a drive after a party where everyone had been drinking. You decided to join them. What are all the possible good and bad things that might happen as a result of your decision?" Subjects were asked to list consequences of the given choice. In some cases, decisions were presented as one-time occurrences, while in others they were presented as recurring activities. For example, "List all the good and bad things you can think are more likely to happen if someone your age drinks beer regularly than if a person your age does not drink beer regularly." This approach to studying decision-making performance, however, is likely to diminish the importance of psychosocial factors in the decision-making process.

Although these studies have provided important information on age differences—or, more precisely, the lack of age differences—in reasoning, it is not clear how applicable the findings from these studies are in explaining how individuals make real-world, real-time decisions in situations relevant to the present discussion of culpability. If emotional and psychosocial influences play a vital role in decision-making outside the laboratory, research that minimizes or controls any such influences may yield incorrect conclusions about developmental differences in judgment. The problem is not simply that hypothetical studies of reasoning may paint an incomplete picture—even advocates of this research admit that this is probably the case—the problem is that these studies likely paint an erroneous one. Indeed, if the most important differences between adolescent and adult decision-making are not due to cognitive factors but to emotional and psychosocial factors, studies that examine cognitive factors in isolation will suggest that adolescents and adults are more similar than is probably the case.

Researchers interested in studying the development of culpability will need to examine judgment under conditions that more closely approximate the situations in which real-world decisions are made. This will necessitate expanding the list of questions asked in this research beyond those that pertain to age differences in logical reasoning. Five sets of questions strike us as especially important:

First, how is judgment affected by psychosocial factors, especially those believed to develop in significant ways during middle adolescence? Our preliminary work indicates that psychosocial factors such as responsibility, perspective, and temperance may indeed influence decision-making, that adolescents and adults differ on these dimensions, and that these age differences may in fact argue for a diminished-responsibility view of young people. Far more research, in both contrived and real-world settings, is needed on psychosocial development and judgment in adolescence.

Second, how is judgment affected by emotional factors such as mood or psychological state? A limited amount of work has examined mood, both positive and negative, and its impact on decision-making, but this work has been restricted to studies of adults and has not to our knowledge been conducted from a developmental perspective. There is also a great deal of anecdotal, if not empirical, evidence that adolescence is a time of heightened volatility in mood. But we do not know whether the impact of mood on decision-making changes with age or whether adolescents are more or less susceptible than adults to the impact of mood on judgment. Similarly, although we know that adolescence is a period during which the prevalence of certain psychological maladies, such as depression, increases, we do not know the effects that such changes have on judgment.

Third, how is judgment influenced by the context in which decisions are made? Laboratory studies provide a basis for assessing decision-making in one particular context: the laboratory. While this is not inherently problematic—after all, there are many advantages to studying certain phenomena within controlled settings—one can legitimately ask questions about the likely generalizability of findings generated in this context to behavior in other settings (Bronfenbrenner 1979). This may be an especially important concern in the study of young people's judgment in antisocial situations, because the context in which adolescent misbehavior most often occurs is markedly different from the context employed in the typical psychology laboratory experiment. Most laboratory studies of judgment test respondents singly, for example, while the decision-making surrounding most adolescent misbehavior occurs in groups. Most laboratory studies are highly structured, but most adolescent misbehavior occurs in settings that are highly unstructured. Most laboratory studies of judgment are conducted under the supervision of adults, and the respondent is generally aware that his or her answers will be read by someone in a position of authority; in contrast, most adolescent misbehavior occurs away from adult supervision, and most young people believe that they will not be caught for their misdeeds. In order to fully understand the development of judgment and the factors that may contribute to diminished responsibility, we need to know whether individuals' decision-making varies as a function of the number and types of people present in the situation, the degree to which the situation is structured, and whether the decision is likely to be revealed to others. We also need to know whether these factors differentially affect people of different ages. To the extent that these contextual factors matter, and to the extent that they matter in different ways or to different degrees during adolescence than during adulthood, laboratory studies that do not take these factors into account may provide a very misleading picture. Research on peer influence, for instance, has found that susceptibility to the pressure of others peaks during midadolescence (Steinberg and Silverberg 1986), and studies of group dynamics suggest that groups tend to reach decisions prematurely, without considering all options thoroughly (Janis 1982, 69–80).

Fourth, how does judgment vary as a function of subject matter? Do individuals demonstrate comparable levels of maturity across different domains of decision-making, or does a person's maturity of judgment vary from one type of situation to another? The prevailing assumption within the study of judgment is that results obtained from studies of decision-making in one domain (such as in medical settings) can be readily generalized to decision-making in other domains (such as in antisocial situations). More likely, however, is that an individual's maturity of judgment may vary considerably depending on the decision at hand, because judgment is affected not only by the individual's decision-making competencies, but by factors such as experience and knowledge. It is not at all clear, for example, that the developmental trends observed in studies of how individuals make medical-treatment decisions (Ambuel and Rappaport 1992; Lewis 1980; Weithorn and Campbell 1982) ought to provide a basis for reaching conclusions about the development of young people's abilities in legal contexts. Similarly, we do not know whether the development of certain aspects of adjudicative competence, such as one's understanding of Miranda rights (Grisso 1980), follows the same developmental pattern as does the growth of various aspects of judgment relevant to considerations of culpability. It is fully plausible, for instance, that the age at which most individuals are competent to stand trial is not the same as the age at which most individuals are competent to waive their Miranda rights, or the age at which they should no longer be assumed to have diminished culpability by virtue of their immaturity.

Finally, does judgment improve with experience? Is it possible to examine the impact of experience on judgment independent of, or in addition to, the impact of cognitive or psychosocial maturation? Do adolescents make more mature decisions about issues they have faced before? Do negative experiences lead to more conservative choices, and do gambles that pay off lead to increased recklessness? How well do adolescents learn from the mistakes of others? Answering such questions is vital if we are truly to understand the dynamics of adolescent decision-making. Not only will the answers have ramifications for the development and refinement of policy concerning adolescent culpability, but they may also provide insight regarding possible treatment and intervention strategies for teens who persistently engage in dangerous and illegal behavior.

Methodological Issues for Future Research

In the preceding discussion of research questions that are important to consider if we are to improve our understanding of the development of judgment and decision-making, we have intentionally avoided the issue of how the effects in question can be reliably studied. We would not be entirely honest, however, if we did not admit that the extension of decision-making research to include emotional, psychosocial, and contextual influences is as difficult as it is important. Three challenging methodological problems must be overcome. First, it is often difficult to replicate, using hypothetical dilemmas, the emotional, social, and contextual factors presumed to influence decision-making within experimental research designs that are ecologically valid. (In psychology, "ecological validity" refers to the extent to which performance in an experimental situation is generalizable to performance in the real-world situation of interest.) Second, conventional self-report measures that ask respondents to describe actual decisions may be subject to significant reporting biases; simply put, it is not clear that individuals actually behave in the ways that they say they do (or say they would). Finally, comparisons between adolescents and adults in studies of decision-making must ensure that the age groups are equivalent with respect to other characteristics likely to affect judgment. Middle-class college students, for example, can not serve as the young adult group against which a demographically heterogeneous sample of teenagers is compared. Similarly, studies focusing on adolescents who have committed crimes must be compared with adults from similar circumstances.

Ecological Validity

One of the most problematic aspects of controlled decision-making studies is that they frequently rely on asking individuals to respond to hypothetical dilemmas (Fischhoff 1992, 133–162). While this paradigm has
been useful in the study of cognitive influences on decision-making, it may
not suffice in the study of emotional, pychosocial, or contextual factors.
Controlled laboratory experiments cannot hope to capture the decision-
making process that occurs when an adolescent is deciding whether to
have intercourse for the first time, whether to abort a pregnancy, whether
to join friends in a shoplifting spree, or whether to rob a liquor store. Responses to hypothetical dilemmas are highly likely to be influenced by
social desirability biases, with respondents giving socially acceptable answers instead of reporting their most likely responses in real situations.
Even in the absence of such biases, however, hypothetical situations lack
important dimensions of real-life situations. Research has shown, for example, that stress has a measurable impact on laboratory-based decision-
making tasks (Janis 1982, 69–80; Keinan 1987; Mann 1992, 201–230). Such
effects are eliminated from most studies relying on hypothetical scenarios.

Furthermore, studies based on hypothetical dilemmas also minimize
the potential effects of psychosocial factors such as responsibility and
temperance. By definition, hypothetical situations do not require an individual to exercise responsibility or self-reliance, because hypothetical
situations have no real consequences. By design, hypothetical situations
minimize the importance of temperance, because subjects in such experiments are well aware that their decision-making is under investigation
and are rarely expected to make decisions in the face of time pressure or
coercion by others. In the real world, adolescents make many decisions
that have serious consequences, often in the company of others and typically in contexts that may evoke impulsivity among individuals with little
self-control.

Designing experimental situations with greater ecological validity is
difficult, but it is not impossible. Examples of the sort of research we have
in mind include work by Ambuel and Rappaport (1992), who studied cognitive competence among teenagers who were visiting a medical clinic for
a pregnancy test, and by Lewis (1980), who examined age differences in
considerations regarding abortion decisions among subjects awaiting the
results of pregnancy tests. Future studies should attempt to examine the
ways in which responsibility, temperance, and perspective come into play
in these and other real-world settings. One important, and researchable,
question is whether adolescents' responses to decision-making dilemmas
are different when they are presented these problems while with peers ver-

sus alone. It would be fascinating to know, for example, whether the influence of group pressure on decision-making—even in the lab—varies as a function of respondents' age.

Self-Report Measures

A second challenge of studying realistic decision-making is that even when studies ask about choices made in actual situations, reliance on self-report data means that social-desirability effects will still be present; it is not clear how accurate even honest attempts at describing one's own decision-making can be. In many instances, the sorts of questions asked of research participants require a level of self-awareness and a sophistication of metacognition ("metacognition" refers to the process of thinking about thinking) that may be well beyond the reach of many adults, much less adolescents. For example, subjects may be given a scenario such as, "You're out shopping with some of your close friends and they decide to take some clothing without paying for it. You don't think it's a good idea, but they say you should take something too. First, suppose nothing bad would happen to you (such as getting arrested) if you took the clothing. Would you shoplift or would you refuse to take the item? Now suppose something bad *would* happen. Finally, suppose you don't know what would happen."

How valid are individuals' descriptions of how they might have behaved if they knew the outcome of different decisions? How accurately can a person estimate the relative importance of peer influence in a particular decision? How much faith should we place in individuals' reports of how much they weighed certain pieces of information but discounted others?

This is not to say that individuals' self-reports should necessarily be discounted as biased or inaccurate. However, research on judgment and decision-making should supplement self-report measures of judgment with other sorts of indices. These supplements might include the reports of third parties, the use of physiological indicators of such phenomena as stress or impulsiveness, and direct behavioral observations of decision-making. Ethnographic studies of adolescents on the street may tell us a great deal about the ways in which group dynamics influence individual decision-making processes.

Sampling Issues

It is also important to pay close attention to how the samples we study are chosen and compared. There is a strong foundation of criminological research on the relations between delinquency and such demographic factors as age, gender, ethnicity, and socioeconomic status. If we are to perform research on decision-making that will be of use to those who deal with delinquent populations, then special care must be taken to ensure that such interrelated variables do not make the findings ambiguous and difficult to interpret. Two implications of this caution warrant further elaboration.

The first implication is that conclusions about adolescent judgment and, accordingly, culpability, must not be generalized beyond the specific population studied. This is extremely important insofar as studies of decisions related to offending are concerned, because the samples of young individuals detained for delinquent or criminal activity are hardly representative of the general population of young people. As Grisso (1996) has argued repeatedly, for example, it is not at all clear that developmental trends in competence that are obtained from studies of community populations of adolescents are generalizable to populations of young offenders, much less young detainees. The "average" adolescent may meet criteria for cognitive or psychosocial maturity at age fifteen; the "average" offender, who is likely both poorer and less intelligent, may not meet the same criteria until several years later. Studies are needed that compare different measures of maturity across populations of young people from very different circumstances.

Similar considerations also apply to comparisons of adolescents and adults. Many such studies draw adolescent samples from heterogeneous middle-school and high-school populations (which contain a mixture of college-bound and non-college-bound youth) but draw adult samples from college campuses, out of convenience. It is not clear, however, whether any observed differences between the age groups in this sort of research design are due to age or to some other confounding factor such as socioeconomic status. Any attempts to draw conclusions about age differences in competence or culpability from experimental research must make sure that age alone is the factor that distinguishes the comparison groups.

This problem is compounded when the adolescent sample of interest is a group of young detainees or inmates. Suppose we wish to ask how this group fares on one or more measures of psychosocial maturity; we are interested in asking whether the concept of diminished responsibility applies to the young people in the group. But what is the relevant comparison group? Other adolescents? Other adolescents who have offended but who are not detained or incarcerated? Adults? Adult offenders? Adult inmates?

There are no simple answers to the comparison-group question. Instead, we encourage other researchers interested in the study of culpability to pay close attention to the need for developing a research design that matches the specific question of interest. This will entail a careful consideration of the methods, measures, and samples used. Research intended to lead to the development of a diagnostic instrument designed to assess diminished responsibility in individuals (a tool to be used by forensic examiners) may well be very different from research designed to inform policymakers about the delineation of broad age distinctions under the law.

Summary

We have discussed recent psychological research relevant to the issue of adolescent culpability, outlined a number of areas in which further research is essential, and described the methodological challenges associated with such studies. Researchers have the potential for greatly improving our understanding of how maturity of judgment develops as individuals progress from childhood, through adolescence, and into adulthood. If properly framed, such studies may serve as useful sources of guidance for those who formulate juvenile justice policy or who are involved in the adjudication of individual juvenile court cases.

In the end, however, how to interpret and apply the results of research on judgment remains a moral, rather than scientific, choice. Even if the developmental progression of mature judgment were, one day, completely and precisely understood, and even if an individual's level of maturity could be accurately determined, the moral issue would remain: where should society draw the line between those who are sufficiently mature to be held fully culpable for their misbehavior (and who should therefore receive full penalties) and those whose transgressions are a reflection of immature judgment? In adult courts, no such distinction is made between immature and mature individuals. Although defendants may claim insanity, pleas of "not culpable by reason of immaturity" are not available for purposes of claiming diminished responsibility for one's actions. When very young children commit violent acts, in contrast, there is little question that they lack the maturity to be held completely responsible for their behavior. Between childhood and adulthood, however, there lies the gray area of adolescence, when the scale tips gradually from certain immaturity to unquestioned maturity.

In our view, the growing body of evidence that maturity improves gradually and at different rates for different people, combined with the lack of a clear cutoff between maturity and immaturity, underscores the wisdom of the juvenile justice system's long-standing emphasis on individually tailored treatment. Under such a system, it may be determined, for example, that an offending teenager who is not yet fully mature but who nevertheless "ought to know better" may be less culpable than an adult but more so than an eight-year-old. Sanctions under these circumstances may rightly be determined as falling somewhere between those for an immature eight-year-old and those for a mature adult. It is our hope that further study of the factors that influence the development of mature judgment will allow issues of adolescent culpability to be resolved more equitably and consistently, and through consideration of the processes behind an adolescent's decisions rather than a reliance solely on the choices themselves in inferring the maturity of an adolescent's judgment.

Works Cited

Alexander, C., Y. Kim, M. Ensminger, K. Johnson, B. J. Smith, and L. Dolan. 1990. A measure of risk taking for young adolescents: Reliability and validity assessments. *Journal of Youth and Adolescence* 19:559–569.

Ambuel, B., and J. Rappaport. 1992. Developmental trends in adolescents' psychological and legal competence to consent to abortion. *Law and Human Behavior* 16:129–154.

Arnett, J. 1992. Reckless behavior in adolescence: A developmental perspective. *Developmental Review* 12:391–409.

Beyth-Marom, R., L. Austin, B. Fischhoff, C. Palmgren, and M. Jacobs-Quadrel. 1993. Perceived consequences of risky behaviors: Adults and adolescents. *Developmental Psychology* 293:549–563.

Bronfenbrenner, U. 1979. *The ecology of human development.* Cambridge: Harvard University Press.

Brown, B., N. Mounts, S. Lamborn, and L. Steinberg. 1993. Parenting practices and peer group affiliation in adolescence. *Child Development* 64:467–482.

Cauffman, E., and L. Steinberg. 1995. The cognitive and affective influences on adolescent decision-making. *Temple Law Review* 68:1763–1789

———. In press. (Im)maturity of judgment in adolescence: Why adolescents may be less culpable than adults. *Behavioral Sciences and the Law,* manuscript submitted for review.

Culver, C. M. 1982. *Philosophy in medicine.* New York: Oxford University Press.

Fischhoff, B. 1992. Risk taking: A developmental perspective. In *Risk-taking behavior,* edited by J. Yates. New York: Wiley.

Furby, L., and R. Beyth-Marom. 1992. Risk taking in adolescence: A decision-making perspective. *Developmental Review* 12:1–44.

Gardner, W., and J. Herman. 1990. Adolescents' AIDS risk taking: A rational choice perspective. In *Adolescents in the AIDS epidemic,* edited by W. Gardner, S. Millstein, and B. Wilcox. San Francisco: Jossey-Bass.

Gottfredson, M., and T. Hirschi. 1990. *A general theory of crime.* Stanford, Calif.: Stanford University Press.

Grisso, T. 1980. Juveniles' capacities to waive Miranda rights: An empirical analysis. *California Law Review* 68:1135–1166.

——. 1996. Society's retributive response to juvenile violence: A developmental perspective. *Law and Human Behavior* 20:229–247.

Grisso, T., and L. Vierling. 1978. Minors' consent to treatment: A developmental perspective. *Professional Psychology* 9, 412–427.

Jacobs-Quadrel, M., B. Fischhoff, and W. Davis. 1993. Adolescent invulnerability. *American Psychologist* 482:102–116.

Janis, I. L. 1982. Decision-making under stress. In *Handbook of stress: Theoretical and clinical aspects,* edited by L. Goldberger and S. Breznitz. New York: Van Nostrand Reinhold.

Keinan, G. 1987. Decision-making under stress: Scanning of alternatives under controllable and uncontrollable threats. *Journal of Personality and Social Psychology* 52:639–644.

Kent v. United States, 383 U.S. 541 (1966).

Lewis, C. 1980. A comparison of minors' and adults' pregnancy decisions. *American Journal of Orthopsychiatry* 503:446–453.

Mann, L. 1992. Stress, affect, and risk taking. In *Risk-taking behavior,* edited by J. Yates. New York: Wiley.

Marks, F. R. 1975. Detours on the road to maturity: A view of the legal conception of growing up and letting go. *Law and Contemporary Problems* 39:78–92.

Meisel, A., L. H. Roth, and C. W. Lidz. 1977. Toward a model of the legal doctrine on informed consent. *American Journal of Psychiatry* 134:285–289.

Murphy, J. G. 1979. Therapy and the problem of autonomous consent. *International Journal of Law and Psychiatry* 2:415–430.

Office of Technology Assessment. 1991. *Adolescent health.* 3 vols. Washington, D.C.: U.S. Government Printing Office.

Rotheram-Borus, M. and C. Koopman. 1990. AIDS and adolescents. In *Encyclopedia of adolescence,* edited by R. Lerner, A Peterson, and J. Brooks-Gunn. New York: Garland Press.

Scott, E., and T. Grisso. 1997. The evolution of adolescence: A developmental perspective on juvenile justice reform. *Journal of Criminal Law and Criminology* 88:137–189.

Scott, E., N. Reppucci, and J. Woolard. 1995. Evaluating adolescent decision-making in legal contexts. *Law and Human Behavior* 19:221–244.

Steinberg, L., and E. Cauffman. 1996. Maturity of judgment in adolescence: Psychosocial factors in adolescent decision-making. *Law and Human Behavior* 20:249–272.

Steinberg, L., and S. Silverberg. 1986. The vicissitudes of autonomy in early adolescence. *Child Development* 57:841–851.

Wadlington, W. J. 1983. Consent to medical for minors: The legal framework. In *Children's competence to consent,* edited by G. B. Melton, G. P. Koocher, and M. J. Saks. New York: Plenum Press.

Weithorn, L. A., and S. B. Campbell. 1982. The competency of children and adolescents to make informed treatment decisions. *Child Development* 53:1589–1598.

CHAPTER THIRTEEN

The Social Cognitive (Attributional) Perspective on Culpability in Adolescent Offenders

SANDRA GRAHAM AND COLLEEN HALLIDAY

The psychologist George Kelly wrote that a good theory has an appropriate range and focus of convenience (1955). By "range" he meant the breadth of phenomena that the theory can address, and "focus" refers to the domains or topics where the theory works best. Kelly offers these distinctions partly to remind the scientific community that no psychological theory can possibly encompass all of the complexity of human behavior, and that a given theory is better suited to predicting some domains of human functioning than others.

In this chapter we hope to make the case that a social-cognitive theory of motivation based on causal attributions can shed light on questions of culpability in adolescent offenders. But the contribution of this theoretical perspective must be evaluated within the constraints suggested by Kelly. The construct of culpability is within the range of convenience of attribution theory. Most of the authors in this volume discuss culpability as the extent to which juvenile offenders should be held responsible (blameworthy) for their offenses and to what degree they should be punished. Inferences about causal responsibility, blame, and punishment deservedness also are central components in attributional analyses. Such inferences help explain the motivations underlying individuals' choices in their everyday lives, including the decision to engage in illegal behavior; they also aid our understanding of how the public evaluates individual culpability. In this chapter we concentrate on individuals' (adolescent offenders') everyday decision making that incorporates attributional principles, although the implications of the approach for understanding how others judge youths' culpability should become apparent.

But we must also acknowledge that the theory and research that comprise this chapter did not emerge from a concern with juvenile justice.

The focus of convenience of attribution theory has been on individual-achievement strivings and on reactions to the needy (Weiner 1995). We are neither criminologists nor juvenile-delinquency theorists and we do not see our work as comprising a theory of adolescent offending. Rather, by taking into account perceptions of causality in self and others, we believe that our approach can shed light on an important but perhaps unrecognized dimension of culpability.

With these cautions acknowledged, our chapter is organized as follows. We begin with a brief overview of the main principles of attribution theory, focusing on those tenets most pertinent to issues of culpability. Next we describe a program of attribution research with adolescent offenders and those at risk for offending that addresses four topics: the attributional biases of delinquent youth, their attitudes about fairness of the justice system, their understanding of the social functions of accounts such as confession, and the relationship between beliefs about control and adjustment following release from confinement. There is an inherent logic (at least to us) to these themes; through them we use our attributional lens to probe the causal thinking of youthful offenders as they penetrate the justice system. We intend to show that many deviant adolescents have a different way of viewing the world and this view shapes their decision making in contexts that put them at risk for criminal offending. In keeping with the theme of this volume, we also will make the case that the way youthful offenders view their causal world reflects an immaturity in decision making that policymakers should consider when determining youths' degree of culpability for criminal transgressions.

Attribution Theory

Attribution theory is part of what might more broadly be defined as a social-cognitive approach to human motivation. Social-cognition researchers study the thoughts, perceptions, and interpretations of events that shape the way people understand their social world (Fiske and Taylor 1991). How individuals process social information is thought to be an important determinant of subsequent feelings and behavior. As a particular kind of social cognition, causal attributions are answers to "why" questions, such as "Why did I fail the test?" or "Why did I get arrested?" Individuals make attributions about other people as well as about themselves. As we were writing this chapter, for example, the American public was riveted by the incidents involving a thirteen-year-old Arkansas youth and his eleven-year-old accomplice who went on a shooting rampage that killed four schoolmates and a teacher. Most of the commentary associated with this heinous crime implicitly or explicitly asked "why": Were the youngsters mentally ill? Had either been the victim of abuse? Were guns too readily accessible? People especially seek answers to "why" questions about themselves and others following unexpected or unusual outcomes.

Causal search can lead to an infinite number of attributions. In the achievement domain, which has served as a model for the study of causality in other contexts, the main perceived causes of success and failure are an ability or aptitude factor, effort, task difficulty or ease, mood, luck, and help or hindrance from others. The dominant perceived causes of adolescent crime tend to be such factors as mental instability of the offender, poor parenting, and poverty (Furnham 1988). The most salient causes of poverty, in turn, are factors such as laziness, substance abuse, or poor management skills, plus social causes such as unemployment, poor schooling, and discrimination (Zucker and Weiner 1993).

Because specific attributional content will vary considerably between domains as well as between individuals, researchers have focused the theory on the underlying dimensions or properties of causes in addition to specific causes per se. Three such causal dimensions have been identified with some certainty. These are locus, or whether a cause is internal or external to the individual; stability, which designates a cause as constant or varying over time; and controllability, or whether a cause is subject to volitional influence. For example, ability is typically perceived as internal, stable, and uncontrollable. That is, low aptitude as a cause for failure resides within the individual, is constant over time, and is not subject to volitional control. This is in contrast to lack of effort, which is also internal but more often perceived as unstable and under an individual's personal control. The main perceived causes of crime and poverty can similarly be classified according to these basic attributional dimensions—that is, whether they are internal versus environmental causes, chronic or relatively short-term, and within or not within the individual's control.

Each of these causal dimensions has both psychological and behavioral consequences. In this chapter we focus on the consequences of perceived controllability, both in oneself and in others. Regarding self-perception, when people attribute their failures to factors beyond their control, they feel helpless or depressed and often display behaviors such as passivity, escape, and withdrawal. Loss of control or the fear of such loss can be a major stress in one's life. Later in this chapter we will elaborate on such causal beliefs when we discuss a particular kind of control belief that is related to recidivism in adolescent offenders.

Controllability is also linked to a set of inferences, emotions, and behavior that involve reactions toward others. Because most behavior takes place in social contexts (this may be particularly true for adolescent offending), how individuals perceive causality in other people can have considerable impact on the kinds of decisions they make. A large body of attribution research documents that when others are perceived as being responsible for negative events (that is, their behaviors are controllable), this elicits anger and the desire to neglect, inflict harm, or punish (Weiner 1995). These principles can partly explain, for example, the behavior of abusive parents toward their misbehaving children, violent spouses in distressed marriages, and conservative legislators who make policy about welfare dependency. Attribution theorists further propose that causal thoughts, feelings, and actions are interrelated in a particular way: our causal thoughts tell us how to feel and our feelings in turn guide behavior.

Individuals constantly use attribution principles in their efforts to understand their environment. Yet even the most competent attribution theorists are not immune to biases, or errors in the way they perceive their causal world. For example, people tend to take credit for their successes and blame failures on external causes, a phenomenon that Miller and Ross refer to as "hedonic bias" (1975); make trait attributions for others and situational attributions for themselves, which Jones and Nisbett call "actor-observer bias" (1972); and have overly positive self-regard, unrealistically high expectations for success, and exaggerated perceptions of control. Such causal illusions are often adaptive, for they appear to be correlated with good mental health (Taylor and Brown 1988). Attributional biases become dysfunctional when they lead to poor interpersonal relationships, ineffective problem solving, or undue hostility toward others. In the next section, we turn to a kind of attributional bias that has these characteristics and may be prevalent in adolescent offenders.

Attributional Biases of Adolescent Offenders

Much of what is known about attributional bias in adolescent offenders has emerged from research with aggressive children. This makes sense inasmuch as childhood aggression is a well-documented risk factor for delinquency in adolescence (Loeber and Hay 1997). A very robust finding in the aggression literature is that aggressive boys display what is called a "hostile attributional bias" (Crick and Dodge 1994). That is, they overattribute negative intent to others, particularly in situations of ambiguously caused provocation. To illustrate, imagine a situation where a youngster experiences a negative outcome, such as being pushed by a peer while waiting in line, and it is unclear whether the peer's behavior was intended or not. When asked whether the peer's action was hostile or benign, aggressive youngsters are more likely than their nonaggressive counterparts to infer that the push occurred intentionally. Attributions to hostile intent then lead to anger and the desire to retaliate. Even among nonaggressive populations the child who believes that another acted with hostile intent can feel justified in endorsing aggressive behavior. This goes back to the basic attribution principle involving responsibility inferences, feelings of anger, and their relations to punitive behavior. The problem with aggressive children is that through some process of distorted social reasoning, they often inappropriately or prematurely assume hostile peer intent in situations of attributional ambiguity.

There is a wealth of data demonstrating that hostile attributional bias is correlated with a number of maladaptive outcomes for aggressive children, including conduct disorder, externalizing behavior, and peer rejection (Crick and Dodge 1994). A common theme underlying these findings is that having a tendency to adopt a blameful stance toward others interferes with the processing of social information (encoding and attentional deficits), anger management (an emotion-regulation deficit), and effective problem solving (social-skills deficits). We know from our own research that attribution retraining, where youngsters learn to infer nonhostile intent in ambiguous situations, has short-term positive effects in reducing anger intensity and aggressive behavior (Hudley and Graham 1993). But on the less positive side, we also know that hostile attributional biases emerge rather early in an aggressive child's life, that they are partly a product of socialization experiences including negative maternal attributions and harsh discipline, and they take on a traitlike quality as they become the preferred method for handling ambiguous provocation (Graham 1997).

Building on findings from childhood-aggression research, there is now a small but growing literature examining hostile attributional bias in adjudicated adolescent offenders. These studies reveal that incarcerated and nonincarcerated adolescents with similar background characteristics can be distinguished according to the extremity of attributional biases, with the incarcerated group showing more evidence of bias (Fondacaro and Heller 1990; Slaby and Guerra 1988). Furthermore, hostile biases may be related to particular types of criminal involvement. For example, Dodge and his colleagues reported that attributional-bias scores in a sample of incarcerated youths correlated with the number of violent interpersonal crimes committed, such as attempted murder, assault, and kidnapping, but not with noninterpersonal and nonviolent crimes such as drug use, fraud, and status offenses (Dodge et al. 1990). Finally, hostile biases appear to distinguish subtypes of adolescent offenders (Dodge et al. 1997). Biases are more characteristic of reactively aggressive offenders—the hot-tempered, easily angered, impulsive youth—compared to proactively aggressive offenders who are more motivated by instrumental gain than by reacting to the perceived threats of others.

We have been studying attributional bias in a group of adolescent offenders who are incarcerated in one of several secure camps in Los Angeles County. Our sample consists of about three hundred boys (with an average age of sixteen years, eight months) of varying ethnicities, but primarily Latino and African American. The boys are serving time for a variety of offenses ranging from misdemeanors (such as vandalism) to serious felonies (armed robbery, aggravated assault). Youthful offenders found guilty of the most violent crimes typically fall under the jurisdiction of the California Youth Authority and are not housed in camps. The youths in our sample tend to be chronic offenders, with an average of three prior incarcerations. When we contacted them, they had served an average of eight months during their current incarceration.

In small group settings, the boys completed a questionnaire packet that included measures of hostile attributions as well as self-reports on a number of psychological variables related to delinquency. To assess attributional bias, respondents were asked to read a series of short scenarios in which they were to imagine that they experienced a negative outcome that was initiated by a peer provocateur, with the cause of the provocation portrayed as ambiguous. For example, participants read the following scenario:

"You are sitting in English class when you are called down to the principal's office. You figure it has to do with a fight you got into at lunchtime. As you approach the door to the office, you see the kid you had the fight with walking in the other door toward the principal's office as well. He enters the door a few steps ahead of you. As you walk in behind him, he appears to be bending down to tie his shoe. But before you realize what he is doing, you trip over him and fall on the floor."

Notice the number of ambiguous causal cues in the story: the provocateur is someone with whom the respondent has a history of conflict, so either the respondent accidentally tripped or the provocateur did it deliberately as retaliation for the earlier confrontation. For each story we then ask the respondent to rate on five-point scales whether he thinks the provocateur acted on purpose and, if so, whether he would feel angry and what the likelihood is that he would aggress against the provocateur. The rating scales were summed and averaged across the four stories to create a response-extremity index, where high scores indicate more extreme attributional bias.

Table 13.1 shows the correlations between attributional bias and other psychological risk factors for adolescent offending. The risk factors are grouped into three conceptually meaningful categories: interpersonal variables, intrapersonal factors, and community risk factors. The first category focuses on interactions with other individuals or one's preferred style

Table 13.1 Correlations between hostile attributional bias and other variables related to adolescent offending

				Correlation with attributional bias					
Interpersonal risk factors		Intrapersonal risk factors		Community risk factors		Offending behavior		Protective factors	
Variable	r	Variable	r	Variable	r	Variable	r	Variable	r
Family conflict	.19**	Self-blame	–.03	Neighborhood disorder	.16**	Early onset of violent behavior (S)	.20**	Family cohesion	–.02
Deviant peers	.28**	Internalizing behavior	–.02	Violence Exposure	.18**	Violent behavior (S)	.21**	Extended kinship	.02
Hypervigilance	.30**					Drug use (S)	.14*	Internal control	–.03
Externalizing behavior	.13*					Chronic offending (O)	–.02		
						Severity of violence offense (O)	.10		

Note: For offending behavior, S = self-report, O = official records

*p < .05 **p < .01

of interacting. Intrapersonal factors are self-appraisals—thoughts or feelings about oneself in relationship to negative outcomes. Community risk factors include perception of neighborhood disorder and one's exposure to violence in that neighborhood. The protective factors in Table 13.1 are those variables whose presence should lessen one's risk for deviance. Finally, there are measures of offending behavior, both self-report and those derived from official police records held by the Los Angeles County Juvenile Probation Department.

While modest overall, the correlations in Table 13.1 reveal a few clear patterns. First, hostile attributional bias is related to all of the interpersonal risk factors. For example, when family conflict is high, the causal variable also is high. We know from our research that mothers who make negative attributions about their children have children who are aggressive (Graham 1997), which underscores the importance of family socialization. Youngsters who are hypervigilant also display more hostile bias. The items on the vigilance scale focus on anxiety about being attacked, belief in a foreshortened future, and the need to be prepared for imminent danger. This is certainly compatible with an interpersonal style of preemptive reacting to another's provocation. The community risk factors also are related to bias, suggesting that one's tendency to view the world as a hostile place is predicted by one's experience and exposure to violence and deviance. Finally, there was some relationship with actual offending behavior, although, not unexpectedly, these correlations tended to be smaller. Patterns of offending behavior are determined by numerous factors other than (and in addition to) social cognitions.

Equally interesting in Table 13.1 are factors that were uncorrelated with attributional bias. For example, the data showed no relationship to the intrapersonal variables, which would indicate that how offenders think about themselves has very little to do with their threshold for blaming others. This is consistent with a great deal of research documenting weak or positive relations between self-esteem and aggressive behavior (Baumeister, Smart, and Boden 1996). The protective factors also were unrelated to attributional bias. Even youngsters who have good kinship relations and a sense of internal control may have low thresholds for perceiving others as acting with hostile intent.

Although not depicted in Table 13.1, attributional bias is also part of a general syndrome of social-cognitive deficits that appear to characterize the way delinquent adolescents organize their social world. Among these other deficits are inattention to relevant social cues, poor recall of those cues, weak perspective-taking skills, impulsive decision making, and a limited ability to generate effective solutions to interpersonal problems (Lochman and Dodge 1994; Slaby and Guerra 1988). We believe that this syndrome of social-information-processing deficiencies can put youths at greater risk for participating in crime. Because the presumed deficits are interpersonal in nature (for example, adopting a blameful stance in reaction to provocation by others), we suspect that they will be more related to (and predictive of) person-directed crimes such as assault, robbery, or attempted murder, rather than noninterpersonal transgressions such as drug offenses, theft, fraud, and the various status offenses (Dodge et al. 1990). For example, consider the context for aggravated assault, one of the most prevalent categories of juvenile crime. It is not difficult to imagine a potential offender who is skeptical about his adversary's intentions, adopts a blameful stance at the slightest provocation, misinterprets benign or prosocial gestures as hostile, is easily angered and therefore unable to attend to relevant information, and has great difficulty generating alternative (noncriminal) strategies for solving interpersonal dilemmas. Public perception of the causes of juvenile crimes such as assault points to environmental factors such as the kind of family adolescent offenders come from or the type of neighborhood where they are reared. Our analysis and the correlational data presented in Table 13.1 intimate that the effects of these demographic risk factors are at least partly mediated by social-cognitive biases such as reactive attributions.

The analysis also has implications for determining the culpability of youthful offenders. The current political climate surrounding juvenile crime is not particularly responsive to the notion that environmental factors such as poor parenting or growing up in violent neighborhoods are mitigators of criminal responsibility. However, one could reasonably argue that social-cognitive deficits relate to reduced responsibility in the sense that one may be less guilty when crimes are committed in reaction to a provocation as opposed to being premeditated (for example, the difference between manslaughter and murder). Furthermore, if youths at risk for adolescent deviance truly have limited decision-making capabilities when confronted with interpersonal dilemmas, this could be perceived as a mitigating factor that reduces culpability.

The strongest case for reduced culpability would require evidence that social-cognitive biases among adolescent offenders reflect immature judgments—in other words, that there is a unique pattern to the way adolescents respond to ambiguous provocation that is not manifested in adults. Unfortunately, developmental data from adolescence to young adulthood on social-cognitive reasoning processes do not exist. We do know that extremity of attributional bias can distinguish aggressive from nonaggressive children and delinquent from nondelinquent adolescents. However, we do not know whether these same biases can differentiate adult criminals and noncriminals, or whether desistance from adolescent offending is accompanied by the emergence of less biased social-information processing. These are fruitful questions for future research.

Perceptions of Fairness

Recent changes in juvenile justice laws, policy, and practice indicate that the system has cycled back to a "get tough" era (Bernard 1992). Lenient options are being replaced with harsher punishments, lowering the legal age for criminal liability has become a national debate, and more youthful felons are being waived to the adult system. The targets of these more punitive schemes are often ethnic-minority males, particularly African Americans, who tend to be as overrepresented in the juvenile justice system as they are in its adult counterpart (Leonard, Pope, and Feyerherm 1995).

The changing features of the juvenile system as well as the relationship between race and incarceration raise the question of whether adolescent offenders, particularly minority offenders, perceive the system as fair. Both criminology and social-psychology research document that people who question the fairness of the justice system often lose faith in its legitimacy and this loss of faith, in turn, can lead to increases in deviant behavior (Russell 1996; Tyler 1990). Thus youngsters who face the adjudicative process with the belief that the system is out to get them may be less likely to be deterred by the severity of their sanction. Furthermore, if they devalue the legitimacy of the system, they may also make decisions about involvement in crime that reflect inadequate attention to the costs of criminal offending. Consistent with this analysis, a national study on incarcerated adolescents by Schneider (1990) reported that beliefs about the certainty or severity of punishment were unrelated to either the intention to reoffend or to actual recidivism, in contrast to a small but significant effect for perceptions of fairness. Youthful offenders who perceived their punishment as unfair were more likely to express the intention to commit crimes again and to actually engage in more criminal behavior following their release from confinement.

We have begun to think about incarcerated adolescents' perceptions of fairness from an attributional perspective. Perceptions of fairness and justice are integrally related to inferences about individual responsibility and the intentionality of actions. The greater the degree of perceived responsibility for a transgression, the greater the punishment deserved. Thus, fair allocations of punishment for criminal offenses are those that systematically use information about personal responsibility and the intentionality of the act (Farwell and Weiner 1996). Of course, using irrelevant information such as race, gender, or group membership in determining punishment or criminal sanctioning would be perceived as unfair.

Guided by this analysis, we recently conducted an exploratory study on perceptions of fairness among adolescents who have had personal experiences with the juvenile justice system. We recruited a sample of eighty-five adolescent offenders, drawn from the same population of incarcerated boys that we described previously. In small group interviews, the boys were presented with four hypothetical scenarios describing a perpetrator who was accused of a crime that resulted in harm to a victim. The four scenarios systematically varied information about perpetrator responsibility and his group status: the perpetrator either committed the misdeed accidentally or intentionally and he was described as either a member of the respondent's in-group or a member of an out-group. In-group perpetrators were portrayed as being from the respondent's own neighborhood, and out-group perpetrators were described as being from a rival neighborhood. For example, one intentional misdeed committed by an out-group perpetrator scenario read:

"Jason, a guy from your rival neighborhood, was assigned in chemistry class to be partners with Charlie, a guy from your neighborhood. One day when they were doing a class experiment, Jason intentionally mixed the wrong chemicals together to cause an explosion. Charlie was standing very close and was badly injured by the explosion. Jason meant to do this and is now being charged with assault."

In the unintentional condition the perpetrator was described as accidentally mixing the wrong chemicals together, and in the in-group scenario Jason was from the respondent's neighborhood and Charlie, the injured party, was from the rival neighborhood. We suspect that this in-group–out-group manipulation was interpreted by our respondents as gang membership since the great majority of youths incarcerated in Los Angeles detention facilities have known affiliations with organized gangs.

For each scenario, respondents were asked to determine how much punishment the perpetrator should receive. These allocations were rated on a seven-point scale anchored at "no punishment" and "the worse punishment for this crime." Respondents were then asked to take the perspective of the judge who would hear the case as well as the perspective of an out-group member, both of whom would similarly allocate punishment. In this way we were able to determine whether incarcerated youths perceive themselves as fair (did they use intent information but relatively discount group membership information) and whether they see judges who represent the legal system and members of out-groups as fair, using these same criteria.

Figure 13.1a (left panel) shows punishment judgments as a function of perpetrator responsibility (intentionality of the misdeed) for the three perspectives (self, out-group peer, and judge). The slopes of the lines indicate how punishment varies as a function of the cause of the transgression.

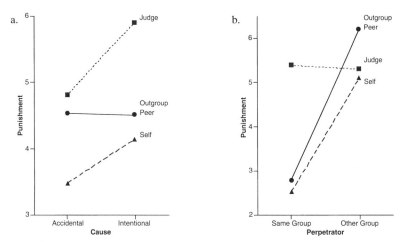

13.1 (a)   Punishment Ratings as a Function of Cause of Offense (Accidental or Intentional) and Perspective (Self, Judge, Outgroup Peer)
13.1 (b)   Punishment Ratings as a Function of Group Status of Perpetrator (Ingroup or Outgroup) and Perspective (Self, Judge, Outgroup Peer)

More fairness would be revealed by greater punishment in the intentional rather than accidental causal condition. There are three noteworthy findings in this figure. First, adolescents perceive themselves as fair, since their punishment allocations are significantly higher when the misdeed was committed intentionally rather than accidentally. Second, judges are perceived as particularly harsh (their punishment ratings are elevated), but also fair since they are thought to use intent-information systematically. Third, out-group members are perceived as completely unfair in that they do not take into account subjective intent when they make punishment decisions.

Figure 1b (right panel) shows the punishment ratings as a function of in-group–out-group status of the perpetrator. Strictly speaking, this perpetrator-status information should be completely irrelevant if punishment allocations are objectively fair. These data show that incarcerated adolescents acknowledge that they do use group membership in their decision making, displaying what is referred to in the attribution literature as in-group favoritism (Hewstone 1989). They viewed the out-group as even more biased in favor of their own group. The judge is again perceived as fair inasmuch as his punishment decisions completely disregard the group membership of the perpetrator.

We acknowledge that our data are simulative and that we have ignored a host of other factors that enter into fairness perceptions. Nonetheless, the methodology does offer a way to study perceived fairness that is less vulnerable to scripted responses that are likely to emerge by directly asking offenders if they think the legal system is biased against them. In our study, the judge was perceived as harsh but generally fair, which somewhat surprised us. However, one wonders if other participants in the adjudicative process, such as police officers, prosecutors, probation officials, or even public defenders, are perceived differently in terms of fairness and impartiality. Police officers seem to be a particularly appropriate target group because their decisions about juveniles at the apprehension stage tend to be highly discretionary (Wordes and Bynum 1995).

The presence of a strong in-group–out-group bias sheds light on when youthful offenders are willing to abandon their principles of fairness. It also raises new issues about relations between attributional reasoning and group membership. Our participants showed strong in-group favoritism and a tendency to distrust the out-group, who was perceived as uniformly unfair. There is a growing literature on intergroup attributional bias, which shows that people attribute the failures of out-group members to dispositional, controllable causes (Hewstone 1989). This group bias therefore has many of the same features and consequences as interpersonal attributional biases that we discussed in the previous section. The main difference is that perceivers define themselves and the targets of their attributions in terms of social identities or membership in social groups rather than as individuals.

For the attribution theorist, these data suggest that when the context for interpersonal crime involves groups whose identities may be in conflict, we should be alerted to look for low thresholds for assigning blame, intense anger, and preemptive hostility—in other words, the same kind of biased decision making that we believe characterizes the offender's responses to individuals whose intentions are perceived as hostile. In light of the importance of peer-group solidarity during adolescence, the significance of gang membership for many deviant youth, and the fact that racial group identity is often made salient by the treatment of offenders, we believe that the study of intergroup social-cognitive (attributional) biases as a potential mitigator of responsibility is a topic that merits further research.

Confessions and Impression Management

Although the rights of due process protect adolescent offenders from self-incrimination, in practice most adjudicated youths admit that they are guilty of the charges against them (Bernard 1992). How the offender explains her guilt and otherwise presents herself before the judge who must make a disposition ruling therefore has important ramifications for punishment severity. For example, does she come across as arrogant and prone to justifying her transgressions, or is she convincingly remorseful and penitent? Attribution research on interpersonal consequences of account-giving is directly relevant to this issue. According to this analysis, accounts are explanations for why a transgression occurred, and when used judiciously they have important impression-management functions. A good example of this impression-management function is in the area of giving excuses. The use of excuses is based on a naive analysis of the attribution linkages that we have been discussing in this chapter. We make an excuse to shift causal responsibility away from ourselves. This mitigates anger from others and the likelihood that they will punish us severely.

Other accounts for transgression identified by sociologists (Scott and Lyman 1968) also are amenable to attributional analyses. Whereas excuses deny responsibility for a misdeed, justifications admit responsibility but reinterpret the act to be more acceptable by appealing to mitigating circumstances ("I committed the robbery to feed my children"). Confessions, on the other hand, are full admissions of guilt and responsibility and are often accompanied by expressions of remorse and offers of restitution (Schonbach 1980).

A number of attribution studies have documented the impression-management functions of excuses and confessions. Not surprisingly, when people offer excuses for their untoward behavior, as opposed to giving no account, perceivers judge them as less responsible and are more forgiving (Weiner et al. 1987). Somewhat paradoxically, confessions have similar ameliorating effects. In our research with adults, for example, we found that when transgressors confessed—that is, when they accepted full responsibility without appealing to mitigators—they were perceived as less responsible than someone who denied the act or offered no account, and they also elicited less anger, more forgiveness, and were punished less harshly (Weiner et al. 1991). Confessions appear to change inferences about the person who violated social norms, including inferences that he was responsible, and they restore beliefs in the person's basic goodness. The social consequences of confession are well articulated by Blumstein (1974) who writes, "Showing penitence, like claiming reduced personal responsibility, splits the identity of the offender. He asserts his own guilt for the act and accepts the momentary blow to his moral character, while at the same time he reaffirms his overriding righteousness (awareness of rules) and acknowledges the offended's right to demand an account."

How well do adolescent offenders appreciate the impression-management function of confessions and other accounts? At least one early sociological theory of delinquency proposed that offenders only know about denials and justifications (Sykes and Matza 1957). But the psychological literature has been virtually silent on this topic. The closest we have come to the issue is our research on aggressive children's understanding of the impression-management function of excuses (Graham, Weiner, and Benesh-Weiner 1995), in which we documented that aggressive youngsters showed less understanding than did nonaggressives. Given a transgression and the opportunity to offer an excuse, the aggressive boys were less aware that perceived responsibility and anger from others go hand in hand, and they were less likely to use this information in the formulation of an account.

Given the similarities between aggressive children and adolescent offenders in the presence of hostile attributional biases, such adolescents also may lack some of the important social skills that enable them to manage other people's anger and negative reactions toward them. This raises the broader issue of these youngsters' general awareness of self-presentational strategies that could allow them to effectively control their environment. Strategic self-presentation involves the individual's shaping of his or her responses in order to be viewed positively by others (Jones and Pittman 1982, 231–262). Erving Goffman (1959) labeled these strategies "performances on the stage of life." People strategically present themselves not only verbally (through altering causal interpretations), but also through physical appearance and nonverbal behavior, including gestures, postures, and emotional displays. Nonverbal behavior, in fact, can be a more powerful presentation tactic than verbal strategies. For example, in one recent study, jurors witnessing a mock trial responded less punitively toward a defendant accused of vehicular manslaughter when the defendant was visibly remorseful (head down, watery eyes) than when he provided the same verbal account but showed no display of emotion (Robinson, Smith-Lovin, and Tsoudis 1994).

The underlying message here is that confessions can be studied not only as evidence (the jurisprudence perspective) or as the product of unconscious motives (the psychoanalytic perspective, Jung 1933), but also as part of a repertoire of impression-management skills. If adolescent offenders lack an understanding of these skills, they may be at risk for being judged by court personnel as unremorseful and therefore more responsible for their crime and deserving of harsh punishment. Thus the study of self-presentation strategies has implications for the study of culpability and its determinants.

Beliefs about Control

In the introductory section of this chapter, we pointed out that self-ascriptions on the controllability dimension have important psychological and behavioral consequences. When individuals believe that they can control their outcomes, they initiate activity, exert effort, and persist in the face of failure or various setbacks. In contrast, individuals who appraise their outcomes as largely uncontrollable tend to withdraw or otherwise become passive, depressed, or pessimistic (Skinner 1995). In this last section we focus on beliefs about control among incarcerated adolescents and how such beliefs might relate to continued engagement in criminal activities. This also is a topic that is pertinent to culpability as the term is used in this chapter. We intend to make the case that many adolescent offenders have maladaptive self-perceptions of control, just as they have biased attributions about the intentions of other individuals or groups. These self-perceptions can then trigger inappropriate decision making that places youngsters at risk for renewed antisocial behavior. Thus maladaptive control beliefs might be yet another set of social-cognitive biases that need to be considered when evaluating the culpability of delinquent youth.

Control beliefs are a particularly relevant topic to study in adolescent-offender populations. Most approaches to control have been formulated to explain what happens in stressful situations where control is either threatened or taken away. In fact, some of the very early studies on locus of control were carried out with adult prison inmates (Lefcourt and Ladwig 1966). Juvenile offenders, of course, also experience enormous stress associated with the loss of freedom and autonomy that incarceration brings. Following release, moreover, probation can place further restrictions on their freedom and choices, including whether or not they live with their parents, where they attend school, what they wear, and where they can go. The unique experiences of coping with incarceration and probation provide a compelling context for studying the effects of control beliefs on adaptive functioning.

Despite the topic's intuitive appeal, there is surprisingly little research that examines control beliefs in adolescent offenders. A few studies with community adolescent samples include perceptions of control as predictors of problem behavior, including delinquency (Jessor et al. 1995; Peiser and Heaven 1996). An even smaller amount of literature compares perceived control in offender and nonoffender populations (Parrott and Strongman 1984; Kumchy and Sayer 1980). All of these investigations suggest that delinquent status is associated with low levels of perceived control, but in none of these studies is the effect of control beliefs very substantial.

Our study of adolescent offenders examined the relations between perceptions of control and both psychological and behavioral adjustment. Here we deviated somewhat from attribution theory. We adopted a conceptual analysis offered by some control theorists who have attempted to explain how individuals successfully adapt when their opportunities to influence their outcomes are severely limited. Relevant to this analysis is a distinction made by Rothbaum, Weisz, and Snyder (1982) between primary and secondary control. Primary control refers to attempts to alter one's outcomes ("I can change how much danger I will face in my neighborhood"). It focuses on changing the environment to fit the self and is most consistent with the way control is typically conceptualized. Secondary control, in contrast, is the sense of instrumentality derived from accepting or adjusting to existing realities ("Facing danger is just the way it is in my neighborhood"). It is concerned with attempts to change the self to fit with the environment—also known as going with the flow. It can involve adjusting expectations for success to avoid disappointment, aligning oneself with powerful others, or reinterpreting negative outcomes in a more favorable light (Rothbaum, Weisz, and Snyder 1982). Although secondary control may at times be accompanied by what appears to be passivity or withdrawal, it is different from relinquishing control altogether, which would involve no attempts to change the self or the environment.

Most researchers view secondary control as an adaptive process in the adjustment to high-stress situations (Heckhausen and Schultz 1995). Accepting one's situation as determined by powerful outside forces might protect the individual from the negative effects and helplessness that often accompany the gradual loss of control. On the other hand, secondary control may be less adaptive or even maladaptive if the individual makes little effort to bring about change in an environment where control and instrumentality are still possible (Band and Weisz 1988).

Our understanding of the literature on control and our experiences working with adolescent offenders has led us to believe that secondary control has maladaptive consequences. Inner-city juvenile offenders come from neighborhoods characterized by widespread poverty, unemployment, and crime. Many youths may accept confronting danger and being involved in criminal activity as features of living in such environments. Accordingly, selling illicit substances or stolen goods may be seen as the only way to earn money, and being involved in violent activity such as gangs may be viewed as the only way to protect oneself. In this manner, secondary control (accepting reality) may undermine attempts to take control of the situation. Much anecdotal commentary and some findings from ethnographic research underscore how adolescent delinquents rationalize their choices as part of accepting the vagaries of their life circumstances (Humes 1996). As one of our research participants, a fourteen-year-old repeat offender, so poignantly disclosed, "That's just the way it is out there. You do what you have to do. If I get locked up, I get locked up."

We interviewed boys in our sample of three hundred incarcerated offenders about one month before their scheduled date of release from confinement. Included in the interview were measures of primary and secondary control. Guided by previous research (Thompson et al. 1996), we asked about the two types of control in a straightforward manner. The respondents were instructed to think about three future outcomes: (a) how much danger they would face; (b) how much trouble they would get into; and (c) what kind of life they would have. Each outcome was accompanied by a question that tapped primary control ("How much control do you have over . . .") and a question that tapped secondary control ("How much do you accept versus try to change . . ."). Each question was answered on a five-point rating scale with appropriate anchors. Data also were gathered on various indicators of adjustment such as self-reported emotional and behavioral problems, feelings of despair, expectations to avoid recontact with the law, and the recognition that continued deviance would jeopardize both personal relationships and career opportunities (Halliday and Graham n.d.). Approximately eight weeks after each participant was released from confinement, we contacted his probation officer, who then completed a set of ratings on the adolescent's adjustment in the community.

Table 13.2 shows the correlations between primary and secondary control and the various indicators of adjustment. It is evident that the two types of control were related to adjustment in a manner suggesting that primary control is adaptive and secondary control is maladaptive. Thus, incarcerated adolescents adjust better when they believe that they can control their outcomes, which replicates most research on perceptions of control. But they show poorer adjustment when they choose to accept their environment the way it is without trying to change it. Note that secondary control also was negatively related to adjustment as reported by the respondent's probation officer.

The boys in the sample are being followed to determine patterns of recidivism. We know from our descriptive data that over half of the participants (56 percent) recidivated by the sixth month following release from confinement. In the next analysis we asked whether primary and secondary control were related to recidivism rates. Information about reincarceration was obtained from probation department records and these data were analyzed using survival analysis. The two types of control were entered into the analysis of survival time (the amount of time elapsed before reincarceration within the first six months), after controlling for background variables and a measure of chronicity of offending.

The analysis revealed that chronic offending was a strong predictor of shorter survival times, such that the more extensive a respondent's history of contact with the law, the earlier he recidivated. There also was an interaction between primary- and secondary-control beliefs. To more closely

Table 13.2   Correlations between primary and secondary control and the adjustment variables

| | Correlation with control | |
Variable	Primary control	Secondary control
Emotional/behavior problems	−.11	.21**
Despair	−.23***	.30**
Expectations	.26**	−.37***
Perceived costs	.23**	−.40***
Probation officer ratings	.06	−.19*

* p < .05 ** p < .01 ***p < .001

examine this interaction, we classified participants into one of four groups based on the level (high or low) of primary and secondary control. Separate survival curves were plotted for each group. These curves are shown in Figure 2.

Figure 2 reveals that the group with high levels of both primary and secondary control recidivated at a higher rate than did the other groups. In addition, most of the differences in rates of recidivism were occur-

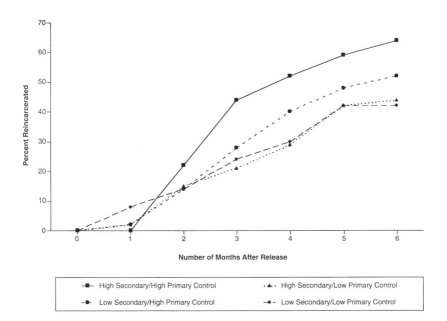

Figure 2. Percent Reincarcerated Over Time as a Function of Primary and Secondary Control

13.2   Percentage reincarcerated over time as a function of primary and secondary control

ring between the second and third month postincarceration. In hazard-probability terminology, for an offender who was high in both types of control, the chance of being reincarcerated during the third month if he had survived up to that time was 28 percent. For the other three groups these probabilities ranged from 7 to 16 percent. This suggests to us that the third month may be a critical point in time for juvenile offenders at risk for reincarceration, particularly those with high levels of both primary and secondary control.

The findings confirm our initial hypothesis that secondary-control strategies, or accepting the reality of one's situation without trying to change it, may be maladaptive, and this is especially true when offenders do believe they have control over their outcomes. The idea of secondary control grew out of recognition that there are realistic boundaries to the adaptiveness of perceived (primary) control, and dynamic-control theorists view successful adaptation as a complex interplay between primary- and secondary-control processes (Heckhausen and Schultz 1995; Rothbaum, Weisz, and Snyder 1982). Secondary control functions as a backup in that it enables the individual to maintain or minimize losses in primary control. But it is maladaptive when it leads someone to prematurely relinquish attempts to shape or alter the environment in ways that enhance their developmental potential. We suspect that many adolescent offenders in our sample believe in their own efficacy—they can influence how much danger they will face or how much trouble they will get into. But for reasons not yet clear to us they have opted to accept the dangers and potential for trouble and to make choices (such as renewed delinquent activity) that are compatible with this acceptance.

These choice patterns guided by perceptions of control (or its absence) may also reflect immature decision making and would therefore have implications for youth's culpability. In general, adolescents have less control over outcomes than do adults, given their status as minors. Youths in the juvenile justice system experience additional constraints on their freedom of choice at a stage in development where issues of control and autonomy take on heightened significance. This creates inordinate tension as these adolescents attempt to cope with both traumatic stress (arrest and incarceration) and the chronic stressors of everyday life. The limited research on adult incarcerated males that examines the role of perceived control suggests that adults have a more balanced perspective on what is changeable (primary control) versus what should be accepted (secondary control) and that perceived primary control is consistently related to better adjustment and coping (Thompson et al. 1996; Thompson, Nanni, and Levine 1994). Thus, the immaturity of adolescents' thinking highlighted here that could be evidence for reduced culpability revolves around their inexperience in coping with stressful life events and with threats to their sense of personal efficacy. To the best of our knowledge, none of the analyses of adolescent development as it relates to decision making and culpability have addressed these dual influences of stress and coping responses.

Conclusions and Implications for the Study of Culpability

By starting with a few basic principles from attribution theory, our goal has been to achieve new insights into how adolescent offenders organize their causal world. The analysis sheds light on: (a) biased attributions about another's intent, which have implications for understanding the causes of interpersonal violence; (b) perceptions of fairness, which are relevant to the individual's responsiveness to judicial sanctions; (c) understanding the social function of accounts, which bears upon the severity of judicial sanctions; and (d) beliefs about control, which may foreshadow desistance versus persistence in deviant behavior.

From our perspective, having a low threshold for adopting a blameful stance toward others, questioning the legitimacy of the justice system, lacking effective self-presentation tactics, and accepting rather than trying to influence reality can all be viewed as ways of perceiving the world that impose limits on adolescents' decision making and their abilities to deal effectively with their environment. We believe that the limits are sufficiently compelling to merit consideration by justice system officials, legal scholars, and policymakers who set the standards by which criminal responsibility and culpability of the juvenile offender are determined.

We also believe that a social-cognitive (attributional) perspective on culpability issues suggests several news lines of needed research. If the case for reduced culpability continues to rest on age-related differences in the maturity of decision making, then clearly we need systematic research on development and change in the use attributional biases, perceptions of the fairness of the social institutions including the justice system, understanding account-giving as impression management, and coping with perceived loss of control. A focal point in this research would be development and change across the critical transition from adolescence to young adulthood. Because social cognition is a relatively neglected topic in developmental research and because the study of age-related continuity and change rarely extends beyond the early adolescent years, the kind of research agenda that our analysis suggests also has the potential to inform the developmental-psychology literature.

These research topics could also promote heightened sensitivity to the fact that disproportionate numbers of adolescent offenders are members of ethnic minority groups. Because these groups are stigmatized and marginalized, members may be particularly susceptible to external attributions and blaming others (this could be self-protective) and may be more likely to view the system as unfair. Furthermore, cultural-display rules no doubt influence strategic self-presentation, including account-giving, and there is a long history of research relating the absence of personal control to ethnic minority status (Graham 1994). Thus the social-cognitive processes that we propose for further study could predict dysfunctional decision making not only because of age-related immaturity of judgment, but also because of the unknown effects of ethnicity on social-information processing.

Throughout this chapter we have focused on culpability from the vantage point of how the youthful offender perceives his or her causal world. To an attribution theorist, however, culpability is also a person-perception issue. It is a causal inference about an actor made by an observer: Is the person responsible? Did they intend for the act to happen? Were there mitigating circumstances? To study culpability as person perception, it would be important to focus on how the major observers in the justice system—police officers, attorneys, judges, probation officers—make responsibility inferences about the offender. In light of the known racial disparities in the treatment of adolescent offenders, we wonder, for example, whether some juvenile justice officials have their own hostile attributional biases about particular types of transgressors, if their punishments would be deemed fair using attributional criteria, and the extent to which they honor the accounts (confessions) of penitent offenders. Our reading of the juvenile literature suggests that little is known about the causal-reasoning processes of those who control the fates of youthful offenders as they penetrate the justice system. From a culpability perspective, these also are fertile topics for future research.

We began this chapter with an observation by George Kelly that reminded us of the boundaries of psychological theory. The social psychologist Kurt Lewin, a contemporary of Kelly's, wrote that "there is nothing so practical as a good theory." We hope that our readers will appreciate the practicality of an attributional perspective for studying juvenile culpability. But we also want to make sure that we do not overstate the importance of what has been presented here. Understanding juvenile crime and the complexities of the justice system encompasses legal issues and relations between race, social class, and crime that are far beyond the range and focus of attributional analyses. What the theory does offer, however, is a framework for asking some of the right questions.

Works Cited

Band, E., and J. Weisz. 1988. Developmental differences in primary and secondary control coping and adjustment in juvenile diabetes. *Journal of Clinical Child Psychology* 19:150–158.

Baumeister, R., L. Smart, and J. Boden. 1996. Relations of threatened egotism to violence and aggression: The dark side of self esteem. *Psychological Review* 103:5–33.

Bernard, T. 1992. *The cycle of juvenile justice*. New York: Oxford University Press.

Blumstein, P., 1974. The honoring of accounts. *American Sociological Review* 39:551–566.

Crick, N., and K. Dodge. 1994. A review and reformulation of social information-processing mechanisms in children's social adjustment. *Psychological Bulletin* 115:74–101.

Dodge, K., J. Price, J. Bachorowski, and J. Newman. 1990. Hostile attributional biases in severely aggressive adolescents. *Journal of Abnormal Psychology* 99:385–392.

Dodge, K., J. Lochman, J. Harnish, J. Bates, and G. Petti. 1997. Reactive and proactive aggression in school children and psychiatrically impaired chronically assaultive youth. *Journal of Abnormal Psychology* 106:37–51.

Farwell, L., and B. Weiner. 1996. Self-perceptions of fairness in individual and group contexts. *Personality and Social Psychology Bulletin* 22:867–881.

Fiske, S. T., and S. E. Taylor. 1991. *Social cognition*. New York: McGraw-Hill.

Fondacaro, M., and K. Heller. 1990. Attributional style in aggressive adolescent boys. *Journal of Abnormal Child Psychology* 18:75–89.

Furnham, A. 1988. *Lay theories: Everyday understanding of problems in the social sciences*. Oxford, England: Pergamon Press.

Goffman, E. 1959. *The presentation of self in everyday life*. New York: Doubleday Anchor Books.

Graham, S. 1994. Motivation in African Americans. *Review of Educational Research* 64:55–117.

———. 1997. Using attribution theory to understand academic and social motivation in African American youth. *Educational Psychologist* 31:167–180.

Graham, S., B. Weiner, and M. Benesh-Weiner. 1995. An attributional analysis of the development of excuse giving in aggressive and nonaggresssive African American boys. *Developmental Psychology* 31:731–740.

Halliday, C., and S. Graham. n.d. *"If I get locked up, I get locked up": Secondary control and adjustment in adolescent offenders*. Manuscript submitted for publication.

Heckhausen, J., and R. Schultz. 1995. A life-span theory of control. *Psychological Review* 102:284–304.

Hewstone, M. 1989. *Causal attribution: From cognitive processes to collective beliefs*. Oxford, England: Basil Blackwell.

Hudley, C., and S. Graham. 1993. An attributional intervention to reduce peer-directed aggression among African American boys. *Child Development* 64:124–138.

Humes, E. 1996. *No matter how loud I shout: A year in the life of juvenile court*. New York: Touchstone.

Jessor, R., J. Van den Bos, J. Vanderryn, F. Costa, and M. Turbin. 1995. Protective factors in adolescent problem behavior: Moderator effects and developmental change. *Developmental Psychology* 31:923–933.

Jones, E., and R. Nisbett. 1972. The actor and the observer: Divergent perceptions of the causes of behavior. In *Attribution: Perceiving the causes of behavior,* edited by E. Jones et al. Morristown, N.J.: General Learning Press.

Jones, E., and T. Pittman. 1982. Toward a general theory of strategic self-presentation. In *Psychological perspectives on the self,* edited by J. Suls. Vol 1. Hillsdale, N.J.: Lawrence Erlbaum Publishers.

Jung, C. 1933. *Modern man in search of a soul.* New York: Harvest Books.

Kelly, G. 1955. *The psychology of personal constructs.* New York: W. W. Norton.

Kumchy, G., and L. Sayer. 1980. Locus of control in a delinquent adolescent population. *Psychological Reports* 46:1307–1310.

Lefcourt, H., and G. Ladwig. 1966. Alienation in Negro and white reformatory inmates. *Journal of Social Psychology* 68:152–157.

Leonard, K., C. Pope, and W. Feyerherm, eds. 1995. *Minorities in juvenile justice.* Thousand Oaks, Calif.: Sage Publications.

Lochman, J., and K. Dodge. 1994. Social-cognitive processes of severely violent, moderately aggressive, and nonaggressive boys. *Journal of Consulting and Clinical Psychology* 62:366–374.

Loeber, R., and D. Hay. 1997. Key issues in the development of aggression and violence from early childhood to early adulthood. *Annual Review of Psychology* 48:371–410.

Miller, D., and L. Ross. 1975. Self-serving biases in the attribution of causality: Fact or fiction? *Psychological Bulletin* 82:213–225.

Parrott, C., and K. Strongman. 1984. Locus of control and delinquency. *Adolescence* 19:459–471.

Peiser, N., and P. Heaven. 1996. Family influences on self-reported delinquency among high school students. *Journal of Adolescence* 19:557–568.

Robinson, D., L. Smith-Lovin, and O. Tsoudis. 1994. Heinous crime or unfortunate accident? The effects of remorse on responses to mock criminal confessions. *Social Forces* 73 175–190.

Rothbaum, R., J. Weisz, and S. Snyder. 1982. Changing the world and changing the self: A two-process model of perceived control. *Journal of Personality and Social Psychology* 42:5–37.

Russell, K. 1996. The racial hoax as crime: The law as affirmation. *Indiana Law Journal* 71:593–621.

Schneider, A. 1990. *Deterrence and juvenile crime.* New York: Springer-Verlag.

Schonbach, P. 1980. A category system for account phases. *European Journal of Social Psychology* 10:195–200.

Scott, M., and S. Lyman. 1968. Accounts. *American Sociological Review* 33:46–62.

Skinner, E. 1995. *Perceived control, motivation, and coping.* Thousand Oaks, Calif.: Sage Publishers.

Slaby, R., and N. Guerra. 1988. Cognitive mediators of aggression in adolescent offenders. Part 1: Assessment. *Developmental Psychology* 24:580–588.

Sykes, G., and D. Matza. 1957. Techniques of neutralization: A theory of delinquency. *American Sociological Review* 22:664–670.

Taylor, S. E., and J. D. Brown. 1988. Illusion and well-being: A social psychological perspective on mental health. *Psychological Bulletin* 103:193–210.

Thompson, S., M. Collins, M. Newcomb, and W. Hunt. 1996. On fighting versus accepting stressful circumstances: Primary and secondary control among HIV-positive men. *Journal of Personality and Social Psychology* 70:1307–1317.

Thompson, S., C. Nanni, and A. Levine. (1994). Primary versus secondary and central versus consequence-related control in HIV-positive men. *Journal of Personality and Social Psychology* 67: 540–547.

Tyler, T. 1990. *Why people obey the law.* New Haven: Yale University Press.

Weiner, B. 1995. *Judgment of responsibility: A foundation for a theory of social conduct.* New York: Guilford Press.

Weiner, B., J. Amirkhan, V. Folkes, and J. Verette. 1987. An attributional analysis of excuse giving: Studies of a naive theory of emotion. *Journal of Personality and Social Psychology* 52:316–324.

Weiner, B., S. Graham, O. Peter, and M. Zmuidinas. 1991. Public confession and forgiveness. *Journal of Personality* 59:281–312.

Wordes, M., and T. Bynum. 1995. Policing juveniles: Is there a bias against youths of color? In *Minorities in juvenile justice,* edited by K. Leonard, C. Pope, and W. Feyerherm. Thousand Oaks, Calif.: Sage Publications.

Zucker, G., and B. Weiner. 1993. Conservatism and perception of poverty: An attributional analysis. *Journal of Applied Social Psychology* 23:925–943.

CHAPTER FOURTEEN

Contexts of Choice by Adolescents in Criminal Events

JEFFREY FAGAN

There is currently renewed interest in the role of criminal offenders as active decision makers in criminal events.[1] This perspective reflects a shift in criminological theory from traditional concerns with the propensities or risks of individuals to a closer examination of criminal events. The latter approach addresses both the motivations that bring individuals to specific events and the transactions or decisions that comprise the event. Recent studies on property crimes (Tunnell 1993; Shover 1995; Wright and Decker 1994), assaults (Oliver 1994; Wilkinson and Fagan 1996), robbery (Wright and Decker 1997), and homicides (Luckenbill and Doyle 1989; Polk 1994) illustrate the confluence of motivation, perceptions of risk and opportunity, and attributes of the setting that shapes the decision to participate in a criminal event.

Conceptual views on decision making in criminal events vary. Although each viewpoint sees the offender as a rational actor, the constructions of rationality are quite different. Econometric perspectives assume that would-be offenders employ a utility curve to assess the costs and returns of a criminal event, even going so far as to include components for taste and preference and moral dimensions of the decision (Miller and Anderson 1986; Kramer 1990; Tedeschi and Felson 1994; Fagan and Freeman 1999). Neoeconometric views recognize the limitations of rational choice, and instead talk about bounded rationality (Clarke and Cornish 1985; Cornish and Clarke 1987). Ethologists contribute foraging models (Stephens and Krebs 1986), where offenders make decisions that are satisficing rather than optimizing.

Social-interactionist perspectives offer a different view of decision making involving "theories of action" (Cornish 1993). In this view, criminal events are dynamic processes in which participants make decisions that reflect the interaction of motivation and social context. That is, criminal events are contingent on either interactions with other individuals, as in the case of interpersonal violence, or the attributes of the setting where a putative event might occur. Sometimes, social witnesses provide an audience that shapes decisions, regardless of whether there is an opponent. Decisions may also be rule bound or even normative, reflecting expected behaviors that are contingent on features of the immediate surroundings. These expectations are set socially and refined through repeated social interactions or observations of the behaviors of others.

In all these perspectives, context is essential to explaining not just criminal behaviors, but a wide range of behaviors (Cornish 1993; Fagan 1993a). Decisions to commit crime are interactive with attributes of the setting. Setting, or place, is a vector with several dimensions: behavioral norms attached to specific situations; opportunities for crime in these locales; provocations, such as drug or gang activity; people present in the setting; and social controls, both legal and informal. The interaction of these factors with individual propensity or motivation produces a situational dynamic that influences individual choices and actions.

Nearly all the research on criminal events involves adults.[2] In this view, violence is a goal-oriented behavior (Tedeschi and Felson 1994; Kennedy and Forde 1999). Adolescent criminality, however, spans a wide range of behaviors in which the adolescents' goals are often closely linked to the unique developmental needs of adolescence. The application of a contextual framework to adolescent criminality must be extended to account for the unique developmental context of adolescence as well as the types of social and situational factors that frame the everyday activities of youths.

This chapter merges these two perspectives to assess the role of contextual factors in decision making by adolescents in criminal events. The framework for decision making assumes that context is a dynamic, not a static, feature of the cognitive landscape. Decisions by adolescents to engage in crime or violence are shaped through interactions with features of their environments, are contingent on responses emanating from that context, and are filtered through the unique lens of adolescence. Rather than assuming discrete and independent components in a decision framework, I assume that decisions are the product of interactions across several dimensions: intrapsychic and personality factors, social cues in the setting, the actions of other persons (bystanders or witnesses, for example), the presence of weapons, and elements of social control in the setting. I will also examine how social contexts influence discrete factors in the natural history of a criminal event: its onset, the course of the event (including decision making), and the actions subsequent to the event.

The chapter begins by defining and decomposing the elements of context into several dimensions. First, specific contexts of adolescent crimi-

nality are identified and their influence is defined, the special case of violence is analyzed, and the contribution of context to adolescent development is discussed. Following that, the next section constructs a framework
for understanding the interactions of individual and contextual factors in
decision making in criminal events. The chapter concludes with a discussion of the implications for law and social science.

Contexts of Adolescent Crime

Adolescence is a prolonged period of stressful development marked by
physical, emotional, and social changes (Hamburg 1974). None is more
important than the increasing use of peers as a critical reference group for
exploration of social roles, exploration of sexual relationships, and changing relations with parents and other adults (Adler and Adler 1998; Steinberg and Avenevoli in press).

The daily routines of this social development occur within several social
contexts: neighborhood, family, school, and peer group. With the exception of family, each of these social interactions occur among groups of similarly situated youths. These contexts proscribe social networks, and daily
interactions within these networks influence social behavior in several
ways. First, these contexts are the theatrical stage for repeated interactions among individual youths. Adolescents see each other daily in school,
on the journey to and from school, in their neighborhoods, and in a range
of social activities such as parties or athletic events. Individuals rank each
other in these contexts through a variety of social comparisons.

Second, on this stage, bystanders are omnipresent as the audience in
these daily contexts of adolescents' lives. They witness and participate in
social interactions, and in turn either confer or withhold all-important social status. From children in playgrounds to adolescents in street groups,
witnesses are a part of the landscape of social interactions and they influence adolescents' decisions on how to conduct social relations and which
behaviors to value.

Third, the neighborhood is a nested social context in which norms
among peer groups and school-based networks develop (Bronfenbrenner
1979). The neighborhood's structure of opportunity and social control
shapes the means by which children and adolescents can obtain social status (Brooks-Gunn et al. 1993). In neighborhoods with high crime rates, social roles are dominated by street-oriented peer groups with limited opportunity for broader participation in community life such as after-school
groups, volunteer organizations, or unsupervised athletics (Anderson
1999; Short 1997). This limits opportunities for developing skills that often bring status in later years, such as vocational or technical skills, analytic

intelligence, or artistic talent. In such neighborhoods, status attainment may instead depend on manifestations of physical power or domination, athletic performance, verbal agility, or displays of material wealth, especially for males (Guerra and Slaby 1990). The continual demand for personal respect, coupled with limited avenues by which to attain it, sets up conflicts that often are resolved through fighting and crime, the most readily available pathways to high status (Anderson 1999; Wilkinson 1998).

This section focuses on how contexts shape adolescents' decisions to engage in crime. First, I describe the dimensions of contexts that influence such decisions. Then I provide illustrations of how some specific contexts influence events in which crimes occur. Next, I place these contexts in a framework to show how the unique demands of adolescence interact with social contexts to motivate decisions to engage in crime and violence.

What Is Context?

Although context is important in both adolescent development and crime, its definition varies widely. Recognition of the role of context stems from a simple fact: people behave differently in different settings, even in the face of similar motivations and emotions (Fagan 1993a, 1993b). For example, Zinberg (1984) examined the primarily social processes regulating drug-consumption patterns, group membership, and behaviors following intoxication. Elliott et al. (1996) showed how neighborhood contexts shaped involvement in crime, after controlling for the effects of individual factors. Sampson and Lauritsen (1994) identified mediating processes within social contexts that shape the interactions between individuals and communities leading to interpersonal violence. These and other recent conceptual views of social context distinguish between the social functionality of behaviors (either their instrumental or regulative functions) and the social processes that we may falsely view as the "determining" influences of setting.

Despite recognition of the importance of social contexts on crime, the definition and components of the social processes within these contexts have been only vaguely specified. Context may refer to spatial or physical dimensions, social aggregations or structural features of a group, or specific situations. Social context may be interpreted as an external condition or as a dynamic process intrinsic to a specific social milieu. It may refer to cultural norms or to microsocial interactions. In short, while everyone may nod their heads at claims that crime is a "socially embedded" behavior, we aren't quite sure exactly what it is embedded in.

Specific conceptualizations of social context vary extensively, and each has some support in the empirical literatures on aggression. Social context may be defined in terms of its structural features. Composition effects refer to population heterogeneity in a specific milieu. This may include the number and types of people, their socioeconomic status, and the gender-age-race makeup of a group that populate a locale (Stark 1987). Spatial effects include the neighborhoods where drinking locations are situated (Roncek and Maier 1991) and their proximities to other social domains where crimes may be prevalent (Cohen and Felson 1979). The physical environment also may influence the behaviors in a location; lighting, crowding, and decor are prominent in the barroom literature as influencing the patterns of social interaction and the prospects for violence (Felson, Baccagglini, and Gmelch 1986).

Other constructions of social context emphasize the normative patterns of belief about violence that are attached to the setting itself. For example, the meaning and purpose of alcohol use in a setting, together with the beliefs about permitted behaviors in the setting, comprise the expectancies about alcohol and violence that are specific to a location. Thus, human "guidedness" (Pernanen 1991) may lead individuals to seek out settings they believe will sanction the behaviors they anticipate in a particular event.

Conceptualizations of social context often are confounded with the presence and salience of both formal and informal social controls in a particular location. Social control comprises a range of constructs, from internalized restraints (for example, the social costs of violence, or one's stakes in conforming to a social order), to the informal social rules and regulatory processes that characterize groups and situations, to the formal rules attached to specific locations. Violence itself has been defined as a process of social control (Black 1983; Katz 1988; Fagan 1992) used to settle grievances or maintain power relationships.

The social cohesion among individuals in a setting influences the strength of these regulatory processes. Zinberg (1984) explained how groups develop and enforce social sanctions, especially social punishments (such as exclusion) that may be particularly salient for would-be violators of the myriad rules of the group and situation. The importance of the collective personality of the group, or what Zinberg called "set," lies in its ability to enforce these codes and modify behaviors using social sanctions. If the group itself is normatively oriented toward violence, social interactions such as disputes may end in violence.

Accordingly, social contexts are both mediating structures and processes that channel the arousal effects of social interactions. Consideration of the effects of context or setting should carefully deconstruct these terms to assess the influences of these components, and particularly the regulatory processes that set and enforce behavioral boundaries. Social context can be conceptualized as a complex web of social controls from multiple sources: external and structural factors, intrinsic attributes of social groups and their aggregate personalities, and the social interactions that occur within groups and between groups and settings.

Social Contexts of Adolescent Crime

Context shapes decisions to engage in crime through the attributes of settings and the interaction of developmental status with the setting in which developmental processes unfold. The following examples show how intentionality and goal orientation are evident in four types of crimes that are common during childhood and adolescence. The goals and functions of these acts are identified, and offer explanations for diversity of outcomes.[3]

Childhood Aggression: Rough-and-Tumble Play

Rough-and-tumble play fighting typically occurs among children and often serves to establish social hierarchies (Humphreys and Smith 1987). The functional value of rough-and-tumble play for younger children is threefold: affiliations and friend selection, development of fighting skills, and initial establishment of one's position in a dominance hierarchy.[4] Moreover, it may even strengthen friendship ties between two fighters. During such play, the roles of dominance and submission are exchanged by mutual consent (Smith and Lewis 1980). However, when rough-and-tumble persists in a pattern of physical aggression in pursuit of domination, it becomes bullying. Bullying is a precursor of stable antisocial and aggressive behavior that may endure into later adolescence and adulthood (Olweus 1993, 1994).[5]

As male children enter adolescence, the forms and instrumental value of rough-and-tumble seem to change—it becomes an important forum for the development of fighting skills. So, for twelve- and thirteen-year-old boys, rough-and-tumble involves both intense and playful fighting (Neill 1976). But the intense fighting often involves hostility, with the potential for injury and other distress for the victim. What was merely playful in a younger developmental stage becomes a more intense, purposive, and consequential behavior that lies at the heart of dominance struggles.

While these struggles ensue on other social fronts as well, rough-and-tumble remains at the heart of social hierarchies among male children as they move into early adolescence, where physical dominance and toughness are valued (Humphreys and Smith 1987). When alternative means of establishing social position are attenuated (success in school or other pro-social activities), rough-and-tumble is likely to continue beyond child-hood. However, its meaning, seriousness, and social value change as ado-lescents enter a developmental context with increased social diversity and competition for status. This transitional period is the stage at which rough play turns serious and transforms into the more consequential violent be-haviors of older adolescence.

Gang Violence

The assignment of status to young males based on toughness and fighting skills is an enduring theme of gang life.[6] Gangs are social groups that value styles of exaggerated displays of masculinity, risk taking, and autonomy, and violence often is part of the collective identity of the gang and its members (Keiser 1969; Padilla 1992). But gang violence is a heterogenous phenomenon, with meanings and functions that vary according to the spe-cific situation. The potential for gang violence results from any number of concerns, including struggles for power within the gang, territorial battles with other gangs, initiation and detachment rituals, material gain, the ex-pression of grievances, retribution, self-defense, defense of the gang, and reinforcement of collective identity. Each of these components of gang vi-olence involves a functional or purposive dimension.

As a social context, the gang is prone to violence because there is fre-quent and repeated interaction among individuals, third parties are read-ily present, status is valued and restricted, there is very low external (le-gal) social control on activity, and violence can help individuals address specific concerns noted above. In addition, violent expression of griev-ances within and between gangs are normative, and cultural values about masculinity are typically strong in the gang context (Oliver 1994; Felson and Tedeschi 1995).

The establishment of social identity and the expression of masculinity are important parts of negotiating and maintaining social position in the gang, and gang members adopt styles to express their manhood in several forms, including violence (Vigil 1988; Hagedorn 1998). Verbal aggres-sion, or violent discourse, among street groups can strengthen group co-hesion (Miller, Geertz, and Cutter 1961). Homophily of friendship pat-terns (Kandel 1985) suggests that gang members will have extensive and exclusive contact with like-minded and similarly situated adolescents, such as risk takers or impulsive actors, reinforcing the central functional role of violence and increasing the opportunities for it.

Finally, gangs often use violence to settle interpersonal and intergang disputes. For example, conflict between two rival gangs often involves violation of territory or perceived insults to the gang, and conflicts within gangs may occur when members jockey for status or when a dispute arises over relations involving girls or money. The expectation of violence in this context is a constant factor: those who violate this rule face expulsion or even violent retribution from other members of the gang.

Female Gang Violence   Although girl gangs often report fighting, they fight less often and fight differently: compared to boys, they seldom use guns, and generally less often use weapons (Hagedorn 1998). But Campbell's (1984) groundbreaking study of female gangs in New York City depicted a world where violence was common and where young women carried guns and other weapons (but rarely used them). Campbell (1990) suggested that many female gangs had moved beyond the stereotypes of auxiliary to male gangs, and female gang members had also rejected the limited roles of carrying weapons, money, or drugs for male gang members.

Campbell (1993, 126) claims that girl gangs often possess many "feminine" qualities while also pursuing instrumental goals through aggression, like males. Girls worked heavily on their reputations for toughness, in the same way that boys did, while also firmly embracing female gender roles: mother, lover, and companion to intimate partners, sister to neighborhood girls. But, like males, girls also sought a social identity and status through toughness and reputation, including outrageous acts to demonstrate "heart" or courage. Many fights among girls reflected disputes involving males: boyfriends are thought of as emotional possessions, and disputes arise over ownership and control (Campbell 1993, 138).[7] Moreover, like males, their pursuit of a tough identity often was designed to ward off attacks from other girls. Taylor (1993) expands on this and places female violence in the context of gender relations. He gives voice to young women whose violence serves to establish their "toughness," which in turn can ward off physical attacks by males. Campbell agrees, citing the high prevalence of girls' victimization experiences from violence at the hands of fathers, the beatings they witnessed of their mothers, and the sexual and other physical assaults at the hands of neighborhood boys or men: "In the context of the routine violence that surrounds them, the attraction of the gang for . . . girls is not hard to see" (1993, 136).

Accordingly, rather than embracing the functions of violence of boys, which emanate from conceptions of manhood and masculinity, female pursuit of toughness and other dimensions of violent identities seems to reflect a rejection of the violence of men toward women and the need for protection of self from men but also from other violent girls.

Robbery: Acquisitive Violence

For some youths, robbery provides a way of "campaigning for status . . . by taking the possessions of others" (Anderson 1999; Wilkinson 1998). Goods obtained in robberies, whether valuable or seemingly trivial, are imbued with a symbolic value for adolescents that far exceeds their material value—they symbolize the robber's ability to dominate another person, control a victim, and gain deference from others (Fagan and Wilkinson 1998b). According to Anderson (in press), while the material returns from robbery contribute socially and extrinsically to the accrual of status, the intrinsic rewards of status and dominance provide comfort, self-respect, and confidence. And it is only through violence, or the threat of it, that these robberies can be successful.

Especially among adolescents, robberies often are unplanned or hastily planned events, the result of a chance coming together of motivation and opportunity (Cook 1991). The goals are acquisitive, but serious injuries also result from many robberies gone wrong (Cook 1980; Luckenbill 1980; Skogan 1978).[8] There are predictable stages for the robbery event, and when the victim's responses fail to meet the robber's expectations, threatened violence may become actual to gain compliance or to get the event back on its planned course (Feeney 1986). The use of force, including firing guns, often is not gratuitous in robberies, unless a robbery becomes a stage for acting out "toughness" or meanness. Although firearms are often present during robberies, their use in the course of a robbery may reflect other contingencies, or what Zimring and Zuehl (1986) call "recreational violence."[9]

Adolescence is a developmental stage when abstract reasoning about the consequences of using guns and the cognitive capacity to read social cues are incomplete (Lochman and Dodge 1994; Steinberg and Cauffman 1996) The adolescent may see only all-or-nothing choices in these situations. During the course of a robbery, the (presumably inexperienced) teenager armed with a weapon becomes an unstable actor in a scenario with an outcome that is dependent on a predictable set of interactions between the robber and his victim. When the initial definition of the situation strays from robbery to a threat, personal slight, or conflict (in the wake of resistance), seemingly "irrational" violence occurs. And if guns are present, the violence may become lethal (Wilkinson 1998).

Dating Violence

Domestic violence often begins with dating violence during middle adolescence (Magdol et al. 1997). As contexts of intimate relationships, dates have meaning both socially and intrapsychically. For example, dating violence may involve sexual assault with the goal of displaying power over women, a form of status tied to sexual conquest and the social status it brings (Anderson 1990). It also may satisfy needs for control (Dobash and Dobash 1992), coercion and maintenance of power (Yllo 1988), or displays of domination or mastery (Makepeace 1989).

Dating violence by adolescents is part of a high-stakes sexual game that governs sexual codes and intimacy among youths (Anderson 1990; Hagedorn 1998). Dating involves the management of gender roles, and identity formation during the critical developmental stage of adolescence requires success in such roles. Having a boyfriend or girlfriend is important for status and identity, and the importance of this form of success can be exaggerated when other means of status or success are not easily attained. When normative patterns of relations devalue intimacy, however, the meaning of dating as a means to status is conflated with other forms of status, identity, and success. Thus, objectification supplants emotional attachment.

In this context, notions of masculinity combine with a material view of relationships to place dating in the context of the struggle for high status (Wilkinson 1998). Males are assumed to be dominant and women subordinate. A violation of these expected gender roles can be interpreted as an insult or threat to respect. When conducted in front of a public audience, the stakes become higher; male violence is perceived as a necessary response to "control" one's girlfriend and to be a "man." Controlling and owning one's intimate partner are mandates of masculinity generally, and these motivations are heightened in a social milieu where taking someone's lover is tantamount to taking his possession. It is an assault to respect, and in many cases mandates a violent response.

In all four types of aggressive activity outlined above, violence has specific functions in meeting the adolescent's needs. It occurs within a shared cognitive framework of purposiveness, where choices are shaped by the interaction of motivation, perception of the situation, and the context of the event.

Social Context and Decision Making

Context seems to be an ideal perspective for understanding the dynamics of adolescent crime. What remains unknown are the dynamics of choice, the circumscribing of choice by social contexts, and the situations that evolve in those contexts. In this section, the concept of context is imposed on a framework of processual dynamics in violent events. In this framework, violence is both rule oriented and normative (Anderson 1999; Wilkinson 1998). It is through these processes and contingencies that individual characteristics such as disputatiousness are channeled into violent events. Violent behavior can be viewed as a method of communicating social meanings within contexts where such action is either expected or at least tolerated. These concepts form the dimensions of an analytic framework that specifies the role of context in decisions to engage in adolescent violence.

Scripts

Decision making by adolescents is not ad hoc for each event, but reflects cumulative knowledge gained through both participation in and observation of violent interactions. This involves socialization processes that begin prior to adolescence and are refined along the way through interaction and practice. This learning may develop into "scripts," which provide a bounded set of choices to be invoked in situations where crime is a possibility. The script framework provides a useful way of understanding the decision-making process, including calculation of risks, strategic decisions, and assessments of available choices.

Wilkinson (1998) suggests several ways in which script theory can explain violence and other crime among adolescents:

1. Scripts are ways of organizing knowledge and behavioral choices (Abelson 1976);
2. individuals learn behavioral repertoires for different situations (Abelson 1981);
3. these repertoires are stored in memory as scripts and are elicited when cues are sensed in the environment (Huesmann 1988);
4. choice of scripts varies between individuals and some individuals will have limited choices (Dodge and Crick 1990);
5. individuals are more likely to repeat scripted behaviors when the previous experience was considered successful (Schank and Abelson 1977); and
6. scripted behavior may become automatic without much thought or weighing of consequences (Tedeschi and Felson 1994).

The development of scripts, the processes of decision making, and the social definitions of conflict and other functions served by crime all form in specific social contexts. These contexts shape normative definitions, imperatives or expected behaviors, and costs and rewards of crime. Many adolescents are likely to look to the streets for lessons on the rules of fighting, for example, or for the definition of a blameworthy target of a crime. But adolescents in conditions of economic deprivation may not develop as complete decision makers. There may be a number of social-interactional, developmental, contextual, cultural, and socioeconomic factors that impinge on the decision-making processes of young adolescents in violent conflicts.

The Social Contexts of Choice

Social context influences decisions to engage in crime through the interaction of individual developmental needs and functional goals specific to adolescence (such as identity, affinity, mastery, and defiance). Competition over limited resources, including social status, respect, and material goods, by violent or other antisocial means is central to this dynamic. When neighborhood and community contexts are isolated and deprived, social interactions are likely to be dominated by street codes that reward displays of physical domination and social approval for antisocial behavior (Anderson 1999, Short 1997). Jessor et al. (1991, 281), for example, show that the joint influences of different psychosocial systems—the environmental system and the personality system—better explain the development of functional problem behaviors such as violence, compared to the explanatory power of either psychosocial system alone.[10]

Street codes that shape decision making are the product of these interactions when summed across individuals. Social identity and respect are the most important features of the street code. Within this context there are clear-cut rules for using violence to gain respect. The public nature of a person's image or status identity often requires open displays of "nerve," including attacks on others, getting revenge for previous situations with an opponent, the protection of members of the group, and having the right props. There is only a limited amount of respect available and the process of acquiring it is highly competitive. Projecting the right image is everything in this context and backing up the projection with violent behavior is expected (Wilkinson 1998).

A social-interactionist view anticipates influences from both personality and situational structures. There are personal motivational structures, predispositions, anticipation of what is likely to happen in a situation (perceived properties of the situation itself), and selective attention to those features of the context. There also are choice-structuring properties of situations, independent of the motivations and perceptions of individuals within those contexts, that shape decisions about who to affiliate with and how and when to interact with them. These situational and individual factors interact to shape the natural course of violent events, including whether violence is avoided even when its likelihood otherwise remains high.

These interactions of perception and individual factors develop over time through the repeated interactions of individuals and settings that have properties perhaps independent of the individuals. That is, while there are contextual cues that trigger normative reactions, individuals may bring these expectations with them based on what Goffman (1983) terms "cumulative baggage."

The question here is whether there are norms in those scenes and contexts, independent of the contributions of actors in these scenes, that shape the outcomes of events leading to violence. Regardless of whether these norms exist in the minds of the individuals in those settings, I believe there are norms that emanate from scenes apart from the people in them, as evidenced in research on contexts and settings (Zinberg 1984; Tedeschi and Felson 1994; Majors and Billson 1992; Kennedy and Forde 1999; Crane 1991; Brooks-Gunn et al. 1993).

When events escalate into violence, it nearly always involves the active instigation of people in the immediate setting, coupled with the expectancy of what is mandated as a behavioral response by the norms attached to these scenes and peer networks within the neighborhood. Some of this is internalized, and is anticipated in terms of the social response when word gets out in the neighborhood about how each actor carried himself in that event. Accordingly, what looks situational may only be partially so, but it also cannot be explained in toto by the personalities of the individuals involved.

The debate between these two perspectives revolves around the question of social- and self-selection. For example, "niche-picking" (Scarr and McCartney 1983) refers to the fact that individuals are not randomly assigned to contexts (niches) but, rather, select them on the basis of their own individual characteristics. The process explains the difficulty of apportioning the effects of individuals and environment or individuals and contexts. Many studies suggest that violent adolescents choose antisocial peers to hang out with and engage in activities more likely to provide the sort of stimulation presumed to increase violent behavior (Cairns et al. 1988; Dishion et al. 1991; Schwendinger and Schwendinger 1985). In each illustration, niche-picking is likely to reflect characteristics of the individual and strengthen the very characteristics that led the individual to pick the niche in the first place.

These processes have been observed among probability samples in longitudinal studies conducted in generally heterogeneous social areas where there is extensive variation in the orientation of the social networks of children and adolescents who live there. But the conditions within areas marked by high violence rates are hardly comparable to nonurban locales. In neighborhoods where adolescent violence rates are highest, choices of social networks and social situations are constrained by patterns of residential segregation, concentrated poverty, and social isolation. The result for adolescents in these circumstances includes attenuated interactions with persons from outside the area and a general cutoff of normative influences and informal social controls from the dominant, mainstream community (Wilson 1991; Sampson and Wilson 1995; Elliott et al. 1996). Accordingly, the social structure of the neighborhood directs the adolescents to only one kind of status-producing niche, causing a narrowing of sources of social identity.

In summary, the interaction of individual and contextual factors in violent events reflects the internalized norms of neighborhoods into individual-level decision making within events, and their influence on scripts and social identity.[11] Perceptions and decisions seem to be filtered through individual and personality variables—such as disputatiousness—to influence the development of behavioral scripts, but the scripts themselves reflect the accumulation of hundreds of social interactions in which violence underlies the exchange of status and identity. Thus, violence scripts and violent social identities become the foundation of developmental capital for children and teenagers growing up in these contexts.

Social Context and Social Identity

Adolescence also is a time of pursuit of some universal developmental goals: social affiliation, mastery, social identity, and autonomy. In an isolated social world where respect and (prosocial) social standing are limited, crime and violence complicate the development of social identity. So, the development of identity is a central and perhaps overarching function of adolescent crime. Teenagers may situationally engage in antisocial behavior to form and/or maintain certain social identities within the broader social context of the neighborhood (Fagan and Wilkinson 1998b). Projecting the right image may have consequences for personal safety, social acceptance, and self-esteem among individuals. Accordingly, social identity has functional payoffs apart from its developmental importance: attaining social status, accruing "props" (respect), and warding off attacks from others (Fagan and Wilkinson 1998b).

Social identities become more salient through repeated performance. The social meanings attached to each performance determine when and how an actor will be known to others in the neighborhood context and, in turn, define subsequent interactions. An individual's social identity can both prevent violence from coming (he won't get picked on) and promote additional violence (other young men will attempt to knock him off his elevated status). These social identities may be temporary or permanent.

Fagan and Wilkinson (1998b) observed three distinct types of social identities tied to violence: being crazy and wild (frequent unstable fighting), holding your own (functional fighting), and being a punk (frequent

victim struggling for survival).[12] Toughness has always been highly regarded and a source of considerable status among adolescents in a wide
range of subcultures, from noncohesive street groups to highly structured
gangs (Whyte 1943; Goffman 1959, 1963, 1967; Wolfgang and Ferracuti
1982; Canada 1995). In some cases, displays of toughness are aesthetic:
facial expression, clothing and accessories, physical posture and gestures,
type of car, use of graffiti, and unique speech are all part of a particular
street style that may or may not be complemented by physical aggression.
These impression-management efforts to convey a "deviant aesthetic"
and "alien sensibility" change over time with tastes, of course, but are evident across ethnicities and cultures (Katz 1988). Toughness requires
young males to move beyond symbolic representation to physical violence. Guns are used to perpetuate and refine the aesthetic of toughness,
and to claim the identity of being among the toughest (Wilkinson 1998).

The "Crazy" Identity

As noted above, at the top of the identity hierarchy of the street is the
"crazy," "wild," or "killer" social identity. Individuals who perform extraordinary acts of violence are frequently feared and granted a level of
respect that others cannot easily attain (Fagan and Wilkinson 1998b).
Some take on this identity temporarily or situationally, while others
describe themselves as always being that way. Their performances are often socially defined as shocking or beyond what may be necessary to
handle a situation. Once an individual gives an extraordinary performance
he may notice changes in the way others relate to him. He may also start
viewing himself differently. This status brings with it a certain level of
power and personal fulfillment that may be reinforced by projecting this
identity. Future violent performances would enable him to maintain the
image of the most violent or toughest on the street. A person who has such
an identity gives the impression that he has extreme heart, is untouch-
able, and does not care about what happens. He has the capability to use
extreme violence and gets respect for dominating others. Others may want
to associate with him to benefit from his high status on the street. The identity itself carries privileges, expectations, and obligations that may open
him to additional opportunities for violence. The powerful identity may
be forced downward by someone else's extraordinary performance.

Holding Your Own

A middle ground involves the "necessary" use of crime to establish a
threshold identity that is functional in a context of identities skewed
toward crime. Wilkinson (1998), based on interviews with 125 respondents

from two high-crime neighborhoods in New York City, described the process of how personal identities formed around displays of "doing what you got to do," or "holding your own" in violent situations. These identities were generally viewed positively on the street and were helpful in obtaining both strategic and functional goals.

Most young men who engage in crime and violence fall into this category (Fagan and Wilkinson 1998b). Individuals who hold their own are respected on the street, although they will eventually face challenges to their ability to "do what it takes" in heated situations, and in all likelihood faced numerous challenges on their way up to that status (Strauss 1996, 90). A person with this identity gives the impression that he has the capacity to use extreme violence but does so only when necessary. This person will face a challenge directly and is respected for that. This identity allows him to be an insider in the street world, but this status can be unstable and may require acts of violence when he is faced with public attacks on his identity.

The Stigmatized "Punk" Identity

At the bottom of the status hierarchy of the street is the "punk," also known as an "herb," "nerd," or "dweeb." In the inner city, those who cannot fight or prove their toughness may be stigmatized either temporarily or permanently. Other guys in the neighborhood will act upon that stigma. The process of "punking" someone, as respondents called it, closely resembles the process of "fool-making" described by Strauss (1996).

Someone with this identity is considered to be fair game for violent attacks. The attacks are motivated by either an attempt to restate the dominance hierarchy or as punishment to the punk for not living up to group norms. Those atop the social hierarchy of adolescence often degrade, dominate, and victimize individuals who have punk characteristics. Gender identity is part of this process; the degradation typically involves a direct or implicit emasculation of the "weaker" males (Fagan and Wilkinson 1998b). Given the intensified acceptance of hegemonic masculinity in the inner-city context, these messages would have a strong negative impact on a person's self-image. Most young men in the street assume that outsiders in the neighborhood (and relevant social network) are punks; the presumed punk must prove otherwise.

Conclusion: Developing and Maintaining Identity

The dynamics of violent events reflect several interesting processes: (1) achieving a highly valued social identity occurs through extreme displays of violence, (2) achieving a "safe" social identity may also require the use of extreme forms of violence, (3) the ready availability of guns clearly increases the stakes of how one achieves status, (4) much behavior is motivated by avoiding being a punk, (5) identities can change from being a punk into a more positive status such as "holding your own," (6) guns equalize the odds for some smaller young men through the process of showing "nerve," and (7) an adolescent can feel like a punk for a specific situation but may not take on that identity. If the street orientation is dominant in public spaces and personal safety is attributed to adherence to the code as Anderson (1994, 1999) suggests, then those who do not conform will be victimized.

Impression management, reputation, and image are necessary to maintain an identity that assures daily survival (Canada 1995; Sheley and Wright 1995). Each crime raises the possibility that identities can be won and lost. These are complex processes that unfold over time and have specific developmental stages. There appear to be ritualistic passages into different social identities that include public displays of violent behavior as a rite of passage.

Finally, identities are won and lost in the responses to identity attacks. Identities are regulated through strict adherence to a proscribed dominance hierarchy in which there are only a limited number of desirable identities to attain. Knowledge of the "players" in the neighborhood is needed to determine what type of action is appropriate in a face-to-face encounter and how respect is to be apportioned. Displays of respect are expected by those who have higher levels of status on the street. Respect in this context may include stepping down from conflict out of deference to the other person's status. Displays of disrespect are also expected in situations where identity posturing is called for. However, shows of disrespect are often an intended or unintended attack on someone else's identity and must, according to the code of the street, be addressed aggressively (Wilkinson 1998).

Implications for Law and Social Science
Contexts, Codes, and Choice

Decisions by adolescents to engage in violence reflect both developmental (social identity, status, and respect) and strategic goals (Fagan and Wilkinson 1998a). The arbiters of respect are peers, the everyday judges who evaluate behaviors and adjust the social hierarchy of the neighborhood. Through the effective channels of rumor, the daily news of who fought who and with what outcome is spread quickly through relevant social networks (Turner 1993).

The use of violence to deter attack illustrates a strategic goal of violence. Status and respect afford protection from attack. In the skewed context of danger and violence, decisions to use violence are expressions of self-help (Goffman 1967, 1983) and social control (Black 1983). That is, adolescent violence often involves the resolution of disputes, the redress of grievances, and even the preemptory strike against a dangerous, hostile, and motivated enemy.

These are functions normally met by legal and social institutions. But in the cities' most dangerous neighborhoods, social control is provided through specific dynamics of social norms among adolescents, norms that are distinct from the ones that shape adult interactions and influence behavior in the mainstream culture. These local codes are actively regulated through the social organization of the street. The reliance on self-help reflects the virtual absence of formal social controls, especially law enforcement, in the most dangerous neighborhoods. Police are a weak presence during violent events, and their efforts to arrest young men involved in violence are not seen as effective (Canada 1995; Wilkinson 1998; Sullivan 1989; Anderson in press).

In neighborhoods with high rates of violence, the imbalance between powerful antisocial contextual forces (and the social norms they raise) exceeds the legal norms developed in (and imposed by) a social and legal culture that lies outside of these inner-city contexts (Meares 1998). Can these contexts create a set of norms, regulated by behavioral controls arising from the dominant social groups within that context, that preempt distal notions of law and fairness? How does law, informed by normative moral values from a distal but dominant society, influence decision making within the inner-city context? These questions are beyond the norms of compliance based on fairness and legitimacy of a legal code; the resolution of these issues requires an understanding of the localized but prevailing code that ensures safety and social standing within the inner-city context (Tyler 1990; Meares 1998).

When normative law is weak, the uses of violence suggest a self-help dimension that illustrates Black's (1983) "self-help" or "crime as social control" dynamic.[13] Law often is a physical and social externality with weak legitimacy for inner-city adolescents (Fagan and Wilkinson 1998a). In areas where legal controls are weak, the externality of law makes legal norms moot, and self-help becomes a codified and normative basis for action. Street codes supplant moral norms that are externalities to the specific contexts of danger. Street codes that are actively reinforced exert a strong locally normative influence on how social interactions are interpreted, how disputes are resolved, and how limited social standing is allocated. Combined with the social and cultural isolation of inner-city life, legal proscriptions of violence are functionally weak compared to a code that values violence and continually defines its strategic value. By conforming to a context-specific code or group character, strategic self-defense goals are met at the cost of a moral code that is salient elsewhere.

Accordingly, the choice to be violent in specific situations may not be a morally good decision, but it is a rational decision based on a calculus of the consequences of other behavioral choices. For adolescents in danger-ous, potentially lethal contexts, threat trumps morality in a context where there is a reasonable expectation of lethal attack. The developmental con-text of violent inner cities shapes a decision-making heuristic among ado-lescents based on their best and immediate interests rather than an ab-stract code of norms that exists only outside the immediate context. When this context involves both safety and social status, two develop-mental needs often unavailable in these contexts of danger, legal compli-ance has doubtful value and low payoff for adolescents. The rule of law takes a backseat to the code of the streets.

Context and Culpability

The concept of contextualized choices can be translated into dimensions of culpability, and raises questions about the blameworthiness of behav-iors when viewed in context. Justification and excuse have always been part of the criminal law's proscriptive norms of conduct (Fletcher 1978). Within this framework, is there room for context as part of the jurispru-dence of adolescent crime?

Theories stressing that inner-city adolescents conform to a normative street code with expectations of violent victimization differ from con-temporary defenses that stress the social toxicity of the defendant's every-day circumstances. Criminal defendants increasingly have claimed that "social toxins" excuse or mitigate their guilt (Falk 1996).[14] Unlike self-defense arguments that typically offer short-term circumstantial or causal explanations for criminal behavior, social-toxin arguments claim that there are long-term, diffuse effects of social toxins on decision making. Such defenses, based on a "rotten social background" claim that social conditions compromise moral decision making, generally claim that be-havioral controls are impaired or that choice is reduced by the actor's so-cial and environmental background (Delgado 1985).[15] While dismissed in the popular press as "abuse excuses" (Dershowitz 1994) or "trash syn-dromes" (Mosteller 1996), these defenses are weak not because they con-tradict normative views of human agency, but because they consistently fail to meet tests of scientific validity.

The Model Penal Code sets forth specific conditions that are necessary to invoke justification or excuse for a criminal offense: an imminent threat, a reasonable belief that the threat is real, an inability to withdraw to safety, and limited alternatives to criminal conduct. To what extent do disputes and other interpersonal transactions within socially isolated inner-city neighborhoods establish these conditions? [16]

To the extent that a street code makes threatened violence necessary and real, adolescents in these social contexts can reasonably anticipate that aggressive action will follow a threat. Fagan and Wilkinson (1998b) describe a constant ebb and flow of identity attacks—physical assaults designed to establish one's toughness—that stem from routine or everyday encounters in some neighborhoods. Disputes are long lasting and often are resolved in violence. So when an adolescent hears that someone has threatened violence against him or her, the threat is perceived as real based on observations of how other similarly situated people in these neighborhoods have made and honored such threats. In a neighborhood context with an active social exchange of violent identities, threats are assumed to be real. To assume otherwise is to risk attack and serious injury.

Are threats imminent in these violent disputes? Threats within the temporal boundaries of a dispute can be viewed as imminent if the other person is carrying a weapon, if he is with friends who are carrying weapons, or if he otherwise has immediate access to a weapon. Weapon carrying is common in some neighborhoods, so such threats must be taken seriously (Fagan and Wilkinson 1998b; Anderson 1999). In other circumstances, the threat may be that the opponent is going to find a gun first and then seek out the adolescent. This threat of retaliation is proximate but not immediate. The "imminence" of these threats is more difficult to judge, and is certainly lacking the probabilities that an immediate threat carries. In inner-city disputes, threats are often carried out at a future time.

Withdrawal usually is not an option. Many disputes are public performances requiring demonstrations of fearlessness and invulnerability. Withdrawal may be possible, but its costs in subsequent fights or disputes may exceed the short-term returns—unless skillfully done, withdrawal invites subsequent attack by weakening social identity and violent identity. Withdrawal in one incident invites attack in a later incident with either the same rival or perhaps someone else. Knowledge of the person's lack of nerve will travel fast throughout the social networks of a community, and younger adolescents seeking to build their status through violent identities may see the withdrawing youth as a worthy target for assault. A negotiated withdrawal takes a great deal of skill, both strategically and verbally. One respondent interviewed by Fagan and Wilkinson called it a "chess game." However, this skill is rare, and is a high-stakes gamble because failure could result in serious injury or death. Accordingly, contexts of high rates of violence among dense social networks of teenagers make withdrawal a last resort. Withdrawal, unless skillfully done, invites subsequent attack by weakening social identity and violent identity.

The relevance of social context to culpability does not require new theories or doctrines of law. These constructs can be accommodated in existing categories of criminal law with little innovation or restructuring of criminal-law theories or doctrines (Falk 1996; Morse 1998). Indeed, expansion of existing doctrine to accommodate new social and scientific knowledge is preferable to the creation of new doctrines (Falk 1996; Mosteller 1996; Morse 1998). One significant dimension of context is its opposition to the subjectivization of reasonableness. Context argues for an objective view of the "reasonableness" of appraisals of threat or duress, but within a spatially bounded world of social interactions, where social meanings are specific to the public stage where they occur.

This conceptualization of context is neither static nor detached from the actions of individuals. Context imparts new causal meaning—indeed, a dynamic causal meaning—to the more static construct of "social environment" (Sampson 1993). It explicitly links environmental contingencies to decision making in situ by adolescents. Context is a stage where social-interactional skills and styles are practiced and learned and internalized into scripts. It is the place where witnesses judge and confer status on actors, thereby shaping social norms and defining the social meaning of interactions, both legal and illegal.

Accordingly, the introduction of a claim of contextual influence in a criminal matter requires attention to three factors: (1) the characteristics and dynamic processes of the context itself, (2) the status and position of the individual within that context, and (3) the interactions of the two (Fagan 1999). The first is self-evident, but the second and third are not. The immersion of individuals within that context determines their exposure relative to other persons in the same setting. This permits a contextualized assessment of "reasonableness" that is not subjective but within the social framework of the specific context.

The examination of interactions can illustrate the adolescent's susceptibility or reaction to the contextual dynamics. Social science is less skilled at determining reactivity compared to network analysis and other indicators of social immersion. This is a significant challenge, since a determination of culpability requires that we parse out the "person" from the "place" in person-place interactions.

Social Context and Social Science

Which rules of science govern the assessment of contextual influences? Evidence thresholds for excusability require that social science establish the precise, rather than the general, dimensions of the social reality that shaped the decision to use force (Mosteller 1996). Thus, research must be able to identify more than simple membership of the individual in the group that is subject to specific processes of social regulation (although this certainly must be established). The evidence must go on to identify the specific contingencies or situational dynamics that proscribe behavioral choices, or that establish clear preferences or mandates for a specific reaction to specific provocations. In the case of adolescent violence, a claim of justification or diminished culpability must show the specifics regarding withdrawal and imminence (Fagan 1999). The studies cited in earlier sections of this chapter go about establishing these contingencies and the social reality of contextualized choices.

Researchers generally hold controlled experiments as the "gold standard" for establishing causal relationships (Fagan 1990). Controlled experiments that show the effects of context on behavior would be extremely difficult; in the measurement of antisocial or violent behavior involving adolescents, experiments would fail several thresholds for the protection of human subjects. Even quasi-experiments, research designs that approximate experimental conditions but fall short of the randomization standard, would fail tests of construct validity by failing to accurately depict the complex conditions and contingencies of social contexts.

A second limitation of experiments, whether natural or controlled, is the hierarchical structure of relationships among independent variables. Context is an ecological variable that affects many persons simultaneously, but the reactions of individuals to contextual influences vary. Social science has rejected analytic methods that place ecological, contextual, or even situational factors within the same variance structure as relations among variables that affect individuals. Recent innovations in the design of studies and the statistical analysis of data address this limitation. These innovations offer analytic techniques that capture effects that span different levels of explanation—from the ecological to the individual—and that distinguish the effects attributable to the context from those attributable to the individual, and then identify the interactions across these levels of explanation (Bryk and Raudenbusch 1992).

A different epistemological approach is necessary to capture the complex processual dynamics that comprise and describe context. Research in this area has primarily used methods of anthropology to construct "thick descriptions" of the actions of individuals within settings, the meaning and influence of the setting, and the adaptation of the individual to the norms of the setting (Geertz 1973). Sociologists have used parallel approaches to study the meaning of social interaction, based on repeated study of events (Goffman 1983). The two unifying characteristics of these approaches are the sampling on the dependent variable, a method widely used when the parameters of the phenomenon are not well known; and the use of narratives to capture recounts of events in the subject's own voice. The analysis of these data results in the development of heuristics or rich descriptive frameworks in which to interpret actions. These methods also are well suited to capture variations in specific responses to different contingencies. For example, Fagan and Wilkinson (1998b) were able to capture the dynamics of both withdrawal and engagement by the same person in a study of violent adolescents involved in putative gun fights.

The validity of these studies is not controversial among social scientists, but the generalizability of this research sparks controversy. The limitation of an approximation of a random sample, and the limitations on comparison groups, are the foci of disagreements over the validity. These studies typify knowledge in this field, however limited. Perhaps most important, its use as evidence in the field of criminal law suggests that the fit of evidence is more important than its scientific validity.

The thresholds for scientific testimony in the Federal Rules of Evidence and affirmed by the *Daubert* decision suggests that any evidence to establish "reasonableness" must be based on a valid and reliable science.[17] Social-interactionist studies that incorporate the perspectives of contextualized street codes may meet that standard by establishing the precise dimensions and causal mechanisms that link context to perception to decision to action.

Conclusion

Traditional social science is focused at two ends of the explanatory continuum: "big science," which establishes the macrosocial forces that create contexts or social toxins, and clinical science, which focuses on the individual, who is often detached from the larger social context. Both big science and clinical assessments defy the paradigm of dynamic contextualism that is intrinsic to the study of social processes and interactions (Sampson 1993). If the study of context is inherently "small science" that focuses on social processes, and the appropriate paradigm is qualitative, this will require a social-science orientation quite different from the contemporary approaches of clinical assessment or large-scale surveys. The negotiation of the scientific threshold for the validity of that science in a criminal proceeding is a process that will take place simultaneously in law and social science (Fagan 1999).

The study of social norms requires analysis of factors that give meaning to actions and shape compliance with normative codes (Meares 1998). What are the implications of a contextualized view of adolescence in conditions of hypersegregation for understanding the law? The perspective of context, bounded rationality, and normative codes suggest the relevance of context to decision making. They also contribute to the elements of both justification, which focuses on the act, and excuse, which focuses on the actor. These are traditional doctrines of the criminal law. Social-science evidence of contexts of violence suggests that the line between justification and excuse may be difficult to draw. Rather than expanding into new doctrines, social science can expand definitions that fall into these existing domains. While bearing directly on the assessment of culpability, these arguments do not address the question of culpability of guilt, or of culpability in the context of determining punishment. An analysis of that determination awaits additional research.

Works Cited

Abelson, Robert. 1976. Script processing in attitude formation and decision-making. In *Cognition and social behavior,* edited by J. S. Carroll and J. W. Payne. Hillsdale, N.J.: Erlbaum.

———. 1981. Psychological status of the script concept. *American Psychologist* 36:715–729

Adler, Patricia A., and Peter Adler. 1998. *Peer power: Preadolescent culture and identity.* New Brunswick, N.J.: Rutgers University Press.

Anderson, Elijah. 1990. *Streetwise: Race, class and change in an urban community.* Chicago: University of Chicago Press.

———. 1994. Code of the streets. *The Atlantic Monthly* (May).

———. 1999. *Code of the street: Decency, violence, and the moral life of the inner city.* New York: Norton.

Becker, Gary. 1968. Crime and punishment: An economic approach. *Journal of Political Economy* 76:169–217.

Black, Donald. 1983. Crime as social control. *American Sociological Review* 48:34–45.

Bronfenbrenner, Uri. 1979. *The ecology of human development: experiments by nature and design.* Cambridge: Harvard University Press.

Brooks-Gunn, Jeanne, Greg J. Duncan, Patricia K. Klebanov, and N. Sealand. 1993. Do neighborhoods influence child and adolescent development? *American Journal of Sociology* 99:353–395.

Bryk, Anthony, and Stephen Raudenbusch 1992. *Hierarchical linear models.* Thousand Oaks, Calif.: Sage Publications.

Cairns, Robert, Beverly Cairns, H. Neckerman, S. Gest, and J. L. Gariepy. 1988. Social networks and aggressive behavior: Peer support or peer rejection? *Developmental Psychology* 24:815–823.

Campbell, Anne. 1984. *The girls in the gang.* New York: Basil Blackwell.

———. 1990. Female participation in gangs. In *Gangs in America,* edited by C. R. Huff. Thousand Oaks, Calif.: Sage.

——. 1993. *Men, women, and aggression.* New York: Basic Books.

Canada, Geoffrey. 1995. *Fist, knife, stick, gun.* Boston: Beacon Press.

Clarke, Ronald V., and Derrick B. Cornish. 1985. Modeling offenders' decisions: A framework for research and policy. *Crime and Justice: A Review of Research* 6:147–186.

Cohen, Albert. 1955. *Delinquent boys: the culture of the gang.* Glencoe, Ill.: Free Press.

Cohen, Lawrence E., and Marcus Felson. 1979. Social change and crime rate trends. *American Sociological Review* 44:588–608.

Cook, Philip J. 1980. Reducing injury and death rates in robbery. *Policy Analysis* 6 (1): 21–45.

Cook, Philip J. 1991. The technology of personal violence. Pages 1–72 in *Crime and justice: An annual review of research,* edited by M. Tonry and N. Morris. Vol. 14. Chicago: University of Chicago Press.

Cornish, Derrick B. 1993. Crimes as scripts. Paper presented at the Second Annual Seminar on Environmental Criminology and Crime Analysis, 26–28 May, at the University of Miami, Coral Gables.

Cornish, Derrick B. and Ronald V. Clarke. 1987. Understanding crime displacement: An application of rational choice theory. *Criminology* 25:933–947.

Crane, Jonathan. 1991. The epidemic theory of ghettos and neighborhood effects on dropping out and teenage childbearing. *American Journal of Sociology* 96(5):1226–1259.

Delgado, Richard. 1985. Social background: Should the criminal law recognize a defense of severe environmental deprivation? *Law and Inequality* 3:9-45.

Dershowitz, Alan P. 1994. *The abuse excuse and other cop-outs, sob stories, and evasions of responsibility.* Boston: Little Brown and Co.

Dishion, Thomas, Gerald Patterson, M. Stoolmiller, and M. Skinner. 1991. Family, school, and behavioral antecedents to early adolescent involvement with antisocial peers. *Developmental Psychology* 27:172–180.

Dobash, Rebecca E., and P. Russell Dobash. *Women, violence and social change.* New York: Routledge, 1992.

Dodge, Kenneth A., and Nicki R. Crick. 1990. Social information processing bases of aggressive behavior in children. *Personality and Social Psychology Bulletin* 16:8–22.

Elliott, Delbert S., William J. Wilson, David Huizinga, Robert J. Sampson, Alexander Elliott, and Bruce Rankin. 1996. The effects of neighborhood disadvantage on adolescent development. *Journal of Research in Crime and Delinquency* 33:389–426.

Fagan, Jeffrey. 1990. Natural experiments. In *Measurement issues in criminology,* edited by Kimberly L. Kempf. New York: Springer-Verlag.

——. 1992. The social control of spouse assault. *Advances in Criminological Theory* 4:187–234.

——. 1993a. Set and setting revisited: Influences of alcohol and illicit drugs on the social context of violent events. Pages 161–191 in *Alcohol and interpersonal violence: Fostering multidisciplinary perspectives,* edited by S. E. Martin. Vol. 24. Rockville, Md.: National Institute of Alcohol Abuse and Alcoholism.

———. 1993b Interactions among drugs, alcohol, and violence. *Health Affairs* 12 (4): 65–77.

———. 1999. Context and culpability of adolescent violence. *Virginia Review of Social Policy and Law* 6(3): 101–174.

Fagan, Jeffrey, and Richard B. Freeman. 1999. Crime and work. *Crime and Justice: A Review of Research* 25:113–178.

Fagan, Jeffrey, and Deanna L. Wilkinson. 1998a. Guns, youth violence and social identity. Pages 373–456 in *Youth violence—crime and justice: A review of research,* edited by Michael Tonry and Mark Moore. Vol. 25. Chicago: University of Chicago Press.

———. 1998b. The social contexts and functions of adolescent violence. Pages 89–133 in *Violence in American schools,* edited by D. Elliott, B. Hamburg, and K. Williams. New York: Cambridge University Press.

Falk, Patricia. 1996. Novel theories of criminal defense based on the toxicity of the social environment: Urban psychosis, television intoxication, and black rage. *North Carolina Law Review* 74:731.

Feeney, Floyd. 1986. Decision making in robberies. Pages 53–71 in *The reasoning criminal,* edited by R. V. Clarke and D. Cornish. New York: Springer-Verlag.

Felson, Richard B. and James T. Tedeschi. 1995. A social interactionist approach to violence: Cross-cultural applications. In *Interpersonal violent behaviors: Social and cultural aspects,* edited by R. Barry Ruback and Neil A. Weiner. New York: Springer Publishing.

Felson, Richard B., William Baccagglini, and G. Gmelch. 1986. Bar-room brawls: Aggression and violence in Irish and American bars. In *Violent transactions,* edited by Anne Campbell and Jack Gibbs. New York: Basil Blackwell.

Fletcher, George. 1978. *Rethinking the criminal law.* New York: Free Press.

Geertz, Clifford. 1973. Thick description: Toward an interpretive theory of culture. In *The interpretation of cultures,* edited by Clifford Geertz.

Goffman, Erving. 1959. *The presentation of self in everyday life.* Garden City, NY: Doubleday.

———. 1963. *Stigma.* Englewood Cliffs, N.J.: Prentice Hall.

———. 1967. The nature of deference and demeanor. Pages 47–95 in *Interaction ritual: Essays on face-to-face behavior,* edited by Erving Goffman. Garden City N.Y.: Anchor Books.

———. 1983. The interaction order. *American Sociological Review* 48:1–17.

Guerra, Nancy G., and Ronald G. Slaby. 1990. Cognitive mediators of aggression in adolescent offenders: Part 2: Interventions. *Developmental Psychology* 26:269–277.

Hagedorn, John. 1998. Gang violence in the post-industrial era. In *Youth violence, crime and justice: a review of research,* edited by M. Tonry and M. Moore. Vol. 24. Chicago: University of Chicago Press.

Hamburg, Beatrix A. 1974. Early adolescence: A specific and stressful stage of the life cycle. Pages 101–124 in *Coping and adaptation,* edited by G. V. Coelho, D. A. Hamburg, and J. E. Adams. New York: Basic Books.

Huesman, L. Rowell. 1988. An information processing model for the development of aggression. *Aggressive Behavior* 14 (1): 13–24.

Humphreys, A. P., and P. K. Smith. 1987. Rough and tumble, friendship, and dominance in schoolchildren: Evidence for continuity and change with age. *Child Development* 38:201–212.

Jessor, Richard, John Donovan, and Frank M. Costa. 1991. *Beyond adolescence: Problem behavior and young adult development.* New York: Cambridge University Press.

Kandel, Denise B. 1985. On processes of peer influences in adolescent drug use: A developmental perspective. Pages 203–227 in *Development as action in context: Problem behavior and normal youth development,* edited by R. K. Silbereisen, K. Eyferth, and G. Rudinger. Berlin: Springer-Verlag.

Katz, Jack. 1988. *Seductions of crime: Moral and sensual attractions in doing evil.* New York: Basic Books.

Keiser, R. Lincoln. 1969. *The vice lords: Warriors of the streets.* New York: Holt, Rinehart and Winston.

Kennedy, Leslie, and David R. Forde. 1999. *When push comes to shove: A routine conflict approach to violence.* Albany: State University of New York Press.

Kramer, Samuel. 1990. An economic analysis of criminal attempt: Marginal deterrence and the optimal structure of sanctions. *Journal of Criminal Law and Criminology* 81(2):398–417.

Lochman, John E., and Kenneth E. Dodge. 1994. Social-cognitive processes of severely violent, moderately aggressive, and nonaggressive boys. *Journal of Consulting and Clinical Psychology* 62 (2): 366–374.

Luckenbill, David F. 1980. Patterns of force in robbery. *Deviant Behavior* 1:361–378.

Luckenbill, David F., and Daniel P. Doyle. 1989. Structual position and violence: Developing a cultural explanation. *Criminology* 27:419–436

Majors, R.and J. M. Billson. 1992. *Cool pose: The dilemmas of black manhood in America.* New York: Simon and Schuster.

Magdol, Lynn, Terrie E. Moffitt, Avshalom Caspi, Donald M. Newman, Jeffrey Fagan, and Phil Silva. 1997. Gender differences in partner violence in a birth cohort of 21 year olds: Bridging the gap between clinical and epidemiological research. *Journal of Consulting and Clinical Psychology* 65 (1): 68–78.

Makepeace, James. 1989. Dating, living together, and courtship violence. Pages 94–107 in *Violence in dating relationships: Emerging social issues,* edited by Maureen Pirog-Good and Jan E. Stets. New York: Praeger.

Meares, Tracey. 1998. Place and crime. Chicago-Kent Law Review 73:669–705.

Miller, J. L., and Anderson, A. B. 1986. Updating the deterrence doctrine. *Journal of Criminal Law and Criminology* 77:418–438.

Miller, Walter B., H. Geertz, and H. S. G. Cutter. 1961. Aggression in a boys' streetcorner group. *Psychiatry* 24:283–398.

Morse, Stephen J. 1998. Excusing and the new excuse defenses. *Crime and Justice* 23:329–395.

Mosteller, Robert. 1996. Syndromes and politics in criminal trials and evidence law. *Duke Law Journal* 46:461–497.

Neill, S. R. 1976. Aggressive and non-aggressive fighting in 12 to 13 year old preadolescent boys. *Journal of Child Psychology and Psychiatry* 17:213–220.

Oliver, William. 1994. *The violent social world of black men.* New York: Lexington Books.

Olweus, Dan. 1994. Bullying at school: Long-term outcomes for the victims and an effective school-based intervention program. Pages 97–130 in *Aggressive behavior: Current perspectives,* edited by L. R. Huesmann. New York: Plenum.

Olweus, Dan. 1993. *Bullying at school: What we know and what we can do.* Oxford, England: Blackwell.

Padilla, Felix. 1992. *The gang as American enterprise.* New Brunswick, N.J.: Rutgers University Press.

Pernanen, Kai. 1991. *Alcohol in human violence.* New York: Guilford Press.

Pikert, S. M., and S. M. Wall. 1981. An investigation of children's perceptions of dominance relations. *Perceptual and Motor Skills* 52:75–81.

Polk, Kenneth. 1994. *When men kill: Scenarios of masculine violence.* New York: Cambridge University Press.

Roncek, Dennis W., and P. A. Maier. 1991. Bars, blocks, and crimes revisited: Linking the theory of routine activities to the empiricism of "hot spots." *Criminology* 29:725–754.

Sampson, Robert J. 1993. Dynamic contextualism. *Journal of Research in Crime and Delinquency* 30:426–450.

Sampson, Robert J., and Janet L. Lauritsen. 1994. Violent victimization and offending: Individual-, situational- and community-level risk factors. Pages 1–115 in *Understanding and preventing violence,* edited by A. J. Reiss, Jr., and J. A. Roth. Vol. 3. Washington, D.C.: National Academy Press.

Sampson, Robert J., and W. J. Wilson. 1995. Race, crime and urban inequality. In *Crime and inequality,* edited by J. Hagan and R. Peterson. Stanford, Calif.: Stanford University Press.

Scarr, Sandra, and K. McCartney. 1983. How people make environments: A theory of genotype environment effects. *Child Development* 54:424–435.

Schank, Richard, and Robert Abelson. 1977. *Scripts, plans, goals and understanding.* Hillsdale, N.J.: Erlbaum.

Schwendinger, Herman, and Julia Schwendinger. 1985. *Adolescent subcultures and delinquency.* New York: Praeger.

Sheley, Joseph, and James Wright. 1995. *In the line of fire: Youth, guns, and violence in urban America.* New York: Aldine de Gruyter.

Short, James F. Jr. 1997. *Poverty, ethnicity and violent crime.* Boulder, Colo.: Westview.

Short, James F. Jr., and Fred L. Strodtbeck. 1965. *Group process and gang delinquency.* Chicago: University of Chicago Press.

Shover, Neal. 1995. *Great pretenders: Pursuits and careers of persistent thieves.* Boulder, Colo.: Westview.

Skogan, Wesley. 1978. Weapon use in robbery. In *Violent crime: Historical and contemporary issues,* edited by James Inciardi and Ann E. Pottieger. Thousand Oaks, Calif.: Sage.

Smith, P. K., and K. Lewis. 1980. Effects of deprivation of exercise play in nursery school children. *Animal Behavior* 28:922–928.

Spergel, Irving A. 1995. *The youth gang problem: A community approach.* New York: Oxford University Press.

Stark, Rodney. 1987. Deviant place: A theory of the ecology of crime. *Criminology* 25:893–917.

Steinberg, Laurence, and Shelli Avenevoli. In press. The role of context in the development of psychopathology: A conceptual framework and some speculative propositions. *Child Development.*

Steinberg, Laurence, and Elizabeth Cauffman. 1996. Maturity of judgment in adolescence: Psychosocial factors in adolescent decision making. *Law and Human Behavior* 20:249–272.

Stephens, David W., and John R. Krebs. 1986. *Foraging theory.* Princeton, N.J.: Princeton University Press.

Strauss, Anselm L. 1996. *Mirrors and masks: The search for identity.* 2d ed. New Brunswick, N.J.: Transaction Publishers.

Sullivan, Mercer. 1989. *Getting paid: Youth crime and unemployment in three urban neighborhoods.* New York: Cornell University Press.

Taylor, Carl S. 1993. *Women, girls, gangs, and crime.* East Lansing, Mich.: Michigan State University Press.

Tedeschi, James, and Richard B. Felson. 1994. *Violence, aggression and coercive actions.* Washington, D.C.: APA Press.

Tunnell, Kenneth. 1993. *Choosing crime: The criminal calculus of property offenders.* Chicago: Nelson-Hall.

Turner, Patricia. 1993. *I Heard it through the grapevine : Rumor in African-American culture.* Berkeley: University of California Press.

Tyler, Tom R. 1990. *Why people obey the law.* New Haven, Conn.: Yale University Press.

Venkatesh, Sudhir. 1997. The social organization of street gang activity in an urban ghetto. *American Journal of Sociology* 103:82–111.

Vigil, James Diego. 1988. *Barrio gangs.* Austin, Tex.: University of Texas Press.

Whyte, William Foote. 1943. *Street corner society.* Chicago: University of Chicago Press.

Wilkinson, Deanna L. 1998. The social and symbolic construction of violent events among inner city adolescents. Ph.D. diss., Rutgers University.

Wilkinson, Deanna L., and Jeffrey Fagan. 1996. Understanding the role of firearms in violence "scripts": The dynamics of gun events among adolescent males. *Law and Contemporary Problems* 59 (1): 55–90.

Wilson, William Julius. 1991. Studying inner-city social dislocations: The challenge of public agenda research. *American Sociological Review* 56:1–14.

Wolfgang, Marvin, and Franco Ferracuti. 1982. *The subculture of violence: Toward an integrated theory in criminology.* 2d ed. Thousand Oaks, Calif.: Sage.

Wright, Richard, and Scott Decker. 1994. *Burglars on the job : Streetlife and residential break-ins.* Boston: Northeastern University Press.

———. 1997. *Armed robbers in action: Stickups and street culture.* Boston: Northeastern University Press.

Yllo, Kersti. 1988. *Feminist pespectives on wife abuse.* Thousand Oaks, Calif.: Sage Publications.

Zimring, Franklin E., and Janice Zuehl. 1986.Victim injury and death in urban robbery: A Chicago study. *Journal of Legal Studies* 15:1–40.
Zinberg, Norman. 1984. *Drug, set and setting.* New Haven, Conn.: Yale University Press.

Notes

1. There has been similar interest in the past, stemming primarily from economists whose theoretical models of the utility curves of would-be offenders portrayed them as rational actors (Becker 1968).

2. Gang research is an exception, where the social interactions of gang life has been central theme for over fifty years, beginning with Whyte (1943) and continuing through contemporary gang studies such as Venkatesh (1997). Each of these studies has examined gang interactions within the social context of their communities.

3. The four illustrations do not imply a developmental progression or hierarchy. These four unique domains illustrate the paradigm of situated transactions. Other domains of violence also can be analyzed from this perspective, including street-corner conflicts, ethnic conflicts, fraternity hazing, sporting-event violence, or sexual assaults (Fagan and Wilkinson 1998a).

4. One of the constants across developmental stages is the ordering of dominance hierarchies among males based on fighting skills and toughness (Pikert and Wall 1981; Humphreys and Smith 1987).

5. Bullying as Olweus defines it involves patterned aggression toward peers, coupled with impulsivity and strong needs to dominate others (1994, 100).

6. Cohen 1955; Short and Strodtbeck 1965; Vigil 1988; Spergel 1995.

7. Campbell describes the violent logic that follows from these disputes. Discovering that a boyfriend has been unfaithful, they see it as the other girl's doing: boys are incapable of turning down an offer of sex, and even if they wanted to, their image and reputation as a man would suffer if word got out. Coming on to one's boyfriend entails both an emotional injury and an assault on her tough reputation (as someone whose possessions and self are not to be messed with) (138–139). The issues seem to be framed in masculine terms, involving intimate partners as possessions, but it is also defined through the lens of their experiences as women and their understanding of gender roles from their families: transgressions of an intimate relation may launch a process of victimization and emotional betrayal. These transgressions are to be stopped and require retribution, often through violence.

8. In Skogan's hypothetical analysis of "life without lethal weapons" he suggests that without them robbers would face more resistance from victims (including fighting back or running away), would have to use an increased amount of physical force to gain compliance, and would need to select more vulnerable targets. But Cook (1980) found that during robberies victims were more likely to be injured by offenders without guns than by offenders with them. He concluded that victims were sufficiently intimidated by nonlethal weapons to more readily comply with the offender's demands.

9. A robbery is considered to be "recreational violence" when the primary pur-

pose is for the entertainment and thrill of the perpetrators above any momentary rewards of the crime. Katz (1988) also discusses this topic.

10. Jessor et al. compared the variance explained in problem behaviors when predicted by the personality system versus the perceived-environment system versus a developmental system that compares these perspectives. The perceived-environment system developmentally situates adolescents in a network of peer influences including friends' approval for problem behaviors and friends' modeling of problem behaviors, plus parent-friends compatibility. The personality system has motivational-instigation components, personal belief structures, and personal controls. Each dimension entails a range of personality and developmental markers, including such factors as value of academic achievement, self-esteem, and religiosity.

11. Goffman (1967) claims that people give staged performances to different social audiences. Individual behavior is scripted to the extent that scripts are used to convey the kind of impression (or situational identity) an actor wanted others to perceive. He argues that different audiences may have different preconceptions of the actor and the actor may have varying degrees of experience projecting alternate impressions in new situations. The importance of status and reputation (impression given off) in this social context influences the scripts an individual may choose when confronted with a dispute on the streets. One could argue that based on whatever limited knowledge is available at the start of the event, an individual will choose a script that casts him or her in the best light.

12. These were the three most common social identities found in the study. Most of the interactions were defined in terms of avoiding being classified as a "punk" or "herb." Respondents also described other violence-related social identities, including "the avoider," "the nice guy," "the beef handler," and "too cool" for violence.

13. Black suggested that the use of self-help, or crime as social control, reflects the weakness of formal legal institutions in resolving disputes (1983).

14. Even under these circumstances, the attribution of blameworthiness or culpability in instances of self-help violence raises ambivalent attitudes, especially when the victims of these crimes are "unworthy" (Mosteller 1996).

15. Judge David Bazelon first articulated a "rotten social background" defense in *U.S. v. Alexander*, 471 F.2d 923, 957–965 (D.C. Cir. 1973, Bazelon dissenting). Also, conformance with a normative code that prescribes violence in response to specific provocation is different from behavior that is the product of "coercive thought-reform techniques," or brainwashing.

16. This line of reasoning on culpability has been most evident to date in defenses of women in domestic homicides toward violent spouses or intimates. These defenses locate the actions of the woman in a syndrome of behaviors that (1) establish the reasonableness of the defendant's actions, (2) provide a plausible mechanism for explaining her failure to use alternatives such as leaving or calling the police, (3) prove that her fear led her to believe that an assault was imminent, and (4) establish her credibility as a witness (Mosteller 1996).

17. *Daubert v. Merrill Dow Pharmaceuticals Inc.*, 509 U.S. 579, 594–595 (1993), holding that FRE 702 requires scientific validity and evidentiary reliability of the principles underlying scientific testimony.

CHAPTER FIFTEEN

Can the Courts Fairly Account for the Diminished Competence and Culpability of Juveniles? A Judge's Perspective

HONORABLE GARY L. CRIPPEN

For most of the century, the juvenile court has been under the indictment of one of its strongest defenders, Harvard Dean Roscoe Pound, who admonished that without "legal checks," judicial authority in juvenile and domestic proceedings is more threatening to children than the powers of the Star Chamber (Pound 1937).[1] Despite Pound's warnings and decades of reform efforts, there is no shortage of literature, some of it reviewed here, demonstrating that adolescent offenders have been badly treated in the courts.

As the first century of the juvenile justice system comes to an end, critics in the tradition of Dean Pound, believing that the juvenile court represents a valuable resource for the protection of public interests, see hopeful signs that the long search for effective legal safeguards is bearing some fruit.[2] The pursuit of a better juvenile system is invigorated by the findings reported in this volume on the competency and culpability of adolescent offenders. In sum, current developments warrant guarded optimism on the future of the juvenile court.

Central Juvenile Court Developments

Two modern reforms in Minnesota illustrate the cause for this cautious but positive portrayal of the juvenile justice system in 1999. Each reflects the realities that juvenile offenders, due to diminished competency, have unique needs when confronted in court with a public prosecution, and that their culpability is diminished by the stage of their development when the offense occurs. And each employs the rule of law to sharply curb the harmful exercise of discretion in the judicial system.

First, three decades after learning that accused juveniles are entitled to representation of counsel, Minnesota, like some other states, has now achieved success in providing meaningful legal services for accused juveniles at all stages of each threatening court proceeding and without the freedom of the court to elicit or accept the waiver of those services.[3]

The nonwaivable right to counsel is at the heart of Minnesota's reform. Simply read, this law provides that the child will have the services of counsel in any proceeding where the court powers include the ability to place the child for confinement in a residential facility. But the reform includes two other elements, the vital guarantee of counsel for juvenile court appeals and the imposition of safeguards on waiver decisions that are still permitted (Minn. Stat. § 260.155 et seq. 1996; Minn. R. Juv. at 3).[4] Reforms such as these recognize the diminished competency of adolescents and are a concerted effort to assist them in the storm of choices they must make when accused.

The second law reform development—making the pursuit of rehabilitation meaningful—squarely responds to evidence of one of the more significant, ongoing misapplications of law in the American courts: the ill-considered and often pretextual choice of "rehabilitative" dispositions in the juvenile courts. For many decades, the courts have unnecessarily confined countless American adolescents in a vast array of residential facilities, predominantly for minor offenses and often before any finding of wrongdoing.[5]

The practice of wrongful placements is heavily driven by considerations of race and gender.[6] The misfortune of many who are confined is simply the circumstance of being a child in a social welfare system that recognizes neither the worth nor the developmental limitations of children who have offended adult expectations. Wrongful placements harm public interests as well as those of children; federal, state, and local governments foot the bill for the bloated system of residential confinement and there is evidence of an elevated rate of repeat offenses by children who have been placed in institutions (Program Evaluation Division 1995).

Modern enactment of laws that permit punitive dispositions for juveniles have largely regarded violent crimes. Literature on these punitive approaches overlooks a vital reality—that the rehabilitative standard remains the lodestar for the bulk of juvenile court dispositions in most states. The history of statutes insisting that juvenile court dispositions be rehabilitative principally traces to a simple but far-reaching provision of the Uniform Law Commissioners in their Model Juvenile Court Act. The dispositional choice, the act provides, must be "best suited to [the child's] treatment, rehabilitation, and welfare" (Model Juvenile Court Act § 31, 9a U.L.A. 51–52 1968). Minnesota's statutory disposition standard is a precursor to the Model Act, and similar mandates for rehabilitative dispositions govern most or all juvenile court dispositions in a majority of the states.[7] Taking into account developmental and child-centered language in juvenile code purpose clauses, only eleven states have codes that contain no language to proscribe dispositions solely aimed at public safety considerations: Arizona, California, Connecticut, Florida, Idaho, Indiana, Maryland, New Jersey, Ohio, Washington, and Wyoming.

The legal system has the means, and policymakers in some states have shown the will, to stem the flood of inappropriate confinements by American juvenile courts. A three-part effort to establish the integrity of the rehabilitation standard includes (a) standard-setting that practically defines the elements of rehabilitation, (b) mandates for trial-court findings of fact to insure that these factors are assessed, and (c) a genuine right of appeal that gives life to the standards and the requirement for findings.

Making the principle of rehabilitation a meaningful rule of law takes account for the facts presented in this volume in two ways. First, a rehabilitative disposition, by definition, is one that excludes consideration of retribution or deterrence of others. To be culpable is to deserve censure, and the prospect for censure is materially reduced when courts do not choose dispositions on the basis of retribution or example setting.[8] Second, a disposition shaped by the rehabilitative needs of the child takes account for both the present and future developmental capacity of the individual.

In this chapter, I will detail these two areas of reform and other efforts to provide essential elements of justice for adolescent offenders in the juvenile court. Also, examining the rationale offered by those who now would abolish the juvenile courts, I will discuss the conflict between these proposals and the knowledge we have about the characteristics of juvenile offenders. Policymakers, I suggest, will find severe flaws in the cases made for abolishing this judicial system. I will conclude by noting the continuing validity of policy considerations lying behind the struggle to develop the juvenile justice system.

Competency and Culpability: A Response

What can be done, in and out of the courtroom, with the findings reported in this volume on the developmental circumstances of youth? My task is to consider this question from the vantage point of a judge, in this instance a generalist with special interest in juvenile law and family law.[9] I confine my focus to rehabilitative efforts in the mainstream activity of the juvenile court, and delinquency adjudications and dispositions, exclusive of the smaller segment of juvenile court activity in transferring severe delinquency cases to adult court.[10]

The Punishment Issue

Some juvenile justice critics, mostly in the political arena, contend that reform efforts should no longer dwell on protection of children, even for the nonviolent offenders who make up the great bulk of the juvenile court caseload.

Calls for punishment sometimes decry emphasis on procedural protections in juvenile court, including those discussed in this chapter, suggesting that the public does not stand to gain by vigorous steps of this kind. To the contrary, the public shares with the accused offender an interest in due process as a means to avoid inaccuracy and to uphold the dignity of legal proceedings. Moreover, the rehabilitative effects of judicial fairness on adolescent offenders bears fruit for children, for their families, and for the public.[11] A procedurally fair and developmentally appropriate system of justice is exactly what should be guaranteed for protection of the public.

Other observers, friendly to the notion of protecting the rights of children, argue that treatment approaches have been ineffective and that they fail to serve the needs of offenders or others who are adversely affected by their misconduct. It follows, these critics suggest, that there is no remaining need for a special juvenile court to deal with adolescents.[12] This criticism of the widespread struggle to constructively help adolescent offenders begs for a thorough social-policy study that can not be attempted in this chapter without unduly enlarging its parameters.

Incompetence to Proceed

The limited competence of adolescents is never implicated more directly than in proceedings to determine whether the child's condition precludes further juvenile court proceedings. Accused children in the juvenile court must be protected, as a matter of law and as a matter of good policy, with the same vigor employed in determining who is incompetent to proceed in criminal-justice proceedings.[13] Because others in this volume are directly addressing this topic, it will not be further explored here.

Reform Priorities

There are two reasons why the reforms I will discuss, highlighted by those on nonwaivable counsel and genuinely rehabilitative dispositions, have unique importance. First, it is my aim to concentrate attention on "hard" reforms—alterations of law and practice that have predictable impact—in contrast to uses of developing knowledge that depend on education, good judgment, and special resources. Second, the "ordinary" huge juvenile court caseload is mostly composed of children who are accused of minor offenses.

"Soft" Justice System Responses

Findings on the reduced competency and culpability of juveniles confirm the insights of those who "invented" the juvenile court a hundred years ago.[14] Unwisely, this historic reform was based on speculation and hope that a cadre of right-thinking special-jurisdiction judges might display unusual restraint and concern to spare juvenile offenders from jailing and other destructive practices they encountered in the criminal justice system, and successfully attract the resources needed to effectively help these offenders. However valid the original conception of the juvenile court, it was evident from the beginning that the hopes of those who created these courts rested too heavily on the goodwill of judges and support staff, backed by an ample level of legislative and private support, with no guarantee that the juvenile courts would not be a venue for abuse.[15]

Thirty years ago, when earnest attention was given to the constitutional rights of adolescent offenders, dramatic results were expected. But this law development often has proved to have limited effect.[16] This is especially true regarding the right to counsel, which remained elusive for adolescents because of the practices of courts and other agencies to elicit waivers of rights by juveniles who were ill-equipped to make those decisions intelligently (Feld 1989).

Although judges and other justice system participants can be trained to better understand adolescent development and conduct, such efforts have been ongoing for a century, and juvenile court abuses continue. Another prospect for reform lies in doing more to develop the tools and practices for assessment of individual adolescents, serving to bring rationality into both dispositional practices and discretionary decisions to refer children for adult-court prosecution. Better assessment practices depend on expensive staffing and are ultimately subject to discretionary judgments of those who prepare and those who use the results of assessments. Although training and assessment are legitimate reform efforts and proper subjects for research and for development of resources, they remain "soft" reforms.

A Realistic Look at the Juvenile Court Caseload and Its Unwarranted Dispositions

My first concern in this chapter deals with the reality that the great majority of accused adolescents, in spite of the serious risk of their residential confinement, do not have assistance of competent counsel. Second, however fitting the treatment approach for adolescents, steps must be taken to correct the abuse and neglect of the rehabilitative standard that has produced a chronic pattern of unjustified orders for institutional confinement. The juvenile court confinement practice often occurs in tandem with the failure to furnish counsel for the child.[17]

One stark reality about the adolescent-offender caseload establishes the significance of these two concerns: nearly all of the misconduct that reaches the courts is in categories of misdemeanors and status offenders, mostly by younger adolescents. Professor Barry Feld's careful study of one state's juvenile court activity, based on 1986 public records, shows that 82 percent of the cases handled by the juvenile courts (even before the upsurge in reference of violent offenders to adult courts) were in the categories of misdemeanor or status offenses, most of them prosecuted against children not over fifteen years of age (Feld 1991a, 172–183).[18] Only 10 percent of the misdemeanor charges were on offenses against a person; the rest were on property offenses (Feld 1991a, 173). Reflecting on these and other like findings, Feld gives critically important advice: "The appropriate response to minor, nuisance, and noncriminal youngsters goes to the heart of the juvenile court's mission and the normative concept of childhood upon which it is based" (Feld 1991b, 700).

Examination of court placements shows occurrence of dispositions and amended dispositions without a hearing and with little or no showing of cause, a problem in some cases that constitutes a deprivation of constitutional rights against wrongful incarceration. It is evident, comparing juvenile court placements with adult sentences for comparable offenses, that the courts have imposed consequences for children that attribute to them a higher level of culpability than that recognized for adults.[19]

The unwarranted preference of juvenile court agents to confine children predates both *In re Gault* (387 U.S.1 [1967]) and the crisis of urban decline that has beset the juvenile courts for fifty years. It has been exacerbated by the growth of family and community problems and by the exploding development of institutional programs that first resulted from "great society" initiatives in the 1960s and then from a widespread fervor for treatment in hospital facilities.[20] Judicial employment of the concept of parens patriae, meant to displace the occurrence of criminal convictions and proven effective in sparing children from some mistreatment, has also given occasion for new risks of harm and neglect.

In 1966, Justice Fortas, writing for the United States Supreme Court, spoke of the worst of two worlds in the juvenile court: the absence of both procedural protections and "solicitous" care and treatment (*Kent v. United States,* 383 U.S. 541, 555–56 [1966]). Dispositional failures, as Fortas knew them, involved the absence of treatment resources. In fact, the second world of Justice Fortas was and remains much more problematic than he observed. Even when they use costly resources in the pursuit of treatment, institutional placements commonly involve severe and unwarranted loss of personal liberties. They are unjust in terms of rights accorded to adults and even more offensive in the context of adolescents with reduced competency or culpability. Too often, especially in removal and placement of adolescents, the offering of goodwill has been pretextual, hiding a punitive course of action no different than any other imprisonment.

Elements of Juvenile Justice

Minnesota law reforms between 1994 and 1996, including legislative enactments and the Minnesota Supreme Court's revision of juvenile court rules of procedure, conform to the facts reported in this volume on the competency and culpability of adolescent offenders. These reforms demonstrate and valuably respond to significant elements of juvenile justice. The content of the reforms is reflected in the following discussion.

Counsel

Because of the risk of a serious loss of liberties and the need for assistance in making vital decisions, an accused adolescent must have a competent lawyer.

Ending Unwise Waivers

As discussed earlier, an effective guarantee of access to counsel has three parts. For any case in which the child may be removed from home, the right to counsel should not be waivable. Waiver in other cases, or the child's choice to have only standby counsel, should only occur after prescribed advisories and should be on the record and confirmed in writing. Finally, the right to counsel must extend to the right of appeal.

Right to Appeal

Special attention should be given to the matter of counsel for appeals. The importance of this law improvement is revealed by noting the rare occurrence of juvenile court appeals in jurisdictions where the justice system does not provide a positive guarantee of effective counsel to assist juveniles for this purpose. Because of the focus in this chapter on unjustified placements of adolescent offenders, I have examined the historic incidence of appeals that challenge juvenile court dispositions in all fifty states. The findings are alarming.

In the history of the nation's juvenile courts, only seven delinquency dispositions, three of them in Minnesota since 1985, have been reversed outright on grounds that they offended governing dispositional standards.[21] Aside from these reversals, there have only been approximately twenty additional instances, seven of them in Minnesota, where appeals courts reviewed application of dispositional standards. In many of these cases, dispositions were reversed due to deficient or misdirected trial-court findings of fact, but with remands that permitted unfettered reconsideration of the case by the trial court. Since 1995, the juvenile court segment of Minnesota appellate law has greatly expanded because of legislation that charges the office of the state public defender with the responsibility to represent juveniles on appeal (Minn. Stat. § 611.25, subd. 1(3) [1996]).

Dispositions

Enforcement of legislative directives for rehabilitative dispositions also requires three elements of reform—the establishment of detailed standards, a requirement of law that trial-court findings of fact address these standards, and an effective right of appeal.

Standards

The law must include carefully crafted dispositional standards that take account for the culpability of adolescents. These singularly will focus on the rehabilitative needs of the child. Put differently, as is emphasized in some state statutes, the ultimate dispositional standard should involve the question of what must be done—what is necessary—in reference to circumstances of the child who has offended the law.[22] The rule of necessity for the disposition should be enunciated in terms of proportionality and need-based cause for any removal of the child from the home or community. Statutes or rules should state the traditional standard of the child's best interest (with exclusion of dispositions that are said to be "best" but are not necessary), specifically including the concept of suitability for any placement program chosen by the court. This standard setting is critical because of the limited culpability and competence of juvenile offenders.[23]

Dispositional Findings

To demonstrate conformance to established dispositional standards and to facilitate appellate review, the law should entitle the child to juvenile court findings of fact that support the court's disposition.[24] This element of justice is an important safeguard against senseless and excessive confinement of children and is especially vital in discouraging consent-dispositions that are thoughtlessly accepted by the child even when he or she is accompanied by parents or counsel. Requiring findings of fact on the juvenile's needs will compel efforts to assess the current developmental circumstances of the child. In addition, legally adequate findings profitably inform the child and the family of the reasons for the disposition.

In the quest for rational judicial action, the law should entitle the child to a separate disposition hearing where all parties can be heard regarding the court's lawful choices (Minn. R. Juv. at 15.04). Statutes or rules should provide similar protections for modifications of a disposition (Minn. R. Juv. at 15.07, 15.08).

Appeal

To make any dispositional law effective, the services of counsel, as discussed earlier, must be sufficient to create a meaningful right of appeal. Without a healthy juvenile court appellate practice, legal rights are often illusory—and given their limited competence, adolescent offenders should be protected by the rule of law with at least the same consistency as that provided for adults.

Research

There is too little precise knowledge about the patterns of placements in the American juvenile courts. Studies show the remarkable volume of placements, and a great deal of anecdotal evidence on casual and punitive placements, commonly in minor cases, has confronted almost every active participant in the juvenile justice system. There is evidence, both empirical and anecdotal, on great variations in placement practice from one jurisdiction to another.[25] As observed earlier, there is evidence showing that minority children and girls are singled out for confinement dispositions. What remains is a need for systematic research to permit a more exact depiction of the cause shown, case by case, for the placements that flow so abundantly out of many courts. Information also is needed on the nature and size of the residential custody industry, including information on intake standards. Finally, comparative studies on placements in other countries would be valuable.

Other Elements of Law Reform

The limited competence of accused juveniles requires additional attention to these other important reform subjects.

Waivers/Advisories

Lawyers and judges must strictly control the waiver of rights, especially the right to trial proceedings.[26] Left on their own to examine and act on their rights, children are largely incapable of making vital courtroom choices. Effective advisories, along with active assistance of counsel, are the major legal tool for avoiding unknowing or involuntary waivers. A sound advisory practice is a major part of the sometimes unexpected reward of due process, that it serves both personal and public interests. Like other procedural offerings, the fair play made evident in a good advisory often serves to gain a constructive response from the child and the child's family, a substantial beginning in the process of rehabilitation.[27] That said, it remains to be determined whether the offering of both counsel and good advisories can be effective in avoiding the inappropriate choices of children to admit accusations, waive the right to trial, and volunteer for suggested dispositions.

Jury

Facing possible institutionalization and desiring that trial proceedings occur before a jury, the juvenile should have the benefit of that process.[28] The need for this right is likely more evident in a poor court system that poses other severe risks to the interests of the child. Even in a good court system, the right to demand a jury trial plays an indispensable part in a system that should fairly assess the culpability of an accused adolescent.

Some observers, concerned about the rights of children, praise what they perceive as the "full panoply" of procedural safeguards in the criminal courts (Feld 1984, 274), and covet especially the jury-trial right and the right to counsel (Ainsworth 1991). But a trade of the juvenile court for the right to a jury trial may not be a fair deal for children. As will be noted more completely in this chapter, it is far from evident that the criminal courts can deliver justice to juveniles. Moreover, juries are infrequently requested in minor offenses, the most predominant subject of juvenile court proceedings, and the meaningful guarantee of counsel may make the jury-trial right much less important for the juvenile. Finally, there have been gains in the quest for recognition of this right in the juvenile court; the battle for this reform is not over.

Prehearing Detention

Evidence shows that unnecessary pretrial detention, often employed for retributive purposes, has been a problem equal in magnitude to the occurrence of punitive, unreasonable dispositions.[29] The same sources report that the threat of detention for minority youth is remarkably disproportionate. Although constitutional attacks on prehearing detention have had limited success, other efforts of detention reform have shown promise. Each is closely related to the developmental circumstances of arrested adolescents. First, rules have been adopted to introduce useable standards into detention decisions. More fruitfully, there have been a number of comprehensive reform efforts in urban areas, largely built around the design of good intake-assessment practices that strictly reject inappropriate detention requests and utilize alternative approaches.[30]

Softer Reforms

In addition to these hard reforms of the rule of law, some other elements of reform need special attention.

The Right to Competent Counsel

The benefits of counsel cannot be guaranteed through disinterested, poorly trained, or overworked lawyers. The poor quality of legal services for juveniles has been recognized as a crisis in the juvenile justice system (American Bar Association 1995, 7–8, 22–27, 46–48).[31]

Because of the need for expertise and independence, legal services for juveniles will be most valuable when lawmakers provide that a permanent staff of public defenders is to provide this representation.[32] The effectiveness of counsel, at least for the appellate process, may require the services of a state public-defender system. It can be expected, as observed in Minnesota, that the guarantee of access to counsel will lead to allocation of more funds for this work.

Fighting the Euphemism Virus

The most vigorous criticism of the juvenile courts is leveled at its dispositional abuses. One observer says of these courts that they are "unconstrained by the rule of law," they intervene with excessive severity, and their dispositions demonstrate "lawlessness" and "idiosyncratic judicial subjectivity"—more specifically, they reflect "indeterminacy, a rejection of proportionality, and a disregard of normative valuations of the seriousness of behavior" (Feld 1997, 91–91).

Minnesota's early experience with newly drafted standards and findings requirements, backed by a sure right of appeal, has provided cause for optimism in the ongoing struggle against dispositions that are nominally shaped by the child's needs but really constitute retribution, deterrence of others, or effortless following of routine.[33] Still, euphemistic use of language on treatment, rehabilitation, or protection remains a deep-seated risk in a system of individualized justice, one that requires continued scrutiny. Lewis (1949) makes a classic commentary on the euphemisms in humanitarian placements for treatment or reform.

Prompt Appellate Review

Because of the exaggerated importance of time for children and the rapid changes in their developmental circumstances, the appellate-court process must move swiftly to be meaningful.

An awareness of the developmental incapacity of adolescents should lead to an anticipation that they will not commonly understand why they might exercise their right to appeal. To be meaningful, the right must be supported by the services of competent counsel, who would give the child information on an appeal and respond to the child's interest in this process. Also, the need remains for research on the ability of adolescents to make decisions on the right of appeal.

Administration of Justice; Caseload Control

Justice in the juvenile court is apt to be defeated if it is administered by judges, lawyers, or court staff with caseloads that compel summary action or other shortcuts. Systems that overlook this reality rarely serve any public interest, either for public safety or for justice to children and families. Similarly, a just system rests considerably on staff training and experience, case management, and management of resources, the latter including a set of practices and skills that make the system accountable in each case. Much more research is needed on the effects of staff behavior and administrative practices, from the conduct of judges to the demeanor of bailiffs.

Excessive caseloads may constitute the single greatest problem in the administration of juvenile justice, both fatal to the proper function of the system and extremely difficult to control without significant enlargement of staff resources for the courts. The need for caseload control is substantially enlarged by the pursuit of essential elements of justice: proper hearings, good advisories, sufficient factual records, and adequate court findings will increase the amount of time required for each case. The need grows still greater when systems conduct proceedings speedily, accounting for the child's sense of time and the quickly changing circumstances of the child. The problem can be resolved with determination and persistence, and some jurisdictions have met the challenge.

Abolition: A Realistic Reform Proposal?

Literature on juvenile justice reform occasionally includes the discordant message that imperfections in the system constitute cause to abolish it, so that prosecution of all accusations against adolescents would occur within the adult criminal justice system.

The call for abolition comes in dissimilar forms, one calling for harsh steps thought to advance public-safety interests, and the other, out of concern for the interests of children, trying to imagine a venue where their liberties are less threatened. The public-safety approach is largely political, evident in campaigns for public office and in legislative proposals. The child-welfare view is evident in a small but significant body of scholarly literature.[34] Both dwell on violent offenders and give little thought to what must be done to justly deal with the vast majority of adolescent offenders who are not accused of violent acts.

Using the findings of this volume on the developmental circumstances of adolescents, flaws can readily be discerned in the rationale for abolishing the juvenile courts, even without examining the value of rehabilitation efforts, the discrediting of which is quite evidently a precondition to the favor of abolition proposals.

Published proposals for an end of efforts to improve the juvenile justice system take little or no account of the competence and culpability of adolescent offenders. One proponent of criminal-court jurisdiction concedes the weight of adolescent-development evidence but nonetheless suggests that the law should focus on the personal responsibility of youthful offenders, offering them only some "discount" of adult-court sentences (Feld 1997, 98–131).[35] Others who propose criminal-court jurisdiction fail to engage in any discussion of the limited capacity of adolescent offenders. For example, Ainsworth (1991) observes a new, constricted view of adolescence as part of the cause for criminal-court jurisdiction over adolescent offenders, and Wolfgang (1982) poses a conclusion based on findings as to the culpability of chronic offenders. The proponents brush aside or totally fail to address the question of whether adolescent offenders, due to their limited competence, need an enhanced right to counsel or other special procedural protections.[36] There are more particular, substantial flaws in their case.

Minor Offenders

Focusing on the occurrence of adolescent violence, abolition advocates uniformly pass lightly over three-fourths or more of the juvenile court caseload—juveniles who are accused of misdemeanors, petty offenses, and status offenses. All but two of the scholars suggesting use of the criminal courts have ignored this topic. Professor Guggenheim gave the topic a single sentence twenty years ago (Guggenheim 1978, 9). Professor Feld, who previously revealed much of what is known about minor offenders in the juvenile court, gives the topic one paragraph in his most recent abolition exposition (Feld 1997, 128–29). Without a thoughtful, workable plan for handling these cases, the abolition proposals are badly flawed.[37] An examination of the few casual observations made by abolition proponents on the handling of minor cases demonstrates that they rest their case on unworkable suggestions.

Professor Guggenheim, posing an adult-court-jurisdiction proposal that he has since abandoned, suggested that "many [status offenders] would not be subject to the jurisdiction of the court in the first place," and "the rest, the minor criminal offenders, would be subject to minimal loss of liberty" (Guggenheim 1978, 9).[38] Professor Feld has gone little further than this analysis, adding only a speculative view that is laced with irony— that legislators and prosecutors, appreciating that the criminal courts are too "over-burdened" to deal with minor offenders, will have to divert or decriminalize these cases (Feld 1997, 128–29).

Proponents of criminal-court jurisdiction speculate that modern legislators and prosecutors will decriminalize a significant number of cases (Feld 1991, 700)[39] As a necessary ingredient in their case, this suggestion should be put at the forefront in presentations of the topic to law-enforcement officials, legislators, and the general public. Proponents no doubt understand that "abolition" sells as part of a "law and order" agenda, and they must know equally well that decriminalization does not.

Those who suggest either decriminalizing juvenile conduct or simply diverting children to some other forum evidently envision that a large number of cases could be directed to the "other half" of the juvenile court, its child-protection function. Where would this shift of jurisdiction leave us? It is evident that abuses observed in juvenile justice cases occur in nearly identical fashion and with equal frequency in child-protection cases.[40] If we enlarge the child-protection topic to engulf half or more of the court's juvenile justice work, the need for juvenile court reform will remain as great as it is today, a challenge that will not be diminished by pushing a number of severe offenders into the adult courts.

Process Reform

The case for abolition also is undermined by the absence of any projection for the kind of procedural reform that would be needed for handling these cases in the criminal courts. The significance of this problem is greatly enlarged if speculation on diversion and decriminalization of cases is unwarranted.

So, for example, attention must be given to the practice of adult-court waivers of counsel and the right to a trial. Progress in reforming juvenile court practice on waivers has been discussed in this chapter. Scant advisories, sometimes to a roomful of accused offenders, continue to be an ordinary part of adult-court processing of misdemeanor cases. There is no evidence on the competence of children to deal with adult-court advisories. There is good reason to expect that adult-court judges will be less oriented than juvenile judges in the nuances of effectively communicating procedural advice to adolescent offenders.

Considerable research is needed before anyone can conclude that the criminal courts will provide counsel more often than the juvenile courts for misdemeanants. Only in felony matters is the criminal justice system entitled to some credit for its guarantee of counsel. Also, observers must learn and reveal much more before there is room to judge that counsel for juveniles can helpfully perform in the criminal justice system.

Thinking of these and many other process patterns in the criminal courts, there is little justification for attributing "enhanced procedural protections" to the system (Feld 1997, 132).[41]

Appellate Practice

Any promise of justice in the criminal courts, for adults or children, has limited significance if not backed by a meaningful right of appeal. What is known about the occurrence of appeals in misdemeanor cases? To what extent is the financial ability to retain counsel the condition precedent to the value of the right to appeal? Without further exploration of this topic, there cannot be a reasoned proposal to abolish the juvenile justice system.

Criminal Justice Sentencing

Abolition of the juvenile court would permit the justice system to contradict what is being learned about the competence and culpability of adolescent offenders. Criminal courts are free to sentence solely for purposes of retribution or deterrence of others. Even when punitive sanctions are discounted for youth, a facially arbitrary accounting for the culpability of a child, they disregard the uniqueness of each child's developmental circumstances.

Felony Sentences

In many states, lawmakers give trial judges unfettered discretion to sentence felons up to the maximum term of imprisonment set by statute. In states that employ sentencing guidelines, courts have less discretion, but observers complain that trial judges have mostly unchecked discretion to deviate upward. There is no reason to assume that the criminal justice system offers rational or controlled sentencing practices, and it is evident that proponents of abolition know that the suggestion is flawed in the absence of criminal court sentencing reforms.[42] For youthful offenders, merely discounting the statutory maximum offense will seldom take account of developmental circumstances.

Misdemeanor Sentences

To understand criminal court misdemeanor sentencing, we need much more research and analysis on the "minimal loss of liberty" once foreseen for juveniles in these courts by Professor Guggenheim, who rightfully lamented abusive dispositions in the juvenile courts. Professor Feld's (1997, 115–21) sentencing-discount proposal requires the same studied comparison between juvenile dispositions and his vision of criminal justice sentences that are somewhat altered for the youthfulness of the offender. Misdemeanor cases are approximately three times more numerous in juvenile court than felony offense cases (54 percent to 18 percent in one study) (Feld 1991, 173). Also, owing to the criminalizing of status and petty offenses, it is reasonable to anticipate enlargement of this class of cases in jurisdictions that become sold on the idea of abolishing the juvenile court.[43]

On misdemeanor sentencing, policymakers need to know more about the typical, maximum criminal justice sentence of ninety-day's incarceration, discounted some in Professor Feld's sentencing scheme. Juveniles in the criminal justice system, Feld suggests, should not be jailed in adult facilities or in "punk prisons," but in age-segregated "correctional facilities," including "existing juvenile detention facilities, training schools, and institutions" (Feld 1997, 130). To what extent will these plans preclude use of secure facilities, and how do those facilities legitimately avoid the label of "kid's jails"? Do we have any information on the question of whether there exists an age-appropriate jail for adolescents? Also, in a legislature motivated to abolish the juvenile court, what are the prospects for limiting the practice of jailing adolescents or developing facilities that would be age appropriate?

Finally, what plea bargaining can be expected in adolescent misdemeanor cases prosecuted in adult courts? Given the limited competence of children, what bargains will they accept when authorities threaten the prospect of jailing? Will children prefer "voluntary" indeterminate placements in the face of the threat of jailing? What recommendations of counsel can be expected in this circumstance? Modern multicount prosecutions that pose the threat, sometimes real and sometimes not, of consecutive jail sentences greatly enlarge the impact of these questions. How much loss of liberty is at stake? Juvenile court critics must carefully explore questions of this kind before any legitimacy will be attributed to their suggestion to put juvenile justice into the halls of the criminal justice system.

Caseload Control and Court Administration

No doubt there are problems of heavy caseloads and assembly-line justice in both juvenile courts and adult courts. But justice system plans should not be advanced with only that knowledge. There is a need to examine comparative caseload problems of courts in urban, suburban, and rural jurisdictions.

There is also a need for studies on other court-administration topics that affect justice for adolescent offenders. How, for example, do adult courts and juvenile courts manage agency resources, public and private, that are provided for offenders?

In sum, there is no reason to believe that the criminal justice system can alleviate concerns about the juvenile courts, especially on the subject of misdemeanors. If we accept speculation as a tool of analysis on this issue, we will do nothing to advance the notion of restrained dealings with offenders whose competence and culpability is diminished by age.

The Juvenile Court at a Hundred Years

One legitimate but incomplete rationale in defense of juvenile court jurisdiction lies in recognizing the perils for juveniles in the criminal justice system (Rosenberg 1993, 173–74).[44] There is ample, alternative cause to recognize the unique capacity of the juvenile courts to do justice in their dealings with adolescent offenders (Scott and Grisso 1997, 188).[45] Moreover, the juvenile courts must be evaluated without losing sight of what can be done to improve them. Those who would overlook the prospect for reform have a heavy burden they have not met, either to show that reforms cannot correct abuses or that policymakers will have nothing to do with these reforms.

Child-welfare advocates who have lost confidence in the juvenile courts persistently fail to accurately recite its roots. In allusions to the "child savers," it is said or implied that those who first conceived the juvenile court model had the haughty expectation that children in these courts, approached with care and treatment, would have no need for due process protections (Feld 1997, 71–72). In the same vein, observers suggest that common law parens patriae is a grab of authority over children premised on an untrustworthy promise of goodwill (Feld 1997, 71–72).

It is true that the promise of goodwill provides little cause for permitting unrestrained authority, especially when fundamental liberties are at risk (Gaylin et al. 1978). Still, the suggestion that an empty promise of social welfare was the sum of past thinking is a misconstruction of parens patriae and early juvenile court defenders. The foremost goal of the parens patriae role is to protect the child, rightfully understood to be in need of more protection than the law gives to adults. Such was the first goal of juvenile court founders.[46] The picture of abuse seen by the original proponents of the juvenile courts was the jailing of kids, a practice they intended to end (Lindsey and O'Higgins 1910, 134–35). They observed that the rescue of children from this practice would itself be the primary step in preventing their further wrongdoing.[47]

Although the juvenile court founders may not have anticipated that the rendering of protection included ingredients of due process and a discipline of restraint shaped by standards and appellate review, these ideas are not foreign to their aims.[48] This is no less true because many of their successors in the judiciary compound the crisis of the juvenile courts, belying both the goodwill of the founders and the rule of law by stubbornly defending the exercise of authority without restraint.[49]

In sum, due process and disciplined restraint fit with parens patriae, and they fulfill the hopes of those who created our juvenile courts. The umbrella of parens patriae is large enough to include both supportive services and the rule of law. Many child-welfare advocates have been too quick to conclude that these elements of protection conflict with one another such that the courts can achieve neither of them (Feld 1997, 93). If rehabilitative dispositions are valuable to adolescents and to public interests as well, there remains room for the vision of a juvenile court that offers children the best of both worlds: "solicitous care and treatment" and (at least) the "protections accorded to adults."[50]

Conclusion

This volume confirms common perceptions that adolescent offenders have diminished competence to participate in proceedings against them and that their limited capacity also makes them less culpable than older offenders. With this evidence, we can identify the elements of justice for juvenile offenders that should be found in the system that deals with their wrongdoing.

Presently, there is no cause to abandon pursuit of the good process and meaningful standards that make our juvenile courts a suitable agent of justice for adolescent offenders. Reformers have defined new approaches that some lawmakers have implemented. This is especially evident with respect to the role of counsel in the juvenile court and the control of the court's dispositions. There is cause to believe that the juvenile court founders would look kindly on these reform efforts and that we do them honor with our successes.

Finally, those who would abolish the juvenile court must replace it. There can be no constructive, reasoned case for the prosecution of juvenile offenses in the criminal courts until we have at hand the research and analysis that shows the better capacity of these courts to employ the rule of law to further justice for juveniles.

Works Cited

Ainsworth, J. 1991. Re-imagining childhood and reconstructing the legal order: The case for abolishing the juvenile court. *N.C.L. Rev.* 69:1083.

American Bar Association. 1977. *Institute of judicial administration: ABA juvenile justice standards; standards for juvenile justice: a summary and analysis.* Cambridge, Mass.: Ballinger Publishing Company.

———. 1980. *Institute of judicial administration: ABA juvenile justice standards; standards relating to dispositions, introduction.* Cambridge, Mass.: Ballinger Publishing Company.

———. 1995. *A call for justice: An assessment of access to counsel and quality representation in delinquency proceedings.* Washington, D.C.: American Bar Association Juvenile Justice Center.

Arthur, L. 1998. Abolish the juvenile court? *Juv. & Fam. Ct. J.* 49:51, 53.

Bureau of Justice Statistics. 1995. *Prison and jail inmates* (NCJ-161132) 10; Washington, D.C.: Bureau of Justice Statistics.

Center for the Study of Social Policy. 1990. *Kids count.* Washington, D.C.: The Center for the Study of Social Policy.

Children's Bureau, U. S. Department of Health, Education, and Welfare. 1954. *Standards for specialized courts dealing with children.* Publication Number 346-1954. Washington, D.C.: Government Printing Office, 63.

Dawson, R. 1990. The future of juvenile justice: is it time to abolish the system? *J. Crim. L. and Criminology* 81:136.

Edwards, L. 1992. The juvenile court and the role of the juvenile court judge. *Juv. & Fam. Ct. J.* 43:1.

Federle, K. 1990. The abolition of the juvenile court: A proposal for the preservation of children's legal rights. *J. Contemp. L.* 16:23.

Federle, K., and M. Chesney-Lind. 1992. Special issues in juvenile justice: Gender, race, and ethnicity. In *Juvenile justice and public policy,* edited by I. Schwartz. New York: Lexington Books.

Feld, B. 1978. Reference of juvenile offenders for adult prosecution: The legislative alternative to asking unanswerable questions. *Minn. L. Rev.* 62:515.

———. 1981. Juvenile court legislative reform and the serious young offender: Dismantling the "rehabilitative ideal." *Minn. L. Rev.* 65:167.

———. 1984. Criminalizing juvenile justice: Rules of procedure for the juvenile court. *Minn. L. Rev.*

———. 1988. The juvenile court meets the principle of offense: Punishment, treatment, and the difference it makes. *B.U. L. Rev.* 68:821.

———. 1989. The right to counsel in juvenile court: An empirical study of when lawyers appear and the difference they make. *J. Crim. L. and Criminology* 79:1185.

———. 1991a. Justice by geography: Urban, suburban, and rural variations in juvenile justice administration. *J. Crim. L. and Criminology* 82:156.

———. 1991b. The transformation of the juvenile court; reporting on minor offenses in juvenile court and the failed struggles for diversion, deinstitutionalization, and decriminalization. *Minn. L. Rev.* 75:691.

———. 1993. Criminalizing the American juvenile court. *Crime & Jus.* 17:197.

———. 1997. Abolish the juvenile court: Youthfulness, criminal responsibility, and sentencing policy. *J. Crim. L. and Criminology* 88:68.

Fine, K. 1983. *Out of home placement of children in Minnesota: A research report;* St. Paul, Minn.: Minnesota House of Representatives.

Gaylin, W., I. Glasser, S. Marcus, and D. Rothman. 1978. *Doing good: The limits of benevolence.* New York: Pantheon Books.

Guggenheim, M. 1978. A call to abolish the juvenile justice system. *Children's Right Report* 2 (June): 1.

Keller, M., and S. Wizner. 1977. The penal model of juvenile justice: Is juvenile court delinquency jurisdiction obsolete? *N.Y.U. L. Rev.* 52:1120.

Lewis, C. 1949. The humanitarian theory of punishment. *20th Century: An Australian Quarterly Review* 3, no. 3:5-12.

Lindsey, B., and H. O'Higgins. 1910. *The beast.* New York: Doubleday, Page & Company.

Lubow, B., and M. Moore. 1997. *Juvenile detention alternatives initiative: Progress report.* Baltimore, Md.: The Annie E. Casey Foundation.

Lubow, B., and J. Tulman. 1995. The unnecessary detention of children in the District of Columbia. *D. of C. L. Rev.* 3, no. 2.

Mack, J. 1909. The juvenile court. *Harv. L. Rev.* 23:104.

Maitland, F. 1936. *Equity: A course of lectures,* 2d ed. Cambridge, Mass.: Cambridge University Press.

McCarthy, F. 1977. Should juvenile delinquency be abolished? *Crime & Delinq.* 23:196.

Melton, G. 1989. Taking *Gault* seriously: Toward a new juvenile court. *Neb. L. Rev.* 68:146.

Office of Juvenile Justice and Delinquency Prevention. 1996. *Juv. justice bull.* Washington, D.C.: Department of Justice.

Olney, J. 1938. The juvenile courts—abolish them. *Cal. St. Bar J.* 13 (April-May): 1.

Pirsig, M. 1960. Juvenile delinquency and crime: Achievements of the 1959 Minnesota legislature. *Minn. L. Rev.* 44:363.

Podkopacz, M., and B. Feld. 1996. The end of the line: An empirical study of judicial waiver. *J. Crim. L. and Criminology* 86:449.

Pound, R. 1905. Do we need a philosophy of law? *Col. L. Rev.* 5:338.

———. 1937. Foreword to *Social treatment in probation and delinquency.* New York: McGraw-Hill Book Company.

Program Evaluation Division. 1995. *Residential facilities for juvenile offenders.* St. Paul, Minn.: Office of the Legislative Auditor, State of Minnesota.

Puritz, P., S. Burrell, R. Schwartz, M. Soler, and L. Warboys. 1995. *A Call for Justice.* Chicago: American Bar Association.

Redding, R. 1997. Juveniles transferred to criminal court: Legal reform proposals based on social science research. *Utah L. Rev,* 709.

Rosenberg, I. 1980. The constitutional rights of children charged with crime: Proposal for a return to the not so distant past. *UCLA L. Rev.* 27:656.

———. 1993. Leaving bad enough alone. *Wisc. L. Rev.* 1993:163.

Rubin, H. 1979. Retain the juvenile court? Legislative developments, reform directions, and the call for abolition. *Crime & Del.* 25:281.

Schwartz, I. 1989. *(In)justice for juveniles.* Lexington, Mass.: Lexington Books.

Schwartz, I., W. Barton, and F. Orlando. Keeping kids out of secure detention. *Public Welfare* (spring): 20.

Schwartz, I., G. Fishman, R. Hatfield, B. Krisberg, and Z. Eisikovits. 1987. Juvenile detention: The hidden closets revisited. *Justice Qtly.* 4, no. 2.

Scott, E., and T. Grisso. 1997. The evolution of adolescence: A developmental perspective on juvenile justice. *J. Crim. L. and Criminology* 88:137.

Weithorn, L. 1988. Mental hospitalization of troublesome youth: Analysis of skyrocketing admission rates. *Stanford L. Rev.* 40:773.

Weldon, M. 1996. Fiscal restraints trump due process: Children's diminishing right to counsel in Minnesota. *Law & Inequality* 14:647.

Wolfgang, M. 1982. Abolish the juvenile court system. *Cal. Lawyer* 2 (Nov.): 12.

Young, D., Jr. 1962. To help children, or to catch them. *Juv. Ct. Judges J.* 12:17.

Notes

1. More completely, Pound concluded: "Child placement involves administrative authority over one of the most intimate and cherished of human relations. The powers of the Star Chamber were a trifle in comparison with those of our juvenile courts and courts of domestic relations. The latter may bring about a revolution as easily as did the former. It is well known that too often the placing of a child in a home or even in an institution is done casually or perfunctorily or even arbitrarily. Even with the most superior personnel, these tribunals call for legal checks."

2. Juvenile court defenders bear a large burden. We find that even a faulty juvenile justice system serves both as a public resource and a venue to promote justice for juveniles. But juvenile court apologists know the failings of this system and hold it to a high standard.

3. In Chapter 4 of this volume, Professor Barry Feld reports the persistent failure of the juvenile justice system to enable juveniles with the right to counsel guaranteed for them as a matter of due process under *In re Gault,* 387 US 1, 18 (1967). See also Puritz (1995) and Feld (1989), reporting on limited representation of children confined to institutions.

4. As documented later in this chapter, appointed or retained counsel have virtually never exercised the right of appeal to compel application of the rule of law. In 1995, the Minnesota Legislature corrected this chronic defect in the child's right to counsel by charging the State Public Defender to assist juvenile offenders in many appeals (Minn. Stat. § 611.25, subd. 1(3) [1996]); that office handled eighty-five juvenile court appeals in the years 1995 to 1997 (staff report to author). See, however, Weldon (1996), lamenting the legislative choice to narrow the definition of offenses covered by public-defender provision. The development of a healthy appellate practice has another reward: trial counsel, openly anticipating appeals, report successes in getting erroneous actions voluntarily withdrawn by the trial courts.

5. See Office of Juvenile Justice and Delinquency Prevention, reporting 152,200 American juvenile court placements in 1994, constituting 29 percent of all delinquency adjudications and 16 percent of all status offense adjudications (October 1996). See also Feld (1991, 183–91), reporting court-ordered placements in 30 percent of cases handled (5,277 of 17,195), and occurrence of 65 percent of these placements (3,426 of 5,277) in misdemeanor and status offense cases—many on the first reported offense of the child; Fine (1983), documenting court placements and still higher numbers of "voluntary" placements—known anecdotally to include placements in lieu of further juvenile court placements; Weithorn (1988), reporting upsurge of placements of adolescents in psychiatric hospitals. In addition, later references in this chapter document the escalating volume of prehearing, secure detention, still including use of adult jails.

6. See Federle and Chesney-Lind (1992). See also Office of Juvenile Justice and Delinquency Prevention (October 1996), reporting that secure detention occurs in 29 percent of arrests of black juveniles, 22 percent of arrests of other minority youth, and 17 percent of arrests of white juveniles; Lubow and Tulman (1995).

7. Dispositional choices in Minnesota are limited to those that are found "necessary to the rehabilitation of the child" (Minn. Stat. § 260.185, subd. 1. 1996). This provision was enacted by the Minnesota legislature in 1959, the source of the language perhaps being in 1954 Children's Bureau standards, which called for a presumption against placement of a child "except where adequate investigation shows this is not to be in the best interest of the child" (Children's Bureau 1954). See Pirsig (1960, 378), explaining documents used by drafting committee.

The Model Act disposition language is found in the juvenile codes of Georgia, North Dakota, Tennessee, and Vermont. Ga. Code Ann. § 15-11-35 (a) (1997 Supp.); N.D. Cent. Code § 27-20-31 (Supp. 1997); Tenn. Code Ann. § 37-1-131 (1997 Supp.); Vt. Stat. Ann. T. 33 § 5529 Cum. (Supp. 1997). Once adopted in Pennsylvania, the standard was abandoned in 1995. 42 Pa. Cons. Stat. Ann. § 6352(a) (Supp. 1998).

Without employing the precise language of the Model Act, Minnesota and sixteen other states have limited juvenile court dispositions to those that serve the individual needs of the child. Ala. Code § 12-15-71(c) (Supp. 1997); Alaska Stat. § 47.12.10(1) (Michie 1996); Ark. Code Ann. § 9-27-330(a) (Michie 1997); Del. Code Ann. T. 10, § 1009(c)(11), (d) (Supp. 1996) (private institution placements); 705 Ill. Code § 405/5-29(1), (2), and § 405/5-23(1)(a)(2) (1998 Supp.) (nonfelony offenses); Kan. Stat. Ann § 38-1664 (Supp. 1997) (defined classes of placements); Me. Rev. Stat. Ann. T. 15 § 3314.1.C (West Supp. 1997) (excepting secure facility placements, adding that dispositions must be appropriate for the welfare of both the child and society, imaginable only in the event that rehabilitation is achieved); Neb. Rev. Stat. § 43-284 (Cum. Supp. 1996) (status offenders); N.M. Stat. Ann. § 32A-2-19 (Michie Replacement Pamphlet 1995); N.C. Gen. Stat. § 7A-647 (1995); S.D. Codified Laws § 26-8C-7 (Michie 1992); Tex. Code Ann. § 54.04(i)(1) (West 1996) (placements); Utah Code Ann. § 78-3a-118(2)(o)(ii) (Supp. 1997) (private institutions); Va. Code Ann. § 16.1-278.8 (Michie Supp. 1997); W. Va. Code § 49-5-13(b)(4) (Supp. 1997) (placements); Wis. Stat. § 938.34(4d)(b), (4m)(b) (Supp. 1997) (custodial placements). See also Idaho Juv. R. 40 (1997) (home-placement plan demand); Miss. Code Ann. § 43-21-605 (1)(g) (Supp. 1997) (training school parole standard).

In addition to the twenty-one states approaching dispositional powers in the same manner as the Model Act, dispositional statutes in six states mandate choices that serve the welfare of both the child and society, which precludes nonrehabilitative dispositions. Mich. Comp. Laws § 712A.18 (Supp. 1998); Mont. Code Ann. § 41-5-1512(2), (3) (1997) (status offenders), § 41-5-1513(1)(c), (correctional placements of misdemeanants); N.Y. Fam. Ct. Act § 352.2 (Supp. 1998) (excepting serious felony cases); Okla. Stat. Juvenile Code § 7303-5.1.A, § 7303-5.3.A.10 (1998); 42 Pa. Cons. Stat. Ann. 6352(a) (Supp. 1998); W. Va. Code § 49-5-13(a) (Supp. 1997). See also N.C. Gen. Stat. § 7A-646 (1995) (in addition to best interests standard, supra).

Four of these twenty-seven states and two others define the legality of a dispositional choice to the one that is least restrictive, which singularly regards the circumstances of the child and the child's conduct, not societal interests in retribution or deterrence of others. Alaska Stat. § 47.12.10(2) (Michie 1996); Iowa Code Ann. § 232.52, subd. 6 (Supp. 1998) (with mandate for return from placement, other than to the state training school, "as quickly as possible"); N.C. Gen. Stat. § 7A-646 (1995); N.H. Rev. Stat. Ann. 169-B:19 (Cum. Supp. 1997) (defined exceptions); N.Y. Fam. Ct. Act § 352.2 (Supp. 1998) (defined exceptions); S.D. Codified Laws § 26-8C-7 (Michie 1992).

8. In a recent decision of the Minnesota Court of Appeals, reversing two short-term placements for minor offenses, the court stated this characterization of the state's juvenile court disposition statute: "Alternatively stated, the legislature established a diminished culpability for adolescent offenders who are the object of a juvenile court disposition. Because the choice of disposition must be driven by rehabilitative needs, neither retribution nor deterrence of others lawfully constitutes adequate cause for the content of a disposition." Matter of Welfare of C.A.W. And L.R.M.B, 579 N.W.2d 494, 497 (Minn. App. 1998). Conceivably, evidence could show reasons why a punitive step would be rehabilitative. Ibid. page 497 n. 5.

9. Although I have always served in general jurisdiction courts, following a general law practice, my attention has been drawn to juvenile and family law developments since watching while in law school the unfolding of juvenile court reform events in the 1959 Minnesota legislature. My experience with children in

courtroom proceedings anecdotally confirms what researchers continue to learn about the developmental circumstances of youthful offenders; thus, for example, I found that advisories to adolescents on the right to trial and to the services of counsel had to be careful, sometimes prolonged, and sometimes accompanied by suggestion or persuasion, in order to avoid the waiver of rights that were, under the circumstances, patently necessary in the pursuit of fair play.

10. The transfer issue involves a central question that parallels my discussion on the nature and worth of efforts to curb judicial discretion in mainstream juvenile court dispositions. See Feld (1978), disapproving judicial role in deciding whether adolescents should be prosecuted as adults—a position paralleling his more recent argument that judicial discretion established in the juvenile court should be entirely eradicated, and compare Redding (1997), criticizing transfers of jurisdiction under offense-based legislative mandates that exclude judicial discretion on waiver.

11. Melton (1989) has criticized the treatment approach but portrays the socialization of youth that agents of the juvenile courts can attain through the guarantee of fair process.

12. Accompanying a review of literature on the treatment topic and noting considerations of law, politics, psychology, and philosophy, Feld (1997), in his most recent statement of cause for abolishing the juvenile court, questions the legitimacy and value of treatment and rehabilitation efforts. He shares the concern addressed in this chapter that punitive dispositions have been a common part of juvenile court history. But he sees this pattern as an inevitable part of a court living under the disciplines of procedural due process, notwithstanding its declaration of social welfare aims (Feld 1997, 68, 86–87, 93–94, 131–34). Feld goes much further in deploring court efforts to bring about treatment and rehabilitation of adolescent offenders, contending: (a) that the absence of punishment (at least when determined by a court) may undermine the value of responsibility (Feld 1997, 91, 121–26); (b) that a social welfare approach is a poor alibi for meaningful reforms that serve all children, including efforts to reduce access and use of firearms (Feld 1997, 91, 93–95, 134–36). Dawson (1990, 141–42, 148–49, 155), viewing juvenile courts as a magnet for social welfare resources that otherwise would not be provided]; cf. also Feld himself, who understands the scarcity of support for social welfare resources, even as needed by the courts (Feld 1993, 256); (c) that court rehabilitation efforts have doubtful value (Feld 1997, 84–86 [n.34], 92, 121–22)— such that it is difficult to justify "the judicial burden and diversion of resources" that they entail. (Feld 1997, 122); and (d) that due process, tied to punishment (in the professor's view) by inviting it, is also tied in the sense of being compromised when punishment is not the pursuit (Feld 1997, 92).

Questions on the worth of treatment, seen from the vantage point of the child, can be found in much earlier legal literature; the Englishman C. S. Lewis, variously a religious apologist, literary scholar, and public-policy critic, authored a matchless portrayal of the liberty interests abused in even the most benevolently designed residential placements (Lewis 1949). Public safety advocates, also critical of treatment approaches, have largely confined their attention to the question of whether rehabilitation efforts tend to diminish repeated misconduct, an issue about which there is very little empirical evidence (American Bar Association 1980).

13. If competency in juvenile court is determined according to the same standards used in the criminal justice system, the competency of adolescents is apt to be less than that of adults with similar cognitive problems, because an assessment of the child's competency necessarily takes into account limitations attributable to their stage of development. Matter of Welfare of D.D.N., 582 N.W.2d 278, 281, n. 3 (Minn. App. 1998).

The incompetency standard, which to date has never been stated differently for adolescents, is an established item of due process law. And adolescents who may be confined in any institution are entitled to due process under *Gault* and its progeny: although Gerald Gault was ordered placed in a training school, the court specifically reasoned that due process was necessary for a child whose liberties may be restrained by institutional confinement, whatever the euphemistic label given to the institution (*In re Gault*, 387 US at 13, 27, 30). Thus, three state appellate courts, the only appellate court voices on the topic, have determined that competency to proceed should be examined for juveniles with the standard employed for the criminal justice system. *In Interest of S.H.*, 469 S.E.2d 810, 811 (Ga. App. 1996); *In re Welfare of S.W.T.*, 277 N.W.2d 507, 511–12 (Minn. 1979); D.D.N., supra; see also *Minn. R. Juv. P.* 20.01, subd. 1 (B) (employing for juvenile delinquency proceedings the same competency-to-proceed standard employed in criminal cases, Minn. R. Cr. P. 20.01, subd. 1).

This view of the law matches the reality, described in this chapter, that great numbers of American children are involuntarily confined by the juvenile courts, putting at risk the liberty interests of most children who appear in juvenile court. Even rehabilitative placements involve significant losses of liberty (Lewis 1949). Hence, the Georgia Court of Appeals observed that juvenile proceedings, just like criminal proceedings, "may result in significant loss of liberties." *In Interest of S.H.*, 469 S.E.2d at 811.

14. As this volume is published, we are a few months away from the centennial, July 1, 1999, for the first functioning juvenile court, opened in Chicago (Mack 1909, 107). Two years later, Judge Ben B. Lindsey altered his Denver County criminal court practice to operate in the fashion that he and others later designated as a juvenile court (Lindsey and O'Higgins 1910, 82). Judges Mack and Lindsey made evident their conviction that the justice system had to deal with most adolescent offenders as adolescents, not simply as offenders.

15. Dean Pound (1937) spoke when many juvenile courts were being formed and few had existed for more than twenty-five years. Judge Mack (1909, 119), in the first decade of juvenile court experience, knew that application of the rule of law in the juvenile courts would be "absolutely essential" to their function. There is perpetual cause to learn what was discovered in the founding of the republic, that a grant of authority cannot be kept in check by the promise of goodwill (Gaylin et al. 1978).

16. See Rosenberg 1980, reviewing development of the law and stating authorities and rationale for extending greater constitutional rights to the accused juvenile than found appropriate for adults in the criminal justice system.

17. Feld (1989, 1236–38), in his documentation of juvenile court placement practices, discovered that over 40 percent of the placements for minor offenses were ordered in cases where the child was not represented by counsel. In some jurisdictions, well over half of the children placed for minor offenses were not represented (Feld 1989, 1238–39).

18. Feld's research also includes a remarkable finding that should compel skepticism about use of juvenile arrest statistics to prove a modern explosion of severe juvenile misconduct. Juvenile court felony petitions were filed for only 18.6 percent of reported FBI Part I felony arrests in Minnesota for juveniles ages ten to seventeen (Feld 1991A, 177).

19. See, for example, cases detailed later in these notes, *Matter of Welfare of J.A.J.,* 545 N.W.2d 412 (Minn. App. 1996); *In re Interest of A.M.H.,* 447 N.W.2d 40 (Neb 1989); *Matter of Welfare of L.K.W.,* 372 N.W.2d 392 (Minn. App. 1985); *State in Interest of Racine,* 433 So. 2d 243, 149 (La. Ct. App. 1983).

20. In 1983, the Minnesota legislature surveyed the state, which had a population of less than 4.5 million people, and found over 235 institutional-care alternatives for adolescents, exclusive of all foster care or group facilities caring for fewer than five children; annual placements had risen to over 15,000 (Fine 1983). On the fervor for hospital care, see Weithorn (1988).

21. In three Minnesota cases, the Court of Appeals reversed dispositions in spite of deference to the breadth of the trial court's dispositional discretion. *Matter of Welfare of J.A.J.,* 545 N.W.2d 412 (Minn. App. 1996) (reversing residential treatment placement following adjudication of indecent exposure offense, employing statutory standard of necessity for disposition); *Matter of Welfare of M.R.S.,* 400 N.W.2d 147 (Minn. App. 1987) (reversing hospital placement following misdemeanor theft adjudication; employing standards on necessity and best interests of child); *Matter of Welfare of L.K.W.,* 372 N.W.2d 392 (Minn. App. 1985) (reversing correction camp placement one year after shoplifting adjudicated; equating necessity standard with demand for least restrictive action and further demand for disposition proportional to severity of the offense; for placements, equating necessity and child's best interests with need to show cause for removal and suitability of placement). See also *Matter of Welfare of J.A.J.,* 545 N.W.2d at 416 (Crippen J., concurring specially) (enumerating statutory standards and substantive due process demands implicated in trial-court detention and placement decisions).

Outside Minnesota, there have been four American appellate decisions that reversed a juvenile court disposition without a remand permitting a reinstatement of the lower court's decision. All but one involved minor offenses. Two reversals, both by the North Dakota Supreme Court, in 1946 and 1981, demonstrate an appellate effort to announce and define a "danger" standard for placements of a child at a state institution. *Egan v. M.S.,* 310 N.W.2d 719, 721 (N.D. 1981) (reversing placement for undescribed "robbery" offense; employing statutory standard of dispositions "necessary" for "welfare" of child and "interest of public safety;" employing previously determined "danger to society" standard); *State v. Myers,* 22 N.W.2d 199, 201 (N.D. 1946) (landmark American case, reversing juvenile court placement for status offense; announcing "danger to society" standard, employed "in a spirit of optimism"). And see *In re Interest of A.M.H.*, 447 N.W.2d 40, 47 (Neb. 1989) (reversing eighteenth-month placement in state institution for driver license offense; employs "reasonableness" standard); *State in Interest of Racine*, 433 So. 2d 243, 249 (La. Ct. App. 1983) (reversing two-year state commitment for stealing property valued at a hundred dollars; employs statutory "least restrictive disposition" standard). See also *Matter of J.H.*, 758 P.2d 1287 (Alaska App. 1988) (reversing secure placement in favor of placement to treatment facility).

22. In its somewhat landmark dispositional statute, adopted in 1959, Minn. Stat. § 260.185, subd. 1 (1996), Minnesota determined that the courts must choose a disposition that is "necessary" for the child's rehabilitation. Delaware and Wisconsin are examples of other states that employ the concept of need in statutory dispositional standards. Del. Code Ann. T. 10, § 1009 (c)(11), (d) (Supp. 1996); Wis. Stat. § 938.34(4d)(b), (4m)(b) (Supp. 1997).

23. This characterization of standards matches a unique dispositional rule adopted by the Minnesota Supreme Court. Minn. R. Juv. P. 15.05, subd. 2 (B)(2); see *Matter of Welfare of C.A.W. and L.R.M.B.*, 579 N.W.2d 494, 497 (Minn. App. 1998) (enumerating elements of rule and companion statute).

The significance of dispositional standards in placement cases is highlighted in a remarkable Pennsylvania appellate opinion that (a) acknowledges the absence of cause for hospitalization of a child under protective standards of the state commitment statute, but (b) affirms the same results as a juvenile court dispositional decision. *In Interest of Green*, 417 A.2d 708 (Pa. Super. Ct. 1980).

24. Legal mandates for findings have ties with due process, evident in the observation of the United States Supreme Court that it might be assumed, for purposes of a rehabilitative disposition, that the court would make "a careful inquiry and judgment" on the possibility of dealing with the child without a placement. *In re Gault*, 387 US 1, 28; see ibid., 19–20 (deploring "inadequate or inaccurate findings of fact and unfortunate prescriptions of remedy" as symptoms of bad process). Both statute and rule require Minnesota's juvenile courts to make detailed findings of fact to support a disposition. Minn. Stat. § 260.185, subd. 1 (1996); Minn. R. Juv. P. 15.05, subd. 2(A). Recently, the Minnesota Court of Appeals had occasion to restate the five principle findings that are needed for a placement disposition, to show why the disposition serves public safety, why it benefits the child, why proposed alternative dispositions were not ordered, why the child's present custody is unacceptable (having regard for the legal preference not to remove the child), and why the proposed program is suitable for the needs of the child characteristics of the proposed program that can be expected to meet the child's needs. *Matter of Welfare of C.A.W. and L.R.M.B.*, 579 N.W.2d 494, 497–98 (Minn. App. 1998). Administrative rulings govern a number of dispositions in some states; administrative action invites like concerns for the right of review and a mandate for dispositional findings of fact.

25. An important piece of this evidence is found in the kinds of trial-court records that are revealed when a healthy appeal practice leads to scrutiny of placement cases. See, strikingly, *Matter of Welfare of L.K.W.*, 372 N.W.2d 392 (Minn. App. 1985) and *Matter of Welfare of J.A.J.*, 545 N.W.2d 416 (Minn. App. 1996).

See Feld (1991, 187–206), studying urban, suburban, and rural variations in placement decisions. And see Center for the Study of Social Policy (1990), showing state by state variations in detention and use of training schools. Anecdotally, there are abundant examples of remarkable placement rate variations from one local jurisdiction to the next, in situations where there is no evident cultural or demographic variation between the jurisdictions.

26. Paralleling restrictions on the waiver of counsel, Minnesota's rules also regulate the waiver of the right to a trial. *Minn. R. Juv. P.* 8.04, subd. 1 (stating an unusually helpful form of advisory of rights for juvenile cases).

27. See Melton (1989), observing the notable rehabilitative effect in offering due process protections. This view was a significant part of the United States Supreme Court decision to bring due process into the juvenile justice system. *In re Gault,* 387 US at 26 (citing views of this kind in the literature of the 1960s).

28. Thirteen states have provided juveniles with the right to a jury trial (Edwards 1992, 7 n.31). Minnesota, now joined by some other states, only provides the jury trial right to a category of quasi-juveniles, serious offenders who (a) have their cases adjudicated in juvenile court, (b) receive a juvenile court disposition, albeit longer than usual, and (c) receive a stayed adult court sentence that threatens their future in the event of recidivism. See Feld (1997, 87–88).

29. See Lubow and Moore (1997), reporting upward detention trends, in spite of a decline in serious offense reports, with current national annual admission numbers nearing 600,000, daily population reaching 25,000, in some 500 secure facilities, with 60 percent of admissions into overcrowded facilities; identifying urban programs successfully reducing detentions, suggesting lack of need for many preprogram detentions); Lubow et al. (1995, ix), introducing published symposium on excesses and control of detention in metropolitan area; reviewing mushrooming detention across the nation, together with summary of consequences, including public cost, overcrowding, and harm to arrested juveniles); Feld (1989, 1254), stating evidence that 65 percent of pretrial detention incidents are for misdemeanors and status offenses; Schwartz et al. (1987, 219, 222), reporting high percent of detention cases never processed in court or used where confinement disposition found unnecessary.

30. See Lubow and Tulman (1995), highlighting need for alternative resources and for objective risk assessment practice). And see Schwartz et al. (1991), reporting on successful strategies for reduction of secure detention in Broward County, Florida.

31. The ABA "Call for Justice" details deficiencies of excessive caseloads and poor performance (American Bar Association 1995, 7–8, 22–27, 46–48). The publication also calls for increased resources and administrative utilization of training, standards of practice, and caseload control (American Bar Association 1995, 67–69).

32. The State Public Defender has responsibility to assist Minnesota juvenile offenders in many appeals (Minn. Stat. § 611.25, subd. 1(3) (1996)). Different Minnesota jurisdictions employ various arrangements for trial court services; a statewide system of district public defenders provides this service in some jurisdictions (Minn. Stat. § 611.14 (4) [1996]).

33. As noted elsewhere, two juvenile court dispositions were reversed in Minnesota before 1995. Since 1995, one disposition has been reversed outright and seven others have been reversed and remanded (or reversed after a placement ended) due to inadequate findings of fact.

34. Public-safety demands have been evident mostly respecting violent offenders, together with adoption in some states of indefinite juvenile code purpose statements that recite public safety concerns. See Feld (1991B, 709), citing this and other evidence of punitive juvenile court dispositions, almost all other evidence being in respect to severe or violent offenses. There are no states where juvenile court delinquency jurisdiction has been completely ended. And among states that have employed a rehabilitative standard resembling the Model Act, discussed early in this chapter, none has altered its law to openly permit punitive dispositions. See 42 Pa. Cons. Stat. Ann. § 6352(a) (Supp. 1998) (abandoning Model Act provision but providing that disposition must be best suited to the child's welfare as well as consistent with protection of the public interest; in added language, calling for attention to community protection and accountability for offenses, but "as appropriate to the individual circumstances of the child's case").

For twenty years, abolition has been addressed by Professor Feld, its most published proponent. In early publications, he only stated an "unanswered question" of whether the juvenile court enterprise would have to be abandoned before it could achieve success in delivering procedural and substantive justice (Feld 1978, 616). Three years later, Feld (1981, 242) found "scant reason" and "little justification" for maintaining a separate juvenile justice system. Soon thereafter, Feld (1984, 276) began active discussion of "the case for abolishing the juvenile court." Four years later, he (1988, 909–15) included in his discussion of abolition the observation that the criminal justice system could do as well as the juvenile court in protecting youthful offenders. Feld's full exposition (1997) on the criminal justice approach to juveniles appears in a publication that coincides with the writing of contributions to this book.

Other early proponents of abolition include: Wolfgang (1982), an isolated observation of Professor Wolfgang that may have been confined to the topic of jurisdiction over chronic offenders; Guggenheim (1978), a proposition, as noted herein, that the professor has now abandoned; McCarthy (1977); Keller and Wizner (1977); Olney (1938, 3, 6), offering the abolition proposal early in the course of juvenile court history; urging adult court prosecution because juvenile courts offer (a) "star chamber sessions in the chambers of the judge," but also (b) a "loophole to the young criminals in their escape from punishment."

In the last decade, abolition and criminal court jurisdiction have been advanced by Professors Ainsworth (1991) and Federle (1990).

35. The idea of responsibility, of course, is foreign neither to the juvenile court nor to its aims. See Mack (1909, 120): "The object of the juvenile court and of the intervention of the state is, of course, in no case to lessen or to weaken the sense of responsibility either of the child or of the parent. On the contrary, the aim is to develop and to enforce it."

36. Professor Feld quickly disregards criticism of criminal court process, and his explanation for this approach is unsatisfactory. Acknowledging flaws in the

criminal justice system, although failing to identify them or to consider their effects on youthful offenders, he faults juvenile court "proponents" for criticizing adult court jurisdiction without defending the juvenile court (Feld 1997, 96). Further explaining his unwillingness to discuss the criminal courts, Feld (1997, 96) retreats for a moment from the role of abolitionist, suggesting that he only proposes a sentencing policy for juveniles. The sentencing policy, of course, has a venue in the criminal courts, and the juvenile justice system, he proposes, need not exist (Feld 1997, 69, 90–91, 95, 131–32).

37. A similar observation was recently stated by Judge Lindsay G. Arthur (1998).

38. Guggenheim now disavows what he recommended in 1978, specifically because he observes that criminal court practice is not a better alternative for juveniles (Rosenberg 1993, 163–64 n. 1, 174 n.66).

39. Feld (1991, 700), contrasting with his current expectation of decriminalization, observed earlier the widespread avoidance of decriminalization by countless public and private agencies, through a "hidden system" of psychiatric commitments and private agency placements.

40. In fact, the greatest prospect for adult court diversion is apt to exist in those cases where authorities seek the indeterminate placement of a child but cannot achieve that result in criminal proceedings, either because they cannot prove a crime or do not believe that a moderate punitive sanction is satisfactory. See *In Interest of Green,* 417 A.2d 708 (Pa. Sup. Ct. 1980) (demonstrating resort in child protection proceedings after failing to show cause for hospitalization under commitment code).

41. See Ainsworth (1991, 1127), in support of juveniles in adult court, noting only the ineffectiveness of juvenile court lawyers.

Feld alludes to the "full" and "full panoply" of procedural "safeguards" of the criminal justice system (Feld 1988, 912; Feld 1984, 274). Another scholar advances these attributions to the adult system in an overstated fashion that few observers will want to defend.

"The abolition of the juvenile court will insure the adoption of a rights-based jurisprudence for children. The elimination of the juvenile system will guarantee that those charged with violating the law will receive the full panoply of protections both constitutional and statutory. Those who participate in such [an adult] court will reinforce the child's rights model. The attorney, who previously saw her role as guardian, will advance the interest of her client regardless of the client's age. The judge will no longer be a parental figure but will be a neutral and impartial arbiter of justice. Charging decisions by the prosecuting attorney will no longer reflect a highly interventionist parens patriae model but one consistent with concerns for community safety. Police behavior will conform to constitutional requisites in the revised system because of its adversarial nature. Finally, sentencing will be proportional to the seriousness of the crime rather than to the attitude of the child" (Federle 1990, 49–50).

Federle (1990, 50) sees so much promise for new justice in the criminal justice system that it will wear off on adults.

42. Adding to other pills of moderation that are preconditions to Professor

Feld's abolition proposal, Feld (1997, 121) proposes that adult felony sentencing must be significantly reformed, to include "presumptive sentencing guidelines with strong upper limits on punishment severity, elimination of all mandatory minimum sentences, and some structured judicial discretion to mitigate penalties based on individual circumstances." These and other Feld proposals will be unattractive to lawmakers who might otherwise be enthusiastic about his proposal to abolish the juvenile court.

43. In his most recent statement on adult court jurisdiction for juvenile cases, Professor Feld (1997, 128–29) speculates that lawmakers are likely to decriminalize offenses to accommodate the caseload in the criminal courts. Yet, in another context, the same author expresses his own concern for legislative pursuit of punishment for juveniles. He is fearful, understandably, that "get tough" attitudes will put in jeopardy the sentencing discounts that he proposes (Feld 1997, 133). And Feld (1993, 230–31) has previously acknowledged evidence that decriminalization of status offenders results in increased prosecution of misdemeanor offenses once overlooked.

44. Without overlooking juvenile court abuses, Rosenberg (1993, 173–74) recognizes that problems of children in the criminal courts would be worse. See also Rubin (1979, 296): "What is noteworthy about the proposals to abolish the juvenile courts is the abolitionists' failure to assess the immense problems in the present criminal court process—problems which have long been taken for granted by criminal defendants and knowledgeable court watchers. Overcriminalization, ineffective defense representation, rehabilitation rhetoric, and severe punishments have characterized criminal courts as well as the juvenile courts." It also is important to note emerging literature on the ineffectiveness of transferring cases to adult court as a means to reduce recidivism. See Feld (1997, 130 n. 163) and Podkopacz and Feld (1996, 489–91).

45. See also Rosenberg 1980, 1993, addressing youthful offender rights. Finally, see Edwards (1992), describing and defending juvenile court practice and reciting adult court deficiencies.

46. "Equity" came, Professor Maitland (1936, 17) reminded us, "not to destroy the law, but to fulfill it." Parens patriae, Dean Roscoe Pound (Pound 1905, 349) observed, "was limited on every side by the maxims of the common law, and the bounds set by the lex terrae." In Judge Mack's (1909, 104) words, parens patriae permits a court to act "for the protection of infants."

Ohio Juvenile Judge Don J. Young, Jr. (1962, 18–19): "The doctrine of parens patriae . . . is a simple and succinct way of saying that children need more, not less, protection than the law gives to adults. No one has a right to rely on this doctrine except with the full understanding of what is included in its broad generality." Judge Young's observation brings to mind current literature suggesting constitutional rights of children that exceed those of adults (Rosenberg 1980).

Judge Lindsey (Lindsey and O'Higgins 1910, 289) boasted in his memoir: "We had founded . . . a Juvenile Court with laws that protected the children from the agents of the System . . ." The purpose of the juvenile court was not alone to be helpful but also "to hurt as little as it can" (Judge Lindsey, quoted in Mack 1909, 121). Judge Mack reported the view of the Pennsylvania Supreme Court, which foresaw no juvenile court prospect for undue invasion of a child's liberty "in the proper administration of the law" (Mack 1909, 110). Mack foresaw that the rule of law would be "absolutely essential" in the function of the juvenile court (Mack 1909, 119). Reciting a standard that later generations failed to honor, Mack observed that placement of a child in an institution "is, as far as possible, to be avoided" (Mack 1909, 116).

47. "The mistake of the criminal law had been to punish these little savages as if they had been civilized, and by so doing, in nine cases out of ten, make them criminal savages" (Lindsey and O'Higgins 1910, 13–35).

Ironically, juvenile jailing practices flourished in the United States through most of the century of the juvenile courts (Schwartz 1989, 69–84). Excluding juveniles held as adults, the number of juveniles in jails has remained steady since 1985 (Bureau of Justice Statistics 1995, 10, reporting 1995 daily count of 1,870 juveniles in American jails).

48. *See* Rosenberg (1980, 707–9). The juvenile court founders are not unlike those who established the American republic. While expecting freedoms, the nation's founders thought that a declaration of personal rights would not be needed to protect them. The Bill of Rights corrected their strategy, and without tearing down the system they had created or the aims that moved them. Similarly, in spite of the skepticism occasioned by learning how race and gender have brought denial of liberty to so many Americans, we trust our capacity to deliver on the promise of equality and to do that without destroying the institution that was created to that end 200 years ago.

49. See B. Flicker, in American Bar Association (1977, 40): "Judges appear hostile to any restraint on their actions; it should be noted that the principle in the standards that all decisions affecting substantial rights be regulated by specific criteria, be in writing, be subject to judicial review, and include reasons for not adopting a less restrictive alternative, is objectionable to the National Council of Juvenile Court Judges (now the National Council of Juvenile and Family Court Judges), as are the positions on proportionality and determinate sentences; all are construed as antithetical to the individualized justice that the National Council considers the foundation of the juvenile justice system."

50. *Kent v. United States,* 383 US 541 (1966) (stating Justice Fortas's metaphor of "the worst of both worlds" to characterize problems in the juvenile court). Thoughts on "the best of both worlds" do not originate here. See, for example, attribution to Salt Lake City Judge Sharon P. McCully in Edwards (1992, 23 n. 169).

EPILOGUE

In the Introduction to this volume, we noted that the MacArthur Foundation Research Network on Adolescent Development and Juvenile Justice, which commissioned this work, has been given an ambitious charge. Its aim is to engage in a process that will eventually provide the information and tools to more effectively address important developmental psychological issues for law, policy, and practice that have been raised by the current trends in juvenile law. Among those issues are the two that the authors of this book were asked to address—adolescents' capacities as trial defendants, and the culpability of adolescent offenders. How have these authors advanced that objective? We believe they have done so in four ways.

First, a measured consideration of the assertions of these authors leaves little doubt about the relevance of a developmental and psychological perspective when addressing the issues that are raised by the recent transformation of juvenile law. Whatever its claims, that transformation has largely ignored the fact that adolescents do not suddenly become adults when they engage in offenses—even serious ones—and laws that treat them like adult defendants alter only their legal status, not their psychological characteristics and developmental immaturity. Placing them in criminal court does not transform them into defendants who suddenly can understand the process they are undergoing, make decisions about their rights, and participate meaningfully in their defense. If this is true, then by automatically prosecuting youths in criminal court for serious offenses, we run the risk of degrading the integrity of the justice system.

Second, while these chapters point out the relevance of a developmental psychological perspective on these issues, they also affirm that developmental psychology currently falls short of providing the information that is needed to guide law, policy, and practice in juvenile justice. The developmental perspective regarding issues of adolescents' capacities as defendants as well as their capacities related to questions of culpability currently is driven primarily by theory and principles that have been supported in basic developmental research. A good theory is essential and usually of some help in uncharted territory, but it is not sufficient. We are not inspired to confidence in social planning until research tests the value of the theory specifically in that area of law and policy to which we wish to apply it.

One of the primary objectives of this volume is to stimulate that research. Several of the authors have provided guidance for both the substance and research methods that will require attention by future researchers in the behavioral and social sciences who wish to pursue their leads. The MacArthur Foundation Research Network on Adolescent Development and Juvenile Justice has embarked on a series of research projects that flow from the insights these authors have provided. We hope that their efforts will help to resolve the issues that this book has raised.

Third, while we await more definitive information from developmental researchers, some of the authors in this volume have provided important information that can be put to use by professionals who are responsible for working with youths every day in the juvenile and criminal justice systems. Some have provided blueprints for improving the quality of lawyering for youths. Others have alerted clinicians to the characteristics of youths that are relevant for addressing their competence to stand trial, as well as methods for identifying those characteristics through clinical evaluations. These contributions can be translated into action now, while we await research information that may eventually reshape more fundamental policies and law pertaining to youthful offenders.

Finally, these chapters collectively make it clear that no progress on these issues can be made without interdisciplinary efforts. Lawyers and courts are not likely to see the relevance of the social sciences for addressing important issues in juvenile justice if they are not aware of the potential of its concepts. In turn, practicing lawyers and law scholars must inform social-science researchers as they develop their research, in order to assure that the eventual results can be translated into meaningful guidance for law and practice.

Much legal thinking and empirical research is needed to resolve the questions raised in this volume. These questions challenge the direction of the current trend in juvenile justice policy, a trend that appears to presume that children are somehow not children if they engage in serious offenses. We conclude, as we did in our Introduction, that this work is dedicated to the evolution of a juvenile justice system that better serves the ultimate interests of society in its efforts to forge a rational and effective response to the needs, challenges, and promise of its youth.

CONTRIBUTORS

Richard Barnum, M.D.
Boston Juvenile Court Clinic
Boston, Massachusetts

Richard J. Bonnie, J.D.
School of Law
University of Virginia

Emily Buss, J.D.
School of Law
University of Chicago

Elizabeth Cauffman, Ph.D.
Western Psychiatric Institute
and Clinic
University of Pittsburgh

Honorable Gary L. Crippen
Minnesota State Court of Appeals
St. Paul, Minnesota

Jeffrey Fagan, Ph.D.
School of Public Health
Columbia University

Barry C. Feld, J.D.
School of Law
University of Minnesota

Sandra Graham, Ph.D.
Graduate School of Education and
Information Studies
University of California, Los Angeles

Thomas Grisso, Ph.D.
Department of Psychiatry
University of Massachusetts Medical
School

Colleen Halliday, Ph.D.
Medical University of
South Carolina

Alan E. Kazdin, Ph.D.
Department of Psychology
Yale University

N. Dickon Reppucci, Ph.D.
Department of Psychology
University of Virginia

Robert G. Schwartz, J.D.
Juvenile Law Center
Philadelphia, Pennsylvania

Elizabeth Scott, J.D.
School of Law
University of Virginia

Laurence Steinberg, Ph.D.
Department of Psychology
Temple University

Ann Tobey, Ph.D.
Youth Advocacy Project
Roxbury, Massachusetts

Jennifer L. Woolard, Ph.D.
Center for Studies in Criminology
and Law
University of Florida

Franklin E. Zimring, J.D.
School of Law, Boalt Hall
University of California, Berkeley

The contributors thank the following individuals who participated in reviews of their manuscripts while they were in progress:

Donna Bishop, Ph.D.
Department of Criminal Justice
and Legal Studies
University of Central Florida

Honorable Jay Blitzman
Massachusetts Trial Court
Boston, Massachusetts

Nancy Guerra, Ph.D.
Department of Psychology
University of Illinois

Janis Kupersmidt, Ph.D.
Department of Psychology
University of North Carolina,
Chapel Hill

Tracey Meares, J.D.
Law School
University of Chicago

Edward Mulvey, Ph.D.
Western Psychiatric Institute
and Clinic
University of Pittsburgh

Norman Poythress, Ph.D.
Florida Mental Health Center
University of South Florida

Michael Wald, J.D.
School of Law
Stanford University

The contributors thank the following persons for their assistance in the organization of this project and liaison with the MacArthur Foundation:

Lynn Daidone Boyter
Administrator
Research Network on Adolescent Development and Juvenile Justice

Laurie Garduque, Ph.D.
Program Officer, Program on Human
and Community Development
The John D. and Catherine T.
MacArthur Foundation
Chicago, Illinois

SUBJECT INDEX

AUTHOR INDEX